The Great Shame

By the same author

Fiction

The Place at Whitton
The Fear
Bring Larks and Heroes
Three Cheers for the Paraclete
The Survivor
A Dutiful Daughter
The Chant of Jimmie Blacksmith
Blood Red, Sister Rose
Gossip from the Forest
Season in Purgatory
A Victim of the Aurora
Passenger
Confederates
The Cut-rate Kingdom
Schindler's Ark
A Family Madness
The Playmaker
Towards Asmara
By the Line
Flying Hero Class
Woman of the Inner Sea
Jacko
A River Town

Non-fiction

Outback
The Place Where Souls Are Born
Now and in Time to Be: Ireland and the Irish
Memoirs from a Young Republic
Homebush Boy: A Memoir

For children

Ned Kelly and the City of Bees

THE GREAT SHAME

A Story of the Irish in the Old World and the New

THOMAS KENEALLY

Chatto & Windus
LONDON

Published by Chatto & Windus 1998

2 4 6 8 10 9 7 5 3 1

First published in Great Britain in 1998 by
Chatto & Windus
Random House, 20 Vauxhall Bridge Road,
London SW1V 2SA

Random House Australia (Pty) Limited
20 Alfred Street, Milsons Point, Sydney,
New South Wales 2061, Australia

Random House New Zealand Limited
18 Poland Road, Glenfield,
Auckland 10, New Zealand

Random House South Africa (Pty) Limited
Endulini, 5A Jubilee Road, Parktown 2193, South Africa

Random House UK Limited Reg. No. 954009

A CIP catalogue record for this book
is available from the British Library

ISBN 1–85619–788–3

Papers used by Random House UK Limited are natural, recyclable products made from wood grown in sustainable forests. The manufacturing processes conform to the environmental regulations of the country of origin.

Typeset by Deltatype Ltd, Birkenhead, Merseyside
Printed and bound in Great Britain by
Biddles Ltd, Guildford and King's Lynn

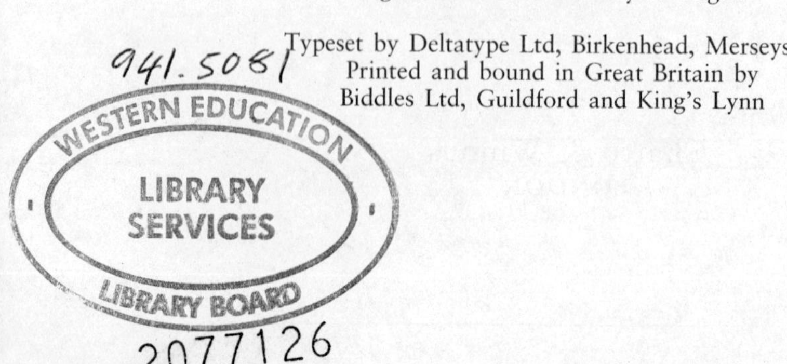

CONTENTS

LIST OF ILLUSTRATIONS

first 8-page section

second 8-page section

third 8-page section

fourth 8-page section

The shooting of Prince Alfred at Clontarf (*Illustrated Sydney News*, Mitchell Library, Sydney)
Labourer's cottage, 1870s (Lawrence Collection, National Library of Ireland)
The convict-built pier, Fremantle (Battye Library, Western Australia)
Grand parade in honour of the amnestied Fenians (J. Clarence Davies Collection, Museum of the City of New York)
The escape of the Fenian prisoners (*Australasian Sketcher*, Mitchell Library, Sydney)
Catalpa's flag (Michael Flynn, Curator, National Museum of Ireland, from its exhibition on Fenianism)
John Goulding's grave on the south coast of New South Wales (Thomas Keneally)
The dry-goods department store of Dillon and Kenealy (Huntington Library, San Marino, California)
John Kenealy in his sixties (Huntington Library, San Marino, California)

PREFACE

After Steven Spielberg's film *Schindler's List* revived interest in the story that I had told in my novel *Schindler's Ark*, I was frequently, to my embarrassment, thanked for having documented on a human scale, through jaunty, disreputable Oskar Schindler, the Jewish catastrophe of the Second World War. I had stumbled on the story, written it with passion because it was a great tale, and now with a delighted and slightly guilty bemusement found that people, particularly the Jewish community throughout the world, were talking to me as if I had done something larger – had to an extent validated the past for those who had lived through it, and had restored their history to their children.

What of my own past? I was born in Australia, and I knew that my name and ancestors were Irish. I knew vaguely that I had some forebears who were convicts, one of them a John Kenealy who served time in Western Australia as a political prisoner. I discovered too that I had married the great-granddaughter of what one historian calls 'a protest criminal', a so-called Ribbonman – sent from Ireland to Australia for life in the decade before the Irish Famine, which began in 1845. This, if it is a boast, is not such an uncommon one in Australia, even if earlier generations of Australians would have suppressed what they then perceived as genealogical stains. I knew that, throughout the nineteenth century, until the last shipload of Fenian prisoners arrived in Western Australia in 1868, and until the last political prisoner had died in exile well into the twentieth century, Australia was the potential punishment that hung over all protest, political activism and revolt in the British Empire – over the Chartists of Britain, the French *habitants* of Lower Canada and the republicans of Upper Canada, but in particular over gestures of protest and rebellion in Ireland.

I wanted to try to tell the tale of the Irish in the new world and the old through the experiences of those transported to Australia for gestures of social and political dissent. The suppression of dissent in Ireland of course marked both Ireland itself, the point of departure, and Australia, the shore of exile. But Australia's place as a zone of sub-Antarctic political punishment would also influence the intense and fatally riven Irish politics of emigrant societies in the United States, Britain and Canada, and I wanted to try to tell some of that tale as well.

Unlike the humble criminal with whom I begin this book, internationally renowned Irish figures serving time in Australia would sometimes be pardoned or, in more graphic cases, would participate in highly organised escapes, arriving again in the northern hemisphere, above all in the United States. There they would exploit in various ways their lustre, and marshal for 'the Irish cause' the sympathy of America and of liberal thought everywhere.

In the twentieth century the reputation of the better known of these prisoners has remained stronger in Ireland and America than in Australia. The famed and tragic Kennedy boys of Boston, for example, would be pointed by Boston's Irish political culture to the speeches of former Tasmanian life-sentenced convict and US general, Thomas Francis Meagher. John Mitchel's *Jail Journal* remains a classic of penal experience, particularly in Ireland. In Glasnevin Cemetery in Dublin, the grave of Terence Bellew MacManus, whose funeral procession – from San Francisco down to the Central American isthmus and across the Atlantic to Dublin – must have been one of the longest funerary events in history, is still honoured and a place for pilgrimage.

But the document which made it inevitable that I should write this book is an obscure one – far more so than any attaching to the spectacular careers of General Thomas Francis Meagher and of John Mitchel, famous friends in Australian exile, famous opponents in the American Civil War. The item which provoked this narrative is a far humbler article than the National Library of Ireland's holdings of the letters of the Irish nobleman prisoner William Smith O'Brien, whose statue stands near Daniel O'Connell's in the centre of Dublin; or than the literary and civic flourishes of the splendid Fenian escapee of 1869, John Boyle O'Reilly, in his adopted city of Boston.

The document which stimulated this book is an 1840 plea from an Irish peasant woman, Esther Larkin, for reunion with her husband. Using the services of a scrivener who knows how to phrase petitions to Dublin Castle, Esther Larkin asks that she and her children should be sent to her husband, who is serving a life sentence in Australia. It is a plea which seemed to me to combine the required feudal subservience with an understated poignancy of loss.

The humble petition of Esther Larkin to His Excellency Viscount Ebrington, Lord Lieutenant General and General Governor of Ireland.

Humbly herewith –

Your Excellency's Petitioner is the wife of Hugh Larkin who was sent out to New South Wales under the Rule of Transportation for life, from Galway Assizes in July, 1833 under a charge of Terry-Altism.

Herewith, Petitioner has two male children one ten years old and the other seven. Petitioner's age 28 years. Under the above circumstances Petitioner begs of your Excellency to look with the eyes of pity on herself and children and order them a free passage to New South Wales and Your Excellency's Petitioner will forever faithfully pray.

her
Esther X Larkin.
mark
Laurencetown, 7th February, 1840

It is this Hugh Larkin from whom my wife and daughters are descended. I hope that, through exploring Larkin and his transported brethren, both the obscure and the more famous, I may show at least some of the experience of the Irish diaspora, and some of the crucial events in the new world's societies. I also hope that through the people of this book some of the causes of the greatest nineteenth-century Irish tragedy will be better understood. For during the course of this narrative, the population of Ireland, between the census of 1841 and the census of 1881, declined to a level barely above half of what it had been – a catastrophe unique in Europe.

It has been delightful to search out these connections, and to live in hope that the reader will be as fascinated by this material as is the writer himself.

Thomas Keneally
Sydney, 1998

NOTE ON THE TEXT

I have retained the nineteenth-century system of capitalising nouns only in official documents and some super-heated newspaper reports, where the use of capitals seems more systematic than random. In quoting from private letters or journals I have for ease of reading taken the liberty of adjusting randomly used upper case to lower case. In other rare occasional instances where sense seemed to cry for it, a comma or a full stop has been supplied. I have avoided scattering the tale with the notation (*sic*) to mark mistaken spellings or variations. For example, in some letters and printed material, the Limerick estate of the convict William Smith O'Brien is spelt Cahirmoyle, in others Cahermoyle. This variation goes unremarked upon. Since Smith O'Brien spelt it Cahirmoyle himself, that is the form used in the body of the account.

Finally, in these pages there are so many people claiming to have had so many adventures that I have avoided as much as possible using the form 'claimed to have had/seen/said/done'. I hope that when the evidence for a particular event is dependent upon one source, such as when Thomas Francis Meagher recounts his experience of being an escapee on an island in Bass Strait, the reader will read a tacit 'claimed' into the text.

IRELAND IN THE NINETEENTH CENTURY
DONEGAL
LONDONDERRY
ANTRIM
ULSTER
TYRONE
FERMANAGH
MONAGHAN
ARMAGH
DOWN
LEITRIM
SLIGO
CAVAN
LOUTH
MAYO
ROSCOMMON
LONGFORD
MEATH
WESTMEATH
CONNAUGHT
Galway
Ballinasloe
Lismany
GALWAY
KING'S COUNTY
KILDARE
DUBLIN
Dublin
LEINSTER
CLARE
Ennis
QUEEN'S COUNTY
WICKLOW
TIPPERARY
Limerick
KILKENNY
CARLOW
MUNSTER
Cashel
LIMERICK
Tipperary
Clonmel
WEXFORD
KERRY
CORK
Waterford
Mallow
WATERFORD
Cork

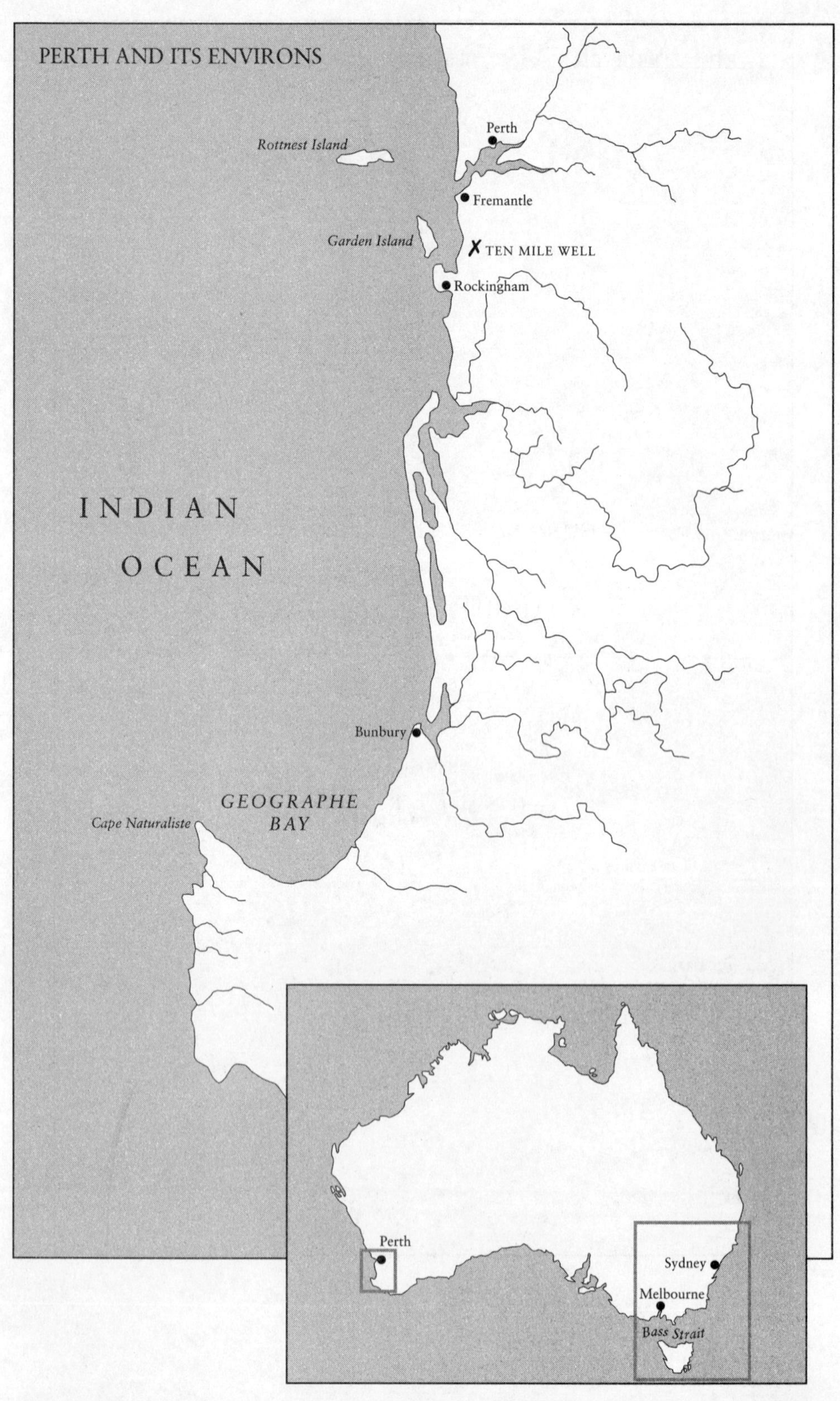
PERTH AND ITS ENVIRONS
Perth
Rottnest Island
Fremantle
Garden Island
TEN MILE WELL
Rockingham
INDIAN
OCEAN
Bunbury
GEOGRAPHE
BAY
Cape Naturaliste
Perth
Sydney
Melbourne
Bass Strait

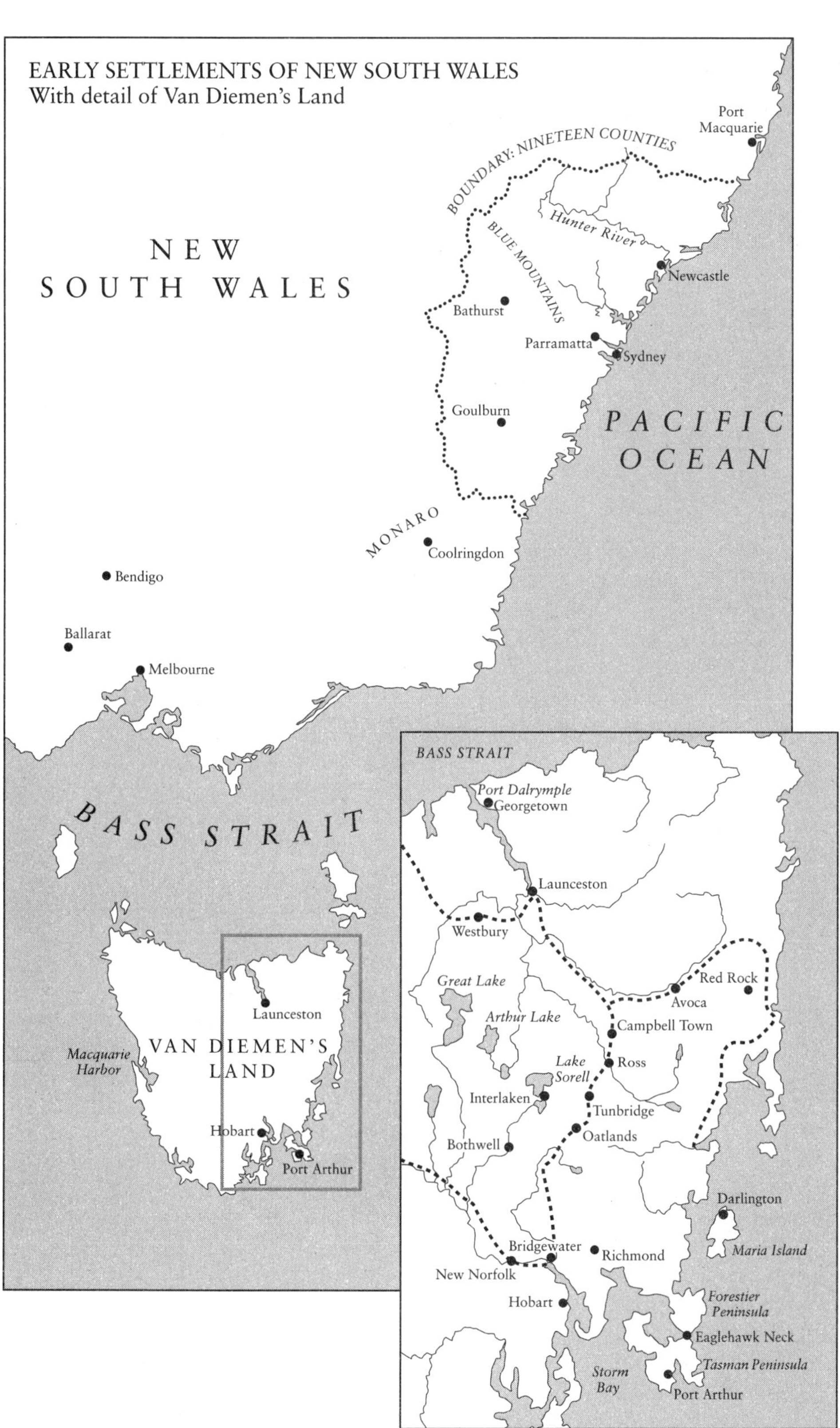
EARLY SETTLEMENTS OF NEW SOUTH WALES
With detail of Van Diemen's Land
NEW SOUTH WALES
BOUNDARY: NINETEEN COUNTIES
Port Macquarie
Hunter River
BLUE MOUNTAINS
Newcastle
Bathurst
Parramatta
Sydney
Goulburn
PACIFIC OCEAN
MONARO
Coolringdon
Bendigo
Ballarat
Melbourne
BASS STRAIT
VAN DIEMEN'S LAND
Macquarie Harbor
Launceston
Hobart
Port Arthur
BASS STRAIT
Port Dalrymple
Georgetown
Launceston
Westbury
Great Lake
Arthur Lake
Red Rock
Avoca
Campbell Town
Ross
Lake Sorell
Interlaken
Tunbridge
Oatlands
Bothwell
Darlington
Maria Island
Bridgewater
Richmond
New Norfolk
Hobart
Forestier Peninsula
Eaglehawk Neck
Tasman Peninsula
Storm Bay
Port Arthur

BOOK I

I

Hugh Larkin's Ireland

> TERRYALTISM:
> Up to the moment we write, there have been . . . about thirty unfortunate individuals convicted under the Whiteboy Act, and therefore destined to spend the remainder of their lives in a clime far, far distant from their native homes – from the land which holds all that is dear to them in the world.
>
> *Galway Free Press*, 31 March 1832

For English and Anglo-Irish noblemen, the post of Lord Lieutenant of Ireland was both a challenge and a reward. The Lord Lieutenant was chief executive of Britain's most ungovernable kingdom but also the British monarch's representative, and the centre and apogee of Irish society. In the bright July of 1833, the Lord Lieutenant happened to be a friendly and reckless 73-year-old womaniser named Richard Colley Wellesley, 2nd Earl of Mornington. He had the benefit of being the elder brother of the Duke of Wellington, conqueror of Napoleon and former Tory Prime Minister. For the mass of Irish peasants, it did not matter a great deal who held the post. The known face of their landlord or his agent, how much land they had to live off, how secure was their tenure, and what they could sell their labour for – these were the intimate and recurrent concerns of their lives. People of quality, though, in towns or on their estates in the west of Ireland, wanted to know about the Lord Lieutenant's movements, levees and recreations.

They read, for example, accounts of that summer's Kingstown (now Dún Laoghaire) Regatta. 'After the morning sailing races, all the Dublin establishment attended a splendid lunch in a huge marquee pitched in the Commissioner's store yard.' Then the Lord Lieutenant and Lord Paget returned to Dublin in separate vehicles, and in Mount Street Paget's horses and vehicle ran into a Dublin urchin. His lordship reined in the horses to prevent his carriage crushing the child, and footmen carried the bloodied child to Mr Burrowe's, apothecary, Lower Merrion Street. There were hopes for the survival of the little sufferer.

The Lord Lieutenant might have enjoyed the opportunity to be of direct effectiveness. He could not have indulged such simple hopes for the health of Ireland as he did for the health of the Mount Street urchin. For in describing the ills of the kingdom of Ireland, commentators of that period rarely knew where to start.

*

In that very same summer of the Lord Lieutenant's encounter with 'the incautious child', a peasant cottier and farm labourer from East Galway named Hugh Larkin was waiting in the county gaol in Galway city. He was to be judged for a gesture of discontent against his landlord, and so against the system represented and protected by the Lord Lieutenant, Dublin Castle and the Parliament at Westminster.

Hugh was twenty-four years old, married, blue-eyed, robust, and 5 feet 7½ inches tall. According to his East Galway descendants, he was the intense, lively, likeable son of a widowed mother. Then or later he became hard-drinking, yet his record would not imply he was reckless or utterly headstrong.

Larkin came from a scatter of houses at a crossroads known as Lismany. This name for the landscape in which he had spent his childhood and youth bespoke pre-British ownership. The Irish name was *Lios Maine*, the fort of Maine, long-ago king of the region called Hy Many. This kingdom was made up of parts of modern Galway, Roscommon and a small slab of modern Tipperary. The Gaelic lords of the region had been dispossessed after the victory of the forces of England's King William III over the Irish at Aughrim, a village north-west of Lismany, in 1691.

During Hugh's childhood people had believed that the old Gaelic system was likely to be reasserted by God in some day of jubilation, but that day now seemed too remote to save him. Hugh's depression in Galway gaol arose chiefly from homesickness for Lismany, his two infant sons, and his wife Esther Tully, whom he had married three years before in the chapel of the Catholic parish of Clontuskert.

That very name, Clontuskert, showed that Hugh's kind of Irish walked the earth with two competing addresses in their heads. For administrative reasons, Dublin Castle had divided the country into Church of Ireland parishes, the smallest local unit, and then into larger baronies, somewhat akin to municipalities. So Larkin's official and English-language address as a member of the United Kingdom was (Church of Ireland) parish of Clontuskert, barony of Longford, County Galway. His emotional and native address, however, was (Catholic) parish of Clontuskert, diocese of Clonfert, Hy Many. Perhaps this double geography the peasants carried in their heads was one of the reasons those in power saw them as sly and duplicitous.

Esther and Hugh, living virtually in the midlands of Ireland, spoke English, the language of government and commerce, when they talked to their landlord or went to market, but courted, sang, praised and mourned in Irish. The courtship of Hugh and Esther had been, if at all characteristic of their society, particularly ardent and poetic, driven by furious longing, observed by an entire rural community which did not countenance fornication, but put a premium on flirtation as an art, and on the extravagant use of the images of desire. Gaelic love verses and songs which have come to us in translation indicate the style of eloquent persuasion Hugh would have been required to use with Esther.

> She could cheat my heart to believe in marvels,
> That no grass would grow, that no moon would shine,
> That the stars are lightless, that she could love me;
> And oh! Christ in Heaven that she were mine . . .
> There is no hill and there's no valley,
> No road, no bog that she passes by
> But is filled with music, heart-breaking music.

The love poetry of a labourer like Hugh was far more elevated than the squalid milieu where love was consummated – the marriage bed for Hugh and Esther was at best a low-lying cot of wooden laths and leather straps, at worst a mass of straw covered by a blanket. Courtship done, union achieved, Hugh and Esther begot and lived with their infant children Patrick and Hugh, and with Larkin's widowed mother, in a stone cottage which stood at the crossroads of Lismany, south of the East Galway city of Ballinasloe and on the road to a village named Laurencetown. A cottage some 25 feet long still stands on the site, and at least its lower walls were part of the home within which Hugh and Esther lived out their short married life here.

Generally, when Galway is mentioned, people envisage the bare grandeur of the western end of the county, the region called Connemara. But the country where Hugh and Esther Larkin lived was a verdant area of gentle downland, broken up by copses, heath thickets and brown peat bogs. The Shannon River flowed to the east of Lismany crossroads, and on fine days Hugh could see the blue Roscommon mountains. The barony of Longford was intersected by the Grand Canal, a wonderful man-dug river of commerce between the Shannon and Dublin.

But Hugh in prison was more than 60 miles from that landscape. The determining fact of his life was that for acts committed a little west of Lismany crossroads he was about to stand trial at the Galway City Assizes, in the stony majesty of the new and august Galway courthouse. On the morning of 29 July 1833, he shuffled, chained, with other prisoners of like background, in the passageway beneath a court he considered alien, and waited to be called up to the dock.

The Galway papers had earlier reported, as a minor item in the tapestry of conflict between small tenants and large landholders, that on 9 March 1832 a threatening notice had been pinned on the door of Hugh Larkin's landlord in East Galway, a Mr Simeon Seymour of Somerset House, 'stating that unless he complied with the Terry Alt rules and regulations, in raising wages and lowering the rent of lands, that he would meet an untimely fate'. Seymour was, according to the notice, to abide by the rules and regulations of the Terry Alt corps (a secret society of cottiers and small farmers) or suffer the consequences. This notice was posted at night, probably by Hugh, and, if not, certainly by one or other of his Terry Alt associates. When there was in Hugh's eyes no improvement in Seymour's behaviour towards his labourers and tenants, the notice was followed up by the action which had now brought Hugh to court.

The grievance of young men such as Larkin was generally to do with land and the insecure nature of their possession of it. The Ballinasloe area was the property of Lord Clancarty of the Trench family. The enormous Clancarty estates were rented out to middlemen, stock farmers of a 'careful, well-educated' class of people who 'in the process of time rose above their station'. But to the south of Laurencetown lay the estates of the Eyre family, around the village of Eyrecourt, and it was Mr John Eyre who rented over 450 acres of pasture, farming land and bog to Simeon Seymour, another 'careful, well-educated' middleman landlord, who in turn rented some of that out to smaller farmers and labourers. It was with Seymour that Larkin had dispute. Seymour had needed the labour of Hugh's late father, and now of Hugh himself, and at some seasons of Esther. For he was a grower of fine wool. The Dublin Society county survey for Galway declared that since the introduction of Leicester rams, East Galway sheep were 'not to be equalled by the general stock of long wool sheep in England'.

Hugh knew from the elders of the region, including his mother and her sisters, that, in the era of his birth and infancy, ordinary people had been able to afford to keep more livestock and eat more broadly. Small tenants could afford butter! This gala period of greater wages, with good prices for pigs and woven cloth, was the time of the Napoleonic Wars. Tenants generally were more vulnerable now than in Hugh's father's day, for in 1829 the Tory government of Great Britain had been persuaded to pass the Act of Emancipation, granting political and religious rights to Catholics and lifting the oppressive net of Acts called the Penal Laws. Now Catholics could hold office, become mayors, magistrates, officers in the army, members of the judiciary and of Parliament. Yet the physical situation of most of them remained appalling.

It was Daniel O'Connell, the Liberator, who had brought about Emancipation. He was the most renowned Irish parliamentarian of Larkin's young manhood, and the first Catholic of the modern era to sit in the House of Commons, as member for Clare. O'Connell was a rare and accidental beast – for he was a Catholic landlord even before Emancipation. His home in the remote glen of Derrynane in Kerry had been inherited from an uncle, Maurice (Hunting Cap) O'Connell. The eighteenth-century O'Connells had saved their land by entering into a symbiotic relationship with the local Anglo-Irish gentry, for whom they smuggled Continental luxuries, particularly brandy.

O'Connell was in his late fifties in the year of Larkin's crime, but ageless to the imagination of Hugh. He was a brilliant demagogue, an instinctive politician with that gift for gesture so beloved in the Irish world. He possessed the open, pleasant, meaty face which would be seen later in the century in Irish-American Democrat party bosses and in which geniality, compassion and opportunism all had equal play. His achievement of Emancipation meant more for the small, energetic, Catholic middle class than for the poorer Larkins and Tullys. But Hugh's family considered Emancipation the foreshadowing of deliverance. They each had for this turbulent, populist invoker of hope a love and piety usually reserved for members of the Holy Family. 'Everything and everybody has a party,' O'Connell had declared, 'save only the people. I go to Parliament to form the party of the people.' This might be considered a flatulent claim, but O'Connell was perhaps the first European to build a mass movement from such sentiments.

During the Emancipation struggle, which Hugh well remembered, a peasant could belong to the Catholic Association, the organisational structure behind Emancipation, by contributing one penny a month. Outside Clontuskert parish chapel after Mass on the first Sunday of the month, Hugh's parents, like Esther Tully's, had in the 1820s donated their minimum penny – 'the Catholic tax', it was named. After Emancipation, people were persuaded to continue the payments towards the Liberator's upkeep as a parliamentarian – 'the O'Connell Tribute', or the 'Repeal tax'. For O'Connell now held out the prospect of the repeal of the 1800 Act of Union between Ireland and England. Unjust rents would be swept away, he argued, tenants would have fixity of tenure, Irish spinning and weaving would be protected and encouraged, the narrow franchise would be expanded, the Chartist-inspired secret ballot would be introduced to prevent landlords terrorising their tenant voters, and Irish landlords would be taxed to support the poor. To such causes, Esther and Hugh, even as Hugh planned his crime, joyfully gave their monthly penny.

What Hugh and others relished about the Liberator was his style. A proclamation of 13 January 1831 from the then Lord Lieutenant, the Marquess of Anglesey, forbade associations under any names. 'I'll make myself an association!' said O'Connell, and tried it, and was arrested. One of his old friends, arrested with him at the Liberator's house in Merrion Square, Dublin, said, 'Please let me have a hackney, I have the gout.'

'No,' O'Connell told him, 'you and I shall walk. And the city shall know that I am arrested like a housebreaker.'

O'Connell was the Chieftain, the King of the Beggars, and held up the palpable vision of Irish independence as the priest held aloft at the climax of the liturgy the all-healing, all-consoling Bread of Life. His rhetoric evoked images of the humblest inheriting the earth – a proposal which fired Hugh.

But, at the same time as Catholic Emancipation, the British government disenfranchised many farmers by increasing the property basis under which the Irish could vote. Previously the holding of a yearly lease of 40 shillings (that is, £2) was the qualification for the right to vote. To vote after Emancipation, a tenant had to hold a lease valued at £10. This reduced the number of voters to a mere 92,000 males, barely more than 1 per cent of the population. It was for the benefit of this 1 per cent that Ireland was largely governed. Most fatally for many small Irish farmers, and indirectly for cottiers like Larkin, it took away the political motives landlords had to keep 40-shilling tenants thickly settled on their land. With a non-secret voting system, the landlord being entitled to look over his tenants' shoulders and see how they voted, 40-shilling tenants had been easy to exploit as a voting block. Now these smaller tenants had lost their political value.

All the more dispensable were people like Larkin, not 40-shilling tenants to begin with. Almost two thirds of all Irish came from such families as his, and in Connacht, Larkin's Ireland, four out of five belonged to what the census of 1841 would call Class III families: people 'without capital, in either money, land or acquired knowledge'. Larkin and his wife were renters from Seymour of conacre, the most casually held, least tenure-secure form of holding land. Larkin and Tully depended on conacre, and were no doubt pleased that they stood, however tenuously, above the very lowest of society, the *spalpeens*, in Irish 'penny-scythes', living on wasteland in the mountains or in bogs, and emerging to get work for a short time in the summer months.

Conacre was generally a little plot of an eighth of an acre, although sometimes as extensive as 2 acres. It was rented for one season to grow potatoes, or sometimes oats. (Its other names were 'dairy land', 'rood land', 'quarter-ground', 'score-ground', 'sniggers'.) The potato was at least an easy crop for those who tended it – 'the lazy crop', it was called, with prejudicial results for the Irish. It did not require people to buy or use any sophisticated reaping or milling tools. It could be planted in 'lazy rows', the seedlings laid in a line and covered with sods from either side of that line. The flowers of the potato bush were sometimes ecstatically praised for their beauty, and the potato itself was all the more lovely for representing survival. It was 'generous and cheerful, laughing at us from the head of the table', recalled one small farmer. The way it was grown permitted men from all over Ireland to plant it and then go away as deck cargo on ships from Galway and Westport to work on the English harvest, coming back in time to dig up their own crop. Hugh Larkin was saved such journeys by the fact that he lived in Ireland's fine wool area, which required hands the year round. His labour for Seymour was fuelled by what grew on his conacre.

Some of the coarser potatoes were grown as stock feed, and therefore in part for sale – potato jobbers were willing to pay the grower out early, to exploit the smallholder's desire to raise money for a wedding, or arrears of rent, or journeys to see a husband or son in his cell in Galway. Apart from a few seedlings needed for the next season's planting, potatoes could be stored in pits, but deteriorated quickly; though easier to grow than wheat, oats or corn, potatoes could not be kept from year to year. Hence the 1837 Report on the Poor of Ireland estimated that even with conacre 2,385,000 persons in Ireland were in a state of semi-starvation every summer, as, with their seedlings planted, they waited for the new potato crop to appear at the end of the season. Conacre (as well as paid labour, and perhaps an item of livestock such as a pig) was essential for the hungry transit from spring to autumn. That little plot lay between Hugh and Esther, and destruction.

Like the small tenants, Seymour and his friends also had a nostalgia for past boom times, and their properties carried debts happily incurred earlier, often by their fathers, and now annually accruing. This caused Seymour and other local landholders, at dinner parties, at race picnics, or within their Masonic Lodges in Ballinasloe, Athlone or Roscommon, to discuss the benefits of clearing the peasantry from as much of their land as feasible, and turning it over to pasture. Ireland in 1833 was thus a country of marginal peasants and squeezed landlords. Breeders of fine wool like Seymour might have been somewhat better off than many, because of the machine-loom factories burgeoning in northern England. And for the present there were social and moral restrictions on savage and widespread eviction – it was considered by most local landholders the sort of callousness which was exercised at arm's length from London or the pleasure spots of Europe through agents and bailiffs by that despised creature, the absentee landlord. But any pretext to be quit of a troublesome, threatening cottier would have appealed to Seymour.

It is reported that when Seymour found out about Larkin's involvement in the local, secret Terry Alt organisation he had dismissed him as a labourer. Larkin had walked away from Mr Seymour in fear that he might now be evicted from his plot of land, which he paid for through his labour and occasional cash. In sacking him, Seymour was threatening to make him a ghost in the landscape, a wanderer upon whom hunger and death attended. An English gentleman who visited nearby Ballinasloe that year, Henry Inglis, found wage rates desperately low for the itinerant labouring class, to which Seymour now threatened to consign Hugh: 'eight pence without diet was the highest rate of wages: and many laboured for sixpence; and even at this low rate, full employment was not to be had'.

Need, anger at an ignored warning, anxiety, pride and peasant politics drove Hugh towards the coming tragedy. But so did Irish history. The defeat of deposed King of England James II and his Irish Catholic allies at the Boyne River in 1690 is the core event in the long struggle between Catholics and Protestants. The victors were the Protestant army of James's son-in-law, King William of Orange, who had been handed the British throne by Parliament in 1688; his reign was confirmed at the Boyne. William's triumph made the final collapse of James's forces inevitable, and to prevent any further Catholic uprising in support of William, a series of Penal Laws were passed in the years following, aimed at keeping the native Irish powerless, poor and stupid. Some of this legislation was not to be repealed until Catholic Emancipation in 1829.

Under the Penal Code the Catholic Irish were barred from serving as officers in the army or navy, or from practising as lawyers – a profession for which they would later prove to have an appetite. They could hold no civic post or office at all under the Crown. At the death of a Catholic landowner his land was to be divided amongst all his sons unless the eldest became a Protestant, in which case he could inherit the whole. A Catholic could not own a horse worth more than £5, was prohibited from living within five miles of an incorporated town and from attending or keeping schools. Hugh, who like most Irish was aggrieved at his own unschooled condition even after Emancipation, saw his ignorance as yet another result of an unjust society.

The practice of the Catholic faith had been proscribed in penal times, too, and even though primitive Catholic chapels were permitted to be erected throughout the eighteenth century, the old, more august churches now belonged to the Church of Ireland, the religion of the Protestant establishment. Hugh was raised with tales of the hunting of priests for sport, and of Masses said by priests on Mass stones – suitable flat rocks – in the open countryside, lookouts being posted to warn of approaching army units. The priesthood was legalised in 1782, but the memory of religious persecution was fresh, particularly in a society in which the aged took energetically to their role as story-tellers.

Edmund Burke, eighteenth-century orator and Member of the House of Commons, fulminated against the Penal Code as 'a machine as well fitted for the oppression, impoverishment and degradation of the people, and the debasement of human nature itself, as ever proceeded from the perverted ingenuity of man'. Despite the letter of the law, a small class of Catholic merchants and professionals had arisen, but, even after Emancipation, men of Hugh's class still felt that something like Penal Laws operated in the countryside in which all relationships were marked one way or another by religious bigotry and in which the court system supported whatever a landlord chose to do. The landlord was upheld by law, was validated in the seizing of livestock and furniture against 'a hanging gale' – a lateness in paying the heavy twice-yearly rent – and was supported if he evicted tenants.

In Hugh's era, one English visitor claimed that *droit de seigneur* – the right of the landlord to deflower the peasant bride before she was handed back to her husband – existed on many large estates. There was also the common requirement before marriage that permission be sought, cap-in-hand, at the big house. The insolence of the gentleman landlord was typified by the practice by which his carriage was often preceded by footmen who whipped peasants and their carts into the ditches to make way for the master. Hugh had also heard of, if not experienced, gentry who required their peasantry to hide before the landlord's carriage came along, lest the gentry should have to look at the facial dirt and hunger of the bedraggled. But whether or not Seymour himself, the substantial pastoralist, followed such feudal practice or not, his rents were considered exorbitant by the peasantry, and to Hugh his face was that of the oppressor, the depriver, the apostate, the occupying power. Thus, in his daily life, Hugh still practised the habits the Penal Laws had created, the habits of powerlessness, masked feelings, apparent subjection, slyness, and dreams of vengeance. Since there was nothing in society to help him towards his rights, since he could seek from neither court nor landlord help in adjusting the balance of the world, he turned to the secret companies of other men, to men of similar mind to himself.

On the night of Hugh's attack against the Seymours, Hugh, Esther and Mrs Larkin ate the accustomed peasant dinner, sitting in a circle on stools or on the floor around a basket of potatoes, with a mug of buttermilk at the side of each of the diners and a little bowl of salt conveniently placed. This sort of meal was commonly called 'dip-at-the-stool'. Hugh and Esther peeled the jackets off the potatoes with their thumbnail, grown long to fulfil the task. 'So expert were the people at peeling potatoes in this way', said one commentator, 'that nobody with a knife and fork could divest a potato of its jacket half so quickly.' Fragments of potato, sips of buttermilk, were fed to infants.

'The Irish diet,' wrote a modern expert, 'while monotonous and perhaps tasteless, was probably richer than all but the most advanced regions of Europe.' Except in summer when potatoes were scarce, an Irish male such as Hugh Larkin had an intake of over 3,800 calories per day from eating potatoes, and was provided with an extraordinary armoury of vitamins, twice the recommended modern intake of protein, calcium and iron, and a low fat content. Potatoes were the only cheap crop which could support life when fed to a peasant as the sole item of diet. They possessed too 'a capacity not to cloy the appetite' and were also suited to the conditions of land tenure, under which the tenant could not afford to build barns or sheds in which to store food.

The choicest varieties of potato, the 'apple' and the 'cup', were the most savoury but were not as enduring or as resistant to the potato disease called curl as was the 'lumper'. But whatever variety, the potato helped combat in Ireland the common scourges of hunger found elsewhere in the world – scurvy, pellagra and malnutrition blindness. Pellagra, a Vitamin B deficiency disease which begins by affecting the skin, was common in the south of the United States, and in European countries where maize was the staple.

A commentator has argued that the potato was looked upon askance in a Protestant country such as Scotland because it had not been mentioned and sanctioned in the King James Bible. In Ireland, where amongst the Catholic peasantry dogma was more important than the King James version, there was no such inhibition.

The family pig, bought each year and fattened on the coarser lumper variety of potatoes grown near the cottage, was also present for Hugh's last meal at home. The young French traveller Alexis de Tocqueville observed of cabins like the Larkins', 'The Irish pig lends himself to the innocent games of his host with a perfect charm. It is not rare to see the children of the house hanging on his tail.' *Paddy's pigs*, as the English music-halls had it! The pig was not a resident of the house for the sake of providing the cottier with bacon for himself and his family, but so that, in the lean summer months, fattened up, it could be sold. With the cash it fetched, the Larkins bought *their* summer oatmeal.

Inside Hugh, the angry intent lay fixed in place. If Mrs Larkin and Esther suspected what he had in mind that night they would have been bent on dissuading him. But Larkin clung to his male purpose and to the brothers of his sworn society. The threatening notice had already been posted on Seymour's door. The next customary level of protest was the armed invasion, and the utterance of face-to-face threats.

Hugh had grown up with the tradition of secret societies of Catholic tenants. Variously named – Whiteboys, Rockites, Ribbon societies – they had existed in his childhood to threaten both the landlord and the bailiff who evicted, and any tenant rash enough to take up an evictee's house and land. When Hugh was ten or eleven years old, the 28th Regiment of Foot was stationed in Woodford, East Galway, to protect landlords, agents and others against the activism of secret rural groups. Leaders of such protests had been hanged or sent to Australia. The tale of the Ribbonman protester Ned Lohan of Ballymacward, three parishes to the west, hanged near his house in front of his wife and three daughters in 1820, would certainly have been canvassed around the hearths of Hugh's childhood.

Now a fresh age of peasant uncertainty had produced a new generation of what were called Ribbon societies in East Galway. The terms 'Ribbonism' and 'Ribbonmen' were titles of convenience, however. The true Ribbon organisation, with its secret oaths, passwords, ribbons and cells of no more than thirty-six men, had had a rough national structure and had been made up of workers from the cities. But in the west of Ireland the word Ribbonism was a portmanteau term for any act or assault arising from peasant or small farmer grievances.

To confuse matters, the *Galway Advertiser* also used the term 'Terry Alts' to mean the same as Ribbonmen. The Terry Alts were a regional branch of Ribbonism, and the name derived from a particular Ribbon assault in 1829 on a landlord's agent named Edwin Synge in Corofin, County Clare. Synge was attacked leaving church, and his servant shot dead. A witness said that the attacker had been wearing a straw hat. An innocent shoemaker named Terry Alt, in the vicinity and wearing a straw hat, was immediately arrested. The local groups of oath-taking young men did honour to the shoemaker by signing their threatening notices and statements with his name.

Indeed, at some stages of 1832 the *Galway Advertiser* had been in a position to fill an entire column of its broadsheet with notices of Terry Alt warnings and attacks.

On the night of 13 March, the house of Pat Morgan, of Clontuskert . . . was attacked by an armed party, who swore him to surrender his present holding to former occupier, and beat him dreadfully for not complying with a former notice . . . the house of Thomas Madden, of Skycur, was attacked by an armed party who fired some shots and demanded money, which they forcibly had obtained for the purpose as they stated of enabling them to employ Council, support witnesses &c. on behalf of unfortunate men, now in custody in Galway Gaol.

It is more than possible that Hugh participated in one of these two local actions. And his wife and mother, who at least suspected Hugh's Ribbon tendencies, must have feared that he himself might soon be in Galway gaol, in need of 'Council'.

Somewhere around Lismany, Hugh had hidden a clandestinely manufactured pike or a musket stolen in a Ribbon raid on a house. On the night, he went out to fetch it, loaded it and started for Seymour's house, barely a mile west across the fields from Lismany crossroads. He lacked shoes, since Ireland was a nation of the bare-footed. He moved with a conviction that his title to Hy Many was better than Mr Seymour's, and that title would be reasserted tonight.

Hugh and his fellow Ribbonmen saw the landlord not only as a potential, individual enemy but as an enemy to culture and religion as well. Though there were some Catholic landlords – the Liberator himself was one – to most peasants landlords were an incarnation of Protestantism, and of the entire threatening order of things. Seymour therefore stood for the other great grievance of Hugh's era: Emancipation had not brought an end to the system of tithes, a tax on the crops, livestock and earnings of Catholics that went to the upkeep of the Established Church – the Church of Ireland and its ministers and doctrines – which Hugh considered heretical. Most progressive British opinion was by now opposed to the system. But the issue was still being fought on the ground in Ireland, and sometimes detachments of the British army were marched off to villages for futile and bloody confrontations about overdue tithe payments. Sometimes, too, the local grandee added his clout to the collection of tithes. 'Lord Courtown's agent', *The Times* correspondent would report in Hugh's last year in Ireland, 'has demanded from His Lordship's tenantry the arrears of the tithes due to the Rev. Roger Owens for the years 1831, 1832 and 1833 . . . In case of noncompliance, he has threatened that ejectments will be served forthwith . . . and the occupants turned out into the road.' The tithe proctors, who represented the local Church of Ireland minister and visited tenants to assess this tax, were oppressive figures in the landscape, agents of the alien system at whose apex stood tonight's target: the landlord.

Our knowledge of Hugh's crime is a little inexact – did he blacken his face, did he wear a white shirt over his head? We would have known all the alleged details of Hugh's 'outrage', including the precise night, had nineteenth-century court records not been destroyed by fire when the

Dublin Four Courts were mined by Republican forces in 1922. As for constabulary reports, it was only after the Royal Irish Constabulary was founded in 1836 that all rural 'outrages' were reported in some detail to Dublin Castle.

But somewhere on the dark walk from Lismany, either back where he collected his weapon or near the small intervening hill called Atteepree-haun or Crowsnest, Larkin met up with other armed Terry Alts, and together they advanced on Seymour's home to put their landlord in his place, entering through a gate in the high garden wall at the rear of the house and gathering themselves in the yard by the kitchen for the imminent uttering of serious threats. Their aim was not the taking of property, but the adjustment of a basic social lesion. Theirs were crimes of protest, very different from the crime of stealing a horse or a pig. Hugh's kind of protest was part of a tapestry of popular and protest movements throughout nineteenth-century Britain and Europe. Under the influence of his subtle peasant culture, and by temperament, Hugh was no member of a criminal class.

The party of Terry Alts arrived at the back of Seymour's property, a two-storeyed, functionally designed structure spacious enough to bear the name Somerset House. Because Larkin had a grievance against Seymour, he was theoretically violating Terry Alt guidelines by participating in this local affair himself, but an intimate sense of personal wrong often guaranteed such violations. Somerset House still stands; the path by which the party came, the gate by which they entered, the back door they approached, all are confidently and credibly pointed to today.

The party broke down the back door. *Assaulting habitation and being in arms* – as the charge against Hugh would have it. The noise and shouts brought servants and the Seymour family to the back of the house, but Seymour himself was not with them. Mrs Seymour faced them – a characteristic landlord's wife, rugged of soul, unlikely to admit her fear. Given the earlier threat hammered to her door, she had pistols handy but may not have seized them up in time. Hugh and others shouted that she was hiding her husband, but that proved wrong. The sight of this familiar woman, of her gestures of command, her body wrapped in fabrics unaffordable by Esther, her mouth full of the threats of the law, very likely betrayed Hugh, however disguised, into angry exchanges. He and the others assured Mrs Seymour that this was the final warning. According to the oral testimony, a male servant of the household, a man named Walsh, recognised Larkin and would later, under threat or inducement, identify him at trial.

The only damage that had been done was the breaking-down of the door. But for Mrs Seymour and her children there had been distress and fear. She would have had some certainty they did not mean her immediate harm. Though there had been a case in the 1820s when a group in Cork had descended on a convoy of coaches carrying soldiers' wives and raped them, an assault against women was alien to Ribbonmen, since they believed that they must act according to conscience. However, as Larkin and the others withdrew across the fields they must have known that they were now in more peril than the Seymours.

When Seymour returned home, and his shaken wife relayed the threats to him, he rode off to swear a charge against Larkin. There was a period in the early 1830s when local 'outrages' required a garrison to be stationed in the village of Laurencetown, some 5 miles down the road. So either to Laurencetown a little way south or to bigger Ballinasloe, a little further north, Mr Seymour went for help. The English visitor Inglis would find 'an encampment of troops from Athlone' in Ballinasloe that year, 'because of recent Ribbon outrages'.

Against Ribbonism of Hugh's brand, the authorities could employ the Whiteboy Acts of 1767 and 1777, which strictly defined and punished illegal assembly and the sort of angry protest Hugh had just made. Punishable too were the administration of illegal oaths and the posting of threatening notices. Of one at least of those charges, it seems, Hugh was also guilty.

A military detachment and county constables marched on Lismany and, surrounding Larkin in the fields, arrested him in a mêlée of roars, blows, punishment with the butts of muskets. They chained him down before a watchful population. Men shouted curses in Irish, the Larkin women keened. In the eyes of Esther Larkin must have risen the awareness that a special kind of widowhood was about to descend upon her – that which derived from execution or transportation.

Hugh's prospects as he was manhandled on to a barge for Ballinasloe – trees suitable for hanging him being pointed out to him along the canal – were not bright. At the recent Kilkenny assizes, two men had been sentenced to be hanged immediately for Whiteboyism; two others were to be hanged on a date to be decided, and twelve more to be transported. Men and women charged by magistrates and on their way to trial would be facing a jury not of their peers, but one selected from the county ascendancy. Even though Catholics could now serve on the grand juries made up of county property owners, the county sheriff could select a jury to his liking, and one very sensitive to Ribbon threats.

Hugh spent weeks if not months in prison in Galway, living a communal life in the stone wards. These county penitentiaries were run by governors under the appointment of the Superintendent of Prisons. In one sense they were private enterprise operations, the governor excellently placed to make deals with the contractors of Galway for the supply of goods, sometimes at inflated prices, or to over-order or pare rations. He could also rent his own apartments, or spacious cells on the debtors' side of the gaol, to affluent prisoners, who were able to furnish them more or less at will. If everyone from the matron of female convicts to the turnkeys and the porters wished to exact bribes and a part of all goods and cash that entered prison, there was nothing to prevent it.

The common criminals in the communal holding pens or wards sat, conversed, ate and slept on straw of varying quality. A prisoner from the country such as Hugh Larkin might have found the companionship of Galway city pickpockets and small criminals in the wards undesirable, but there were many men from the country, and other Ribbonmen from areas and protests different from Hugh's. These included a young man named John Hessian and two brothers, the Strahanes, gamekeepers, all future Australians.

Waiting, the common prisoners conversed in Irish, for in western Ireland more than 80 per cent of the people still spoke the native language. In Irish, the Gaelic language, men from one ward might cry to women in another. Their cries of grief and separation rose up the walls.

The annual crisis of 12 July, the Glorious Twelfth, on which the Orange Lodges paraded, celebrating the Protestant victory of the Boyne in 1690, came round as Hugh Larkin awaited trial. Sir William Gossett, Senior Constable of Ireland, this year tried to dissuade the Lodges from marching. But Orange fear of a Papist takeover of civic institutions, sustained in Ulster into modern times, energised the Orange Lodges to march in the July of Hugh's imprisonment, celebrating their ancestors' valour with banging of drum, jauntiness of pipe and flute, and some gestures of threat.

The robust Orange pipe music, behind which lay a ferocious pride and anxiety, would have penetrated the stones of the county gaol as Hugh filled his time with regret and discreet, impotent promises to Esther, come 35 miles at great expense to see him, and to his widowed mother and Esther's brothers. In his straw-strewn ward, he may have been jigging one of his infant sons for the last time on his knee as Orangemen processed rowdily in Galway.

On 18 July, the *Times* correspondent attributed the general peace of the day to the 'prudent advice of Roman Catholic clergy'. But an affray developed in Coote Hill, County Cavan. There the Orange procession turned riotous and four Catholics were killed. As often happened in Ireland, the police magistrates had gone missing from the town on the day of the march, and remained in hiding for some days after. Three days later, the 12 July killings of Catholics were dismally avenged. 'An innocent Protestant' was beset by 200 Catholics and beaten to death.

The Englishman Inglis, travelling in Ireland that summer, talked of 'the military air' of courts: 'the armed police in military uniform, guarding the avenues, and stationed throughout the court'. Justice, after the waiting, was brisk though. The young French nobleman de Tocqueville, journeying in Ireland two summers later, wrote in some astonishment: 'The same man was often indicted by the Grand Jury, found guilty by the Petty Jury, and condemned by a judge in the course of an hour.' Larkin seemed to get that sort of treatment, and after the jury had found him guilty of 'assaulting habitation and being in arms', Justice Torrens, presiding judge at the Assizes, whose journeys around Ireland for court-sittings permitted him to indulge a passion for fox-hunting, told Hugh that his behaviour deserved a lifetime sentence of transportation. By comparison the manslaughterer Bartholomew O'Donnell was sentenced to only twelve months' hard labour, and the disparity seems at first confusing. But O'Donnell had been implicated in a faction fight: the death of a participant at an all-in brawl between clans, rival parishes or baronies at a county or local fair was often considered bad luck and a result of exuberance. 'An English murder is a private act,' said Inglis, 'perpetrated by some ruffian for the sake of gain.' In Ireland, homicide was committed 'by a crowd of demi-barbarians . . . who have no other reason for fighting, than because one half of the number are called O'Sullivan and the other O' something else'.

Justice Torrens, inured to the grief of the relatives of prisoners, to the keening of women like Esther and Widow Larkin, and to the closed hostile faces of men, noted that the number of prisoners had been small, and that there seemed to be diminished unrest in Galway compared to the previous summer.

The nationalist *Galway Free Press* of Wednesday 31 July remarked, after mentioning Larkin, that 'There were no other trials or convictions of any importance with the exception of one, wherein a man named Hessian was found guilty of Terry-Altism and sentenced to immediate transportation for life'. The *Free Press* continued: 'After sentence was pronounced he [Hessian] was instantly removed from the dock and conveyed under strong escort of the 60th Rifles, to Gort.' But Larkin and the Strahanes remained in Galway. Removal of Hessian to the orderly garrison town of

Gort might have occurred owing to the risk of disturbances and even rescue attempts by his friends and family.

Because of the contempt of the Irish peasant for the court system, the accusation that one man might have informed on another was, and is to this day, a serious matter. According to a modern member of the Larkin family, in one version of Hugh's story a shadow of that accusation hangs over Hugh himself. In this account, a well-regarded Terry Alt named John Lohan is said to have fulfilled his oath in the case of Hugh's grievance and come down from Ahascragh, well to the north of Ballinasloe, to attack Seymour's property. For Ribbon oaths might include a clause like the following: 'I hereby swear to go 15 miles on foot or 21 on horseback, when called upon by a brother upon lawful occasion or unlawful.'

I was told that Larkin was the junior member of what could be called a troika of East Galway Ribbonmen: Lohan, Coonahan, Larkin. Ribbonism was an abomination not only to landlords but to the parish priest of Hugh's parish of Clontuskert, the Pope having condemned such secret societies in a decree of 1825. Thus, according to this version, in 1832 Coonahan was sent to the army in Ballinasloe with a note from the priest, and on arrival was shackled, marched back home and lynched in his garden.

Lohan is said to have been a party to an earlier Whiteboy outrage. An apparently empty house had been set afire, and a servant in a rear room had been accidentally killed. Afterwards, Lohan spoke to Larkin about the incident and expressed guilt and regret. When Larkin were captured, transported in chains by canal barge to Ballinasloe, struck, bruised, threatened with imminent lynching and revenge against his family, news of Lohan's involvement in the earlier house-burning was forced from Larkin. On Hugh's evidence then, Lohan was at some stage taken back to his village of Ahascragh and hanged, and then Hugh himself received a life sentence. 'I wanted to make sure you knew what a terrible place Ireland was then before I told you this story,' a modern Larkin explained to me.

But there is no evidence for this account. No Coonahan was hanged in the early 1830s – it would have made the Galway *and* Dublin papers had he been. If a Lohan from Ahascragh accompanied Larkin to the back door of Somerset House, there is no record of his trial or of his public execution, as again there would certainly have been. He is absent from Hugh's Assizes and those for the previous year. Some Ribbonmen of course simply vanished, summarily conscripted into one of the overseas battalions of that very 60th Regiment of Foot which provided the escort for Hessian on the way to Gort. But they were not put into the 60th if they had caused a death.

And the idea generated by this story that Larkin was one of a small body of East Galway Ribbonmen is not borne out by the facts. In April 1833, there was so much Ribbon activity in the barony of Longford, Hugh's neighbourhood, that Lord Clancarty, the Church of Ireland Bishop of Clonfert and the local magistrates sought the imposition on the area of the Coercion Act, enabling summary arrest and punishment. In Eyrecourt, only six miles from Lismany, the rebellious feeling of tenants was described as 'formidable if not checked in time'.

It is possible that the tale of the East Galway Ribbonman Ned Lohan, condemned to death at the Galway Assizes of August 1820 and hanged in his own village, was grafted over time on to the Larkin one – and an Irish historian I spoke to told me that similar graftings occurred in oral history. Therefore, Hugh's record, however sullied from Justice Torrens's point of view, remains utterly unblemished from the point of view of Terry Alts.

Hugh was by now aching for familial squalor. He would never again feel the warmth of cottage peat smoke or smell the turf fire, turf being a large element in the peasant view of earthly paradise. Turf or peat, cut with spades called loys, is composed of ancient trees, fallen into Ireland's primeval swamps and partially carbonised, on their way to becoming coal. There was a bog a short walk to the south of Lismany, and a succession of them near the Lawrence estate of Belview, not more than 3 miles down the road from Larkin's cottage, near the village of Laurencetown. Convivial turf warmed the Irish family in a land where the woods were owned by landlords and unavailable as legal fuel. It filled Hugh's chimney-less cabin with smoke, rendering clothing disreputable. De Tocqueville remarked that he would have thought himself back in the company of his friends the Iroquois of Upper New York, except that the interior of the Iroquois habitations had a smoke hole: 'which gives a decided advantage to the architecture of the Iroquois'.

But all of it, house, fire, peat-reek, pig, child, song, sportiveness, painfully dear to Hugh! His condition was captured in a Gaelic song about an imprisoned Ribbonman:

O a year from tomorrow I left my own people,
I went down to Ardpatrick, the ribbons in my hat.
Some Whiteboys were there then, they were fighting the English
And now I'm sad and lonely in the jail of Clonmel.
My bridle and saddle are gone from me this long time,

My hurley long hidden behind my own door,
My slither's being played by the boys of the valley
The one I could hit a goal with as good as another.

One of the central rituals Larkin was leaving and might miss most was the wake of the dead, of which modern Irish wakes are merely a shadow. In an early chapter of a didactic novel published in Dublin that year, *Irish Cottagers*, a Scots land steward asked an Irishman whether at a particular wake there had been a lecture from a minister of religion. He was told instead that first and foremost the dead were honoured with drink and games named Five and Forty and Hunt the Slipper, and that the wake was held as much for the sake of courting as for mourning. The Scot asked whether all this profligacy went on in the house where the dead man lay. He was told a 'dead wall' was placed between the corpse and the party. As for the widow and family in their grief, no one 'hindered them from crying their full . . . and a good right they had to cry'.

Two years past, the Archbishop of Dublin had forbidden 'disorderly vigils for the dead' but said that 'they are to be gradually abolished'. That unusually lenient adverb, 'gradually', indicated how endemic was this great ritual of riotous mourning, song, licensed drunkenness, sexual playfulness and renewal. Some of Hugh's and Esther's courting was inevitably conducted at wakes, 'where the young of both sexes meet, and the night is generally consumed in drinking whiskey, smoking tobacco and playing different games of romps, etc.' A wake game named Flimsy-flamsy, in which girls sat in turns on a man's knee and were asked, 'Flimsy-flamsy, who's your fancy?' was singled out for special clerical condemnation, but Hugh and Esther were likely to have played it.

Of another game named Boat, the antiquarian Prim wrote that it 'was joined in by men and women who all acted a very obscene part which cannot be described'. In Drawing the Ship out of the Mud, men appeared before the rest of the group totally naked. Mock Marriages, Building the Fort and Hold the Light were other games Hugh and Esther may have played when separated from the dead by a mere screen.

Larkin was to be deprived of a landscape of mysteries too, some kindly, some more threatening, but all familiar. A spirit world – quite separate from the spiritual cosmos of Catholicism – abutted upon the seen world of pasture, wood, bog and farmland. Hugh and Esther knew which types of bush were believed to be sacred to the fairies and to be left severely alone in the midst of cultivated fields. Johann Kohl, a German visitor, noticed that although the Irish would remove wood from a landlord's plantation, they never took wood from the growth that covered 'fairy-mounds', pre-historic mound tombs. The water of holy wells protected the individual soul from curses or fairy tricks, and from *Geasa Dravidacht*, the sorcery of the Druids.

Hugh's cherished landscape did not lack known perils then. A person betrayed into praising a child or an animal needed to add, 'God save him', and spit immediately after. Women incurred ill fortune if they did not sweep the floor towards the door; candles were not to be lit before making the sign of the cross; an oatcake was not to be consumed before a piece was nipped off and thrown away. The worst danger was that changelings, homunculi or imitation humans might be left in the place of children who had been abducted by fairies. To 'put the fairy out' of a child required harsh treatment. Eight-year-old Ann Moorhouse of Rathvilly, County Carlow, would die in 1837 as a result of bluestone administered to her by a servant who believed her to be a fairy. But all these – curses, fairies, changelings – were *known* risks and they could be wisely combated.

And through tales of other places carried home to Ireland by old soldiers, sailors or itinerant workers, a man like Hugh implicitly knew that whatever his conditions of land tenure were, a peculiar grace reigned at the Irish hearth, while the outer world was vicious. O'Connell had reflected on this when he said that despite the crowded conditions of the Irish household, incest was extremely rare – any man accused of it became ostracised and universally condemned. In Lismany Hugh knew where he was with sexual morality. Despite all the concerns of reforming visitors to Ireland about earthy liberties at wakes, the famed traveller de Tocqueville, dining with the Catholic Bishop of Ossory, was told that twenty years in the confessional had made the bishop aware that sexual misconduct was very rare, and amongst married women almost unknown. Yet de Tocqueville would find that virtue was exercised with a high degree of rustic informality. Of the west of Ireland he would write: 'I have seen young girls bathing naked in the sea a short distance from young men.'

Now Hugh suspected that, in passing on a ship through some blazing latitude, he would lose the balance of good order and good fun, the complex of teasing ardour, wild games and securely fixed behaviour. And lose too the outward sign of that viability, the sacraments of the Church, and all the markers of his year. He would lose 1 February, St Brigid's, when crosses of rushes or straw were hung over any small outhouse or *scalp* that contained seed, and also in the cabin for health and fertility of humans and livestock. He would lose 1 May, when tenancies began and ended, and cattle and sheep were joyfully transferred from their byres to the open fields. He was slated for a Christ-less place where all these customs and calendar references, sacred and profane, would be either reversed – summer being winter – or meaningless.

On a Monday morning, 19 August, Hugh and 21 others were taken in the clothes in which they had been arrested out of their wards, chained at wrist and ankle and then to other weeping, cursing or bewildered transportees, and placed in four carts, all under the supervision of a detachment of the 30th Regiment. Like a similar procession witnessed two years before in the square outside Galway gaol, the procession of carts moved slowly, the military escort crowded in by weeping relatives, wives and children, wives being permitted to raise infants for a last paternal kiss, but all others being kept back, moaning and cursing and crying farewells. The hope Esther had harboured that a ship would not be available to take Hugh off proved futile. In fact the carts of the Galway men were merely joining an already existing convoy of Mayo transportees from the gaol at Castlebar.

Sometimes wives tried to walk along with the column, persuading constables and soldiers to permit a last tearful intimacy. But the Esthers of Ireland soon enough had to turn back, to go back to their landlords, work and children. Returned to her parish of Clontuskert, Esther needed to go on labouring for the Seymours and sometimes for the Lawrences of nearby Belview, from whom Laurencetown took its name. Hugh's mother and wife had not been thrown out of their cottage, a sign both of humanity on Seymour's part, and maybe even of a fear of Ribbonman reprisal.

That same summer and early autumn cholera had appeared in Connacht. The New South Wales emigration agent for Galway, Mr Logan, competing with the far greater, mass-volume emigrant trade to the United States, chose this season of epidemic, hardship and political turbulence to advocate emigration to Australia. He submitted letters, supposedly written by Australian settlers, which spoke of fine weather, prime beef costing only 2 pence a pound, and an acre of land 5 shillings. But Hugh was facing involuntary emigration.

Larkin and his company travelled about a hundred miles south to the Cobh of Cork. Apparently Hugh's longest journey yet, these miles were minor compared with the distances which waited to be traversed. In Gort the convoy of carts had collected young John Hessian. Already in the carts were the two brothers Strahane, John and Michael, twenty-four and twenty-two years, both single, guilty of the Ribbon offence of illegally storing arms – as Galway gamekeepers, they had been conveniently placed to do so. Patrick Qualters, 28-year-old father of two, who had posted a Ribbon notice, was also on the chain, with Darby Goode, a farm servant, and Patrick Kelley, both of whom had stolen firearms. The sentences of these five were only seven years each: they might have had the notion of an ultimate return to Galway. But they must have known in their blood that the resources required for a return over that global distance were not within their reach.

Others amongst the chained Galway men had committed minor and conventional crimes. James McKeon, 34-year-old shoemaker, had received stolen goods; John Allen, groom, and an English cabinet-maker named George Botham had stolen cloth and flannel. John Concannon took a sheep (life sentence); Patrick Healy, unemployed weaver and father of two, likewise. Edward Coghlan was a young forger; 14-year-old farrier and groom Timothy Cusack had lifted cash; George Hefferman, a butcher, carried a life sentence for manslaughter; and William Kelley, a shepherd, life for stealing a horse.

Their path skirted the limestone desert, the Burren of Clare on one side and the Slieve Aughty Mountains on the other, through Ennis itself, past the Gaelic ruins of Bunratty, and over the Shannon. At night they were accommodated in county or city gaols. Their jokes, curses, coughs and prayers were absorbed by the stone walls of counties previously unknown to most of them. They were by turns watchful for improbable escape, cowed by the guards, chastened by the miles of the journey, and the harm chains did to wrist and ankle. And though Cusack the 14-year-old farrier must have affected worldliness, he needed the protection of older men. There is a mass of evidence that Irish rural first offenders did not practise gaol rape. But blows, ironies, cruel songs and harsh mockery to cover one's own loss of a place in the world – these were common.

A large scar on Hugh's inner ankle was reported by a ship's surgeon at the end of this journey. But any pain from the wound merely put a further edge on inner uncertainty.

At last the party of convicts were in Cork's large county, and crossed the Lee at the fashionable spa town of Mallow, favoured by Ireland's wilder young gentry. Then their way took them down pleasant country lanes, by the distant ruins of Blarney, into wonderful Cork city, probably the biggest town Hugh had seen, and so to the port of Cobh. Within sight of the waterfront and steep-hilled town of Cobh itself, the broad reaches of the harbour stretched out, protected from the sea by the bulk of Great Island, within which sat Spike Island, a low fortified rock; prisoners awaiting ships to Australia were housed either in its barracks-like prison, older and darker than Galway gaol, or in an old hulk, a retired British naval ship, anchored offshore. On the prison decks of this old vessel, men were chained ankle-to-ankle. Wood rot and unpumped bilge water added their sourness to the air. Years later John Mitchel confessed that beneath the impressive walls of Spike Island, he was first overwhelmed by feelings of a hopelessness 'language was never made to describe . . . I will forget what the fair, outer world is like.' Here Larkin and the others gave up their civilian clothes, carrying at least in their fibres the peaty smell of home, and put on Spike Island's brownish, inadequate canvas prison clothes. The prison diet – 'non-stimulating and anti-scorbutic', as the authorities said – consisted of small measures of milk, bread and oatmeal, with a too occasional portion of fresh meat or vegetables. Scurvy and dysentery were both common in the island and its hulk.

2

The Shipping of Ireland, and the Exile of Chains

> Between decks a strong grated barricade, spiked with iron, is built across the ship at the steerage bulkhead. This gives the officers a free view of all that goes on amongst the prisoners. Bunks for sleeping are placed on each side all the way to the bows . . . There is no outlet but through a door in the steerage bulkhead, and this is always guarded by a sentry.
>
> Commodore Charles Wilkes, USN,
> after visiting a convict ship, Sydney, 1839

By October 1833, the barque *Parmelia*, 443 tons, had arrived in Cobh from Gravesend, its convict decks empty. The master of *Parmelia* was James Gilbert. The commander of the guard of soldiers who had boarded in Gravesend was a Major Joseph Anderson of the 50th Regiment of Foot, a 53-year-old Scot, who had survived the Spanish Peninsular campaign against Napoleon's armies twenty years past, carried a Napoleonic wound, and had now been posted by the War Office to the undramatic duty of guarding felons for the duration of the journey, and of then swelling the garrison of New South Wales. Mrs Anderson was also adventurously on board, accompanied by four of the Andersons' near-grown children. An ensign was the only other officer aboard, and there were twenty-nine other ranks. Eight soldiers' wives were to travel too, and fifteen soldiers' children. Major Anderson now observed the detachments of convicts come aboard in Cobh, amongst them Larkin. Mustered on deck and quick-stepped below, these men experienced for the first time perhaps the suck of the tide aboard a vessel big enough by the standards of the time, yet also in its way a fragile, shifting world.

Gilbert was no virgin captain in conveying such people as these to the nether world. We know little enough of him – which is in a sense one way of saying his voyages were efficiently managed and therefore attracted little official scrutiny from either the governor of New South Wales or the Navy or Transport Board of Great Britain. His first journey to Australia had been as master of the female convict transport *Edward* from Cork in 1829. In 1831, in the same vessel, Gilbert brought 153 male convicts from Cork to Sydney, losing 5. The prisoners below were to a certain extent the fall-out from the discontents of the hungry summer and the rent strife of the early autumn, when evictions were high. Many were in a weakened condition from their confinement on Spike Island, but the loss of life on both voyages of the *Edward* was considered fairly standard. James Gilbert had then commanded the first journey of the much younger, A1 Lloyds-registered, Quebec-built *Parmelia*, on its first excursion from Sheerness with 200 English prisoners, of whom 4 died of cholera. And now it was returning to Australia a second time, with Hugh and around 200 other Irish males.

It was an irony of civilisation that the despised, the ejected Ribbonman travelled in better-found and -regulated ships than most emigrants sailed in to Canada, New York, Boston or Baltimore. The convict transports were required to meet a standard. Eight-year-old *Parmelia*'s present classification of AE1 meant that it was still considered a first-class ship but was not quite sufficiently refurbished to maintain an A1 certificate. A certain lack of recaulking could be painful for Larkin and his fellows, for in the tropics the exposed tar often melted in the seams and dropped from overhead. There would, however, be much worse ships than *Parmelia* in the Atlantic. Below A lay E, I and the barely seaworthy O.

Anthony Donoghoe, the surgeon-superintendent for this new voyage of *Parmelia* to Australia, was on his first trip and would later make something of a career out of the convict run. He was a strong soul, which was not a bad thing. For it was upon him that the survival of the prisoners depended.

Before being inspected by the surgeons of convict ships, the prisoners were often warned by their gaolers to look smart and cheerful, an injunction prisoners heard with irony and muttered curses. In preparation Hugh and the other Galway Ribbonmen and thieves were given a communal bath and dressed in fresh clothing. Many prisoners did their best to simulate good health, though many others pretended to illnesses as a means of staying in Ireland. The medical examination often occurred on the deck of the convict ship, from which the prison surgeon frequently absented himself so that the surgeon-superintendent was not able to question him about the marginally healthy.

Despite the chain-induced ankle injury, Larkin was passed by Donoghoe for the voyage. He was allotted a ship number, 35 – the Galway men had numbers ranging from 27 to 44 – which indicated that he and his fellow Galway boys were loaded aboard fairly early. There was a strong tendency in Irish prisoners to divide themselves into regional groups, such as 'Cork boys' and 'North boys', and Larkin's Galway group were now able to choose where to establish themselves as a rowdy bloc on the as yet uncrowded deck, perhaps away from the taint of the privies or heads.

Ordered and urged down the companionway, and entering the prison deck by its barred bulkhead, Hugh observed two rows of 6-feet-square sleeping benches running down the port and starboard lengthwise, each bench, as an observer said, 'calculated to hold four convicts, everyone thus possessing eighteen inch of width to sleep in . . . The hospital was in the fore part of the ship, with a bulkhead across, separating it from the prison.' Claustrophobia was relieved by the sight of scuttles – portholes – above the benches. They could be opened but only in the stillest weather.

Even if lost to all other counties, the prisoners were not yet lost to Cork. Major Anderson was touched to see convicts' relatives brought out daily to the ship by local boatmen. They called up to their lost ones exercising on deck, or at the portholes. Such tortured, delicious, futile conversations went on for hours, and Hugh must have looked at the wives and families standing in the boats, laughing, weeping, and both envied and pitied the Cork men. The sound of soldiers' children from the upper deck was also likely to fill him with complicated longing and disabling regret.

Fortunately for the survival of desolated Hugh and his brethren, by the 1830s, under the influence of Quaker prison reformers and of British progressives generally, the Transport Board put considerable responsibility on Captain Gilbert and on Surgeon Donoghoe. The contractors had to place a bond of £1,000, to be withheld until the governor of the penal colony had issued 'certificates of the true and just delivery of all the provisions . . . and of the proper conduct of the Masters and Surgeons'.

All requests the master received from the surgeon regarding the convicts were to be entered in the logs, as was the daily expenditure of rations and water. One log-book was to be handed to the governor of New South Wales or the lieutenant-governor of Van Diemen's Land on arrival in either of those places, and the second copy was to go to the Transport Board office on the ship's return to Great Britain. The contractors fitted out the ship with everything from galley fires enclosed in brick to an Osbridge machine, a series of colanders for filtering and sweetening water. The charter also required masters to travel to the penal station as quickly as they could, touching in at intervening ports only as necessary.

Larkin wore the clothing of a transportee. He had been issued three shirts, flannel or cotton, two pairs of duck trousers, and a novel item: a pair of shoes. He had a Guernsey smock, a woollen cap and neckerchiefs. There was an official prejudice against woollen clothing, because of the risk of lice, and so the damp of the convict deck often brought on colds and catarrh and respiratory illness. It seems though that Larkin, inured to cold both by rustic and penal experience, did not need attention from the surgeon. Hugh's name would not occur in Donoghoe's log as seeking medical treatment for any serious complaint.

Linked below now with a chain which ran from one convict ankle to another via ringbolts on the sleeping platforms, Larkin must have privately felt that he had been buried amongst unnameable perils. It was partially true. Until 1835, tonnage laws taxed ships on the basis that the depth was equal to half the beam. So slim-beamed, tall vessels were in favour, and *Parmelia* had to carry a large quantity of ballast to sit right in the water. Hugh, who had not seen the open ocean before, would be required, on the basis of a tax anomaly, to face the world's worst seas in a ship less than well designed for the purpose.

In the period spent waiting for the prison deck to be filled and the winds to come right, Donoghoe had more leisure to make notes on the ship's muster beside the name and number of each prisoner. He did not yet, in case death rendered the task irrelevant, fill in with ink all the details. But when Larkin was marched into the hospital for assessment, O'Donoghoe saw before him a fairly typical husky peasant, a good height, with the dark brown hair and blue eyes beloved of Esther, and a 'ruddy and much freckled' complexion. Donoghoe also listed: 'A scar on back of right hand. Wart on inside middle and fourth fingers of left hand. Scar on back of fourth finger of left hand. Large scar over inner ankle of right leg.'

Hugh's age at sentencing was noted as twenty-four years, and he was credited with possessing reading but not writing. His writing would nonetheless appear on a number of later documents. The young Larkin had been taught a certain amount then in some so-called 'hedge school', classes taught in the open, often by a hedge in summer, or in a barn or a loaned cottage in winter, by volunteer, itinerant schoolteachers. Peasants sent their children, paying the schoolmaster with small amounts of cash or food, to ensure that they learned something of the Sassenach language – English – which would give them some leverage in dealing with the establishment. The hedge schools also taught Irish and mathematics and even a smattering of Latin, history, geography – the Liberator himself had attended one before going to the Continent to study. Hedge schools were clearly a brave reaction to the Penal Laws that excluded the native Irish from education, and would not be transplanted until a National School system was established following Emancipation. The masters laboured under an acute shortage of books, and standard reading texts included *Irish Rogues and Rapparees*, *A History of Witches and Apparitions* and the biography of Freney the Highwayman, a literary diet which commentators believed contributed to Irish lawlessness. But the hedge schools had their impact in the summer of Rs (Reading) and Ws (Writing) which Donoghoe would place beside the names of *Parmelia* convicts.

Donoghoe listed Hugh's fellow Ribbonman John Hessian as twenty-one years of age, farm labourer, single, no prior convictions, and 5 feet 3¾ inches, ruddy and freckled. The Strahane boys were dark, sandy-headed, muscular, average in height. Cusack, the 14-year-old, was 5 feet 1 inch, and he carried three scars which might have derived from either horse-shoeing or imprisonment. Donoghoe's notations of heights and scars and colours of eyes would, if any of these prisoners escaped captivity in New South Wales, be used to track them down.

As soon as he took them aboard, the surgeon was required to exercise the prisoners in small numbers in a barricaded exercise pen on deck. Prisoners could savour the autumn air, see the sky and – by craning over the high walls – the shore, and envy birds, but rifle loops were cut through the wood, to enable the soldiers of the 50th to fire into the crowd of exercising felons if there was a riot. A few sheep and goats – to provide goat's milk for the soldiers' children – were brought aboard and confined in their own pens on open deck, near the exercise area. Men with pastoral backgrounds like Hugh's were given the pleasant task of feeding and tending them.

As the *Parmelia* filled up, Donoghoe exercised the pragmatic wisdom built up by previous surgeon-superintendents. He had the prisoners choose their own mess captains, responsible for drawing the rations and keeping their section of the prison deck clean. Donoghoe also appointed convicts to act as deck captains, rather like prefects in a schoolyard, and he selected hospital attendants, cooks, water-closet attendants and barbers. There had to be barbers: short hair promoted health.

As Hugh looked from his sleeping berth along the lines of ankle-chained men on port or starboard, he saw some familiar but also some unexpected faces. An Oxford student, Archibald Turnbull, had been reduced to sharing this deck with the spade men, the vagrants, the Irish speakers, by having stolen a horse in Cork. He was the convict deck's only gentleman. Of the others, more than a quarter came from the west – Clare, Galway, Mayo, Sligo and Leitrim. Only four prisoners were Dublin residents, and the others would have been pleased by this, since Dubliners possessed such a vicious repute that rustic convicts on many ships felt obliged to arm themselves with rocks tucked into the toes of stockings.

One surgeon of this period noticed that at night, when mustered below deck, the mass of convicts recited the Rosary. It was an act of communal identity from which the fifteen Protestant felons were excluded by choice and conviction.

A Durham-born soldier stationed in Limerick, Thomas Gibson, sentenced for habitual insubordination and drunkenness, was the last to be assigned a number. Amongst the prisoners were now three English soldiers, one Scottish and two Irish. Two were guilty of desertion, and two more of habitual drunkenness and insubordination. Most Ribbonmen aboard remembered army brutality, and here, in Privates Gibson, King, Grahame, Kelly, Ryan and Warden, was the cut-down-to-size visage of their tormentors.

By mid-October *Parmelia* was filled with 220 men, 62 of whom had committed crimes of Ribbonism. They included a father and son, the Brennans, coal-miners who had issued a threatening notice. Apart from the Ribbonmen Strahane there were two other teams of brothers, the McGrath boys of Wexford and the McNallys of Mayo. Grievance inevitably ran in families.

John McCauliffe, a farm servant, had threatened society in another way – a transient, he had been sentenced to seven years for vagrancy, along with his two sons, John, a Cork errand boy thirteen years of age, and 16-year-old Jeremiah McCauliffe, a shoemaker's boy. Ten men altogether had been sentenced for vagrancy. Travelling with these least criminal members of the company were eight men guilty of murder, whose sentences had been commuted, again bespeaking deaths resulting from the fury of faction-fighting. So too were the sentences of the twenty-two men aboard found guilty of manslaughter. Twenty-seven had stolen livestock, whereas only eleven had stolen cash, and only one bank-notes. Clothing, hats, caps, a saddle, shoes, a bag of grain, butter, were amongst other items stolen by various of Hugh's shipmates. Only seventeen were guilty of taking property by force, and only one of being a pickpocket, James McCarden, a sickly 16-year-old errand boy from Waterford who would die in hospital in Sydney within months of his arrival. One of the more interesting crimes might have been that of 27-year-old John Kelly of Roscommon, a tailor who was accused of sacrilege.

At night the boots of Anderson's sentries beat against the decking like the hammering of a heavy, human clock. As the boatload of felons ached towards departure, there was little chance of an uprising from the hold. Generations of convict ships had made their way to the antipodes without one mutiny succeeding. Any escape by launching oneself into the massive oblivion of the sea was attended by fear of the fire of Hell. Hugh had by now heard that, under some circumstances, wife and children might after many years be shipped to join a convict. So each tale and impulse neutralised the other as Hugh sat below in ferment.

When the state of the winds and of *Parmelia* itself permitted Captain Gilbert to consider sailing, he was required to sign the Lord Lieutenant's warrant, which attested that various persons having been found guilty of crimes against the laws of Ireland, and sentenced to be transported,

'Service of the convicts is hereby transferred unto the Governor of New South Wales.' The list of convicts was then signed by Gilbert and Surgeon-Superintendent Donoghoe and the documents sealed in a tin box and dispatched to Dublin Castle. A copy of warrant and list was sealed inside a second tin box for delivery to the governor of New South Wales.

Hugh and others, though not previously seafarers, could nonetheless make sense of the racket of weighing anchor, the new urgency of orders, the bugle calling the entirety of the guard on deck, the thump of feet and military boots, the crack of canvas, creak of shrouds, howling of timber. *Parmelia* had intentions for the open ocean. In the echo chamber of the prison deck, the prisoner was overwhelmed, and had the options of shocked silence, praying, curses, tears and full-blown frenzy. The guards at the companionways heard this primal racket within the prison. But to most on deck, where squeezebox and fiddle had now combined with more businesslike yells and riot, the prison deck seemed appropriately voiceless.

Parmelia left Cork on 29 October, a season of dimness and squalls. The seasick, demented, embittered, grieving, cowed, were still restrained by the ankle chains running the length of their prison deck. *Parmelia* sailed past the old Head of Kinsale, out to the deeper reaches of the Celtic Sea and into the Atlantic. To the protests of the few who were not seasick, men writhed and vomited where they sat. The hatches were battened down, producing in addition to the noise of sea and the shriek of timbers under stress a sense of being helplessly chained up in the whale's belly. Some of the transports were wet ships; water seeped through the seams. Prisoners reported being washed from their bunks by water accumulating in the bilges and forming waves. Conditions were scarcely better for the families of the soldiers of the 50th, but at least the well were able to escape to the deck for a brief gasp of clean air. *Parmelia*'s convicts had ahead of them a 124-day dose of that mighty ocean so celebrated in Irish ballads.

A few days out into the North Atlantic, the surgeon and captain, after a consultation with the officer of the guard, struck the leg irons permanently off. The well-behaved could now move free of chains until Sydney. It was for all parties an act of normalisation. Routine would carry the inhabitants of *Parmelia* all the way to Australia, and in honour of the power of routine Surgeon-Superintendent Anthony Donoghoe's log maintained a level, functional tone, though he would complain that some of those sent aboard showed debility and emaciation.

The regularly managed days at sea muted if they could not do away with Hugh's sense of loss. Sometime between 4.30 and 6.00 a.m., convict cooks were admitted on deck and began working up the fire in the galley. At sunrise, in suitable weather, the prison doors were thrown open, and prisoners came up the companionway. In the ever-dramatic ocean daybreak, in good weather Hugh and all the others washed in tubs and were rinsed off with buckets of sea-water. Twice a week at this time convict barbers began to cut hair and shave. At six o'clock, rations were served out in the storeroom to the mess men for the six convicts each represented, while volunteers swabbed the decks, glad of the exercise. Below, the sleeping benches had been raised and all bedding, each man's mattress and blankets tied with sennit string, was brought up on deck and stowed beneath canvas hammock cloths, which in open sea might not be adequate to protect them from rain or spray. At eight o'clock, everyone below again, the mess men served breakfast out of buckets and pannikins at the central table running the length of the convict deck. Then the prison deck was cleaned by teams using lumps of pumice stone. On most ships there were classes, offered by some well-instructed convict or crew member; Archibald Turnbull might have turned his Oxford knowledge to use. An anti-scorbutic mixture called sherbet – lime or lemon juice with sugar – was served just before noon, or else a few mouthfuls of wine. The noonday meal was usually 4 ounces of salt pork or beef, 4 ounces of suet pudding, a few ounces of biscuit; or sometimes pea soup and bacon instead.

When laundry was done on deck, and clothing spread out in the rigging, the ship took on the normal aspect of crowded vessels of the age: a floating tenement. The bedding was taken below at sunset, prisoners were mustered below and the prison locked up. Supper was a hot drink and left-over biscuit. Climate and mutinous behaviour could vary all this, but the daily timetable brought both solace and a hypnotic tedium.

Men slept crowded together on their platforms. In practice surgeons often took a less than interventionist interest in what prisoners, male and female, did for sexual solace. We do, however, possess some broad indicators in the case of ships like the *Parmelia*. Governor Gipps of New South Wales wrote a decade later to Lord Stanley, British Colonial Secretary, that sodomy was realistically estimated as involving somewhere between one in eight and one in twenty convicts. 'The Crime is said to prevail almost exclusively amongst prisoners of English birth,' wrote Gipps, rightly or wrongly, '. . . and the Irish are (to their honour) generally acknowledged to be untainted by it.' Certainly Irish social and religious restraints made an uneasy milieu for homosexuality. But the idea that homosexuality did not manifest itself at all on the prison deck beggars modern belief.

The same Irish conditions which had now rid Ireland of John Hessian, the Strahane brothers and Hugh Larkin had already produced a large free emigration to the new world. Between 1825 and 1845 the total number of

Irish emigrants to North America alone was said to be in excess of 800,000. In the late 1820s and early 1830s, Canada attracted two thirds of the Irish emigrants to North America. A high proportion settled in Nova Scotia and Newfoundland, which straddle the approaches of the St Lawrence River, or in New Brunswick. But others made their way down the St Lawrence itself to Lower or Upper Canada, Quebec and Ontario. Amongst them were a strong emigration of Ulster Protestant tenant farmers, who looked upon leaving home hard-headedly as an opportunity rather than an exile. One of them would write of the independence farmers enjoyed in London, Upper Canada: 'I may say I never wrote anything of this country but the truth and I am sorry at nothing so much as that I did not come sooner to it.'

After 1835 the United States became the preferred Irish destination, and would from then on absorb three out of five Irish emigrants. Emigration to America is the stuff of romance and folk-song, but there was also a considerable invasion of English, Welsh and Scottish ports and cities, notably Glasgow, Liverpool and Manchester – half a million Irish would be living in Britain by 1843. Karl Marx would ultimately write that Ireland got its vengeance on England 'by bestowing an Irish quarter on every English industrial maritime or commercial town of any size'.

Perhaps less than 5 per cent of pre-Famine emigrants from Ireland voluntarily committed themselves to the long voyage to Australia, which Hugh had now no choice but to make. Amongst the emigrants to the Australian colonies were again Ulster Protestant tenant farmers and their families, adventurous people with means to last them the longer journey, and carrying in their luggage astonishing reports of opportunities for free settlers. British government assistance and emigrant societies helped Irish tradesmen emigrate, and in the next two decades single young women were sent out as domestic help, and to adjust the imbalance of the sexes. But Australia was the opposite of handy Nova Scotia. In the Irish imagination, it was synonymous with the worst kind of exile, the unchosen one; the exile of chains.

Parmelia traversed the Bay of Biscay and passed the north-western capes of Spain. As the weather began to moderate, the Madeiras showed remotely to port, and then the Azores to starboard. Within two weeks, the ship was in temperate waters. Hugh had never known such weather or such sights. The idea of relaying all this – the porpoises, the light, the range of men met – to someone beloved probably flared in him. Surgeons liked to see their convicts sing and dance, and Donoghoe had provided pipes and fiddles for use in this balmy air, these calm seas. It was thought the lethargy of scurvy could be combated by jigs and reels.

The Canaries were distantly sighted, and ahead lay the Tropic of Cancer and the Cape Verde Islands off Africa's westernmost point. By then, in a zone of stillness, the weather turned torrid. Even with the scuttles open, the prisoners experienced a deadly heat. In the *Hive*, Anthony Donoghoe's next ship, prison deck temperatures reached 100° Fahrenheit on a regular basis. He would have sixty men sleep on deck at a time, changing them every four hours. He probably used the same method on *Parmelia*. If a third of the men were on deck, he estimated, the temperature below fell by between 5° and 8°.

Far out in the Gulf of Guinea, as *Parmelia* crossed the breathless Equator, Larkin entered the southern world. He must have been occasionally at least astonished that the powers and principalities he had offended were capable of punishing him with such climes and distances. The Christmas he had anticipated spending in the parish of Clontuskert he now spent with the desert south-west coast of Africa to port and Napoleon's St Helena far away to starboard.

'The convicts behaved well,' wrote Major Anderson, 'except on one occasion, when one nearly murdered another by striking him violently on the head with a pumice stone used for scrubbing the decks.' The offender was placed in heavy irons, 'and next morning the whole of the convicts were paraded on deck, and with my detachment under arms and loaded on the poop and in the cuddy, the prisoner was brought forward, stripped, and tied to the rigging, and there received the severe corporal punishment of one hundred lashes'. This rite of discipline was considered neither exceptional nor a blot on *Parmelia*'s record.

Surgeon Donoghoe, who was treating for dysentery James McGuire, a 25-year-old Dublin shopkeeper who had stolen clothes, found his patient 'heartily irritable'. Eye infections had broken out too amongst the private soldiers and spread to the prison deck. Thomas McCaffrey, number 24, suffered pernicious diarrhoea, having in Donoghoe's opinion been too long in Spike Island. He had lain in the ship's hospital for six weeks after he first boarded, and had never fully recovered. Donoghue recorded that by December McCaffrey was 'suffering hunger, considerable debility, and strongly marked with Scorbutic'. Ulcers appeared on his hips and thighs. Calomel and ipecacuanha were used to dose him. His death occurred on 12 January 1834, and he was committed to the sea south of Africa.

Here the Atlantic Ocean met the Indian. The air became colder again, as *Parmelia* reached down for the edge of the Southern Ocean that surrounded Antarctica, and the global band of winds called the Roaring Forties. They made the transit between South Africa and Australia a fast but uncomfortable one. Donoghoe noted in his log that at 48° south the convict deck was full of men coughing and rasping with catarrh. They suffered because their clothing, though lice-resistant, was 'nothing calculated to resist cold'. The hospital forward filled up with cases of pneumonia.

An unfortunate man named John Gleeson, rural thief, was one day swept overboard in the violent Southern Ocean and sank in a second with a bitter cry to mercy in his mouth. Gleeson's details – age, literacy, crime, place of trial, marital status – would not be finally inked in on the muster; no need existed to do so for the Sydney authorities. In Donoghoe's log his loss was recorded in a brief paragraph of slanting handwriting.

Larkin endured as *Parmelia* was swept past the unoccupied sub-Antarctic islands of Crozet and Kerguelen, and towards its encounter with Van Diemen's Land. That island's stormy west coast was at all costs to be avoided. Then a last great turn at Southeast Cape, and the Van Diemen's Land convict establishment at Port Arthur, brought *Parmelia* on the final long reach north for Sydney. It was March, late summer, and under electric blue skies off a long New South Wales coastline of noble headlands, brilliant beaches and blue coastal mountains, they were back in kindly air. Tacking up the coast against northerlies, or else zooming along before a southerly, they passed the wide mouth and low headlands of Botany Bay. This inlet which Captain Cook had made famous more than sixty years before was popularly used in the British Isles as a synonym for New South Wales, but Sydney Harbour itself was 7 miles north of it.

Parmelia had been at sea for 124 days.

3
Assigning Ireland

> Convicts embarked in Ireland generally arrive in New South Wales in a very healthy state and are found to be more obedient and more sensible to kind treatment during the passage than any class. Their separation from their country is observed to make a strong impression on their minds.
>
> Report of John Thomas Bigge,
> Special Royal Commissioner, 1819

When, on 2 March 1834, the *Parmelia* entered through the august sandstone headlands which were the gate to Sydney, and the great, accommodating stretch of Sydney Harbour spread away to its south, the scuttles on the convict deck were opened fully on the pleasant, humid late summer day. *Parmelia*, avoiding the mid-harbour rocks named the Sow and Pigs, anchored well down-harbour. From the deck and ports, what the travellers could chiefly see was not the half-penal, half-free town itself, for it lay in its own little deep-water cove some miles upstream. For the moment, Larkin beheld stretches of coastal hill and headland, covered with deep-green foliage of plants from before the Fall, and the yellow of the harbour beaches. It was a landscape without familiar saints and presences. Hugh could also see the scatter of buildings of South Head (lighthouse, signal station), the shacks of convict fishermen at Watson's Bay, the first anchorage inside the harbour, and the fires of the natives on Middle Head rising into a bright godless sky. *Parmelia* was not immediately rushed by officials or news-hungry colonists. The *Fairlie*, a larger ship with more than 300 English convicts, had recently arrived. The officers went ashore both to report and to taste the raw, boozy pleasures and limited civilised intercourse of Sydney. The convicts would not be landed for some days, for their existence, their behaviour and the skills of those eligible for employment had to be advertised. The garrison of *Parmelia* were landed four days after arrival and marched 30 miles inland to the town of Liverpool. Major Anderson did not go with them, however. The governor had another task for him, one that would endow him with Australian penal notoriety.

The *Sydney Gazette* of 6 March told the readers of Sydney that the prisoners of *Parmelia* 'appear to be a healthy, robust set of men'. But on 18 March, *Parmelia* was still 'lying in the stream' with convicts aboard.

Larkin's boredom and anxiety to land must have begun to transcend any doubts he had about penal life ashore.

In that waiting time, the convicts were brought on deck and inspected by the Colonial Surgeon, the Principal Superintendent of Convicts and other officials. These shipboard inspections in theory gave prisoners the opportunity to lodge complaints. Another opportunity came when at last, sometime before 25 March, the convicts were landed at the dockyard on the western tip of Sydney Cove itself, and the governor or his deputy inspected them and explicitly asked for complaints.

Sydney had seen exiled Irish trouble-makers already in its history of forty-five years. Amongst the first Irish to be transported were members of the loosely knit society named the Defenders, founded to counter attacks on Catholics in the North. After an armed resistance to the burning of Catholic homes, the so-called 'Battle of the Diamond' in Armagh in 1795, the Defenders were sentenced in job lots. Some were pressed into the Royal Navy, others sent to New South Wales. They were the first to bring the Irish language to Australia, where it generated great official suspicion.

In the same decade, Irish Protestants of the professional classes and the gentry involved themselves with their poorer Catholic brethren in a revolutionary organisation, the United Irishmen, which pulled against the more inward-looking Orange Order. The United Irishmen, and indeed women, a movement whose saints included Voltaire, Tom Paine, Washington and Jefferson, had been enlivened by the successful revolutions in North America and France, and by the chance of fraternity across the divide of Irish sect and class. Larkin knew and venerated, like every member of his class, the names of the Protestant United Irish martyrs of 1798 onwards. They were passed around like smoothed and lucky stones amongst the poor. The name of Lord Edward Fitzgerald, dead of wounds inflicted during his capture. The name of Wolfe Tone, who, in an act of self-destruction which a merciful God understood, cut his throat with a razor smuggled into his cell by his brother. These men had shown a passionate philosophic sympathy for their powerless Catholic fellow countrymen. Some United Irishmen fled into exile – Thomas Addis Emmet, for example, to enjoy a career as a New York jurist and state Attorney-General. But Robert Emmet, his brother, attempting to revive rebellion in 1803, was publicly hanged and then torn apart in Dublin. His speech before the hanging judge, Lord Norbury, was much quoted by hedge schoolmasters and hence familiar to Hugh. 'Let no man write my epitaph . . . When my country takes her place amongst the nations of the earth, then and not till then, let my epitaph be written.'

United Irish were shipped to Australia on six vessels which arrived between 1800 and 1806. Of these prisoners, one of the best known was General Joseph Holt, a Wicklow farmer, United Irishman, Presbyterian, who came as an amnestied prisoner aboard the *Minerva* in 1800. Holt had become for a time commander-in-chief of the remnants of the rebel army at Glenmalure in the mountains south of Dublin, and in Wicklow generally, taking command of 3,000 or 4,000 men gathered by a young United Irishman, Michael Dwyer, the Wicklow chieftain, another transportee-to-be. Holt and Dwyer had entertained great hopes for the success of a French army under General Humbert, which landed in Mayo late in the summer of 1798. But the French-Irish Republic of Mayo collapsed in October. A further French fleet which had set out from Brest to invade Ireland was in part destroyed, in part captured, and Wolfe Tone captured with it.

Holt surrendered to an amnesty offered by the Lord Lieutenant of Ireland, Lord Cornwallis, who had had experience of rebels when his British army had been surrounded by Washington's forces at Yorktown, Virginia, in the War of American Independence. In 1800 Holt would be permitted to travel as a gentleman detainee with his wife and children on *Minerva*, where below decks there were many rebels, summarily tried by court martial, and placed aboard without proper warrants.

Hundreds of such unrepentant Irish seditionists full of savage memory and unsettled scores reached Australia in the first decade of the nineteenth century. The survivors brought to New South Wales a virulent memory of the instruments of torture which had been used against their forces and supporters: the shears for docking ears, the triangle for flogging, the pitch cap – a cap of tar put on suspects' heads and lit to burn flesh and boil brains.

In 1804, the transported rebels rose against their captors at a place to the west of Sydney which the rebels inevitably named Vinegar Hill after the site of the battle in Ireland on 21 June 1798 in which Irish rebels fought the British. Major Johnston of the New South Wales Corps pursued the Sydney and Parramatta rebels, capturing the two leaders while a parley was in progress in the bush. Dozens of the rebels were hanged, and Holt was sent to Norfolk Island, 1,000 miles off the New South Wales coast.

In Ireland, near Christmas 1803, Emmet's uprising having deplorably failed, legendary Michael Dwyer, just thirty-one years old, having continued fighting a guerrilla war with thirty or so rebels, threw himself on the mercy of the government. To his own surprise, he was given the promised amnesty and came to New South Wales above decks with his wife Mary and four young children on the *Tellicherry*. Governor Bligh, of *Bounty* renown, needing the support of the loyalists for his battle against a clique of army officers in the colony, sent Dwyer to Van Diemen's Land. Returned to the Sydney area in 1809, Dwyer helped to police the turbulent Irishtown district near the present Sydney suburb of Bankstown.

General Holt sold his Sydney property in 1811 and returned to Dublin. Dwyer remained, his name lustrous through song and legend to most Ribbonmen transported to Australia later in the nineteenth century. Larkin was in no way consoled, however, by the prospect of adding his ultimate dust to that of Dwyer, who had in 1826 died in New South Wales in 'respectable prosperity'.

As every visitor to Australia remarked, here in the time capsule of the antipodes lived plants and animals that had vanished from the rest of the world. And yet the passions of men and women, and the politics of the place, would remind Hugh that despite the distances travelled he had brought the old world with him.

Hugh's new, ultimate master, the governor of this immense territory of New South Wales, was an Irish soldier and landowner in his late fifties, Major-General Sir Richard Bourke. Bourke was a cousin of Edmund Burke, parliamentary orator and attacker of Lord North's policies in North America and Ireland. Bourke would have liked to have been a parliamentary orator himself, but a jaw wound suffered as a young man fighting the French prevented him from being a forceful public speaker. Like Larkin, he had been created by Irish problems – he had inherited an estate at Thornfield in County Limerick, and bad seasons and uncertain markets meant that he had been forced to seek government offices as a means of paying debts. He had a liberal attitude towards the peasantry of Ireland. Two of his chief colonial officers, the Crown Solicitor John Hubert Plunkett, and Roger Therry, Commissioner of the Courts of Requests in New South Wales, were friends of O'Connell.

In his first vice-regal appointment to the Cape Colony in South Africa, Bourke had been accused of being a radical defender of the Kaffirs. In New South Wales, while showing perplexed concern in the cruel destiny of the Aborigines, he was devoted to the proposition of full civil status for emancipists, pardoned convicts. These men and women and their children had a voice in organs like the *Sydney Gazette*, and were so often associated with demands for an end to transportation, and for colonial self-rule and equal political rights, that Bourke himself was portrayed by enemies as the creature of barely reformed felons. While enjoying the benefits of convict labour, exclusives – those wealthy free settler landowners who believed that political influence should be restricted to themselves – accused Bourke of raising in the emancipists a dangerous expectation of power.

Bourke was also considered by the exclusives to be dangerously soft on serving convicts like Hugh. He had reduced the power of magistrates in remote areas of the colony to inflict punishment on convict servants. Property owners were always reporting in their paper, the *Sydney Herald*, as proof of Bourke's 'soothing system for convicts', the impudence and unruliness of their servants and labourers. On 10 March, for example, while Larkin and the others still 'lay in the stream', the readers of the *Herald* were told by a colonist of the way female convict servants had helped through their insubordination to hurry the late Captain Waldron to an early grave: 'not only my own female prisoners, but those assigned to my neighbours, have dared us to send them to court. "What do we care," they say, "for the **** Court, or the old magistrates either?" '

As for Irish convicts, they were seen as very dangerous but also as comically incompetent and unruly. The day after *Parmelia* arrived, the *Sydney Herald* had carried a characteristic tale characteristically told.

> Eliza Burns, a native of Hibernia, favourites whiskey and potatoes, whispered to the bar, that . . . she did on Friday last, in Castlereagh-street, commit an assault with a pair of tongs of some value on the person of Mrs Griffiths. Mrs Griffiths . . . said that the defendant on Friday last, sans provocation, threw some water on her, and fetching a pair of tongs from her house, threatened to lay hold of that useful portion of the face, vulgarly termed a proboscis, or smeller.

Mrs Griffiths had objected that she would 'be deprived of the only pleasure, (except a drop of the cratur occasionally) which rendered life desirable, namely that of the taking of sundry quantities of snuff'.

The comfort in all this was that Larkin and his fellows would find plenty of their compatriots, bond and free, ashore, amongst the upwards of 30,000 prisoners then in Sydney and the bush. Added to this number and still bearing the stigma of former imprisonment were the time-served and pardoned emancipists, who numbered as many again. Both Bourke in Sydney and the British government in Whitehall had schemes to encourage free immigrants, and the population would come close to doubling during Bourke's 7-year rule, from 1831 to 1837, but the ratio between bond and free was only marginally adjusted. Liberals and improvers, including the children of convicts, cried that Australia should refuse to accept that British penal requirements were the colony's reason for existence. Free artisans would come in numbers only when they no longer had to compete with cheap convict labour. At the time of Larkin's landing, however, convict transportation, the order of the colonial past, seemed established as the order for the future as well.

The town of Sydney, to which Larkin and the others were enjoying their first introduction, ran raffishly inland along gentle hills either side of Sydney Cove, one of dozens of anchorages in the remarkable harbour. The settlement retained the narrow streets of the original convict camp of the late 1780s. Most houses were cottages with little gardens in front, and clung in random clusters to the sandstone ledges of the Rocks. But they took on a more ornate, orderly character in the streets Pitt and Macquarie, to the eastern side of town. The landed prisoners, chained to one another and on their way to their depot, heard the catcalls of old lags. The momentous earth seeming to rock beneath their feet like *Parmelia*'s deck, the new men staggered uptown past St Phillip's Church on its hill, past the Colonial Treasury, the Barrack Square, and saw the town's theatre on the left. Barracks and the offices of government were being built of Sydney's honey-coloured sandstone, forming the most splendid structures of this eccentric seaport.

The town abounded with canaries – convicts in government employ, in sallow-coloured jackets and pants – and free dungaree men, poor settlers and occasional tradesmen, who wore cheap blue cotton imported from India. The lean, dishevelled children of convicts, called 'cornstalks' or 'currency urchins', ran wild, grown healthy by the standards of Europe on colonial corn doughboys, salt beef, fresh vegetables. Convict women on ticket-of-leave, a system of probationary freedom available once a convict had served a number of years, stood in gardens or outside public houses smoking Brazil twist in *dudeens*, clay pipes sometimes scarcely half an inch long. 'Laggers' or ticket-of-leave men wore blue jackets, or else short woollen blue smocks, and the hats of both convict and free were unorthodox, some of plaited cabbage-tree fronds, some of kangaroo skin. Soldiers and police were much in evidence in front of Customs House, Commissariat Office, Treasury, post office, and all government offices. But side by side with this martial formality, male and female sexual services were full-throatedly offered in a manner visitors said was more scandalous than the East End of London. 'A Wapping or St Giles in the beauties of a Richmond', as one Englishman described Sydney, contrasting squalid behaviour to the strange natural beauty all around. The abnormal imbalance between male and female gave the flesh trade an added fever, as did dram-drinking – the downing of Bengal rum out of wineglasses.

Hugh's line were offered nothing and had to be content to see Government House off Bent Street, the turrets of Government House Stables near the Botanic Gardens, and then the School of Industry and the General Hospital, called familiarly the Rum Hospital, built by three Sydney merchants in exchange for a monopoly on rum imports. On one edge of the dusty green named Hyde Park lay St James's Church and the courthouse, both splendidly designed by the convict architect Francis Greenway, a Bristolian transported for forging a contract. Across from St James's were the outbuildings and chief barracks of Sydney's convict depot, Hyde Park Barracks.

The superintendent of the Hyde Park Barracks at the time Larkin and the other *Parmelia* prisoners arrived was a young, recently retired military officer of the 40th Regiment, E. A. Slade. By the time Larkin marched into Slade's barracks, the superintendent was an enemy of any programme of leniency, and so an enemy of Governor Bourke. Bourke would soon remove him from the magistracy for having abducted a young immigrant woman ashore and for living illicitly with her. Though thought a libertine in his personal life, he was nonetheless an exacting official with convicts, taking pains to ensure that lashes at the barracks were properly given. He would report three years later, in London before the Select Committee on Transportation, 'When I had the lash inflicted, I never saw a case where I did not break the skin in four lashes.' He was proud to declare that he had standardised the cats used for lashings throughout New South Wales.

Larkin, Hessian, the Strahanes and other *Parmelia* men were fortunate in being not long enough in the barracks to attract more than a cursory glance from E. A. Slade. Many have argued punishment in Australia was no greater than in the British army or navy and less than was employed against slaves in the American South. But floggings were commonly ordered by magistrates throughout the 1830s. The possibility of moral and physical destruction hung over each man, over Larkin himself. Father Ullathorne, an English Benedictine priest in Sydney, believed that the Irish were vulnerable in the face of flogging, which disoriented a man and altered for ever the balance of his soul. The young Polish explorer John Lhotsky, a doctor, was outraged at the harm done to a convict's heart and lungs by flogging on the shoulders. The use of lashes clotted with infected blood from earlier victims, he feared, helped spread venereal disease.

But some commentators of the day saw the fact that flogging could be administered only on a magistrate's order as an absurd nicety. Masters in Britain were still permitted to beat apprentices, husbands beat wives as of right, masters of ships were able to flog their seamen. But convicts, less worthy than spouses, apprentices and seamen, were restricted to a maximum of fifty lashes. Yet it was not as if the lashes designed by E. A. Slade went unused in New South Wales. In 1835, there would be 7,103 floggings amongst some 30,000 convicts in the colony. So though Larkin, Hessian and the Strahanes were for now sorted into the sheep and not the goats of the penal system, their good fortune could prove impermanent.

The reason Larkin and the other Ribbonmen needed to spend so little time in barracks was that they had been transported at a period of some prosperity. The Australian countryside was experiencing a spate of lushness. In the area called the Nineteen Counties, the beachhead region which government serviced, and in the huge outer regions where unauthorised grazier-entrepreneurs occupied hundreds of square miles and ran their flocks, there was a demand for agricultural workers. Larkin would be spared the chain and work gangs – described by liberals and emancipists as Egyptian slavery – by this boom in the bush, by a hunger for fine wool in the mills of northern England, by a colonial hunger for mutton and beef. He would be saved too from Sydney, that great Babylon of convictism.

Perhaps his rural experience in East Galway counted, and the fact that he had clearly swallowed his fury and was watchful now. But then so did the nature of his crime. Experience had told employers that first-offender criminals who had made some vaguely political or industrial protest or other were good workers. Of 1,078 so-called protest criminals, including United Irishmen and Ribbonmen, sent to New South Wales between 1800 and 1840 and studied by one historian, not one had previous convictions, and none would commit crimes in the colony. Some English rural labourers who had destroyed threshing machines which they feared would take their jobs had arrived in New South Wales in 1831, and were in tranquil employment. Why should Ribbonmen not prove similarly useful?

In the year of Larkin's arrival in Sydney, a young man named Wakefield, recently released from prison in London for the statutory misdemeanour of eloping, published a tract named *England and America*, in which he called the sort of assignment under which Larkin would soon be labouring 'slavery in disguise'. The Polish explorer John Lhotsky, journeying in 1834 from Sydney into the very area where Larkin would be sent, came away pitying assigned servants. The prostitution of women prisoners by their masters shocked him.

The system spread Hugh Larkin's friends from Galway gaol all over a vast colony. John Strahane was assigned to a Captain Oldsey, who owned a property called Broulee in St Vincent, one of the southernmost of New South Wales's Nineteen Counties. By contrast his younger brother Michael was claimed by a settler at Richmond, not more than 50 miles to the west of Sydney. John Hessian went to a Dr Foster of Brush Farm near Bathurst, 150 miles or more inland. Larkin had been applied for by an entrepreneur and pastoralist named William Bradley. To be employed by Bradley, Larkin had to undertake a journey of nearly 130 miles to the inland town of Goulburn, in the county named Argyle, and thereafter might be consigned more deeply still to the spacious bush.

William Bradley was an energetic man in his early thirties who, unlike most masters, had been born in New South Wales. His father, Jonas Bradley, a sergeant of the New South Wales Corps, had been given land grants around Goulburn, grew tobacco, acquired further grants and bequeathed them to his son. When the line of the Nineteen Counties had been drawn, with an extra county later added to the north around beautiful Port Macquarie, it was considered that the five million acres therein contained and open for settlement were more than enough for the inhabitants of the colony. Though a mere sliver of the Australian continent, the area was as large as many nations and three times the size of Wales. It ran 250 miles along the coast and to a depth of 150 miles inland, where the Lachlan River formed a natural boundary. It included rich, well-watered coastal valleys and plains, the timbered Great Dividing Range, and beyond it grazing country. One commentator said of the late 1820s: 'The Nineteen Counties, to all intents and purposes, meant Australia, and the government decreed that they should be viewed as if the sea flowed all around, and not merely to the east.' These limits were given a name with a ring: the Limits of Location.

William Bradley was approaching his thirty-fourth birthday when Larkin went to work for him. He already owned a fine property called Lansdown Park near Goulburn and had built a large residence on it. But like others, he had begun putting livestock and convict labourers on land well to the south of Goulburn, beyond the Limits of Location, in a huge upland plains area then named Maneroo. Maneroo is the modern Monaro, and includes the site of the present Australian national capital, Canberra.

By 1834 Bradley was running more than 10,000 sheep both around Goulburn, within the limits of settlement, and beyond, in the Monaro to the south. So, on the assignment documents of 1834, Hugh was noted as being sent to Mr Bradley of Goulburn within the Limits. But the convict muster of 1837 said frankly that he was working for Bradley in Maneroo outside them.

Embarking on his journey to Goulburn with a small cash advance against his wages from Bradley, Larkin travelled, it seems, in his shipboard clothes and without chains. He moved out of Sydney up Brickfield Hill through the late summer bush, eucalyptus trees and acacia and tea-tree scrub, along the Parramatta road and then, at a fork a dozen miles out of the town, turned left, to the south-west. He might have travelled on a wagon behind Bradley himself, a rider and a renowned bushman, or else with a convict overseer of Bradley's returning to Goulburn after delivering wool or collecting goods. However accompanied or conveyed, Hugh was entering a hinterland in which unexpected passions, enthusiasms and melancholies would descend on him.

The land itself was like an argument against remembrance, utterly removed from anything he was familiar with from his Irish manhood. Its trees perversely bloomed in any season and were not stripped by autumn. Yet the strangeness also sharpened the loss of Esther and his sons, and produced the typical chastened wistfulness recorded in 'The Exile of Erin' by an anonymous Irish convict, who had laboured at the penal station of Emu Plains in the 1820s.

> Oh! Farewell, my country – my kindred – my lover
> Each morning and evening is sacred to you,
> While I toil the long day, without shelter or cover,
> And fell the tall gums, the black-butted and blue.
> Full often I think of, talk of thee, Erin –
> Thy heath-covered mountains are fresh in my view,
> Thy glens, lakes and rivers, Loch Conn and Kilkerran,
> While chained to the soil on the Plains of Emu.

Larkin may have seen enough of Irish canaries in chain gangs in the plains beyond the small inland town of Liverpool, then on the mountain terraces and through the passes opening on the interior of the country, to feel dismally lucky. Moving with newcomer wariness, he may have evoked a level of mockery and howls of irony and dark lust from some on the chain. He was instructed at night on the complexities of convict existence, when in the camps amongst Australia's lanky, irregular trees, ticket-of-leave wagoneers drank pannikins of tea with freshly assigned men and were pleased to pass on tales of Gothic hard luck and the randomness of the system. Twentieth-century historians argue that the success or failure of a convict was not as haphazard as was popularly believed, but campfire talk amongst the convicts themselves took a more melodramatic line, with the system an insensible Moloch of a machine, willing to grind all flesh. During a life sentence, a man could by small folly or mere technicality end up a beast on a chain.

Liberals in New South Wales and in Britain, however, believed that the convict system was a national disgrace, particularly the road gangs which some of Larkin's comrades would have to survive. But they considered worst of all the arrangements at Norfolk Island, the exquisite basalt plug, lovely in nature, humanly appalling, nearly a thousand miles out in the Pacific. Bad luck, a false step, an angry word, could take Hugh there yet. Larkin had by now heard that while *Parmelia* waited 'in the stream' to unload its convicts, a mutiny had occurred on Norfolk Island. Most of the mutineers were Irish convicts. The acting superintendent of Norfolk Island at the time, a petty man named Captain Foster Fyans of the 4th Regiment of Foot, and his superior Morisset, had helped catalyse the outbreak, and to the annoyance of the exclusives, Bourke pardoned sixteen of the thirty convicts found guilty and sentenced to death. In appointing a replacement for Morisset, Bourke may have been impressed by the fact that on *Parmelia* Major Anderson had flogged only one man. Anderson was given the administration of Norfolk Island, and instructions to reduce the regularity of floggings and hangings.

He was in place on Norfolk even as Hugh travelled west, but his presence would not improve Norfolk Island's repute. Later, Anderson spoke of his time there as a period of 'humble endeavours'. The number of average lashings, he argued, was reduced to seventy or seventy-five cases a year, and the individual sentence was between 50 and 300 lashes, 'whereas in Colonel Morisset's time they always exceeded a thousand'. Yet amongst the punishments he inflicted on the prisoner William Riley were 100 lashes for saying, 'Oh my God!' while chained up following the mutiny, and a further 100 for smiling on the chain. Anderson also reported without embarrassment how he rode his horse over the 'impertinent Daniel Shean', formerly a soldier of the 50th Regiment, a man who was apparently so reformed by the experience that he returned to service with the regiment, and was – said Anderson, as if this death confirmed his redemption – eaten alive by an alligator in the Ganges. Hugh and the men he met on the trail did not yet know of these exploits of Anderson's – some of them still in the future. But they would not have been surprised. To everyone in mainland New South Wales, Norfolk was hell's core.

Hugh carried in his jacket a 'private employment ticket', to be produced on the irksome demand of soldier or constable. The trail of British law ran to a degree he found awesome along roads of red clay and dust even in this remotest sector on the planet. Lying on his blanket in late summer air, he knew he could abscond – that was the official verb – and live a marginal and unstable life, a bushranger subsisting by theft of livestock, ultimately driven to raid settlers' homes, and then to be hunted down, hanged, or sent to Norfolk Island. The authorities had emphasised this message in the week *Parmelia* arrived by executing three absconding convicts or bushrangers, the 'Hunter River desperadoes' – William 'Blue Stockings' Johnson, William Gills and William Elliott – who had fatally wounded a policeman. Well educated now by the limits of past impulsive action at Mr Seymour's door, he had like many others resolved not to consider bolting. The system which could mangle him was also the machine which could deliver him safely at the end, and might even deliver Esther and his sons.

Yet as he tramped over Towrang Hill down to the inland town of Goulburn, like other Irish convicts he secretly though futilely retained his Ribbon attitudes, his willingness, like the absconding Irish bushranger Jack Donahue, to see any act of rebellion he was driven to as part of an ancient resistance, that of 'the Emmets, the Tones and the Moores', as Bold Jack Donahue put it. But Donahue had been shot and somewhat kinder possibilities might exist for Larkin. Bradley was a sort of Tory, but of the less virulent colonial-born variety. He had a native flexibility. A large man, he could strip off his shirt and stand beside a convict and shear a sheep. He would serve on the New South Wales Legislative Council's select committees on Aboriginals, land and economic conditions, committees which admittedly gave scope to his economic interests but were also concerned with social improvement. Ultimately, he appeared before the House of Commons to speak on the question of colonisation of Australia by the people of Ireland as a necessary boon for both countries. While others of his class abhorred Irish immigration to New South Wales, Bradley would give support to the plans of Caroline Chisholm, an English widow who devoted herself to bringing unmarried women from the British Isles, especially from Ireland, to Australia. 'He told me that he approved of my views,' Mrs Chisholm said of Bradley before the House of Commons Select Committee on Colonisation from Ireland, 'and that if I required anything in carrying my Country Plan into operation I might draw upon him for money, provisions, horses.'

Larkin may have worked for a little at Lansdown Park, Bradley's pastoral headquarters near Goulburn, but he was soon sent south to become a shepherd, stockman and labourer. Monaro was a relatively high inland plain enclosed by hills covered with eucalyptus trees and hardwoods, and scattered in its higher reaches with boulders left behind by a vanished glacier. An Englishman, William Brodribb, looking for land to settle in Monaro soon after Larkin was assigned to Bradley, wrote of it with enthusiasm. 'I crossed the boundary line separating the *County of Murray* from the *Maneroo* squatting district . . . passing east through a delightful plain called Michelago – on my right the lofty ranges, through which the Murrumbidgee ran.' On his east the coastal range named the Tinderies towered into the sky and 'the scenery altogether was magnificent, although in the depth of winter'.

As Larkin travelled south into this country where land had no protection and no price, where a settler's capacity to stock it with sheep and convict labour was the only question, he met increasing numbers of the nomadic Australian Aborigines. Many had been reduced to fringe-dwelling status in towns, and worked for the police as trackers, or for stock bosses as stockmen. Others still lived tribally and travelled their traditional ground, carrying their kangaroo or opossum rugs and cloaks, their weaponry, and their gourds and calabashes and bark dishes. Though in their travels they followed a calendar of food-gathering and ritual events of intricate subtlety, they were judged to be aimless. The Irish, so passionate on land questions themselves, did not inquire whether the indigenes had any ownership of this ground.

In 1834, the year Larkin began working for Bradley, as the southern winter began, severer in that part of New South Wales than nearly anywhere else in the colony, Bradley was running 800 cattle and some sheep at a place called Bullanamang near Bredbo, nearly 300 miles south-west from Sydney. Over the next ten years he would consolidate his runs into a vast inland property stretching from Michelago near the then non-existent Canberra down to the present border of the state of Victoria. Bradley's ultimate pastoral holdings here would be close to 3,000 square miles, and would stand beside his other assets, his brewery in Goulburn and his ultimate interest in the Sydney-to-Parramatta railway.

Bradley – already, in 1834 – occupied beyond the Limits more land than most Irish lords, and yet on his bush rides he slept on a sheet of bark wrapped in kangaroo skin. He and other settlers lacked any title to their Monaro holdings. There were no fences. The boundaries of runs or land grabs were often marked informally with tree-blazes or an occasional cairn of stone. Bradley's class of occupiers saw themselves as enterprising and respectable British gentlemen doing the sort of earth-inheriting expected of them, and sent into the bush according to God's plan for humankind. The term squatter was in 1834 applied to absconders living in scrubby country beyond the Nineteen Counties. But because even 'respectable' settlers in these regions were technically breaking the law by being here, 'squatter' gradually became attached to bush gentry like Bradley.

Ultimately, in 1836, two years after Larkin made his first acquaintance with this odd, immense bushland, Governor Bourke would yield to the reality of these highly capitalised occupations, and assent to imposing licence fees, legitimising Bradley's and others' informal occupation of the outer reaches of New South Wales. The British Home Office gave grudging consent to this arrangement.

Beyond the Limits, the pastoral system Hugh found was unlike anything around Lismany. There was a central homestead area, where the master or his overseer lived with the cattle grazing about, often moving up into the mountains. Early in Larkin's transported career, this chief homestead was located near the point where the Bredbo River flowed down its narrow valley and joined the broader valley of a river named the Murrumbidgee, about 170 miles south of Goulburn. From this central area, flocks of sheep were sent off in a number of directions under the care of teams of convict shepherds, nicknamed hatters (since isolation might render them eccentric). Unless he was instantly recognised as a good offsider or homestead worker, this was Hugh Larkin's first occupation in the bush. Eight or ten miles from the homestead, screened off by wooded hills and flinty ridges, a bark hut would be built as an outstation for two shepherds and a hut-keeper. A tree Larkin had never previously encountered, the red beef-wood, was best for producing sturdy uprights. Bark panels to make walls and roof were easily stripped from gum trees. A flue of bark and a flour or cracker barrel on top provided the chimney Larkin had never had at home.

Alexander Harris, the 'Emigrant Mechanic', as he called himself, spoke of sleeping in such a bark hut barely more than 6 feet square and looking up at the stars through the gaps in the roofing. Occasionally, Harris said, the floor became so infested with fleas that the hut-keeper would drive all the sheep into the place, the fleas transferring themselves *en masse* to the livestock. But for many rustic convicts, bark huts were not much different from the cabins of Ireland, except that the hearth fire of fallen eucalyptus branches possessed a redolence different from a turf fire.

Who were Hugh's companions in his trial period as a shepherd, and what did they talk about? Larkin heard from fellow shepherds the regional accents of Ribbonman Ireland, the voices of Cockneys, Scots, Welshmen, some among them Erse or Welsh speakers. But a shepherd might sometimes be a fallen student of the Edinburgh College of Surgeons, a cashiered lieutenant in the Buffs, a hard-up French count caught running confidence scams in London, or a quiet, literary old man with a haversack of English magazines and reviews. One squatter described his collection of shepherds as machine-breakers (they had attacked mechanised weaving machines), drunken and insubordinate British marines, small thieves or horse stealers, but no major criminals. They were 'safe guarded from the defects of their character by their isolated life'.

This then was Hugh's early routine: from the hut every morning, each of the two shepherds would walk out with his sheep in an opposite direction to the other, and graze his separate flock in solitude amongst the strange, gargling bird calls and in the massive quietude of the bush. Hugh found the unpeopled bush a drastic contrast to the crowded, sociable countryside of Ireland, and in its fearful spaciousness an encouragement to a morbid revisiting of the personal rashness, the unchanged grievances, which had landed him here.

Some of his fellows became so unhinged by the endless thinking-time that they moved through the bush with dogs chained to their waists at each side, to bark away ghosts and remorse. Others communed with stones, saw incarnate devils in their flocks or believed the boulders were an audience watching them. Hugh distracted himself from madness: he must have noticed, for example, that it took more pasture here than in East Galway to support a sheep, and yet the flocks grew splendidly.

The predominant colours of this country were brown and olive green. It made few concessions to the Irish eye in terms of subtleties of weather, of light and landscape. In the winter, beginning in July, the morning ground this far south would crackle underfoot from frost, just as in Lismany, and there was sometimes snow. For Hugh had been assigned to a rare Australian region, where snow was no novelty. Summer, he would find, was sometimes soft breezes and pleasant air, but at other times a baking dome of sky, unrelentingly blue. Irish convicts began tentatively to salt the strange country with Celtic names: Cashel Rock, Burren Downs, Tipperary. But it remained unapologetically itself.

Returning at dusk to the vicinity of the hut, the two shepherds rejoined the hut-keeper, who had spent the day resting in the bark hut, cleaning, and cooking mutton and damper, a bush bread of flour and water. The three convicts would count the two flocks into temporary folds made of brushwood hurdles. Four dozen or so of these hurdles, light, easily constructed, 6 feet long, stacked by the hut, were set up each night, sometimes some distance off. A little coffin-like portable box, handles at either end, was put in place between the two flocks and there the hut-keeper spent the night, to protect the livestock from the native dogs or dingoes, or from Aborigines. Dingoes possessed preternatural courage and cunning which would establish for them an especial place in settler mythology, and one dog could kill five or six dozen sheep without being heard. Men who lost too many sheep were returned to the convict depot and work gang, beaten by the overseer or flogged at a magistrate's order.

The shepherds and hut-keepers were forbidden to communicate with their convict neighbours, miles off in the next outstation, in case the flocks were 'boxed' or mingled, and the delicate balance of wethers, ewes and rams Bradley had selected was thrown out. The three minders in each set were meant to console themselves with dark tea sweetened by gum-manna – a sort of fructose resin collected from eucalyptus trees – and with sucking on their clay pipes. In return for this isolated care of flocks, a convict shepherd could earn – if paid in money instead of kind – £12 or more a year, and authorise his master to bank money against his ultimate release. Men who could ride and herd cattle were also needed and paid. Everyone, at homestead and outstation, lived off mutton, vegetable gardens, and supplies of flour brought in once a year by bullock wagon.

In Larkin's first lost year beyond the Limits of Location, in a brisk

Monaro June, lambing brought a spate of activity and the reassurance of the familiar. It was of course his chance to show competence. The lambs needed to be weaned, dressed, castrated and branded with pitch. Sick lambs might be brought into the hut, to the fire. Then, as the weather turned warm in October, the shearing commenced at the homestead. The shepherds brought in their flocks to shearing stations alongside the Bredbo, Numerella or Murrumbidgee Rivers. Larkin and other men stood waist-deep in the spring flood as the flocks were run through the river; each animal was passed along from man to man and ducked. Larkin rubbed at the Bathurst burrs caught in the wool, at the excrescences which had accumulated on the sheep's back during the weeks of grazing. But he noticed the quality as well: this wool was about to beat the wool of Saxony and East Galway for strength of fibre and length of staple.

Beside the shearing shed was a rough wool press of split timber. The fleeces were packed in there, the weight being a large glacial stone roped to a pole. It is hard to connect these rough operations to the huge fame Australian wool was then achieving in Europe. In helping bring a new and more sought-after wool to the world market, Larkin was devaluing the product of his nemesis, Seymour.

In the end, the stupefaction of the bush may well have consumed him in a routine of spring sheep-washing, of October shearing, of droving sheep to Goulburn or from Goulburn to the high country of Monaro. Men shared the solace of moonshine distilled by the few gaunt-faced absconders hidden in the hills above, who occasionally descended in coats of kangaroo skin and on horses stolen from some other station to visit huts, trade and complain that they were being crowded out by settlement. To Larkin, these rare contacts with men of no future, who would die alone in the bush or on the scaffold, or vanish to Norfolk Island, were a sobering and reconciling business. They were frequently Irishmen who shared Larkin's politics. Unlike them, however, Larkin certainly knew now that after eight years' good behaviour, he could petition for his family to be sent to New South Wales. He had a tenuous colonial future. To maintain that hope, he had the wit never to be given on a magistrate's order what cynics called 'a present of a red shirt' – a flogging. The chance of reunion with Esther, the only partner permitted to him by Irish custom and Catholic doctrine, became a powerful motive for 'good behaviour'. So in Sydney, clerks began to count the years, as the convict tallied sheep. It was nearly an endurable life.

We do not know what convict servants such as Larkin, drinking black tea by the fires of their huts, wrapped in coats of skinned possums or kangaroos, listening to the high winter winds of Monaro, said of Bradley.

But the remoteness of his holdings probably influenced his treatment of them. Bradley's pastoral headquarters in Monaro lay more than 100 miles south of the nearest police magistrate. If Bradley wished to take legal vengeance on one of his workers, it would require a journey of three or four days' duration. If he or his overseer executed punishment informally with fist, knout, or stopping of rations, they had to be sure that it was all seen as appropriate by the convicts, or else risk that their workers would rebel or abscond, and livestock be harmed.

Alexander Harris, a footloose young Englishman who worked in Australia for seventeen years, saw how pastoralist and convict shepherd might compromise. A master visited a hut and noticed without creating a fuss an illicitly killed and hung sheep. That, he thought, made the master a sensible man. And yet Harris also visited a farm where the convicts told him they had been starved. On the Goulburn plains, wrote Harris, 'the masters seem generally to be in very bad odour with their men, *excepting only the young natives* who have land there'.

It was masters, rather than semi-literate convicts, who left what comments we have on the relationship between master and assigned convict. One vocal employer of convicts, James Mudie, who owned a pretentiously named property, Castle Forbes, was influenced in everything he had to say about his convicts by hostility to Governor Bourke. A number of Mudie's men had absconded, and one had fired at him during a raid they made for supplies. When they were recaptured, Roger Therry, friend of the Liberator, defended them. A number of them told Therry and the court that they would rather die than be sent back to Mudie, and one showed his counsel the scars of Mudie's punishments. The bench of magistrates, friends of Mudie's, would not let this evidence be presented, however. In the end, two prisoners were hanged at Castle Forbes, three – including a boy of sixteen – were executed in Sydney, and the sixth was sent to Norfolk Island for life. With someone like Mudie for master, Hugh could have been similarly destroyed.

Bourke had ordered an inquiry into Mudie's behaviour, but removed him too from the list of justices of the peace. Mudie began writing a book, *The Felonry of New South Wales*, designed to embarrass Bourke before a proposed Select Committee of Inquiry into Transportation, in London. 'It is notorious', wrote Mudie, 'that, during the administration of seven successive governors of New South Wales, transportation to that colony was so far from being regarded as a severe punishment by the major part of the criminals in England, that numerous avowals have been made by convicts of their having actually committed the crimes for which they were tried, for the express purpose of being sent out to a land of promise.'

Hugh, argued about by Tories and improvers, kept his counsel in a huge, strange country. Australian-born currency lads might on Australia Day in Sydney toast, 'The land, boys, we live in!' It was unlikely that in the huge natural pastures of the Monaro Larkin drank that toast or thought himself more than an exile. But as surely as the immigrant to North America was making and being made by that society, Larkin was – in the great Australian stillness – himself making, and being made.

4
The Limits of Location

Thy father is a chieftain!
Why that's the very thing!
Within my native country
I too have been a king . . .
But rebels rose against me,
And dared my power disown –
You heard, love, of the judges?
They drove me from my throne . . .
The bush is now my empire,
The knife my sceptre keen;
Come with me to the desert wild,
And be my dusky queen.

Colonial song,
'The Convict and his Loubra'

If assigned to the main homestead, Hugh and the overseer – and even Mr Bradley on visits from Goulburn – were housed democratically close together, the master in one rough hut, the overseer and man or men in the other. Everyone slept on a sheet of bark with bedclothes of sheepskins and opossum rugs. The door was often a curtain of hessian wool packs. A pannikin filled with clay and mutton fat provided the lighting. Near the wall stood the standard medicine for all ailments, the sole remedy other than alcohol – a blue box of Seidlitz powders.

Larkin's convict clothing had by now been replaced by the standard bush uniform supplied by masters – leg-strapped trousers, blue Crimean shirts, and a cabbage-tree hat of plaited leaves. A few kangaroos provided material for a warm coat. Hessian-style boots and spurs were worn for rounding up livestock on horseback. Mustering strayed cattle, riding up escarpments through the great verticals of eucalyptus trees, the Ribbonman might have been mistaken for the master.

The relationship was closer and more democratic still when tyro settlers found remote land and brought into it the few resources they could afford. One of Bradley's protégés in the Monaro area was a man the same age as Hugh Larkin, William Adams Brodribb. Brodribb's father had been an English political prisoner, a lawyer who in youth had belonged to a republican cell and who was given seven years for administering illegal oaths. Brodribb senior had finished out his sentence as a ticket-of-leave attorney in Hobart Town, Van Diemen's Land. He became both a farmer and a shareholder in the Bank of Van Diemen's Land.

The younger Brodribb had come to Tasmania as a child in 1818, with his mother. The boy grew up in respectable Anglo-Scots colonial society, in which it seemed that everyone did his best to forget Mr Brodribb senior's modest foray into republicanism. William Adams Brodribb arrived purposefully in New South Wales in 1835, when Larkin had been working for Bradley for a year. 'In those days,' Brodribb would remember, 'it was no unusual thing for a squatter to claim 200 or 300 square miles; land was no object; there was plenty for new squatters.' One stockman tending flocks in a hut in Monaro – it could have been Larkin, or any other of Bradley's fifty other assigned convicts scattered throughout the bush – promised to show Brodribb 'a good cattle station, unoccupied, not far from his master's station, provided I should thereafter feel disposed to settle in that squatting district'. Brodribb's run lay in a deep corner of the Monaro, in a plain made bare perhaps by the fire-stick hunting methods of the natives who came here in summer, perhaps by other causes. Wooded hills and snow-streaked alps rose above the pastures.

Larkin was loaned indefinitely by Bradley to young Brodribb. Some years later Brodribb stated in an official document that he had employed and known Larkin since 1834, a slight exaggeration, since Brodribb himself did not arrive in the Monaro until 1835. But in Brodribb's first year in the Monaro, with a convict shepherd, probably Larkin, and 'the assistance of a few Aborigines, I washed and sheared my 1,200 ewes'. Here the wool press was far more primitive even than the one Hugh had seen at Bradley's. Brodribb confessed, 'My hut-keeper pressed the wool with a spade, in a rough primitive box made by ourselves on the station.'

After the settlers' runs were given some legitimacy, flamboyant officials named commissioners of Crown lands rode out in green uniform, hessian boots and braided cap, trailing a few mounted police through the mists or heat hazes, to decide where Bradley's and Brodribb's properties and grazing rights began and ended. But boundary lines were still drawn with the same informality – natural springs, an Aboriginal tumulus of stone, tree-blazes, ant heaps, isolated she-oaks, all served as markers. Settlers were to pay £10 for every 20 square miles of country they occupied, and on top of that a halfpenny for each sheep.

Hugh, now a servant of Australian beef and wool, but distracted by labour, distance and adequate diet from any clear impulse of rebellion, probably had his journeys too. When the wool had been loaded on its wagon in later spring, that is, October–November, a settler like Brodribb started out with a reliable man to bring the load overland to Goulburn. From there they eased it up the Razorback range and down through endless hills to the place called the Black Huts on the Liverpool Road, where Sydney wool buyers posted themselves. In good years, buyers would in fact advance far up the road towards Goulburn on fast ponies. The buyer would cut a slash in an ordinary bale, take out a handful of wool, hoping he had picked a representative sample, and make a bid. These were primitive but significant dealings. On them depended the colonial prosperity with which settlers consoled themselves, to make up for their distance from Britain. What slave cotton was to the American South, convict wool would be to Australia. The mills of Britain had an illimitable hunger for both.

There were a number of hostelries in the area where the roads from both Sydney and Parramatta met – the Farmer's Home, the Square and Compass, the Woolpack and Old Jack Ireland's – at which the squatters and dealers argued and struck a price, while the Larkins of the system went amongst the wagons looking for someone shipped more recently than they, to hear news of that most distressful country. The wool from Monaro, bought at the Black Huts, would be taken on to Sydney by the dealer, be shipped to London and turn up at Garraway's Coffee-House in Change Alley, Cornhill, where by the light of guttering candles early Australian fibre drew bids based on an unprecedented enthusiasm.

The returns his master achieved must have raised in Larkin the teasing prospect of becoming a grazier and landholder in his own right. To establish a station, capital was needed, £5,000 for a well-balanced flock, wagon and convict shepherds. But some determined former convicts, starting with small flocks, managed to become the living exemplars for the character Magwitch, the English convict who left his fortune to Pip, in Charles Dickens's novel of 1861, *Great Expectations*.

Larkin heard at some stage of Ned Ryan, a Ribbonman who twenty years before had been involved in 'assaulting habitation' in one of the early tithe outrages at Ballagh, Tipperary. He had got his conditional pardon in 1830 and settled land near the present town of Boorowa beyond the Lachlan River. He called his station Galong Castle, and eventually went on to build a castle there and be reunited with his wife and three children, one of whom would serve in the Legislative Assembly of New South Wales. The Etonian, classicist squatter might find that his neighbouring pastoralist was a former sheep thief from Ireland or Scotland, or even a former opponent of the British system. Though rare, the convict who returned home rich, like Orpheus ascending from Hades, would become one of the stock figures of popular literature, and sentimentally implied what many liberal-minded folk believed: that there was no criminal class; that in the right milieu the convict became laird.

If Hugh daydreamed along these lines, there were factors which might make him think twice. In the winter and early summer of 1837, inadequate snow fell on the alps above the Monaro to fill the rivers. This was Hugh's first experience of that recurrent but assured Australian phenomenon, drought, the most severe until then experienced by Europeans. There would be five to six such years of blazing suns and poor rainfall. The Murrumbidgee River dried up. Hugh and other convict stockmen had horse races in the dry bed. He would rise up in stifling air to see huge walls of flame moving down the wooded slopes, set off by lightning or an Aboriginal hunting fire. Hugh Larkin's Australian education was proceeding apace, and heat and fire annealed him further in this inescapable landscape.

Hugh's bush limbo had its complications. The day came when, out on his own, he watched in edgy wonderment as the tribespeople, old men and warriors ahead, women and children behind, came down out of the screen of forest on the hills to hold discourse with him and perhaps to trade. Matters in the Monaro had not yet reached the stage where Hugh was armed with one of Brodribb's carbines. He knew these people speared sheep and, if a shepherd objected too strongly, killed him with spears or a blow to the back of the head with one of the hardwood clubs or stone axes they used to finish off kangaroos. The young native men of Monaro in fact carried a variety of purpose-designed hunting spears and two designs of the stunning and felling boomerang. The women came behind carrying their dilli bags and finely wrought nets of kurrajong fibre for catching insects. Later, when anthropologists visited the area, the Ngarigo were accorded an international scholastic repute for the latter.

Because these early contacts so frequently befell men like Larkin, there exists too little of a European record of them, but Hugh would have been a remarkable fellow if he had seen communal cause between himself and these opossum-skin-cloaked elders, the watchful younger warriors, the women (*lubras* or *gins*, as they were commonly called), and the children who did not know that in this conversation between Ngarigo and English-Irish lay the ruin of their world.

The Ngarigo had occupied for millennia this side of the Australian Alps between the Murrumbidgee and the Snowy Rivers. They had ritual and marriage relationships with people named the Walgalu and the Ngunawal to the north, towards present-day Canberra, and with the Bidawal to the south. They encountered in summer the Djila Matang from the western side of the Alps, and traded for shells with the coastal Djiringanj to the east. Virtually until the year Hugh arrived in the Monaro, these had been the borders of their feasible world.

They wintered to the north, but came south to the higher Monaro in spring, to feast on the nutty, protein-rich Bogong moth, *Agrotis infusa*, 'animated fat-bags' settling inches deep on trees and in rock crevices to breed. It was probably in the time of the Bogong that Hugh met them. He brought to the encounter convict and settler myths, likely to cause the European to daydream of some bush liaison with the prescriptive 'dusky maiden'. Aboriginal monogamy was based on blood laws, and was therefore as strict as European morality, and in terms of legal sanction stricter. Observers claimed that sometimes a casual sharing of a wife was permitted, as long as it was with a man inside the husband's kinship group. But the white convict shepherd lay outside the bloodlines and so outside the moral universe of the natives. He was a chimera, and so not a forbidden contact.

One commentator spoke of 'black women cohabiting with the knowledge and consent of their sable husbands, in all parts of the interior, with white hut-keepers'. It was often the armed or lustful convict shepherd, the rejected of Europe, who was guilty of the founding tragedies of the contact between Europeans and natives. But the blame was regularly sheeted to the inferior morals not of Europeans but of the natives. 'Although the *gins* cherished some of their children, they certainly kill many, and almost invariably, the male half-breeds,' wrote an observer in 1849.

There were other versions: the natives found that

> their *gins*, or daughters, are taken from them; and the diseases of the white man, extended without remorse, destroy and daily diminish the race of Aborigines as the squatter advances . . . I am told it is no uncommon thing for these rascals to sleep all night with a Lubra . . . and if she poxes him or in any way offends him perhaps shoot her before 12 next day.

Hugh Larkin may have been utterly innocent of the grossest of these crimes. He had the memory of Esther, but an Esther impossibly remote. He had the taboos of his own religion and culture. But he was removed from the landscape of his customary morality, and hard-used men can themselves be hard users. It was at least likely that Hugh shared liquor, distilled in one of the bush's plentiful illegal stills, with tribal people. And in protecting his livestock, both because that was the European thing to do, and because it was what his master expected of him under pain of punishment, he would eventually have instigated or witnessed the collision between European and native, the explosion of the relationship into spear-throwing on one side, the firing of carbines on the other. Some shepherds, it was claimed, would potshot natives as if they were pigeons.

Larkin became aware too of the shifts of policy designed by anxious governors to protect the natives. After Governor Bourke went home in

1837, the new man, Sir George Gipps, would appoint 'Protectors of Aborigines', usually Anglican clergymen, to patrol remote districts and try to regulate the treatment of the native people within their regions. These men often came to Australia in answer to an advertisement in the *Church Times*, and saw themselves as living with their wives and children in a manse amongst white-robed natives. Instead they were given a dray and dispatched into the interior. Hugh saw one such man moving bewildered through Bradley's and Brodribb's holdings. Like his secular brethren, the protector found the nomadic quality of Aboriginal life an affront, and tried to keep Aboriginal peoples near his hut by supplying them with flour, sugar, tea, tobacco.

In 1842, even the system of protectors would be abandoned, but the squatters complained that Governor Gipps himself acted as Supreme Protector and generally blamed problems of violence on settlers and their shepherds. Gipps founded the border police to keep order in the remoter bush, and insisted that every native killed should have the same form of inquest as a European. As one commentator complained, Gipps 'ignored the hundreds of miles that made absurd any comparison between a crime in George Street and a murder in the outer bush'. He put eleven men on trial for the shooting and burning of twenty-eight natives at Myall Creek, hundreds of miles north-west of Sydney, and seven were hanged. He wanted to punish Major Nunn of the mounted police for killing too many natives while clearing the Namoi country. Squatters told improbable stories of natives warning settlers that if they responded to native impudence they would be hauled off to Sydney and hanged. They blamed Gipps and not themselves for the seven or eight years of terror and warfare between 1837 and 1845. The natives would kill whites, one of them complained, 'for no reason at all save their isolation!' And Hugh saw himself as possible victim of a sporadic war he had not chosen.

Helena, the capital of the state of Montana, would on the face of it be a strange reference point for the careers of Australia-bound Irish felons. But on a terrace before the main entrance of the granite Legislature stands a massive statue of a mounted Union general, riding parallel to the Rockies, which can be seen to the west, beyond the Helena airport. This towering figure on its large plinth faces north, as if marching towards Canada, an enterprise in which some Irish would during the century involve themselves. Around the massive monument's base are samples of the general's oratory: in Ireland as a youth, in Van Diemen's Land as a prisoner, or in the United States as a defender of the Union. The man represented here is Thomas Francis Meagher, an Irishman and, for a time, Australian convict.

He was born in Waterford on 23 August 1823 into one of that small number of Catholic mercantile families who, despite the Penal Laws, could be found in the big ports, supplying shipping and imports, needed by the landowning establishment. The family wealth derived from his grandfather, who had left farming in Tipperary in the previous century, and emigrated to St John's, Newfoundland, establishing an import-export business with Waterford. At one stage – in a foreshadowing of the melodramas of his grandson's life – he was captured by a French privateer.

Meagher's father, also Thomas, had been put in charge of the Waterford end of the family's business, and ran it until August 1820. That year he married Alicia Quan, daughter of Thomas Quan of Wyse, Cashen & Quan, one of the largest trading companies of Waterford. Thomas Francis Meagher's birthplace was an elegant pierfront home on the west bank of the River Suir. It was a household of excellent Irish linen, and furniture and draperies from England and France. In February 1827, when the boy was less than four years of age, his mother died, leaving a husband with three children – one daughter and two sons. The boy retained for life the questing intensity of a child too early deprived of a mother.

His father, Thomas Meagher senior, was a member of O'Connell's Catholic Association, 'a silent, steadfast man held in general respect'. His austerity of character would always distance him from his flamboyant son, although his lifelong generosity was often exercised across a gulf of incomprehension. Elected first Catholic mayor of Waterford in 1829, he would later hold a seat in the House of Commons. Like many wealthy Catholics, he distrusted the Establishment's Trinity College, Dublin, and looked to the Jesuits of Clongowes Wood in County Kildare to supply his son with the attainments and tastes of a nineteenth-century Catholic gentleman. Thomas Francis Meagher was sent there in the year of Hugh's trial, 1833. (Much, much later, Clongowes would also give the young James Joyce a childhood home and education.)

Meagher's fellow student and lifetime friend on three continents, Pat Smyth, later remembered it was never Meagher's ambition to win the regard of the priests. 'I have known him in a football match to let fly deliberately at a master's shins.' He was no doubt practising for whacking his father's shins, the shins of Westminster, and ultimately those of the man nearest to God on a secular level, O'Connell.

In the years of Larkin's early vast detention in Monaro, the Jesuits were refining if not tempering the ardent, husky Meagher. While he had saving intellectual and artistic enthusiasms – he would begin to play the clarinet, and join the Debating Society – in retrospect he saw Jesuit Clongowes as an ill-assorted place, not fully possessing either Irish roots or English validity. 'Architecturally considered,' he wrote, 'it is a curious compound.' What he was taught he believed similarly mixed:

they talked to us about Mount Olympus and Vale of Tempe; they birched us into a flippant acquaintance with the disreputable Gods and Goddesses of the golden and heroic ages; they entangled us in Euclid . . . gave us a look, through an interminable telescope, at what was doing in the New World; but, as far as Ireland was concerned, they left us like blind and crippled children, in the dark.

There were, Meagher remembered, sacred Irish sites around Clongowes. The boys went out on rambles under the care of Jesuits, 'without a finger to mark them on our memories . . . Ireland was the last nation we were taught to think of, to respect, to love and remember.'

There is no reason to doubt the claim he would make, decades later, at the Irish Immigration Society of St Paul, Minnesota, about the 'one scene I witnessed in the morning of my boyhood which left upon my memory an impression that can never be effaced.

That scene was the departure of an immigrant-ship from the quay of my native city of Waterford . . . On the deck of the ship were huddled hundreds of men, women and children – the sons and daughters of Innisfail . . . Young as I was, I had heard enough of the cruelty that had, for years and years, been done to Ireland, to know that her people were leaving her not from choice but from compulsion; that it was not the sterility of the soil, or any other unfavourable dispensation of nature, but the malignant hostility of laws and practices.'

At the same time as the boy Meagher tussled and took instructions from the Jesuits, a young man subject to apparently different Irish influences, another future Australian convict, was running his estate in Limerick, and participating in the national political debate. This man's name was William Smith O'Brien, a tall young aristocrat already thirty years of age at the time of Larkin's sentencing. (He like Meagher would have his statue, but his would be at the heart of Dublin, in O'Connell Street.)

O'Brien's birth date was significant, 1803, three years after the abolition of the Irish Parliament and the Union of Ireland and England. He would grow up a formidable enemy of that Union. His birthplace was Dromoland Castle in County Clare, on the O'Brien estate of Dromoland. He was a direct descendant of Brian Boru, who in the tenth century had fought his way across Ireland, absorbing allegiances until recognised as High King. Boru had died at the Battle of Clontarf in 1014, when his forces defeated a combination of Irish and Danish opponents. Saving Ireland seemed to be a genetic responsibility for O'Brien. But so was saving family land. In the sixteenth century Murrough O'Brien had submitted his crown to that of Henry VIII for the sake of retaining ancestral land. Young William Smith O'Brien had written in the 1820s:

'The lapse of more than three hundred years which has taken place since that humiliation was inflicted upon our family does not reconcile me to it.'

Sir Edward O'Brien, baronet, O'Brien's father, had in the 1820s converted the old house at Dromoland into the 'baronial castle' seen today. But the O'Briens were characteristically encumbered with debt, especially from the renovations. Sir Edward had followed as a young man the normal stratagem: to marry the daughter of a financially secure commoner. No Gaelic fervour marked such marriages. But undertaken dutifully, they produced contentment. Sir Edward O'Brien married Charlotte, daughter of William Smith, a lawyer and landlord who had held mortgages over the Dromoland estate and who waived them in time for the wedding.

Given his grandfather Smith's name out of family piety, William Smith O'Brien was the second son of Sir Edward and the forthright Charlotte. He experienced the benefits of the upbringing of his class, which should have ensured that he would never have fellow feeling even with Meagher, let alone Hugh Larkin. He went to preparatory school in Kent and then to Harrow and Trinity College, Cambridge. But: 'From my boyhood I have entertained a passionate affection for Ireland . . . I have never witnessed the miseries and indignities which its people still suffer without a deep sentiment of indignation.'

By 1828 O'Brien had graduated from Cambridge, and was admitted to the Bar after attending Lincoln's Inn. He was by then a tall young man, a good, austere speaker, but certainly without Daniel O'Connell's common touch. He possessed a thorny sense of honour and astounding energy. For the sake of an active life, he thought of entering the Royal Navy. Instead, almost immediately he was 'brought into Parliament by my father as member for the borough of Ennis – a closed borough to which our family possessed an alternating nomination with the late George Fitzgerald'. In other words, he inherited a so-called 'rotten borough', a parliamentary seat to which men were not so much elected as virtually appointed, and he served until such anomalies were swept away by the Reform Bill of 1832. He was considered slightly dangerous, the sort of Protestant establishment figure who supported Catholic Emancipation on grounds of equity. He shocked his mother, Lady O'Brien, by joining O'Connell's Catholic Association.

Then to her further horror, when Daniel O'Connell so cunningly forced the issue, O'Brien voted for Emancipation. Though a Catholic and by law ineligible, O'Connell had decided in 1828 to stand for County Clare, the O'Briens' own county. This was an election in whose result shoeless and voteless Irish like the Larkins and Tullys were engrossed. Wellington and Robert Peel were compelled now either to deny the election or confirm it by granting Catholic Emancipation. The young O'Brien was delighted, though he believed O'Connell had brought it about in a cheap, vulgar way, and was not even a Clare man to begin with, but an outsider from Kerry.

Some of O'Brien's statements about O'Connell's opportunism led to a duel between O'Brien and O'Connell's lieutenant, Tom Steele. Duelling was a regular mechanism for relieving political pique and gentlemanly honour in Ireland. Both men survived – according to a gracious legend, it is said that one of Steele's seconders made a private plea to O'Brien on behalf of Steele, who was no marksman, and, after Steele had fired and missed, O'Brien himself – to the applause of a large, open-air audience – turned in his loaded weapon. If so, it was an act of crushing contempt for which Tom Steele would never forgive him.

Then when Lucius, Smith O'Brien's brother, contested Clare at the next election, this same seconder, one Mahon, voiced some insults against the O'Brien household which led to another duel. This contest was conducted before a large crowd at Ennis racecourse. Mahon fired and missed, and O'Brien's pistol, improperly prepared by his seconds, failed to fire at all. By some Irish gentlemanly formula not immediately clear, this settled the affair. Such confrontations naturally suggest that beneath O'Brien's external reserve lay an intense temperament. His brother Lucius was aware of it: in 1830 he extricated William from an affair in London, during his sojourns at Westminster, with a woman named Mary Anne Wilton. She would bear O'Brien a child, but she was not marriageable by O'Brien standards, and Lucius, on the basis of discussions with his father, Sir Edward, promised the young woman in return for silence an annuity of £50 for life. 'With this proviso that if ever at any time this affair be brought before the public . . . my promise shall be void.'

O'Brien, still representing Ennis, was now steered towards marrying a loyal, genial, loving young woman, Lucy Gabbett. Lucy's father was a liberal-minded landlord of High Park, who had been mayor of Limerick, and she was part of a large Church of Ireland and farming family. Like O'Brien's mother, Lucy never understood William's politics. O'Brien, who had already inherited one of his grandfather's estates named Cahirmoyle in County Limerick, persuaded his mother to let Lucy and himself live in a handsome but dilapidated Georgian house there. It was a delicate request. Lady O'Brien said that her father had 'in fact let the whole place go to ruin by giving it to Bridget Keevan for a dairy and letting the cows into every part of it'. Keevan had been her father's mistress.

Though Smith O'Brien loved women and charmed them with a quiet ease, Lucy would, in politics as in prison, be his lodestar. And in the first year of Larkin's labour in Monaro, tall, earnest Smith O'Brien seemed to be safely rusticating at his estate of Cahirmoyle, in the renovated estate house with Lucy and their three young children. But in 1835 he was easily enough persuaded to stand as an independent Liberal candidate for the County of Limerick.

His large family were still ambiguous about his politics. Of his earlier published pamphlet on disestablishing the Church of Ireland, his father Sir Edward wrote: 'You certainly would destroy the Protestant religion altogether in Clare when you would give but five clergymen to our population of 5,000 persons.' It all savoured, said Sir Edward, 'of the O'Connell school'.

Now, after a hard campaign on the narrow franchise then in existence, Smith O'Brien was elected to the House of Commons by a constituency he described as a progressive landlord or two and the humbler end of the £10 leaseholders. He would hold that seat for fourteen years, crossing to England by ship for sittings of Parliament, travelling to London by coach and later by rail, a regimen of which many other Irish MPs soon tired. He was careful with the expense all this demanded, but at some level he devoutly desired this demanding life. Lucy, aware that he was careful about money, wrote to him from Cahirmoyle, 'I wish you were settled in nice, clean and elegant lodgings. Pray do not spare upon yourself but make yourself comfortable. I hope you will go to many literary evenings and it will beguile the long and lonely evenings.'

Because a fire had gutted the chamber of the Commons in Westminster Palace, Parliament then met in the less than cosy St Stephen's Chapel. Here, Smith O'Brien voted with the Whigs under a succession of Prime Ministers beginning with Lord Melbourne. Unlike the Irish masses, though, he still found great O'Connell, and the relatives O'Connell swept into the House with him, vulgar and populist and grandstanding. Yet though he disapproved of the fashionable house they kept while in London, he pursued the same issues as they did, and voted with them frequently. He pressed particularly for an Irish Poor Law, under which absentee and other Irish landlords would be required to provide the funds for the relief of the evicted, the landless, the widowed. But he wanted relief to be distributed on an outdoor basis, not through the institution of the workhouse, as was the British model. Irish poverty, he told the Parliament, was a different beast from British poverty.

Despite his aristocratic aloofness, his friends and enemies admired him. Here was a fellow who could have stayed at home, farmed, collected botanical specimens or invented irrigation systems, coming to the House of Commons to be what Tories considered an independent radical, busying himself in Westminster without any hope of, or ambition for, office. That was his stated position – he would not let himself be neutralised as a spokesman for Ireland by offers of Cabinet or other posts. Yet he was conscientious to the point of exhaustion in attendance at parliamentary sessions, paying boy runners to rouse him at night from his lodgings in Westminster if a debate he had an interest in came on.

He did go to many interesting evenings, including an occasional dinner with other politicians, Lord Melbourne, Lord Palmerston, or Lord John Russell, the leaders of the Whigs, and with writers like Thomas Carlyle and the just emerging, witty, but far from Irish-sympathetic, William Makepeace Thackeray. To these tables he brought a passion for statistics and a strong gift for reasoning rather than graphic leaps of imagination and imagery, and he enjoyed the *frisson* of political discussion with handsome, Whiggish women. But he did not pay court to Cabinet ministers.

And if there was any hubris in the distance O'Brien kept from the Liberator, it was balanced by an endearingly modest view of his own gifts. Later, he would reflect that had he not been true to his principles, he would probably have been given a place in the British Cabinet, but then he did not think that was saying much for a man's honour *or* talents.

Even when he came home, after hours if not days in a coach, there was no rest. His young sisters Grace and Anne were promoters of what Wakefield called 'systematic colonisation', both as a means of rescue for the people and also, cynics said, as a means of relieving estates of squalid encampments of tenants-at-will. Grace was, more than anyone else in his family, Smith O'Brien's soul-mate. The two of them founded in an office in Limerick the Emigrant Friends' Society to provide the Irish of Limerick County with information on colonies, sources of emigration funding, landowning opportunities in the new world, shipping, available employment in distant places, and so on. With his brother Henry O'Brien, ten years younger, Smith O'Brien set up in Limerick and Clare temperance societies whose chief purpose, said O'Brien, was to allow the peasantry and the town worker a pleasant environment in which to study at night. The societies were devised to act too as savings banks-cum-credit unions. The little reading rooms in Ennis and Limerick, rented at family expense and stocked with pamphlets, newspapers and books, were unjustly suspected by Catholic labourers as dens of heresy.

The Irish Poor Law came up for its first reading in Parliament in 1837. A plentiful potato crop in that year ensured people like Esther Larkin, and her infants Hugh and Patrick, a further year's margin and survival. But, O'Brien asked in the Commons, was a margin enough?

5
Ireland and the *Whitby* Women

> The women from the Irish counties, on the other hand, were more frequently first offenders, and more likely to come from a background of distress, poverty and destitution from loss of husband or loss of employment.
>
> Portia Robinson, *The Women of Botany Bay*

By October 1838, the Irish establishment, sometimes mockingly called 'the Garrison', congratulated themselves that nearly a decade of Emancipation had not brought the horrifying shifts of power, the fall from Protestant enlightenment to Papist barbarism, they had feared. Their enemy Dan O'Connell was in a slough. The Dublin *Protestant Guardian* crowed:

He confesses to the people of Ireland, to the Roman Catholic millions, that for thirty years during the whole of which he has hallood them on to treason against the state, and to outrage and pillage of the Protestant Church, yet nothing has been done! yes, nothing! . . . the tens of millions of your hard-earned cash, the tribute which he extorted from his abused and deluded followers, have been idly spent!

Hugh Larkin had been working in the bush more than four years when at the City Court of Sessions in Limerick thirteen Irish labourers and servants, of a section of society that had unwavering faith in the Liberator, were unremarkably sentenced to seven years' transportation each. One of them was an auburn-haired, small-boned, handsome young woman of twenty-two years named Mary Shields, who had stolen wearing apparel from a Timothy Reardon.

The readers of the *Limerick Chronicle* would have found utterly predictable the published list in which Shields's name appeared. Other women sentenced at the same Hilary session by magistrates and recorders were Catherine Mongavan, who had stolen £5 13 shillings, a third of the average yearly wages for the Kingdom of Ireland; Martha Walker, who had stolen a sheet; and Rosanna Daly, who had shoplifted ribbon from Todd & Company. The rest of the potential transportees sentenced at that October session were males.

Details of Mary Shields's crime are as obscure as those of the mass of Irish convicts. We do not know what cash value the jury may have put on the clothes Mary Shields took from Mr Reardon. But there were some indicative lighter sentences: Mary Brennan, stealing soap from the shop of James Kelly, was given one month's hard labour; Patrick Farrell, stealing £1 15 shillings from Timothy Collopy, received three months. Was Shields's theft greater in terms of quantity or did she take more expensive clothing? Since her occupation was given as that of servant, she may have been Mr Reardon's servant, and the magistrates and jury perhaps saw her theft as a betrayal of a supposed 'good master', a man like themselves. It was recorded also that she was a native of Tipperary. So she and her parents belonged to the masses of landless or evicted peasantry who wandered into cities and took what work they found.

Accepting that Mary committed the crime, there are a number of grounds that justify our asking if it was a crime of malice or a crime of need, or both at once. Could it even have been – not unknown amongst low-paid, ill-used servants – a crime of industrial vengeance? This young woman, 5 feet 1¼ inches in height, bore the indications of want. She was also mother of a small son and an infant daughter. She had been married at eighteen in May 1834 to a man named John O'Flynn in St John's Church, Limerick. The first child was baptised at St Michael's Church, Limerick, in October 1835, and was named Michael after the saint. A daughter, Bridget, named probably in honour of a close friend, Bridget Purcell, listed as baptismal sponsor, was baptised in December 1837.

Though there had been some recent prison reforms, Limerick city gaol – strictly the county gaol for the city of Limerick – was not much different from Larkin's prison in Galway city. Limerick gaol too was run under contract issued by the county's Chief Constable. Parents, husband, relatives like Annie Moloney, godmother to the infant Bridget, and friends like Bridget Purcell, came tentatively into the corridors of the women's ward to see Mary, hoping she had not been scarred or misused. They reproached, commiserated, argued, wept, made arrangements about the infants. They gave Mary tobacco for her short clay *dudeen*, and heard her utter the hope there would be no ship available. If so, she might serve her time companionably in Limerick where they could see her face and she could keep her children.

Children often accompanied their parents to prison. Mary's son Michael was of an age, about two years old, to want to be with his mother, and was, at least part of the time, in the wards of the gaol with her. In purely physical terms the conditions of her imprisonment may in fact have been no worse than the crowded room in a city hovel where she and O'Flynn lived with their families. But she missed bitterly what Hugh had missed, the hearth, the familial caress.

*

Like most of the women who were to accompany her to Australia, Mary Shields had no previous conviction. In this and other aspects of her transportation, she fitted fairly precisely the same picture of the Irish female first offender given us by a modern historian who has studied convict women of a slightly earlier generation, up to 1828. More Irish female convicts – as compared with convicts from the rest of Britain – were married women, more were mothers of young families, more came from the country. Apart from Dubliners, few were described as 'of the Cyprian tribe', that is, prostitutes. Fewer, too, had been found guilty of crimes of violence such as assault or highway robbery.

The date of Mary Shields's trial, in the autumn of the year, suggests that her crime was committed in the summer. The potato did not last after early summer, and the new crop was not harvested until September. Shields was at least a city woman, receiving a cash salary. But with the price of food rising as the summer advanced, one infant at the breast but the other growing wizened, and a husband, parents, sister, facing the customary hunger, it is not fanciful to claim that Mary's motive for her first and sole lifetime offence was to convert stolen clothing into cash for bread, oatmeal, a luxurious piece of bacon, and – God knows – some liquor.

The bill for an Irish Poor Law passed into law on 31 July 1838, three months before Shields's trial. Home Secretary Lord John Russell greeted its passage and the establishment of Irish workhouses 'as a measure of peace, enabling the country to prohibit vagrancy'. The hope that the Poor Law and the workhouse would lever the poorer Irish off the land had caused O'Connell to oppose the new legislation unless it was accompanied by the broader Irish reforms he sought.

There were as ever special Irish problems with a Poor Law. In England, rudimentary conditions within the workhouse stimulated inmates to seek employment in the outside world. A Poor Law commissioner, George Nicholls, wrote that such a stratagem could not be used with the Irish. 'The standard of their mode of living is unhappily so low that the establishment of one still lower is difficult.' Ireland was now to be divided into Poor Law unions based on the administrative units called baronies, and a workhouse was to be established in every barony, paid for by a poor rate levied amongst landlords and leaseholders. The workhouses – 'all mere decoration being studiously excluded' – were of a pattern, severe in structure, with a small entrance lodge through which the inmates approached the main three-storey building of comfortless neo-Gothic stone.

The Limerick workhouse, costing nearly £13,000 and covering 11 acres, would not be ready to receive its poor until May 1841. But the probable truth is that had the workhouse existed as a safety net in her day, Shields would still have committed her crime. To many people, even after the workhouses were in place, a minor crime committed to deal with a needful emergency would prove preferable. Smith O'Brien had warned in the Commons that the workhouse would prove alien to the Irish. They feared not only the indignity of make-work stone-breaking, or the endless pushing of the spoke of a mill wheel, both characteristic labours associated with the workhouse, but also, above all, the separation of women from men and children from parents. William Makepeace Thackeray, visiting the North Dublin Union workhouse in 1843, noticed that 'Among the men there are very few able-bodied, most of them, the keeper said, having gone out for the harvest time or as soon as the potatoes come in'. It would take a cataclysm to make the Irish approach these grim institutions in any numbers.

When Mary was moved out to Dublin, she took her son Michael. What became of Mary's infant, Bridget? The child may have died in infancy. Death being then considered a family matter, most Irish priests did not intrude upon it by marking down the date of death or burial. But Bridget might well have been still alive. Some infants reached the transports if there was no one to leave them with, but it was always at their peril. So it was possible that the baby stayed with Mary's parents, Daniel and Ellen Shields, or her sister, or with John O'Flynn, or with her godmother Anne Moloney. It is possible too that Bridget grew, experienced the coming Irish catastrophe, and emigrated to England or Canada or the United States, where Mary's blood lives on in some unguessable place.

The departure of Mary and her son Michael with six other Limerick women from the county gaol in Limerick occurred in late autumn or winter, an obscure penal event no one took the pains to record. Were they hurried away by cart in the early morning to avoid a scene, or did the Shieldses and O'Flynns find out, and the normal prayers, screams, plaints and improbable promises of reunion steam up into the autumn air?

Though chained at wrist, waist, or even at ankle, and guarded by soldiers detailed from the Limerick garrison, the resultant group of felons could hardly have seemed much of a threat to the social fabric. Catherine Bourke, housemaid, a cloak-stealer, as well as being sixty years of age, was only 5 feet tall. Rosanna Daly, the 19-year-old cook and laundress who had shoplifted, carried pockmarks on her face and was only 4 feet 10 inches. Bridget Lonrigan, a 25-year-old single kitchenmaid and clothes thief, also reached less than 5 feet.

And it was a harsh business getting to the ship. Some years before, the English women of the *Roslin Castle* came on board at the Downs after having travelled in winter 150 miles or more chained up on the outside of coaches. The surgeon found his charges aching with chilblains, and one woman crippled by frostbite. Shields and other Limerick women imprisoned with her would be conveyed in bitter air not to Cork, 50 miles away, but 120 miles across-country to Dublin, a destination which could be approached not only by road but by canals. From Tullamore in County Offaly, they would have been put on the decks of a barge, and subject to the mockery and occasional kindnesses of bargees as they traversed the canal locks along the Grand Canal to Dublin, to august Kilmainham gaol by the Liffey on the edge of the city.

At some time in this sequence of walking, riding, trying to keep herself and Michael warm and safe from molestation in Kilmainham's cellars; somewhere amongst the mists and damps of an Irish early winter spent in unhealthy places, turnkeys and soldiers were certain to have meanly slipped her the horrific news of Atlantic storms, unspeakable catastrophes at sea and unguessable destinations. She heard of the *Neva*, which left Cork in early 1835 with 150 Irish women convicts and over 50 of their children. Four months from departure, in July, on the far side of the earth in Bass Strait, between the Australian mainland and Van Diemen's Land, *Neva* struck on an unmarked rock which ripped her rudder out. The stanchions on the prison deck gave way. All but twenty of the female convicts and all their fifty-nine children were drowned.

Mary's potential *Neva* was the bark *Whitby*, a ship of 431 tons, registered A1 at Lloyd's. Throughout January and February, 130 prisoners and 24 of their children were rowed out through the misty estuary of Dublin Bay and put below in piercing cold on the damp prison deck. In the struggles for space, rations and warmth, Michael was both burden and protection. Not that the other women were hardened criminals. Only three of them had done serious prison time. Whatever their slyness, sullenness, loudness, they were identifiably normal, powerless women, most of them in grief.

On 16 February 1839, Captain Thomas Wellbank signed the Lord Lieutenant's warrant, acknowledging the 'several bodies' he had received on board, and the prison shifts, jackets, petticoats, caps, stockings, shoes intended for their use. 'Twenty-four children accompanied the above Female Convicts supplied with two Suits of Clothing each.'

The surgeon-superintendent on *Whitby* was the naval man John Kidd, who found Mary to have brown hair, brown or chestnut eyes, ruddy complexion. Kidd noted also 'marks of scrofula under the chin or right jaw'. Called the King's Evil because it was believed that the touch of a monarch could cure it, scrofula was something she caught by her parents' hearth, while drinking buttermilk from a cow infected with bovine tuberculosis. Tuberculosis of the lymph glands had imposed high fever, agony of the joints, and swelling and ulceration. The scars remained.

Surgeon Kidd would note that, like Larkin before her, she had Reading but not Writing. As a small girl, then, she too had got a taste of a hedge school.

Many of the children aboard were young and delicate, said Kidd, and 'several of the women old and infirm'. But he kept the women busy with sewing and exercise on deck, and the noise of some crewman's fiddle and the distant thump of jigs was probably heard through the mists by occasional winter promenaders ashore.

The time of anguish and noise came on 18 February. *Whitby* left in much more severe climatic conditions than had *Parmelia*, and in their chains some of the women held and nursed infants. Panic was diminished only by the onset of seasickness and exhaustion. The sickest young woman aboard, Mary Hennessy of Cork, mother of an infant son, had entered the sick bay even before sailing, and continued to suffer from dysentery with anal bleeding – 'the bloody flux'.

A veteran surgeon, Peter Cunningham, who made six journeys to Australia, frankly recommended cohabitation between convict women and sailors or guards. He proposed that these sexual alliances were to the benefit of all parties. They provided the women, he said, with extra comforts – tea and occasional spirits – and provided the sailor with washing, sewing and cleaning. Other more evangelical surgeons kept a stringent eye on the behaviour of all parties. As ever, the little island of a women's ship left in the record more questions than answers, carrying within it its own net of accommodating secrets. And how could the letter of the Admiralty's and Transport Board's regulations always run in the unsupervised Atlantic, and the cold reaches of the Indian and Southern Oceans? Kidd's journal gives not the slightest *direct* information on what arrangements were permitted or suppressed aboard *Whitby*. We have the consistent observations of visitors to Ireland, from Arthur Young to Sir Walter Scott to de Tocqueville and the German Kohl, on the strict virtue of Irish women in their communities. But these women were mislocated, and whether or not they would have welcomed new associations, they had only the surgeon and the far-off regulations to protect them from abuse. Sailors may well have considered them savages. They carried the stain of proven criminality, their Irish raucousness, and – in most cases – their Catholic religion. Many had the further disadvantage of being a speaker of Gaelic.

In kersey jackets, or frocks and woollen caps, the twenty-four children of the convict deck, solace to their mothers, may also have reminded other women of children left behind, deliberately or because of the random policies of the various counties. A 22-year-old needlewoman named Elizabeth Byrne, who had stolen two tumblers in Carlow, was noted as having male and female children. If so, none of them appeared on *Whitby*'s list. But Mary Doyle, a potato-thieving kitchen maid of Dublin who had a previous sentence, was accompanied by a 7-year-old son. There were many such poignant disparities.

But it was surprising how many of the prisoners were going to a reunion. Amongst others, Eliza White of Dublin travelled in hope to her convict husband, Christopher Reilly. Jane Ramsay, a Protestant kitchen maid, was also on her way to her husband, and Mary Carroll, a 39-year-old dairymaid, wanted to show her convict husband her 2½-year-old John Carroll whom he had never seen. But then a 60-year-old, Ann Murray, also had a relative on his way to New South Wales, a son, John Colquhoun, aboard the *Waverley*, a ship for males which left from Dublin a week after the *Whitby*. Had any of these women committed crimes specifically to achieve reunion?

In the turbulent currents south of Africa, Mary Hennessy was mortally ill in heart and body, as was her infant, John Hennessy, six months old at the time of embarkation. Hennessy's lassitude, characteristic of scurvy and heartbreak both, annoyed Kidd: he told her to collect herself and mind her child. The infant died on 21 May off the southern tip of Africa. The keening from the convict deck competed with the particular thunder of those freezing westerlies, and the pitiless discourse between *Whitby*'s timbers and a strenuous sea. Not long after, Hennessy herself died. She was twenty-seven when she expired and was committed to the sea to the south of Amsterdam Island, a plug of granite claimed by France, roughly half-way between Africa and the west coast of Australia.

In harsh June, Shields found the blankets skimpy and too damp to combat the sub-polar cold. The flux was a common complaint on *Whitby*. It did not always aid sisterhood or composure in such limited space. Women cursed and pitied each other as on stormier days the heads became fouled and faecal stench suffused their pitching world. They knew the harsh diet was the problem. So did the new governor of New South Wales, Sir George Gipps, who had taken over from Governor Bourke. He had written to Whitehall about the inferior quality of rations on ships coming from Ireland. Gipps was a studious army engineer with a taste for research. Early in his New South Wales career, he had ordered a more modest study made of the rationing of two ships, the *Diamond*, which had arrived from Cork in March 1838 with females, and the *William Jardine* from Dublin with males. 'A simple perusal of this report will, I hope,' he wrote to Colonial Secretary Glenelg, 'induce Your Lordship to cause an inquiry to be made into the mode of victualling these ships.' But plain tastes, and the fact that hunger was no stranger, equipped most of the *Whitby* women to survive be-weevilled flour and the rancid barrels of bony and unsavoury beef and pork.

As Captain Wellbank rounded the southern tip of Van Diemen's Land and reached up the New South Wales coast, he fell into company with a sloop from Sydney called the *Freak*. *Whitby* and *Freak* sailed in company through the sandstone headlands of Sydney Harbour. The drag of sea slackened. Mary heard raucous Australian birds call from the bushy heights above Watson's Bay.

6
The Lass from the Female Factory

> So agreeable a retreat, indeed, is the *Factory*, that it is quite a common thing for female assigned servants to demand of their masters and mistresses to send them there and flatly, and with fearful oaths, to disobey orders for the purpose of securing the accomplishment of their wish.
>
> James Mudie, evidence before the
> Select Committee on Transportation, 1837

Even the *Sydney Gazette*, edited by emancipists, former convicts, had fallen into the significant mannerism of reporting human cargoes as if they were equivalent to inanimate ones. The *Gazette*'s shipping news the following Tuesday stated *Whitby*'s cargo to be 'female convicts', and without so much as a paragraph break listed another ship, *Tybee*, from Boston, as carrying a cargo of 75 hogsheads of rum, 155 boxes of refined sugar, 18 oars, 122 kegs of tobacco, etc., etc.

The magnates of Sydney and the bush still wanted convict labour and were determined to maintain the convict cargoes and the assignment system. The report of the British Select Committee on Transportation, sitting in London, however, had the year before, 1838, recommended an end to assignment – it generated a convict peasantry, 'one more strange and less attached to the soil they till than the negro slaves of a planter'. The Colonial Secretary of New South Wales said too that assignment of females produced 'grave evil to the women themselves from their frequent change of service, especially in Sydney'. Though Governor Gipps said he found it administratively and fiscally impossible yet to take all the assigned servants back into government labour, all these forces at play helped ensure that Mary's was one of the last half-dozen women's transports to New South Wales, although many more would be sent to Van Diemen's Land.

Unlike Hugh, Mary had not arrived in Sydney in a prosperous year. The price of sheep had begun its 6-year crash from 60 shillings to 1 shilling. Private coaches or other luxury items were offered for a sixtieth of their value. Some free labourers cleared out on trans-Pacific vessels to Valparaiso, Chile, and poorer settlers and their families were lean enough to look familiar to Irish eyes. The names and skills of the *Whitby* women, advertised in the *New South Wales Government Gazette*, brought relatively light demand, and none for women with children. So on 1 July, with perhaps this or that sailor dwelling on a woman's face and regretting her loss, the women and their infants were rowed down-harbour and landed on the western side of Sydney Cove at the dockyard. Lined up unchained, they were lectured by a number of colonial wives, members of the Ladies' Committee, who gave them sisterly though sometimes highly evangelical advice on the perils and possible rewards ahead of them.

It was unlikely that, on their way to the women's barracks at Hyde Park, they much resembled Mudie's description of newly arrived women convicts: 'a herd of females of all ages, and of every gradation of vice, including a large proportion of prostitutes of all trades . . . All who can carry with them the whole paraphernalia of the toilette, with trunks and boxes stuffed with every kind of female dress and decoration.' *Dulcineas*, he said, whores, were the commissioned officers of these rabbles of women. But the demographics of *Whitby* makes unlikely the concept of a flaunting cavalcade of debased colleens, laden with boxes of dresses and trinkets from home.

Five Irish Sisters of Charity had come from Cork the previous December to look after and protect their convict sisters. Mary would have been astonished to sight two or three of them at the women's section of the Hyde Park barracks. The others she would encounter at Parramatta, acting as visitors at the Female Factory, which was to be her home. Much later, a visitor to the barracks said that the sisters 'spread a monastic sphere of quietness, gloom and silence throughout the place', though it is unlikely that they had managed to do so within their first six months of residence in Babylon-on-the-Pacific. In any case, Mary's detention in Sydney was brief. The *Whitby* women and children were brought back down to the water, put into whaleboats by constables and rowed up the Parramatta River, a broad waterway with islands, inlets and fine juts of sandstone, and, further up, broad mangrove swamps.

It could be a pleasant journey even in Sydney's mild winter. In the intimacy of a whaleboat, something like normal male society was now temporarily restored to Mary. The constables and oarsmen were all former or serving convicts, some honourable men, some rascals. The Colonial Secretary of New South Wales *had*, however, taken measures to ensure that reliable fellows had the post. The journey was only 14 miles as the crow flies, somewhat more by the bends of the river, and many fine picnic places lay along the way. Until the 1830s the trip to Parramatta had sometimes taken constables and women three days. Liquor travelled with the parties, and in camps set up early – so it was surmised by the Colonial Secretary – evening bush orgies had been the pattern. These days the journey was meant to take only one long day, or in exceptional circumstances two, and the presence of children would in any case have helped mute wilder behaviour. Boats still generally stopped for refreshments at Squire's Public House, a large slab-hut inn at Kissing Point, above a beach surrounded by sandstone ledges and bush. Here was a sand bar which boats *kissed* against, but it had a repute too for convict sexual recreation. Squire's inn provided Mary with her first Australian drink and social occasion, and she was partial to both.

The Female Factory, opened in 1821 at Parramatta, was built on 4 acres on the river bank, and was judged necessary because of the perceived fallen nature of the women, but also because of the degraded nature of society. The disproportion of male to female in convict society – 100 male convicts to every 17 women convicts – had called the place into being, to save females from prostitution. So the Factory would always have an ambiguity of intent – was it a haven or was it a gaol, was it workshop, hospital, marriage bureau? Certainly the latter, since ticket-of-leave men called there, on their way to the bush, to look for a wife. It had been designed for all possible purposes by the talented convict architect Francis Greenway. Behind its 9-feet walls, it was three storeys high, and was meant to house 300 women.

Within a year of Shields's arrival there, it held 887 women and 405 children. Since free immigration for deserving poor spinsters from the British Isles was taking jobs once given to convict women, women accumulated in the Factory. Before he even left England the new governor, Sir George Gipps, had sought and received permission to extend the Factory. But although he built more cells, he did not expand accommodation for women like Shields who were not serving sentences for colonial misdemeanours.

In some ways the Factory was an extended, land-based version of the convict deck. In the dormitories, women competed for space through sly stratagems and by maintaining a phalanx with those from the same ship and county. *Whitby* women stuck together against women from earlier-arriving ships such as *Lady Rowena*, *Diamond*, *Sir Charles Forbes*, *Surrey* and *Planter*. The English women from these last two ships had their own encampment in the Factory's long dormitories, but the Irish had a larger one, and many of the arguments over space and food were conducted with that Irish raucousness which would become an Australian characteristic, but which polite people wrongly mistook for lowness of soul. The Sisters of Charity did their best to mediate, but may have understood better than male officials that the Factory made a woman edgy and assertive. Those who lost the fight would wither under melancholia, die, or be sent to join the mad at Tarban Creek.

A few months before Shields's arrival at Parramatta, Governor Gipps had as part of his new initiative dismissed a tipsy matron and a strait-laced and incompetent superintendent. All Gipps could fall back on was a pragmatic but venal couple, the Bells, earlier sacked, who returned now to the jobs of matron and steward as the only people willing to manage the place. The chances for corruption inherent in such an institution were lustily embraced by George and Sarah, who, during Shields's time at the Factory, were its day-to-day managers.

The Bells had in their care three categories of women. Category I consisted of women like Mary who were eligible for assignment, had the right to go to church on Sundays, could receive friends at the Factory and earned wages if there was something for them to do. Single women in this category were sometimes 'drawn up in a line for the inspection of the amorous and adventurous votary, who, fixing his eye on a vestal of his taste, with his finger beckons her to step forward from the rank'. There was a colonial song about this extraordinary process:

> The Currency Lads may fill their glasses,
> And drink to the health of the Currency Lasses,
> But the lass I adore, the lass for me,
> Is a lass in the Female Factory . . .
> The first time I saw the comely lass
> Was at Parramatta, going to Mass . . .

etc., etc. The Factory's Sunday clothes were designed perhaps to attract the attention of a newly pardoned drover or shepherd in church: a white cap, straw bonnet, long dress with a muslin frill, a red calico jacket, blue petticoat, grey stockings, shoes, and a clothes bag to store all these in between Sundays. For weekday wear the women had plainer garments: calico cap, serge petticoat and jacket, and an apron.

Category II women were those who had been returned by masters as unsatisfactory, sometimes because of pregnancy. 'In fact,' the jaundiced James Mudie had told the Select Committee a few years before, 'it is a common joke in Sydney, that it is not a factory, but a lying-in hospital.' These women ate Indian cornmeal instead of wheaten bread.

Last of all, Category III inmates had committed crimes in the colony, and were in the strictest sense prisoners. They resided in cells which Greenway had designed at a tight 5 feet by 7.

When it came to quality items, beef and vegetables, at least in theory the daily ration for Category I was more than twice that of Category III, and included such luxuries as salt, brown sugar, a ¼-ounce of tea (considered very precious by Irish women) and a ¼-ounce of yellow soap. Michael O'Flynn was entitled to a ration equivalent to half his mother's. But the

Bells, who had few airs and too willingly drank with convict women, also engaged in short-weighting, of which Bell had already in his earlier occupation of the post been accused.

The facilities of the place were as erratic as the rationing. When Gipps had first inspected the Factory, he found that the four huge dormitories in which most of the women lived had broken windows and inadequate mattresses and blankets. To prevent rain penetrating the dormitories, the women would pile up mattresses against the shattered window panes. Gipps had been horrified to find too that the women were completely idle, apart from cooking and washing for themselves. The year before Shields arrived, the governor decided that he would introduce a supply of New Zealand flax which could be picked by the women and turned into mesh for fishing nets and screens for fruit trees. From 18 October in the year of Mary Shields's arrival, 1839, the public was informed too 'that Needlework of all sorts is performed at the Female Factory in the best possible manner and at very moderate charges'. The Colonial Secretary set a scale of prices – slips 1 shilling and 6 pence; shirts from 1 shilling and 10 pence; baby gowns upwards of 6 pence. None of the Factory's operations was particularly profitable for government, but Gipps favoured them for their rehabilitative aspects. Any woman who produced more than the requisite nine items of clothing per week received 9 pence for every extra article.

Lady Gipps, daughter of a British major-general, had some of the best-behaved of the Factory women visit Government House, Parramatta, to receive lessons in needlework, which she conducted in the parlour with the help of a housekeeper. Mary Shields walked up the driveway of the vice-regal residence to attend these sessions, and breathed the urbane air of a civilised household. The classes were interrupted in the early 1840s by Lady Gipps's bad health.

With whatever skills she possessed, Mary was motivated to maternal vigour to ensure her son's rations. When he reached the age of five, sometime in 1840, he was taken from her, and sent to one of the orphan schools in Parramatta, probably the one founded by the Sisters of Charity. Contact between Mary and Michael would of course have been permitted, especially on Sundays. The boy was growing up amongst the children of other convicts, yet the orphanages of Parramatta did not seem to be schools for criminality. Michael would not come to manhood lawless.

More or less the same period as Mary Shields resided under the discipline of the Female Factory, Thomas Francis Meagher of Waterford spent at a privileged male version of the same: Stonyhurst, a Jesuit college in Lancashire founded by leading northern English Catholics. To it a number of the sons of wealthy Irish, and even the children of Spaniards and

French, were sent to receive a comprehensive British education with Thomistic philosophy and theology thrown in. Tom Meagher, flirtatious, sociable, stylishly outfitted, and better suited in many ways to a worldly university like Trinity, was driven through drenched fields to the sombre front of Stonyhurst at the age of seventeen in October 1840, when Mary was already a second-year veteran of the Factory. Not excessively tall, well-muscled and sweet-featured, a good friend and a gifted hater, he was definitely an Irish nationalist by now and was set to give the English Jesuits a hard time.

Later in life, he liked to recount well-rehearsed anecdotes of the cultural edginess of Stonyhurst. The English Jesuits, he said, attacked his 'detested Irish brogue' – particularly so the Reverend William Johnson, under whom he studied in the school of rhetoric. The sweetest words, said Meagher, 'uttered with an Irish accent, uttered with the rich roll of the Milesian [native Irish] tongue, was enough, and more than enough, to give hysterics or nausea to the Reverend William Johnson, Professor of Rhetoric'. When Meagher rehearsed the part of the Earl of Kent in *King Lear*, Reverend Johnson struck him on the back of the head with a manuscript copy of the play: 'That frightful brogue of yours will never do for Shakespeare . . . I must degrade you from the Peerage. . . . You'll have to be a common soldier.' Meagher later commented that 'it wasn't the first time the brogue entailed the forfeiture of title and estate'.

In 1842, while still at Stonyhurst studying Thomas Aquinas, he wrote 'a little record of the proceedings of his favourite Society', that is, the Debating Society of Clongowes. This was his first published work and according to Meagher's adoring friend, Pat Smyth of Dublin, the demigod Liberator was, that autumn at Clongowes, shown a copy of it and remarked prophetically that 'the author of such a work is not destined to remain long in obscurity'.

It was while on vacation as a student in the summer of 1843, touring Germany with some other students, that Meagher boarded a boat up the Rhine to visit the new nation of Belgium, whose successful revolution against the Dutch in 1830 still stood as a glamorous European exemplar. 'From that time,' wrote Smyth, 'Belgium became in his mind a model of what Ireland should be.'

By the time Meagher, a Celtic-Byronic figure, stood pulsating on Antwerp's ramparts, Mary had spent a largely unrecorded four years in the Factory's rowdy sorority. Though no notable misdemeanour or illness raised Shields to public notice, she suffered from the way the prison-cum-refuge was run. Embezzlement of funds, over-ordering and short-rationing were the *modus operandi* of steward and matron, Mr and Mrs Bell. News of Factory dissatisfaction reached Governor Gipps, and he agreed to meet a delegation of convict women. 'They represented that they'd been sentenced to be Transported, but not to be imprisoned after Transportation.' They contrasted, 'I must say, with great force and truth', their treatment with that of women in prison in Britain and Ireland.

About the time of the appeal to Gipps, two women detained in a small cell started a fire, and their screams were heard throughout the Factory. A hundred women packed into one of the dormitories broke their door down to get to their threatened sisters. But the constables, the Bells and their sub-matron, Mrs Corcoran, got there first and rescued the two women. Abuse and recriminations were exchanged between the two sets of rescuers. Bell used colourful insults, and the women began breaking doors and windows. A detachment of military arrived at the double, but the insurgent women subjected them to a volley of stones and pieces of broken furniture. Eighty of the rioters were arrested and confined at the Factory or Parramatta gaol.

It was reported that some women, not wanting children hurt in a general riot or in the retribution of police or military, came to the assistance of Sub-matron Corcoran. Since Mary was soon to be included in a list of the 'best conducted', she was obviously not imprisoned as a rioter, but was one of those who, whether or not Corcoran deserved it, stood by her. By now the commissary officials of the colony were investigating Bell, and had found that, for the past two years, 'Mr Bell's expenditure appeared to be inconsistent with any means he was known to possess'. The Bells and Mrs Corcoran had also been depositing money in the savings bank beyond their means. Mrs Corcoran, however, was now willing to give evidence that Bell had been withdrawing rations for 100 more children than the Factory contained, and that Mrs Bell had often kept money paid for needlework. To avoid questions by the visiting surgeon, Bell had once ordered Corcoran to pound to powder a secret hoard of soap. Corcoran claimed the prisoners were never issued meal, and the supply of bread to the children was intermittent. Mr Bell liked the women's company too, and took a number of the prisoners to town on drinking sessions, and so on. The matter of the Bells, reported now to the Colonial Secretary, Lord Stanley, drew a passionate statement from Stanley's permanent secretary, Charles E. Trevelyan, a young man who would later have so much to do with hunger in Ireland itself. Unlike Ireland, the Female Factory was distant and based on simple propositions. It was easy to bring the appropriate thunder down on it. Trevelyan ordered that provisions must be of the 'best quality' and come from 'clean, sound colonial wheat, barley, or maize'. The fresh meat was to be delivered alternately in fore- and hind-quarters – Bell had been reserving the best cuts for himself and possibly for the black market. 'The matter', said Trevelyan, 'was at last brought to light only by the loud complaints of the females on the occasion of the Governor visiting the Factory in person.' So the voice of Mary Shields and of other *Whitby* women had reached the consciousness of a man who would later hold starving Ireland in the palm of his hand.

The Colonial Secretary told the Factory's visiting justice on 3 March 1843 that Governor Gipps had approved a scheme to place some of 'the best conducted women' with reputable employers. Shields was due for her ticket-of-leave that year, after four years of her sentence, so it is mystifying that her release was cast in official papers as part of this plan of reward.

In any case, by April 1843, twenty-two women – largely from the ship *Margaret* – were selected for the scheme, and then in June a further eleven were added, amongst them a number of the *Whitby* women with children, including Mary, who sat on her cot assessing the glory and the peril of being advertised as promising in the *Government Gazette*. Applications from potential employers were to be accompanied by references from clergymen or magistrates, and the Colonial Secretary took the trouble to draft at the time a special set of rules for the employment of these women. They were to be paid between £8 and £10 sterling per year – Gipps had said he wanted this group to have purchasing power from the day they left the Factory. 'Women discharged from the Factory with Tickets-of-Leave are in very many cases absolutely friendless, and it is scarcely possible for them by any honest means to maintain themselves without assistance, during the first few days of their liberty.' Money the women had earned was to be sacrosanct and not taken by the police.

Middle-aged Cecily Naughton and her children were to go to Campbelltown, no more than a day or two's ride away. Mary Carroll, who had a convict husband, was to remain as close as Penrith, barely 15 miles. But another *Whitby* woman, Anne Morrow, was to be sent by ship to distant, beautiful Port Macquarie, 250 miles up the coast, and Mary Smith and Mary Gallon to Yass, a remote town in the interior at the limits of the old Nineteen Counties.

Three women were to travel initially to the inland town of Goulburn – Mary Shields, a Bridget Conelly, who had arrived on the *Diamond* from Cork in March 1838, and Margaret Carthy, whose transport the *Sir Charles Forbes* had put into Sydney on Christmas Day 1837. Shields herself had been applied for by William Bradley of Lansdown Park, Goulburn. The other two were off to similar employers in the County of Argyle hinterland. There is every reason to believe that Michael O'Flynn, now eight years old, travelled with his mother, bearing his reading and writing into the bush.

Each of the three women carried on her person her ticket-of-leave, indicating that she was permitted to stay in the district of Goulburn. The women were to present their papers on demand to magistrates and police along the way, in the knowledge that any dallying or diversion from their approved route would be reported. This was their first extended and open experience of a society which was said to be the most debased on earth, and a landscape in which any European woman was a rare sight likely to release male frenzy. How they negotiated it, how they evoked protection and respect from some men to balance the savage intentions of others, we can only surmise. Ticket-of-leave men driving wagons or droving sheep watched them pass, and there were also crowds of English and Irish convicts in road and timber-cutting gangs. Unhappy and angry felons, some in chains, brushed their eyes over the travellers in sullen desire. That these three came from the Female Factory was evident in their well-kept clothing, and women from the Factory possessed a certain *éclat*.

By day, they travelled on their own recognisances on the outside of coaches, which transport consumed part of their 10-shilling advance, or took rides on wagons, walking up the steeper grades. They took pains to look like nobodies' fools, not that they could have seemed an impressive company. Margaret Carthy was the squat worldling, a Dubliner, 5 feet 1, with light blue eyes. Her nose was remarked to be broad at the point, and she was older than the other two, in her early thirties. Brown-eyed Bridget Conelly, the marks of smallpox on her face, tallest of the three at 5 feet 3 inches, was from Galway and therefore an Irish-speaker. The offences of all three women were identical: stealing clothes.

We do not know how much contact Carthy, Conelly and Shields chose to have with men in the camps along the way, or whether they wished to answer Gaelic endearments shouted from campfires. But the authorities did not want to see women molested or prostituting themselves around the night encampments, and police magistrates assigned them shelter in empty cells or unused police shacks. To the Factory women, a roof was welcome, for the Australian winter nights were growing frosty, and in the mornings a skin of ice needed to be broken on the washing pails.

The browned, dusty country through which Mary Shields, Carthy and Conelly journeyed was, however, beginning to revive after some hopeful winter rains and to show an occasional burst of green now that the biblically long drought was ending. In this countryside, drought and land speculation had obliterated a great number of William Bradley's fellow entrepreneurs and squatters. William Brodribb, Hugh's immediate employer, had had to abandon his pastoral lease in the Monaro and was pleased to be given well-paid work managing Bradley's ever-increasing squatting leases beyond the Limits of Location. The Bank of Australia also failed that year of Mary's release, and some of the oldest free settler families were swept away by this disaster. The emancipists' bank, the Bank of New South Wales, survived, underpinned by the massive trading deposits of the late Samuel Terry, 'the Botany Bay Rothschild', a convict who had been transported for stealing 400 pairs of stockings in Salford, Lancashire.

One of the chief signs of the recent economic crisis which the three women bound for Goulburn noticed from the start of their journey was the stench of boiling-down works in the bush and on the outskirts of every settlement. Earlier that year an Irish settler from Mayo named Henry O'Brien decided that the few pence value bankruptcy sheriffs put on sheep could not be a correct assessment. He conducted an experiment in his premises in Fort Street, Sydney, boiling down sheep for the tallow used in the manufacture of candles and soap. O'Brien reasoned that a sheep could produce 12 to 15 pounds' weight of tallow even if starved. Eight hundred tolerably fat sheep would cost £109 to boil down and deliver to London, where the tallow would sell for £350. O'Brien calculated thus that – boiled down – a sheep was actually worth 6 shillings. So there *was* a bottom value to livestock. It could be said therefore that a Mayo man had saved European New South Wales from economic devastation – but at an environmental price. As flocks of sheep were driven to tallow houses and boiling-down vats, the foulness of the process pervaded the country, increasing the suspicions of the native people that these white ghosts were an accursed and poisonous race.

Having crossed the Razorback and then sloped down Towrang Hill, the women approached the Goulburn police magistrate, who arranged for them to be delivered to their employers. Mary, at the end of her institutional existence, said goodbye to the last of her Factory comrades. She went in the first instance to Lansdown Park, Bradley's home near Goulburn, a fair imitation of a British country estate, which employed dozens of convicts and former convicts. Recently elected to the new Legislative Council of New South Wales, representing the County of Argyle, Bradley had left management of his business within the Limits to a young Englishman, John Phillips, to whom Mary would at first have presented herself. She was not to stay long here in the defined regions, however, but was slated to work as housekeeper or servant in the Monaro bush with the manager of the huge Bradley sheep-runs further south, Mr Brodribb. In the meantime, serving and sewing for Mrs Emily Bradley, daughter of the explorer William Hovell, and her five daughters at Lansdown Park, Mary – over a clay pipe of tobacco and a mug of *tay* taken with other Irish women – got what useful advice she could about remote stations.

When Mary and her son Michael went off on a wagon to the far south, they still had to travel about the same distance as already covered, and in wilder and less administered country. It was of course possible, in view of what developed, that the wagon-driver was Hugh Larkin, now himself a veteran of the system, come to Goulburn for supplies. If so he would have received heavy warnings from Phillips as to his demeanour towards the woman from the Factory. The wagon advanced over the Limestone Plains and gradually upwards into the broad, grand, windy, stone-strewn, mountain-rimmed reaches of Monaro, where European women became a rarer and rarer phenomenon, and where men might feel liberated by suffering and distance from restraints they accepted in the churched and sainted world. Again Michael served as something of a protection as mother and son took their rest in rough company, in overseers' and shepherds' huts along the way.

The homestead at which she arrived at last, her Factory neatness jaded by distance, lay beyond Cooma Creek at a place named Coolringdon. The approaches to the modern Coolringdon homestead lie along an avenue of fir trees planted to cut the wind, but that avenue did not exist when Mary arrived. The main house was not much more elegant than the habitations she had visited along her track, and certainly nothing like Lansdown Park. Brodribb planned to marry, though, and to introduce refinements. Inside the slab timber and bark walls, on the packed earth floor, Mary found an occasional excellent item of furniture, and good linen and silverware, and bound editions of the Latin and Greek classics as well as volumes of sermons, histories and even novels.

The bark kitchen where Mary fulfilled some of her duties was separate from the house. The huts of the workers on the station stood about, of no more elevated construction than that of the master. In one of them resided her future lover, Hugh Larkin, whose Irishness and humour were, she clearly felt, close to her own.

Larkin, one of the Great Dan O'Connell's most distantly placed admirers, had by the time of Mary's arrival at Coolringdon served ten years of his life sentence. Eighteen months earlier, on 21 December 1841, he had filled out a form he got from the police magistrate in the new village of Cooma, 25 or so miles away. It was an application to have Esther and the children sent to Australia at the British government's expense. 'The Petitioner is desirous of being reunited to the family from which he was separated at the time of his transportation.' Brodribb certified that 'the Petitioner above named has been in my service since the month of March 1834, during which period his conduct has been such, that I respectfully recommend his Petition to the favorable consideration of His Excellency'. Hugh's application was signed too by a police magistrate and a clergyman.

Esther's own appeal to Dublin Castle in 1840 implies that there had been some letters between Hugh and herself, and that Hugh was operating on the basis of Esther's stated willingness to cross the mighty ocean. Esther Tully of Lismany, Galway, of the Parish of 'Cluntowescirt nr Lawrencetown', was listed in his own handwriting as spouse, and the children named as Patrick, ten years, and Hugh, eight. The referees Larkin nominated in his arduous, broad-stroke handwriting were Walter Lawrence, Esquire of Belview, Laurencetown, County Galway, Ireland, and 'Right Reverend Thomas Cowan, Bishop of Loughrea, County Galway'. Hugh could have found out these men were alive and willing to be referees only from Esther. In her late twenties in 1840, she hiked by road to Loughrea to bespeak the bishop, or lobbied him while he was in Clontuskert parish on a pastoral visit. Similarly, she took a short walk south through country in which she knew every cabin, face, nuance of stone and mound and field, and up the long avenue to Belview House, to ask Mr Lawrence for the use of his name so that she might be removed from the familiar to an Australian future. For still she and her sons worked at Somerset, still she must find a space for herself within the ambiguous relationship with land and landlord. Hugh's application would be her ticket out of a connection which, at the large house, in the cabin, in the field, poisoned the spirit.

Having filled in the form, Larkin must have enjoyed the heartiest Christmas yet of his Australian exile. From assignments all over the Australian bush, other men also applied for reunion. James Doolan, a shipmate aboard *Parmelia*, wanted his wife, Margaret Egan, and two children to join him. Stephen Doyle of the *Lady McNaughton*, serving seven years for a Ribbon crime, had applied for his wife, Jane McCone, of Newry Street, Banbridge. But he had been flogged in January 1839, for losing sheep on Patrick's Plains. A year later he was flogged again. His application would be marked, 'Not Recommended on account of punishment'.

Hugh's petition needed to make its way by bullock wagon and mail coach to Sydney, where two months later a Colonial Secretary's clerk checked Larkin's record and wrote: 'Nothing recorded.' On that basis, Governor Gipps himself inscribed the petition: 'Allowed.' In May 1842, the Colonial Secretary in Sydney told the Superintendent of Convicts to apprise the successful applicants.

Dependent on shipping availability, the approving document would have reached Ireland in the summer of 1842. There was no problem with the way Hugh had addressed the petition. Laurencetown was a well-known market centre, Lismany a few miles north of it. Since she was still in the parish of Clontuskert, in Laurencetown or Lismany, under the eyes of relatives and the clergy, it was not likely that a lover delayed her. In early 1840 she had been more than willing to go, in fact desperate to. If she *did* receive the invitation to travel, it may have been an elderly and ailing parent who halted her departure – it may even have been Hugh's mother. Or perhaps when it came down to addressing the journey, Esther found she did not have the financial means to travel with her sons to the port of embarkation, or acquire the food and range of clothing required for the journey. Or maybe she never received the approval: sometimes, for reasons of inefficiency, laziness, malice or loss of documents, the papers were never delivered.

The most likely, most pathetic explanation for Esther's failure to reach Australia was the success of the anti-transportation movement. Convict transportation to New South Wales had been ended by a Royal Order-in-Council in August 1840. But the wives of convicts could receive free passage only on convict vessels. Even when Esther Larkin made her petition in February 1840, it was already nearly too late to link up with the last women's ship, the *Margaret* from Dublin.

The Reverend John Dunmore Lang complained that 'the knot of squatters in the Legislative Council' wanted to revive transportation. To supply labour needs, hill coolies, natives of the mountains north of Calcutta, labourers from the indigo factories of Calcutta, were imported, and Chileans too, who pervaded the bush with the sound of guitar. The renewal of transportation was Esther's best hope. About 1848 arrangements *were* made for convicts' wives to travel on emigrant ships. But all these adjustments would be too late. There were still transports travelling to Hobart. But it was probably assumed by a bureaucrat within the Castle that Esther, landed in Hobart without connecting transport, might be reduced to prostitution. So, for lack of a ship, Esther remained, and all inquiries and demands she made at barrack gates in Ballinasloe and at constabulary posts in the countryside were futile.

The Colonial Secretary in Sydney had signed Hugh's ticket-of-leave on 1 June 1843. But near-freedom brought no hope of an Australian hearth. The dream of showing Esther the bush, of introducing sons to its particular grandeurs and squalors, of eating meat and damper with them in quantities to make them cry out in wonder, could no longer be entertained without pain. By the time Mary Shields and her son ascended the slight slope where the homestead of Coolringdon stood, Hugh was entitled to go out and seek employment where he chose; to set up in business in his own right if he wished. He chose to remain in this isolation, in the rawness and splendid space of that rising plain. He might never get his conditional pardon if he went off to some district more administratively fussy, or fell foul of new masters. Larkin knew Brodribb, Brodribb knew him. Even so, the arrival of Mary may also have been a cause of his sticking with Brodribb.

One thing can be said for Hugh Larkin at this time of his exchanging flirtatious jokes in Gaelic and English with Mary: in his involuntary service Larkin had experienced empire-making adventures on the Sydney side of the Australian Alps, and on the far side too, where tangles of hills, lagoons, rivers, billabongs and thickets ran away towards the town of Melbourne on Port Phillip Bay. For someone who had worked as Brodribb's man from the mid-1830s onwards, the tedium of bush life would have been interspersed with remarkable excursions. These he would ultimately have a chance to relate to Mary Shields and to children yet unborn, as well as – in ultimate freedom – to other men in pubs and shebeens in Goulburn.

As drought hit Brodribb's pastures in the Monaro in the late 1830s, he decided livestock could be moved west over the mountains to pasture in what is now the state of Victoria. He started out from his station with a considerable expedition: two bullock drays, 1,200 head of cattle, 3,000 sheep and 40 horses, and a number of his assigned servants. Though, as in the Americas, cattle stockmen despised shepherds, trusted men became proficient in both areas. They could both shear sheep and ride up into the mountains to chase and herd at breakneck pace wild *bushians*, wandering herds whose young bulls had never seen a rider before. Brodribb's men now drove the livestock up through the Port Phillip Pass in the Alps and, after a miserable time on short rations, were still 200 miles from Port Phillip Bay. Brodribb knew that recently Mr William Faithfull of Goulburn had been attacked by Aboriginals in this location near the Hume River – nine of Faithfull's men had been killed and a large number of his sheep destroyed. In shared peril, convicts kept the same watches as Brodribb, and carried carbines, which must have struck Hugh as a divine satiric turn. At last, on the Broken River, in hilly, heavily wooded country not yet much marked by Europeans, Brodribb found natural pasture suitable to fatten his stock. Two shepherds were put with each flock of sheep, armed with short carbines, and the stockmen tending the cattle were armed too. It was from the weapons of these hair-trigger dispossessed of Europe that the natives received the thunderous news of their own coming dispossession.

Brodribb himself made his way back over the mountains and the headwaters of the Murrumbidgee, and found that plentiful rain was falling in Monaro. In his absence, two Port Phillip men had ridden out from Melbourne and turned up at the station Brodribb had started at the Broken River, and now wrote to him offering to buy it. At once Brodribb saddled up for another journey from Monaro, over the mountains, with two horses, a gig, and one assigned convict, to conclude the deal in Melbourne. This assigned convict – Hugh, if Hugh was not already on the Broken River? – rode with Brodribb to the small, shambling town of Melbourne, whose few thousand Europeans had recently been joined by its first shipload of Scottish immigrants. The first architectural office of what would become, after the discovery of alluvial and underground gold more than a decade later, a stylish and renowned city of the British Empire, had been opened. But when Brodribb and his assigned convict visited the outpost, the idea of impending glory seemed unlikely in streets hazed with summer dust, in Collins Street with its open sewer in mid-thoroughfare. While in town, enterprising Brodribb negotiated a further deal on 'breeding cattle, sight unseen', to be delivered to Melbourne.

So most of Brodribb's assigned men from the Broken River now rode back over the mountains to Monaro, and prepared again a herd for Melbourne. This time Brodribb's brother Frank, with his own party of drovers, met him on the Melbourne side of the mountains and helped him on his way. Brodribb still needed to use 'every vigilance'. There were three watches during the night, 'three men and myself took the first three hours . . . Large fires were kept burning all around the cattle.'

This was in 1839, and while Brodribb, having made his delivery, was still in Melbourne with some of his men, an explorer appeared from the east in the streets of the town. Count Paul Strzelecki's interest in remote places had derived in part from a failed elopement in his Polish boyhood. He had named the stretch of country he had just crossed, a good way to the south of the track Brodribb had taken, Gippsland – after Mary Shields's benefactor and his own patron. Strzelecki told Brodribb that if cattle and sheep were shipped from New South Wales to Gippsland, they could be driven from there to Melbourne, fattening along the way. The problem was to find a route from Melbourne to coastal Gippsland. So Brodribb called a Melbourne meeting of entrepreneurs, who decided to charter the 300-ton vessel *Singapore* to find a harbour on the Gippsland coast to and from which livestock could be driven. Brodribb and his companions in the enterprise, along with their various assigned men, began exploring the area of great coastal lagoons east of Melbourne. Finding a decent anchorage, Brodribb, son of a once-radical republican political prisoner, called it Port Albert, to honour the queen's consort.

It was the first European contact for most of the local Aborigines.

Exploring the thick coastal forests around Port Albert with his men, Brodribb encountered a large party of natives. But he would not let them come within a hundred yards of the communal hut. As a warning, the men fired rifles at marks on trees, or at empty bottles suspended in the air, to show that they had arms to defend themselves. 'We brought with us a small cannon, which we loaded and fired off towards the bay, and they saw the double shot strike the water.'

Brodribb next had to find a track through Gippsland to Melbourne. He left a party of three men and an overseer at Port Albert, well-armed, not least with the 'little cannon' on its pivot. Six rode to Melbourne, a hungry and hard ride enlivened by the birdsongs of 'native warblers'. Brodribb named rivers they met – one, the Latrobe, in honour of Lieutenant-Governor Latrobe of Port Phillip, from whom Brodribb's consortium hoped to get land grants in and around Port Albert.

The scrub took nine days to get through. Charlie Tara, a native guide from the Monaro, saved them from famishing by catching tree sloths. At last they reached a cattle station in the area of Western Port, the last great coastal indentation before Melbourne's Port Phillip. But the trail they had survived would have killed cattle, and Brodribb was distressed that their failed research journey had cost £2,000, 'including the wages of the men and their rations'.

Larkin no doubt heard Brodribb complaining that the local authority, Lieutenant-Governor Latrobe, was overridden in his decision to grant the development of Port Albert to Brodribb's group. Governor Gipps in Sydney sent a surveyor to prepare maps for the development of Gippsland on Sydney's terms, which did not include allowing Brodribb's syndicate any of the 20,000 acres immediately around the port. 'The pioneers of this beautiful country,' wrote Brodribb, 'instead of receiving *encouragement* from the local government for their arduous, spirited, and expensive undertaking, every obstacle was thrown in their way.'

Ultimately the recession hit Melbourne too, put an end to rewards for overlanders of cattle and sheep, and so set a limit to the adventures of Brodribb and his assigned convicts. Both Brodribb and Larkin went off now to work for Bradley, to be in place for Mary's arrival at Coolringdon in the late southern winter of 1843.

7

Ireland Young and Old

> The car-boy who drove me had paid his little tribute of four pence at the morning Mass. The waiter who brought me my breakfast had added his humble shilling. And the Catholic gentleman with whom I dined, and between whom and O'Connell there was no great love lost, pays his annual donation out of gratitude for old services and to the man who won Catholic Emancipation for Ireland.
>
> William Makepeace Thackeray

In 1843, as Mary Shields exercised her new Australian freedom, Thomas Francis Meagher, home from Stonyhurst at nineteen years of age, settled not in Waterford but in racy Dublin. Obviously he did not see himself as a merchant; he and others were persuaded he would make a lawyer. He enrolled in the Inns of Court, his application signed by his father's friend, O'Connell, the Liberator himself. The florid young man took rooms in the fashionable south-east segment of Dublin between the Liffey and the Grand Canal, around Lincoln Place, and went to Dublin soirées with eagerness and an air of nervous striving, which made an impression on people of being foppish. Yet he was not unaware of the Liberties slums a little to the west, of the claustrophobic misery of older Dublin, between the Castle and the river, the stench, the washing-hung crevices of streets, and windows patched with paper. He was always a lusty fellow and was likely to have made early excursions, for curiosity and out of a Jesuit-repressed taste for low life, to Peter and Bride Streets.

He did not spend time reading case law in the law libraries at the Inns or the Four Courts. Almost immediately on settling in Dublin, he joined the Liberator's 'Loyal National Repeal Association', founded three years before and headquartered for the time being in the Corn Exchange building on the Liffey quays. Repeal's glittering aim was at one with his own: the legislative independence of Ireland. In his splendid coats and elegantly cut trousers, Meagher became a volunteer apparatchik, willing to attend Repeal rallies all over the country. He would please his eminent father by achieving election to the Repeal Parliamentary Committee, which liaised with Irish politicians serving in the House of Commons. In that way, he first sighted in some Dublin drawing-room the austere, well-regarded Smith O'Brien. But Meagher was as yet tentative, awkward with great men, willing to chase any stick the Liberator threw him, trying to adapt his schoolboy debating arts to real politics.

Meagher had arrived in Dublin after the close of O'Connell's lord mayoralty of Dublin, which had begun in 1841 with Repeal getting control of the Dublin corporation. But the predominant gestures of that mayoralty were still being talked about in a Dublin part loyalist, part nationalist. Lord Mayor O'Connell would bellow to the crowds who mobbed his carriage outside the Mansion House: 'Boys, do yez know me now?' And the roar would come back: 'Ah, sure, aren't ye our own darling Liberathor?' 'Does the hat suit me, boys?' he would ask, slanting his hat comically on his head. There would be a frenzy of cheering. But behind the posturing, there was substance: the Liberator was administratively gifted.

The talkative youth Meagher, watchfully attending Repeal meetings with his handsome schoolmate from Clongowes, Pat Smyth, was aware too that O'Connell had recently been preoccupied by a large non-Irish issue: American slavery, the plausible serpent at the heart of that republic's Jeffersonian Eden. In 1841, when the liberated slave Charles Lenox Remond visited England and Ireland, he felt entitled to ask the Lord Mayor O'Connell to sign a petition calling on Irish Americans to join the abolitionists. The result in America was an education for the Liberator. On one hand, abolitionists, brave Anne and Wendell Phillips and blazing William Lloyd Garrison, travelled from Boston to Ireland to greet him. By contrast, most of America's Irish, including miners in Pottsville, and Bishop Hughes of New York, superintendent of a slave plantation in Maryland in his youth, resisted the concept that they had a unique duty to unite with abolitionists, and to oppose decent men and women in the South who had been friendly to them. Didn't the Liberator know that Irish workers were America's true slaves? Didn't he know some slaveholders in the South used Irish to clear their swamps rather than risk the lives of valuable slaves? So O'Connell performed mental and oratorical somersaults to keep Repeal money flowing from America.

He was now nearing sixty-seven, but he still possessed a resilient soul. His beloved wife and cousin, Mary O'Connell, had perished five years before of a respiratory disease. He bore great financial burdens, and was particularly exercised to secure the futures of his three sons. Maurice O'Connell, member for Tralee, was – a little like his father – an energetic philanderer; Morgan had served in Devereux's Irish Legion under Simón Bolívar in South America but was now Assistant Registrar for Deeds; and John, member for Athlone, increasingly took over the administration of Repeal. The Liberator spent spacious sums on marriage settlements for all his sons, and his three daughters, Ellen, Kate and Betsey.

It was to maintain the O'Connell Repeal machine in Dublin, and meet the Liberator's and other Repealers' parliamentary expenses at Westminster, that Esther Larkin, leaving Mass at Clontuskert chapel, paid her Repeal 'rent' on the first Sunday of the month to local association wardens.

Some young Repealers were beginning to feel that the movement needed a new voice to complement other Repeal newspapers such as the highly Catholic, O'Connell-controlled *Pilot.* And so it was that a handsome, muscular, pensive young Protestant, Thomas Davis, five years older than Meagher and already admitted to the Bar, walked out from the Dublin quays to the thickets and open lawns of Phoenix Park, one day in 1842, taking along two interesting companions. One was John Blake Dillon, a Catholic contemporary, an extremely handsome and eloquent man from the Mayo–Roscommon border, a former Maynooth seminarian and a graduate from Trinity. The other was a talented young Monaghan-born journalist from the *Belfast Vindicator* named Charles Gavan Duffy. Under a large elm opposite Kilmainham the three junior Repealers paused, and here, Duffy claimed later, a jointly owned weekly newspaper was proposed to be an aggressive voice for Repeal.

It was decided to call the paper the *Nation.* Davis wrote a prospectus that spoke of the new nationality, which would draw on Catholic, Protestant, Milesian (native Irish) and Cromwellian. In the *Nation*'s rented office in 12 Trinity Street, Thomas Davis and Gavan Duffy quarrelled constructively over whether the Belfast Protestants would ever take anything but a hostile attitude towards Repeal. But hope, excitement and fervour impossible to recapture marked the new paper's appearance on 15 October. Duffy, recently married, was its managing editor, and – without family wealth – needed it to succeed. So it carried race results from the Curragh of Kildare and from Kilkenny, and advertisers such as the United Kingdom Life Assurance Company and Paul's Everyman's Friend for Corns and Bunions. Its first printing of 12,000 copies sold out by noon, despite the high cost of 6 pence per copy. It excited readers, particularly young Irish adults, by calling on them to be done with 'rubbish nicknames . . . With all the nicknames that serve to delude and divide us – with all their Orangemen and Ribbonmen, Tory men and Whig men . . . there are in truth but two parties in Ireland: Those who suffer from her National degradation, and those who profit by it.'

As a safeguard, contributions on political matters would be printed unsigned, itself a confession that liberty of expression could not be relied on. But most observers could work out who wrote what. Duffy's opening editorial complained of Ireland's 'mendicant spirit'. Dillon attacked Irish landlordism. Davis criticised British policy everywhere, finding in the invasion of Afghanistan parallels to British occupation of Ireland. He also fervently attacked the touted option of emigration as any cure for Ireland. Equity, not emigration, was ever his line.

Duffy's poem 'Faugh-a-Ballagh' (Irish for 'Clear the Way') also set the *Nation*'s tone:

As your fears are false and hollow,
Slaves and Dastards stand aside –
Knaves and Traitors, Faugh-a-Ballagh.

When he first heard Duffy's verses, Davis himself was catalysed to write a poem to be published in the same edition. The sentiments of Davis's verse may seem merely workmanlike from this distance, but to his contemporaries he appeared to imagine Irishness for them in song, and their gratitude would be massive. His 'Lament for the Death of Owen Roe O'Neill' appeared, a ballad which did for Meagher what the Jesuits had failed to do: it connected the struggles of the Irish past with the aspirations of the present. Owen Roe O'Neill, leader of Gaelic forces against the Cromwellians, had died in circumstances bespeaking treachery in 1649.

Your troubles are all over, you're at rest with God on high;
But we're slaves, and we're orphans, Owen! – Why did you die?

The young men of the *Nation* still saw themselves as faithful votaries of great O'Connell. They published his *Repeal Catechism*, a series of questions and answers between an Agitator and a Farmer:

Farmer: By what means then, was the Union carried?

Agitator: The means were three-fold – atrocious fraud, the vilest corruption, and the most profligate exhibition of military violence.

In the House of Commons, where he presently represented Cork, O'Connell controlled for now a loosely allied Irish party of between twelve and twenty members, depending on what issue was being voted. Smith O'Brien was still only sometimes with him. A former duelling opponent of O'Connell's, the Tory Sir Robert Peel, was Prime Minister with a massive and hostile Tory majority, and was still a personal enemy. A quarter of a century before, in 1815, Peel had accepted a challenge from O'Connell first to fight in Kildare, then in Ostend. In the latter case, Peel was accused of arranging for O'Connell's arrest by the Home Office on his way through London. O'Connell's political instincts, bitterly personal and sweepingly universal, told him to make some unanswerable and climactic mass gesture against Peel and Westminster.

He decided that three million Repealers would be recruited in 1843, and Repeal would be carried by moral force. He planned to hold what *The Times* would dub 'monster meetings'. The idea was said to have come originally from a pug-faced Tipperary lawyer, Michael Doheny, who wrote in the *Nation* under the pen-name 'Eirenach'. These vast 'moral force' gatherings were designed as peaceful meetings which also served to indicate the potential size of the forces behind Repeal.

One of the more important crowd-gathering devices for the monster meetings, in the midst of which the law student Meagher found himself that summer, was the procession which preceded the meeting itself. Among the floats that passed in front of O'Connell at the start of the Cork procession was one that featured two boys, one painted black, the other white. The black figure bore the label *Free*, since Westminster had abolished slavery in the West Indies. He displayed to the crowd his broken chains. The white figure, representing the Irish, wore intact chains, and a label round his neck which proclaimed: *A Slave Still!*

Varying estimates exist for the numbers who attended these great events. The meeting at Castlebar in Mayo was stated by the Repeal press to be somewhere from 150,000 to 400,000, although a British army officer put the same crowd at 15,000. Esther Larkin, beginning to age under her unyielding widowhood, would have walked in a mass of farmers and peasantry to witness the Messianic entry of the Liberator to Tuam, the Galway monster-meeting venue closest to her, or else to the Athlone event in Westmeath, some 20 miles by road or River Shannon. It was possible that she, or her boys, attended both. Waiting for harvest or lambing, peasants had some time to spare in summer, and an independent Ireland under the Great Dan would surely bring her husband home.

The mass parades Esther and her sons experienced resembled moving forests, since marchers carried the green bough of liberty – some even entire trees – in their hands. Given that these needed to have been taken from landlords' woods, the carrying of a bough was itself a political statement at which the Repeal wardens, O'Connell's security force, were forced to blink. Other members of the crowd carried their membership certificates on the end of sticks, or strapped around their hats, coats or necks by green ribbons.

When Esther reached the place where the platform for the speeches had been set up, she might have glimpsed the Liberator over the shoulders of masses of frieze-coated peasants and farmers, and beheld the banners stitched in red on green: *Erin go bragh* and *Ireland for the Irish*. The

Repeal wardens, nicknamed 'Repeal cavalry', led by Tom Steele, O'Connell's chief warden, patrolled the perimeter of the crowd, giving it unity, and all around were the carriages of better-off supporters, and stalls for the sale of food and non-alcoholic drink. Irish-speaking spectators often turned home now, satisfied to permit the Liberator to deliver his speech to those close enough to hear and take note.

By Athlone, on 24 June that year, O'Connell was under pressure to show that his movement was not traitorous. He attacked Peel, who 'had the audacity to assert that Her Majesty had expressed herself against Repeal. It was a lie (immense cheering) . . . Oh, God bless the Queen. Three cheers for her. (Tremendous cheers).' But then he went on to promise the crowd what he always promised, and what they desired: the rule of just law from a sovereign Irish legislature.

As massive as the monster meetings were, there were parallel meetings in the new world, at one of which in New York, attended by Governor Seward, a motion had been passed: 'That it is the opinion of this meeting that, if England invades Ireland, she will do it with the assured loss of Canada by American Arms.' Repeal members in America included some notable citizens, people from both sides of the slavery issue. One was James Buchanan of Pennsylvania, a future President. The *New York Tribune*'s Horace Greeley was notable in Repeal, and an abolitionist. But the chief of United States Repeal was the son of slave-holding President Tyler.

Other monster meetings occurred in the summer and autumn of 1843 at Dundalk, Wexford, Castlebar, and elsewhere. But the meetings which particularly captured the enthusiasm of Repeal's young foot-soldier, Thomas Francis Meagher, were the ones held in legendary locations. The Hill of Tara in Meath, where the O'Neill kings ruled until the eighth century, was the scene of a meeting on 15 August, feast day of Our Lady, all within sight of the sloping churchyard where Croppy rebels had been slaughtered in 1798. In September the Rath of Mullaghmast in Kildare, a fort where in 1577 Irish chieftains were assassinated by Elizabethan forces, was used.

As the summer ended, the *Nation* reported massive Repeal rents. The rent for the week ending 4 September was £1,097. Throughout 1843 it came to total over £20,000, which helped pay for the newly decorated headquarters of triumphant Repeal, opened before the end of October on Burgh Quay, and named Conciliation Hall. The high tide of Irish confidence caused by monster meetings was never to be matched again in that century. But the axe was being sharpened. Peel had been informed by observers that at Mullaghmast in Kildare in late September, O'Connell had been crowned king of Ireland. O'Connell's speeches had regularly defied Peel and British power. In Kilkenny he had roared, 'Wellington never had such an army. (*Cheers*) There was not at Waterloo on both sides as many brave and determined men as I see before me today.' In Mallow in June, Peel heard, O'Connell had uttered what became known as the *Mallow Defiance*. 'In the midst of peace and tranquillity our Saxon traducers are covering the land with troops.' Someone in the crowd called, 'We are ready to meet them.' To which O'Connell replied, 'Of course you are. Do you think I suppose you to be cowards or fools? . . . We were a paltry remnant in Cromwell's time. We are nine millions now!'

Now the thirty-second meeting for that year was planned, a culminating monster to be held on 8 October at Clontarf on the north side of Dublin Bay. Clontarf was the scene of Brian Boru's defeat of the Danish invaders and of his death in battle in 1014. The meeting would attract Irish from England, Scotland and Wales. Terence Bellew MacManus, a young Dublin woolbroker, had founded a business in Liverpool trading East Galway's fine wool to the textile mills. He chartered four steamers to bring Repeal supporters from England. Thomas Davis asked if, with 45,000 Irishmen in the British army, the government would dare call on the Irish to suppress the Irish? This rhetoric bespoke the fatal belief of Irish activists that numbers could somehow equal military organisation.

Though recently O'Connell had been deliberately moderating his speeches, in Downing Street they did not understand that rhetoric and imagery were to some extent ends in themselves for the Irish; the uttering of violent metaphor a prayer for legislative equity. Far from being lawless, the meetings had in fact been heavily policed throughout by the corps of wardens. But in the notices of the Clontarf monster meeting posted throughout Ireland and in Merseyside and Glasgow, the Repeal officials had made the mistake of referring to 'Repeal cavalry'. When O'Connell saw the notice he denounced the phrase, but it provided Peel with an opportunity. He ordered that the Lord Lieutenant of Ireland proclaim the meeting illegal. British warships appeared in the bay off Clontarf, and troops with artillery massed at Pigeonhouse fort on Dublin Bay. At 3.00 p.m. on the day before the meeting the proclamation proscribing it was pasted on walls. O'Connell had two hours before dark to decide whether to cancel or risk a collision between his cheering multitudes and the British army, in which every serving Irish private was, after all, only one man caught in a mighty machine! At Conciliation Hall, amongst his followers, there were some voices in favour of defiance. Meagher accepted O'Connell's decision to cancel as the right one. But any attempt to arrest O'Connell should be grandly resisted!

On the day of the proposed meeting then, the 'Head Pacificator', Tom

Steele, helped the 60th Rifles and the 5th Dragoons turn away the few brave spirits who came to Clontarf. The Repeal rent defiantly increased afterwards, but the day after the failed meeting, warrants were issued for the arrest of O'Connell, his son John and seven others, including Gavan Duffy, editor of the *Nation.* The young men of the movement, Duffy, Davis, a young solicitor named John Mitchel of Banbridge, County Down, who was just emerging as a *Nation* feature writer, and the acolyte Meagher, all now expected that O'Connell would call on them to resist the arrest. At the time touring Mayo, Davis wrote:

> We promised loud, and boasted high,
> 'To break our country's chains or die';
> And should we fail, that country's name
> Will be a synonym of shame.

But O'Connell ordered his disciples not to oppose the arrest. That ensured there could not be massed resistance. The seven men, nicknamed the Traversers, were flatly arrested, brought to Green Street courthouse and charged with conspiracy before a packed jury. In various of the young men, an unease grew at this avoidance by O'Connell. There was an element of lost nerve, they thought, which sharpened other grievances they had. O'Connell, said the *Nation* set, was too Catholic. And the Repeal rent, coming from the shoeless people, instead of maintaining O'Connell and his lieutenants in undue style, ought to be fed back to the poor in widespread Repeal reading-rooms, where tenant and artisan could educate themselves.

In the light of O'Connell's arrest, however, William Smith O'Brien at last sent from his house at Cahirmoyle in Limerick a £5 subscription to the Repeal Association, together with an application for membership. His accompanying letter expressed his scepticism about the policy of British governments since Emancipation. 'Fourteen years have elapsed since that event, and the experience of each succeeding year has tended to show the fallacy of these expectations, and to dissipate those hopes.' From summer travels in France, the Netherlands and Germany, O'Brien believed that Ireland suffered from unique levels of poverty, and he considered the moral pressure represented by O'Connell's meetings to be legal and honourable.

O'Brien's widowed mother Lady O'Brien, reading that her 40-year-old son had joined Repeal, wrote from Dromoland Castle telling him she wanted to 'clasp your knees and hold you fast until you gave a promise that you would separate yourself from these ungodly men'. Indeed, joining Repeal was by some lights the fatal decision of his life. His loyal wife Lucy suspected as much, and her husband's alliance with O'Connell passed like a shadow over the nurseryful of young O'Briens in Cahirmoyle. By late January 1844 O'Brien would come forward to chair a session of the Repeal movement at Conciliation Hall as the most visible and esteemed Protestant convert of all to Repeal.

At liberty on bail, O'Connell continued to call for utter calm. 'Keep the peace for six months, at the utmost twelve months longer, and you shall have the parliament in College Green again.' But in February, four judges directed an all-Protestant jury to find the 70-year-old O'Connell and the other Traversers guilty. They were all permitted to remain at large, however, pending sentence. In the interim between verdict in February and sentencing in May, a meeting of the Repeal Association was held in which the shaken and despairing O'Connell proposed to disband the organisation. Under the candlelit columns of Conciliation Hall, Duffy and Smith O'Brien argued against the idea. In compromise it was voted that all the newspaper editors – Duffy of the *Nation*, Barrett of the *Pilot* and Dr John Gray of the *Freeman's Journal* – resign from the Association so that any indiscretion of theirs might not rebound on the Liberator and Repeal.

When O'Connell returned to the Green Street court for sentencing on 30 May he was cheered and applauded by Repealers, including Meagher, in the courtroom, and many members of the Bar stood as he passed. He was sentenced to twelve months' imprisonment and fined £2,000. Duffy and the other Traversers were sentenced to nine months. The Liberator's lawyers got leave to appeal to the House of Lords, but in the meantime the prisoners were taken in a police cart to the south side of the river, to Richmond bridewell – a prison for civil cases such as debt – which Gavan Duffy found surprisingly pleasant. The governor and his deputy were allowed to sublet their houses and gardens to the prisoners.

The edition of the *Nation* which appeared the week Duffy and O'Connell went to prison was printed in green ink.

In O'Connell's absence, Smith O'Brien's was for the moment the face and voice of Repeal. At weekly meetings and at speeches in his home area, his level, statistical tone and honourable demeanour attracted more people to Repeal than did the Liberator's son John O'Connell. The Repeal rent surged to £3,000. This was due to the influence of O'Brien in attracting affluent Protestant nationalists, and to the imagined penal hardships of the Liberator. Between Westminster and Conciliation Hall, O'Brien, living in Dublin in economical lodgings in Westland Row, now had little time for the idyll of Cahirmoyle, for Lucy and his young family.

On the evening of 13 September 1844, as the prisoners assembled for dinner in Richmond bridewell, they were told that their appeal to the

House of Lords had succeeded. Next morning, after a celebratory breakfast, the Liberator was driven to his house in Merrion Square in an ornate triumphal car 30 feet high. It was a characteristic O'Connell event – 200,000 men took part, it was claimed. But gaol had shaken the Liberator, and now freedom did not favour him.

As O'Connell grew uncertain, Meagher began to gain a greater presence within Repeal, and to become more vocal on some of the proposals O'Connell and his son John now brought before the committees of Repeal. The organisation, said John O'Connell on his father's authority, should work not for total Repeal but for Ireland to become a self-governing unit within a federal Great Britain – what would be called, later in the century, Home Rule. Taking a lead from adored O'Brien, dandy Meagher despised the idea. All the Liberator and his son seemed to be offering was a timid constitutional nip and tuck. It would need more than that. Meagher had taken fire as O'Brien introduced him to the dreadful statistics of the decline of Irish linen manufactures, and the quantities of Irish produce – grain, dairy products, livestock – exported each hungry year. These wrongs grew directly out of the Union with Britain. And Meagher had recently read Carlyle's *The French Revolution* and absorbed the idea that the sovereignty of the people would one day soon irresistibly assert itself. Yet he was still boyishly uncertain, as a later confession to Gavan Duffy seems to show. 'Flaunting and fashionable as I sometimes was,' said Meagher, 'I thoroughly hated Dublin society for its pretentious aping of English taste, ideas and fashions, for its utter want of all true nobility, all sound love of country, and all generous and elevated sentiment.'

The loose alliance of writers, orators and activists associated with the *Nation* began to be referred to as 'Young Ireland'. It is not certain where the term came from – there were 'Young' movements throughout Europe; Mazzini's Young Italy was the foremost instance. 'Young Ireland' may have been attached to the *Nation* group by the *Warder*, the Northern Unionist paper, which also suggested the term 'middle-aged Ireland' when talking about Smith O'Brien. Young Ireland wanted total Repeal, and to achieve it many of them were willing to accept the idea of armed uprising.

The *Nation*'s occasional swipe at Repeal headquarters was very mild, but O'Connell's touchier supporters complained about Davis's series of articles, 'Letters of a Protestant on Repeal', which argued that Protestant power was so strong that nationality could not be achieved without it. Protestantism's hold on Ulster was weakening, claimed another Repeal paper, the *Pilot*, with blithe inaccuracy. Sectarian perception, ever Ireland's poison, began to do its work between the *Pilot* and the *Nation*.

As John Blake Dillon's law practice absorbed his efforts, and as management of the paper, and the building of circulation and advertising absorbed Duffy's, Davis became editor. He had by now become something akin to an outcast in polite Protestant circles, but was too passionate to notice.

One of the most renowned members of Young Ireland was the young Unitarian lawyer John Mitchel. Mitchel possessed blazing eyes, had great charm and was intense in a more absolute way than the playful Meagher. He had been born in Derry in late 1815. His father, the Reverend John Mitchel, who had been associated with the United Irishmen of the 1790s, had seceded from the Orange-dominated wing of the Presbyterian Church in Derry when his son was still a child, and had found a Unitarian post in Newry, County Down, the town on the estuary of the Bann. At school in Newry, young Mitchel met an older, milder boy, another Northern Protestant, John Martin. They would go together to Trinity, into Repeal, into Young Ireland and on into shared exile and long years of struggle, sharing a friendship that was to last half a century.

Mitchel and Martin were both at Trinity in the days of Davis, graduating in 1834, and John Martin studied medicine but was saved from the practice of it by inheriting a modest but profitable estate named Aston near Loughhorne, County Down. Like O'Brien then, he was a landlord. Mitchel in the meantime worked in his uncle's bank in Derry, hating it. He was an asthmatic, and had the toughness and fixity of purpose that often characterises those who habitually struggle for breath. In Newry, as he was studying under a solicitor, he sighted a beautiful 16-year-old named Jane Verner, a student of Miss Bryden's Select School. His sister Matilda, Matty, arranged an introduction and provided chaperones for their walks together. But in the winter of 1836–7, Captain Verner intended to take his daughter to France on an educative tour, and rather than be parted from her, Mitchel suggested an elopement. The young couple hired a boatman to take them from Newry harbour out to the Liverpool steamer, and then, upon landing, went on by coach to Chester to seek a marriage licence. Waiting for the licence at their hotel, in conditions of the most stringent chastity, Mitchel was reading Jenny a novel by a young English Tory named Disraeli, when the Verner parents and a policeman broke into the room. Returned in custody to Newry, he was released after two days when a judge dismissed charges of abduction. The Verners had by now hidden their daughter with friends in the countryside, but Mitchel tracked her down, fell back on his limitless eloquence and pursued a more conventional courtship. If the Verner parents had realised the shifts and griefs through which John Mitchel would lead Jenny, they would not have been won over, but the marriage took place in February 1837. His meek schoolfriend John Martin stood by him at the altar in an austere Presbyterian church at Drumcree, and would be a reliable friend to both parties and to the children of the marriage.

In 1839, when O'Connell visited Newry, Martin and Mitchel were already devout believers in Repeal, were on the dinner committee, and were captivated. They joined the Repeal Association just before Meagher in May 1843. After the *Nation* began publication, Mitchel went down to Dublin to introduce himself to Davis at the *Nation*'s editorial offices, and contributed to the paper from his law office in Banbridge. His father the Reverend John Mitchel died in O'Connell's Repeal year, by which time Jenny had given birth to two sons and a daughter at Dromalane House, the Mitchel family home. Needing to support Jenny and his babies by his law practice, John Mitchel could contribute for now only intermittently to the *Nation*, but when he did, as in his article 'The Anti-Protestant Catholics', he generally managed to upset the Liberator.

In early 1845, Thomas Francis Meagher came into Conciliation Hall out of the spring air above the quays to witness one of the bitterest Repeal meetings to that point. Sir Robert Peel, the Prime Minister, had offered to establish colleges in Belfast, Cork and Galway, where Catholics and Protestants could study together. But the Catholic bishops had already decided Peel's colleges to be 'dangerous to faith and morals'. O'Brien spoke for the colleges, but in a two-hour speech the Liberator condemned the Colleges Bill as 'a nefarious attempt at profligacy and corruption'. When Davis replied, the Liberator said that everyone knew the national bard considered it a crime to be Catholic! 'There is no such party as that styled "Young Ireland",' cried the Liberator in what Gavan Duffy called a 'tipsy rhodomontade'. 'There may be a few people who take that denomination on themselves. I am for Old Ireland . . . I shall stand by Old Ireland; and I have some slight notion that Old Ireland will stand by me.' Smith O'Brien asked the Liberator to withdraw the slighting nickname 'Young Ireland', and faced with O'Brien's moral authority, the Liberator did so. Davis, relieved and filial, rose to applaud him, and, to everyone's astonishment, burst into tears before he could finish speaking. There was a temporary reconciliation, with Davis weeping and shocked, and O'Connell holding him by the hand and crying, 'Davis, I love you.' In the judgement of the lawyer Michael Doheny it was this bitter meeting from which 'the Association never recovered'.

Young Ireland wished to create a meeting ground away from the Liberator's 'rough demagoguery'. So the '82 Club was founded, in part as a social group where ideas could be uttered without the rancour that now typified Repeal meetings, and in part as if to create a highly informal officer corps for some coming national resistance. A uniform was devised for members, for in its name the Club looked back to the Volunteers of 1782, predominantly Protestant gentlemen who had mustered on College Green and successfully demanded an Irish Parliament. Even sober Smith O'Brien wore the '82 Club uniform. He declared in a Kilkenny speech, 'I am not sorry that the Government should feel that the dress we wear wants nothing but the sword attached to it to constitute us as officers of the Irish people.' In their sashed uniforms the '82 Club met at the Rotunda, where in the Pillar Room dinner was served and – John Martin, gentlest of members of the Club, would remember – young Meagher, the emergent orator, wore his tailored green and gold Club uniform splendidly. Mitchel thought Meagher's accent marked by Stonyhurst. But: 'In speaking of Davis, his Lancastershire accent seemed to subside; and I could perceive, behind the factitious intonations of Cockaigne, the genuine roll of the melodious Munster tongue.'

The morning after an '82 Club affair, Mitchel, who had been offered a job on the *Nation*, met Meagher at the editorial office (which had by now moved to D'Olier Street, very close to Repeal headquarters). 'We walked out together . . . almost into the country, near Donnybrook. What talk!' Mitchel said that Meagher spoke fervently of politics, 'but had much to say concerning women and all that eternal trouble, also about Stonyhurst and his college days'.

As Old and Young Ireland grew apart, in Australia Mary was becoming inured to her work in a slab timber and bark homestead. Had she heard anything of her husband O'Flynn and of her lost child Bridget? If living, Bridget would now be six or seven years. Where was O'Flynn? Was he dead, or serving in the British army in the West Indies or India; was he an itinerant Irish labourer, a servant, an industrial worker in Manchester, or an emigrant to North America? Had letters been received? Had he perhaps perished, cancelling out the *M* beside her name in the convict records? Or did she anticipate ultimately filling out the same application for reunion as Hugh had? In courting her, did Hugh break the news that that would not work?

Apart from the bush flies, ants, large but not particularly vicious spiders, and the occasional hut-intruding brown or red-bellied black snake, a particular terror to the natives of snake-free Ireland, the homestead must have seemed habitable, and freer and more pleasant than the Factory. As the Australian spring came on, in the rush of activity around shearing when excitement, talk and the flow of liquor were at their peak in the Monaro, Larkin and Shields took each other as partners. The following July, screaming at a bark ceiling, she gave birth to a boy on a bed of saplings and leather strapping. Though an observing Anglican, Brodribb seemed philosophic about these liaisons between felons; such flexibility, shocking to visitors from Britain, was not considered extraordinary in New South Wales.

Brodribb himself was to be married that year, 1844, and bring his wife, Eliza Matilda Kennedy, to Coolringdon. She was a cultivated young woman who had grown up on her father's pastoral stations. In the bush's natural democracy, her children when young would play around the woolshed with such convict children as the Shields-Larkin son, or under the care of Michael O'Flynn, the boy from *Whitby*, now nearing ten years of age.

The new child was baptised Thomas by Father Walsh at the end of August 1844. The priest gave the couple the usual talking-to for begetting an Australian bastard. If wise, Hugh took this in silence. After all, Mary's sentence would be fully served by October the following year. She would then be free to live and marry as she chose. And one day he would get a conditional pardon, making him his own man within the colony's borders. Besides, like other convicts, Hugh must have thought that if authority could make his marriage to Esther a dead letter, he was in return entitled to be indifferent to the letter of authority, even to the Canon Law.

8

A Fond Farewell to the White Potatoes

> A fond farewell to the white potatoes, pleasant it was to be in their company; generous and cheerful, laughing at us from the head of the table. They were 'the nurse that kept us amused at meals, daytime and night-time'.
>
> Peatsaí O'Callanáin, Craughwell, East Galway

That last, most hopeful autumn before blight and Famine changed all Irish propositions, Duffy, the manager and publisher of the *Nation*, tended his tubercular, pregnant young wife, Emily, and received a note too that Davis was ill. 'I have had an attack of some sort of cholera,' wrote Davis, 'and perhaps have a slight scarlatina.' The invalid was in love – he had met a young woman named Annie Hutton, the daughter of a Dublin Presbyterian couple. Courting Annie, Davis had the disadvantage that nearly all her loyalist clan were appalled by his furiously nationalist poems. A considerable number of these ballads and lyrics are still sung in Ireland and in Irish communities throughout the world, but they were not likely to appeal to the Huttons.

'The West's Asleep', for example, had celebrated the Mayo uprising of 1798 and raised the proposition so favoured by young Tom Meagher that if the lost battles were remembered, they would accumulate in the end into a won independence.

> But – hark! Some voice like thunder spake:
> '*The West's awake, the West awake*' –
> Sing Oh! hurra! Let England quake,
> We'll watch till death for Erin's sake!

Now Davis lay at his mother's house at Baggot Street. MacNevin, a lawyer and a member of Young Ireland, ill himself at the time, wrote to Davis wishing him a speedy recovery and reproving him for being so unpatriotically stricken with 'English cholera'. All the jokes turned sour when, within a week, at dawn on 16 September 1845, the 30-year-old Davis died. As he expired, the air over Ireland was filling with the spores of a mould which would work a ferocious change. Old and Young Ireland, with Annie Hutton and Davis's desolated family, followed his corpse to the family burial plot in Mount Jerome Cemetery, Harold's Cross. In the same few weeks, Gavan Duffy's pregnant young wife perished in giving birth to a second Duffy son. But in Duffy's *Autobiography*, written decades later, it was the death of Davis which carried the emotional, the national, weight.

After Davis's death, Mitchel was offered the editorship of the *Nation*, and accepted. Thomas Carlyle, who had recently visited Dublin and met Mitchel, described him as 'a fine elastic-spirited young fellow with superior natural talent'. Full of zeal, Mitchel departed each morning from his wife Jenny, his mother, his small children and his 'frugally elegant small house and table' at 8 Ontario Terrace near Charlemont Bridge, for the *Nation* offices. There he wrote a series of articles on railways, including advice on the way Repeal wardens should deal with the spread of railroads throughout Ireland. Should they be used to move troops, it was easy, said Mitchel, to break down an embankment or lift a mile or two of rail. Rails and sleepers could be used for making pikes and barricades. 'But sooth, 'tis a dream,' he wrote, as if that would save him. 'No enemy will put us to realise these things. Yet all understand what a railway *may* and what it may not do.'

A disgruntled O'Connell himself called into the *Nation* offices and protested to Mitchel and Duffy about the first railway article. He was outraged that *his* Repeal wardens should be called on to destroy property. Amongst themselves, the Young Irelanders were cynical about the complaints, attributing them to the fact that the Liberator had invested some Repeal rent and become the first shareholder in the Dublin and Cashel Railway. At the end of November 1845, Duffy, as publisher, was arrested for allowing the publication of the railway articles, taken to College Green police station, and charged with sedition.

Esther Larkin, sitting at some neighbour's fire and hearing the articles of Mitchel read aloud by a hedge-school teacher or pupil, may have looked at her sons and felt a pulse of fear and excitement. But a curse she knew nothing of already lay over these cabins and the companionable potato patches beyond the doors; the fury of God was already moving on the late summer breeze.

The first account of the onset of a potato blight had come to the government at Westminster from the fields of England. There had been a slightly earlier rumour from Belgium of a blight which turned the potato flower and stalk black and which caused the tuber itself to putrefy. Sir Robert Peel did not at first believe the report from across the Irish Sea. 'There is such a tendency to exaggeration and inaccuracy in Irish reports that delay in acting on them is always desirable,' he wrote on 13 October 1845. But the Royal Irish Constabulary reports of 15 October told the administration unambiguously that everywhere in Ireland potatoes were rotting. Esther and her adolescent sons were party to this horror. Someone in Lismany, as elsewhere, 'went out to the garden', to quote one tale of the onset of blight, 'for potatoes for a meal. He stuck his spade in the pit, and the spade was swallowed. The potatoes turned mud inside. He shrieked and shrieked. The whole town came out.' This blight may have reached Europe by way of produce in the holds of ships from America. In return it would generate a vast emigration to North America and elsewhere, altering for ever the character of the new world.

After the initial shock, the sense of being orphaned by the Deity, the peasantry received advice from experts of the day about how to dig a potato pit secure from contamination by moisture. One man, a Church of Ireland minister, the Reverend M. J. Berkley, correctly diagnosed the mould on the plants as a 'vampire' fungus. Forty years later it was identified as *Phytophthora infestans*. It could be treated by spraying with copper compounds, and so was reduced to the level of an agricultural nuisance, rather than what it was here, a momentous force.

Esther's sons dutifully dug dry pits to save the crop, but the fungus spores were carried by wind and washed into soil by soft rain. Everyone was amazed that the potato itself, safe in the earth, could have been so heavily attacked. But fungus spores borne on the air and burrowing into soil attacked the meat of the potato as well as the plant, and leaf and fruit alike fermented, blackened and rotted.

In November 1845 O'Connell, in receipt of awful intelligence from Repeal branches all over the country, went with a delegation to visit Lord Lieutenant Heytesbury in Dublin Castle. O'Connell pleaded for a suspension of the export of grain and provisions, and a prohibition on distilling and brewing from grain. He also urged Heytesbury that the ports be opened to the free import of rice and Indian corn from British colonies. For Irish ports were not open now, but subject to the special provisions of the Corn Laws, laws designed to peg the price of local grain at the highest possible level and to keep out other, cheaper grain until the entire British crop had been sold at that artificially pegged price. The Liberator also asked that paid labour be provided on public works for those whose staple food had rotted before their eyes. If these things were not done, said O'Connell, millions would have nothing to eat throughout the winter except decomposed potatoes, seedling eyes cut out of the diseased tubers, and family pigs. The Liberator wrote to Smith O'Brien of 'the frightful certainty of an approaching famine; and you know pestilence always follows famine, the prospect is really frightful'.

Sir Robert Peel considered what was to his party the unutterable: the repeal of the Corn Laws. The champions of the Corn Laws argued that if foreign grain was admitted freely into Britain and Ireland, the price would collapse, and millions of labourers whose livelihood was dependent upon the growing of grain would go without work. But the Corn Laws worked as a spur to ill-paid employment of peasants on next year's harvest only if the peasant had not starved to death before then. Peasants *were* starving in Ireland, and in parts of the Highlands of Scotland. Prime Minister Peel's motives in amending or repealing all Corn Laws were humanitarian but also profoundly conservative. The fact was that these laws had pushed the price of food beyond the reach even of English labourers. For the end result of such bad laws, he argued, one had only to look at the French Revolution.

It is remarked in every Famine history that the lives of millions of Irish peasants were in the hands of men on both sides of Parliament who believed in market forces, in what was called political economy. Most members and most bureaucrats were influenced also by the theory of Benthamite utilitarianism, which took its name from the late political reformer Jeremy Bentham. His principle that legislation was unjustified except where it answered a clear need to achieve the greatest happiness of the greatest number gave a licence for inaction. And legislated pain could be admitted 'so far as it promises to exclude some greater evil'. In the name of greater possible evils, Ireland's pain was to be sanctioned.

Leaders on both sides of the House were men too who were fatally impressed by the Reverend Thomas Robert Malthus, the population theorist. Malthus had written a considerable amount on Ireland, which he never visited. In 1817, he had stated to one correspondent: 'The land in Ireland is infinitely more peopled than anywhere else; and to give full effect to the natural resources of the country, a great part of the population should be swept from the soil'. A doctrine which favoured rationalisation of Irish population by some 'dreadful resource of nature' was fashionable with leading Tories and Whigs. An Irish catastrophe was considered scientifically inevitable and, though few could bring themselves to say it until the disaster was well advanced, even desirable. Whatever alliances O'Connell made in the House of Commons, he could not talk his English allies out of their Malthus.

So the Famine, whatever its other causes, would be seen as a visitation upon the Irish themselves, a corrective to their over-breeding, and their over-dependence on the potato. If Esther Larkin and her Irish brethren were to perish, that reality was governed by great and immutable factors beyond the scope of government.

These sincerely held principles are seen in the writing of the four-square young bureaucrat Charles Trevelyan, elevated from dealing with such questions as the Parramatta Female Factory at the Home Secretary's office and now Assistant Secretary to the Treasury in Whitehall. Trevelyan was a high-minded and decent member of the Clapham Sect, a group of progressive Evangelical Anglicans, and was married to the sister of the historian Macaulay. Some twentieth-century Irish historians complain that Cecil Woodham-Smith had in her 1962 classic *The Great Hunger* demonised urbane Trevelyan; had made him a byword for administrative callousness. But a fair reading of Trevelyan's own tract on the Famine, published in 1848 and prematurely declaring the Famine ended, shows that he went to some trouble to demonise himself. The Irish smallholder, wrote Trevelyan,

> lives in a state of isolation, the type of which is to be sought for in the islands of the south seas rather than in the great civil community of the ancient world. A fortnight for planting, a week or ten days for digging, and another fortnight for turf cutting, suffice for his subsistence, when, during the rest of the year, he is at leisure to follow his own inclinations without even the safeguard of those intellectual tastes and legitimate objects of ambition which only imperfectly obviate the evils of leisure in the highest ranks of society.

And though, said Trevelyan, it was argued 'in Ireland that the calamity was an Imperial one . . . the disease was strictly local, and the cure was to be obtained only by the application of local remedies'.

A virtually widowed Irish peasant such as Esther Larkin would have laughed at the concept that her life that autumn and winter of 1845 was a South Seas idyll translated to East Galway. As for her supposed vices, one of which would be declared to be early marriage, she had not – in terms of Europe – married recklessly young. Studies of contemporary Western European records, says a modern historian, show that Irish women married on average at 26.3 years, as against a Continental average of 25.7 years for females. And though Hugh and Esther had two infants by the time Hugh was twenty-four years, such a family as theirs would not now be considered either abnormally fertile or appallingly young.

Before the final collapse of his government, Peel had ordered the purchase of £100,000 worth of corn, to be sent to Ireland and warehoused in British army commissary stores throughout the poorer regions. It was to be sold off to the hungry only when the price of meal rose to an 'unreasonable' level. The Indian corn which was to save, in extremity, Esther and all her sister Irish women was the same which in the southern United States produced the food called hominy. It was corn so hard to crack that it had to be chopped in steel mills, and there were no such mills in Ireland. A circular was issued to the local relief committees suggesting that corn could be sold unground as long as it was subsequently cooked. But it was very difficult to cook and, if improperly done, caused severe and even fatal bowel disorders.

The first to seek recourse to the yellow cornmeal which the Irish called 'Peel's brimstone', *min déirce*, beggar's meal, Indian buck, were the people of the extreme west and south-west, where food was soon exhausted and where there existed few stores and chandleries. In the wool-breeding areas of East Galway, Esther Larkin and her fellow peasants were used to buying foodstuffs in the summer if they had the cash. The large, well-planned town of Ballinasloe lay only a little to the north of Esther. The *Galway Mercury* at first reported failures in other areas but said that there was no 'ground of apprehension in this neighbourhood'. The potatoes which were sold at the Ballinasloe market, and which normally fetched from 2½ pence to 3 pence per stone (14 pounds), were fetching 4½ pence per stone, so that there was as elsewhere a momentary surge of prosperity. Even on 11 October 1845 the *Galway Mercury* was still sanguine. Within a fortnight, however, widespread reports of the appearance of the blight in some local potato crops led the *Mercury* to recommend that not all grain should be exported from Ireland to England. There was now a panic. People crowded into town from the countryside, and vendors of bread raised the price by reducing the size of the loaf. By 8 November 1845 the *Mercury*'s headline read: THE THREATENED FAMINE. No further hopeful editorials appeared.

The time had begun to which the Irish applied the name *an Gorta Mór* – the Great Hunger, or simply *an droch-Shaol* – the Bad Life, the Bad Times. Esther and her neighbours had at first tried to eat diseased potatoes, by grating, boiling and squeezing them in a cloth, and making them into *boxty* or potato cakes. The result was stomach cramps and diarrhoea, or dysentery with bleeding from the anus, sicknesses from which her robust sons recovered but which carried away a first toll of the aged and infants. In mid-February 1846, the survey of the destitute population of five townlands in the barony of Longford near Lismany found that 211 persons in the district were 'absolutely starving'. They were correctly seen as the apex of a pyramid of hunger in the area, and reduced in some cases to the skeletal condition where the body feeds necrotically on its own substance, they had only a poor chance of survival. The government was advised by local officials 'to distribute Indian meal at reasonable prices as the most immediate form of relief'. But by the spring, distress in the barony of Longford was 'alarmingly great and uneasing'. It was accompanied by calls from landlords for a new Coercion Bill to be passed, suspending Habeas Corpus and allowing for summary punishment, since rural outrages had increased in East Galway with the coming of this most extreme want since 1822. The proposed new bill would make it possible for magistrates to have men arrested on suspicion, and label the bearing of any kind of arms a transportable offence. Esther nagged her sons Patrick and Hugh to remain indoors at night and abstain from Ribbon oaths, threatening notices and secret meetings of disgruntled men. According to a Lismany source on this matter, at least one of the boys did have Ribbon tendencies.

But a visitor to Ballinasloe after this terrible winter saw a people on the road leading into the town who still seemed to possess their souls. 'The poor labourers were going to their work, smoking or singing, their tattered garments but an apology for clothing. As I passed the wretched cabins, now and then the happy voice of some child singing a merry song greeted my ear.' For Esther, of course, diet was neither as reliable nor as varied as that of Mary Shields in the Monaro a world away. In modern terms, one would need to visit a distressed area of East Africa to see a woman who possessed as lean, as agelessly hollowed, a countenance and as chancy a hold on life as Esther had in the late winter of 1845–6. But she still held normal hope of finding labour in the spring and of an unblighted potato crop at the end of the summer, and it was on other roads than hers, and in other baronies of Galway, that travellers would already have commonly seen full-blown and terminal malnutrition, and an accumulation of corpses in ditches and by hedges.

In increasing numbers, the peasants found Repeal irrelevant to this visitation, or could no longer afford to support it. Outside Mass, O'Connell's Repeal wardens were rebuffed, and Repeal rent collapsed. The minds of Esther and her neighbours ran confusedly for explanations of what had befallen them. One Famine song asked whether the disaster was God's punishment for 'the shame of a Queen who counted the nation's people', a reference to the supposed arrogance of the census of 1841. Strictly political explanations seemed remote. The Repeal rent published in the *Nation* on 24 January was a mere £367. There was residual faith, however, and on 14 March the *Nation* printed a poignant letter from the priest at St Mary's, Clonmel, Tipperary. 'With famine staring us in the face, the enclosed £10 from the parish of St Mary's, Clonmel, is rather a substantial proof of our devotion to the cause of nationality. The money would afford a temporary relief, but self-legislation would confer lasting prosperity.'

In the late winter, sooner than in many other parts of the country, Esther saw the emergence of what people called Black Fever, *fiabrhas dubh*, known by physicians as typhus. By February 1846, T. Harrison, medical officer of the dispensary of Ballinasloe, wrote that 'fever has been more prevalent within the last three months than in former years'. The Loughrea dispensary, a little to Esther's west, reported that in six weeks there had been an increase of 308 patients, all due, said the resident medical officer, to 'heavy rains, want of food, and bad clothing'. Marching side by side with hunger, typhus darkened the swollen faces of the victims, and finished them. During the spring and summer of 1846, Esther Larkin saw people collapse from it in fields and on roadsides around Lismany. She recognised it. There had been a terrifying outbreak when she was a child, in 1816–17.

Lice infected with *Rickettsia*, the bacteria of typhus, communicated the disease from sufferer to sufferer. The mere squashing of an infected louse on the skin permitted invasion by the minute bacteria. The excrement of the louse contained *Rickettsia* also. The extension of a helping hand to the ragged elbow of a sufferer's coat could release the invisible and fatal powder of dung. Hence, clergy, nuns and doctors who tended fever patients, handled their tattered clothing, comforted them with a hand to wrist, shoulder or forehead, readily became victims. In Clougheen, East Galway, the doctor, the apothecary and three priests all died of it in the space of ten days. Many witnesses mentioned the mousy stench of the disease, how it drove one backwards when the door of an infected house was opened.

A deadly relapsing fever emerged almost simultaneously. It was sometimes named Yellow Fever, *fiabrhas buidhe*, because it produced a jaundiced appearance. Relapsing fever was also transmitted by lice, but the bacterium was carried on the body and limbs of the louse, not in the stomach. This fever raged five or six days, but then passed. But after perhaps a week it hit again. There could be as many as three or four relapses, any of them fatal.

Both fevers between them carried a generic name: Famine Fever. Under their attack, it became apparent that a fever hospital needed to be set up in every Poor Law union. Ballinasloe Poor Law union would in the first instance provide accommodation for fever-convalescent cases in its idiot wards, until a fever hospital to accommodate sixty-four patients could be built. The progress of disease amongst the people around Esther would render both arrangements inadequate.

The gentlemen of the *Nation* tried to convey to their better-off readers a panorama of a disastrous west, Connacht, that is, and of parts of Munster. Galway and Cork were counting deaths, but the *Nation* had heard, as Esther had, of proud families pledging themselves to starve rather than beg. Hundreds of thousands waited for typhus to deliver them 'from the griping horrors of want'. For there was a powerful sense that 'worse is coming. Hospitals yelling with delirious starvelings – churchyards fattening – drugs at famine price – doctors at fault – and parish coffins at a premium – to this state will the Government permit this country to be reduced.'

At the end of the first winter of the Famine, O'Brien told his friends in the '82 Club that he was going back to the spring sitting in Westminster merely to fight the Coercion Bill the Irish landlords wanted, and to urge more positive options. 'A year of warfare', O'Brien later argued in line with his attitude that spring, 'would cost England a far greater amount of money than would have been sufficient . . . for the whole number of those who have disappeared from the register of our population.'

In London, in the chilly House, pale, tall, intense O'Brien's methods of delaying a new Coercion Bill to crush rural outrages were to make endless speeches, call for divisions on small amendments to clauses, rally a small group of Irish parliamentarians to engage in interminable discussions of every possible clause. The Speaker had in the meantime appointed him to a House of Commons Select Committee on Scottish Railways. On 3 April, O'Brien told the Speaker he refused to serve until Ireland's problems were addressed by something more effective than a Coercion Bill and an occasional sale of inedible Indian corn.

In the previous session of the House, Daniel O'Connell and his son had announced the same intention, not to attend select committees. The Liberator was by now, however, moving in another direction. He saw the chance of an alliance with Lord John Russell's Whigs, and decided to serve on committees after all. To the young men he yet again seemed to have given ground. Smith O'Brien, who was not a ground-giver, still wanted 'outdoor relief', not the workhouse system which would soon be shown to be horrifically inadequate. Outdoor relief was to be paid for by a tax upon all landowners, including absentees; that is, a tax on O'Brien's own class.

The Speaker warned O'Brien that a failure to serve on committees would put him in contempt of Parliament, for which he could be imprisoned. Images of the Tower of London rose in O'Brien's mind, but he held his ground. On 30 April 1846, while the House was deliberating O'Brien's case, O'Brien stood by the Parliamentary Library door, 'in a state of great excitement, frequently clasping his hands together in a very agitated manner'. The vote went against him. The Speaker committed O'Brien to the Sergeant-at-Arms for an unprecedented imprisonment. The two rooms which were to serve for his detainment were not in the Tower downriver but off an open passageway between the House of Commons and the House of Lords. The first room was a cramped anteroom, the second 'a low small (15 by 8 and 7 feet high), damp-looking and miserable room, with a trestle bed and a little deal table'. Although he was permitted to go for short walks in the passageway, and could sit in the anteroom door reading, this was not nearly as cosy an imprisonment as the Liberator had enjoyed in Richmond bridewell. O'Brien found the rooms cold, with coconut matting on the stone floor, and because he refused to pay the daily fine imposed by the Speaker, the food seems to have been tea and dry toast. Though he did not know it, O'Brien was practising for coming steely disciplines of imprisonment.

That past winter O'Brien had seen people near Sixmilebridge in Limerick eating potatoes an Englishman would not feed to his hogs. Now he had leisure to read of end-of-winter evictions. In East Galway, for example, in the area of Ballinglass on the Galway–Roscommon border, a Mrs Gerrard had evicted more than 60 tenants, nearly 300 people, for unpaid rent. The eviction, carried out by a detachment of the 49th Infantry and numerous constabulary, was described by a bystander 'as the most appalling he had ever witnessed – women, young and old, running wildly to and fro with small portions of their property'. That night the ejected families slept in the ruins; their neighbours were warned on pain of eviction against taking them in. Like the evicted throughout the country, they had now to live in *scalps*, burrows roofed over with boughs and turf, or in *scalpeens*, holes dug in the ruins of a 'tumbled' house. The nightmare which Hugh, years before, had tried to prevent in his own case had come.

The *Nation* denounced Mrs Gerrard and publicly applauded another landlord, the imprisoned O'Brien. But the other Repeal newspaper, the *Pilot*, dismissed O'Brien's demonstration, and Tom Steele refused three cheers for O'Brien at the Repeal Association meeting in Dublin on the Monday following his imprisonment. 'I cannot disguise from you', Smith O'Brien wrote from 'his coal-hole', as *The Times* described it, 'that the conduct of the Repeal Association has deeply disappointed me.'

Mitchel, his friend John Martin, Meagher, the lawyer Doheny, another Young Ireland lawyer named Richard O'Gorman, and the young woolbroker Terence MacManus all joined an '82 Club delegation to go to visit O'Brien in London, to signify their support and respect. After their arrival, O'Connell met the group in his London lodgings and distracted and disarmed them by exchanging some banter with his adored infant grandson. 'Meagher was obliged to push his chair back a little,' Martin would later remember, 'and to stuff his handkerchief in his mouth.' When the delegation got to the point, asking O'Connell to accompany them to the House of Commons, the Liberator declined. The party went on without him. When at Westminster Palace, inside O'Brien's dim, cramped anteroom, Meagher mentioned that the Liberator had declined to join their party, O'Brien merely smiled. O'Connell himself did in the end visit O'Brien, but it was unofficial, and arranged only after the Young Ireland delegation had left London. O'Brien was released by order of the Speaker after twenty-five days' incarceration.

On 6 June that year, as Ireland endured its summer, Daniel O'Connell, with his son John and other Repeal MPs, visited the house of Lord John Russell in London. Rumours quickly got around Conciliation Hall and all the newspaper offices in Dublin that a new alliance was planned between the Liberator's Repeal MPs and Russell's Whigs. To the Young Irelanders it seemed the sort of alliance which had served Ireland poorly in the 1830s and which would ensure that Repeal became a dead issue. The *Nation* attacked the alliance, beginning on 13 June and continuing for months. 'NEVER TRUST A WHIG . . . Dream not that those Whigs are going to save you from your landlords; but pray that the Almighty might put it into your landlords' hearts to save you from the Whigs.' At a weekly Repeal meeting at Conciliation Hall, more strenuously and more vocally than the newly released 43-year-old O'Brien, the 22-year-old orator Meagher found his authoritative and, said some, patricidal voice. Reluctantly recognised by the chair, he uttered a most thoroughgoing attack on the alliance, a speech which one of the Liberator's lieutenants could describe only as 'malevolent'.

Meagher believed in oratory as the supreme artful weapon, a matter of style, cadence and the application of controlled but massive energy. The genial but yearning dandy had studied the styles of Carlyle, Lamartine and Emmet, and possessed an exceptional gift: he was potent in imagery but he was sparing of the indulgent rage which is a trap for young activists. Meagher, said Duffy, 'was at that time a youth of twenty-two, who had scarcely heard his own voice in a college debating society, and had not written a line for the public beyond one feeble copy of verses in the *Nation*'. But now, 'he began to address the Association in language such as it had never heard – the language not only of conviction . . . but of passion, poetry, and imagination'.

Meagher demanded:

what was the condition of the people – what was the condition of the country – during the reign of the late Whig government? Your commerce – did that thrive? Your manufactures – were they encouraged? Your fisheries – were they protected? Your wastelands – they were two million acres – were they reclaimed? How fared the Irish artisan – how fared the Irish peasant? Where one pined, as he yet pines, in your beggared cities, the other starved, as he yet starves, upon your fruitful soil.

The sneers of Steele, the disapproval of Ray, the hostility of John O'Connell, could not halt the boy. The Poor Law Commissioners, Meagher said, mainly Englishmen and Scotsmen, were examples of Whig mercy. They had been authorised to impose upon the Irish an alien form of relief. 'The poor houses were soon stocked with vermined rags, and broken hearts, with orphan childhood, fevered manhood and desolate old age. Whilst those coarse specimens of the Tudor Gothic were being thus filled, your custom house was drained – and now it stands upon your silent quay.' His attack turned to an easy target, Dublin Castle. There was gaiety in those courts, he said, and brilliance amongst the visitors. 'But were there bright eyes, and happy hearts, and busy hands, in the tenements of the Liberties?' So, he called with desolating irony:

Name your terms to the Whigs ... Lease them your vote for another experimental session ... pat down your demands to their crippled powers of concession – unite with them in their oppression of the Orangemen, who are your brothers – give over your notions about self-governance ... speak no more about the Irish genius, the rearing up of Irish art, the planting of an Irish flag ... sustain the new police. Be tactful, that is, be partisan – be sensible, that is, cease to be honest – be rational, that is, conceive the poorest possible opinion of your country.

Meagher had referred during his oration to the late Davis as 'our leader and our prophet', and in the uproar of applause and dissent which followed his Promethean speech Steele moved a motion that the Irish people acknowledged no leader but O'Connell. The Liberator in London was assured that the sentiment of the meeting, once 'the fascination of Meagher's speech was off', was entirely against Young Ireland. But throughout the country thousands of Irishmen and women who still had a mind for politics were grateful to Meagher for so powerfully and bravely stating their own misgivings about O'Connell and Lord John Russell.

Later in the summer, when O'Connell's support for the Whigs *had* brought Russell to the prime ministership of Great Britain, the Liberator compounded the sin of the Whig alliance by favouring Russell in an especial manner – agreeing not to run a Repeal candidate in the northern seat of Dungarvan against the Prime Minister's candidate. Meagher's new, heady, almost loving rage was cemented in place by this decision:

Go into the churchyard – write *Fool* upon every tombstone that commemorates a Volunteer – and thank your God that you live in an age of common sense, with philosophy and starvation. Aye, write the sarcasm upon the gravestone of a Volunteer ... the Citizen soldier of 1782 was a fraud! He did not sign petitions for outdoor relief but levelled his gun with *free trade.*

Older cynics in Repeal said that for all occasions florid young Meagher had a sublimely metred, extempore speech carefully written, which he delivered with rehearsed spontaneity, and more intensity than grace. But there were grounds for passion that summer. Meagher's oratory coruscated across the Irish scene as had Davis's verse earlier, but the Ireland it cast light on was a skeletal presence, tall and ravaged, loosened by malnutrition from all politics, and from all allegiances except grief and the dream of the succulent, blood-enriching, vanished potato.

Everywhere, particularly in the west and south-west, the coastguard and the commissary were disobeying their superiors and yielding to the pleas of scarecrow Irish. Authorised or not, during June and July the Limerick depot sold 500 tons of Indian meal per week, while in Cork 600 tons were sold weekly.

Esther and her sons had probably used every culinary dodge and food source to avoid using the yellow meal, Peel's brimstone. That was a matter of pride, for they were still afflicted with hope. Esther found it impossible to imagine that the blight had survived the previous winter and retained any power to strike the new crop. In many areas people had survived to this point by selling off their peat-smoky clothing or anything of value. High-price oatmeal or low-price corn had prevented their buying the yearly pig. In millions of cases their only reserve was the new potato crop. Waiting for it, hundreds of thousands had spent the summer on Board of Works projects, building for wages roads which went nowhere, hauling down hills as a make-work, digging railway cuttings for railways which would never come. All this was authorised by the Board of Works lest the peasantry develop a sense of entitlement. In the limestone wilderness of the Burren of Clare can still be seen Famine roads of limestone chippings, beginning nowhere discernible, going nowhere discernible. Beside them lie piles of rock fragments where family groups signed up by the Board of Works supervisor in the area sat down to break stones. In the Lismany area, some of the public works available to Esther and her sons included making a new road in the direction of Somerset House and digging drainage-ditches around the Belview estate. Daily output was measured by surveyors. It was not easy work for a woman of forty, whose best hopes for life had already been defeated.

In the *Nation*, John Mitchel published his own gloss on all this.

In the first year of the famine, then, [he would write] we find that the measures proposed by the English government were, *first*, repeal of the Corn Laws, which depreciated Ireland's only article of export; *second*, a new Coercion Law, to torment and transport the people; and *third*, a grant of £100,000 to certain clerks or commissioners, chiefly for their own profit, and from which the starving people derived no benefit whatever. Yet, Ireland was taunted with this grant, as if it were *alms* granted to her. Double the sum (£200,000) was, *in the same Session*, appropriated for Battersea Park, a suburban place of recreation much resorted to by Londoners.

Whatever their politics, Lucy at Cahirmoyle and the O'Briens at Dromoland felt bound to exercise stewardship towards their threatened people. In that, they were like the debt-ridden Liberator, whose son Maurice managed the Derrynane properties of the O'Connells. Maurice had sent the family sloop to Cork to buy produce to sell to their people for cost. In a different spirit from that of Trevelyan, 'I wish you to be as abundant with the people as you possibly can', O'Connell would write to his son.

Even for the itinerants drifting along the road from Ennis to Newmarket, the O'Briens claimed to have some responsibility. Their initiatives towards their own tenantry included leniency on rent, feeding people outdoors, participation in public works and, later, relief committee work, encouragement of well-conducted emigration schemes and – especially in the case of Sir Lucius O'Brien – frequent letters to the decision-makers. He tried to enlighten Bessborough, the new Lord Lieutenant appointed by Russell to deal with the crisis. He wrote to Redington, the Under-Secretary, who had been to Harrow with his brother William Smith O'Brien, Routh the Commissary-General in Dublin, and members of the Cabinet at Westminster, about the true condition of Ireland. A public works project started under the aegis of Sir Lucius was the 9-mile stone wall which still surrounds Dromoland estate. Certainly, it benefited the estate, but would not have been of priority to the O'Briens. Sir Lucius seems to have seen it as an exotic though useful enterprise whose chief worth was that it provided work for hundreds, but he was shocked by the poor health and weakness of some who presented themselves for work.

Later, in 1847, when she was dealing matriarchally with the results of a second potato crop failure, Lady O'Brien would assure her son William with what appears to have been some truth that people 'in this neighbourhood are so well taken care of that there is nothing like starvation, though no money has yet been asked for from Government'. The people themselves may not have felt as rosy about their condition. But a daily ration of soup or gruel *was* handed out by a member of the Dromoland household – notably by Grace O'Brien – near two ash trees on either side of the road leading to Newmarket-on-Fergus. At Moohoun, Lady O'Brien organised a woman named Mary O'Grady to sell rice porridge at a penny a quart to save people going into Newmarket or Ennis futilely looking for food.

Another example of a paternal landlord in that area of Ireland – the estuary of the Shannon – was Lord Monteagle, Thomas Spring-Rice of Mount Trenchard, who had been a Whig Chancellor of the Exchequer in 1835. Meagher satirised him as a devotee of the benefits of the Union with Britain. But when during the Famine the local Office of Public Works ran out of money to pay people on public projects, Monteagle advanced £4,500 of his own; he reduced rents; and for his benefit and that of his tenants, he caused those still in arrears to emigrate.

He did not operate in this way entirely at his own expense. From funds acquired in part through the sale of Crown land in Australia, the British government was willing to assist and even pay for the emigration of Irish settlers to leaven their convict brethren. The first group of Monteagle emigrants had been sent on the *Aliquis* in 1838. Most of them were more or less landless peasants of Hugh's class, and a number of them settled in Goulburn and its surrounding country as farm labourers or maids. In the Cathedral of St Peter and St Paul, Goulburn, they would in the end occupy the same pews on Sunday as Hugh Larkin and Mary Shields.

When the emigration schemes revived under the pressure of the Famine in 1847 and 1848, groups of thirty or forty of Monteagle's people at a time arrived as free settlers in Sydney and Melbourne. Monteagle told his tenants, 'Have your assets valued. I will take what they realise, forgive you the difference, and help you to emigrate. Otherwise, I shall be forced to evict you.' He spent some money ensuring their humane passage, and even wrote ahead to colonial officials seeking their assistance for his former tenants. This was forced emigration, but to possess paternal landlords like the O'Briens, the O'Connells or the Monteagles was to be more fortunate than some hundreds of thousands of others.

Towards the end of summer, as the peasantry observed the winsome flowers of their potato crops bloom in apparent health, the Liberator was in torment at the way famine had altered all politics. If early reports of another blight in some areas were correct, the idea of a 'physical force' rebellion might appeal to Young Ireland. Gavan Duffy was already about to go on trial for publishing in the *Nation* John Mitchel's infernal articles on the railways. He would be acquitted, but his very arrest had made the young men combative and resentful of the Liberator. Duffy's aged chief counsel, Robert Holmes, who had defended United Irishmen at their trials after the 1798 uprising, declared before the court that, the Irish light having been 'extinguished by the foulest means that sword and tyranny ever practised . . . any attempt to rekindle it is to be treated as sedition'.

To counter these sentiments, O'Connell found it necessary to say at a general meeting of Repeal in Conciliation Hall one evening in mid-July, 'If I were a Quaker I could not abhor violence more than I do.' Meagher, though still reverential towards the Liberator, asked why, if the Liberator favoured the constitutional route over physical force, Repeal had not stood its own candidate in Dungarvan. Why at its first test had it knuckled under to Russell? Why had Repeal softened to some vague concept of ultimate federalism within Britain? John O'Connell moved, to boos from Meagher's friends, that 'the language of Mr Meagher was not language that could be safely listened to by the Association'. Smith O'Brien, in London at the time, received a letter from a friend saying how amazing it was to see 'Mr Meagher, a stripling, pitted against the great O'Connell'.

It was to deal with the oratorical challenges of remarkable Mr Meagher, and the journalistic ones of Mitchel, that O'Connell finally drafted two peace resolutions to present for the approval of Repeal's over-large, dozens-strong committee at Conciliation Hall the next week. The press and public turned up to watch, with the galleries full of fashionable and nationalistic young men and women. The Liberator himself was bravely present, his authority as Ireland's redeemer at stake as he asked Young Ireland to vote for and accept his two principles. The first proposition declared Repeal's task to be 'the amelioration of political institutions by peaceable and legal means alone'; the second, that it would pursue its aims while 'abhorring all attempts to improve and augment constitutional liberty by means of force, violence or bloodshed'. In the Liberator's febrile mind, lives, and the continued flow of succour from Lord John Russell, depended on acceptance of both proposals.

Meagher and Richard O'Gorman both objected to the use of the verb in 'abhorring all attempts'. John Mitchel deferentially asked the chair if this proposition to which O'Connell wished to bind Ireland applied to other countries. After all, the Liberator had fellow feeling for armed rebellions elsewhere in the world. Mitchel asked, could George Washington, one of O'Connell's heroes, have acceded to the Liberator's proposals?

O'Connell replied improbably that Washington's war had been a defensive one and therefore just. Then, said Mitchel, either you acknowledge the abstract possibility of such a defensive war in Ireland, or else you should embody Quakerism and the turning of the other cheek in the Association rules. In the end the committee voted to refer the propositions to a meeting open to full membership later in the month. Obviously, thousands would attend, and dilute the voices of Young Ireland.

Tireless Smith O'Brien was back in Ireland. But though a committee member, he was at the time of the inconclusive meeting giving an earlier-arranged speech in the town hall of one of the worst-afflicted towns,

Kilrush, County Clare, as hapless country people drifted in from shattered cottages to the neo-Gothic Kilrush workhouse. Looking at the national ruin, O'Brien told his audience, it was impossible to condemn outright the option of physical force in all circumstances. This was reported and interpreted as a warning to the Liberator that O'Brien would not stand for the expulsion from Repeal of 'the young men'.

He made sure he attended the climactic meeting, which took place at Conciliation Hall over two evenings at the end of July. But O'Connell himself chose to avoid the turmoil and was in London, awaiting reports. His son John represented him. The gallery around the hall was again packed with observers and the young men and women, from families at least physically immune from famine, who were Meagher's preferred and stimulating audience. An O'Connell lieutenant named Captain Broderick was in the chair, and O'Brien, under attack for what he had said in Kilrush, was called on early to speak. O'Brien argued that Young Ireland had merely embraced ideas which the Liberator had expressed in the monster meetings. And while it was easy enough for both sides to tie each other up in the knots of rhetoric, with hungry and fevered Ireland not far removed from the door of Conciliation Hall, the need to chase abstractions with the aged Liberator and his supporters annoyed and frustrated O'Brien. 'The factions of Jerusalem struggling for the upper hand at an hour when the catapaults of Titus were beating down the gates furnish a stock example of national folly. But Ireland, it was plain, was about to encounter a worse calamity than siege or sack.'

The next evening supplied the moment of the debate best remembered, endowing Meagher with a soubriquet which would serve him on three continents. The Liberator's Repeal-warden-in-chief, Tom Steele, stood up to challenge the young orator for his chronic ingratitude to the Liberator. Stop equivocating, he said, and stand up and repudiate violence outright, except for defence.

To Meagher this served as invitation to make the clarifying and focusing speech he had prepared. He rose to catcalls and interjections from older men, and began by restating his principles. 'A Whig minister may improve the province – he will not restore the nation.' By the clear gleaming of Conciliation Hall's candelabra, Meagher refused to accept Steele's accusations of ingratitude. 'No, my Lord, I am not ungrateful to the man who struck the fetters off my arms, whilst I was yet a child, and by whose influence, my father – the first Catholic to do so for two hundred years – sat for the last two years in the civic chair of an ancient city. But, my Lord, the same God who gave to that great man the power to strike down an odious ascendancy in this country . . . gave to me a mind that is my own.'

Meagher, with a Davis-like romantic ignorance of war, hailed the sword 'as a sacred weapon; and if, My Lord, it has sometimes taken the shape of the serpent and reddened the shroud of the oppressor with too deep a dye, like the anointed rod of the High Priest, it has at other times, and as often, blossomed into celestial flowers to deck the freeman's bow'. He conjured up three instances of recourse to the sword, all of them ones the Liberator had praised. First, the rebellion early in the century of Andreas Hofer, an old-fashioned Tyrolese patriot who drove the Bavarians out of a traditionally Austrian area; then the American rebellion; and thirdly, that of the Belgian patriots. 'Abhor the sword – stigmatize the sword? No, my Lord, for at its blow, a giant nation started from the waters of the Atlantic and by its redeeming magic, and in the quivering of its crimson light, the crippled Colony sprang into the attitude of a proud Republic – prosperous, limitless and invincible. Abhor the sword – stigmatize the sword? No, my Lord, for it swept the Dutch marauders out of the fine old towns of Belgium – scourged them back to their own phlegmatic swamps and knocked their flag and sceptre, their laws and bayonets into the sluggish waters of the Scheldt. My Lord, I learned that it is the right of a nation to govern itself, not in this Hall but upon the ramparts of Antwerp. I learned the first article of a nation's creed upon those ramparts, where freedom was justly estimated, and where the possession of the precious gift was purchased by the effusion of generous blood.'

'This', said Duffy, 'was thrilling music.' A spate of oratory, ensuring for the young man almost instantly the initially mocking but ultimately heady title of *Meagher of the Sword*, seemed to shift the earth beneath Conciliation Hall. John O'Connell was panicked into interrupting, causing the speech to remain unfinished, like some valiant bugle call when in mid-chord the bugler is cut down. He was convinced, said John O'Connell, 'that it would not be safe for the Association to allow Mr Meagher to proceed . . . The question was not should a young man be put down? But should a young man put down the Association?'

O'Brien made a short, final, withering protest, no flashiness to it, and all the more scarifying to those listening. 'You are charged', he told the Association, 'with being a people who will never give fair play to an adversary. You are charged with being willing slaves to any despot who may obtain the reins of power at a particular moment.' Then he simply walked out, silencing some, causing others to scream abuse. He was followed by Meagher himself and most of the Young Irelanders, including Meagher's schoolfriend Patrick Smyth, John Mitchel, Gavan Duffy, and a number of women from the gallery.

Meagher was pursued out on to the Liffey quays by Captain Broderick, who had been in the chair, and there was a scuffle. In Broderick's mind, it was malicious for Meagher, the spoilt youth who spoke like an angel both of light and division, to have induced the man nobody could afford to lose, Smith O'Brien, to vacate Repeal.

Reacting to the stand of Thomas Francis Meagher, one of Gavan Duffy's trio of young women poets, versifying under the pen name 'Speranza', wrote:

> Unbought – unsold – unstain'd, undoubted man!
> Stand fast – take breath – time shows who Will and Can.

In her early twenties, Speranza, whose real name was Miss Jane Elgee, was the daughter of a Protestant lawyer long deceased, and her verse had made her already a national figure. The poet W. B. Yeats would later recount how she had been influenced to begin writing by the death of Davis. Gavan Duffy found her tall, elegant, with 'flashing brown eyes and features cast in an heroic mould'. The name Elgee, she believed, was a derivative of Alighieri, and she suspected she bore Dante's blood, toying with the idea that the great poet had re-found his voice in her.

She would later marry the surgeon Sir William Wilde, but that did nothing to temper her unfeigned outrage. Like her dresses, her poetry might be sometimes over-elaborate, favouring quirky metres, but she excited Irish readers of her day to such a degree that in the future her son Oscar Fingall O'Flahertie Wills Wilde would find it hard to achieve a literary presence independent of his mother's.

'Liberty's torch is bright!' read a poem typical of her tendency to gild the lily of metre:

> The light
> May mock our tyrant's scorning,
> For millions of hearts will be kindled ere noon
> And the freedom we dreamed of in darkness, full soon
> We'll achieve in the light of the day.

Another of Duffy's stars who reacted to Meagher's speech was an adolescent girl, Mary Anne Kelly of Killeen near Portumna, East Galway about 10 miles from where Esther Larkin lived. Mary Anne, known as 'Eva', was the brave, pretty, well-read and naïvely yearning daughter of a prosperous, austere but nationalistic gentleman-farmer, and had been fifteen when her intellectually vivacious mother and sisters had first persuaded her to send Duffy verse.

Down, Britannia, brigand down!
No more to rule with sceptred hand:
Truth raises o'er thy throne and crown
Her exorcising wand.

When the soft maiden of Killeen opened her mouth, fire came forth. Like Speranza, Eva was a literary sensation, but she remained in Galway for some years yet.

'Young Patriot, bend thee lowly,' she wrote now, apostrophising Meagher:

A mighty spirit silently
Breathes o'er thee true and holy.

The *Nation*'s third muse, a woman in her early twenties, Miss Ellen Downing from Cork, who wrote under the name 'Mary', later to become a nun, also approved of Meagher, as did the leading male poet, the alcoholic librarian Mangan.

The walkout of Young Ireland, praised as it might be by rhymesters, was now lambasted by Catholic and Protestant press alike. But definite news of a blight more sudden than that of the year before, and universal throughout Ireland, overshadowed the quarrel. Father Matthew, the Capuchin monk who was the champion of Irish temperance, wrote to Trevelyan: 'On the 27th of last month [July], I passed from Cork to Dublin, and this doomed plant bloomed in all the luxuriance of an abundant harvest. Returning on the 3rd instant I beheld with sorrow one wide waste of putrefying vegetation. In many places the wretched people were seated on fences of their decaying gardens, wringing their hands and wailing bitterly.' Esther again found her East Galway potatoes reduced to muck. Putrefaction of the crop might well now be the norm for the future, a permanent curse. Young men raged, but many older people wondered if God had found out their secret sins and imposed an endless, annual punishment.

The East Galway farmer Peatsaí O'Callanáin, who lived not far from Esther, knew by heart a Famine ballad, '*Na Fataí Bána*', 'The White Potatoes', in which one verse refers to a sudden total obliteration of the potatoes by 1 August that year. The refrain might credibly be put in Esther's mouth:

It is my woe and misery that potatoes are blackening in every corner of the world, the stalks are old and withered from the 1st of August, flowerless and lifeless as if it were November . . . It is just one thousand and eight hundred years, two score and six more, since our Saviour descended from Heaven, that the potatoes of the world were destroyed . . . The hospital and the poorhouse are full, and the people are being buried deep in the clay; and our only food is yellow meal morning and evening.

The secretary of the Killimor Relief Committee (Killimor being some 7 miles south-west of Laurencetown) put the problem more prosaically when he wrote to Sir Randolph Routh, Commissariat General, at Dublin Castle in a letter on 10 October 1846:

There has been no oatmeal sent into this market and as for potatoes I regret to have to state that there is scarcely a potato for miles around. The consequence therefore is that the poor are obliged to travel to either Ballinasloe or Loughrea, a distance of twelve miles, for a few stone of meal.

On whose authority could Esther now counsel her sons? The countryside was full of young men prepared to raid even by daylight canal barges carrying produce for sale and export, or to ambush the wagons, loaded with grain or livestock on their way to ships, passing through the Laurencetown area. Such gestures of traditional grievance and corrosive fear were still labelled 'outrages', and they tripled in number in the first full year of Famine. Hugh Larkin might be lost to his family in a region whose name was not even known to the landlords of East Galway, but the conditions of the time ensured that the landscape was full of his hungry reincarnations.

John Eyre, the East Galway landowner who had signed Esther's petition to the Lord Lieutenant in 1840, and who owned the prime estate of Eyrecourt south of Laurencetown, would on 27 October 1846 request military protection for the boats carrying provisions on the Grand Canal from Ballinasloe to Shannon Harbour *en route* for Dublin. More concerned about attacks on wagons, Walter Lawrence, resident magistrate in Laurencetown, named on Hugh's New South Wales application for reunion, echoed Eyre's request for protection. Lawrence recalled that 'during the Terry-Alt disturbances in this county, a military party was stationed at Laurencetown'. The need was more acute now, as Laurencetown was 'a great thoroughfare' for the transit of provisions to other parts of the county.

9

A Thousand Farewells to You, Island of St Patrick

> A thousand farewells to you, island of St Patrick. It was there we grew up and our ancestors before us; it was the potato blight that drove us abroad to Baltimore, to earn a living.
>
> Gaelic ballad, Famine era, Irish Folklore Commission

Spacious Miss Elgee, remarkable Speranza, had been a witness to the debates in Conciliation Hall, but also to the irregular army of phantoms drifting into Dublin, while detachments of soldiers marched off to protect grain shipments coming into Dublin from the direction of Wicklow, Kildare and Meath. She famously wrote:

> 'Weary men, what reap ye?' 'Golden corn for the stranger.'
> 'What sow ye?' 'Human corses which wait for the avenger.'
> 'Fainting forms, hunger-stricken, what see ye in the offing?'
> 'Stately ships to bear our food away, amid the stranger's scoffing.'
> 'There's a proud array of soldiers – what do they round your door?'
> 'They guard our masters' granaries from the thin hand of the poor.'
> 'Pale mothers, wherefore weeping?' 'Would to God that we were dead –
> Our children swoon before us and we cannot give them bread.'

At the *Nation*, Mitchel rushed this technically awkward but politically urgent poem into print, for he knew the truth of it, having revisited a village first visited two years before.

> There is a horrible silence; grass grows before the doors; we fear to look into any door . . . for we fear to see yellow chapless skeletons grinning there; but our footfalls rouse two lean dogs that run from us with doleful howling, and we know by the felon-gleam in the wolfish eyes how they lived after their masters died. We stop before the threshold of our host of two years before, put our head, with our eyes shut, inside the door-jamb, and say, with shaking voice, 'God save all here!' – No answer. Ghastly silence, and mouldy stench, as from the mouth of burial vaults! They are dead! The strong man and the fair dark-eyed woman and the little ones, with their liquid Gaelic accents that melted into music two years ago; they shrank and withered together until their voices dwindled to a rueful gibbering, and they hardly knew one another's faces; but their horrid eyes scowled at each other with a cannibal glare.

Mitchel would have acknowledged, though, that for its effect on British opinion the horrifying journal of one Dr Donovan published in the *Cork Southern Reporter*, not a Young Ireland organ, and reproduced in newspapers in England and the United States, was more potent.

The following is a statement of what I saw yesterday evening on the lands of Taureen. In a cabbage garden I saw (as I was informed) the bodies of Kate Barry and her two children very lightly covered with earth, the hands and legs of her large body entirely exposed, the flesh completely eaten off by the dogs, the skin and hair of the head lying within a couple of yards of the skull, which when I first threw my eyes on it, I thought to be part of a horse's tail . . . I need make no comment on this but ask, *are we living in a portion of the United Kingdom?*

The winter of 1846–7 was climatically savage. In country atypically choked with snow, Esther and her neighbours lived off yellow meal, cabbage leaves, an occasional captured bird, whatever charity came from Belview or from Somerset House. Oats, rising in cost, were probably beyond the reach of what they earned on public works, but she may have had some anyhow, filched from barges on the canal or from the wagons going south into Tipperary. She and her sons, appearing barefoot that steely season at the gale-swept public works, by the flooded ditches and the snow-flecked cuttings, would have been surprised to hear that for now they lived in a less severely affected area of Ireland. By November, 286,000 people were trying to make wages out of the public works, and depending on each labourer, some of whom were children, were three, four or more other people. As public work ran on into the summer of 1847, no one was planting the coming year's harvest.

The arguments between Young and Old Ireland were remote from Esther. Her interest was to get close to the turf fire, God's one remaining blessing. In the Monaro Hugh rode beneath blazing skies, listening to cicadas sizzle in the forests of eucalypt. She knew, from early letters, that some such contrast existed, and it is remarkable that she did not break under the sardonic weight of that.

It was not fever and dysentery alone that hastened the famishing end of some of her neighbours. Virulent scurvy was also common – black leg, as the Irish called it, since it caused the vessels under the skin to burst. Famine dropsy, seen widely today in the distended bodies of African famine victims, also took its share. Another dietary disease made hair fall from children's heads but grow in patches on their faces, so that one of the Society of Friends working in Skibbereen said that the starving children looked like monkeys.

But typhus was still the supreme killer. During the winter, Thomas

Burke of Roscommon, not so far from Esther, wrote to his emigrant sister in Australia, 'They are dying like the choler pigs as fast as they can bury them and some of their remains does not be burid for ten or fifteen days and the dogs eating them some buried in mats others in their clothes.' Esther and her sisters could lose the strength and motivation to fetch water in quantity, and they did not have the means to boil large amounts for washing what clothing they still owned. People huddled together by any turf fire, and lice and typhus travelled from one to another. By day, the roads were full of desperate travellers who conveyed the infected lice from place to place. In late February and March 1847 nearly 3,000 were dying every week in Ireland's workhouses. The Board of Guardians in Fermoy, Cork, reported by March what other Poor Law guardians around the country were observing. 'Every room is so crowded that it is impossible to separate the sick from the healthy . . . thirty children labouring under disease were found in three beds.' Esther Larkin and her sons saw a shadow and a distancing fall over kinships they had till now taken for granted. They became wary and grudging. The families of sufferers would themselves often vacate the house where fever brought down a sister, a parent, a spouse. 'It was not desertion so much as quarantine,' says a historian, 'for once or twice a day these people would feed the ailing one inside by tying a can of water and a bit of hot gruel to the end of a long pole.' When there were no more tugs on the pole, the house would be pulled down on top of the corpse and burned, an unprecedented method of disposing of a body.

Did Esther ever face these impossible options, considered mortally sinful by those who carried them out? Or did she ever find herself isolated and at the end of the pole, and emerge at last to see the evasive shame in the faces of her kinsmen?

She and all her peers meant to avoid the workhouse at all costs. The Poor Law commissioners spoke with some dismay of the reluctance of people in the areas of Loughrea and Ballinasloe to use the available relief, the shelter, food, clothing, medical and spiritual consolation within the workhouse, and the willingness instead to suffer 'the worst privations'. It was better to appeal for some miraculous intervention than approach that neo-Gothic standardised gatehouse beyond which lay hell.

> O King of Glory, hear and answer us,
> From bondage save us, and come to our aid,
> And send us bread, as we cry in misery,
> And may the poorhouse be in ashes laid.

The reaction against the workhouse would become even more markedly the last option when in June 1847 an amendment was made to the Poor Law. Proposed by the Galway landlord William Gregory, it was commonly known and cursed as the Gregory clause, and it denied access to relief to any person and his or her children who still tenanted more than a ¼-acre of land. To enter the workhouse or the fever hospital, a family had to abandon their land, and could expect their cottage to be tumbled in their absence. Esther may have held as much as a ¼-acre of conacre, but, if not, a holder of even smaller amounts of land was often equally vulnerable to a law whose purpose was to clear the tenantry.

Some of the images of the Famine which would reach the world through journals such as the *Illustrated London News* were of people, as an Irish song said, like 'young crows, with death in their throats'; of women and children nearing an end, of passive, skeletal hopelessness. These illustrations did not indicate how cleverly, how determinedly, the portrayed scarecrows struggled to avoid being so reduced. Apart from outdoor relief and public works, apart from whatever it was men were able to take at peril from barges and wagons, Esther Larkin and her compatriots were engaged in a huge national hunt for any half-workable food source. Coastal people in the west dealt with hunger by catching fish, winkles and mussels. They gathered seaweeds named *crother* and *dulaman*, the second of which was not edible until after the first frosts of winter and caused diarrhoea. In Mayo, seabirds were hunted. Men were lowered over cliffs by rope and stole eggs, fighting off large ferocious mother birds.

A Wicklow farmer saw groups of men cornering cattle, to cut a vein in the neck of a beast and pour off a few pints of blood into a jar. They would repair the incision with a pin and a swatch of hair cut from the animal's tail. The blood would be salted then and fried in a pan. People fought over the blackberries before they had ripened. When the fish in the Ow River in Wicklow had all been caught, people ate the pencil-thick worms from the bottom of the stream. A landlord, afraid that all the birds of the country would be exterminated, paid a bounty of 2 pence each for every live bird brought to him. Rats which had eaten of the dead were fair game. In Mayo in the spring of 1847, 3,000 people of the parish of Island Eady intended trying to live through the summer on chickweed. One recipe in common use in Galway was to boil nettles, sorrels and dock leaves with a spoon of meal on top.

Then there was soup. In fact, for fear of the impact of the sale of cheap corn on the market, Trevelyan had ordered that from now on sales would occur only in the extreme west and south-west. The Ballinasloe corn depot was closing down. But in February 1847 a new Act of Parliament provided for the immediate establishment of local relief committees to dispense soup from premises outside the workhouse, to sustain the Irish and encourage them to plant for the harvest. The soup kitchen also gave official form to some of the individual, already existing gestures of landlords like the O'Briens in Clare and Limerick, and of Maria Edgeworth of Edgeworthtown in County Longford, who had been distributing soup or porridge locally. The Society of Friends of Cincinnati had read of Maria Edgeworth's ministrations to the 3,000 starving of her area, and consigned to her $180 worth of cornmeal to be used in stirabout, that is, corn porridge. The Friends had already entered the soup business in Ireland before outdoor relief became official. From their three-boiler soup plant in Cork city, they made and distributed 2,500 quarts of a full-bodied recipe including meat, vegetables and barley.

It took a little time that spring for new relief committee kitchens to be established throughout the country, and ordinary people, however hungry, had a resistance to them too. There was the matter of personal pride. And then charity of this nature had generally in the past been dispensed by such bodies as the Protestant Colonisation Society, which attempted to combine generosity with a demand that the peasant also climb out of the spiritual pit of Papism and convert to the Protestant faith. But need came to override any reluctance. By the summer of 1847, for nearly three million people, half the population of Ireland, the transition from stirabout to soup from the soup kitchens had been accomplished. Some modern commentators claim that much of the soup was too watery to help famine-bloated bodies. But there was no doubting the goodwill of Alexis Soyer, the French chef from London's West End, who in the spring of 1847 opened in Dublin a series of model kitchens in which fashionable volunteers worked to feed the masses. No doubting it unless one saw the soup kitchen at, say, the Royal Barracks, Dublin, from the same point of view as John Mitchel of the *Nation*. He wrote of:

> the piteous ranks of 'model' paupers, broken tradesmen, ruined farmers, destitute sempstresses, ranged at a respectful distance till the genteel persons had duly inspected the arrangements, and then marched by policemen to the place allotted them, where they were to feed on the meagre diet with *chained spoons* – to show the gentry how pauper spirit can be broken, and pauper appetite can gulp down its bitter bread and its bitterer shame and wrath together.

As operated in Ballinasloe itself, outdoor relief catered for all but unmarried men. Lord Clancarty, the local landlord, considered that 'a system of demoralisation had become very general among the poor and their industrial habits had been altogether interfered with'. To give young men soup was to foster indolence. But from 1847 onwards, the degree of need in the Union of Ballinasloe was such that people were impossible to control even when relief was being distributed. A report to Dublin Castle declared that the scenes at the two soup kitchens in the town of Ballinasloe were beyond description, with the hungry competing for the next available bowl. There or in the countryside to the south, Patrick and Hugh tasted the thinned-down soup of charity.

But as well as displays of individual desperation, acts which would cause fits of shame amongst survivors, there were also displays of solidarity amongst the masses of people of the margin. In March 1847, for example, in a Roscommon procession headed by a man carrying a loaf of bread on a pole, a large body assembled in order to speak to the gathered relief committees of the nearby parishes. But licit protest was itself considered an outrage. The leader was taken into custody and armed troops were set to patrol the streets.

On the first day of 1847, a meeting had been held at Rothschild's offices in London to establish a British Association for relief of distress. Baron Lionel de Rothschild, Lord Monteagle and Mr Abel Smith were founder-members. The association was catalysed by the magistrate Nicholas Cummins, who, after a visit to Skibbereen in West Cork, had written to the Duke of Wellington a letter published in *The Times* on Christmas Eve, 1846. Coming from such a reliable source, it was above all the communication that galvanised British compassion. In Skibbereen's hovels were scenes

such as no tongue or pen can convey the slightest idea of. In the first, six famished and ghastly skeletons, to all appearances dead, were huddled in a corner on some filthy straw, their sole covering what seemed a ragged horsecloth, their wretched legs hanging about, naked above the knees. I approached with horror, and found by a low moaning they were alive . . . four children, a woman and what had once been a man . . . Suffice it to say, that in a few minutes I was surrounded by at least two hundred such phantoms . . . My clothes were nearly torn off in my endeavour to escape from the throng of pestilence around, when my neckcloth was seized from behind by a grip which compelled me to turn. I found myself grasped by a woman with an infant just born in her arms and the remains of a filthy sack across her loins, the sole covering of herself and baby.

Trevelyan made a personal donation of £25, as people from throughout the British Isles and the world sent money to the newly founded association. But Trevelyan warned that 'Feeling in London is so strong against the Irish, that I doubt if much progress will be made in subscription until further horrifying accounts are received.' Queen

Victoria donated £2,000, though an Irish myth still has it that it was a lesser sum – £5 is often nominated. The amounts raised would be distributed through regional agents of the association, but – as generally occurs in famines in any century – under government directive. The February 1847 articles in the *Illustrated London News* by sketcher-journalist Mr James Mahony, whose frank but non-partisan tales of his journeys in West Cork, and whose sketches of stricken villages, hasty and pathetic burials and wasted people, would become some of the most frequently invoked images of the Famine, also appalled and moved Britons.

The same reports and illustrations caused a number of American cities and committees to raise money for Ireland, independently of the British Association, from fêtes and other events. Tammany, the American Democrat headquarters in Lower Manhattan, wisely entrusted what it raised to the Society of Friends. Individual Catholic dioceses sent money – the parish churches of Brooklyn raised an initial amount of $19,000. Boston as a whole may have sent as much as $150,000. The Choctaw Indians contributed an amount in excess of $100. Southern railroads carried food donations freight-free. The Irish Relief Committee of Philadelphia sent three barks loaded with aid, one to Londonderry, one to Cork, one to Limerick, all in care of the Society of Friends. The citizens of Boston and the Irish Relief Committee of New York had shipments of grain for the Society of Friends in Cork; the United States navy provided the sloop *Jamestown* to deliver Boston's grain and the aged, formerly British frigate *Macedonian*, moored in Brooklyn, was seconded to the New Yorkers.

At the Fever Hospital in the County of Dublin infirmary, an assistant surgeon and Young Irelander, Kevin Izod O'Doherty, treated the rampant fevers which took the lives not only of Dubliners and refugees from the countryside but also of some of his colleagues. Though he must have carried fever with him into the councils of the Young Ireland movement and the meetings of the '82 Club, he and the others were well fed, and fortified against disease. O'Doherty's late father, a conservative Westland Row lawyer who did not sport the Celtic O' before his name, had provided O'Doherty with a robust constitution. He was the same age as Tom Meagher, but had a calmer presence, and was less exorbitant in dress and manner.

In the Irish mass he treated, many cried, 'Let us reform with Jesus's help and place our trust in the Lord above; and we will have potatoes again.' But to O'Doherty at the Dublin infirmary, the sick were victims not of their own sins but of those of others. 'The potato-blight', wrote Gavan

Duffy in terms O'Doherty agreed with utterly, 'had spread from the Atlantic to the Caspian, but there was more suffering in one parish in Mayo than in all the rest of Europe.' O'Doherty came to Young Ireland about the time it was deciding to give itself a formal structure, to turn itself into a political party. The '82 Club, being largely a social group, was not adequate. An Irish Confederation, the official organisation of the Young Irelanders, came into existence at a meeting in the Rotunda in Dublin, on the evening of 13 January 1847. The participants in that first Confederation meeting were delighted to be joined by Smith O'Brien, who warned the young men that the Confederation should be driven in this awful hour by the need to unite all the Irish parties, including aristocrats and Repeal. The organisation would at its peak have 10,000 members, less than the 11,000 pay clerks, gangers and inspectors employed by the public works. And the Confederate Council of thirty-nine people now proposed – of which clergy, members of parliament and justices of the peace were *ex-officio* members – seemed almost as top-heavy as the committee of the Repeal Association.

Splendidly attired Meagher, no longer inhibited by his relationship to the Liberator, was called upon to coruscate at that Rotunda meeting. He achieved an astounding authority of presence for a man of twenty-three. 'Sir, there was a levee at the Castle this morning. Our gentlemen went there to pay their respects to the representative of Royalty. We have met here this night, to testify our allegiance to liberty.' He held up a fistful of papers. 'I hold in my hand a statement of Irish exports from 1 August to 1 January. From the statements you will perceive that England seizes on our food whilst death seizes on our people – total export of provisions from the ports of Waterford, Cork, Limerick and Belfast, from 1 August 1846 to 1 January 1847: pork, barrels, 37,123; bacon, flitches, 222,608; butter, firkins, 388,455; ham, hogsheads, 1,971; beef, tierces, 2,555; wheat, barrels, 48,526; oats, barrels, 543,232.' And so with barley, oatmeal, flour, live pigs, cows, and sheep. 'From this table, Lord Monteagle would expatiate for nights upon the benefit of the English connection . . . From this table, Mr Macaulay would surely conclude that Irish opulence was a sound reality – that Irish famine was a factious metaphor.' Meagher appealed then to his Protestant fellow citizens. 'Let not the dread of Catholic ascendancy deter. If such an ascendancy were preached, here is one hand that would be clenched against it. Yes, here are four thousand arms to give it battle!' Then he turned to Smith O'Brien: 'Sir, you who are the descendant of an Irish king – go to the English Commons, and tell the English Commons what you have seen this night . . . Tell the Commons, that these citizens decide that the destiny of the Union shall be the destruction of the Union.'

The ageing and ailing Liberator at once denounced Meagher's speech as inflammatory, and was accused in return of 'felon setting', that is, trying to plead for Meagher's arrest. But despite all the rhetoric, there was still co-operation. Repeal and the Confederation supported the one candidate in the Galway by-election in February. John Martin would later remember how he, the sober Protestant, and Meagher, the dandified Catholic with no aversion to a drink, 'travelled all night through the flat snowy wastes of Roscommon', to be in place for electioneering. In the Theatre Royal, Galway, before a mixed crowd of supporters and detractors, the Young Tribune thundered again:

The struggle, begun this morning upon the hustings of your old town, is not a struggle between two men – it is a struggle between two countries. On the one side, the side of the Whig candidate, hangs the red banner beneath which your Senate has been sacked, your commerce has been wrecked, your nobility has been dishonoured, your peasants have been starved. On the other side – the side of the Repeal Candidate – floats the green flag, for which the artillery of 1782 won a legitimate respect – beneath which your Senate sat, your commerce thrived, your nobility were honoured, your peasants prospered.

The Liberator and his son John blamed the narrow loss of the Repeal candidate on the inflammatory speeches of Young Ireland. Smith O'Brien blamed it on his fellow landlord, Lord Clanricarde, who threatened all his tenants in the Claddagh of Galway with eviction, to compel them to vote for the Whigs.

That same February of the Galway elections, the distracted, grieving Liberator made what proved to be his last speech to the Commons. He was a profoundly distressed old man. He had great personal debts, and only £30 a week was coming in to Conciliation Hall. Maurice O'Connell had not proved a competent administrator of his estate at Derrynane, and the O'Connell family had much capital tied up in the Derrynane food stores. Apart from that, the Whig alliance had been a disaster, and the millions of humbler Repealers were dying of it. Now, scarcely able to stand in the House without trembling, O'Connell, the 'Big Beggarman' as he was called by *The Times*, could utter only a plea. He told the house that the Irish 'were starving in shoals, in hundreds – aye, in thousands and millions. Parliament was bound, then, to act not only liberally and generously – to find out a means of putting a stop to this terrible disaster . . . He solemnly called on them to recollect that he predicted, with the sincerest conviction, that one-fourth of her population would perish unless Parliament come to their relief.'

The Liberator's doctors and his chaplain had in the meantime told him to go to sunnier places for his health's sake, to the South of France and on to Rome. His biographers are not utterly specific on the cause of his illness, but from his tottering gait and sense of doom, on top of ravaged hopes, it may have been cardio-vascular. In Paris, Lyons and Genoa, the old man became increasingly panicked and fearful and dependent on his chaplain, Father Miley. 'By night all his griefs and terrors are on me – for he will not be satisfied unless I am by his bed,' wrote Miley. The pilgrimage of healing he had planned to fulfil in Rome was now an impossibility. He died in Genoa in agony of soul one evening in May 1847.

Throughout Ireland those who had paid the Catholic and Repeal rents were travelling down the same path or else trying to outdistance death by emigrating. When O'Connell's embalmed body was returned home later in the summer, it would pass ships full of the refugees of Famine. The Confederates of Young Ireland were not invited to the funeral. They were the heedless youngsters who had killed an irreplaceable father. Many of them, Meagher in particular, were abused in the streets of Dublin for having shortened the Liberator's life: assassination by oratory. Richard O'Gorman, John Mitchel and Meagher himself, emerging from the Rotunda, had to run from a mob and hide in a grocer's shop. Tom Meagher's dreams must have been uneasy, but it was clear by daylight reasoning that the Famine and the Whigs had done more to destroy O'Connell than had the young men who had challenged his policy.

The leaving of Ireland had until now been seen by most small tenant farmers as a more grievous destiny than death. Esther had earlier thought of it at a time when her special circumstances prevented it from being seen as perverse. But as the pestilent summer of 1847 approached, people were passionate to quit, and did so in less comfort and security than had characterised Hugh Larkin's *Parmelia* – without benefit of chains certainly, but also without surgeon-superintendents.

Some tenants left in the middle of the night, without telling anyone. Back in Ireland, on the public works in the barony of Longford, names were called out but no answer was heard. In Irish experience this was an unprecedented flight. Women whose grip on the jambs of their hovels a year before would have needed dragoons and constables to relax it now willingly fled the hearth. One song concerned an emigrant who symbolically renounced Ireland by jettisoning his hurley stick, an icon of Irish sportiveness and identity. 'He was a fine lad. He brought his hurley and ball with him on board, and he tapped the ball upwards twenty-one times with the hurley; then, next time as it came down, he doubled on it into the ocean and threw the hurley after it.'

To Esther Larkin, migration must have seemed a huge alteration of her area. Even so, it was not as massive a phenomenon as in Mayo, Connemara, Clare and West Cork. It seems that through lads like Esther's sons, the people of Lismany and Laurencetown benefited still from being close to the Shannon and the Grand Canal, and the produce which moved there. Was it her resourceful sons, not the pathetic and shrunken chance of New South Wales, which kept her in place in Lismany instead of on a boat to the St Lawrence or Liverpool?

Once in the ports, country people were sadly duped. Sold nautical instruments and equipment they were told they would need aboard, in many cases they paid their last money for forged tickets. But there was an impetus to board any ship and go from the isle of nettles, fevers and corpses. Ships little bigger than schooners tried to crowd passengers aboard in ports such as Ballina and Killala, Westport, Tralee, Kinsale, offering cramped passage to the cornucopia of the Americas.

Perhaps all the poorest of emigrants could afford for the present was deck passage to Liverpool, though many ultimately had North America in their minds. 'Hordes of paupers, bringing want and disease with them, are cast on the English shore,' the *Illustrated London News* told the British public. The result of Irish immigration to the north of England had become already apparent to Friedrich Engels, who believed the powerless Irish at least had the power to debase:

> the most horrible spot lies on the Manchester side, immediately south-west of Oxford Road, and is known as Little Ireland . . . The race that lives in these ruinous cottages, behind broken windows, mended with oilskin, sprung doors, and rotten doorposts, or in dark, wet cellars, in measureless filth and stench . . . must really have reached the lowest stages of humanity.

British North America, Canada, was the closest American landfall to Ireland. Even so, many Irish emigrants landed at Quebec, took a barge down to Montreal and walked south over the border into the United States. The back door to the great republic was necessary because, in terms of cubic space per passenger, rations, fresh water and medical attention, United States Passenger Acts demanded more of emigrant ships and their captains than did the similar British Acts. The American restrictions were not all humanitarian – the States wished to receive skilled and healthy immigrants, not wasted refugees. In February and March 1847 Congress passed two new Passenger Acts especially for the coming immigrant season. The number of passengers per ton of burthen was reduced by one third, and the minimum fare to New York rose to £7. New York State, sensing the coming flood, founded a Board of Commissioners of Emigration, six of whom belonged to the benevolent society called the

Friendly Sons of St Patrick, and were equipped to succour newcomers until they were on their feet.

It was in a sense all futile. Despite the regulations governing the shipping, landing and processing of immigrants at Castle Garden, a water-girt pleasure dome and immigrant clearing centre on the Hudson, despite the quarantining of ships with fever at Staten Island, and the guarantees ships' captains had to give as to the capacity of passengers to support themselves ashore, just under 850,000 Irish would enter the United States via the port of New York in the years between 1847 and 1851: that is, the same number as entered the entirety of North America – all the ports of Canada and the United States – in the previous two decades. Obviously not every one of those had paid £7 per passenger, so in various ways the new Passenger Acts were subverted. The impact on the city would be enormous. Irish navvies had made New York what it was by digging the Erie canal, which turned the port into a great outlet for the produce of the Midwest. Now, entering into the New York Irish traditional trades of digging, cartage, saloon-keeping and politics, the refugees of the Famine would give it its cheap labour, augment its particular character and influence for ever its politics. Philadelphia, Baltimore and Boston were to be similarly rushed, and the United States faced unprecedented challenges to public health and civic imagination.

As for Canada, the first ship of the season, *Syria*, arrived in the St Lawrence carrying eighty fever cases. By late summer a never-before-seen armada of immigrant ships crowded up that river. Most of the immigrants landed without supplies, even the 7 pounds of provisions supposedly required under the British Passenger Act. Thousands of them lacked the steamer fare from Quebec upriver to the Irish enclaves of Montreal.

When the St Lawrence iced over in the autumn of Black '47, ships continued crossing the Atlantic to the Maritimes and to United States ports. The United States complained that they were becoming the year-round dumping house for European paupers.

Robert Whyte, a Dubliner who travelled cabin class on the *Ajax* from Dublin in June 1847, left a classic account of the travails of country people from County Meath who travelled in steerage to the new world. The steerage passengers of *Ajax* bravely formed a committee to try to deal with the shifts and dangers of their journey, but fever and other diseases had come on board with them, and would spread exponentially. Not long at sea, the captain was alarmed at an outbreak: 'Having shown itself in the unventilated hold of a small brig, containing one hundred and ten living creatures, how could it possibly be stayed without medicine, medical skill or even pure water to slake the patients' burning thirst?'

On 23 June, at sea, a poignant attempt was made to observe the Nativity of John the Baptist: 'Some young men and women got up a dance in the evening regardless of the moans and cries of those who were tortured by the fiery fever.' Of a woman whom he had earlier noticed, Whyte wrote: 'Her head and face had swollen to almost unnatural size, the latter being hideously deformed'; *cos dhubh*, the famine dropsy. He remembered 'the clearness of her complexion when I saw her in health, shortly after we sailed . . . as the sun was setting, the bereaved husband muttered a prayer over her enshrouded corpse which, as he said Amen, was lowered into the ocean'. Two brothers died of dysentery, leaving a third to mourn. The third then died and 'left two little orphans, one of whom – a boy, seven years of age – I noticed in the evening wearing his deceased father's coat'. There was an even greater tragedy in that than the bacteriologically uninformed Whyte knew.

The ship had now bypassed Newfoundland to starboard and Nova Scotia to port, entered into the Gulf of St Lawrence and was becalmed by the Iles de la Madeleine. But when the breeze revived, *Ajax* crept up the Honguedo Passage to the head of the St Lawrence estuary and then south between the lovely banks of the broad river. As soon as the inspecting surgeon, in straw hat and leather coat, stamped across the deck to the companionway into the hold, he was able by the stench to announce, 'Ha, there is fever here,' but told Whyte he was free to go on to Quebec if he wished. There *Ajax* herself, with a fleet of other immigrant ships, would have to stand to before the quarantine island, Grosse Ile, which was screened from the city of Quebec by the huge wooded Ile d'Orléans.

In May, within four days of the quarantining of the first ship at Grosse Ile, eight others had arrived carrying fever cases. 'I have not a bed to lay them on or a place to put them,' wrote Dr Douglas, the valiant physician who administered the station. Nine days later, thirty vessels with 10,000 immigrants on board were waiting at Grosse Ile. Brave assistants like Dr Benson, an Irish doctor who had arrived on the *Wandsworth* and volunteered to work with Douglas, died of typhus, and others were overwhelmed by fever or fatigue. By 5 June, with summer barely begun, 25,000 Irish had been quarantined on Grosse Ile or in ships anchored nearby.

By the time *Ajax* arrived in full summer, the fever wards and tents ashore were impossibly overcrowded with 2,500 fever cases. Death came quickly, so that the 2–3,000 ashore one week bore little resemblance except in symptoms to the population of the previous week. In stupefying heat the dead on the quarantined ships were lifted out of the holds with hooks and stacked like cordwood on the shore. A Special Committee appointed by the Canadian Assembly found that because of lack of personnel and space, patients lay in their own excrement for days. Receiving water only once a day, they shared beds overnight with corpses, since there was no staff to move the dead at night.

Whyte wrote of the continuous line of boats, each carrying its freight of dead to the burial ground. 'Some had several corpses so tied up in canvas that the stiff, sharp outline of death was easily traceable. Others had rude coffins constructed by the sailors from the boards of their berths.' As *Ajax* waited out the quarantine, the wife of the chief of the passengers' committee perished. One of the sailors told Whyte that after the grave was filled up her husband took the shovels and placed them crosswise upon it, and calling Heaven to witness said: ' "By that cross, Mary, I swear to revenge your death – as soon as I earn the price of my passage home, I'll go back and shoot the man that murdered you and that's the landlord." ' Significantly, unlike Young Ireland, he did not curse the Whigs.

Partridge Island off St John, New Brunswick, a nearer landfall to Ireland, was another ill-starred quarantine station. It received 17,000 Irish from ninety-nine vessels, of whom more than 2,000 died on the voyage or in quarantine. But apparently healthy immigrants took the disease ashore and into the town of St John. And Grosse Ile similarly afforded the citizens of Quebec and Montreal only slight protection. Many immigrants who seemed healthy in Quebec died on their way to Montreal on board the river steamers, and those who sickened in their progress were received into the fever hospital in Montreal. The Immigrant Hospital of Montreal contained by August more than 3,000 dying patients, both passengers and infected citizenry. Many of the surviving Irish settled in Montreal's tenements, creating an instant and much-resented Irish constituency.

Some who survived this second sifting of fever were sent on to Kingston, 180 miles further south, and from thence to Toronto or over the border, every city and town being anxious to be rid of them as soon as possible. At St Catherine's, 600 miles from Quebec, 'I saw a family who were on their way to the western part of the state of New York. One of them was taken ill and they were obliged to remain by the wayside with nothing but a few boards to protect them from the weather. There is no means of learning how many of the survivors of so many ordeals were cut off by the inclemency of a Canadian winter.'

So between St John, New Brunswick, and the borders of New York perished the peasantry whom both O'Connell and Meagher loved so much and understood so little; their very journey an index of the failure of O'Connell's alliance with the Whigs. Saved by ice, at the end of October the quarantine station of Grosse Ile was closed down, and Father McGoran, a priest who had left two brothers dead of fever there, was last to leave, boarding the final ship of the year, the *Alliance*. Aboard it, he gave last rites to six of the passengers who died before Quebec.

Those stricter passenger statutes gave some protection to the United States. The Boston City Council established a quarantine station at Deer Island, at the entrance to Boston Harbor. But the penalties for landing fever-carriers ashore were such that captains of fever ships tried to avoid Boston. The number of patients on Deer Island between June 1847 and the following February was about 2,500, whereas Grosse Ile harboured as many as that every week. The Irish who were healthy enough to land in Boston occupied in particular the Eighth Ward in North Boston, where huge, fire-trap tenements dwarfed Paul Revere's House. The *look* of the ragged, hungry, verminous Famine immigrants unleashed much anti-Irish hysteria, as from New York to Baltimore Irishmen and women were suddenly begging on the icy streets of the eastern United States. In New York Irish immigrants settled downtown, notably in the Sixth Ward, which took in the East River waterfront, the Bowery, Broadway, and from below Canal Street down to City Hall. New York's quarantine station on Staten Island was served by a steam ferry, so that families settled as healthy in Sixth Ward rookeries could go to Staten directly or indirectly from the city. There were officially 1,300 deaths in New York from typhus.

The *Nation* had already warned its readers that Irish arriving at New York will be met by 'runners of the boarding houses, who try . . . to get possession of them and their luggage, and when once obtained, they charge what they like for that entertainment'. The *Nation* urged immigrants to see the agent of the Irish Emigrant Society, founded in Manhattan in 1841, which met all arriving ships. In its office in Lower Manhattan, immigrants could seek advice on jobs and lodging, and report swindlers and unjust captains. Through the society, they could also send passage money back to Ireland, and valid pre-paid tickets. The Emigrant Society offered the Irish arrivals their first tentative gestures of leverage and power, so that they felt for the first time that they had indeed entered a new world.

Now that ceaseless tragedy was the daily order of Ireland, those transported earlier lived lives almost of banal well-being in their distant quarter of New South Wales. Hugh Larkin and Mary Shields did not escape the average, bitter nineteenth-century bereavements, though. In December 1847, a second child, Mary, was born and lived only eleven days. Hugh performed his own baptism of her, pouring the waters of Monaro over her head, having been trained since childhood in the importance and potency of baptism. With Mary still ailing, he took the

A line of convicts at the Hyde Park Barracks, Sydney.
Despite their brutal depiction, was Australia redeeming them?

The convict shepherd, in his bush stupor, meets the natives.
This style of bark hut is typical of the outstations in which convicts lived – a barrel provides the chimney Hugh Larkin never had in Ireland.

Thomas Meagher's indulgent father, Lord Mayor of Waterford and Member of the House of Commons.

The Liberator, Daniel O'Connell.

O'Connell comes home from prison, 14 September 1844 (p. 100).

William Smith O'Brien.
From a daguerrotype.

John Mitchel,
clear-eyed revolutionary.

O'Brien's birthplace: Dromoland Castle, County Clare,
in its modern incarnation as a hotel.

Gentle John Martin,
otherwise Knox, the unlikely rebel.

Eva Kelly, newly married
to Kevin Izod O'Doherty.

TICKET OF LEAVE.

No. 42/1457 13 June **1842**

Prisoner's No. 34/574

Name .... Hugh Larkins

Ship .... Parmelia (2)

Master .... Gilbert

Year 1834

Native Place.........

Trade or Calling ...

Offence ....

Place of Trial ...... Galway

Date of Trial ...... 29 July 1833

Sentence .... Life

Year of Birth ......

Height ....

Complexion ....

Hair ....

Eyes ....

General Remarks...

24 Oct 1842

Allowed to remain in the District of Goulburn

On recommendation of do **Bench.**

Dated Feby 42

NEW SOUTH WALES.

CONDITIONAL PARDON.

L.S.

48/1221

By His Excellency Sir Charles Augustus Fitz Roy, Knight Companion of the Royal Hanoverian Guelphic Order, Captain General and Governor-in-Chief in and over Her Majesty's Territory of New South Wales and its Dependencies, and Vice-Admiral of the same, &c., &c., &c.

WHEREAS, by an Act of the Imperial Parliament of Great Britain and Ireland, passed in the Sixth Year of the Reign of Her Majesty Queen Victoria, intituled *"An Act to amend the Law affecting Transported Convicts, with respect to Pardons and Tickets of Leave,"* it was amongst other things enacted, that, after the taking effect of the said recited Act, in any place to which Felons and Offenders had been or might be transported by Law, the Governor or Lieutenant-Governor should, from time to time, by an Instrument in Writing, under his Hand, recommend such Felons or other Offenders as he should think fit to be recommended, to Her Majesty, for an Absolute or Conditional Pardon; and in case Her Majesty should, through one of Her Principal Secretaries of State, signify Her approval of any such recommendation, it should be lawful for the Governor or Lieutenant-Governor to grant an Absolute or Conditional Pardon, pursuant to such Instructions as should be sent to him by the Secretary of State, by an Instrument in writing, under the Seal of his Government, which should be deemed from the Day of the Date thereof, to have within such Place or Places as should be specified in such Pardon, but not elsewhere, the same effect in the Law, to all intents and purposes, as if a General, Absolute, or Conditional Pardon, had passed on that Day, under the Great Seal of the United Kingdom: And Whereas the said recited Act has taken effect in the said Colony of New South Wales: And Whereas Hugh Larkins whose Description is hereunto annexed, having been indicted and convicted at Galway on the twenty ninth day of July One thousand eight hundred and thirty three of the Crime of Attacking Habitation was, in pursuance of the said Conviction, sentenced to Transportation, and was accordingly Transported to the said Colony, for the period of his natural life: And Whereas, in consideration of the good conduct of the said Hugh Larkins since his arrival in the said Colony His Charles Augustus Fitz Roy as such Governor of New South Wales, recommended the said Hugh Larkins to Her Majesty for a pardon, to take effect in all parts of the World, except the United Kingdom of Great Britain and Ireland: And Whereas Her Majesty has been graciously pleased to signify Her approval of such recommendation, through Her Principal Secretary of State for the Colonies: NOW KNOW YE, that I, SIR CHARLES AUGUSTUS FITZ ROY, in pursuance of the Power and Authority so in me vested by the said recited Act and of Her Majesty's gracious approval so signified, and of the instructions of the said Secretary of State in this behalf, do hereby grant unto the said Hugh Larkins a Pardon for the Offence, in respect of which such Sentence of Transportation was passed as aforesaid, which shall take effect in all parts of the World, except the United Kingdom of Great Britain and Ireland PROVIDED ALWAYS, and it is hereby expressly declared to be a Condition of this Pardon, that if the said Hugh Larkins shall, at any time during the continuance of the term of his said Sentence, go to, or be in, any part of the United Kingdom of Great Britain and Ireland then this Pardon shall thenceforth be and become wholly void, as by Her Majesty's Commands expressly limited and directed: And all Her Majesty's Officers and Ministers of Justice, and all other, Her Majesty's Subjects, are hereby required to take notice accordingly.

IN TESTIMONY WHEREOF, I have caused these Letters to be made Patent, and to be sealed with the Seal of the said Territory.

(*Above*) Hugh Larkin's conditional pardon rules out a return to any part of the United Kingdom of Great Britain and Ireland.
(*Left*) Hugh Larkin's ticket-of-leave.

Famine burial.

Woman begging at hard-hit Clonakilty in Cork, 1847.

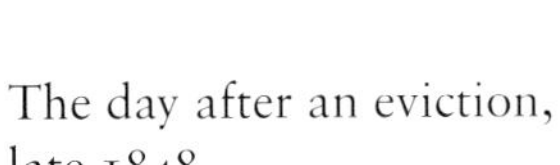

The day after an eviction, late 1848.

The Famine endures: a house at Fahey's Quay, Ennis, County Clare. The widow Connor and her dying child, 1849.

Famine desolation: the village of Tullig, 1849.

Judy O'Donnel's habitation under the bridge at Doonbeg, County Clare, 1849.

One thread of smoke remains in the village of Moveen, 1849.

The central soup depot, Barrack Street, Cork.

Miss Kennedy, daughter of the Poor Law Inspector, distributes clothing at Kilrush, County Clare, 1849.

Bridget O'Donnel of West Cork, and her children, in the Famine's fourth year. Illustrations such as this activated the British liberal conscience.

small coffin and his dead child by cart to burial somewhere in that immense country. Mary had now lost both daughters she had given birth to, O'Flynn's Bridget and Larkin's Mary, and that must have weighed heavily on her.

It was apparent to her that they must marry for the sake of young Tom Larkin, now three years old. On the one hand, there was no doubt that Hugh and Mary, being now in some senses and not by their own choice dead to the old world, could not countenance marrying outside the Church. But the priests were not as easily convinced. In their eyes the fact that wives or husbands in the northern hemisphere were unreachable did not justify new unions at the earth's extreme south. An Attorney-General of New South Wales, Roger Therry, who lived thirty years in the colony, was well aware of the marriage stratagems of some of his convict brethren. He told of how a man transported from Cork had left his wife and two children behind in Ireland. On becoming free, he wished to marry within the colony. He was able to produce a letter, complete with a Cork postmark forged in Sydney in red ink on the corner of the envelope. The letter, purporting to be from his brother in Ireland, indicated that the man's dear wife had died in the bosom of the Holy Catholic and Apostolic Church, a touch which worked well, said Therry, with the clergy.

In the end, Hugh and Mary managed to marry just before Hugh's conditional pardon was granted, when in theory he still needed permission from the Convict Department. This wedding prior to Hugh's freedom could have occurred only if Esther Larkin or John O'Flynn, or both of them, had died in Ireland – and the oral record says Esther did not; or else Hugh and Mary used some device like the one mentioned by Therry. The ceremony took place on 16 March 1848, the eve of St Patrick, at the Cathedral of St Peter and St Paul at Goulburn. The invocation of St Peter and St Paul would have comforted the couple – it was a pledge that they were re-entering the Communion of Saints.

The marriage came at the end of an Australian summer and of another fatal Irish winter. News of the immutable Famine was in every paper they flinchingly read to each other, or had read to them. The Famine fell over their plentiful bush table, and made its claim upon them at dead of night, when they were released from distracting labour and lay together, as spouses in this hemisphere, wondering what was happening in the parallel universe.

There was now a new governor in New South Wales. Well-meaning Gipps had left in 1846 in a state of failing health and with the general disapproval both of the progressives, who saw him as too much a servant of the Crown, and of the squatters, who believed him too lenient on Aboriginals and indifferent to their own problems of tenure. The new governor, Sir Charles Augustus FitzRoy, had fought at the age of sixteen years in the Battle of Waterloo, and had had experience of colonial government in both St Edward's Island in Canada and in the Leeward Islands.

It was FitzRoy who on 1 June 1848 signed the conditional pardon of Hugh Larkin. In this ornate document, towards the bottom of its page of print and penmanship, lay the clause: 'Provided always . . . that if the said Hugh Larkin shall, at any time during the continuance of the term of his said Sentence, go to, or be in, any part of the United Kingdom of Great Britain and Ireland, then this Pardon shall thenceforth be and become wholly void.' He could not do a Magwitch, and take his dark, knowing benevolence even temporarily back to Galway.

Hugh and Mary did not settle permanently in Goulburn until after the conditional pardon, but Hugh had an intention now to give up the remote stations. He and Mary left that boulder-dotted high plain, going away as their own people, possessed of freedom of movement and the rights of ambition. In late October 1848, he bought for £25 a town allotment in Cowper Street, Goulburn, and set to work to build a house upon it. An infant, Anne, born of Mary Shields/Larkin on 30 November 1848, was healthy and like her elder brother Tom, now five years old, would live on into another century.

Mary and Hugh, townspeople now, heard regular reports of Ireland from the pulpit of St Peter and St Paul. The offerings plate came around for Famine relief. The voices of their bush children, speaking in a potent, crow-harsh Australian accent, confirmed their distance from the Irish disaster, but also evoked other children who spoke more liquidly in Limerick or Galway.

The future seemed promising for these convicts' children, but utterly limitless for the children of the employer, Brodribb, the two young Brodribb daughters and a small son. But in the middle of 1849, when Hugh and Mary were establishing themselves in Goulburn, Brodribb's wife fell ill, and almost at once his daughters. It was diphtheria. The doctor from Cooma 'had their hair cut off, and cold applications applied to their heads'. At the end of July 1849, in the same room where her mother and sister lay, Brodribb's eldest daughter died. Brodribb rode by phaeton 25 miles to Cooma for a coffin. Eight days later the second daughter died in great suffering. Mrs Brodribb recovered but the 'loss of our daughters weighed heavily on her mind'.

William Bradley, Brodribb's employer, also suffered grief. During his journey to Europe, he lost his sickly wife Emily, whom Italy was meant to cure.

But for the moment, Hugh Larkin's wife and children bloomed.

*

In March 1849, the Goulburn magistrates' bench authorised the final release to Hugh of £47 5 shillings and 6 pence deposited in his name in the savings bank. When handed to him by an officer of the bench, it was without any doubt the biggest sum of money he had ever seen at the one time. He bought another town lot in Grafton Street, from which he decided to conduct the business of chandler or hardware dealer, and where he and his family now lived. His behaviour bespoke confidence, and some ambition.

The Goulburn in which he and Mary were emancipists was a township of 3,000 people, but served an immense hinterland of hamlets, farmers and settlers. It was very likely to seem a pulsing metropolis to a man who grew up in Lismany and had been in Monaro for so long. Though lit by evil-smelling oil lamps, it had an urban brightness. Hugh had gone into the bush in 1834, fifteen years earlier, when the newspapers had been full of the names of felon absconders and complaints about convict behaviour. The Australia into which he emerged now had proceeded beyond the lambasting of felons and emancipists. The *Sydney Morning Herald* of 5 July 1848 announced that of the now 220,000 settlers in Australia, an auspicious 80,000 were females. The *Herald* took delight in a colony 'thus blessed with the political liberties for which the millions of Europe are dying, and with those material comforts without which political liberty is an empty name'. The political liberties of New South Wales were as yet more in prospect than in reality – the franchise was property-based, and the larger land-grabbers occupied the Legislative Council. But progressives had definitively ended transportation to New South Wales. The attempted landing of shipfuls of 'exiles', trusty prisoners from British prisons, was resisted by mass meetings at Circular Quay, Sydney. The exile ships were forced to go elsewhere, the *Hashemy* to Port Phillip, the *Mount Stewart Elphinstone* to Moreton Bay, now Brisbane, far to the north.

Yet though anti-transportationists had brought transportation to New South Wales to a stop, they were at the same time champions of the rights of emancipated convicts. It was in itself a triumph of New South Wales democracy that the Larkins were not placed in the position of an underclass. They drank clean water, ate well and opened the door of their Grafton Street, Goulburn, chandlery business for passing trade, seeking to serve in particular the large Irish community of Goulburn and its broad hinterland.

10

Fiasco and Noble Gesture: The Rebellion of Young Ireland

> The position we stood in; the language we had used; the promises we had made; the defiances we had uttered; our entire career, short as it was, seemed to require of us a step no less daring and defiant than that which the Government had taken.
>
> Thomas Francis Meagher, July 1848

Young Ireland had spent the winter of 1847–8 in hectic certainty that their poorer fellow countrymen and women would not lie resigned to their fate. The Young Ireland Confederation, inaugurated at the Rotunda a year past in January 1847, spawned enthusiastic Confederate clubs throughout Ireland which, unlike the highly social '82 Club, had no quasi-military uniform. But they were more purely political, and took some interest in potentially bearing arms. Young lawyers, journalists, merchants, joined in numbers – and some landowners. They represented the network necessary for so-called *spontaneous uprising*.

Young Ireland had not been forgiven their defection from the Liberator. When, in September 1847, O'Brien, Meagher and others went to Cork to address Confederate clubs there, they had to talk their way in through the stage door of the Theatre Royal. From the galleries in the theatre Old Irelanders screamed at Tom Meagher, 'Who killed O'Connell?' Then in November, when O'Brien bravely went with Meagher and Mitchel to Belfast, to argue the Confederate cause with both Protestant and Catholic Repealers at a rally at the Music-Hall, they found themselves besieged by furious Old Irelanders, and rocks shattered a number of windows.

And already Dublin Castle, centre of the British administration, had a spy in Confederation. His name was John Donnellan Balfe, four years older than Meagher but another graduate of Clongowes. He was one of the corps of 400 protectors who accompanied speakers like Meagher and O'Brien to their homes after Confederate meetings in the Rotunda or the Dublin Music-Hall. The Irish Confederate leadership gave Balfe the sensitive task of liaising with the English Chartists, but even when he was seen talking to English detectives in the London Inn near Confederate headquarters he for the moment explained away any suspicions.

Against a background of continuing mass desperation, there had been one hopeful sign – the potato harvest of 1847 came up at last unmarred but in desperately small quantities, most seed potatoes having been eaten.

If Esther and her sons had managed to plant the previous spring they were in a minority. But the apparent end to blight caused Trevelyan to decide in the spring of 1848 that the emergency and the need for relief were at an end. This increased the grim, radical conviction of John Mitchel, the editor of the *Nation*, that matters were so bad that a popular revolution would occur in Ireland at harvest time, 1848. The masses would not watch their crops shipped out once more.

Mitchel was about to be heavily influenced by a new voice, however. From the area of Tinakill in Queen's County (now Laois) came articles written on a farmhouse table by a 'deaf, near-sighted, ungainly, and deformed' young man, suffering from a congenital spinal disease. His name was James Fintan Lalor. He came of a farming family who had been engaged in anti-tithe politics, and he despised the ideas both of Repeal and of Carlyle, the concept of revolution as a form of spontaneous combustion. 'I would never contribute one shilling,' he told Mitchel, 'or give my name, heart, or hand, for such an object as the simple Repeal by the British Parliament of the Act of Union.' The matter of land – that was what counted. 'A secure and independent agricultural peasantry is the only base on which a people rises.' The deformed young man in Tinakill chastised Mitchel for believing a successful rebellion would occur without planning. 'I want a prepared, organised, orderly and resistless revolution,' wrote Lalor. 'You would have an unprepared, disorderly and vile jacquerie.' The farmers, said Lalor, were ripe to rise, but Young Ireland wasted energy on questions of 'defensive' or 'offensive' wars and did nothing to prepare or train potential battalions. 'Ireland', mocked Lalor, 'are ready to strip for battle, and none flinched but the fire-eaters.'

Smith O'Brien spent the early new year of 1848 drafting a peaceable charter for the Irish Confederation in his study at Cahirmoyle. He set out on the train from Limerick to deliver its charter at the Rotunda, believing that Mitchel and his allies, chief amongst them that unlikely radical the Ulster landlord John Martin, must be prevented from leading the Confederation into an under-planned revolution. Meagher's defence of the *concept* of the Sword was reasonable. But Mitchel, most of the moderates believed, was unrealistic: 'The peasantry of the South, at that time unfamiliar with arms, and accustomed to rely chiefly upon their shillelaghs, he represented to himself as Calabrians or Tyrolese, with rifles always in their hands and ammunition in their pouches.'

While Ireland perished or fled, some of the most decent and least physically discomforted gentlemen tried to resolve how Esther Larkin's mass of fellow sufferers could best be rescued from powerlessness. In a series of meetings at the Rotunda in January and February of 1848,

Mitchel's small group pushed one of Lalor's strategies – a rent strike by the smaller tenants, 'the frieze-coats', and a poor-rate strike, a refusal to pay the tax which kept the workhouses going, by all sympathetic landowners. These devices, said Mitchel, would produce an ugly display of authority by the British government, sure in itself to generate revolution. On one hand, Mitchel said, he was not suggesting that oppressive landlords or their agents be shot down from hedges, but something had to happen. When it came to Smith O'Brien's fellow aristocrats, he would give his right arm if class unity were possible, but it was not. As for constitutionalism: 'There is no opinion in Ireland worth a farthing that is not illegal.'

The lawyer Richard O'Gorman nicknamed Mitchel's faction 'Infant Ireland'. But young Meagher plaintively wished Thomas Davis was alive to guide everybody. Duffy said of Meagher that he 'would have gone to battle for Ireland more joyfully than to a feast' but 'refused to consent to a policy which he considered rash and hopeless'. Though Tom Meagher had invoked the most intense martial images, he believed the Confederation and the redemption of Ireland would succeed along the lines proposed by O'Brien. For the Confederation's strength lay in the reality that it was not corrupt like Repeal, sought no money, did not condone thuggish methods, permitted the broadest spectrum of Irishness.

Young Ireland expended huge and futile energy on these arguments, the night-time debates sometimes not ending until weary Confederates stumbled out of the Rotunda to their carriages at three o'clock or later. And the main resolutions were very like the peace proposals of the Liberator, which two summers ago Meagher had countered with his withering Sword speech. At ten o'clock on a raw Saturday morning in early February, with John Martin in the chair, the Confederates voted for O'Brien's moderate principles by 318 to 188. Rifle clubs, which Mitchel wanted, were also voted down. But even those who opposed Mitchel, like Richard O'Gorman, forced Duffy to promise to publish Mitchel's apologia for his position in the *Nation*.

It was between Duffy and Mitchel that the greatest rancour now existed. Mitchel could no longer work at the *Nation*, and so had no prospects of income. He went back to 8 Ontario Terrace, where, amidst all this turbulence of opinion and threats of guerrilla war, 28-year-old Jenny Mitchel was raising their three sons and two daughters as well-washed, well-mannered, well-instructed young Dubliners from the Presbyterian tradition.

Mitchel was supported by Jenny, for she knew that John, wheezing and orating, was always the sort of man whose first reaction to disaster was to publish. Now his schoolfriend John Martin suggested 'a new weekly Mitchelite paper', financed in considerable part by Martin. Mitchel thought at first he would need to go to Cork or Belfast to begin a new paper, that there was something vaguely dishonourable about confronting Duffy's *Nation* in its own city. But Martin and the young journalist Devin Reilly dissuaded him. Why abandon the capital to equivocal voices? So Mitchel, Martin and Reilly found an office in Trinity Street, not far from the *Nation*, and began the *United Irishman*, named to honour Mitchel's father and the principles of 1798. The first issue emerged in February 1848, and included material from the Young Ireland priest Father Kenyon and Eva of the *Nation*. She had not renounced the *Nation*; most Young Irelanders did not see Mitchel and the *Nation* as being so far apart.

The *United Irishman* was a grand success, though it would run for only a few issues. 'The man in Dublin', said the Tipperary lawyer Michael Doheny, 'who did not read the first number, might indeed be pronounced a bigot or a fool.' Mitchel's 'Letters to Ulster Protestants', published over four issues, created a sensation. 'Lord Enniskillen, the Irish nobleman, for his part cautions you earnestly against Popery and Papists . . . My Lord Enniskillen does not say a word to you about what is, after all, the main concern – the *tenure* of your farms.' Protestants invoked in song and prayer their rights. But 'Outdoor relief is our main institution at present – our *Magna Carta* – our Bill of Rights'.

In pursuit of the plan to provoke the government into action oppressive enough to ensure revolution, he addressed defiant editorials to 'Butcher Clarendon'. 'You will resort to court martial, and triangles, and free quarters? Well, *that*, at last, will be the end of "constitutional agitation".' In dedicating each issue to Lord Clarendon not only as 'Butcher' but as 'high commissioner of spies', Mitchel begged a reaction.

Thomas Francis Meagher, the Young Tribune, had failed to win a Waterford by-election in which his own father felt he must stick by the Old Ireland candidate. For now he was consoled and teased by the fact that a spontaneous and nearly bloodless revolution occurred in France! The overthrow of King Louis Philippe's government had been partly achieved by methods borrowed from the Liberator. Bourgeois reformers, the French equivalent of Mitchel or Meagher, had arranged a series of banquets to demand a responsible ministry. The government had banned the culminating banquet, just as Peel had banned the Liberator's Clontarf meeting. Troops then fired on a peaceful demonstration outside the Foreign Ministry, and young intellectuals and working-class men and women began side by side to build barricades in the centre of the city. The French National Guard joined the revolutionaries. Seeing the democratic ferment outside the Tuileries, King Louis Philippe, in his mid-seventies, abdicated in favour of his grandson and left for London.

Most of the members of the new republican Cabinet had quoted passages from the *Nation* in their own journals. Alphonse de Lamartine, in effect president, was the author of a book on the Gironde faction in the original French Revolution, a work devoured by Meagher and other Young Irelanders. Above all, this new French revolution, as well as involving little violence, promised justice, admitted members of the working class to the Cabinet, yet left the entire social order intact – an impulsive, stainless, responsible, ideal revolution. Under the influence of the French phenomenon, even Duffy was now writing like Mitchel. 'Ireland will be free before the coming summer fades into winter. All over the world – from the frozen swamps of Canada, to the rich cornfields of Sicily – in Italy, in Denmark, in Prussia, and in glorious France, men are up for their rights.'

Tom Meagher spoke of French and Irish events before a huge and excited crowd at Dublin's North Wall on 21 March 1848. But it was O'Brien's speech that alarmed the Castle. 'The Confederation would invite all classes . . . to inscribe their names on a roll of persons willing to serve in a National Guard.' A Council of Three Hundred would be elected to represent all sections 'of the National party authentically . . . For foreign policy they must fraternize with English Repealers, of whom there are millions, and, above all, with the people of France.' Secretly, the Confederation had elected a committee of twenty-one as a sort of revolutionary directory. Meagher and Father Kenyon had been the two most popular men elected to this council, with thirty-one votes each, Smith O'Brien polling thirty, along with Duffy, Dillon and O'Gorman. Pat Smyth, one day to volunteer to descend into the nether world to rescue Smith O'Brien and Mitchel, was also elected.

Lord Lieutenant Clarendon had now stationed 12,000 troops in the city of Dublin in strategic positions: not only in such places as the Royal Barracks and at the Royal Military Hospital at Kilmainham, but also in Trinity College, at the post office and the Old Parliament. He called on 'the striplings of Trinity College, the elderly antiquaries of the Royal Dublin Society, and the clerks in the Bank of Ireland to arm themselves'. On the evening of the event at the North Wall, he ordered that Mitchel, O'Brien and Meagher be arrested. The constables who presented their warrant to Meagher were respectful, and as a first experience of arrest and imprisonment it was less a punishment than an intoxicant, with the police at College Green police station ready to supply anything the gentlemen needed. The next morning the prisoners' wagons were followed by crowds of supporters. The three were charged at Green Street with seditious libel by court officers who could hardly hear themselves for the hubbub from the gallery. O'Brien and Meagher were charged for the speeches they had made at the North Wall, and Mitchel was indicted for the Butcher Clarendon letters he had written in the *United Irishman*. He was also charged with three articles written by others, including one by his assistant Devin Reilly suggesting that vitriol could be thrown from windows on government troops.

O'Brien was outraged that the government was attempting to identify him with extremism by trying him along with Mitchel. He regretted the heedless and fiery metaphors of the hour. 'It became conventional', O'Brien later complained, 'to assert that the time for words had passed before launching into yet another four-column diatribe.' All three prisoners were released on bail subscribed by members of Young Ireland, and the freed Mitchel announced that 'Sedition was a small matter, but he intended to commit high treason'.

At the end of March, Confederate delegates, including the bailed Smith O'Brien and Meagher, O'Gorman and John Blake Dillon, sailed for France and travelled to Paris to visit Lamartine. The delegates entered the glittering rooms of the Tuileries in elation and hope. Lamartine, former diplomat and deputy, was in his late fifties, at the height of his powers, and elegance of language and person were in him so combined with populism that two million voters had given him their approval. But he was already steeled for the *realpolitik* of this situation. His government needed British recognition, and the British minister, Lord Normanby, had already told Lamartine that if he encouraged armed resistance in Ireland the British would withdraw their embassy. After effusive praise of the Irish people, and polite inquiry about the progress of Famine, Lamartine depressed the delegation on the far side of his desk by saying that nothing could be done by France: Ireland was an internal British question. O'Brien, Meagher and others went home disconsolate, leaving the lawyer O'Gorman to study the operations of the French National Guard. Meagher returned to Dublin with a gift, however – a committee of Frenchwomen presented him with a tricolour in Ireland's colours: orange, green and white. When Meagher brought it to a Confederation meeting, Mitchel – in favour with everyone again now – was reported to have said, 'I hope to see that flag one day waving as our national banner.' It would prove to be the future flag of the Irish Republic.

In the House of Commons, O'Brien attempted to offer a personal explanation for having visited republican France, but was subjected to ten minutes' abusive yelling. Parliament had just been shaken by a great Chartist march in London, Englishmen carrying a monster petition for parliamentary reform and male suffrage. The procession had been surrounded and muted by the police and dragoons, who intimidated the marchers and caused them to melt away in the spring rain between Kennington Common and Westminster. Westminster was ready now to crush the other anti-authoritarian wing, the Young Irelanders.

But the sedition trials of O'Brien and Meagher before a Dublin Commission of chosen judges in Green Street were both unsuccessful for the Crown. It was very hard to prove the case from their reported speeches. O'Brien was acquitted on a Tuesday in mid-May, Meagher the following day. Mitchel's trial still pended. To ensure Mitchel did not avoid the fairly narrow trap of seditious libel, the Whig government in Westminster rushed through a scandalous piece of legislation, the Treason-Felony Act. It made prosecution easier; any mere statement that the Crown of Great Britain might one day lose sovereignty over Ireland was an offence punishable with a gaol term. Two days before he was to come to court, Mitchel was respectfully seized at home and charged afresh under the new legislation. He was detained in Dublin's antiquated Newgate prison, near Green Street courthouse. At night in his cell he could probably hear the howling and grief of Irish women convicts slated for a destination similar to the one that lay ahead of him.

On 26 May, he was led by tunnel to the notorious court, where a crowd of Confederates, including Meagher, Dillon and O'Gorman, gathered to await his entry into the dock. Jenny was present too in John Martin's company as Mitchel entered, a gentleman-martyr, 'lifting, as he advanced, the glazed dark cap he wore during his imprisonment, as gracefully as if he entered a drawing-room'. The Sheriff, he complained, 'skilled in the arts which corrupt justice at its source, and enraged by two defeats, had taken the panel in hand and packed it'. Mitchel was defended by the octogenarian Robert Holmes, who was willing to risk being indicted himself. He mounted a powerful defence but was defeated by the breadth of the Treason-Felony legislation and the hostility of the jury. The railways articles were Mitchel's, and were all that was needed to convict.

Mitchel, asked the next day for his comments before sentencing, got up and swept the gallery with his Old Testament eyes, crying out in a voice in which the effects of Newgate's damp were audible: 'The Roman who saw his hand burning to ashes before the tyrant, promised that three hundred should follow out his enterprise. Can I not promise for one, for two, for three, aye for hundreds?'

To the young medical assistant in the gallery, Kevin O'Doherty, how close the revolution must have seemed as Mitchel cried for supporters, and received in answer a torrent of shouts of approval! How close when the exquisite young Galway poet, Eva, should respond from Killeen:

For one – for two – for three –
Aye! Hundreds, thousands, see!
For vengeance and for thee
To the last!

The sentence pronounced on Mitchel was fourteen years' transportation.

Jenny, Mitchel's mother Mary and Martin rushed above ground to Newgate as John himself returned to his cell through the tunnel. They suspected correctly that the authorities wanted to get him quickly out of Dublin. It was rumoured that the ship assigned to move him was already in Dublin Bay. In his rooms at Newgate he said goodbye to his womenfolk, and then to his baffled children. John, the eldest son, was barely ten, and the youngest, Willie, was an infant. Little Henrietta knew just enough to weep. Mitchel consigned them all to the faithful care of John Martin.

Some Dublin Confederate clubs had proposed that on the way to his ship in harbour he should be rescued. Indeed, at the Castle's urging, the governor of Newgate brought Mitchel a document to sign, denouncing all attempts at rescue, but Mitchel refused to put pen to it. Meagher, though uneasy, favoured a rescue effort. Mitchel could be transported only in a sea of blood, he is reported to have told others. Duffy urged a calmer look at the state of readiness of the Dublin clubs and the size of the Dublin garrison. And it was Duffy whom Mitchel blamed: 'if the city of Dublin permitted any Irishman to be put on board a convict-ship under such circumstances, the British government could have little to fear from their resentment or their patriotism afterwards.'

Mitchel's *Jail Journal* opens with an intractable sentence: 'May 27th, 1848. – On this day, about four o'clock in the afternoon, I, John Mitchel, was kidnapped, and carried off from Dublin, in chains, as a convicted *Felon*.' In departing Newgate for the ship, he was aware of the tension of his guards. They lacked time to put both fetters around his ankles. 'Here, take the other in your hand, and come along.' Outside, in the street, he stood on the steps a moment, pleased to be causing the government all this fuss: 'the black police omnibus – a strong force of the city constabulary occupying the openings of the streets hard by. I walked down the steps; and amidst all that multitude the clanking of my chain was the loudest sound.'

The crowd who had gathered around Newgate rushed off to the North Wall, to watch the arrival of the police vehicle there. Escorted by dragoons with drawn sabres, the covered police carriage careered around the North Circular Road, a detective sitting on either side of Mitchel, one displaying a capped pistol ready for firing. On arrival at Dublin Bay, he was marched to the quay wall between two ranks of infantrymen. The government steamer *Shearwater* awaited him, and he descended into the ship's boat and sat in the stern.

As soon as Mitchel was on board the *Shearwater*, the naval officer beside him conducted him to the cabin, ordered that his chains be taken off and provided him with a sherry and water. The officer, Captain Hall, was the captain of the *Dragon* steam-frigate, a man-of-war which would guard the *Shearwater* on its way out of Dublin. He was amused to tell Mitchel that by an irony he was due to have dinner with Lord Lieutenant Clarendon that very evening. Until dinner at the Castle was over and both ships could weigh anchor, Mitchel sat in the cabin of *Shearwater* chatting with detectives.

The day after, *Shearwater* moored in the Cobh of Cork, within 500 yards of Spike Island with its white-limed barracks pressing down to the shore. Landed, Mitchel was greeted by a prison official and taken past several sentries and through gratings to a large vaulted room comfortably furnished. Nonetheless, at locking-up time, 'I flung myself on the bed, and broke into a raging passion of tears . . . tears of wrath, pity, regret, remorse.' Waking, he was presented with brown prison clothes.

Edward Walsh, song writer and balladist, had a job teaching child convicts on Spike Island, and managed to meet Mitchel on his second day there while he was sitting in the sun in the yard. 'Ah!' he said. '. . . You are now the man in all Ireland most to be *envied*.' The Inspector of Prisons came up to inform him that he would be leaving almost at once for Bermuda on a man-of-war, ominously named *Scourge*, arrived that day in Cobh. In the meantime, the inspector said, he had orders from the Castle directing him to treat Mitchel differently from 'a common convict', to let him wear his own clothing and not to put him in irons. Though relieved to be excused the brown canvas of Spike, Mitchel did not possess adequate clothes for the journey – only an old brown summer coat, old shoes and the glazed cap he had worn at his trial. One prison official bought him a few changes of linen from a store in Cobh.

On his last evening he was asked to sign some autographs which the surgeon of Spike Island had promised a certain young woman in the town. It was an old pattern: Ireland emasculating its heroes, then passing autograph books to them through the bars. Next morning, 1 June, a mere four days after sentencing, he and his small bundle of clothes were collected by the first lieutenant of the *Scourge* and taken out to the ship. Once up its side and on board, he was introduced to Captain Wingrove, a cheerful soul, Mitchel thought. The prisoner, *Scourge*'s only convict, looked at that long, unbroken but crowded deck – there were 180 men and boys aboard – and at the large field-piece in the stern, four small cannon or carronades. *Scourge*'s sole present purpose was to part Mitchel from Ireland.

Esther and her sons were still eating soup the spring of Mitchel's arrest, advancing in line to a counter to use the same bowl and spoon as the person before. Even in those lines of what Mitchel called 'pauper appetite', it was known as an evil omen that Mitchel had been transported like an ordinary Ribbonman. It was almost as if his expulsion made it less likely that ordinary people could in the autumn claw their way back to that plateau of accustomed, manageable want they had occupied in the years before the Famine. It also released in younger men sundry vows to seize the coming harvest by force. So there was confusion and fever in heads and homes.

In Dublin, Mitchel's *United Irishman* was succeeded by two briefly flaring, briskly suppressed papers. One was the *Irish Felon*, named in honour of Mitchel and edited by his friend and the mentor of his fatherless children, John Martin. It would manage to produce four copies. The other was the *Irish Tribune*, written and edited by two eminently civilised young men – Kevin O'Doherty, aged twenty-four, the surgical assistant from the fever hospitals, and the poet Richard D'Alton Williams.

An auction of Mitchel's goods had been reported in the first issue of the short-lived *Irish Felon*. A sword and two pikes belonging to the hero sold for a guinea each. Martin wrote, 'The transportation of a man, as a felon, for uttering sentiments held and professed by at least five-sixths of his countrymen, seems to me so violent and so insulting a national wrong, that submission to it must be taken to signify incurable slavishness.' And in case the main game were forgotten, the *Felon* reproduced information from around the country, such as an account from the *Castlebar Telegraph* in Mayo, whose correspondent went to the workhouse there.

We were induced to take this step from having previously seen hundreds of persons marching in (or crawling) from the direction of Balla, with asses carrying in baskets starved children and crippled old women and men. Some of the quadrupeds bore burdens of four to six children, crammed into turf baskets, with long hair growing on their shrivelled features from actual want of food! . . . We afterwards, at the dead hour of night, saw hundreds of these victims of landlordism and Gregoryism [the results of Gregory's quarter-acre clause] sinking on our flagways! We saw the inhabitants with lighted candles in their hands administering stimulants to the wretches, as they lay on the streets, emitting green froth.

Of John Martin, the *Irish Felon*'s unlikely editor, Duffy said that he was upright, simple-minded, in feeble health; 'as unfit to play a part in a revolution as in a pantomime'. The *Felon*'s edition of 8 July, largely put together by young Devin Reilly, reported an attempt to arrest Martin on a charge of treason-felony at the offices of the newspaper. But Martin hid in the suburbs, since a special judicial commission had been appointed to deal with the rash of radicalism, and he wanted to make it adjourn for lack of men to sentence. By using couriers, he and Devin Reilly managed to produce a further edition of the *Felon* on 15 July.

After the judicial commission had adjourned, Martin drove up to the College Green police station, was quickly indicted by the grand jury, and refused to take bail. Bail money, he said, might better be used on Famine victims. In an attempt to help Martin, Lalor wrote to Under-Secretary Redington, assuring him that the articles with which Martin was charged had been written by himself and by Devin Reilly.

In Newgate Martin found Gavan Duffy already installed. For as Duffy was walking to dinner at his home in the suburb of Ranelagh on the Saturday evening of 9 July, a party of detectives had arrested him too. The staff of the *Nation* still managed to get the edition on to the streets. 'On this Saturday evening Mr Charles Gavan Duffy, the Proprietor, was arrested under the New Felony Act for the articles in pages 441, 2, 3.' The articles nominated by the authorities were ironically very Mitchel-ite, the page 443 article being 'How To Break Down a Bridge or Blow One Up'. Also in residence at Newgate, Martin found, were the *Tribune* editors, O'Doherty and D'Alton Williams, and their printer Hoban. One of the articles for which they had been arrested had been entitled 'Blood for Blood', a reference to 1798 that also had a ring of which Mitchel might have been proud. 'Every ditch has its corpse, and every lordling Moloch his hecatomb of murdered tenantry. Clearly we are guilty if we turn not our hand against the enemies of our race.'

As these gentlemen in their common room at Newgate discussed the chances of transportation, the last edition of the *Nation* for the present was on the streets. For it Margaret Callan, Duffy's sister-in-law, wrote a famous article – '*Alea Jacta Est*' ('The Die Is Cast') – stirring Irish men to rebellion. 'Now, indeed, are the men of Ireland *cowards* if this moment for retribution, combat, and victory, was to pass by unemployed. It finds them slaves, and it would leave them infamous.' Because some thought Speranza wrote it, it would figure in her mythic repute.

There was appropriately a verse in that edition from teenaged Eva, urging men to follow Silken Thomas, a reference to the original 'Silken Thomas' Fitzgerald, Earl of Kildare, who had led resistance against Henry VIII, but also to Tom Meagher:

Our silken Thomas may be seen, all glorious from afar.

This poem was one of the last printed effusions of Young Ireland's intent.

Smith O'Brien was still trying to make a national front, but his negotiations in Dublin with John O'Connell were destroyed by new events in Paris. In a rebellion against Lamartine's republic, 100,000 workmen marched into the centre of Paris and demanded a socialist state. Unlike the earlier, praised rebellion, there was an enormous slaughter of soldiers and insurgents. The crucial death, however, was that of the Archbishop of Paris, who went to the working men's barricades as a negotiator and was shot dead. Some Dublin press asked of O'Brien and Meagher, 'Would not they too murder Archbishops if they got the opportunity?'

So be it, thought the young men of the Confederate clubs. In Dublin they elected a further 'secret' executive committee of five, Dillon, Meagher, O'Gorman, Devin Reilly and a talented and elfin boy journalist, D'Arcy McGee, to prepare the Confederate clubs for harvest time and its uprising. Above all, Michael Doheny and Tom Meagher had planned for the weekend of 16 and 17 July an event which aspired to be like the monster meetings of O'Connell. It was to be held atop Slievenamon Mountain in County Tipperary, a location which possessed, as had the site of the Liberator's meeting at Tara, a mythic significance. Its ancient name, Sid ar Femin, was associated with the warriors of Finn MacCool, the Fianna.

On the Tuesday before the meeting on the mountain, Meagher was club-visiting in Waterford when a troop of the 4th Light Dragoons and three companies of the 7th Fusiliers appeared on the waterfront and formed up outside Mr Thomas Meagher's residence. Police entered the house and Thomas Francis Meagher was arrested on a charge of having uttered seditious language at the town of Rathkeale. As Meagher was taken by carriage to the police station, the news of his arrest spread through Waterford. Church bells were rung and a special corps from Waterford Club, 'the Ballybracken men', hurried to the centre of town and on to the quays. Club men intended to rescue him immediately, barricade the wooden bridge over the Suir, the route to Dublin, and take over the city.

At last the Young Tribune, a little relieved to find that he had been arrested for harder-to-prove sedition rather than for treason-felony, was brought out from the Waterford police headquarters, and placed in a locked police carriage which set off for Dublin guarded by his escort of dragoons and fusiliers. As he neared the blocked bridge Tom Meagher could hear the angry citizens shouting at the escort. The officers commanding the infantry and cavalry units unlocked the back door of his carriage and appealed to Meagher to restore order. Tom Meagher, tickled to be asked, climbed on to the roof of the wagon to thunderous cheers, and ordered the crowd to wait for word from Dublin. 'We fear you will be sorry for it, sir!' a man in the crowd cried. It would later be argued that a good chance for a successful uprising was thrown away here by Meagher. But he had been warned by his captors that three warships, the *Dragon*, the *Merlin* and the *Medusa*, lay in the estuary, and would take less than an hour to reduce the town to dust.

After a night in a police cell in Dublin, Meagher was moved by train to Limerick, close to Rathkeale, the scene of his seditious speech. Like Mary Shields ten years earlier, he appeared before a Limerick grand jury in that town and an indictment against him was found. But Dublin Castle, alarmed at the popular reaction if he were refused bail, ordered he be allowed it. Doheny, held in Nenagh on the Limerick–Dublin road, was also bailed. He rushed back to Tipperary, travelling all night, on horseback and on foot, and in a hotel in Cashel met up with the inexhaustible Meagher. The two of them, with supporters from the clubs, rode south through fields of barley and oats to Slievenamon followed by 50,000 men 'under a scorching July sun'.

Though less than 3,000 feet high, Slievenamon rises above the Tipperary farmlands with the assurance of a Kilimanjaro, and with all the presence of a peak inhabited by deities. Lord Clarendon feared the insurgents would begin operations in the triangle of Kilkenny, Waterford and Tipperary – Slievenamon marking one of its corners. Thousands climbed the hill that weekend, Meagher on horseback making a brilliant figure in his tricolour sash and gold-braided cap. 'Wending their way up the side of the mountain from the direction of their various locations', a journalist wrote, 'might be seen the men of Cork, Waterford, Wexford, and from all sides the "Boys of Tipperary" . . . At four o'clock Messrs Doheny and Meagher, headed by the Cashel band, arrived at the mountain, when the huzzas commenced like the rumblings of a thunder storm.' Doheny, an unpretty, unfashionably dressed but generous man, told the mass of men and women that they had a right to the coming harvest on the plains below. 'The potato was smitten; but your fields waved with golden grain. It was not for you. To your lips it was forbidden fruit.' Before leaving the summit the next day, Sunday 17 July, the Young Tribune, Meagher of the Sword, issued his own proclamation on the rights of Irishmen, which many Confederates on their way home pasted up over a new seizure-of-arms proclamation from Dublin Castle.

Hearing that a crowd of supporters who had not reached Slievenamon were in the town of Carrick, Meagher and Doheny rode to visit them. In late afternoon, they found a crowd in the market square, so urgent in their cries for action that they insisted on escorting them on to Waterford. The procession did not arrive in Waterford until three o'clock the next morning. From an upstairs window Meagher and Doheny addressed the mass of men, women and flaring torches. How achingly close Ireland's deliverance must have seemed in those wide-awake night hours. Meagher believed that in the face of the great popular demonstrations, no sane government would continue with the charges, or rig a jury against Duffy, O'Doherty, John Martin and the others.

From Waterford, Meagher felt some urgency to get to Dublin and tell his fellow executive committee how ripe Ireland was:

> in the evening, between seven and eight o'clock, I ordered a covered car . . . Whilst the car was getting ready, I ran up to the drawing room, where my father and aunt were sitting at the time, to wish them good-bye. I put on my tricolor sash – green, white and orange – buckled on my sword-belt, cross-belt, cartouche-box – and, flourishing a very handsome sword which belonged to a grand uncle of mine in the days of the Merchant Corps of the Waterford Volunteers, gave myself up to the gay illusion of a gallant fight, a triumphal entry, at the head of armed thousands, into Dublin, before long!

His father, he remembered, was 'mournfully serious'.

Arriving in Dublin by hired carriage the next day, Meagher told Dillon, Smyth, O'Gorman and others at the *Nation* office and the Confederation council rooms that 'The crowds had been restrained with difficulty and would re-emerge when the word was spoken'. O'Brien, recently returned to Dublin too, reported that 'at Cork he met ten thousand Confederates as capable of effectual action as any troops in the Queen's service'. After an intoxicating day, that Friday night Meagher slept at Pat Smyth's family house, Mount Brown near Kilmainham. He had meant to rise early, but slept till noon. Pat Smyth let him rest, but at midday came to his schoolfriend's bedside with the news that the House of Commons had voted for the suspension of Habeas Corpus in Ireland. This would enable Dublin Castle to issue warrants for the immediate arrest of all Young Ireland leaders.

Young Ireland had presumed that they would have another three or four weeks before harvest to prepare themselves and the people. 'There is nothing for us now,' Meagher told Smyth, 'but to go out; we have not gone far enough to succeed, and yet, too far to retreat.' Taking a hackney coach into the city they met up with Dillon and others. Dillon suggested that he and Meagher should pursue Smith O'Brien, who was in Wexford visiting Confederate clubs, and refer all plans to that sage's judgement: 'It struck us', said Meagher, 'that the smallest victory . . . would be a very great influence on the spirit of the country at large'. Young D'Arcy McGee had already left for Glasgow to gather volunteers, intending to seize merchant vessels in Scotland to transport expatriate Irish back to the west of Ireland. This was characteristic of Young Ireland's rough plan for a revolt in the provinces. Years later in exile, Meagher still believed that departing the city was the correct choice. A Dublin uprising would have been 'stifled in a pool of squandered blood'. Similarly, Doheny left Cashel and rode to a farmer's house below Slievenamon, a place known to Meagher, to await communication from the unquestioned leader, O'Brien.

On their mission to find O'Brien, Meagher and Dillon caught the five o'clock train on the newly built railway line to Kingstown and then on to the seaside resort of Dalkey, where they caught a trap to the hotel in Killiney where Mrs Dillon was staying. The Dillons were said to be the most striking couple in all Ireland, yet for once picturesqueness was not on Meagher's mind. During dinner they all discussed whether they should accept arrest, try to escape, or instigate an uprising. Brave Mrs Dillon agreed on the last.

So her husband and Meagher must catch the coach to Wexford, in hope of intercepting O'Brien in Ballinkeele, where he was rumoured to be. They ordered two inside seats, but thought it safest to walk some miles out of town to get aboard in the dark. They proved to be the only inside passengers. Small farmers and peasants in sundry states of health hung to the outside of the vehicle as the young gentlemen slept within. In the small hours, getting down in Ballinkeele, they found Smith O'Brien had gone on with a friend, John Maher, who lived in Wexford. It was at first light on the morning of 22 July that Meagher and Dillon, on a cart, caught up with O'Brien at Maher's house and told him he was a fugitive. O'Brien turned to Mr Maher and asked him to 'have breakfast made for me and send us on our way'.

On that first morning, Smith O'Brien had wanted to go to New Ross, scene of a battle of 1798, and the location of a strong Confederate club. But Meagher urged they go to Kilkenny, where the Royal Agricultural Society Show was then in progress. 'With some hundred head of the finest cattle in the island, we could have managed admirably behind the barricades for three or four days.' Worthies could also make good hostages. O'Brien agreed that he should test the Kilkenny area first – to check whether there was a high level of support.

Heading south, Meagher and Dillon attended Mass at Enniscorthy in County Wexford, where they discovered many of the churchgoers weakened by hardship, and unprepared to fight in an insurrection. They were prepared, however, to protect the Young Irelanders from arrest. But travelling on, having met up with O'Brien, the three rebels were mobbed by the people of Craiguenamanagh, who were ready to fight. O'Brien was not sure, however, if he yet had an adequate picture and, continuing in a trap through the pass between Mount Leinster and Blackspur's Mountain, the three came in the rain to the city of Kilkenny.

In steaming clothes, they went at once to the house of a Dr Cain, a Confederate. There they were told to their chagrin that there were not – as earlier reported – 17,000 club members in Kilkenny but only 1,700, of whom only one in four had arms. As they emerged into the street, a number of famished townspeople and farmers told Tom Meagher to find a priest who would consecrate the resistance. For it was the truth, one of them told Meagher, that ordinary people were sick of staying quiet and dying day to day. Though Meagher sent off messages to presbyteries, no Kilkenny priest turned up at Cain's house.

The path the Young Irelanders now took is confusing. Basically, they would spend the next week swinging across the south of Ireland, through Waterford and Tipperary, raising the populace; but no sooner did they succeed in doing so than the clergy would use their influence to disperse the gathered force. But despite all disappointment, these men were committed to rebellion by the warrants out for them, to a rebellion chaotic in its shifting schemes, sweeping in its intent, massive in its possibilities, brave in its execution, disastrous in its effect and, to some people at least, laughable in its form. It would confirm O'Brien and Meagher as two of the most admired Irish figures of the nineteenth century and feed an Irish sense that it was always the irrepressible myth, not the potent battalion, which conquered in the end.

A relatively obscure member of Young Ireland, Patrick O'Donohoe, a Dublin law clerk with a weakness for drink, married and with one adored little daughter, had discovered that his name too was on a warrant. A member of the Grattan Confederate club in Dublin, he had received from the imprisoned Gavan Duffy a note to be passed on to O'Brien.

O'Donohoe travelled the first leg by train, but got to Kilkenny after O'Brien had already left. Inquiring after the great man at hotels, he found himself visited by a group of militant Young Irelanders who sombrely told him they would take him to O'Brien, but if O'Brien did not greet him his safety could not be guaranteed.

O'Brien and the others had by now moved on to the town of Callan, County Kilkenny, where a crowd materialised in the market-place as a band struck up the old Jacobite tune 'The White-Cockade'. Some 8th

Royal Irish Hussars applauded as O'Brien addressed the people. Meanwhile, Tom Meagher, riding ahead and already entering County Tipperary, ran into men who had been on Slievenamon. They told him that there were hundreds ready to join him. Meagher said of the countryside and towns of Callan and Carrick as they were that day: 'It was the Revolution, if we had accepted it.'

O'Brien caught up with Meagher in Carrick, Tipperary, that night, and the local leader, a stripling named John O'Mahony, led O'Brien and the other leaders to a house where refreshments were served and a confused meeting developed between the leaders and local supporters. 'One was for commencing, there and then,' O'Mahony later wrote:

> Another proposed that . . . the morning should be ushered in with the volleying of guns and the gleaming of pike heads. A third suggested . . . that the elections of the Council of Three Hundred should take place with as little delay as possible, and that the delegates should proceed immediately on their election to the Rotundo, each escorted by a thousand armed men.

A wearied O'Brien stepped up to the window the following morning to remind the crowd waiting outside that many had pledged to struggle and die with Young Ireland if need be. 'We are here to demand the redemption of the pledge, in the name of our enslaved country.' In the street, local clergy and other voices began to ask, 'Why should Carrick be selected?' The longer the debate continued the more diffuse the intentions of the populace became.

Ultimately disappointed, the party left town and headed west for Cashel, Doheny's town. Meagher himself, dispatched by O'Brien, arrived on horseback at Doheny's hiding-place at the bottom of Slievenamon, and moved on with him to other areas, rallying people, seeing pikes being forged in village smithies. He rode back even into his home town of Waterford, and had to leave at the gallop to escape patrols of the British army, which for the moment was concentrating itself in the major cities. The countryside would be left open for several days to Young Ireland's reconnaissance.

For the Young Irelanders, the story was everywhere the same, even in Cashel. The police lay low, waiting to gauge rebel strength. But Confederate clubs proved not as numerous, organised or well-armed as they had sometimes boasted to headquarters in Dublin. There was no question that the peasantry and much of the middle class wanted revolution. But no sooner did that sentiment emerge than other voices, particularly those of the clergy supported by Old Ireland aldermen, advised the call of conscience, asked people to think of the vengeance that would descend on the first town to rise.

On a country road outside the town, O'Brien, his party retreating in two carts, had been joined by some leading Young Irelanders from Dublin, including Meagher's schoolfriend Pat Smyth. James Stephens, a Kilkenny bookseller's son, one day to command an international Irish revolutionary body, also turned up, with the awkwardly earnest Dublin law clerk Patrick O'Donohoe, who was grateful to be greeted by O'Brien, and thus have his life redeemed. Some thought the best move now was to arrange escapes to America or France. O'Brien and others would be fêted in New York or Paris, and be able to apply the heat of world opinion. But even after Cashel, O'Brien was committed to resistance, and had decided to head east to the inaccessible hilly country which ran north–south between Cashel and Kilkenny. If things continued to go less than splendidly they would be able at least to hide until the export of the new harvest unleashed the rage of the people. In all this frenzied movement through the summer countryside, the Young Irelanders moved in a wakeful fever of expectations or a grind of disappointment. Nor did they seem to realise that many of their countrymen and women were so Famine-struck and deranged as to be more unfit for action than any other peasants in Europe.

From this point on, an inner nucleus of O'Brien, Dillon, O'Donohoe and Stephens moved around a rectangle of villages in eastern Tipperary, while others, including Doheny and Meagher, ranged widely in a number of directions but always returning to make occasional contact with O'Brien.

As O'Brien's party travelled towards the network of villages in and on the edge of the Tipperary collieries, unbidden crowds gathered and again hope flared. On their entering the village of Mullinahone, for instance, the chapel bell was ringing and thousands gathered in the market square. O'Brien stood in his carriage, a spectacular figure in his paramilitary cap and trim suit, and addressed the mass of people. Though the local police waited outside their station, nodding approval, again two Catholic clergymen of the town 'appeared by his side, and openly resisted his advice'. But after the priests left the square more villagers still came. Amongst the 2,000 enthusiastic men, said the law clerk O'Donohoe later, some bore muskets, pikes and pitchforks, and others promised to procure them.

Perhaps 3,000 people remained bivouacked in the square and around the commons of Mullinahone that night while, like a soldier-king from Shakespeare, O'Brien went walking from one campfire to another, the nobleman face to face with the peasant for the rare fraternal purpose of rebellion. And then the clergy would follow behind him. Whatever their motives, the priests would be accused of dispersing the risen people because they did not want an annual parliamentary grant to the seminary at Maynooth to be threatened; nor did they want to encourage the red republicanism which had left the Archbishop of Paris dead.

Yet O'Brien would prove a most scrupulous rebel. It was not until the day after he entered Mullinahone and found half of his overnight army vanished that he barricaded the road and walked over with Blake Dillon, O'Donohoe and others to the Mullinahone police station. There he was met by five policemen whom he called to surrender their arms. But a senior constable announced through the stone doorway that if he and his fellows gave up their arms to a small number of men they would be dismissed, and then, in Famine time, where would their families be? To O'Donohoe's amazement, O'Brien let the police persuade him that if he came back with thirty men, they would willingly give up. While O'Brien and a disbelieving Dillon and Patrick O'Donohoe set out to attend to these niceties, the police escaped from the station back door, taking their weapons with them.

Next day in nearby Ballingarry, O'Brien climbed on to the chapel wall and addressed the gathered people. His terms had become more modest by now. He asked that they protect him long enough for the harvest to come in. He told them to respect property, and urged married men to remain at home and labouring men to stay at work. He wanted no man who could not bring with him three days' provisions of bread or biscuit. One can imagine his hollow-faced army incredulously telling their families that O'Brien required of them three days of bread and biscuit. This was not their old dream of the bread taken from the mouth of landlords and given to their children.

At a conference in a farmhouse at night, over mutton chops and water, 'Mr Doheny asked, hypothetically,' the boy O'Mahony remembered, 'if Carrick were taken, should the bank be seized and the money be carried off?' O'Brien was horrified, and asked if Doheny wanted to destroy the character of the movement.

It was in Ballingarry that the young woolbroker from Liverpool, Terence Bellew MacManus, caught up with O'Brien. This apparently wealthy young merchant (some would later say his business was in trouble) was dressed in the fashion of 1848 European rebels – a cap, green with a gold band, on the back of his head, riding boots and a black leather bandolier. So MacManus was in place to see another example of O'Brien's war-making. It was at dawn on the seventh day of the march across the south that O'Brien, up early after resting in a farmer's house, met young men running into town to say cavalry was coming. Blake Dillon, James Stephens the bookseller's son, and O'Donohoe began to erect barricades of spare wood, drays, old furniture generously loaned by local people, to block either end and the middle of the main street. A troop of hussars, light cavalry, travelled right up to the first blockade, and an officer in command, a Captain Longmore, asked could he be allowed to pass? Blake Dillon told him he could not. A wild cheer was heard from the largely unarmed people who were coming from side-streets to man the second and third barricades. O'Brien ordered O'Donohoe and Dillon to let the troop pass if the officer gave his word of honour not to arrest any of them. 'Whereupon a space was opened in the barricades and the officer and his men passed on. There is no doubt if a collision had taken place we would have killed or captured the entire troop.' With that O'Brien's second chance of revolutionary success galloped away. Soon rain began to fall and the rebels took dismal refuge in a hut on the road to Urlingford colliery.

Elsewhere, in a farmhouse on the southern side of Slievenamon, Meagher had interviewed the presidents of a number of clubs and concluded that, though the rising was four or five weeks before the harvest, it could work now if O'Brien took some decisive action. Everyone wanted to prevent O'Brien's capture, but they were also waiting for him to manifest himself. The bloodless seizing of the police station at Mullinahone and the dismounting and disarming of the cavalry unit would have served as a good start in this direction.

Meagher, O'Mahony, Devin Reilly, Doheny and others arrived in Mullinahone later that day as a lively party in an Irish jaunting car. Rebels saw them coming and discharged pistols and waved hats and green branches. Now a final council of war took place in a public house in a mining village a little way west. O'Brien reiterated that when the garrisons of the big towns emerged, as they soon would, he would not skulk – he would be visible to the people even on Slievenamon, he said. Doheny again suggested genuine revolutionary steps, urging O'Brien to issue a proclamation 'confiscating the landed property of the country and offering it as the gage of battle and reward of victory'. Doheny also suggested a war order 'directing the people to live at the expense of the enemy'. But, O'Brien answered, only an aggressive act on the part of government could justify 'such a sweeping proceeding'. It was the Liberator, not John Mitchel, who cast a long shadow over rebel deliberations in that hotel.

O'Brien was to stay for now in this area, a region in which there were at least people who would intervene to prevent his arrest, while other leaders were to disperse and generate an appearance of strength, of a countryside in revolt, by lighting beacon fires on the surrounding mountaintops.

Tom Meagher was eager and unexhausted. Ordered to Waterford once more, for a last attempt to raise men, he started off on a hard ride over the lovely Comeraghs. After visiting Waterford, it was in these mountains that Meagher was to take up a post, and have regular fires lit and maintained. Doheny was to keep an eye on the town of Clonmel and warn O'Brien of any movement of the garrison there. Mitchel's young journalist friend, Devin Reilly, was to go to Kilkenny on the same sort of mission as Meagher's.

Saturday 29 July was the day that settled everything. After a few hours' sleep in the colliery public house, O'Brien and his party took their cart back to Ballingarry, where, priest or not, there were some ordinary people willing to fight. MacManus, riding ahead, arrived in the main street as a young man rushed up to his stirrup to tell of an approaching police column. Surrounded by townspeople, he called on them to build a barricade across the main road on the edge of town. O'Brien himself stationed some of the men who had guns on hillocks of mine slag either side of the road. In the ditches he placed others, including women, usually obedient to the priest but obeying now imperatives of their hungry situation, armed merely with stones and pikes. Of 200 people serving in this ambuscade, the Young Irelander Patrick Kavanagh says that two thirds of them had no weapons.

From behind the barricade, Young Ireland saw a strong body of armed police cresting the hill to the east outside the town. Forty-six men, under the command of a Sub-Inspector Trant from Callan, came to within 600 yards of the barricade, formed a line and advanced. O'Brien's army uttered their contempt and rage from the slagheaps, ditches, windows and barricade. The force of police were about a hundred yards from the barricade when without warning they turned at the double up a lane to their right. Believing they were fleeing, the rebels began to race across country to cut them off. MacManus complained, 'All we could do or say was of no avail and in about two minutes we were alone.'

The Young Irelanders now followed their runaway supporters and found that in fact the police had taken possession of a small two-storeyed, two-chimneyed house surrounded by a stone wall, on land named Boulagh Common. They were barricading the windows, and Kavanagh could see in each of them 'six or seven long dark tubes ready to blaze away on us at any moment'. O'Brien and MacManus and about a dozen men took shelter behind a haystack – a *haggard*, as it was called – at the back of the house, and MacManus suggested heaping hay around the door and lower windows and setting it afire. O'Brien refused. For one of his rebel army told him a Widow McCormack owned the house, was away at the time, and her five children, all under ten years of age, were within.

Mrs McCormack returned a little later to find her windows barricaded with furniture and bristling with carbine barrels. At the front of the house MacManus stood up with O'Brien and two unidentified 'brave fellows' to accompany Mrs McCormack through the gate in the fence, through her cabbage patch, and around the corner of the house to a partially clear window, to inquire after the infants. O'Brien called, 'I want you to give up your arms. We shall not hurt a man of you – you are Irishmen.' Grotesquely, a number of policemen stretched out their hands to shake O'Brien's. But while O'Brien was up at the sill, said MacManus, 'ruffians' on the rebel side began hurling stones from behind the wall, and suddenly forty carbines were discharged at the besiegers. O'Brien was at the time standing about 3 yards from the house, MacManus about 7. Two men fell beside MacManus, one dead, the other wounded. MacManus fired, and then all the rebel musketry, perhaps a little more than two dozen guns, broke out. O'Brien, MacManus and the howling widow retreated through the rage of fire.

O'Brien understood quite clearly that this *was* the revolution, begun, full of promise, morally feasible. An excellent cache of pistols and carbines could come out of it, and a stylish victory enlarged upon in retelling around a cowed Ireland. To pursue this prize, Patrick Kavanagh, the Young Ireland youth, left his position to move up to the house, heard a crash, and fell. A bullet had passed through his thigh, 'grazing the main artery'.

Then MacManus and a few of the proletarian rebels thought it time to edge their way up to the back door with bundles of hay. A pikeman lifted up a load of it, a musketeer knelt down, laid the musket along it and fired. The hay would not burn. Meanwhile, the firing from within the house was orderly and concentrated. The pikemen, scythe-bearers and stone-throwers began to retreat before it. 'I found the entire mob', said the militant MacManus, 'had been drawn off with the exception of about twelve brave fellows who still lined the wall and kept up a straggling fire.' MacManus led these musketeers to a place of safety at the gable end of the stables, and went back to O'Brien by the fence and insisted he should leave the field. 'This he refused to do and returned again and again under the fire of the windows, declaring he would rather perish than turn his back on the enemy . . . he was the last man who left.'

After further exchanges, two priests came up the hill, one of them Father Fitzgerald of Ballingarry, who knew the names of the fallen and would give them the last rites once the firing stopped. 'When I was entering the wicket in front of the house,' said Fitzgerald, 'one man, John

Walsh, was lying outside the gate on his back, quite dead. Another young man, named Bride, a widow's son, was dying outside the wall, having received his death wound from a bullet in passing over it.'

There would be commentators on both sides of the conflict who believed it might have been a mercy had O'Brien been fatally wounded with Walsh and Bride, and witnesses stated that he was indeed courting death. Perhaps the police marksmen inside went to trouble not to shoot him, and at last he was persuaded to walk away. At the bottom of the hill MacManus and others encountered a mounted policeman and took his horse from him. O'Brien walked on to the point near the original Ballingarry barricade, where the 'well-clothed, well-mounted' priest had collected retreating peasants. 'O'Brien addressed them and tried to rally them, but the spell was on them.' MacManus got the policeman's horse, put a man on either side of the bridle and told them to take O'Brien, dazed by failure, back through Ballingarry. MacManus took a short cut across the field to the village 'but to my mortification on turning round I again beheld him returning to where the young priest and the mob were standing'.

MacManus located O'Brien's rented carriage parked in the village, and drove it up to the bottom of the hill to get O'Brien away. He could find no one. A new body of police estimated at 100 were lined out along walls and ditches and were firing at the junction where the priest and his parishioners had been. The few remaining foot-soldiers of the uprising told him that the young Confederate from Kilkenny, James Stephens, had been one of the wounded. MacManus rode towards Slievenamon, marvelling that the casualties had been so light, particularly since the range was so short, about 12 yards between wall and house.

The *Illustrated London News* correspondent, on the scene within twenty-four hours, told his English readers, 'The story of Smith O'Brien creeping away among the cabbages is only a story . . . In the eye of any military man his positions and conduct were censurable for their indiscreet daring.' Indeed Father Fitzgerald, who had no reason to praise O'Brien, later wrote that the rebel leader 'had no protection from the constant fire'.

The *Times* correspondent was able to report by Monday that the green at Ballingarry, where O'Brien drilled his rebel forces, 'is to-day a "tented field" for the soldiers of Her Majesty the Queen'.

Richard O'Gorman of Young Ireland had already been in Limerick visiting clubs at the time of Young Ireland's foray through the south. He held rallies in towns and villages along the Shannon and was sheltered in rural homes at night. The people of the town of Abbeyfeale declared for immediate resistance, and seized the Limerick and Tralee mail, taking possession only of official dispatches and passing private letters unopened on to the local postmaster. But when the news came from Ballingarry of the disaster there, the Abbeyfeale force dispersed in 'sullen despair'.

Meagher had earlier assured young D'Arcy McGee that if he collected 400 to 500 Scots and landed them in the west, he would be as famous as the American privateer John Paul Jones. But while McGee was making arrangements in Edinburgh, a mechanic who had previously lived in Dublin recognised him by his small stature and his strangely African features, and reported him to the police. The Scottish Young Ireland committee told him to make immediately for the west of Ireland and prepare to receive the invasion force there. He took a train to Carlisle, and found himself sitting opposite the Grand Chaplain of the Orangemen, Thresham Gregg, who, McGee claimed, knew him but said nothing.

Crossing to Belfast, he found the newspapers contained Lord Clarendon's wily letter to the Catholic primate of Ireland, Archbishop Murray, offering to alter the new Colleges Act to the liking of the Catholic bishops and to remodel the Bequests Bill to their benefit. McGee headed for Sligo. There were only 100 British soldiers in the area, he was told, and the barracks in Sligo were protected by a thin 8-foot wall, which the Confederates felt could be easily breached. McGee was put in contact too with the Sligo Molly Maguires, Ribbon-like societies which would later make a transatlantic crossing and establish themselves in the coalfields of Pennsylvania. Their local leader told him, 'Bring us this day week . . . assurance that the South has risen, or will certainly rise, and we will enrol two thousand men before the week is out.' Exaggerated or not, in that statement lies some hint of the potential significance of Ballingarry. McGee was sheltered in the country around Ben Bulben, and got news from Scotland that, though 400 had been ready to land in the west, their movement had been cancelled by the news from Ballingarry.

Had all these forces been brought into play at the same time, Britain and Dublin Castle would have faced not something as contemptible as the 'Widow McCormack's Cabbage Patch', but a widely spread uprising, inchoate, and hard both for Dublin Castle to combat and for O'Brien to manage. And if O'Brien had authorised a famished and deprived people to attack the property of landlords and to commandeer resources, would clerical appeals to conscience and virtue have still worked to temper events? The image of O'Brien shaking the policemen's hands through the windows of the Widow McCormack's house is an abiding symbol not so much of minor vanity as of an unwillingness to declare any Irishman his thorough enemy: 'He could never quite forget, as Mirabeau and Lafayette forgot,' wrote Duffy, 'that he belonged to the caste of gentlemen.' O'Donohoe declared in imprisonment some years later, 'A vicious man with the talents and prestige of O'Brien's name would have overthrown English dominion in Ireland.'

Patrick O'Donohoe, having found a horse, met Meagher riding up from the direction of Waterford. O'Donohoe, who had behaved with valour during the siege, trying to direct the rebel musket fire, told the Young Tribune the dismal news. However uneven O'Donohoe's temperament proved to be, Meagher would be a loyal friend to the older man. The two of them travelled along country roads towards the Keeper Mountains to the north-west of Tipperary, hoping to make a junction with O'Gorman and other Confederates in Limerick. At every step they were recognised, and men presented themselves, voicing support, but they now knew what value to put on that. O'Donohoe the penniless clerk and fashionable Tom Meagher were forced to ride up into the hills and take to complicated glens whenever they sighted the army and police patrols and checkpoints, or were warned of them by peasants. The military had sallied out of the garrison towns and were now everywhere.

MacManus tried but failed to find Meagher in the Keepers. He climbed one mountaintop to light a beacon and was answered from twelve other summits by the beacons of supporters, and descending to a crossroads was joined by a thousand men, but armed with nothing but pikes or stones. Bandolier-less now, MacManus was on the run for five weeks, making his way towards Cork, finding a welcome in houses but retreating to the mountains when the valleys filled with police and redcoats. 'Between the Keepers and Cork,' he would say, dealing briskly with the history of those weeks, 'I was three times in the hands of the police and three times escaped.' Friends in the Cork City Confederate clubs sheltered him for weeks and booked him a passage on a New York-bound steamer, *N. D. Chase*. On 7 September, when he was waiting in his cabin for departure, he was identified and put under arrest during the final police search of the ship. Though he would never ultimately recover from this arrest, at no stage, then or later, did he voice any regret.

It was rumoured that the warrants for the arrest of Smith O'Brien and the others had in some cases been read from Catholic pulpits. *The Times* of 4 August said, 'We imagine the king of Munster is at the moment wandering about from one unsavoury boscobel to another in the shape of coal-pits, bogs, dung heaps and ditches.' In fact O'Brien was in hiding in the mountains which lay in all compass directions from Ballingarry. When he descended at night, his direction was westwards, towards Limerick. An uprising by the Limerick people was possible, and if not that, escape to Europe or the United States. But the authorities had by now turned up the heat on potential protectors. Wherever O'Brien halted, he recognised 'the utmost alarm' in his hosts.

Perhaps unwisely, since the railway was watched, he decided to enter the town of Thurles and, wrapped in a coarse cloak, catch a train home. He had bought a second-class ticket and was waiting on the station when a railway guard named Hulme made a citizen's arrest on him. O'Brien struggled, but resistance was soon quelled by the arrival of police and soldiery. The prisoner was handed straight over to the military, who in the south were under the command of a General McDonald. Locked up in the police station at Thurles, he could hear the people gathering outside and making eloquent protests. The mass of Irish, though they had not marched with him the previous month, admired him and did not want him arrested. Indeed Hulme, who had nabbed O'Brien in hope of promotion and reward, became a pariah and had to move away and live under another name.

In order that he would be able to change his linen before being moved to Dublin, O'Brien was permitted to send a note to Mrs Michael Doheny in Cashel asking her to forward a portmanteau he had left at her place. He believed that General McDonald and other authorities would not invade the privacy of his possessions. But the portmanteau ended up at Dublin Castle. O'Brien was appalled, especially since his old school and parliamentary friend Under-Secretary Redington seemed to be a willing party to this action. Every fragment of paper in the portmanteau – down to visiting cards – was numbered, initialled and sent to the Crown Solicitor's office.

11

Young Ireland on Trial

> Nothing new at Clonmel. The trial of Meagher is going forward and I hear that the courthouse is full of priests today. It is said that Meagher has given Whiteside and Butt full leave to bring out all about the priests that they like in this trial . . . A visiting clergyman states that the young patriot appeared as cheerful and buoyant as in the days of his boyhood.
>
> Grace O'Brien to her sister Anne Martineau, October 1848

The uprising had come and gone without the participation of John Mitchel, the first victim of the Treason-Felony Act, who in June 1848, less than a month after his sentencing in Green Street courthouse, arrived in Bermuda aboard *Scourge*. He had enjoyed on board both the leisure and the degree of isolation to savour *Two Years Before the Mast*, and to write a hostile analysis of Macaulay's *Essays*. Since it was the government's intention to keep him quarantined in all circumstances, he was helped, and perhaps tormented, by his voracious mental powers. When permitted on deck, he took note of everything, flying fish and dolphins and the flotillas of Portuguese men-of-war on the waves under 'opaline sails of purple and rose-coloured membrane'.

Then on 20 June, one of the mulatto pilots of Bermuda boarded and took the *Scourge* past the main port of Hamilton, with its white houses, scraggy cedars and low hills. 'If I am to be allowed some moderate liberty here, say the range of one of the islands, I might bring out all my flock, and we could cultivate arrow-root, oranges and potatoes, dwelling primitively in a white-roofed cottage.' *Scourge* came to anchor off the dockyard on the northernmost island, ironically called Ireland, inside the crescent of breakwater, where three naval ships were anchored: 'great clumsy *hulks*, roofed over, and peopled by men in white linen blouses and straw hats, were visible'. He hoped that he would not be put amongst these men, on whose clothing the broad arrow was visible. Waiting to hear what his precise treatment would be, Mitchel was able to comfort himself by reading the *Morning Post* of the day after his sentencing. Edmund Burke Roche, a parliamentarian, had challenged Sir George Grey, the Home Secretary, about Mitchel's 'unjust and disproportionate sentence', but Mitchel thought Roche a blockhead – the nature of the trial was the issue, not the severity of sentence. It would always be an ungrateful task to be Mitchel's advocate.

Two boats approached, manned by men in white blouses. 'The hulks, then!' he concluded. 'No seaside cottages or cedarn valleys for me.' The Superintendent of Convicts boarded with the master of the hulks and told Mitchel he had been assigned to the one anchored furthest out, the *Dromedary*. He was allowed his books and his portmanteau, would be free to walk on the deck and on the adjacent breakwater, and would not be required to wear convict clothes. Mitchel packed his belongings, bade the captain and discreetly kind officers of *Scourge* goodbye, and was rowed across to his hulk. Here his cell below decks proved to be a 6-by-6-feet compartment, created by the space which had once boxed the mainmast. A hammock was slung diagonally, and occupying it on his first night he found the walls alive with brown cockroaches nearly 2 inches long.

To the deck forward, where the convicts were kept, he had no direct access. Each morning, he was permitted to descend stairs to a platform from which he bathed silently in the sea with the others, but apart from that he was meant to seclude himself. Hearing no Irish accents during his dips in the sea, he learned from an illicit chat with a steward that before his arrival some eighty or ninety on that hulk had been swapped for Englishmen. After a week's asthmatic wheezing on board, he was given a better cabin, 6 feet high and 14 feet in length, with a spacious barred porthole and bookshelves. He would for a time be transferred under the care of the medical officer, Dr Warner, to the hospital ship *Tenedos*, 'moored about a quarter of a mile from land, in a most beautiful bay'. Sometimes, aware that hunger possessed Ireland, he felt disgraced at the enjoyment he found in his spacious two-portholed cabin on *Tenedos*. But soon he was unexpectedly moved back to his original hulk, the *Dromedary*, because of New York newspaper reports that the Irish were considering arming a vessel for a rescue attempt.

From the window of his cabin on *Dromedary*, he could see the dockyard, the barracks and the parade ground. The 42nd Regiment of Highlanders was stationed there, and he watched them march up to their barracks with bagpipes playing Scottish airs. Opposite the parade ground on the breakwater the convicts mustered, sometimes to witness floggings. By late July 1848, as O'Brien marched through Tipperary, the command on board *Dromedary* had clamped down severely upon his access to newspapers. He saw others – guards, stewards – reading them, and consoled himself with a trunk he had been allowed from home, including daguerreotypes of John Martin and Jenny. He read Homer. 'Weather delicious. Have also been swallowing autobiographies – Gifford's, Thomas Elwood's, Captain Crichton's *autobiography by Dean Swift*.' He watched the other convicts during church services on deck, when they stood holding their palmetto hats reverently in hand. 'Closer examination makes you aware that many of them have evil countenances and amorphous skulls . . . burglars and swindlers from the womb.'

O'Brien would have to be removed, the authorities decided, from disaffected Tipperary to Dublin. Cavalry was used to clear the streets of Thurles, and shopkeepers were ordered to close their doors; when some disobeyed, General McDonald himself threatened severe and summary reprisal. On 7 August, the authorities got O'Brien through a shuttered town to the railway station, but the engine driver refused to take the train on to Dublin. An officer produced a pistol and told the engineer he would blow his brains out. For had the departure of the train been delayed, Young Ireland sympathisers would have had time to pull up the lines.

As O'Brien's train pulled out of Thurles, Meagher was still on the run with the Cork man, Denny Leyne, and with Patrick O'Donohoe, 'sometimes sleeping in hay lofts on bundles of straw, and other times in miserable cabins, with the most wretched and sickly of the peasantry, and once or twice by the ditchside'. Uncomfortable billets, they seemed to release in Meagher a zany jollity. In one whitewashed farmhouse, Meagher was visited by a clergyman who proposed that they should all surrender on condition of being allowed to leave the country. Meagher consented to try this on condition that everyone in the movement would be offered the same facility. He wrote a letter outlining these terms, which was then carried to Dublin Castle. The reply was that the lives of Meagher and his immediate associates would be guaranteed if they pleaded guilty to high treason, and if the arms from all disturbed districts were delivered up. This offer, conveyed back to Meagher, was rejected. Too few rebels were covered by it, and there was unreality in the idea that the leaders of the rebellion had any control over its arms. 'A cruel perversion of Meagher's generous proposal appeared in some of the newspapers,' said Duffy. 'It was reported that he offered to surrender, if his life was spared.' To protect his reputation, Meagher walked out of hiding towards Cashel, intending either to be taken alive or to try one last appeal to arms. On 13 August, he and O'Donohoe were arrested by a roadblock of police north of Thurles, Tipperary. They were taken unchained in a cart to the town, and then, before news of their capture could get around, quickly by train to Dublin, to join O'Brien in Kilmainham. Supplied with fresh linen, Meagher posed beside a serenely seated Smith O'Brien for a photograph taken in the prison governor's garden.

By then, Michael Doheny, fleeing west, saw from the top of the Comeraghs the black patches of putrefaction in the fields below. The blight was cruelly facing those like Esther Larkin who had for three years tried every stratagem. Now, again, there was no guarantee that from August 1848 until the end of time the Irish would not be yearly mocked with this seasonal rot of their hopes.

O'Brien's younger brother Robert, justice of the peace for both Limerick and Clare, brought Lucy to Dublin, and from Morrison's Hotel wrote to his wife, Ellen De Vere, 'I sat up late last night going over all William's speeches and indexing them for Whiteside' (O'Brien's senior counsel) 'and have been struck when one comes to put them together at the noble spirit they evince.'

Only a few days after O'Brien's arrest, Gavan Duffy and other journalists, including John Martin and Kevin O'Doherty, stood trial for treason-felony. Duffy, standing in the Green Street dock, was told by a regular counsel of Irish rebels that a letter incriminating him in high treason had been found in O'Brien's portmanteau. High treason was a hanging, drawing and quartering offence.

Twenty-four-year-old Kevin O'Doherty's trial started the same day. Articles from the *Irish Tribune* of 1 and 8 July were put forward by the Attorney-General as proof of guilt. One article, 'Our Harvest Prospects', after asking the usual question about whether livestock and grain would again be shipped out of a passive Ireland, cried, 'No; the strong men of this land . . . will gladden our eyes by saving the coming harvest and easing their longing thirst deep, deep in the blood of the English foe.' In leading O'Doherty's defence, 35-year-old Isaac Butt admitted the articles were seditious, but his client was not being tried for sedition. To convict him, said Butt, the jury would have to believe that in the recesses of his soul he intended treason.

No portion of handwriting had been produced to show that the articles were O'Doherty's. Butt now referred to O'Doherty's behaviour during the present typhus epidemic, for which he had been praised by a number of the medical profession. The young man had treated the famous physician John Curran when Curran himself had been felled with fever. In fact, as Butt spoke, many of the jury selected with a bias towards a guilty verdict could understand if not condone the sense of outrage behind the open features of this decent young man who in a saner time would make a splendid surgeon. When, on Friday night, 11 August, the chairman of the jurors declared that a verdict seemed impossible, they were ordered to be locked up without 'food or easements'. But even a night of discomfort did not bring a verdict.

O'Doherty was held in a cell near Duffy's and Martin's in the debtors' section of the prison. The prisoners were able, if they chose, to have their own beds from home, French maple in O'Doherty's case, and other furnishings. They shared a common room where they could receive visitors. Here O'Doherty and the others had been visited by a supporter named Miss Bruton, who brought with her the young East Galway contributor of verse to the *Nation*, Mary Anne Kelly, Eva. Just eighteen years old, Eva had come up to Dublin to visit her editors, Duffy and Martin, in prison, and to attend their trials with Miss Bruton as her chaperone. The heroic, near-operatic situation in which she encountered the valiant young physician O'Doherty must have intensified the sentiment felt by these two glittering children of the revolution. Pat Smyth, who was at the time in the process of escaping to the United States, knew Eva and would later describe her at this stage of her life as 'tall, with daydreamy eyes and wonderful black hair reaching to her knees'. O'Doherty and she fell in love.

One of the tales she was able to tell O'Doherty as she formed a lifelong attachment to him was to do with John Blake Dillon's escape. Dillon had arrived at Killeen House one evening as a fugitive: 'He had only gone off a short time when we were that night invaded by police and the magistrate. Our house was ransacked from top to bottom.' Dillon had escaped to America from Galway dressed as a priest, so well disguised that Pat Smyth, travelling under an assumed identity on the same ship, wondered why this cleric kept staring at him across the deck.

Though so young, Eva was still a maiden of rigorous views. 'The rising misnamed,' she wrote later, as an ageing woman. 'No rising. No plans or order – no leader.' She always believed that the time for striking the blow had come and gone when Mitchel was brought as a convicted felon through the streets of Dublin. 'The people were then ready – were filled with rage and enthusiasm.'

O'Doherty's second trial began five days after the first hung jury. His counsel uttered the normal complaint that out of the panel of 150 selected as potential jurors, only 30 were Catholics. But the Crown had a new document and a new witness. A fellow medical apprentice of O'Doherty's, McKeever, was asked under oath to look at a manuscript copy of 'Our Harvest Prospects' and swear that the handwriting was O'Doherty's. He did so. Isaac Butt again took up the question of O'Doherty's motives in establishing the *Irish Tribune*, pleading that his noble-hearted client's 'nerves were shocked' in the fever sheds. For Eva, watching from the gallery, there was now no *Nation* in which to publish the verses forming in her, verses in which the beloved accused's face became identical with the visage of the noble, misused nation. Amidst the venal faces of judges and lawyers who had made their accommodations with the ruling power, O'Doherty's features shone with an inspiring probity. After five hours out, the jury chairman declared that not only was there no verdict but that two jurors were ill. Pending a third trial, however, O'Doherty was refused bail.

The trial of Mitchel's gentle friend John Martin, editor of the *Felon*, had in the meantime already been held at Green Street courthouse before O'Doherty's first no-verdict. The jury was a long time out but returned to find Martin guilty on the basis of an article advising people to retain their arms. As with Mitchel, the catch-all nature of the Treason-Felony Act gave Martin little chance. The jury recommended him to mercy, since the articles had been written in disturbed political circumstances. Martin stood up to the trial with a calm courage which his delicate appearance had not prepared some observers for. Called upon to state his principles, he expressed sentiments closer to O'Brien's than Mitchel's: 'My object in all proceedings has been simply to assist in establishing the national independence of Ireland for the benefit of all the people of Ireland – noblemen, landlords, clergymen, judges, professional men – in fact, all citizens, all Irishmen.'

On his sentencing day he was brought at the rush from nearby Newgate prison into court and condemned to be transported beyond the seas for ten years. He was moved in a black carriage south of the Liffey to Richmond prison, which backed on to the Grand Canal, to await transportation. Here he had rooms on the better side of the gaol. His health was not robust and he must have despaired of his life. His brother would administer his inherited land in County Down, and, given that the blight and hardship had hit Down harder this autumn than in previous years, he was oppressed by the fact that he would not be in a position to give any succour to the local populace around his estate of Aston.

With Martin in the bag, the Dublin Commission into the State prisoners closed on 19 August, needing now to go off to Clonmel, Tipperary, to try O'Brien and his associates, leaving O'Doherty, Duffy and D'Alton Williams waiting in Newgate for the next sittings to begin on 2 October. During the week after the commission went into recess, O'Doherty was visited by a parish priest, the Reverend Dr Ennis – 'a pious corporal', said Duffy. Sent by Lord Clarendon, Ennis told O'Doherty that if he would plead guilty, he would not be called up for judgment. This proposal caused O'Doherty to consider the realities. Transported, he would not be able to finish his studies or marry adored Eva. One afternoon, in the garden at Richmond, he discussed the matter with the 'fair poetess of Portumna' herself. Possessed of all the absolutism of an untempered soul, she told him to be true to Ireland, and in return she, Eva, would be true to him. O'Doherty rejected Clarendon's offer.

By late September, O'Brien, Meagher, MacManus and O'Donohoe were gathered from Kilmainham and transported secretly by train in a jovial bunch back to face the grand jury in Clonmel, southern Tipperary's county town. In Clonmel gaol, they awaited trial for high treason. O'Brien's enlightened sister Grace, coming there to visit her brother, feared 'the cry for blood from some of the tyrannical landlords'. Sir Lucius worried as well about the influence of his brother's failed rebellion on Westminster – the government now had a pretext to ignore the latest seasonal disaster. Lucius had read in *The Times* an editorial which rang like a death sentence: 'In no other country have men talked treason until they are hoarse, and then gone about begging for sympathy from their oppressors.' Sir Lucius wrote what he hoped were instructive letters to Cabinet ministers and to those Dublin newspapers that belittled the sufferings of the countryside. He pleaded with Lord Bessborough not to suspend road works in Clare: a thousand people in the Ennis and Newmarket area would starve. 'What am I to say to them?' But in the wake of O'Brien's rebellion, the government had run out of mercy, and the British Association out of cash. The commissariat closed its depots for good and left Ireland in August. Trevelyan announced a special new poor-rate levy, to be collected from the almost universally money-short landlords and landowners, to deal with the new potato failure. For these new severe policies, most of them based on decisions taken long before Ballingarry, Smith O'Brien had to face the reproach, in veiled and in more naked form, from visitors and relatives and in a mass of gently chastising mail from his peers.

His sister Anne Martineau had now travelled from Wales to Clonmel to be close to him. 'We have had a levee all day . . . Mama seems quite up to it, and I do not think will suffer. She saw William at twelve o'clock today and bore it pretty well . . . Lucy cannot walk through the town at all as she is known and the poor prisoners' wives follow her.' Going to the abbey church with Lady O'Brien and Anne, Robert O'Brien was appalled that 'A great number of people . . . ran out to see my mother, as we drove by no man touched his hat and no woman curtseyed or said God speed. Such are the persons for whom a man of honour has sacrificed life, property, wife, children, friends.'

Smith O'Brien had adequately furnished his rooms in stony Clonmel, but Meagher decorated his own with typical stylishness. A young man named William Lyons remembered being collected from a handball game by an elder and taken to see the Young Tribune in his cell:

> we found ourselves at the end of a long corridor . . . 'That is mine,' said Meagher . . . Imagine a little room, about the size of an ordinary pantry,

lighted from the top by a large skylight, with bare whitewashed walls . . . A warm crimson cloth lined the walls, and at once removed the fever-hospital look of the place. Handsome French prints hung in rich profusion . . . a pretty sofa bedstead completely filled the farthest end of the cell. Around three sides of it were arranged well-stocked bookshelves, just within reach of his hand; he thus lay nestled in books . . . There were keepsakes as well, many of them sent by women, and a dressing table with flowers on it.

The Clonmel prisoners were, however, deprived of seeing the indictments against them until 21 September, the first day that the Judicial Commission, headed by Chief Justice Blackburne, assembled. The charges against O'Brien and his three confrères consisted of a number of counts of high treason. They were claimed 'to have levied war on our Sovereign Lady the Queen in her realm'. They had marched 'in a warlike manner through diverse villages, towns, places and highways and did maliciously and traitorously with great force and violence march to a certain dwelling house in which a large body of constables then were lawfully assembled'. They were also accused of traitorously building barricades across the highway. They had by implication attempted to destroy the Constitution and compass the death of the queen. Before a standing-room-only gallery in Nelson Street court, Clonmel, the grand jury found that the prisoners had a case to answer, 'which, in the strange jargon of criminal pleading, declared that, moved and seduced by the instigation of the Devil, they had treacherously assembled, with divers other false traitors, at Ballingarry'.

Observed by parties hostile and friendly, by correspondents from *The Times* and the Irish papers, by artists from the pictorials, on 29 September O'Brien was the first to go to trial. Bare-headed, he rose from his holding cell into a courtroom which not only had a crammed floor but a crowded and emotionally engaged public gallery. Applause greeted him. He seemed composed. James Whiteside, QC, chief counsel for O'Brien and the others, who had defended O'Connell in his prosecution after Clontarf, had no input into jury selection and complained that the panel of jurors was taken from the grand jury list which had already found O'Brien had a case to answer. A hundred possibly sympathetic men had been struck off the panel. In a recent English case against a Chartist named Frost, the jury had been taken from the panel by ballot, and Mr Whiteside asked that this be the method of proceeding in Clonmel. But Attorney-General Monahan, who had the jury he wanted, did not consent.

The prosecution produced against O'Brien a letter from Duffy, the one found in O'Brien's seized portmanteau. Written a few weeks before the uprising, it urged O'Brien to more decisive action. Duffy was dubbed by the Solicitor-General a 'diabolical tempter'. He was offering O'Brien a lifeline – to agree to the mitigating factor that Duffy had had a seductive effect on him. To tears and shaken heads from Lucy and Lady O'Brien, William refused to seize the chance. 'I must say that it is wrong,' O'Brien told the court, 'at a time that gentleman himself is awaiting his trial, to take this opportunity of prejudicing the public mind against him.'

A policeman was brought forward and told the Solicitor-General that when the police at the Widow McCormack's refused to surrender, O'Brien said, 'Slash away, boys, and slaughter the whole of them.' O'Brien cried, with an 'abrupt vehemence', 'Don't you know you are swearing falsely when you swear that, sir?' Grace, staying in Golden Cottages in Clonmel, and coming every day to court to see her brother, wrote, 'I become every day more alive to one fact – it was not so much because the Young Ireland Party ministered to William's vanity that he was taken by them' (as her mother believed) '. . . as that among them alone he found that deep sympathy in the dreams of his youth that he found nowhere else.'

Whiteside's defence of O'Brien began and was eloquently managed. He urged that O'Brien's behaviour was based on a desire not to be arrested, 'and not in pursuance of a universal design'. He made much of O'Brien's family – O'Brien had heard from his father how Union with England 'was carried with corruption. That father recounted to my client what Plunket, Bushe and Grattan spoke on the last memorable night of our national existence.' And other family considerations were invoked by Whiteside. 'A venerable lady, who had dwelt amidst an affectionate tenantry, spending her income where it was raised, diffusing her charities and her blessings around, awaits now, with trembling heart, your verdict . . . Alas! More dreadful still – six innocent children will hear from your lips whether they are to be stripped of an inheritance which has descended in this family for ages.' At this point, O'Brien suffered a storm of grief. The correspondent of the *Illustrated London News* said: 'The prisoner shed tears towards the conclusion, and on the faces of many . . . the same evidences of deep emotion were visible.'

Character witnesses for O'Brien, including parliamentarians Sir David Roche, Sir Denham Norreys, and an old parliamentary friend Mr Monsell, brother-in-law of Harriett O'Brien, the prisoner's sister, had been produced to prove that throughout his parliamentary career O'Brien's opinions had been 'favourable to constitutional agitation and to the monarchy, and opposed to Republicanism and Communism'. And the supreme character witness was the handsomest and most heroic officer in the British army, Sir William Napier, a Scots Irishman. Napier had considered taking up arms in support of the Reform Bill of 1832, which had broadened the electoral system of Great Britain. A Whig prime minister, Lord Melbourne, had arranged secretly with Napier that if the

Tories blocked reform, he should take command of the artisans of Birmingham. Napier was not only willing to give potent testimony to O'Brien's uprightness of character, but answered questions about his own involvement in what he called 'Reform agitation'. It was all in a letter, he testified, written to him by Mr Young, private secretary to Lord Melbourne. The prosecution appealed to the court to disallow a question about the contents of this letter, and Justice Blackburne agreed.

O'Brien's trial lasted a mere eleven days, considered short given the complexities and penalties attaching to the charge of high treason. Prosecution concluded, the jury retired, but came back not in days but in a few hours with a guilty verdict, coupled with a recommendation that O'Brien should be spared the statutory brutality attached to high treason. Judgment calmed and stiffened O'Brien. Following the verdict, he manifested a 'self-possessed countenance'. When the court adjourned overnight, O'Brien ate a normal gentleman's dinner with Meagher and the others in the common room in Clonmel prison, and spent the normal talkative hours. They surmised that things might go badly for MacManus and O'Donohoe. But Meagher had not been at Ballingarry. Because of all his galloping around rallying people in Waterford, Callan and on Slievenamon, he had not so much as directed a muzzle at the Crown.

The next morning, a Monday, Lucy's blood must have run cold at the economical and impenitent speech O'Brien made before sentence was imposed. 'My Lords . . . I am perfectly satisfied with the consciousness that I have performed my duty to my country; that I have done only that which, in my opinion, it was the duty of every Irishman to have done . . . Proceed with your sentence.' There were huge cheers from the gallery. Journalists prepared for the dash to the telegraph office, but so did many laypersons who simply wanted to send the grievous news off as soon as the statutory sentence was uttered.

> The sentence is, that you, William Smith O'Brien, be taken from hence to the place from whence you came, and be thence drawn on a hurdle to the place of execution, and be there hanged by the neck until you are dead; and that afterwards your head shall be severed from your body, and your body divided into four quarters, and to be disposed of as Her Majesty shall think fit. And may the Lord have mercy on your soul.

A profound sensation followed. Friends rushed forward to bid O'Brien farewell. He leaned down from the dock and shook hands. 'Several women ran to the gates shrieking and throwing up their arms in violent grief.' Despite the family bemusement, Robert O'Brien felt it had to be admitted that the 'trial was fair and the verdict just'. Robert possessed a particular view of why his brother had been seduced into high treason. 'Sad indeed is the contemplation of what a person may be driven to by allowing his mind continually to foster a feeling of discontent of everything about him.' So Lady O'Brien saw vanity in her son, and Robert a maiming melancholy in his brother.

Later, when Lucy and Lady O'Brien visited him in the room where the State prisoners received their guests, their mouths were twisted with similar loving incomprehension, and O'Brien comforted them softly but intractably.

On 9 October, MacManus almost routinely stood trial. 'MacManus's achievements in Tipperary were proved by the Crown,' Duffy succinctly wrote, 'and the only answer it was possible to make was to exhibit his personal and commercial character in the favourable light they deserved.'

One of the documents presented against MacManus was a letter from Philadelphia, dated 10 May 1848, signed by Robert Tyler, son of President Tyler, offering the support of American citizens in the coming struggle 'in any mode they think proper to designate'. The jury quickly found MacManus guilty, and sentencing was held over. And so next, hapless O'Donohoe, who through the support of the other prisoners, notably of Tom Meagher, had the same excellent counsel. Isaac Butt argued that although O'Donohoe had been present at Ballingarry he was 'ignorant of treasonable intent'. He was found guilty on 17 October, and he too was held for sentencing.

Adored Tom Meagher was now to stand trial, beginning on 18 October. 'I understand that four hundred of the Rifles are ordered to this town immediately,' the *Times* correspondent told his readers. In contrast to the number of O'Briens in Clonmel, an eloquent absence was that of Thomas Meagher the elder – even though it was largely his money which had guaranteed Meagher and O'Donohoe a gentlemanly incarceration and a good defence. Thomas Meagher senior certainly disapproved of his son's summer rashness, but did not believe these men should be tried under the severe rubric of high treason by an administration which had so unjustly and typically suspended Habeas Corpus.

The trial begun, the *Times* correspondent in Clonmel reported 'the court was greatly crowded and the majority of those in the galleries were ladies. The prisoner had frequent demands for autographs.' The case against Meagher was weakest, but the Attorney-General reminded the jury that in treason there was no such thing as an accessory – all the persons engaged were principals. Meagher's speeches were used as evidence. Butt argued that most of them had been made at least six months before Ballingarry, and words on their own could not constitute high treason. If the jury pronounced Meagher guilty, their verdict would mean that on their oaths they found that he *had* appeared in arms at Mullinahone and erected barricades, etc. Meagher did not seem to lose any standing at all amongst his fellows through his lawyers having used such a defence. 'You may be well assured,' wrote Gavan Duffy, 'that this contention had not Meagher's assent.'

The Attorney-General now produced an elderly police sergeant whom Meagher had met on Young Ireland's progress through Callan, and the old man proved less than willing to swear that in conversation Meagher had uttered traitorous sentiments. Whiteside asked the old man what his conversation with Meagher had been.

Sergeant: 'Only I told him I was at his grandfather's funeral.'

Whiteside: 'Then, sir, the sum total of your connection with Mr Meagher is that you told him you were at his grandfather's funeral?'

Sergeant: 'Why then, that's all; and I agree with the Learned Counsel, that much is not much.'

This reply, said to have produced 'convulsions' in court, showed Meagher had his admirers even amongst the police. As for the clergy, contrary to expectations Meagher did not use the trial as a forum to express his disappointment in them.

On 22 October, the jury returned a verdict of guilty against Meagher with a recommendation of mercy on account of his youth. Sentencing of MacManus, O'Donohoe and Meagher occurred at once. In the customary pre-sentence speech MacManus said that he placed his life, and, above all, his honour, in the hands of his advocates, and faced the sentence which awaited him with a light heart and a free conscience. He had passed some of the happiest and most prosperous years of his life in England, and his actions did not bespeak enmity to England but love of his own country. Both MacManus and O'Donohoe were briskly sentenced to death, and waited serenely in the holding cells under the dock for Meagher's sentencing.

Had Meagher in particular pleaded for mercy, it might have been given. But he believed it would be spiritual death, and death of honour, to do so. His speech from the dock proved of the same character as Smith O'Brien's, equally likely to seal the prisoner's fate, but it was of course more overtly eloquent – prepared and delivered as if he fully expected that in short order it should be printed up on handbills; as if he foresaw the generations of fair and freckled Celtic children who on St Patrick's Day concerts from Derry to Montreal, from Butte, Montana, to Sydney, would recite it. He had no enmity against the jury, he said, for Chief Justice Blackburne had left them no option but to find him guilty.

To the efforts I have made, in a just and noble cause, I ascribe no vain importance, nor do I claim for those efforts any high reward. But it so happens, and it will ever happen so, that they who have tried to serve their country, no matter how weak the efforts may have been, are sure to receive the thanks and blessings of its people. I am here to regret nothing I have already done, to retract nothing I have already said. I am here to crave, with no lying lip, the life I consecrate to the liberty of my country . . . To lift this island up – to make her a benefactor to humanity instead of being the meanest beggar in the world – to restore to her her native powers and her ancient constitution, this has been my ambition, and this ambition has been my crime. Judged by the law of England I know this crime entails the penalty of death; but the history of Ireland explains this crime, and justifies it . . . I hope to be able with a pure heart and perfect composure to appear before a higher tribunal – a tribunal where a Judge of infinite goodness, as well as of justice, will preside, and where, my Lords, many – many of the judgments of this court will be reversed.

This conclusive spate of oratory, thunderously cheered from the gallery, brought the Confederate prisoners to the close of a trial in which they had all behaved well. Blackburne and the other judges put on their black caps and Justice Doherty told Meagher that with MacManus and O'Donohoe he too would be drawn on a hurdle to the place of execution, to be there hanged by the neck, et cetera. Meagher's fellow prisoners, expecting him to be acquitted, waited for him to come down the stairwell from the court, from the enraptured and weeping gallery to the holding cells. 'We received him at the end of the corridor, and through the iron gateway grasped his hand. He laughed quietly when he met us. "I am guilty and convicted for the old country . . . Come into the cell, and let me have my dinner."'

It became known in Clonmel that the four condemned were to be conveyed to Dublin under an escort of dragoons. The prisoners were ordered to pack and hurried out of the gaol at three o'clock in the morning, and were far on their route before daylight. Several young men were arrested by the military earlier that past night while holding a secret but premature rescue meeting in a glen outside the town.

While the Clonmel trials were in progress, Duffy in Newgate had been brought by one of his visitors a sturdy rope ladder. He had raised with O'Doherty the idea of escape to America. Through some of their visitors, Duffy and O'Doherty arranged for a small vessel to be hired, and a date in late October was given for an attempt at escape, to be made from a prison courtyard at midnight.

But at noon on the day of the proposed escape, O'Doherty saw the governor and deputy-governor of Newgate, and an official from the Castle, conversing earnestly with a guard Duffy had thought sympathetic to the escape. Duffy tried to run with the ladder to the 'jakes', the latrines, and drop it in. The governor and his colleagues got to his cell door before he could do it. In punishment, Duffy and O'Doherty were moved out of their rooms and locked in a stone cell under a double guard. The traducing guard, Hutchinson, displayed the near-pathological duality of loyalties within the one breast, the duality many considered the true national disease. He told the authorities that though he had co-operated in preventing the escape, he remained a devout Confederate. Dublin Castle, having first rewarded him, now sacked him.

Kevin Izod O'Doherty, beloved of Eva, was tried a third time in Green Street, on 30 October. 'On this occasion the jury were more securely packed,' said Duffy. They found him guilty but strongly recommended him to mercy. The panel of judges sentenced him to ten years' transportation. O'Doherty's fellow editor D'Alton Williams was found not guilty. His servant swore – a Catholic witness swearing on the King James Bible – that Williams had been ill for the two weeks before his arrest, and could not therefore have written the articles to which the Crown took exception.

O'Doherty was now moved from Newgate prison across the river to a cell in Richmond bridewell, a prison for civil cases, where Martin was already in place. He found the Clonmel condemned – O'Brien, Meagher, MacManus, O'Donohoe – were exalted by the support and outrage of their fellow countrymen. Even the *Warder*, organ of Orange-ism, complained that O'Brien savoured 'his delicious immortality' with 'the irrepressible complacency of a gratified coxcomb'. The Young Irelanders had, by the nature of their sentence, been 'divested of their farcicality'.

Lady O'Brien was not as grateful as others for her son's services to the Irish people. She sent him nineteen closely written pages marked *Political Duty*. 'Persons are in very great error who suppose that men may disturb the country to promote political changes without being morally guilty.' But sweeter missives came in, a typical one from an Irish doctor named O'Hanlon in Wisconsin: 'How I would like to be your ordinary medical attendant in the fertile and happy territory of Wisconsin . . . where souls are free and tyrants taint not nature's bliss.'

O'Brien would always ruggedly maintain that his resistance was not a moral violation but a crucial gesture of defiance. There would be many references in his later journal to Thermopylae, Artemisium, Salamis and Platea, physically lost but morally won battles of antiquity. If these threw an improving light upon the Battle of Ballingarry, as winter came on in Richmond he refused to renounce the impulses of the summer of 1848. The apology to the British government for which his family waited, as a prelude to possible official mercy, would never be offered.

Nor was he the only unrepentant Irish prisoner that autumn. In Mayo, Mr Michael Shaughnessy, the Assistant Barrister, a court officer who travelled on circuit with judges, complained that many of the children he interviewed pleaded with him for sentences of transportation to Van Diemen's Land. Since the suspension of transportation to New South Wales, Van Diemen's Land had received thirty-one Irish transports between 1840 and 1848. Shaughnessy noted that the children of Mayo were 'almost naked, hair standing on end, eyes sunken, lips pallid, protruding bones of little joints visible'. At Westport, one such youth, Dominick Ginelly, a 17-year-old charged with stealing hemp rope, said he would do it again if only he could be transported. The judge obliged by giving him a 7-year sentence. John Austin, 12, and Charles Ruddy, 15 years old, were 'honest people's children from Clare Island', where more than a third of the population had died. The boys were found guilty of sheep-stealing and transported for seven years. Michael Gavin, Thomas Joyce, Martin McGinty, John McGrene, John English, all about seventeen, pleaded with Shaughnessy to be transported. A youth named Owen Eady said that even if he wore chains he would have something to eat. Mr Shaughnessy wrote, 'I am satisfied that they have no alternative but starvation or the commission of crime.'

Many of Mr Shaughnessy's boys were transported to Van Diemen's Land, though one, Michael Gavin, perished in Spike Island. Dominick Ginelly, the hemp rope thief, and Thomas Joyce, after a considerable wait in prison, arrived in Hobart in March 1851 aboard the *London*. Martin McGinty was on the *Blenheim* which put into Hobart in July 1851. Eady travelled on the *Rodney* from Cork and did not arrive until December. Their descendants are at large today in Australia.

In Lismany, in that season when Mayo boys pleaded with the court, Esther Larkin had like a million others at first thought herself lucky. The potato flowers had been in expected, normal bloom. But when her sons drove their spades into the earth for the tubers, the fruit was again reduced to a black rotten mass by contact with the air. So began what was for her and her region the worst year of that Famine Trevelyan said had ended. Over this coming winter and on into the summer of 1849, Esther, unless saved by a financial input from Hugh, would witness what was for the country south of Ballinasloe a new level of hunger and thus of disease amongst locals. There would in fact now be a higher death-rate than in those previously stricken regions, West Cork, Mayo, Connemara, which no longer possessed enough population to figure as highly in the statistics.

By this stage the resources of many proprietors such as the Seymours were near exhausted. The Marquess of Sligo, a 28-year-old progressive, had to borrow to pay the poor rate and was rumoured to be living off rentals of the family box at the Covent Garden Opera. Lord Clarendon at Dublin Castle applied to Lord John Russell for a loan from the Treasury to meet the new emergency of the 1848 blight. Lord John replied negatively, 'the reason being rage against Ireland on account of its faction, its mendicancy, its ingratitude'.

This effect of the blight of 1848, extending bitterly into the following year, had brought what modern aid bodies call 'compassion fatigue' in British donors. But Patrick and Hugh, if able to get seeds, may, like other East Galway people, have planted a few turnips as a hedge against potato blight. Rural society had fallen into two camps, turnip growers and turnip thieves. In the barony of Longford, people had to stay up at night to guard their turnips from frantic men and women who came to dig them up with spades muffled with cloth. The thieving of vegetables was a matter of shame, social and moral, and for both parties. Before the Famine, a man or woman gave away food to show they had a stake in the earth and were agents of Christ's charity. Now man-traps were dug in turnip fields.

Esther was forced back on whatever little store of yellow meal she retained from the now closed Ballinasloe commissary. This despised foodstuff was the perverse sacrament of the Famine: once you were forced to consume it, death began to make its claim! Even to throw something more accustomed, a cabbage head say, into the mess of beggar's meal – a combination named *brawlum* – redeemed a person from utter shame and terror. Some in this earth of gentle hills and peat bogs were furtively eating ashes, and asking God's forgiveness for making such a foul choice.

Since October 1847 the British Association had been feeding 200,000 orphan children under a scheme devised by its chief agent in Ireland, that remarkable Count Strzelecki, who in his avocation of explorer knew the same line of country as Hugh Larkin. Paul Strzelecki, now nearly fifty years of age, and still living off modest income from family property on the Polish-Russian border, had at first involved himself as agent of the association for the district of County Mayo. Like modern aid administrators, he quickly saw how a lack of storage facilities made hunger worse. The town of Clifden, he observed, 'exhibits a most astonishing absence of the common agencies by which, in towns and markets, food is concentrated, stored, and redistributed'. From Westport, Mayo, he had assured Association headquarters in London, 'You may now believe anything which you hear and read, because what I actually see surpasses what I ever read of past and present calamities.' On Ireland's disastrous western fringe, he had devised a scheme for feeding children warm broth and rye bread through the agency of local schools.

By the summer of 1847, Strzelecki had become the chief agent of the British Association in Ireland. He extended his system of feeding children broadly throughout the so-called 'distressed unions' and beyond, and the cost of doing this he estimated at one third of a penny per child per day. Throughout Mayo, in Ballina and Swinford, schools sprang up in profusion, chiefly to act as feeding centres under the supervision of local clergy. Captain Mann of the Kilrush Union wrote to the association on 14 February 1848, 'I cannot tell you how much benefit is derived from feeding the destitute children at the Schools; it prevents the little creatures from starving, and improves their habits, and leaves the parents free to seek for their subsistence.'

In late 1847, the British Association in London passed resolutions acceding to Trevelyan's demand that a limited list of 'distressed unions' be drawn up, in which all further relief would be concentrated. The names of twenty-two unions were selected by Strzelecki. In practice his children's scheme and aid to Poor Law unions continued in many more unions than that, until in the summer of O'Brien's uprising he began to run out of funds. Lord John Russell promised that the government would take up the burden of feeding children, but only in the unions on the list of twenty-two.

The admirable expenditures of the British Association, founded at the start of 1847, came to £603,535 8 shillings and 2 pence as at 25 December 1848. Between October 1847 and July 1848, when his funds for the purpose ran out, Strzelecki's children's and Poor Law unions' operation distributed £249,386. In the same period the British government expended £156,060 on relief.

As the British Association's resources gave out, it was warned by the newly knighted Treasury Secretary Sir Charles Trevelyan not to devise any new programmes 'which would produce the impression that the lavish charitable system of last season is intended to be renewed'. In disbanding itself, the association gently attacked the critics of aid to Ireland: 'Any evils which may have accompanied its distribution have been far more than counter-balanced by the great benefits.'

Strzelecki himself refused payment for his services to the British Association. But in Lismany's harshest season, he – like the world – was turning to other causes and possibilities.

12

Shipping Young Ireland

> Below decks, chairs, casks, books, basins, trunks, jugs, hat cases, spoons, every conceivable article of dress and furniture . . . all came cracking, crashing, spitting . . . in one miscellaneous heap together, mingling and interweaving with coats, tablecloths, suspenders, Scotch plaids, shirt collars, slippers and pillow cases, utterly effacing all signs and tokens of our life, and burying us alive, like the citizens of Pompeii, beneath the complicated ruins of commerce, conviviality, literature, and the fine arts.
>
> Thomas Francis Meagher,
> on a storm aboard *Swift*, 1849

In Van Diemen's Land, Britain's furthest penal colony of all, the ramrod governor Sir William Denison received a dispatch from Earl Grey, Secretary of State for the Colonies, dated 5 June 1849, which told him that the British government had decided to commute the sentences of the condemned Irish State prisoners and send them to him. The miscreant journalists John Martin and Kevin O'Doherty would also be sent. The dispatch instructed Denison that, with consideration of the prisoners' superior rank in society, they were not at first to be subjected to hard labour, for that would aggrieve domestic and international opinion. If the captain of the ship which brought them to Van Diemen's Land reported well on their behaviour, Denison was to offer them special paroles, tickets-of-leave, 'placing them as far as you can in separate Districts at a distance from the Capital'. If they misbehaved, they could be 'thrown back among the ordinary offenders'.

Denison was a strong-willed military engineer who had at one stage worked in that same dockyard at Ireland Island, Bermuda, where John Mitchel had lately been a prisoner. He had also been involved in the building of the Rideau Canal in Canada. A scholar in matters to do with forestry, geology and natural history, he had a two-dimensional attitude to the penal system: talk of reform was 'maudlin sentimentality'. In his robust mid-forties, his soul-mates were his mother in London, to whom he confided all his administrative problems, and his wife Caroline, a vigorous helpmeet who agreed thoroughly with his principles. She already thought that 'if, indeed, he might put them into grey jackets and send them to wheel barrows on the wharf, or break stones on the roads, like any ordinary convict, it would simplify the matter very considerably'.

*

The subjects of the dispatch had been living many months in Richmond bridewell. There Meagher's exuberance the previous autumn was unbounded when he received news of the escape of Michael Doheny, safe in New York. Meagher wrote to Doheny, 'I made the infernal corridors ring with a shout of glee – and in this manifestation I was ably assisted by fourteen other voices amongst which Smith O'Brien's was thrillingly effective.' O'Brien reported to his sister Anne Martineau in Wales that the end of autumn and the stony environment had brought him lumbago. But though the costs of *Queen* vs *W. S. O'Brien, Esq. MP* were £381 18 shillings and 4 pence, about half of what was considered a gentlemanly income, stately O'Brien was able to live frugally well in Richmond. He was permitted to occupy two rooms in the residence of the governor and had the use of two courtyards with gardens. A servant from Cahirmoyle was provided by his wife Lucy, and his food was supplied amply from Dromoland, Cahirmoyle and the Dublin markets. His lawyers had of course filed a writ of error before the House of Lords. Meagher and MacManus did not join in this appeal in case they might be thought afraid of a martyr's death. But O'Brien, driven both by principle and the acute fear of forfeiting his estate, his children's inheritance, to the Crown, wanted to test the legitimacy of the concept of *treason* in occupied Ireland.

During their confinement, Meagher read in his book-lined cell; MacManus had got a box of tools and was turning out knick-knacks; and O'Doherty, who had not received a death sentence, was studying huge medical tomes for a surgical future. O'Donohoe was able to live like the others through the generosity of O'Brien, Meagher and various Confederate supporters. He fell into depressions, though, about what would befall his wife and child. Unfortunately O'Brien and MacManus found his fits both of depression and manic exuberance irksome. He was awkward in drink.

In windy December in Bermuda, three convicts from John Mitchel's hulk had tried to row away to North America but were recovered and flogged. Mitchel watched the ceremonial punishment administered before lines of convicts and soldiers on the breakwater, and felt oppressed; another fillip to the asthma which kept him awake at night. Dr Hall, medical superintendent of the entire convict establishment, advised him that he would not get better in Bermuda. 'I assure you many hundreds of men have died here who need not have died.' Mitchel could be moved out if he would consent to petition the colonial governor. The absolutist Mitchel declared, 'I will never, by throwing myself on the mercy of the English Government, confess myself to be a felon.' But after further vicious bouts, he decided to apply to the governor of Bermuda. His appeal had not been answered by Christmas Day, 1848, when there was a service on deck, with the entire hulk reeking pleasantly of plum pudding.

A jolly enough Christmas 1848 was spent by the Richmond prisoners. William Smith O'Brien dispatched a charming note to his mother, Lady O'Brien, inviting her to dine at three o'clock with the family 'at our Christmas table'. Grace O'Brien, as ever, found Meagher amusing, and Lucy did her best to chuckle while having at her breast the recently born seventh child of the O'Briens, a son. O'Brien was not as worried about his land as he had been, she noticed. On the advice of his lawyers, O'Brien intended to place his property in trust, to secure it for his family, should he be executed, Cahirmoyle being managed for his eldest son, Edward, by his brother and trustee Robert. Lucy and the children would live at Dromoland Castle, which was huge enough to absorb the brood. It seemed a wise provision at the time.

Some 12,000 miles removed from Richmond prison and Lismany's bleak crossroads, Mary and Hugh faced each other over ham and poultry in the normal sweltering but enthusiastically celebrated Australian holiday season, and doused memory and imagination in rum, ale and the bounty of the country, all at a table where their first Australian child Tom sat, and their newborn infant daughter Anne was at Mary's breast, and where a strapping adolescent Michael O'Flynn, who had learned to ride and crack a whip and rope steers in Monaro, had a seat as well.

O'Brien's brother Robert, managing Cahirmoyle, wrote to his brother in February 1849 with restrained compassion both for William and the local peasantry. 'I regret your absence for the sake of the poor as well as for your own account . . . The men called able-bodied who are evidently stumbling with fever, dysentery and the course of famine are now refused all relief.' The local overseer of public works had told Robert that two thirds of the men on these works were suffering from dysentery.

In East Galway in those early months of 1849, a new epidemic of cholera descended as the Famine's final deft killer. By March 1849 it dropped people in their tracks in Lismany and Laurencetown. Peasant women who had always dressed elegantly for Sunday Mass were now clothed in shreds. One of Ballinasloe's two hated pawnbrokers, William Hines, told the Poor Law commissioners: 'Latterly wearing apparel has not been much afforded; instead articles such as blankets and sheets were being pawned indicating a more advanced stage of distress.'

Cholera increased the number of cremations, some of which Esther beheld with a numbed horror. 'Michael Garvey got the cholera, and he and the entire household succumbed . . . He had a daughter, and had she survived she would have been the finest girl in the parish of Dún Chaoin.

Somebody went to their cottage door, and could see that they were all dead. All they did then was to set fire to the thatch on the cottage, burn it, and knock in the walls.'

Because people were now without remaining resources to take into the summer, in June 1849, about the time Earl Grey was writing to Governor Denison of Van Diemen's Land, the highest number of people ever were sheltering in Irish workhouses – 227,000 inmates. The following month the highest number on outdoor relief occurred: 800,000. So, in the summer of 1849, over one million people would be in receipt of relief, despite the fact that close on two million were already dead or emigrated.

In seeing her community shrink, Esther suffered like others a peculiarly daunting sense of being in a cursed place in which the populace was subject to a bitter culling. She had until about 1846 lived in a world of natural increase in population. Not any more. Even the bare facts for the barony of Longford supported her perception. At the start of the Famine there were nearly 6,000 habitations. By the end of the decade there were less than 3,900. The population similarly fell from more than 33,000 to 21,000. The smaller electoral division of Laurencetown dropped from 1,650 people to just over 1,000.

But there were to be no further universal blights for now. In an altered Ireland, hunger and fever imperceptibly relaxed their fierce disciplines. At the end of the attrition, Esther, according to local memory, was still standing, and her sons certainly were, already knowing more of humanity than was safe. At some time in the 1840s Seymour's lease on Somerset House expired and was taken over by a Scots family named Pollack, who gained a local reputation as ruthless evictors. Esther continued to walk to work, however, for the Seymours, who took over a local property named Grove Hill, and she laboured a few years there until her sons were fully grown and took over her care.

Gavan Duffy, the man most likely to share Mitchel's exile, would be tried on the present charges five times without a verdict being reached, the last trial closing on Good Friday, 1849: '*Dies Irae* but with the hope of resurrection'. At midnight, with the court 'as crowded as a theatre on a command night', the Sheriff announced that the jury could not agree. 'A shout of triumph, that made the roof ring, burst from the audience . . . Bankers, magistrates, manufacturers, desired to pronounce a verdict of not guilty. They were locked up all night, and twelve hours reflection added one more to the number for acquittal.' The Attorney-General admitted him to bail, and it was clear Duffy would not be further prosecuted: 'So I saw the daylight again. I walked out amongst stalwart men whose manly faces were wet with tears.'

The writ of error against the finding of high treason which O'Brien had taken was heard in the House of Lords in May 1849. It was based on a claim that the statute of Edward III had defined treason as levying 'war against the King in his realm'. Ireland had not been a realm of Edward III. But the Lords dismissed the writ, and their judgment caused not a ripple of agitation in Thomas Meagher, who was planning parties. 'My dear O'Farrell,' he wrote to Michael O'Farrell, junior counsel to O'Loghlen and Butt, 'we shall have a little Soiree here on Monday evening, and we all jointly unite in requesting the very considerable pleasure of your company . . . The Governor has most kindly given us the use of his apartments, and desires me to intimate to all our friends his wish that they *should ask at the hatch* [that is, at the outward gate] *for the Governor*.'

Mitchel had heard at last, in his cell in a Bermuda hulk, of the death sentences against O'Brien and the others, and complained in frustration that a 'mighty game of sixty years' was beginning, and yet he would have 'through all these crowded years of life, to sit panting here . . . and rot among Bermudian blattae beetles'.

But there was now a chance he might escape the beetles. A committee of officers selected Mitchel amongst men to be sent to the Cape of Good Hope, South Africa. This new penal venue had been chosen because the populace of New South Wales had balked at receiving more convicts. '*Me vel extremos Numidarum in agros, Classe releget*,' wrote Mitchel. 'He banishes me therefore by sea to the furthest fields of the Numidians.'

The transport for Africa, *Neptune*, 700 tons, arrived in Bermuda on 5 April that year. Its officers socialised on the hulks. Though Mitchel was delighted to find from the newspapers brought by them that Duffy had been released, he thought Duffy's defence was 'wretched work'. Duffy had Father Matthew in court to say that he was pious, the novelist Carleton to say that he was a solid citizen, and he had also pretended that the articles for which he was prosecuted were written by someone else.

Members of Parliament, Mitchel also discovered, had been asking questions about his kindly treatment. Was he convict No. 2014, it was asked in the House, or was he not a convict at all? Mitchel himself saw the logic of these questions; he despised the policy of pretending he was a convict but making special accommodations for him. But as the cedars of Bermuda receded, he found perhaps that some special accommodations also marked his time on *Neptune*. At sea he was permitted to walk the poop deck, but in silence, while far forward the other prisoners in their Bermuda uniforms swarmed over the deck. The captain and mates would not risk talking to him. The biblical instructor, a Glaswegian, immune to fear of parliamentary questions, loaned him books.

By July 1849, *Neptune* had tacked back and forth three times across the Equator looking for winds. The drinking water aboard 'has grown very bad, black, hot and populous with living creatures'. Seven prisoners had died. The transport turned towards Pernambuco in Brazil to re-provision. When, off the hip of South America, rain came, 'I went out to the gangway, stark naked, and stood there awhile, luxuriating in the plenteous shower-bath'. Soon there was the added pleasure of mooring in Recife, Pernambuco province's chief port. From his strolling place on the poop deck, Mitchel was delighted after the monotony of ocean to see the vigorous vegetable life on the mountains, and the sides of fresh beef, panniers of yams, limes and oranges, being brought aboard. Most significantly, watching, he beheld for the first time 'a slave in his slavery – I mean a merchantable slave, a slave of real money-value, whom a prudent man will, in the way of business, pay for and feed afterwards'. The state of the slave carrying the fruit and beef aboard seemed preferable to that of Irish peasants. 'Is it better, then, to be the slave of a merciful master and a just man, or to be serf to an Irish land-appropriator?' It was a question that in time would harry him and devour his sons.

The same day Earl Grey was drafting the Denison dispatch, 5 June 1849, O'Brien, O'Donohoe, Meagher and MacManus were called out of their rooms at Richmond prison into the yard to hear a letter from Sir Thomas Redington announcing that the death sentences had been commuted to transportation for life. O'Brien still thought a pardon a possibility and did not consider transportation a legal option. In Van Diemen's Land too, he would be removed not only from the comfort of his family, but from the support, comfort and faith of the Irish. Immediately he sat down to write a letter to the Sheriff of the city of Dublin, advising him 'that it is not compellent for the Government to cause me to be transported without my own consent'. A further letter to Sir Colman O'Loghlen asked him to obtain a writ of Habeas Corpus, it having by now been restored.

Descending the staircase from O'Brien's rooms that day, Sir Colman O'Loghlen and the young counsel Michael O'Farrell met Lady O'Brien and William's sister Grace ascending. 'Oh my son, my poor son,' exclaimed Lady O'Brien. Grace told them in passing, 'He will be transported at seven o'clock tonight.' Indeed, a transport named *Mount Stewart Elphinstone* had arrived in Cork, and it was intended the prisoners be sent to join it. The immediate and engrossing game for O'Brien and the others was to ensure *Elphinstone*, also loading general convicts from Spike Island, left without them. O'Loghlen and O'Farrell rushed off for Dublin Castle to find Redington, but it was Saturday evening and they could not. O'Loghlen surmised the authorities had chosen a Saturday to act because it would not be possible to get a writ of Habeas Corpus out of any judge on a Saturday night or Sunday, by which time the prisoners would be on a steamer to Cork.

Going back to the prison, O'Farrell found a police van in the courtyard and the prisoners – his friend Tom Meagher calling out something whimsical – lined up to enter it. As the prisoners and O'Farrell argued for a delay, an order came to postpone the movement. The escorts of dragoons and mounted police trotted away. Towards midnight Butt, O'Loghlen and O'Farrell raced along to the Merrion Square house of Baron Pennefather, a friend of the O'Brien family. When a servant admitted them, Pennefather descended the stairs in his dressing gown, consulted Redington's order, heard the arguments of the lawyers, and at once issued a writ. The Whig government would now need to pass an enabling Act to make it lawful to transport the condemned men to Australia. Though O'Doherty and Martin were not protected by this technicality, for the moment they were also spared a sudden move.

O'Brien's friends in the House of Commons, including Chisholm Anstey, a Young Irelander, and Sir Lucius O'Brien, were assigned the job of trying to delay the enabling bill, since transportation meant their rebellion had been branded a felony. In the meantime, while Governor Denison of Van Diemen's Land awaited him, young Meagher expatiated on his politics to a visitor of uncertain identity who took notes. This supposed red republican showed a sentimental leaning towards an Irish monarchy of the old Gaelic type. He considered a republic the highest order of government, but one which required a nearly impossible level of intelligence and virtue amongst the citizens. However, 'Had the Irish people fought and been victorious,' this unspecified visitor wrote, 'Meagher would have insisted upon a republic as a compensation for their blood, and in honour of their heroism.' At the end of all his speeches he was like O'Connell in trying to avoid being closely identified with the atheistic or deistic revolutionary movements of Europe. 'He did not desire to *import*, as he often said to me, any of the "raw modernisms" of the Continental Revolutions.' This view of Meagher, no doubt reasonably accurate, was nonetheless intended for ultimate publication and designed to exculpate him with all those who considered him a red and a heretic.

Kevin O'Doherty and John Martin were roused at five o'clock on 16 June, given an hour to pack and say goodbye, and, without a chance for O'Doherty to scribble something to Eva, taken at the gallop across town attended 'by a nearly complete regiment of dragoons', and put aboard a warship, the *Trident*, for Cork. There they were transferred straight to the conventional convict transport, *Mount Stewart Elphinstone*, which already had on board 163 English prisoners from Pentonville, Millbank and the hulks at Woolwich, and 70 Irish convicts loaded at Cork. The captain's orders, O'Doherty and Martin were told, were to deliver the entire penal *mélange* to Sydney, and receive further orders there from the governor, FitzRoy. While O'Doherty and Martin were certainly bound for Van Diemen's Land, it was correctly suspected that the others were all to go to the convict settlement of Moreton Bay, more than 600 miles north of Sydney.

On *Elphinstone*, a number of cabins had been specially built for the State prisoners, each of which contained a mahogany sofa. O'Doherty and Martin expected that the rest of the State prisoners would join them in this space. In the meantime, Captain Loney permitted O'Doherty to receive last letters and poetry from his pure, betrothed, heroic Eva. He read them for comfort and was cheered by Martin, who would prove adept in dealing with the younger man's depression. But no one else would be joining them. The debate on the enabling bill, and its passage through the Commons and Lords, occupied weeks.

In Richmond MacManus now gleefully told the young lawyer O'Farrell, 'You will doubtless be surprised to hear that we have a new ally – Viz the cholera – There are three cases on board "The Elphinstone" yesterday . . . Would it not be well for some member to move an amendment that we should be allowed to transport ourselves, and that the money it will cost the Govt. be applied to the relief of the dying in Connaught?' Four days later, on 28 June, the *Elphinstone* weighed anchor without O'Brien and the other three – a victory of sorts. As the ship sailed out of Cobh, the guns of Spike Island and from moored naval vessels thundered out a salute for the anniversary of Queen Victoria's accession. Already, in fact, Clarendon the Lord Lieutenant had been informed that despite cholera in Dublin, the queen, her consort and family would visit Ireland, as an antidote to the virus of subversion.

O'Doherty and Martin, isolated aft by a nervous master and by Surgeon Moxey, were permitted access to the deck once the ship left Cobh, but had to retire to their cabins by nine, and only the master and the surgeon were to address them. Fortunately the Catholic physician and the slightly desiccated Newry Protestant landowner liked each other greatly. They gave each other nicknames – 'Saint Kevin', the rigorously chaste saint of Glendalough, for O'Doherty, and 'John Knox' for the Presbyterian Martin.

Elphinstone was far gone out into the Atlantic when the House of Commons voted the enabling bill through. Sir Lucius, having lost the legislative fight, crossed to Dublin to see his brother in Richmond and console him with the fact that Earl Grey had given assurances 'to the effect that no indignity should be offered to him on the passage or afterwards'. Devoted Lucy wrote to Redington to ask whether O'Brien would be able to receive drafts of money in Van Diemen's Land, and was wrongly reassured that of course he could.

Tom Meagher was still talking politics with his visitors. 'Walking one evening with me in the garden of Richmond Prison,' wrote Meagher's unnamed recorder, 'the week of his transportation . . . he said, "Should our country be born again, she must be baptized in the old Irish Holy Well."' Meagher, who loved a nice image, would find that this one – despite the term 'baptized' – ran him into trouble with the clergy. What was this 'old Irish Holy Well'? It seemed to the clergy to bespeak Celtic myth, and no doubt French deism, the European belief that an architect God had made the earth but abandoned its further functioning to human reason.

Lucy and Grace had proposed coming on to Van Diemen's Land by passenger vessel to keep William company. He wrote his response to Lucy in verse.

> Yes! I forbid our children dear
> To share their father's lot
> Nor fear however lone and drear
> To be by them forgot.

Meagher had no women of his family in a position to make similar offers, but was typically well prepared for transportation. He paid Henry Fitzgibbon over £19 for clothing, including a rifle-green cloak. From Wright & Foxley he equipped himself with feint-ruled notebooks, pencils, indiarubber, envelopes. He had also ordered a rug and counterpanes, and paid £9 for chests. From Stephen Phelan, bookseller, he had ordered a mini-library – *The Life of Petrarch*, *Punch's Almanac of 1846*, Shelley's *Essays*, a multi-volume history of Germany, Kohl's *Ireland*, *Coningsby* by Disraeli, Carlyle's *Sartor Resartus*.

On 9 July, at nine in the morning, the prisoners were informed that they would be leaving for Van Diemen's Land at twelve noon. For Patrick O'Donohoe, the meeting with his wife and children in the prison yard that morning was a dismal affair. He left for Van Diemen's Land with only 11 shillings and 6 pence to his name. Lady O'Brien, Grace and Lucy were there to say goodbye, but soon all four State prisoners were seated, a little stunned, facing each other in a wagon rolling out of a back entrance of Richmond prison towards the port of Dublin. Fifty mounted police with carbines and pistols, three troops of dragoons, and a company of the 6th

Carbineers escorted the prison wagon. As the vehicle neared Pigeon House, a fortress by the harbour, the prisoners were able to observe through a small window that artillerymen were standing by their cannon and boatloads of armed sailors had landed from naval vessels. The four State prisoners were rushed down steps to ship's boats, which pulled away immediately towards the 10-gun brig *Swift*, their ship. O'Brien wrote that after the long eight months in Richmond prison, 'in monotonous though not disagreeable residence', and despite 'the pain incidental to departure' he felt a 'short-lived sentiment of release'.

The junior counsel O'Farrell, who knew 'the head of the Prison Department', rode with him to the harbour, and was allowed to travel in the same boat as Meagher and the captain of the *Swift*. Once all the prisoners were aboard *Swift*, Smith O'Brien handed O'Farrell a 5-word message for Lucy. A number of supporters who had set off in boats parallel to the course of the ship's boats were at first headed off by naval cutters, and spectators ashore were ordered not to wave handkerchiefs and hats. Ultimately, though, the navy could not hold back a flotilla of well-wishers, and O'Brien 'was surprised and delighted to find my sister Grace and my brother Henry', whom Captain Aldham had permitted briefly aboard.

After these brief farewells the officers ushered the State prisoners to their cabins aft, to the space which was to be their mess, and they were not permitted on deck again until the boat was towed clear of the lighthouses of North Bull and Poolbeg by the *Trident* steamer. The banishment of O'Brien and the others now left Ireland a kingdom fit for a royal visit.

Smith O'Brien derided the man-of-war *Swift* as being 'greatly in want of paint' and more 'like a collier than a man-of-war'. The positive-minded Meagher, however, saw *Swift* as 'a spritely, handsome little brig'. Whatever the ship's condition, on the late afternoon of 9 July, when *Swift* had left port, the young and splendidly named Captain W. Cornwallis Aldham acquainted the State prisoners in their mess with the regulations for their management. They were to live as gentlemen under guard, though only two were to be on deck at the one time. They could use their saloon or mess at will. Baths would be restricted to salt-water bathing with buckets of water, but during calms they could take the option of being lowered overboard on the end of a rope.

Three of the State prisoners were accommodated on the starboard side in small cabins with high bunks beneath which were three drawers. The bunks were reached by a step – 'that he can sit on', as O'Brien would say in a diagram he would draw for his children. Smith O'Brien, Meagher and MacManus were in these three cabins, and Patrick O'Donohoe had a small cabin on the port side attached to the officers' quarters. The prisoners shared a chamber, near the officers' quarters, which O'Brien would in his drawing label the *State Prisoners' Mess.*

Some miles down the Irish coast, Smith O'Brien was allowed on deck again, and saw with some nostalgia 'the beautiful vale which lies between Killiney and Bray', where Lucy and he had the year before spent a delightful two weeks. He had already begun his journal for Lucy. 'Today,' he boasted in it the next morning, 'I made my bed for the first time in my life and I am resolved to continue the practice throughout the voyage.' By evening that second day, the Irish coast, pleasant in its summer light, was fading away, and the regrets normal in a failed revolutionary rose in him – 'Had we been contented to allow ourselves to be carried to prison under the suspension of the Habeas Corpus Act, instead of making an appeal to the country for which it was not prepared, we should probably have been at this moment masters of the public opinion of Ireland.' But there was an extent to which in any case they were masters of opinion.

At first the prisoners were given two thirds of the officers' ration, but O'Brien and charming Meagher made representations on the matter, and Captain Aldham made an adjustment. Dinner, served at an ungodly 5.00 p.m., was 2 pounds of hard beef divided between all four men, some biscuits, a jug of water and two glasses of wine each. O'Brien approached this harsh food as an experiment – to test whether he could ignore its scantiness. To Meagher, it provided a source of jokes. But Meagher was not restricted to comedy. Throughout the usual spate of seasickness in the North Atlantic, he was particularly kind to O'Donohoe, drawing the venetian blinds over the portholes to exclude light from his fellow convict's aching eyes. On 11 July, O'Donohoe noted, 'After dinner, whilst I lay sick, Mr Meagher read to me *Digby's Compendium.*' As the weather settled, while 'Meagher read a portion of the Scriptures from the Catholic Douai Bible', O'Brien 'read simultaneously the same chapter in my German Protestant Bible. I hope thus to continue my German biblical studies which were commenced in Richmond Prison.' Recovered, O'Donohoe was cheered up when he learned the identity of a youth aboard. 'A young gentleman, a midshipman, about thirteen years of age, named Lord Ockham, mounted the rigging for the first time today. He is a grandson of Lord Byron.' O'Donohoe, an enthusiast for Byron, had found that the poet referred to Midshipman Ockham's mother as, 'Fair child, Ada! Soul daughter of his home and heart.' O'Donohoe apologised for the shaky hand with which he wrote all this for his wife's information, and advised, 'You may tell Bessy I have thrown away the dirty old wig.'

They had been at sea ten days when in the mess Meagher announced to his fellow prisoners that henceforth, and until and unless he was liberated, he was to be addressed as O'Meagher. It was the eve of the anniversary of

Ballingarry, and *Swift* was becalmed in mid-Atlantic. Edging across the Equator in early August, they watched the initiation of officers and crew who had not previously crossed. But the winds were so low that, searching for them, *Swift* was at one time little more than 200 miles from Brazil, in fretful air which caused O'Brien to admit, 'I am by no means so indifferent as I believed myself to the luxuries of the table.' He had already made a resolve to touch no alcohol until Ireland was free, and had to mix lemon acid and raspberry vinegar with the nearly undrinkable water. And his *bête noire* was Marine Sergeant Perry, who insisted on turning out the prisoners' lights – as per regulation – at a preposterously early hour. O'Brien wrote with a dryness lacking from his serious verse:

> Fat Sergeant Perry comes at nine
> And robs us of our light.

Swift arrived off Cape Town on 12 September that year. Captain Aldham and the officers, permitted to land, were told that the *Neptune*, with Mitchel aboard, was so long overdue that it might have been lost at sea. Despite his political differences with the man, O'Brien was saddened at the possibility and wrote in his journal, 'Poor Mitchel! What a fate! Poor Mrs Mitchel!'

They were all drawing personal hope, however, from the news of the resistance of the colonists of Cape Town to receiving transportees. If Hobart, like Cape Town, opposed the landing of prisoners, the authorities might have no practical choice but to grant an early pardon. Wary Cape Town settlers agreed to re-victual *Swift* only on condition that Captain Aldham sailed the next day. While the *Swift* was moored in the harbour overnight, a settler who had been a childhood friend of O'Brien's rowed out to try to see him exercising on deck, and wrote to Ireland to spread the news that he appeared well. There was no time for a follow-up reconnaissance. At one o'clock in the afternoon of 13 September, the *Swift* weighed anchor and left Africa behind.

During the voyage, O'Brien wrote a considerable quantity of awkward verse, which he then showed to Meagher, receiving a deal of applause in return.

> I have sinned oh my Country! But not against thee
> Proud England I have sinned, but my conscience is free.
> I have sinned against thy Laws, I have sinn'd against thy might,
> But no sin have I sinn'd against Justice and Right.

Lying on a plank one day, oppressed by his lengthening distance from

Lucy, he felt his head gently raised to allow a sailor's coat to be slid beneath it as pillow: 'a tear started in my eye . . . I turned around and perceived that I owed it to an Irish sailor . . . May his head never want a pillow, may his heart never want rest.'

On the arrival of the *Mount Stewart Elphinstone* with O'Doherty and Martin in Sydney in early October, after ninety-seven days at sea, the Irish community of the city called a meeting at the Lighthouse Hotel on the corner of Sussex and Bathurst Streets at which it was agreed that the unlanded Irish politicals were national heroes and not criminals. It was further resolved that a committee of citizens should now be formed to supervise the treatment of all State prisoners by the colonial authorities.

Members of this committee sought to board the *Mount Stewart Elphinstone*, talk to O'Doherty and Martin, and give them a collected sum of £94. But on 20 October, both men were transferred directly across the harbour of Sydney to the brig *Emma* for Hobart. After a lively passage down the east coasts of New South Wales and Van Diemen's Land, they sailed up the ample estuary of the Derwent to Hobart to find that the *Swift* had arrived the day before.

Swift had entered the River Derwent on the afternoon of 27 October, and Meagher was delighted with the scenery, the 'bold cliffs' to the left, and to the right 'the green lowlands of Tasman's Peninsula, sparkling in the clear, sweet sunshine of that lovely evening. The town swept into view, and behind it massive Mount Wellington with snow on its brow.' At anchor off Hobart Town, Meagher was cheered to hear Irish voices – 'warm whispers of the old Irish heart' – from passing boats, asking how the gentlemen were. Hungry for sights, the prisoners looked ashore through a glass. 'And even the poor dog we caught playing amongst the bales and baulks, the casks and spars, upon the wharf in front of us was followed through all his windings, tumblings, twists and twirls, with the keenest curiosity.'

Though O'Donohoe might have been a difficult, fallible man, he did try to look on Van Diemen's Land, its rugged geography and its complicated society, with some bravery and determination. There was in fact a great deal of sympathy ashore for the exiles. Progressives in the colony resented the Viceroy Denison for delaying the wish for Van Diemen's Land's, or, as they preferred to call it, Tasmania's, sovereignty. To them, O'Brien was a noble soul, and there was no question that he was seen as the moral leader of the group. Even from this deeply placed exile, he realised his demeanour might be reported back to Ireland and have a political impact there. But the *Hobart Town Courier* advised him before he even landed to refrain from local politics. 'They [the State prisoners] cannot aspire to the honour of a Washington . . . If these gentlemen are wise they will study botany, poetry, metaphysics, anything but colonial faction.'

On 29 October, the Assistant Comptroller of Convicts, William E. Nairn, came aboard the *Swift* at mid-afternoon and met the prisoners in their saloon. With typical piquancy, Meagher described Nairn's actions: 'First of all . . . he disengaged a yard or so of thin red tape from a bundle of large, thick-wove, blue paper; and in so doing exhibited an easy dexterity of finger, and a deep-water placidity of look.' Nairn presented the prisoners with the conditions of their special paroles or tickets-of-leave. They were to be allotted separate districts, where they could lodge and within which they could have freedom of movement, but from which they were not to roam. They were to report their residence to the police magistrate, and from then on present themselves to the magistrate once a month. They were not to be absent from their residence after nine o'clock at night, nor have any contact with each other, and their districts were to be 'rural inland districts'. None of them was to be permitted to live in Hobart Town. To receive this ticket-of-leave, they had merely to give their parole, a promise not to escape. O'Brien loyally raised the matter that O'Donohoe was a legal draftsman, needed to make a living, and could not make one in a rural district. Nairn took a note of that.

Smith O'Brien had already decided that he would not accept the terms. 'I could not make any pledge that I would not attempt to escape.' O'Brien was refusing to accommodate Earl Grey's hope that he would disappear into a pleasant, torpid oubliette, a velvet hole in which he would soon be forgotten by Ireland and the world. The woolbroker MacManus decided not to accept the parole conditions either, until he could be told whether he would be put into a district where he could work for a merchant. O'Brien, perhaps knowing he would need some of his group to communicate with the world, urged Meagher to accept his ticket-of-leave, as he did 'for a limited period – say for three or six months'. Denison was affronted that Meagher accepted the ticket-of-leave provisionally. Did he want to reserve the right to escape after he had studied local conditions? Wherever Meagher settled, the local police magistrate would be ordered 'to lay his hand on him as soon as the six months are over; and either make him renew his engagement, or place him under restraint'. Lady Denison noted that O'Donohoe 'thankfully accepted the Government terms, and only begged that he be allowed to live in town'.

Throughout the following day, many persons on *Swift* tried to talk O'Brien into accepting Denison's terms. Nairn had by now returned to tell them paroles had been granted to O'Donohoe and to Meagher, but O'Brien and MacManus were to be sent to convict probation stations. The letter he bore had the ominous, sparse bureaucratic tone to which O'Brien would become accustomed. 'The Assistant Comptroller has now to acquaint Mr O'Brien . . . that the Lieutenant Governor has decided Maria Island should be the place of such confinement.'

Maria Island was a lovely but remote offshore island along the east coast of Tasmania, a place beyond the horizon of the world, a sub-Hades. MacManus was slated to go to the Salt Water River penal station on the Tasman Peninsula, an extraordinarily beautiful, forested jut of earth which was connected to the Tasmanian land mass by a series of narrow land bridges. But by now, MacManus, possibly under the persuasion of O'Brien, had decided to accept his ticket-of-leave. Lady Denison wrote, 'So O'Brien is now the only victim.' She could still not understand why her husband was subject to such vexation. There was no need for indulgence. 'It is true that the punishment of transportation would fall more heavily on the gentleman than on one belonging to the lower classes.'

Before the prisoners were disposed of, there were sympathetic visitors to the ship. Father Dunne of Van Diemen's Land, who would become later a firm friend of O'Brien's, came aboard. So did a Mr Carter and his son, progressives and merchants who owned stores throughout VDL, as people often called the colony. Carter was in a way a litmus test of VDL attitudes to the State prisoners. He was a visitor to Government House and knew the Denisons, but clearly did not see O'Brien and the others as average transportees.

It was during that same afternoon of arguing with O'Brien that O'Doherty and Martin arrived on the sloop *Emma*, and looked over to the *Swift* in the hope of seeing their friends. They did at last spot MacManus 'strutting about the *Swift* with a telescope in his hand and sending great demonstrations of friendly salutations across the water'. Salutations were, however, brief. At three o'clock in the morning on the last day of October, Meagher was rowed ashore in a guard boat with his belongings. His coach for Campbell Town, the chief town of the area to which he had been assigned, 100 miles north of Hobart, left at half past three, and he was compelled to move straight across Hobart's stone wharfs on uncertain sea legs to board it. But once the sun rose, 'At last, there was the heart of the country itself, with its beautiful hills, rising in long and shadowy tiers, one above the other, and the brown foliage of its woods, and the blackened stumps of many a tough old tree, and mobs upon mobs of sheep, and the green parrots, and the wattle birds!' The island he was entering was eerily beautiful, characterised by dramatic and dangerous coastlines, tangled western mountains, great plateaux which the Vandemonian population called tiers, and settlement chiefly spread in the north–south basins of farming land created by the Derwent, on which Hobart Town had been established, and the Tamar, on which the northern town Launceston stood. Van Diemen's Land was colder than the Australian mainland, since it lay in that great band of westerlies called the Roaring Forties, though sometimes winds from the continent's hot interior swept down across it. To Meagher and other Irish State prisoners, however, it would seem more temperate than Ireland.

Nairn had now been to the *Emma* to offer O'Doherty and John Martin the same arrangements offered the day before on *Swift*. Both prisoners accepted. An Assistant Registrar recorded their appearance; O'Doherty's, when taken together with his character, made of him a fitting object of devotion for Eva of the *Nation* – 5 feet 11½ inches high, complexion fresh, hair and whiskers brown, forehead broad, mouth and nose medium, and chin small. In Ireland in September, the *Nation* had begun publishing again under the editorship of much-tried but now freed Gavan Duffy. Here was the outlet for Eva's verses, compounding grief for the national loss with grief for loss of the beloved.

How I glory, how I sorrow,
How I love with deathless love –
How I weep before the chilling skies,
And moan to God above!

Meagher found, on dismounting from the coach after an all-day journey, that little Campbell Town had only one street and three side-lanes. But at least in Mrs Kearney's hotel the main parlour was decorated with pictures of Brian Boru and Daniel O'Connell, and she herself was sitting up and honoured to provide him with a dinner. It was proof that if the official British Empire could spread its sway over such fantastic distances, so too could the unofficial Irish empire, its icons no more diminished by distance than were the potency of the lion and unicorn above the door of Government House, Hobart. Meagher did not greatly like Campbell Town – it 'has too much of the vulgar upstart village in it; contains too much glare, dust and gossip'. Three days later, with the police magistrate's permission, he was driven by cart a little south to the town of Ross, which he described to O'Brien as an Elysian location. For a while Meagher rented two front rooms from a couple, though he sometimes took residence in Hope's Hotel. One of his first plans was to hire a horse and explore the limits of his district, 35 miles long and 15 miles wide. He would in the meantime make a drama even out of his negotiations with his landlords, a Wesleyan couple:

an amiable woman of stupendous proportions, and proportionate loquacity. Her husband is Wesleyan too, a shoe-maker by trade, and a spectre in appearance; so much so, indeed, that the wife may be styled, with the strictest geometric propriety, his 'better half' and three-quarters.

'Sir,' said Mrs Anderson, sticking a pin into the sleeve of her gown, and spreading down her apron before her . . . 'You see as how it is, me and my husband be Wesleyans, and we don't like a'cooking on Sundays . . .' [Meagher told the husband he didn't mind cold meat, but] 'Potatoes, you know, Mr Anderson, are very insipid when cold' . . . A moment's consultation sufficed – a new light descended on Mr Anderson and, yielding to the inspiration, he pronounced it to be his opinion that a boiled potato would not break the Sabbath.

The evening of the same day of Meagher's journey to Campbell Town, MacManus was landed from *Swift* with orders to travel a little north-west of Hobart to the town of New Norfolk, on the banks of the same Derwent River, and O'Doherty and Martin were landed from *Emma* with orders to catch the Launceston night coach to Oatlands. This was to be O'Doherty's area; for the immediate future he and Meagher were to be neighbours without rights of visit. Martin was to continue on north-west from Oatlands to a village named Bothwell. The Irish editor of the *Hobart Guardian*, John Moore, promised O'Doherty and Martin a dray to bring on luggage behind the coach. Now, before departing Hobart, they went to the post office in Moore's coach to make arrangements for the redirection of their mail, and then on to the Albion Inn, terminus for the New Norfolk coach, where they were excited to find MacManus waiting for transport. A crowd of sympathisers gathered, and took the three Irish heroes to a reception room in the inn, where they were called on to make speeches. MacManus, O'Doherty and Martin had landed to an '82 Club kind of warmth in the capital of their province of exile.

When the coach delivered Martin and O'Doherty that night at the Oatlands Inn, they discovered that it was owned and operated by a Tipperary man, John Ryan. Ryan provided O'Doherty with a rent-free stone cottage, Elm Cottage, which still stands. After their first breakfast on land, Saint Kevin and John Knox reported to the Oatlands magistrate, and then Martin climbed aboard a gig belonging to a settler, and set off to pick up the westward road to Bothwell.

It had been decided between Governor Denison and the Comptroller-General of Convicts, Dr Hampton, a youngish man with a specialty in tropical diseases, that O'Donohoe be permitted to live in Hobart Town. O'Brien had generously forced five sovereigns into O'Donohoe's hands before he landed. For a while he lived in a hotel, but his resources were so restricted that at last he rented a back room from a Mrs Ludgater. The priests of Hobart opened their homes to him. Bishop Willson, the Catholic bishop, a former Nottingham farmer and friend of O'Connell, who had devoted himself particularly to care of the insane, of whom there were many amongst convicts, also offered open house to O'Donohoe. O'Donohoe was, however, spiky about accepting charity.

Smith O'Brien's immediate destiny was the most dramatic of all. He was taken from *Swift* at seven o'clock on the morning of 31 October, and was rowed across the port of Hobart to the *Kangaroo*, a neat little 52-ton steamer. He found the journey out of the Derwent and up Van Diemen's Land's east coast impressive – Cape Pillar in particular reminded him of the Giant's Causeway. 'The outline of this coast resembles much some parts of the highlands of Scotland and the mountain regions of Ireland.' Maria Island itself looked nearly as mountainous as the mainland coastline it echoed. By nightfall the *Kangaroo* dropped its anchor off Darlington Probation Station on the north shore of the island, and Mr Lapham, the superintendent, a Kildare Irishman ten years younger than O'Brien, came aboard with the visiting magistrate to call on their famed prisoner. O'Brien took a liking to Lapham, and Lapham in turn showed the awed respect the son of a middling Irish Protestant farmer should to the descendant of Irish kings and huge landowners.

By the light of next morning, O'Brien saw the white-limed settlement of Darlington, standing on a spit of land beneath its twin mountains primly named the Bishop and the Clerk, and noticed a substantial prison. 'To find the gaol in one of the loveliest spots formed by the hand of nature . . . creates a revulsion of feeling which I cannot describe.' There were about 130 convicts in Darlington, some of whom, O'Brien noticed, wore grey, and others yellow chequered with black – the magpie suit reserved for second offenders. Lapham's instructions were that O'Brien was not to be subjected to 'coercive employment' nor to be made to wear prison clothing. He should have 'a little house' to himself. Brought ashore now, Smith O'Brien was greeted on landing by Patrick Lynch, a young Irish convict, assistant to the Catholic chaplain, who had worked for his father on the Dromoland estate. O'Brien then walked up the small hill into the shallow protected valley where the settlement lay, and was introduced to his convict overseer, a former soldier named George Miller.

The main settlement was laid out to make an oblong with administrative buildings at either end, and the long sides made up of the chapel, a series of convict and military barracks, and a row of connected cottages, each with a little garden behind it. One of these cottages O'Brien was given, 'about the size of one of the smallest bathing lodges at Kilkee surrounded by a few borrowed articles of the rudest furniture'. It had two rooms, and an attic which had a chimney opening to serve as a midget fireplace. Here, as sub-Antarctic winds combed the island, he could write his letters and his journal.

Things did not at first look utterly dismal. Given that Captain Bayly, visiting magistrate, and Lapham and his deputy were all Irish, and considered O'Brien distinguished company to be enjoyed, there were reasons for comfort. Lapham permitted O'Brien to make excursions – he 'rode with Captain Bayly and some of the other residents to Long Point', a probation station about 6 miles south of the main station. He was also allowed to walk around the northern end of the island, an area of open grassy shore, populated by Cape Barren geese, and dotted with the huts of the storekeeper and religious instructor. On this slope above the sea he could visit the cemetery, the graves of soldiers' wives and children, and that of a Maori chieftain, Hehepa te Umoroa, who had died on the island after offering too good a resistance to Governor FitzRoy and sundry British regiments in New Zealand.

He began writing verse again, his first Australian poem being dedicated to a walking-stick Captain Aldham had given him, made of a vine branch cut on the Elysian Fields near Naples. It was such a twig which enabled Aeneas to climb out of the underworld.

> Say – to this rod is equal power given?
> Say shall this rod uphold my faltering steps
> Whilst I retrace the path to Liberty?

Letters to Lucy he would not write while they were subject to official scrutiny.

13
By Order of Great Denison

> This attempt to mortify my vanity and to degrade me from a position in society which the officials of Hobart Town can neither give nor take away has been as unsuccessful as was their attempt to vex my corporeal organs by withholding from them the fare to which they have been accustomed.
>
> Smith O'Brien, to Thomas Francis Meagher, Maria Island, December 1849

Dr John Stephen Hampton, Comptroller-General of Convicts, believed that if O'Brien had too sociable a time on Maria Island, he would find it easy to avoid giving his parole. Until that parole was extracted, O'Brien would have the twin benefit of appearing a martyr to the larger world, while enjoying the congenial company of Mr and Mrs Lapham, their charming daughters, Captain and Mrs Bayly, the Catholic chaplain Father Woolfrey and Surgeon Smart, the island's physician. During a brief visit to the island soon after O'Brien arrived, Dr Hampton made it clear to Lapham that not only was O'Brien forbidden to enter the house of any official, but they were not to speak to him except in performance of their duty. 'The system of petty persecution which I have been led to expect has commenced,' wrote Smith O'Brien in his cottage. He had been receiving the hospital ration, but was now to receive the regular convict ration of flour, meat and vegetables with small amounts of tea, coffee, sugar, salt, soap, vinegar, and milk. It was enough to live on, but monotonous and less in quantity than Captain Aldham had allowed him on board the *Swift*.

Even on Maria Island, and in something like solitary confinement, O'Brien knew how to use his world audience, writing after lock-up to former friends, telling them of the tyranny under which he was being held. His regular correspondents included his friend Chisholm Anstey, middle-aged Irish Member of the House of Commons, who had lived in his youth in Tasmania, and the Reverend Charles Monsell, the Church of Ireland minister married to O'Brien's sister, Harriett. Both Anstey and Monsell were friends of a rising Whig politician, William Gladstone, and Hampton – perhaps for fear of questions in the House of Commons – let those letters through. In the minuscule upper room of his hut, while Tasmanian gales nudged his windows, O'Brien, who had never in his crowded life been so lonely, also favoured his brother Sir Lucius with mail. 'Every human being – man, woman, and child – is forbidden upon pain of instant removal from this Island to hold any intercourse with me,' O'Brien told Lucius.

But letters to the other prisoners and citizens within Van Diemen's Land were easier to seize or censor without having to face complaints in the House of Commons. Part of a confiscated letter to Meagher enclosed a whimsical poem.

> By order of Great Denison
> To solitude consigned
> I'm learning now a lesson
> That will instruct my mind.

Letter-writing was O'Brien's release as well as his strategy. He wrote to Archdeacon Marriott of New Norfolk, a friend of his mother. Marriott – something of a High Church, Romish-ritual rebel – was no approver of seditionists and urged O'Brien to accept the parole. With better results, O'Brien communicated with Mr Reeves, a Hobart hat merchant who had offered his services. Meanwhile, Hampton removed the convict Patrick Lynch, once a kitchen servant at Dromoland, in the hope of coercing O'Brien further to parole. The nobleman O'Brien nonetheless was strangely proud of his new skills in domestic matters. He told his brother Robert, who was running Cahirmoyle, 'I am becoming very skilful in washing plates, cups and saucers and other earthenware. I make my own bed and perform other unmentionable duties.' That is, he was required to get rid of his own night waste, a job reserved in Cahirmoyle and Dromoland for the lowliest servants. His chief indulgence was that his shoes were polished for him once a week, his room was cleaned, and his rations were sent in already cooked.

In mid-November O'Brien was moved to a slightly more commodious house next door to the one he had been occupying. His morale still seemed robust, for he had time to set down in the journal for Lucy's ultimate information a complete summary of Tasmania from the *Tasmanian Kalendar* of 1849. It covered everything: the seasons, the officers of colonial government, courts, imports, exports, shipping, post office, newspapers. He was interested in questions of land tenure, since they had lain at the base of all Irish discontent. But as convict work gangs went forth past his front windows to garden, fell timber, work on the breakwater, or scrape out rudimentary tracks along the coast, he envied their activity and apparent camaraderie. He possibly heard Irish conversations which evoked the image of harvesters walking to work at Dromoland or Cahirmoyle. He lived hardly more than 200 yards from the barracks of many of them, but they received little mention in his journal or letters. They were on another penal planet.

He tried to vary his rations, and wrote in November 1849 to Mr William Carter in Hobart, with whom he had already deposited money, to send him 7 pounds of rice, a bottle of curry powder 'of moderate size', 3 pounds of coffee and 7 pounds of lump sugar. Carter wrote back and said that sadly the government would not authorise such a purchase. This limitation also drove him to mock-heroic verse:

> Such is the system of *Control*
> In Mary's Isle applied
> Thus the Comptroller daunts a soul
> And lames a rebel's pride.

Christmas approaching, O'Brien marked his letters '6/7 week of my solitary confinement'. Some of these were apparently smuggled off the island in Father Woolfrey's mail, or else the Convict Department was sloppy in its censorship, for he sometimes got away with criticising the administration. 'While one eye looks towards home, the other must be directed to Hobart Town and when I desire to express the sentiments of my heart to those whom I love I am compelled to frame my diction in such a manner as to avoid giving offence to the official inspectors.'

Some letters got through to O'Brien from the other prisoners. Meagher, in his spiky handwriting, detailed how in and around Campbell Town he was enjoying 'a delightful solitude'. He was a source of reading matter too – he sent O'Brien his *History of Germany* by Kohlrausch, a *History of Switzerland* by Vienssent, Carlyle's *Miscellanies*, a book of Irish Jacobite poetry. In one of his rides in the bush near Ross, Meagher told O'Brien, he had met a settler named Adam Robinson, a comfortable, wealthy farmer who always asked after Mr O'Brien. Robinson's father had been steward to Sir Edward for many years. To read of such familiar names was balm to an isolated prisoner.

Questions on his health *had* begun to be asked in London and in Ireland, and ten days before Christmas, Denison sent Dr Dawson, chief of the Medical Department, to visit Maria's most famous felon. Dr Dawson, whose manner seemed confiding, gave the Denisons a 'rather amusing account' of his meeting O'Brien. O'Brien, thought Lady Denison, 'is evidently under the delusion that his case is exciting great interest and sympathy here'. Some modern commentators have joined Dawson in taking a slightly derisive view of Smith O'Brien's attempts to achieve a moral victory by enlisting influential allies. What else was a revolutionary leader, trying to turn political imprisonment to advantage, to do? Denison was playing the propaganda game just as energetically as O'Brien, and wanted an obeisance from him. O'Brien was surely justified in enlisting the world's help to avoid such a genuflection?

The Scots Dr Smart, Maria Island physician, who had been given permission to raise O'Brien's ration if there seemed to be any decline in his health, did so almost as soon as Dawson left the island. But Christmas Day saw O'Brien's struggle unresolved. His solitary Christmas and his plain dinner contrasted sadly with the imprisoned Christmas dinner of the year before, which he had spent in Richmond bridewell with his mother, his wife, and five of his then six children. By 4 January he again confessed, 'I feel that Dr Hampton's recipe for extinguishing an Irish patriot is beginning to do its work.'

'The other prisoners, meanwhile, are . . . setting up a newspaper here,' wrote Lady Denison in Hobart, 'to be called "The Irish Exile and Freedom's Advocate".' In fact, the paper was to be all Patrick O'Donohoe's work. Meagher sold some subscriptions in Ross, Martin contributed a series of letters, 'The Case for Ireland', but apart from that the other Young Irelanders kept remote from it. And Denison might have been secretly tolerant of O'Donohoe, despite his publishing the standard Irish rhetoric, because of certain remarks he made soon after landing about the hypocrisy of the free-settler gentry. They, he would say, condemned the baseness of convicts yet were willing to impregnate convict women, and to deny land and opportunity to emancipated felons. Their opposition to transportation was duplicitous.

Consoling his wife Anne by letter in the weeks before the *Exile* was published, O'Donohoe gave an unflattering view of Hobart, the target of his proposed journal: 'I suppose the earth could not produce so vicious a population as inhabits this town; vice of all kinds, in its most hideous and exaggerated form, openly practiced by all classes and sexes.' It was a place where people 'think nothing of hanging 5 or 6 people of a morning; some of them, if old offenders, on very trifling charges'. Yet it was a city of plenty: 'Why, the greatest wretch in a chain-gang gets beef and mutton to eat every day, while the purest and most virtuous of the Irish race rot in the ditches.' In a letter to his friend O'Doherty, Martin reported that at a recent picnic – Hobart abounded in lovely picnic spots – O'Donohoe (nicknamed 'Denis') 'got lost in the bush; and, by a remarkable coincidence, the hostess of the party got lost too, at the same time. Now the lady, by Denis's own account, is very pretty. Hem! Well, the "Tasmanians have it as table-talk that one of the Irish rebel rascals, vampire-like, took that woman into the bush and there by force of arms, pikes and so forth, illegally and unconstitutionally detained her."' Martin was quoting from a letter from O'Donohoe, who seemed perversely proud of his picnic assignation.

The next time Denison sent off dispatches to Earl Grey, he enclosed a copy of the first issue of the *Irish Exile* – significantly dated for the anniversary of European occupation of Australia, 26 January. The founding circulation of O'Donohoe's ardent, quirky little paper was 800, of which 300 subscribers were in Van Diemen's Land, and the rest on the mainland, in Sydney, Maitland, Melbourne, Geelong and Adelaide. The *Exile* was ironically well supported by those advertisers of Hobart who disliked Denison. *Hats! Hats! Hats!* cried the advertisement of P. O'Reilly's Hat Warehouse, just as Marsden the Butcher's cried *Meat! Meat!! Meat!!!*

O'Donohoe's prospectus, republished in the first edition, was conciliatory both to government and to the Irish community. O'Donohoe did, however, exhibit a traditional Irish willingness to adopt firm views on local politics within a short time of arrival. 'The political aspect of Van Diemen's Land has now assumed that conspicuous character, which requires a far different view to be entertained concerning its destinies.' He thanked his clients: 'Irish, English, Scot and Native, have vied with each other, in rendering us their aid, and calling out, "Fair play, a free stage, and no favor".' As expected, he expressed editorial mistrust of the high tone of the anti-transportationists, Mr William Carter, merchant, and John Compton Gregson, barrister. 'We have no sympathy with those Colonial Pharisees who are so often to be heard proclaiming the moral depravity of the convict population, by way of proclaiming their own moral purity.'

In its early months, the *Irish Exile and Freedom's Advocate* provided O'Donohoe with a living and congenial engagement with Hobart people, something denied the other prisoners. But it exposed him to greater peril. The matter which caused the most trouble between the *Exile* and the Denisons was the case of Smith O'Brien. On 2 February 1850, O'Donohoe reported, 'We have learned with inexpressible anguish, that owing to the severity of treatment inflicted on this virtuous and noble hearted Patriot, his health is rapidly declining.' In the next edition, O'Donohoe admitted he had received threats from Denison to leave the subject alone. 'Innumerable communications have reached me respecting this great and good man's health. I am not at liberty to insert any of them, or to make *note, or comment on any act whatever connected with the Government*.' Gagged, he fell back on simpler causes: that of a freed prisoner of political background named Patrick McDonnell. McDonnell had sent for his wife and children to join him, but while they were at sea, had been crushed to death by a tree. 'The widow of McDonnell is now alone, unprotected, unprovided – she and her orphans are wanderers in this land of strangers.'

He also recorded straightforwardly the mania with gold strikes in the American West. And despite the ban on publishing anything directly on Smith O'Brien, he did quote from local and home newspapers on the matter.

At the anniversary dinner of the Limerick Literary Institute . . . it was announced by the Secretary, Mr Potter . . . that he had strong hopes that, before twelve months passed away, the company would have the pleasure of BEHOLDING MR SMITH O'BRIEN ONCE MORE AMONGST THEM.

By early new year, Lapham, to whom O'Brien would always owe a debt, adjusted Hampton's regulations and seemed gradually to permit officers and members of their families to talk to O'Brien. Both sides of the arrangement benefited. He was able also to roam widely again: 'If Maria Island were placed near the west coast of Ireland I should be quite contented to make it my abode for a long time – provided I was surrounded by my children.' He was getting some of his spirit back.

'*Numquam mihi gratia*', he felt expansive enough to write educatively to his eldest son Edward, '*fuit memoria officiorium ab amicis perfunctorum quam nunc huic solitudine relegato*.' ('Never will the memory of the kind offices performed by my friends bring me more gratification than it does now that I am relegated to this solitude.') And he needed also the energy to deal with occasional business letters from the Ireland of estates and tenancies. One, from Lady O'Brien, who gave advice to Robert O'Brien now managing Cahirmoyle, concerned rent abatement on a property called Cappaculhane. The farmer at that place was ready now to pay off his rent in the form of butter and milk. Would O'Brien approve of the man's having his two cows back? O'Brien assented to this arrangement. In a postscript of a letter to the Reverend Gabbett, Lucy's brother, he asked that an enclosed, banal but, in the circumstances, touching poem might be passed on to his wife.

For as from thee I farther go
Me thinks 'twill cheer thy heart to know
That dearer far to me than life
Is my incomparable wife.

Lucy herself was not above smuggling letters to her husband through Dr Nixon, Anglican bishop of Van Diemen's Land, a friend of Lady O'Brien's. Lucy senior went for solitary walks around the estate, and cherished 'a secret tree and valley'. He found it sweet consolation too that his birthday had been celebrated at Dromoland the previous October, and a delightful letter written that day by his daughter Lucy confessed all the fragmented enthusiasms of childhood. 'Baby is a very nice little fellow he is always laughing when he is with Mamma. I am reading the history of Egypt in Rollins ancient history . . . The thrush that we got at Richmond is at Limerick, it was become very impudent and runs after us pecking at our clothes.'

The Lapham family residence lay perhaps 45 yards diagonally across the square from O'Brien's little cottage. (Both buildings still stand.) Clearly, exchanges were not only likely but nearly unavoidable. O'Brien wrote a poem in acknowledgement of a rosebud presented to him by the superintendent's younger daughter, Susan Lapham, whom he thought a splendid, lively, generous girl. Even with his keeper, Miller, he had discourse. On their strolls, Miller related entertaining military anecdotes, and in return O'Brien might sit with Miller on the huge fossil limestone cliffs just around the northern end of the island and read aloud from Schiller, Byron, or Carlyle. But the relaxed conditions prevailed only on Maria, and it did not take long for a further grievance against the Convict Department to arise. £50 had been sent to O'Brien care of the Bank of Australasia. O'Brien was notified: 'Will be delivered W S O'Brien when he is eligible by law to hold property.' O'Brien wrote to Grace, 'Though I profess no admiration for Lord Clarendon and his Government, I yet cannot believe that he would condescend to encourage my wife in a season of great pecuniary difficulty to procure for me a little money in order that it might be subsequently kidnapped *in transitu* by an official in VD Land.'

Everyone had by now discovered that Mitchel's ship had not been wrecked on the passage from Bermuda to Africa, merely blown about the Atlantic and delayed by perverse calms. In September the year before, after the *Swift* had departed South Africa, *Neptune* at last arrived in Simon's Bay off Cape Town.

In the Atlantic's slack airs, a sergeant's wife, a Mrs Nolan of Clare, chatted with Mitchel every day on the poop deck. She told him there were nearly 200 Irish prisoners on the prison deck, many of whom spoke not a word of English. 'I seldom hear their voices,' wrote Mitchel, 'except when they sing at night on deck.' They were 'the famine-struck Irish of the Special Commission'.

Ashore, as the British authorities and the locals waited for each other to give in, *Neptune* was left swinging at anchor. Mitchel became very ill with asthma in December 1849 and January 1850. When Earl Grey's dispatches arrived at last to tell the captain of *Neptune* what to do with his cargo, 'the men poured aft as far as the gangway in gloomy masses;

and when Captain Bance unfolded his papers the burliest burglar held his breath for a time'. The ship was to go immediately to Van Diemen's Land, and all convicts aboard, in compensation for the hardships of their long passage, were to receive conditional pardons, except 'the prisoner Mitchel'.

Neptune slipped away from Cape Town on 19 February, and Mitchel wrote that for more than a month thereafter, in the squally southern latitudes, as he looked down from the poop on his walks, 'the convicts look at me with a sort of respectful pity; and doubtless think my crimes must have been enormously villainous indeed to merit the distinguished consideration of being singly excepted from their universal emancipation'. He had been nearly a year aboard *Neptune* when in early April the ship lay off Bruny Island, Van Diemen's Land, in calm water, waiting for the Hobart pilot to come aboard. On 6 April, the *Hobart Town Courier* announced *Neptune*'s arrival, though the editors were more concerned with its hundreds of felons than with Mitchel. 'New South Wales rejected them, New Zealand rejected them, South Australia rejected them, Port Phillip rejected them – and therefore Van Diemen's Land, which has long suffered under an accumulated load of evil, must bear the penalty.'

He found he was to be permitted to reside at large in any one of the police districts he might select, subject to the normal parole and terms. He was troubled: he had heard a rumour that the others were discussing the possibility of surrendering their paroles. Dr Gibson, the surgeon of *Neptune*, saved Mitchel from his absolutist tendencies by telling him frankly to take the offered ticket-of-leave, since confinement on Maria Island or any other penal station would finish him. Mitchel wrote a letter to the Comptroller-General accepting comparative liberty. Waiting for an answer, he heard from Patrick O'Donohoe, 'informing me that he has established a newspaper called the *Irish Exile*, enclosing me a copy of the last number, and proposing that *I should join him* in the concern . . . The thing is a hideous absurdity altogether.'

Mitchel was in fact permitted to join his schoolfriend, Martin, and four days after landing, relished sitting 'on the green grass by the bank of the clear, brawling stream of fresh water. It is Bothwell, forty-six miles from Hobart Town, from the *Neptune* and the sea, and high among the central mountains of Van Diemen's Land. Opposite sits John Martin, sometime of Loughorne, smoking placidly, and gazing furiously on me with his mild eyes.' According to Martin, Mitchel reached Van Diemen's Land 'a wretched-looking asthmatic . . . And now he can ride his forty or fifty miles a day, or walk a score with perfect ease and pleasure.'

The two old friends shared rented rooms in Bothwell, and their attentive landlady lost no opportunity to say that she 'came out free', which Mitchel says 'is the patent of nobility in Van Diemen's Land'. In physical terms the town, a thousand feet above sea level, was delightful. The fragrance of the gum trees filled the air, which was 'illuminated by the flight of parrots of most glowing and radiant plumage, that go flashing through the arches of the forest like winged gems'. The settlement contained some seventy houses, a church where clergymen of the Churches of England and of Scotland performed services by turns, four large public houses, 'much better supported than the church'. There was also a police barracks, headquarters of the police magistrate, whom Mitchel would get to know well. Below Bothwell the Clyde River surged over a waterfall to the settlement of Hamilton, which Mitchel was pleased to find was settled chiefly by Scots immigrants.

Meagher quickly tired of his quarter of the bush. No elections to fight, no speeches to give, no rallies to galvanise. He early complained to O'Brien, 'Between a prison and a district, I have discovered there exists just about the same difference as one may observe between a stable and a paddock.' Ross had thirty or forty houses, and a military barracks 'before the door of which two soldiers yawn and smoke all day'. Here there were 'more indications of Morpheus than of Mars or Bellona'. He relieved his ennui by riding and hunting. 'Dashing through woods, clambering up hills, clearing fences; and with a smart rifle cracking at everything that comes across you, is a great relief from the stagnation of a miserable little village.' His generous companion in some of the expeditions was a Dr James McNamara from County Clare.

He had retained his normal taste for mischief. He went to discuss the boundary of his territory with his magistrate, and was told that it was Blackman's River between Ross and Oatlands. So the Young Tribune satirised this official arrangement by inviting Kevin O'Doherty to meet him at the stone bridge over that river, on the edge of a village and convict station called Tunbridge. On four or five successive Mondays an impudent meeting between Meagher and O'Doherty occurred here. A table from a local public house was placed at mid-bridge and, each prisoner sitting on his appropriate side, they were served lunch by an Irish publican from O'Doherty's side of the river, watched by amused locals. 'To be sure,' wrote Meagher, 'the passage through the air, for upwards of five hundred yards or so, condensed the steam of the potatoes and solidified the gravy somewhat; but the old salmon-coloured inn was not to blame for that. In all these cases, the Home Office spoiled the cooking.'

Tiring of that stunt, Meagher ordered a skiff from Hobart, and it was brought up by bullock team, O'Doherty legally escorting it through his territory, along a rough path through the Western Tiers towards Lake

Sorell, a high mountain tarn, 3,000 feet up, where most of the State prisoners' districts converged. There Meagher planned to launch it on St Patrick's Day, 1850, naming it *Speranza* in honour of the *Nation*'s famed woman versifier. A number of supporters and friends from various towns were invited to attend the launch and to fire a volley into the air to mark the occasion. Such exorbitant festivals would always be Meagher's style. On the day, O'Doherty did not turn up, and Martin, who was illicitly present, was anxious that something had befallen him. 'I am afraid you are sick or suffering from some accident.' O'Doherty was indeed suffering in Elm Cottage, Oatlands, from lassitude and dejection. Eva, now a 19-year-old bard, was publishing in the pages of the revivified *Nation* a string of verses designed to rally Ireland and to express her yearning for O'Doherty, and she would temporarily cheer O'Doherty when the verses at last reached him.

> Yes, pale one in thy sorrow – yes, wrong'd one in thy pain,
> This heart has still a beat for thee – this trembling hand a strain.

But Eva's beloved had not received them yet, and he found the interruption to normal courtship tormenting. He remained a loyal celibate devoted to an ethereal Eva, and being so famously betrothed he did not have the liberties of flirtation, the wooing or even seduction of colonial women which Meagher did. He was also concerned about shortage of money, though he earned a tiny stipend as assistant surgeon to the Irishman Dr Hall, the government surgeon in Oatlands, a good and generous mentor.

At the end of summer on Maria, a man who had been kindly to O'Brien, Captain Bayly, the 50-year-old visiting magistrate, dropped dead of 'paroxysms in the heart', leaving a widow and four young children. O'Brien joined the straggle of mourners to the grave where Bayly still lies, as Lapham and Dr Smart went on taking risks in being lenient towards their prisoner, lest O'Brien make the same journey as Bayly. They must have known at some level that the hard men ashore might one day judge them for it. In the meantime, they were charmed by O'Brien's conversation, his tales of great parliamentary figures and his memories of literary men who were to them merely names in late-arriving newspapers. Lapham may have felt O'Brien would win his battle with the administration anyhow. O'Brien had already written to Robert Pitcairn, a Scots lawyer in Hobart, and one of the champions of anti-transportation, asking whether a writ of Habeas Corpus could be obtained which would force Denison and Dr Hampton to show under what statute they kept him in solitary confinement. Pitcairn told O'Brien that he planned to speak to two Hobart barristers, a young man educated at the Middle Temple, Thomas John Knight, and the combative and democratic Geordie lawyer John Compton Gregson.

Gregson's 'Case for Opinion' was sent to O'Brien, who must have rejoiced in it. 'My opinion is that Mr O'Brien . . . might by suing out a writ of Habeas Corpus returnable in the Supreme Court procure such relief as would secure him from close confinement in the future.' But O'Brien did not immediately act.

In London, Earl Grey arranged for Chisholm Anstey, O'Brien's brother Lucius and William Monsell, O'Brien supporters in the House of Commons, to peruse the Denison dispatches on O'Brien at the Colonial Office in Whitehall. Sir Lucius may have felt in some ways a sneaking sympathy for Denison, for he knew what an astute and unyielding prisoner his brother was. Anstey was pleased to see that O'Brien was again receiving rations as a hospital patient. But, like Lucius, he wanted O'Brien to take his ticket-of-leave. Anstey's letter of persuasion is fascinating because he understood O'Brien so well, knowing that because of Ballingarry, not despite it, O'Brien had assumed as a burden the role of Ireland incarnate and exiled. But O'Brien, said Anstey, was not the author of the insurrection. 'You only joined it . . . I say nothing therefore of the morality or prudence of that Insurrection – that Cause, as we may agree in terming it. I only say that you are not . . . its representative; that all the world is now aware of that fact.' Anstey sternly told O'Brien that he had achieved credibility on

> the one great article of national belief and conduct, Repeal of the Legislative Union between Ireland and Great Britain. Many Protestant, nay, protectionist and Orange partisans, listened favourably to the overture because it came from *you* and because they knew that *you* were much nearer to them than to the Whigs, and, in fine because they confided in *your* honour . . . Let me add that those days are past – those hopes extinguished – *and forever*. The Rebellion hath done this!

In his effort to convince O'Brien to succumb, Anstey threw doubt on the loyalty and judgement of O'Brien's fellow prisoners and former associates. O'Brien's lieutenants, said Anstey, had intended to depose him as soon as the rebellion was successful, but since it had failed, left him with 'the sad and doubtful onus of chiefship'. Anstey even argued that two of the lieutenants were in favour of 'putting him to an immediate and violent death'.

Though there is no evidence that any of the rebels considered shooting

O'Brien, O'Brien himself in his little, increasingly cold cottage by the rough parade square of Maria had no resources for checking. We are left to wonder whether he wavered a fraction as Anstey urged him against 'an useless and a too late persistence in wearing the aspect of chief criminal'. No wonder that he found the long evenings desolate.

It is dark at four o'clock and as I do not go to bed till ten o'clock you may conclude I do not enjoy my winter's evenings as much as Cahirmoyle where a merry little party assembled around the tea table and one of my children claimed the privilege of putting sugar into my tea while another insisted upon the right to add cream to it.

O'Brien had already heard from John Martin that he had met Meagher illegally at Lake Sorell, 'where his district, O'Doherty's and mine all touch each other'. Indeed, at one of the State prisoner meetings on the shore of Lake Sorell, as Meagher would tell the world through a letter sent to the *Nation*, it was agreed: 'I should write a respectful remonstrance to Sir William Denison, stating the facts I had heard in regards to O'Brien's health . . . In case no alteration took place, it was further agreed upon we should throw up our "tickets of leave".'

'Here we dine,' O'Doherty himself recorded of a reunion he attended here in a hut of the ticket-of-leave stockman Cooper. 'Whilst the preparations for the dinner are going on, whilst Mr Cooper is splitting chops, shelling peas, washing onions, and melting himself away in a variety of labours by the log fire, we are rambling along the shores of the lake, talking of old times, singing the old songs.' Despite all rumours of John Martin's delicacy of health, the frail, beak-nosed Ulsterman loved to ride up here, in between looking for a job in his Bothwell district.

By mid-April, Martin, jobless but reunited with Mitchel, thought his friend's health good enough to take him on the exciting ride to a Lake Sorell meeting. On the appointed day Martin had his grey pony, but Mitchel set out on a horse rented from a man in the village. It rained, and Mitchel soon found that the autumn weather of Tasmania could resemble that of Ireland. Beyond the home of Martin's friend, Mr Russell, a Scottish settler, the rain changed to snow. Mitchel insisted they ride on, and so they passed through 'a scene of such utter howling desolation', amongst rocks and trees. Martin promised that if the weather continued bad, they would turn back when they were half-way. High up they came across open country, a plateau between the two lakes. With snow coming on again, they reached the small hut of round logs, thatched with grass, of the former convict Cooper. Cooper told them that Meagher and a reinvigorated O'Doherty had been up to see him that day and were now at

Townsend's – another, more commodious, hut 4 miles further on. Mitchel was too exhausted to ride any further; 'so Cooper took one of our horses and set off to Townsend's.' In the last of the light, Martin and Mitchel heard three horses outside, and Meagher's unique laughter. 'We *laughed* till the woods rang around; laughed loud and long, and uproariously, till two teal rose, startled from the reeds on the lake shore, and flew screaming to seek a quieter neighbourhood.'

Mitchel had barely met Kevin O'Doherty in the past but found him a noble-looking young man, his face bronzed. Cooper provided a splendid meal of damper and mutton chops, as the other Young Irelanders told Mitchel more distressing news – Smith O'Brien had been deprived of his usual supply of cigars, sent him from Hobart Town. 'To a man all alone, and already goaded and stung by outrage and wrong, even such a small privation as this may be a serious grievance.' The next morning they all rode along the peninsula which ran out into Lake Sorell, the Dog's Head Peninsula. Snowy mountains lay beyond the western side of the lake, and here Mitchel felt his soul breathe. He returned to Bothwell from the ride delighted to have found that all his friends were '*unsubdued*'. Now he became a devout excursionist. Exploring to the west of Bothwell, he met families of Scots Highlanders, Erse-speakers, refugees from the same potato blight that had descended on Ireland. He and Martin also enjoyed the 'pleasant parlour of Ratho, the home of a most amiable and accomplished Edinburgh family'. Their name was the Reids, and Ratho a fine stone house of the kind successful settlers built early in Tasmania, structures very different from the ones occupied until recently by New South Wales pastoralists such as Brodribb. Mr Reid's widowed daughter, Mrs Williams, whose officer husband had died in India soon after her marriage, was personable, of lively intelligence, and barely twenty years old.

Mitchel had on his travels begun to notice the impact the Australian wilderness had upon the convicts. 'The best shepherds in Van Diemen's Land are London thieves – men who never saw a live sheep before they were transported; and what is stranger still, many of them grow rather decent – it would be too strong to say honest – by their mere contact with their Mother Earth here.'

One of his rides took him illegally to the homestead of Mr and Mrs Connell, Gaelic-speaking Irish settlers of Glen Connell in the foothills of the Western Tiers. They were generous and expansive hosts, and Meagher himself often went hunting and riding in the wild country above with their Australian son. Martin liked them so thoroughly that he sent them books – in his opinion, the highest gift of all.

In the *Sydney Morning Herald* early in April 1850 appeared a letter, painful to O'Donohoe, signed 'A Friend to Erin's Exiles':

I beg to assure those who feel an interest for the 'Irish state prisoners' now in Van Diemen's Land, that those gentlemen endeavoured to *dissuade* Mr O'Donohoe, one of their number, from the publication of his newspaper . . . the other State Prisoners are much displeased with Mr O'Donohoe's conduct . . . the character of some of his 'new associates' make his 'compatriots' blush for him and wish that HE had never been amongst THEM.

We can merely guess at who might have been the Hobart associates who made his compatriots blush.

O'Donohoe gamely republished the hurtful sentiments in the *Exile*. Driven by the need to show public loyalty for their fellow rebel, three of the State prisoners wrote a letter of support for him, though each danced round the point of applauding O'Donohoe's *Irish Exile*. From the town of Bothwell, Mitchel chose to attack the anonymous writer for claiming that O'Donohoe's fellow felons were ashamed 'of being associated with you in our pious Felony. I know not one amongst us who engaged in it with truer and more disinterested devotion than you.' John Martin followed the same line: 'You have sacrificed your property and your family affections, and you offered your life in that cause.' Meagher, who was probably the best friend O'Donohoe had, declared, 'Never have I blushed for the brave, generous, devoted friend – the sharer of my watchings and my wanderings – the sharer of my anxieties, privations, and calamities.' O'Donohoe, touchingly pleased, enthusiastically published all three letters, and fought on.

On Maria Island, after the triangle of iron was rung to signify lock-up time for O'Brien and the convicts in the long barracks further down the square, the nights were now lengthening. Hampton had notified O'Brien he *would* be allowed to buy clothing, but only if he endorsed a letter of credit the registrar would send him, the registrar being thereby authorised to honour drafts in payment of O'Brien's bill. O'Brien did not acknowledge the registrar's right to have any management of his money. 'I wrote in answer to say that I must decline to endorse the order.' He may have been as stimulated as exhausted by these arm-wrestles with the administration, and understood that Hampton's bureaucratic procedures could be made to seem like tyranny when conveyed to sympathetic listeners in Europe. 'What will be the next move?' asked Smith O'Brien with a trace of relish. But the little fights diminished him too, and he had reached the stage of composing, whether in daydream or despair, an inscription for an urn, containing his heart, which was to be deposited in the Church of

Ireland Cathedral of Limerick after his death. '*Cor patria moriens exsul commisit O'Brien / Quod fuit et fidum patria dum vita manebat*.' ('Dying, the exile O'Brien committed to his homeland a heart which, while life remained, kept trust with the nation.')

The northern hemisphere's reaction to his imprisonment on Maria Island, inevitably delayed, was by now potent. The revivified *Nation* announced on 1 June 1850: 'They are killing Smith O'Brien by slow murder on Maria Island.' That utterance in itself ensured O'Brien's victory in the Irish mind. 'He is caged in the closest solitary confinement. His food is scanty and loathsome . . . He never sees the face, or hears the voice, of a friend. He is denied the common requisites of decency. For months he has not been allowed a change of raiment, or permitted to cleanse his dress.' Irish Members in the Commons would ask questions. On 22 June, reaction to the treatment of O'Brien was quoted by the *Nation* from the Irish regional papers. The *Sligo Champion* asked: 'Who can contemplate unmoved this descendant of a line of kings . . . this man of warm and loving heart, subjected to such vile torture?' The *Cork Examiner* had to defend Sir Lucius from those who thought he was not exerting himself enough on his brother's behalf. 'I am in a position to know that the fate of his brother has preyed on his mind to such an extent that his health is giving way under it.'

The *Nation* reprinted a letter O'Brien wrote to Isaac Butt from Darlington Penal Station: 'An amiable Catholic clergyman inhabits the adjoining cottage, and though his garden is separated by a low fence from mine, he is not allowed to exchange a syllable with me.' Against such heart-breaking assertions, the Denison couple had no answer. Meetings of protest and support were held in London, Cork, Limerick, Dublin, Ballyhaunis and Kerry. A group of a thousand met in New York with newspaperman Horace Greeley in the chair. Michael Doheny, the Young Ireland escapee, struck a militant attitude for his old friend. 'If you wish to send comfort to Smith O'Brien,' he cried, 'tell him there are a hundred thousand Irishmen in America ready to fight the battle of freedom.' This myth of an Irish-American army ready to apply themselves at once to the old battle took no account of the claims the new battle made on the Irish, as they applied their immigrant skills to the mills and mines and navigation canals.

Against the wall of his cottage O'Brien had tacked a view of Dromoland Castle sent to him by his eldest son, Edward, now an adolescent. O'Brien was if anything more anxious than he would have been at home to ensure Edward got the education he, Smith O'Brien, considered appropriate, rather than the one Sir Lucius and Lady O'Brien wished the boy to have. Edward had forgotten to tell him, he wrote, 'to what school you are to be sent'. O'Brien himself wanted St Columba's, the school of the Protestant establishment, founded in Dublin since the time O'Brien himself had attended the Sassenach school of Harrow. And Edward was not to slack: 'You may acquire before the age of 23 a competent knowledge of 7 languages.' He listed them – Irish (that was essential), English, Latin, Greek, French, German, Italian. And then a proficiency with abstract, experimental and natural sciences. He was concerned that his entire family should see Ireland as the central location of their souls and schooling. 'Your education would be completely stopped if you were to come to this country,' he warned his daughter Lucy.

And his wife too was so instructed, now that Hampton had given an official guarantee that his letters to her would not be opened. He had a chance to praise her resignation and fortitude, but they were to go on being exercised at home.

I sometimes feel not a little melancholy when I think that our young rebel Charles Morrough will not know his father when he sees him, and I feel that Charlotte and Donough will also have forgotten me, but painful as are these feelings I cannot in the least agree to consent to the removal of my children to Australia – I wish you to consider Ireland as your home and the sphere of your duties and of your affections.

The botanical friendship between O'Brien and the young Lapham women flourished. Anne Lapham, fifteen years old, gave O'Brien a cutting for his garden, for which he recompensed her with the expected verse.

Take back this stem its flower is thine
Though nurtured by my care
For gladly I thy gift resign
That thou its bloom may'st wear.

Smith O'Brien considered this verse innocent enough to have a place in the journal he was preparing for his family to read at a later and happier date.

Not long after midday on 18 July, a Convict Constable Hamerton was playing with a 6-inch telescope in front of the coxswain's cottage on the hill a little to the south of Darlington. He was in the company of the coxswain Griffiths and of another constable, Rogerson. Constable Hamerton would later claim to have seen through the telescope, from a distance of 400 yards, O'Brien and the younger Miss Lapham, Susan, twelve or thirteen ears of age, embracing in an enclosed back garden on the sea side of the Lapham residence. Hamerton would swear before Dr Smart:

I saw Smith O'Brien reclining on a garden seat and Miss Susan was close to him. I positively declare I saw O'Brien's flies open in front and that I saw Miss Susan's hand in his trousers. Smith O'Brien had on his cloak and tried to conceal himself by drawing it around him . . . I have seen them kissing. I have repeatedly seen them together after dark.

Hamerton passed the telescope to Coxswain Griffiths. Griffiths would claim to have seen what Hamerton saw, and so the telescope was passed to Convict Constable Rogerson. Rogerson claimed he rushed down the hill to alert Mrs Lapham, who was resting in a front room of the Lapham house. 'I told her to call her daughter from O'Brien immediately from the Garden or she would be ruined and I would tell Mr Lapham all about it when he came home . . . Mrs Lapham made me promise I would tell no one and I did so.' She summoned Rogerson back later in the day. 'Mrs Lapham said now I depend on you for Mr Lapham has an appointment at Port Arthur and if the Comptroller General was to hear anything of this the family would be ruined for life.'

Convict Constable Hamerton also paid Mrs Lapham a visit, was seen near the Lapham house by the Scots Dr Smart and, questioned by him, was forced to make a sworn statement, with which the surgeon confronted O'Brien. O'Brien and Dr Smart exchanged a number of angry letters across the little Darlington station square. Smart, said O'Brien, had 'brought into question the name of a young lady . . . by giving countenance to the reports of a mischief maker who I understand states that he saw through a telescope doings which he could not have seen had he been within ten yards . . . but as this want of prudery arose from a kindly desire to mitigate the loneliness of my solitude you ought to be the last person to condemn it'. Smart answered that unless the imputation was withdrawn, he would authorise a public inquiry. Smart read both his own letters and O'Brien's to Mrs Lapham, including the one in which O'Brien withdrew any sentiment which might hurt Smart's feelings, since 'it will be an act of wanton cruelty towards as amiable and excellent a girl as ever existed to make it a matter of public investigation'.

So the matter seemed settled, though the shame did not give O'Brien, guilty or innocent, much rest. Dr Smart did not take an affidavit from Rogerson and Griffiths until 12 September, nearly two months afterwards, when the Convict Department happened to see the affidavit he had taken from Hamerton, and demanded more information. Between 23 July, when Hamerton swore his statement, and 12 September, Rogerson and Griffiths had plenty of time if necessary to ensure their stories did not clash with Hamerton's.

Smart's ultimate report to Comptroller-General Hampton had it that a very ill and fraught Mrs Lapham admitted that O'Brien had 'taken liberties with her daughter . . . A great part of Mrs Lapham's anxiety was to keep all knowledge of the affair from Mr Lapham', who was 'subject to violent attacks of illness'. Smart, only thirty-four years old and with a career to make – he would ultimately become mayor of Hobart – deflected blame from himself to Lapham by claiming Lapham had said 'that the Comptroller General was perfectly aware of all the liberty Smith O'Brien enjoyed here, and he was perfectly pleased with all parties'.

In summary Smart, though guilty of being indulgent himself, made Mrs Lapham seem a very strange mother, Mr Lapham a perverter of Hampton's orders, and Smith O'Brien a perverter of the young. But neither Hampton nor Denison used the incident against O'Brien. Possibly this was from sensitivity towards the girl's reputation. Possibly it was because the governor and comptroller suspected the affidavits and the reliability of Dr Smart's self-saving report.

A defender of O'Brien could of course argue that twelve years was Ireland's marriageable age. But if the incident happened, quibbles of this nature could barely lessen the guilt and betrayal. There were never, however, any further accusations of such abuse at any other time of O'Brien's life, and at first hearing it was hard to believe that a man of such punctiliousness and stubbornness of will could have so betrayed the Laphams. Yet O'Brien confided to his journal: 'It is beyond measure painful to one who is sincerely desirous to do right . . . to feel that he has been led by the frailties of his nature into acts which have brought with them consequences not only disastrous to himself but most detrimental to others.' Those who choose to could read this ambiguous statement as an admission.

After the event, Smart chastised O'Brien's minder, Miller, and ordered Constable Hamerton 'never to lose sight of Smith O'Brien'.

In the Australian winter of O'Brien's supposed fall from grace, Terence Bellew MacManus, former wool broker, had been permitted to move from New Norfolk north to Van Diemen's Land's second port, Launceston. Here he took up residence at the home of Dean Butler, an English priest, found work as a clerk in a warehouse, and settled urbanely into the life of the little port. Southwards, in wilder terrain, Meagher meant to build a Gaelic refuge on the Dog's Head Peninsula on Lake Sorell. He was given land for it by a friend he had made in Ross, a middle-aged English settler named William Clarke, to whom Meagher seemed colourful and amusing. Clarke, who would found a politically powerful Tasmanian clan, already possessed extensive pastoral leases in Victoria and New South Wales, Bradley-style, and was known as 'Big Clarke' or 'Moneyed Clarke'.

Meagher and his assigned Irish convict Egan now moved up into this high, cold, grand country on the lake-shore, and built a timber cottage on a stone foundation. Near the makeshift pier Meagher built, the oared skiff he had ordered from Hobart, *Speranza*, was moored. By *Speranza*, Meagher and Egan, antipodean Noahs, transferred a small quantity of livestock to a grassy and wooded island offshore, 70 acres in extent.

Saint Kevin O'Doherty was more mundanely stuck in his little stone cottage in Oatlands, waiting for a disapproving brother in Dublin to send on his Irish medical certificates so that he could sit for the Van Diemen's Land Medical Board examination. In fact he had not heard at all from his family, and his chastising mother and two brothers might have been punishing him by not writing and by withholding funds. O'Doherty wondered too whether the Medical Board's fussiness was a hint 'to attempt no further intrusion'. But in the region around Oatlands, living with a convict midwife, there was 'a self-styled Doctor' whose qualifications were much shakier than Kevin's.

In August 1850 O'Doherty's superior, Dr Hall, was transferred from Oatlands to Ross. In a panic, without a job or money, he believed he must surrender his ticket-of-leave. By the time Dr Hall was packing, a further mail ship had arrived from Ireland without letters or money, not even from Eva. Saint Kevin felt he was lost at the bottom of a pit. Against the advice of his police magistrate, he decided he must resign his ticket-of-leave and be fed and lodged by the government. But Bishop Willson urged him to apply for a transfer to Hobart or Launceston where he could at least work as a pharmacist.

Bishop Willson and Patrick O'Donohoe both now promoted to Dr William Crooke of the Tasmanian Dispensary in Hobart the idea that O'Doherty's presence as a pharmacist would bring in Irish customers. Kevin received approval for a transfer to Hobart. By then a further Eva poem had been published in the revived *Nation*, and sent to cheer O'Doherty.

Come, wild deer of the mountainside! Come, sweet bird of the plain!
To cheer the cold and trembling heart that beats for thee in vain!
Oh! Come, from woe, and cold, and gloom, to her who's warm and true,
And has no hope or throb for aught within this world but you.

As O'Brien lamented the second anniversary of his capture, 6 August, Queen Victoria gave royal assent to a Bill allowing representative government in South Australia, Victoria and Van Diemen's Land. O'Brien reflected that these were benefits long denied to Ireland but granted readily to remoter British possessions. The new Act meant that anti-transportationists like Mr William Carter could rise to power in the Legislative Council of Van Diemen's Land, there to battle Denison.

But O'Brien looked to possible rescue. Already, an Irish physician, Dr J. C. McCarthy of Hobart Town, had had a meeting with Meagher at which Meagher insisted that O'Brien's life might well be ended by some random act of oppression. Whereas, if O'Brien escaped, he would resurrect the validity of the rebellion itself, the Irish would be consoled and emboldened, and the claim of treason reduced to a mockery. Meagher showed McCarthy an unsigned letter that he had received from New York, from the Irish Directory, a secret organisation of which Michael Doheny was a member. The letter implied 'that there would be no hesitation in America to honour any demands' for organising O'Brien's escape. If necessary, Meagher could depend on his father as well. McCarthy agreed therefore to outlay in the short term the large amount required to finance a rescue of O'Brien.

Patrick O'Donohoe was told to make contact with Captain William Ellis, rakish master of *Victoria*, a small vessel which sometimes supplied Maria Island. Father Woolfrey was contacted on a visit to Hobart and was given the job of asking O'Brien whether he favoured escape. It was ascertained that O'Brien did, but he wanted it clear as a matter of personal pride that his family could not be expected to carry the expense. In the near term it would need to be borne by others, and then O'Brien himself could recompense them after escape.

The prisoner received a message to be ready on or about 10 August, and to keep watch when out on his daily walks. On 10 August, no ship appeared during O'Brien's exercise, and likewise there was nothing on 11 August. But the next day, as he set out southwards with his unwitting daily companion, Convict Constable Miller, 'between 1 and 2 o'clock p.m., I observed a vessel in the distance bearing towards the point of the shore on which I was walking'. He had also spotted Constable Hamerton in the trees on the steep slope above, 'but did not perceive that he was armed with a gun'.

He sat down to eat his lunch of biscuit and beef, took out his book 'and continued to read to my keeper as had been my usual practice in our rambles'. Despite a shower of rain, O'Brien – by occasional standing and shifting of position – made sure he was visible to the oncoming vessel, which was soon within half a mile of the shore, and which sent out a boat towards the beach. O'Brien read on until 'when the boat was within fifty yards of the shore I dashed into the sea'. He was soon out of his depth, but he could swim, and expected to be dragged aboard by the men in the boat at any time. In fact, an armed constable, probably Hamerton, emerged from the bush and covered the men in the boat with his gun. Weighed down by garments and books and other items he carried in his pocket, O'Brien had to be dragged ashore on an oar.

As the boat was beached, Smith O'Brien jumped into it and refused to move. The constable with the gun punched a hole in the timbers. But O'Brien would not walk back to the station. William Denison reported to his mother: 'The three men who had come to rescue him were made to carry him. Was not this a most absurd termination?' But O'Brien yielded, 'not wishing to annoy men who had already exposed themselves to some risk on my account'. He walked very slowly, however, perhaps to allow another boat from the ship to intervene. By the time he reached Darlington he was appalled to find that the government boat was towing the *Victoria* into Darlington Probation Station.

It was later widely believed that Captain Ellis had betrayed the escape plans. A ticket-of-leave man, having earlier been sentenced to fourteen years for piracy, he seemed to have made a deal with Hampton for absolute pardon. Yet it was obvious from Sir William Denison's letters and his wife's journal that the escape attempt came as an utter surprise at Government House. Nor did Ellis seem to benefit from his bargain – he and his first mate Hunt stood trial and were fined £60 each, which the supporters of the escape attempt, not yet aware of Ellis's treachery, felt bound to pay. Dr McCarthy was by now severely out of pocket. But things were to get worse – on the night following their fine, Ellis, Hunt and their crew stole *Victoria* and took to the open sea. Perhaps permission to do so was part of the contract with Hampton. But the owners held McCarthy responsible, and in time O'Brien would need to help Meagher and McCarthy in paying for *Victoria*.

Marched back to his cottage on Maria, Smith O'Brien mourned for the lost possibility: 'If the wind had brought the vessel nearer to the shore and if there had been a little more resolution on the part of the boat men and perhaps less promptitude and fidelity on the part of the Constable . . .' To compose his mind, he wrote an essay on his escape attempt abstractly considered, drawing upon St Paul's escape from Damascus by being lowered from a window in a basket. He was concerned by indications that admirable Lapham might be the scapegoat for the attempt. That would be unjust. His prisoner had given no guarantees. Every and any day, O'Brien was entitled to try to get away.

He was a little surprised to be told that Denison did not 'propose to take any special notice of his recent attempt to escape from custody. The Assistant Comptroller is to warn the prisoner that any second attempt of the kind will . . . place him in the position of an ordinary convict working in a gang.' O'Brien acknowledged this forbearance. But he was certain to be moved from Maria. The Laphams were due to leave also, to take up their new posting at Port Arthur. O'Brien, confined to his house, had been kindly treated by the superintendent; 'though in truth I should not have been much surprised if he had displayed some excitement and vexation'. By the eve of his departure for Port Arthur at Hampton's orders, O'Brien was edgy from isolation and anxious to go. He had been writing letters assuring the authorities that both Lapham and Miller, his keeper, had been utterly ignorant of his proposed escape.

Before O'Brien left his cottage on Maria Island, his goods were searched by Mr Lapham. The superintendent found £10 12 shillings and, according to regulation, confiscated it.

14
Young Ireland and the Profane Colonists

> But my prayer, my fond entreaty to you . . . is to keep out of the hands of these men as you would out of the clutches of the very demon himself . . . I am treated as a common convict, obliged to sleep with every species of scoundrel, and to work in a gang from six o'clock in the morning to six o'clock in the evening – being all the while next to starved, as I find it wholly impossible to touch their abominable 'skilly'.
>
> O'Donohoe to Meagher, January 1851

'I have been told that Port Arthur', O'Brien confided in a letter to his sister Anne, 'is as near a realization of a Hell upon earth as can be found in any part of the British dominions except Norfolk Island.' The penal establishment of Port Arthur lay in the corner of Van Diemen's Land, a handsome, well-wooded, well-watered port. If one travelled south-east from Hobart, first a very narrow neck of land connected the bulk of south-eastern Van Diemen's Land to bulbous Forestier Peninsula, and eventually a further narrow string, Eaglehawk Neck, connected the Forestier to the massive Tasman Peninsula, Port Arthur's site. Notorious Eaglehawk Neck, the land approach to the Tasman, was some hundreds of yards across and guarded by a line of chained mastiffs, a collective Cerberus barring the gates to hell. Through its flimsy geographic connection to the nether world of Van Diemen's Land, the Tasman Peninsula with Port Arthur became a yet further nether world.

O'Brien, unchained, made the journey down the coast from Maria Island to Port Arthur in a 25-ton cutter, on which Lapham and his family travelled too. O'Brien's relationship with them seemed still cordial, but there was little conversation between them. At midnight they were off Cape Pillar, and ill winds held them back from entering the Port Arthur penal station until dawn. 'Its appearance is very picturesque as seen from the water. It is surrounded on every side by wooded hills and looks more like a pretty village.' O'Brien's new quarters ashore were a small two-room house, free-standing unlike his little Maria Island cottage, furnished with a bookcase, a cupboard, tables, a washstand, and 'four chairs with very hard seats being such as are used in kitchens in Ireland'. A garden was behind the house. Nearby stood a majestic stone gaol, three storeys high, a fine chapel, a stone barracks and other well-designed outbuildings, all solid on this last jut of earth before Antarctica. O'Brien was pleased that his garden, full as it was of thistles, was 50 yards long by 30 wide, for he would not be permitted beyond it. An armed soldier of the 99th Regiment was always in the garden. During his one hour of exercise in the morning, his one hour in the afternoon, 'The sentry constantly paces backwards and forwards within the garden walls . . . Two powerful lamps throw light round my dwelling at night. At seven o'clock in the morning my door is unlocked by the Acting Superintendent.'

Lapham stayed distant, or was ordered to do so. There was not a sight of the Lapham women. At first O'Brien was pleased that the Assistant Superintendent, Irvine, was an Irishman, and the surgeon also, as was the officer in command of troops, Brevet Major Philip Smyly. But these three were too scared to carry on more than basic, administrative conversations. O'Brien's rations were 'barely sufficient to satisfy my appetite though compared with the allowance of Indian meal which Lord John Russell said was enough for an Irish peasant they are indeed superlatively rich and abundant'.

On Sundays only, attending church, he saw other convicts, some 200 Protestants of the station, and, as Mitchel had in his solitariness, made a scholarly assessment of their features. 'They seemed to be almost all Englishmen of the lowest class . . . and I cannot but think that a craniologist would find in the study of this collection of heads much to confirm the theories of his science.' A natural generosity did assert itself: 'It is possible that this impression may be unfounded.' In fact it was the moral squalor of officialdom rather than of his fellow prisoners which depressed him. An officer who gave a cook a leek to go with O'Brien's vegetables was chastised by Irvine. O'Brien was told that instead of his allowance of 1 pound of potatoes he would from now on draw 4 ounces of leeks, since they were what he desired. He sought solace in Tasso, Virgil, and W. B. Stevenson's *A Historical and Descriptive Narrative of Twenty Years Residence in South America*.

Lapham was judged severely by an inquiry into the attempted escape, and was removed from the superintendency at Port Arthur. O'Brien's sense of debt to this dismissed official, like his debt to those who paid for the failed escape, grew mountainous in his solitary mind. For the first time he began to consider the possibility of accepting a ticket-of-leave, to delight Denison and take the pressure off Lapham. He wrote to Dr Nixon, the Anglican Bishop of Tasmania, declaring a willingness to improve Lapham's chances by accepting a 1-year parole. Bishop Nixon passed the letter directly to Denison, whose response was hostile. Smith O'Brien would take his ticket-of-leave 'if the Government will pardon the Superintendent whose negligence allowed him to make the attempt! A modest proposal, is it not?'

The dismissed Lapham and his family left Port Arthur on 19 September – as it turned out, the O'Briens' wedding anniversary. William wrote to his brother Lucius, imploring him to intercede on Lapham's behalf. His utter powerlessness at Port Arthur led him to write directly to Hampton, offering what he had earlier offered through Bishop Nixon. He asked too whether he would be permitted to live in Hobart Town or Launceston for the sake of employment.

On 2 October, Assistant Comptroller-General Nairn wrote to O'Brien to tell him that he could not be allowed to reside in Hobart Town or Launceston, 'but that he may reside in any country district not already selected by one of his fellow prisoners'. There was not a mention of Lapham in this. 'As I do not propose, except in the event of Mr Lapham's restoration to the Superintendency of Port Arthur, to accept a ticket-of-leave on these conditions, I must now reconcile myself to a protracted incarceration in my present abode.' So he celebrated his forty-seventh birthday, in solitary servitude.

O'Donohoe in Hobart, in the process of moving his newspaper office from Macquarie Street to Collins Street, was gathering a petition calling on O'Brien unconditionally to accept his ticket-of-leave. Simultaneously, MacManus, at work in a warehouse in Launceston, and Mitchel from Bothwell urged Smith O'Brien to take the means to liberate himself. Terence MacManus reached back to a classical education for an argument: 'Cato might do without Rome, but Rome not without Cato.' Then at the end of October a public meeting was held in Hobart Town in which an address calling on O'Brien to take the ticket-of-leave was signed 'by upwards of 500 persons'. The communal desire to free O'Brien was so great that O'Donohoe had to warn his readers in early November against a confidence man, operating under the name of Baron de Bhere, who was visiting supporters, asking for money towards a rescue attempt.

The document with 500 signatures arrived in O'Brien's little house in Port Arthur on 9 November. 'It is written in good taste, earnest and simple,' said O'Brien. He was moved to sit down at once to write to Denison. 'Sir, I hereby engage not to attempt to escape from this colony during the ensuing six months namely from the 9th Novr, 1850 to the 9th May, 1851.' He wrote to Lucy, 'Until now I have never felt myself thoroughly beaten by English power.' Yet he knew that the purpose of his exercise in endurance had already been achieved. The world had been drawn into the matter of his treatment, had identified him with every ailing man and woman of Hibernia. Governor Denison could embrace his wife in exaltation and clap Hampton on the back. In petty terms, he could be said to have worn O'Brien down. In world terms, the triumph would prove to be O'Brien's. To the Irish, including those in America, and amongst sympathisers in Van Diemen's Land, Smith O'Brien emerged not as a man subdued, but as a man who had yielded to the humane concerns of a worldwide multitude of admirers.

His offer was accepted. Waiting for transport to Hobart, he took hikes, one of them to Point Puer, where child convicts had recently been kept, another to the top of Mount Arthur. At six in the morning on 18 November, he left Port Arthur by a railway between the port itself and the north coast of the Tasman Peninsula at Eaglehawk Bay. This line saved ships from Hobart the trouble of rounding the Tasman Peninsula's complex coast to Port Arthur, and shortened the passage to Hobart. The motive power of the little coaches was, however, human. 'I was then placed in a little waggon and impelled along the railway by four men . . . the labour of pushing the waggon up the inclined planes is very severe.'

At the end of the rail, he was put on a steamer, which made calls at a number of penal stations on the way to Hobart. At the Cascades station, he noted that as a result of public protest the treatment called 'ring-bolting' had been suspended: the victim had been hung spreadeagled from four ring-bolts set in a stone wall, while a wooden gag with a breathing hole was strapped in his mouth to prevent screams. 'The Superintendent was, I believe, reprimanded by the Governor but while Mr Lapham was being dismissed for the exercise of humanity the Superintendent at Cascades has been retained in his situation.'

From the deck of the steamer approaching the dock at Hobart Town that evening, O'Brien could see some hundreds of people gathered at the wharf. A Mr Reeves, a progressive hatter, entertained him at dinner and accompanied him the next day in a promenade through the town. Dinner the next evening at Mr William Carter's house at Newtown, 3 miles from Hobart, was the first time for nearly two and a half years that Smith O'Brien had eaten at a family table. But next morning he was required to set out upriver for his district, New Norfolk, a pleasant few hours away. As soon as the coach carrying him pulled up in the main street of that town, he was greeted by the former Catholic chaplain on Maria Island, Father Woolfrey.

O'Brien liked the aspect of the valley here very much, and chose to stay on the far side of the river in the well-provided stone structure named Elwin's Hotel at a rent of £6 per four weeks. From the front of the hotel, 'in every direction Highlands covered with forest bound the horizon, but I fear I shall find but little attraction in the scenery of this district as it is wholly destitute of historical associations and is rather monotonous in character'.

The prosperous settlers of this section of the Derwent were, he wrote to Lucy, 'plain unpretending men, with neither more nor less polish than belongs to that class of gentleman in England or Ireland'. Typical of affluent settler families were the Fentons, who occupied a fine house named Fenton Forest. Captain Michael Fenton, Irish-born, had served in India until 1828, and at Fenton Forest, although a temperance man, he was involved in hop-growing. He was also one of the new members of the Tasmanian Legislative Council. His wife, Elizabeth, was handsome but 'a shocking bigot'. O'Brien was grateful to the Fentons, however, for their kindnesses and the company of their lively daughters, who entered the gap in his affections left by the departure of the Lapham sisters.

Early in his life at New Norfolk, MacManus, O'Doherty, Meagher and O'Donohoe all arrived at Elwin's Hotel to see their captain. These were illegal calls and would have evil results. On his way to Elwin's from the Launceston coach, MacManus – a resident of New Norfolk for a time – was spotted by a hostile local named Mr Jordan, who challenged his presence. MacManus replied, 'Do you think we want to steal your sheep and cattle?' O'Donohoe came from Hobart by coach with his printer and fellow publisher, John Moore. Both of them had drunk their way up the Derwent at inns at each coach stop, and no doubt visited the Old Bush Inn of New Norfolk before crossing the bridge to Elwin's Hotel. Arriving, they began throwing punches at each other over some business matter right in Elwin's driveway, and were arrested by the constables of New Norfolk who had been trailing them. After a night in cells, O'Donohoe appeared before Magistrate Mason and was fined 10 shillings for being drunk and disorderly. Sobered and in pain, he cursed himself for having offended O'Brien, from whom he had always sought to find favour.

Meagher made a more discreet but equally dangerous visit with a young Irish friend named Keane. Mr Elwin interrupted the visit to warn O'Brien that police were advancing on the hotel, someone having spotted Meagher as he rode through the town. When the police arrived in the hotel hallway, a waiter went up and told the three men that Mr Meagher was to report downstairs. It was Keane who presented himself and was arrested, putting himself in a position afterwards to claim false arrest. Ten minutes after the police went off with Keane, a New Norfolk Irishman brought a horse to Elwin's Hotel to allow Meagher to escape. Keane returned home to Ross only two hours after the Young Tribune. This had been a delicious trick.

O'Donohoe returned to Hobart from his New Norfolk fracas in poor health, caused by alcohol and the damaged ribs suffered during the brawl at Elwin's Hotel. He was placed under armed guard until fit to appear again before Mr Mason on the more serious charge of being outside his district. O'Doherty and MacManus were also summoned to appear before Mason. But on the day of their hearing, Mason reprimanded them and sent them home again. He knew there was sympathy for the exiles even amongst some of the English and Scots gentry of the region. Perhaps this encouraged his lenient judgment. But it did not endear him to Denison.

Overriding Mason, Denison revoked the tickets-of-leave of O'Donohoe, O'Doherty and MacManus. The decree went out to the men on Christmas Eve: MacManus was to serve three months' hard labour at the Cascades, O'Doherty three months at Impression Bay, O'Donohoe at the Salt Water River. For O'Donohoe this was a disaster – he would have to close the *Irish Exile*, or transfer it by deed to others. A deed was being prepared, he told Meagher, assigning interest in the newspaper to Mr McLaughlin and Mr O'Donnell, two Hobart businessmen.

For overriding the magistrate's decision, Sir William Denison was, to his wife's amazement, 'very much abused in the colonial papers'. Even the *Courier* asked, 'Can we be surprised that any of them should have felt a wish to visit Smith O'Brien for a few hours, after a long captivity?' On Christmas Day, Meagher wrote to O'Brien asking for guidance on whether he too should abandon his ticket-of-leave 'to a government capable of acting in so coarse, so imperious and brutal a manner?'

He hoped the answer would be 'No!' For at the time, he had good reason not to surrender his parole. He had fallen in love with a young Australian woman of Irish parentage. It had happened thus. Walking in the countryside near Ross one day, Meagher had come across a broken-down carriage around which stood in bewilderment Dr Edward Hall, the recent mentor of O'Doherty, Mrs Hall, their six children, and their governess, Catherine Bennett. Catherine was barely nineteen years old, daughter of an Irish emancipist, Brian Bennett. Meagher repaired the broken wheel and from then on began to visit the Halls regularly. The governess was not of Meagher's background – her father was closer to the Hugh Larkin end of the Irish spectrum. In his twenties, Bennett had held up the mail coach in Trim, County Meath, and was transported to Van Diemen's Land in 1818 on the *Minerva*, prior to the policy, operating in the 1820s and 1830s, of excluding Irish felons from VDL. By Christmas 1850 he, his wife and his large Australian brood, who lived on 100 acres at New Norfolk, had the exhilaration of knowing that the Young Tribune was contemplating marriage with their Kate. Not only that, but over the next few years the greatest Irishman, Smith O'Brien, would occasionally walk down from Elwin's Hotel to their place for tea.

An Irish band performed outside the Hobart Prisoners' Barracks every night for MacManus, and also played outside the recuperating O'Donohoe's lodgings in Collins Street. An unrepentant Terence MacManus, waiting for transport to the penal station, refused Meagher's offer of surrendering his ticket-of-leave in protest. 'I am off in the morning by 7 o'clock, per steamer,' he told Meagher, 'to the "Cascades" convict station. You'd laugh, my dear fellow, to see me in my grey uniform, with a little bundle already tied up, containing a few pairs of socks and a flannel shirt – all other necessities supplied by the Government.'

When Patrick O'Donohoe reached Salt Water River on 8 January, he was too weak for hard labour and was taken on to the hospital at Port Arthur for two weeks. One traveller reported seeing him there, 'lying on his iron pallet in the common ward, and in the ordinary blue flannel hospital dress'. The Hobart journalist 'Veritas' noticed him later, a little recovered. 'I never saw a man in more cheerful spirits – when he sits down to his scanty repast of brown bread and skilly, he has all the convicts round him in roars of laughter.' Recuperating from his broken ribs, O'Donohoe was placed on relatively light duties. 'Making brooms and other menial work, getting up at four in the morning; and occupied in many ways until half past eight at night. When he was locked up with the vilest of the vile', a brutal overseer named Booth, three times convicted, harassed him at every opportunity. On 24 February he was happy to be sent now to the Cascades probation station.

Earlier at the Cascades, MacManus felled timber and dragged it to the saw-pits. He assured his friends that he was becoming a true 'backwoodsman' and that he was already anticipating his release on '1st April, quail-shooting day'. In fact, he envisaged a much earlier date.

Meagher had the easiest job: wooing Catherine Bennett, even though the idea drew the disapproval of John Martin. Catherine, literate herself, was the child of parents who came from the semi-literate Irish masses for whom John Martin, like the rest of the Young Ireland leaders, was willing to risk death, but whom he could not contemplate a friend's marrying. For Martin and the others might at the sharp edge of their politics be rebels, but in their social dealings their manners were those of British gentlemen. 'I am unable to discover any grounds of confident hope that any of his sanguine expectations from the marriage project will be realized,' wrote Martin. But Meagher felt reinvigorated by his love for the governess. Catherine had awoken in him 'the proud and generous nature that was sinking, coldly and dismally, into a stupid and sensual stagnation . . . I am myself again.'

O'Brien, still concerned about repaying debts and being a financial drag on his family, was tempted by a job offer from Dr Henry George Brock, an Irish naval surgeon who had settled in a remote valley in north-east Tasmania. O'Brien was to tutor Brock's sons in return for £60 per annum plus board and lodging. His plan was to live off his tutoring fees and use the money his family remitted to pay off to Dr McCarthy £200 outstanding from the failed escape. He was not perhaps aware that Meagher had undertaken to pay the owners of the *Victoria* for their loss, a total of £550. 'The adventure in which you risked so much had been excessively improvident and fruitless,' wrote Meagher senior to his son, but, as ever, covered the bill.

When the Launceston coach carrying Smith O'Brien to his new teaching post called in at Ross, O'Brien was welcomed by Meagher, who took him into the coaching inn and introduced him to Catherine Bennett. The daughter of an Irish highwayman was entitled to possess high colour, but O'Brien saw her as a muted presence. 'She is in person and manner very pleasing but in a worldly point of view the connection cannot be considered advantageous for him.' Arriving by way of the town of Avoca at Brock's remote wing of the country, O'Brien faced up to the healthy and active 13- and 10-year-old sons of Dr Brock, future colonial men of action, unreceptive to the classics. It was 'not a little humiliating to think that . . . after having acquired experience which ought to enable me to rule nations, I am reduced to a position in which nearly my whole time is consumed in teaching two boys the elements of languages which they could learn with equal advantage from some pedagogue'. He found it 'not a little provoking to think that I am drawing a salary little exceeding that which is paid to the governess of my daughter'.

Before being shipped off to the Cascades to haul logs, MacManus had employed a young solicitor, Adye Douglass, to try to have him released on Habeas Corpus. Douglass in turn commissioned the barrister Knight. Knight issued a challenge to the very transportation law itself, as it applied to all Irish convicts in Van Diemen's Land, and to Terence Bellew MacManus, prisoner at the Cascades. Lady Denison was flabbergasted: 'The lawyers have set up the most extraordinary pleas on this occasion: first, that the Government has no right to subject an Irish convict to the same treatment to which the English convict has to submit; second, that . . . the Queen herself, has no right to coerce, or compel to work, any convict here at all.' To Denison's chagrin, the Supreme Court agreed to hear the case, and the Convict Department was thrown into a panic after a writ of Habeas Corpus was granted for MacManus. The demented government lawyers found they did not have on file certificates of conviction for MacManus and thousands of other Irish convicts, and that they did not possess copies of any of the Irish statutes on transportation. If

MacManus were discharged, every transported offender from Ireland for whom there was no certificate could also demand discharge!

MacManus was brought back by steamer from the Cascades and escorted into court in Hobart in his grey penal uniform. Friends crowded in to shake his hand as he entered the Supreme Court, a short march from the docks. The arguments were put, and while MacManus waited at the convict depot, the judges took a week to consider their decision. At last, on 21 February, the Chief Justice announced, 'We are of opinion that T. B. MacManus cannot be remanded and that we have no power to detain him and he is now free to go out of this court.'

'I am not, I think, in a fit state to write to you to-day,' Lady Denison told a friend, 'for I am in a tumult of evil passions . . . whereas he is known to have been sentenced to death, they have no legal evidence that he was pardoned . . . They have no legal evidence that he was not hung!!' Denison blamed the home government for the missing documentation and statutes, and issued an order for MacManus, who had already caught the coach to Launceston, to present himself to the barracks there for rearrest. Lady Denison feared that her husband 'may be incurring a great responsibility; and yet in truth the state of things seems so desperate that one does not know what he can do better, for he cannot leave all his prisoners at large'.

MacManus's coach stopped in Ross, where a bearded Meagher, dressed as a bushman in large hat, flannel shirt and strapped trousers, handed him a note. 'On Sunday the wedding takes place. No gloves, no cards, no cake. Everything very quiet.' MacManus was able – illicitly – to attend in the home of Dr Hall the marriage of Meagher of the Sword and Catherine Bennett, a ceremony performed by Dr Willson, Catholic Bishop of Tasmania. With glittering eyes, Brian Bennett committed the care of his eldest daughter to Meagher. He did not sense as clearly as some of the gentlemen prisoners or as Dr Hall that it was an improbable marriage. Now the Meagher couple intended to live on the shores of Lake Sorell, an idyll which would be easier for Catherine, with her bush-born hardiness and higher tolerance of rural tedium.

The Monday after the wedding, MacManus travelled on and reached Launceston, where a number of sympathisers briefly celebrated his release with him. According to a report spread about the town, 'he sank on his bed in a state of high fever'. In fact, MacManus's parole had not been reimposed on him since he left the Supreme Court, and an elegant escape was in progress. He went into hiding in the home of Dean Butler, while an Irishman, John Galvin, a gentleman farmer who came from the same vigorous genetic stable as MacManus – long face, lean frame, curly hair – took to MacManus's bed in the home of a sympathetic Launceston merchant named George Deas. Galvin acted out the symptoms of fever so well that Dr Grant, a private physician, and Dr Gavin Casey, government surgeon from the Royal Hospital at Launceston, were both convinced that he could not be moved. Dr Grant 'had found it necessary to bleed him copiously, and adopt other treatment'. A more sceptical Denison asked the Chief Medical Officer of Van Diemen's Land, Dr Dawson, to call in at Launceston and report on the illness of MacManus. On 28 February, Drs Casey and Grant obtained from the pseudo-MacManus a 'distinct and solemn promise that he would not, whilst under our . . . charge make any attempt to escape, or act in any way tending to compromise us'.

From Dean Butler's house, the true MacManus, supplied with money, had already rushed down the Tamar River estuary to George Town, a village from which he was smuggled by rowboat aboard the *Elizabeth Thompson* after the ship had been searched.

The *Elizabeth Thompson* sailed towards Hawaii and San Francisco. MacManus gone, Galvin sat up and confessed the imposture. It was useless to bring him before a magistrate, for he would be defended by passionate counsel. Lady Denison remarked on 'what a mistake it was to treat these men so differently from ordinary convicts'.

Hard labour at Impression Bay had been trying robust Kevin O'Doherty also, but he sustained himself with readings from and meditations on the mystic Thomas à Kempis's *Imitation of Christ*. Patrick O'Donohoe at the Cascades might equally have been sustained by thought of what his penal experience might add to his editorials in the *Exile*. But in his absence that journal had continued its decline, which had begun before he was imprisoned. It published a notice: 'The late proprietor of this Journal, Mr P. O'Donohoe, being now a Probationer Prisoner of the Crown, it is hoped that all persons indebted to the *Exile* . . . or otherwise, will forthwith discharge the same.' Returned to Hobart, O'Donohoe was not permitted to stay in town but sent on to Oatlands. He asked the current manager, Mr McSorley, and the current editor, Mr John O'Donnell, bootmaker, for any income due him, but they could offer him nothing; 'O'Donohoe had the *honour* of being the owner of a journal for three months, without deriving the slightest benefit from it.' Ownership of the *Exile* was still in dispute when McSorley unilaterally closed down the paper, its last issue appearing on 19 April 1851. O'Donohoe was to stay in Oatlands and – as he put it himself – 'starve at leisure'.

Kevin O'Doherty gave an indication of what O'Donohoe had been through, saying of his own time at Impression Bay, 'I was treated with more vigour and harshness than the worst amongst them, having been put in the hardest labouring gang on the station, and refused the poor privilege of obtaining credit (that is, shortening my time by increased industry).' Transferred to shingle-cutting, he 'worked like a Trojan and speedily became a professional hand at the art'.

As it happened, his sentence was shortened as a result of a petition, so he returned to Hobart much sooner than O'Donohoe and began working in the dispensary again. But he wanted to practise medicine, to escape the tedium of the pharmacy. Soon he gave up work in Dr Crooke's dispensary – it was said he had got word of an inheritance from an uncle in Ireland. Though his brothers would try to block his access to the money, he planned, Medical Board-certified or not, to go into a practice of his own in some small town.

In Bothwell, John Mitchel had long since decided to bring out his family, and had written to Jenny about it the previous July. 'Pray God, I have done right.' He was influenced by 'my experience of the good-breeding and intelligence and honorable character of many Colonial families . . . in this remote, thinly-peopled and pastoral district, engaging in some sort of farming and cattle-feeding, and mingling in the society of the good quiet colonists here, we might almost forget at times, the daily and hourly outrage that our enemies put upon us'.

For whether by the appearance of a platypus in a stream on one of his rides, or by the shrill call of kookaburra or laughing jackass – 'a noisy bird so named by profane colonists' – he was perpetually reminded that this beautiful place was not Ireland and rather the home of strange fauna, 'profane colonists', and worse. 'We overtake on our track homeward, a man and woman – the woman, a hideous and obscene-looking creature, with a brandy-bloated face, and a white satin bonnet, adorned with artificial flowers. She is a pass-holding servant, just discharged from some remote settler's house, and she is going to Hobart Town in custody.'

Jenny Mitchel and the children were on their interminable way to John when in May 1851 he was permitted to go to Hobart to await his wife's ship. While in town he was able to meet up with O'Doherty. 'St Kevin is sometimes gloomy and desponding.' The problem was the thought of Eva: 'a fair and gentle lady, with hair like blackest midnight; and in the tangle of those silken tresses she has bound my poor friend's soul; round the solid hemisphere it has held him, and he drags a lengthening chain'.

For Mitchel, even waiting for Jenny and the children became a complicated matter. After some days in Hobart, he had a letter from Adelaide. Mrs Mitchel, her five children and a servant had arrived there in the ship *Condor* from Liverpool. They had not known till the ship was at sea that she was to touch first at Adelaide in South Australia and discharge cargo, which would take an extra month. A ship's captain, who had just come from Adelaide, found Mitchel in his lodgings and told him Mrs Mitchel meant to take passage on a brigantine for Launceston. But after ten days' waiting at Launceston, most of it with a schoolfriend from Newry, now a flour miller, he received a letter from O'Doherty; the brig *Union* had arrived in Hobart Town with Jenny and his family. So he turned south, sending a message that his adored Jenny and the family should catch the stage north. He would meet them at Green Ponds, where the road to Bothwell left the main stage route.

Two days later, his journal entry was uncharacteristically succinct. 'Today I met my wife and family once more. These things cannot be described. Tomorrow morning we set off through the woods for Bothwell.' Their ride was joyous, though rain mixed with snow was falling across their track. Thirty-year-old Jenny enjoyed a sense of solid arrival and the promise of normality. His younger daughter Minnie had been alarmed at the isolation of the bush, the narrow, bushy trail, but was quickly reassured. Mitchel rode Fleur-de-lis, a horse he had stabled at Green Ponds for the past two weeks precisely for this last leg of the journey. Beside him, the family travelled in a spring cart, 'to the comfortable hotel of Mrs Beech – incomparable cook of kangaroo. Knox was waiting for us; and we spent such an evening as seldom falls to the lot of captives.'

The few rooms Mitchel and Martin had shared in Bothwell were inadequate for the family. By the end of August, they had all moved 3 miles from Bothwell to a more spacious though far from palatial house, Nant Cottage. It sat, and still sits, on a 211-acre farm Mitchel and Martin intended to work. From its upper windows, the Mitchel family and their closest friend enjoyed a noble view stretching for 3 miles north to Quoin Hill. In theory at least, Mitchel adored the rural life, and began stocking the farm with sheep and cattle.

Mitchel heard from Jenny how John and James and Willie had loved the crowded passage out and had spent their evenings at Irish parties in steerage. They took to the bush with the same enthusiasm. 'Four hours every day are devoted to the boys' lessons,' said Mitchel, 'then riding, or roaming the woods, with the dogs.' Later events would cast a poignant light over the image of these three boys in hallooing chase after wallabies in the Australian bush, at play in the valley of the Clyde at the world's end. Jenny Mitchel wrote enthusiastically about the farm near Bothwell to her childhood friend Miss Mary Thompson. 'I am now perhaps happier than I would have been had I never known trouble.' Two months of seasickness on her way to Mitchel, her recuperation lying on a mattress on the poop deck, were all but forgotten. She now had the normal pleasures of gossip. 'You will have heard before this of Mr Meagher's marriage to one of the beauties of this country. It is a pity on the whole (between ourselves). I fear his father will be very wroth with him.'

Jenny, a Van Diemen's Land householder now, employed convict servants, including a Tipperary woman convicted at Clonmel at the time of O'Brien's trial. But despite her own willingness to become a colonial wife, Jenny would later have to tell Miss Thompson that John insisted on calling their house a 'lodging . . . for John will not have me use the word "home" in this country. But the sweetest little spot it is you ever saw.' So she was willing to cry *Home!* and raise her children there. She visited and liked a number of the local families – the Reids of Ratho, the McWilliamses, the Pattersons, the Wilkinsons, the McDowells. 'Not an Irish family among them,' said Jenny with a trace of her father's Orangeism.

In Dr Brock's house the VDL winter laid up O'Brien with lumbago. Kept awake at night by pain, he distracted himself by reading *My Prisons* (*Le mie prigioni*), an account by the Piedmontese poet Pellico of his imprisonment under the Austrians. He left his lessons with the Brock boys to weep secretly in his room at news that his cherished brother-in-law the Reverend Charles Monsell, husband of Harriett, had died in Ireland – 'perhaps the most amiable man whom I have ever known'.

As he travelled into Avoca in the rain to report to the police magistrate, he became aware that a huge Australian shift had developed. Gold had been discovered outside Melbourne, and many men of capital were rushing there. Australian colonial governors were believed to have quashed many other earlier gold discoveries, understanding the impact a gold rush would have on the stability of the convict system and of society generally. Count Strzelecki and the other Polish explorer Lhotsky had encountered auriferous rocks on their explorations in the 1830s. A boy named Chapman had turned up in a jewellery store in Melbourne in 1849 with 35 ounces of gold found in the bush. A clergyman found alluvial gold outside Melbourne, but kept quiet about it for godly reasons. But a man called Hargreaves, who had mined in California, chose not to be quiet when he found gold in June 1851 near Bathurst, where John Hessian, former Ribbonman, had served out his time. Gold made further transportation to New South Wales or the Port Phillip area absurd. The British poor might seek transportation for a minor crime, achieve an early ticket-of-leave and become miners, all at government expense!

In another golden venue, San Francisco, Terence MacManus landed at Front Street on 5 June 1851, to a raucous welcome amidst the civic stench of stagnant water, tar and sewage. The population of San Fastopolis, as wits called it, had trebled since 1849. Around the old Plaza, saloons and casinos operated twenty-four hours a day to serve gold-diggers. MacManus himself, for whom every Irishman wanted to buy a drink, was not immune to the crass charms of the Plaza, although he seemed to be less readily attracted to women than Meagher and O'Brien. Sentimentalists said that he would never marry because he was wed to Ireland. His chief vice, encouraged here more even than in VDL, seemed to be drinking, the sin most easily forgiven in mad San Francisco, where, it was said, one quarter of the population drank to celebrate luck and three quarters to comfort themselves for its lack.

In the week of MacManus's arrival, an Australian – perhaps an escaped ticket-of-leave man or a discharged felon – was hanged by a mob for trying to steal a safe. A gang of former convicts – the Sydney Ducks – were of particular concern to citizens. So a publicly proclaimed Committee of Vigilance was formed to regulate punishment for crime. Some order *was* needed in a town where 500 or 600 ships cluttered the waterfront, and hotels slept eight people in an 8-by-10-feet room, behind walls of flammable canvas painted brick. Although MacManus saw the results of a massive recent fire in the centre of the city, the San Franciscans took these disasters with composure, and had time to plan a number of public receptions to greet 'Brave MacManus'. On the night after his arrival, a levee was held at the Union Hotel. MacManus, no Meagher when it came to oratory, said he found it difficult to express his exhilaration when three months earlier he had been wearing grey felon's clothing and chains. He knew with delight now that he would live the rest of his life under the American flag. Ecstatic applause greeted his short oration.

The following night, at a committee meeting and further reception for MacManus at the Union, the crowd was so thick that the floor gave way and the entire assembly fell into the cellar in a state of what MacManus called 'beautiful confusion'. Picking its way good-humouredly out of the Union's cellar, the meeting now moved out into the old Plaza of San Francisco, where, on the permanent rostrum, MacManus said that wherever the Star-Spangled Banner needed a soldier, there he would be found.

Official America (including two US generals present) rejoiced in the escape of a Young Irelander. The extradition treaty between Britain and the United States was considered by American judges not to apply to political prisoners, and rejoicing was not restrained by transatlantic diplomacy.

MacManus's arrival was celebrated not only in San Francisco but in every Irish centre of influence throughout the United States. He was given a dinner *in absentia* in Boston, and an Irish-American militia regiment in New York was named the MacManus Invincibles. As the fury of welcomes diminished, MacManus tried to come to terms with a mercantile life in San Francisco, setting up as a shipping agent, a task at which he was no rival for the Yankees.

The escape of MacManus had produced joy amongst British liberals and ecstasy in Ireland itself. On the Australian mainland, amongst those who rejoiced in MacManus's feat were those humbler Irish ex-prisoners such as Hugh Larkin and his wife to whom such a resurrection was improbable and glorious. So it was also to Irish free immigrants with whom Hugh did business. There was much delighted counter-thumping in Hugh's store. The Goulburn, Braidwood and Yass areas were full of Lord Monteagle's former tenants from Limerick – Culhanes, Ezburys, Quiltys, Kenellys and Kenealys, Connells, Daltons, Sheahans, Burkes, all discreetly congratulating themselves on MacManus's adroit flit.

But there was no flitting for Hugh. Another child, John, had been born in 1850. As a small trader and paterfamilias, he saw his town grow by several thousand settlers, particularly after the gold discoveries at Turon Creek in 1851. By now, Michael O'Flynn, Mary's first son, was a robust young man of sixteen, working as an agricultural labourer in the high-priced labour market around Goulburn, or else trying for gold. For the same fervours which had earlier seized San Francisco now marked the bush. There was a sense of movement and spaciousness.

For the Larkins, it was a cause of pain to think that the demigod O'Brien had been subjected – as many Irish and anti-transportation newspapers implied – to the same indignities as they had. But new heroes in New South Wales politics claimed their attention as well. A New South Wales Constitution was about to be framed. There had been argument about whether it should contain a hereditary House of Lords, a concept the Australian populace mocked, and there was already intense debate on the connection to the British monarch. One of the leading republicans, an 'extreme Liberal' activist, had moved to Goulburn to work as a journalist and barrister. His name was Dan Deniehy, and he was the sort of fellow who would have fitted very well into the '82 Club and Young Ireland. In his early twenties, he was a dishevelled but handsome little man and a dazzling orator. Dan Deniehy's father Henry had been one of the humblest of felons, transported to Australia for seven years for vagrancy, but had become a produce merchant in Sydney. Dan's mother Mary McCarthy had also received seven years for some minor crime. Larkin saw in Deniehy a man of similar background to his own who yet spoke and wrote with all the vivacity and scholarship of a Meagher. Deniehy wrote in the *Goulburn Herald*:

I have adjourned to this good town, a remarkably thriving place, for the purpose of recruiting my health, of scraping together a little of that prime element of social and political power – money . . . This, even partially done, my eye is fixed on one point – the doing my duty in establishing Republican institutions and advancing in every genuine method, my native land.

This young man of great gifts, speaking for the democratic, anti-squatter elements, would in early 1854 mock Sydney's narcissistic fear that Russians would seize the colony once the threatened war between Britain and Russia broke out in the Crimea.

I can only say that if that Roosian Ketchikoff does land, I only hope he may try travelling upon the Goulburn road. I have a notion that he would undoubtedly regret such a step; and further, if the few gentlemen that are studded here and there about our district (like ornaments on a twelfth-cake) be a sample of what is really understood to be the genuine article, why rather than thirty of 'such gentlemen', I vote for Ketchikoff.

One can without too much effort imagine Larkin and Mary, listening to such pungency, doubled over in laughter.

It does not appear that in between children, the store, and watching Deniehy grow in grandeur, Hugh went looking for gold in a persistent way. He stuck to commerce, such as it was, to home, and to Goulburn's familiar pubs, probably avoiding Mandelson's, the swankiest, the least like a shebeen – unless, of course, brilliant Dan Deniehy was orating there. He might still have been remitting money to Esther, but whether Esther knew of his Australian family there is no way to tell.

The authorities had had the good grace now to give Mitchel and his family total liberty within Van Diemen's Land – the sort of liberty enjoyed by all other ticket-of-leave men other than O'Brien, Meagher, O'Donohoe and O'Doherty. Under this impetus, Mitchel decided to visit O'Brien, and set off with Mrs Jenny Mitchel on horseback cross-country towards Oatlands. This is even now hard, hilly terrain, and the journey stands as a tribute to Jenny's sturdiness as well as Mitchel's. Jenny, letting her horse drink in the Jordan River, was full of enthusiasm for this country her husband would not let her call home. 'Anything to exceed the beauty of our drive that day through the bush I never saw.'

In Oatlands they boarded the coach northwards, Mitchel still taking a sour view. 'Every sight and sound that strikes eye or ear on this mailroad, reminds me that I am in a small, misshapen, transported, bastard England; and the legitimate England itself is not so dear to me that I can love the convict copy.' As they travelled, they sensed the excitement of Van

Diemen's Land's first election under the new Constitution. Political rosettes were attached to the ears of coach horses. Denison did have some supporters, particularly the *Hobart Town Advertiser*. The proprietor of this paper was John Donnellan Balfe, a former infiltrator of Young Ireland, who had been rewarded for his spying with a post and land grant in Van Diemen's Land and wrote under the pen-name 'Dion'. Balfe and pro-transportationists wore red ribbon as their emblem, but the coach the Mitchels travelled on was full of blue-ribbon wearers, supporters of a Mr Kermode, the anti-transportation candidate in north-east VDL. At a hotel in Avoca, the five-starred flag of the Australian League was flying, and Mitchel noticed that Mr Kermode, the candidate for the Avoca area, had used Meagher to write his election address. 'The sharp pen of the hermit of the lake pointed every sentence: in every line I recognised the "fine touch of his claw".'

Mitchel and his wife were in the hotel parlour taking refreshment when they saw Smith O'Brien pass by on the street. 'We met him at the door as he entered; and our greeting was silent . . . his form is hardly so erect, nor his step so stately; his hair is more grizzled, and his face bears traces of pain and passion. It is sad to look upon this noblest of Irishmen.' They finished breakfast together, and Smith O'Brien suggested a stroll up the valley of the South Esk. They wandered for hours, talking of '48. With Mitchel, Smith O'Brien felt thankfully free to attribute failure in great part to the behaviour of the priests. O'Brien said he had by now despaired of any revolutionary action in Ireland; Mitchel would never do so.

When the Mitchels and O'Brien parted on 16 October, the eve of O'Brien's birthday, Jenny cried. 'We stood and watched him long, as he walked up the valley on his lonely way.' Seeing Jenny had made O'Brien yearn for his own family, but he still resisted the idea of 'placing my wife and children under the control of the brutes who govern the prisoner population'.

On the way back to Bothwell, Mitchel and his wife travelled a little way up the Macquarie River to that point called the Sugarloaf, the home of John Connell and his wife. Connell had already fetched their horses for them from Oatlands and he and his wife diverted Mitchel with stories of their early life as settlers: 'A wild forest to tame and convert into green field – wilder black natives to keep watch and ward against – and wildest convict bushrangers to fight sometimes in their own house.' Mrs Connell, who had a thick Munster accent, seemed to be the characteristic Irish *vanithee*, or woman of the house, and was locally famous for having once defeated four bushrangers in an exchange of fire.

John and Jenny now turned west, towards Lake Sorell. Mitchel was leading the horses up a sharp slope 'when we suddenly saw a man on the track above us; he had a gun in his hand, on his head a cabbage-tree hat, and at his feet an enormous dog'. This man and Mitchel exchanged Australian 'cooees', a bush-dweller's yell. The bushman above was Meagher. 'The next minute, instead of commencing our descent into a valley on the other side, we are on the edge of a great lake.' They followed a path cut amongst the trees, 'at the head of which, facing one of the most glorious scenes of fairy-land, with the clear waters rippling at its feet, and a dense forest around and behind it, stands our friend's quiet cottage'.

'I must say', Jenny wrote of Catherine Meagher, 'that his wife seems a handsome, nice, amiable girl.' The Meaghers' ticket-of-leave man, Tom Egan, offered to sail the Mitchels across on the skiff *Speranza* towards that large island in the middle of the lake, where oats and potatoes had now been planted. But the wind became contrary, and they were pleased to get ashore and indoors. 'Pleasant evening, of course; except when we spoke of Ireland and the miserable *debris* of her puny agitators.' The fire gleamed red on gaily bound books cramming the shelves. The Mitchels rode home carrying in a burlap bag a small kangaroo, a present to his children from the Connells. 'John Knox and all the children are walking the field with the dogs . . . and there is joy at Nant over the little kangaroo.' 'Notwithstanding all my exercise,' wrote Jenny, 'I continue stout – a new feature in my case, but a decided improvement.'

The elections proved a triumph for the Australian League. 'There is a large majority of anti-transportation returned,' Jenny wrote. 'Would that our poor brethren at home could be induced to unite for their rights – it does seem there is some spell over them which they cannot overcome.'

A sad William Smith O'Brien renewed his parole and engaged not to escape between 7 November 1851 and 7 May 1852. Throughout October and November there was continual rain, and he felt his low spirits dragging his physical health down. His efforts to be tutor to Brock's sons still suffered from a certain futility. He and his friend Brock agreed the arrangement was not working, and O'Brien sought leave to return to New Norfolk. Ten days before Christmas, he left the Avoca area 'without experiencing the slightest desire ever to return to it'. At Campbell Town, travelling south, he was met by Meagher, apparently settled, but with a firm intention to escape. Marriage had failed to provide him with a focus for his energies. There was every indication that, as other Young Irelanders had said, he and the 20-year-old colonial Catherine were ill-matched.

The next evening, O'Brien caught the night coach to Hobart, where he was permitted to do two days' business before returning drearily but comfortably to his old home, Mr Elwin's Hotel in New Norfolk. But from

Major Henry Lloyd of Bryn Estyn estate, an excellent stone house with even more excellent English-style stables, he received a welcome invitation to spend Christmas. He stayed on in comfort until the New Year, and then moved downriver to Fenton Forest, home of his friend Captain Michael Fenton, newly elected member of the Legislative Council. As for his Australian-born daughters, O'Brien confessed he delighted in their singing. But he told Lucy he was reluctant to praise them 'lest you may imagine that I am desirous to comfort myself for the loss of your society by that of other daughters of Eve'.

At Fenton Forest a strange event occurred, indicative of the sort of society O'Brien lived in. A man in animal skins presented himself at the Fenton house and explained that he was an absconded convict and had lived 8 miles from them in the bush for the past seven years. The man was Philip Markham, a convict whose escape had imposed a form of solitary confinement on him: 'As long as he was engaged in making improvements his life was tolerable but as soon as he ceased to find employment for himself he became haunted with visions.'

Catherine Meagher was entering her last trimester of pregnancy. Nonetheless, with a young man's heedlessness, Meagher was bent on escape, and believed Kate would come to term and bring the child to join him after his escape. In this he had her enthusiastic blessing. The Connells of the Sugarloaf had undertaken to provide horses and escorts and to signal readiness by a bonfire.

The signal fire was lit a few days before Christmas. All the gentlemen involved in easing Meagher's escape had finished their arrangements. Rather than leave the matter entirely to a column of smoke, Connell sent his son to tell Meagher as well. Catherine said goodbye to her husband and went down the mountain to her parents and sisters in New Norfolk, perhaps glad to leave solitude and marital bemusement at the lake. She had faith that soon she would be following Meagher into a larger world. After Christmas, a number of friends from the locality of Ross rode up the hills to join Tom Meagher in his mountain cottage. There, on 3 January 1852, he composed a note to the local police magistrate, who happened to be the same Mr Mason who had been overridden by Denison in the matters of O'Donohoe, O'Doherty and MacManus. The letter gave the magistrate twenty-four hours' notice that Meagher was withdrawing his parole, and unless apprehended in that time, he would feel free to go his way.

Getting Meagher's letter by messenger, Mason ordered two officers to Lake Sorell to make the arrest. They rode up the Dog's Head Peninsula and, according to them, found Meagher's house empty except for his servant. What happened then is subject to contradictory report. Meagher was on horseback in the thick bush around the promontory and said that he rode up within yards of the officers at the hut, challenged them to arrest him and announced that he intended if possible to escape. The officers made no move.

They would later claim, however, that Meagher did not present himself, nor could he be found around his house. Witnesses support Meagher. An unnamed neighbour and friend of Meagher's said that he was 'on a visit to Mr Meagher', a formula to avoid accusation of being actively involved, and in the house awaited the arrival of the constables on the afternoon of 3 January. Meagher in the meantime strolled and chatted with his companions in the bush around the house. At 8.00 p.m. a constable called Durieu and one other policeman arrived to take Meagher into custody. 'Later they went to the stables to attend their horses. While there, Meagher cantered into the yard, an open cleared space ten yards from the stable, and sent one of his servants to tell Durieu he was waiting to speak with him. I myself heard the servant deliver the message.' Durieu, in this account, moved from the stable, returned to the house, and again visited the stables. 'All this while Meagher patiently awaited an answer to his message . . . the constable scrupulously remained in the stable.' Given the police unwillingness to recognise his presence, Meagher 'went off amidst the cheers of his party in the full conviction that he had fully discharged every obligation'.

Five years later in New York, another eye-witness told his version in defence of Meagher – how Meagher went up to the police in the company of the writer, a Tipperary man, and three other riders including Keane, who had once been mistakenly arrested in New Norfolk in place of Meagher. 'Seeing the police coming towards him from the lake, Meagher cried, "I am Meagher. No longer fettered by my parole, I am about to escape if I can – and your duty is to take me into custody if you can, etc."' When there was no response, says this witness, Meagher felt free to go. There would be endless argument about whether he should have.

Meagher rode round the lake northwards, stopping to shave off his moustache at the hut of a man named Old Job Sims. At that same time, in Bothwell, Mitchel had spent a day hunting kangaroos with his sons – before getting in his hay 'with the aid of two or three horrible convict cut-throats, all from Ireland – and all, by their own account, transported for *seizing arms*'. This was a Ribbon crime, and Mitchel confessed only that these chatty, sociable workers, who dossed in his barn at night on possum-skin rugs, 'were not half so bad as the Queen of England's Cabinet Councillors'. Johnny Mitchel had killed a diamond snake, snakes being

Jenny's one phobia. In the ferocious heat the boys bathed daily in the river, but Jenny hesitated for fear of serpents, who were said to be able to swim.

Meagher's escape, when the Mitchels and John Martin heard about it a few days later, seemed of a questionable nature to them. Jenny wrote, 'We do not like the way the thing was done.' She related to Miss Thompson the story of one constable who had refused Mason's order to go to arrest Meagher, had been fined £10 and dismissed, and so had simply gone to the Port Phillip diggings. 'I wish I were a man,' said Jenny, 'to go and dig.'

John Martin mentioned 'serious embarrassments' which had oppressed Meagher. Martin had earlier reported to O'Doherty that Dr and Mrs Hall objected to Meagher's treatment of Catherine. 'The best consideration is that his wife is quite on his side. But I am vexed beyond expression at the vile entanglements he gets himself into – he has hardly any common sense in some respects.' We can only speculate whether some of these 'vile entanglements' meant that Meagher was seeking out women in Ross and Campbell Town. Martin also reported, 'We knew that for several weeks he had been suffering from serious embarrassments and we had vague fears of some horrid crisis or other.' The seemingly frail Martin was worried enough after the escape to ride up to Cooper's hut. Cooper related how he had seen a large party of horsemen, Meagher in their midst, pass through by moonlight. 'The sad truth is that . . . though O'Meagher . . . sent a message by his servant to Durieu to the effect that he wanted that officer and was waiting for him, and that, after waiting 8 or 10 minutes (near the tree where "Ross" is generally chained), he called out, "Good bye" so loud as to be heard by Keane who was outside the house, yet O'Meagher was not actually in the presence of Durieu.' Had Meagher 'staid in his own house awaiting the constables, and received them there, and been arrested there, and been rescued either there or down near the *tier* . . . and *then* dashed away to the sea-coast . . . what a consolation at least for him and us there would be in the welcome of the Yankees and the baffled spite of the English'. Martin's impression of two of Meagher's abetters was that 'both regard the transaction much as Mitchel and myself'.

On 19 January, two weeks after the escape, Mitchel asked Smith O'Brien whether they should all publish an appeal to Meagher, asking him to return. 'This seems romantic and absurd: yet I do believe if your judgement on the whole matter coincides with ours, and he be made aware of that, he will come.' O'Brien, though not entirely easy, did not think such a step necessary.

If he recaptured Meagher, Sir William Denison said, 'I will send him to Port Arthur and make him "bottom sawyer" under a very good "top one".' Unaware of the debate, Meagher was sheltered in houses around Westbury, a town north-west of Lake Sorell. Here solid English and Scottish citizens willingly offered him rest, and he responded with his disarming charm. But Westbury was also useful to him as a region thick with Irish-speaking settlers. There was no shortage of volunteers to ride with him down to the estuary of the Tamar River, where he was put in the care of the Barrett brothers, who fished Bass Strait in a boat of their own construction. They were to take him to a rendezvous with a ship, the same *Elizabeth Thompson* MacManus had escaped on, in Bass Strait. After last Tasmanian farewells, Meagher stepped into the boat, and the Barretts set their sail and rowed out into the strait for Waterhouse Island, 40 miles or more along the coast.

Meagher's later published account of his escape was graphic and, some say, exaggerated, and no one would be surprised if Meagher's taste for high-coloured narrative caused him to gild events. The Barretts beached after four hours in a quiet cove on Waterhouse Island, ate smoked herring, ship's-biscuit and cheese, and drank sherry. They found the figurehead of a wrecked ship and encountered a Newfoundland terrier, probably a survivor. 'Made a fire on beach of pieces of the wreck, made a tent of oars, mast and sail and lay on an opossum skin rug for mattress and another above for blankets.' The wild dog rested near their fire.

The Barretts had brought provisions for two days, and on the morning of the third day, with no sail in sight, they needed to return to the mainland. So that they would not be suspected of cowardice or foul play, Meagher wrote a note 'for the gentleman who had engaged the boat and under whose patronage the expedition had set out'. (This was the good-hearted merchant Deas, who had helped MacManus.) For writing materials, he knocked the bottom out of a tin pannikin, wrenched off the handle and, flattening out the remaining metal, blackened it over the smoke of the fire. Then he wrote his letter on it with the point of a penknife. 'In three quarters of an hour I was alone on that morose island.'

Meagher spent ten days there, waiting for his overdue ship. He saw a number of passing vessels, lit signal fires and waved his coat. One misty morning an eight-oared boat arrived from the direction of the mainland. 'Thought it was all up – the police must have seen the fire.' The oarsmen were civilians, though. He informed them for cover's sake that he was there prospecting for gold. They winked at one another, pitched a large tent, lit a huge fire. Over the flames they swung an immense black pot into which they poured crabs and shellfish they found along the beach, some mutton, onions and potatoes. They were escaped convicts from Hobart, on their way to the gold rush in Port Phillip. 'I had the best and the most of everything going, the snuggest corner of the tent – the rarest morsels of the daily stew – the choicest pipe full of tobacco – the last drop of Holland's in the locker.'

After some thought, Meagher confided his problem to the escapees. 'The third morning after the arrival of the pirates I was as usual on the lookout when through the blinding mist I spied a sail . . . The ship was standing in close to the island and shortening sail. The stars of the Australian League were gleaming at the mizzen peak.' From the deck a signal gun was fired, then a second gun and a third. His friends the gold-seekers manned the boat and pulled him out through a furious sea. 'I leapt . . . from the stern sheets of the boat and was on the quarterdeck a second after. I had promised the gallant fellows who had brought me from the island to have their stores replenished but there was no time for it. The wind was fierce, the sea too rough, the ship too near the breakers . . . I emptied my pocket of all the money in it and handing it down to the leader of the gang, bade them farewell forever.'

At her father's farm, Stonefield near New Norfolk, under the care of her parents, Kate Meagher wrote to a friend, 'I got . . . just a few pencilled notes the moment before he stepped into the boat which was waiting for him . . . I have great hopes that he is far on the sea before this . . . our days of separation, I earnestly hope, will not be long.' The *Elizabeth Thompson* was carrying fine wool to England, which meant that Meagher would need at some stage to transfer to a ship of different destination. Captain Betts, 'small, chubby, round-faced, cozy, active, convivial, humorous', commanded a very mixed crew. Many competent sailors had deserted ships and headed for the goldfields, and men who were eccentrically immune to that lure, or who could not afford to remain in Australia, made up the crew. They were six weeks crossing the Pacific, rounding the Horn and reaching Pernambuco in Brazil. Meagher landed in Recife without taking from it any Mitchel-like lessons on slavery, and booked aboard the American ship *Acorn* for New York.

In February, Catherine was delivered of her child at New Norfolk – a boy whom she named, according to Meagher's instructions, Henry Emmet Fitzgerald Meagher, baptising him thus by the name Henry into the Church about whose senior clergy her husband had doubts, and by the names Emmet and Fitzgerald into the Irish struggle.

15

Locked Within the Pyramid

> Here's the clime that suits your bosoms
> Here awhile you may repose
> Till you rise to free old Erin
> From her tyrants and her woes.
>
> *Irish American*, welcoming
> Meagher, 30 October 1853

Making for New York aboard the ship *Acorn*, Thomas Francis Meagher was approaching a land which was not indifferent to his fate. In 1851, the US Senate had heard a motion read by Senator Henry Foote of Mississippi which called on England to free O'Brien, Meagher and their immediate associates, and offered the prisoners 'sanctuary on American shores'. Even President Millard Fillmore, a Whig, suspicious of the Irish, who acceded to the presidency after the death of Zachary Taylor in 1850, had asked his Secretary of State, Daniel Webster, to exert pressure for Young Ireland's release. He had stated too that America would offer the Irish exiles 'safe asylum and full protection'. The day after Christmas 1851, while Meagher was still on the shores of Lake Sorell, Webster advised US Ambassador Lawrence in London that he should make discreet representations on the matter with the British government, always taking account of 'the many natives of Ireland now in this country, and the influence, more or less, which they exercise over the policy of the Government'.

A new surge of diplomatic activity had begun in February 1852, while Meagher was at sea, when Lord John Russell's ministry, the government under which the Young Irelanders had been sentenced, fell from power. On 7 February, Senator James Shields, Irish-born Democrat, detailed in the Senate the sufferings the State prisoners had endured, and Senator William H. Seward of New York declared on the same floor that 'Ireland was guilty of one crime . . . and that was the crime of proximity to England'.

On 15 May, the *Pilot* in Boston announced that Thomas Francis Meagher had escaped from Van Diemen's Land and was expected on the Atlantic coastline. 'In him,' said the *Pilot*, 'the Irish in America will find a chief to unite and guide them.'

Knowing nothing of his being awaited, on 27 May Meagher sailed up the long approaches into New York aboard the *Acorn*, and landed at the depot at Castle Garden, in the Hudson off Lower Manhattan, like any other foreign arrival. Looking up a city directory in one of the emigrant aid offices, he sought mention of his friends from Young Ireland – lawyer Michael Doheny, with whom he had once led masses of men up Slievenamon; journalist and Clongowes schoolmate Pat Smyth, who had escaped from Galway on the same ship as John Blake Dillon; and Dillon himself, his companion in the search for O'Brien in 1848. Dillon was listed as living in Houston Street, but on walking with anonymous delight uptown, Meagher discovered his friend had moved to Brooklyn. And so he booked a room at the United States Hotel, and was not noticed until he set out next morning for the law firm of Dillon & O'Gorman at 39 William Street, the latter partner being Richard O'Gorman who had led the rebels in Limerick.

In the William Street law offices, placed between the trade of Fulton Street and the capital of Wall Street, 'A distinguished looking stranger, with a bronzed and ruddy countenance, having all the appearance, in his dress and movements, of a US Naval officer, presented himself in the corridor and was heard enquiring for his friends.' There was an immediate eruption of enthusiasm. By nine o'clock that evening, the entire Irish population of New York were in the know, and some companies of the 69th Regiment, New York State Militia, mustered and marched to Richard O'Gorman's house in Lower Manhattan. Accompanied by the Brooklyn Cornet Band, the 69th serenaded the escaper, as a crowd of 7,000 gathered to cheer him. When invited to step out and speak, he said that he could not do justice to his feelings, for he was exhausted by the long journey. 'He could not account for their enthusiasm,' he was reported as saying in the *New York Herald*, 'as he had been in no battles in Ireland . . . he was grateful beyond expression for the honour of their welcome, while he confessed, his heart was filled with sorrow to think that he was there alone to receive it. O'Brien, and Mitchel, and O'Doherty, were still in fetters.' The *Irish American* reported that an Englishman who lived nearby threw up his window and played 'God Save the Queen' 'on, we suppose, a very cheap piano'. To escape the frenzy, Meagher stayed that night in Dillon's house in Dean Street, Brooklyn.

As days passed, interest grew. The *New York Times*, usually cautious about Anglo-American relationships, declared significantly that Meagher's arrival 'has created universal satisfaction here'. The Democratic *New York Herald* spoke of his youth, his military appearance, his slight stoutness of build, his good looks, 'always a favorite with the ladies'. According to the *Herald*, he was a better orator than Kossuth, the stellar Hungarian patriot who was visiting the United States seeking recognition for an independent Hungary! The paper even went so far as to give instructions on how to pronounce his name, and said that the normal American pronunciation, *Meagre*, was wrong; *Mah-er* was correct.

It was clear at once to Meagher, liberated again to enthusiasm, that the Irish in America, despite their uncertain status, had achieved exceptional leverage. This was in part because of weight of numbers. Throughout the 1830s and 1840s, there were each year more than three Irish immigrants to every English immigrant. In 1850, out of a total population of twenty-four million, the United States had four million citizens of Irish birth or parentage. They did not necessarily possess economic power; many of them lived downtown in unspeakable fire-trap tenements either side of Broadway. Cartage and labouring were the usual occupations for males, domestic service and garment-making for females. The sons and daughters of Innisfail could also be found above 59th Street, living with their domestic pigs on irregular streets in wooden huts under conditions hardly advanced on what they had known in Ireland. They were enthusiasts, however, in a way not possible at home. They were both exploited and given hope by the powerful party machinery of the Democrats. An Irish political brio, suppressed in Ireland, was let loose in America.

On guided tours of the official and unofficial city, Meagher saw that the locale of Irish political power under Tammany was the saloon. It served both as bank and political meeting-place. The saloon was also where favours, contracts, city and state jobs were dispensed by emergent Irish political bosses. The august court system was also exploited by the Irish: local Democrat bosses illegally naturalised the newly arrived Irish with the help of Democrat judges. The way politics was played here and in other cities was everything the Irish enjoyed: intimate, them-against-us tribal, and based on getting one's own people – brothers-in-law, nephews, the children of friends – into some, *any*, public post. The law attracted many of the clever, since it required what many self-taught Irish could provide: the gifts of oratory, a passion for reading, an artful mind, and a furious but not always uncritical belief in the righteousness of any claims their fellows might bring. Taught by O'Connell in the villages and townlands of Ireland to expect political results, the Irish were wringing slowly from America what they had historically craved, a place in the landscape.

On the morning of 29 May, a levee was held for Meagher which was attended by the most prominent local Whig and Democratic politicians. Mindful of his recent allegiance to the Australian League, the anti-transportation forces in the Australian colonies, he told the audience that the convicts of Australia were a very low lot, but that the free colonists deserved a much better comment. That evening he visited Mrs Mary Mitchel, John Mitchel's mother, who had moved from Newry to Brooklyn with Mitchel's sister Matilda, and his ten years younger brother, William, who was attending classes at Columbia and devoting himself to a characteristic American vocation, that of inventor.

Subject to no police magistrate, Meagher also went out to Glen Cove, to a summer house provided by an Irish merchant friend of O'Gorman's, Dillon's and Doheny's. Here he rested and was advised to wait to be offered 'public entrée' by several authorities. While he vacationed, little D'Arcy McGee came down from Boston to invite him to make an appearance in that city.

Meagher might indeed have taken a lesson from McGee, who had arrived in New York a young hero after escaping from Ireland following Ballingary. A natural newspaperman, McGee had initiated the *New York Nation*. He quickly made an enemy of the Catholic Bishop Hughes of New York by attributing the failure of 1848 to the strength of British garrisons in the towns and to the malign influence of the clergy in the countryside. He had also shown sympathy for the Garibaldian rebels who had forced the Pope to flee Rome. After his *New York Nation* was denounced from altars, McGee had gone to Boston at the invitation of a remote relative, the Bishop of Boston, to edit the *American Celt*.

But drinking coffee by the shore of Long Island Sound, the boyish McGee, scarcely twenty-five years old, was undergoing a total reversal of the opinions which had recently got him in so much trouble. The national movements in Europe were godless and secular, he would soon be writing, and a danger to Catholic faith and morals. Many Boston Irish found his new politics too pious and sales of the *American Celt* declined for exactly the opposite reason those of the *New York Nation* had. In his four years in America, McGee had offended nearly every constituency on which his living depended.

For the moment, Meagher was in no danger on that score. A fury of approbation raged round him. Governor Lowe of Maryland, an old schoolmate from Clongowes Wood, urged a visit to Baltimore. Governor Wright of Indiana sent an invitation, as did the corporations of Detroit and Macon, Georgia. In Charleston a sympathy meeting was held to applaud him on his escape.

In a letter received by Meagher, Catherine said Smith O'Brien had been to see her frequently at her parents' home – a remarkable example of O'Brien's loyalty. Now she devoted herself to building up the baby's strength for the sea journey ahead. But on 8 June, Meagher's 4-month-old Tasmanian infant died in the hamlet of Richmond, where Catherine was visiting friends to say farewell and to show off the hero's son. 'Poor Mrs Meagher lost her baby,' Jenny Mitchel wrote to Miss Thompson from

Bothwell. '. . . She has had a very pleasant letter from her father-in-law lately, the first time since her marriage. Also very handsome presents from Mr Harry O'Meagher.' There was a tacit proposition here: the Meagher family growing closer to Catherine as Meagher himself grew more remote.

Since he did not yet know of the death, no cloud hung over the honour given him at the city's premier hotel, the Astor House, where he was waited on by a committee of the Common Council of New York. Meagher pleaded, 'Gentlemen – had the effort in which I lost my freedom been successful, the honours now tendered me would not surprise me. But it was otherwise.' He made it clear that he did not seek any planned public receptions in New York or throughout the east, and the *New York Times* declared that this would 'confirm and strengthen the favorable impression that he has already made upon the public mind'.

Nonetheless the newly founded Meagher Club of New York presented him, at the law offices of Dillon & O'Gorman, with exquisitely bound American classics – Sparks's *Life of Washington* and Bancroft's *History of the United States*. In July he accepted *in absentia* an honorary doctorate of Laws from Jesuit Fordham College in the Bronx. And a gala martial event was planned at the end of July. On the appointed morning, Meagher emerged from O'Gorman's house with his refound schoolmate Pat Smyth, and walked down to the Battery to review the Irish regiments of New York – the 9th, 69th, Emmet Guard, Shields Guard, Irish American Guard, New York Irish Dragoons and Mitchel Light Guard. This event was attended by an immense number of the Irish population. Michael Doheny, now a New York militia colonel as well as an attorney, stepped forward to call on Meagher to communicate to his friends still in bondage 'that day and night their honourable deliverance is the first thought of their armed countrymen in these Free States'. Facing continuous and frantic applause, Meagher invoked the light from the bayonets of the Irish militias the way he had invoked the light from the sword. 'They penetrate and disturb the clouds which overcharge the present hour – revealing to us, in the light which quivers from them, many a fragment and monument of glory.'

The hero had by now made his home in the extremely comfortable Metropolitan Hotel at Broadway and Prince Street. He enjoyed its utter modernity. It was serviced by 12 miles of gas and water piping, and featured upper-floor sky parlours from which ladies and their escorts could look down amazed on the activities in the street below. There, large shuttle coaches carried shoppers across the slippery Belgian-block pavement of Broadway, and respectable people walked on the west – not the disreputable east – side of the thoroughfare. Looking down in the company of splendid young American visitors, he felt the shadow of his

Vandemonian marriage, adequate for a Lake Sorell solitude, but perhaps not for complex New York.

The letter which marred the year was placed in his hands in late summer or early autumn. Meagher was not particularly explicit on his grief for his lost son. But there was now flesh of his flesh which would never escape Van Diemen's Land.

The *New York Herald*'s editor, Irishman James G. Bennett, boasted that election season that 'All the Irish leaders – all the Irish exiles banished from their home by a persecuting government – have either come out in favor of Pierce, or remain silent from delicacy'. Millard Fillmore was no choice – he was trying to curry votes by attaching himself to the widespread, nativist, anti-Irish Know-Nothing movement, so named because its early members, questioned about their anti-immigrant, anti-Catholic policies, structure and membership, always claimed to know nothing about such things. Tom Meagher himself certainly took an instant and avid interest in the coming presidential elections and in the Democratic candidacy of General Franklin Pierce. But Meagher's chief work as the elections came on was to prepare for the lecture season which began in the fall in New York, and for which his opening lecture – 'Australia' – was to be at Metropolitan Hall. The organising committee pitched the entry price at 50 cents in hope of a mass audience. They were not disappointed. Though the doors would not open until seven, by five o'clock in the afternoon of 25 November the hall was surrounded by people, and by six the pressure of the crowd was so great that the management opened the doors in any case. From backstage Meagher could hear that exciting anticipatory murmur of a mass of people bigger than most VDL townships. 'The number present could not have fallen far short of six thousand,' reported the *New York Times*, unlikely to exaggerate numbers for Democrat darlings like Thomas Meagher. Meagher had appeared on stage with two significant aids, a map of Australia and Robert Emmet, nephew of immortal Emmet, and for two and a half hours recounted to an enthralled audience the tale of his escape, going on 'to consider the position Australia would yet assume as a Republic'. Knowing his audience, he concluded with a coruscating passage in praise of America. In a field by the Hudson, he said, he had been struck by the bounteous harvest. '"That seed," said one who stood by, "came from Egypt." It had been buried in the tombs of the kings – and lain with the dead for two thousand years. But, though wrapped in the shroud and locked within the pyramid, it died not . . . And thus it is that the energies, the instincts, the faith, all the vitalities which have been crushed elsewhere, have been entombed elsewhere, in these virgin soils revive, and that which seemed mortal becomes imperishable.'

The *Irish American* recorded that the T. F. Meagher Lecture committee presented the lecturer with a cheque for $1,650. Given that he had a wife and future family to provide for, Meagher went afield lecturing. It suited his desire to see the sprawling United States. His first series of hinterland speeches was made at Albany, Schenectady, Auburn, Utica and Rome. The *Utica Evening Telegraph* believed the Schenectady crowd 'showed about as much admiration as would be exhibited in the tail of a defunct rat'. But it admitted that in Utica itself the reception was better.

Meagher spent his first Christmas at liberty speaking in St Louis, where one member of the audience gave a toast: 'The Five Stars in the new constellation in the Hemisphere.' Meagher declared that he could not let the occasion pass without saying, 'Hurrah! Hurrah! And Amen! to that sentiment . . . the worst thing the British officers in Australia had to say against the flag is, that it "looks devilishly Yankee".' But after a lecture he gave in the last days of 1852 in Cincinnati, he was urged by Catholic papers to clarify his attitude towards the clergy, and to explain his admiration for anti-clericals like the Italian Mazzini, who wanted to unify Italy and sweep away the Papal States, and for Kossuth, former radical governor of Hungary and political prisoner, now agitating in the United States on his country's behalf. The *Freeman's Journal*, the *American Celt*, the *Shepherd of the Valley* and the *Boston Pilot* printed tales of Meagher's red anti-clericalism. 'I spoke favorably of Kossuth and the European movements for liberty,' he later wrote to O'Brien, 'and that was the whole of it. For this I was denounced from the pulpits and through the bigoted Catholic press, and in highways and by-ways.'

After Meagher's getaway, O'Brien fretted and felt entrapped. If he accepted a pardon on Britain's terms, he told Lucy, he would 'probably feel myself morally bound to abstain during my life from seeking to overthrow British Rule'. His gentle brother Henry ran into the problem of his impenitence when drawing up a Memorial petitioning a pardon. 'You will observe', wrote Henry depressingly, 'the absence of many names which I had hoped would have been attached to it.' But at least, said the Reverend Henry O'Brien, at prayer times in St Columba's, when the boys were called on in the Litany to pray for all captives, 'I know your son Edward and your nephews are in the habit of connecting your name with this petition'.

One anxiety bred another. He told Lucy he had received some money from Robert and had discharged some but not enough of his escape-attempt debt. And as frankly as an innocent, he raised his anxiety over

Lapham and 'his amiable family'. He was dependent for any joy in life upon small favours. He felt poignantly relieved when an honest maid at Elwin's found a lost locket Lucy had given him. But that was offset by doubts about how his family would treat his raw colonial friends. 'I hope you will ask Mrs Meagher to visit you at Cahirmoyle.'

And though O'Brien considered Lucy a paragon, he scolded her for not being a model of the Irish rebel's spouse. On his forty-ninth birthday, 17 October 1852, he remarked that Mrs Dillon, 'a six months bride', joyously committed her husband to the rebellion, 'bidding him die for his country rather than live for her. But you breathed no word of encouragement in the crisis of Ireland's fate.' When he thought of what she and his children had had to suffer for a cause they either did not feel, or were too young to feel, sympathy for, 'I am tempted to exclaim – Maidens, beware of patriots!'

There was a maiden who had not bewared. Mrs Kate Meagher was about to sail off to join her husband by way of Ireland, where she would visit Thomas Meagher the elder. This was as good a route to New York as any through the Americas, but the prospect awed her. A father like Brian Bennett was familiar, hearty, possessed of a warm colonial vulgarity. From her husband she would have got a very different picture of Thomas Meagher senior – sage, authoritative, disapproving of his son's excesses, one of which he might consider to be this colonial girl.

Since leaving his penal station on the Tasman Peninsula to live in Oatlands, Patrick O'Donohoe had had a vexing time, but had now been permitted to go to Launceston. Here he was greeted at the coach and looked after by Dean Butler. He tried to achieve redemption, financial and spiritual, by writing a manuscript on Port Arthur, but the printers to whom he entrusted it decamped to the Victorian goldfields. This was but one of many disasters and follies to afflict the increasingly alcoholic O'Donohoe. In January 1852, he staggered tipsy into the watch-house in Launceston and gave up his ticket-of-leave. Though he took it back the next day, he was sentenced to fourteen days on the treadmill in Launceston gaol. Convicts called this mechanical corn-grinder, designed for the dissipation of criminal energies, the 'everlasting staircase' or the 'cockchafer'.

Then in August that same year, John Donnellan Balfe, the Young Ireland informer, was explicitly accused of treachery by the *Nation* in Dublin and by papers in Van Diemen's Land. While defending his behaviour, Balfe took time to describe Meagher's escape from Van Diemen's Land as dishonourable. Loyal O'Donohoe rebutted Balfe in a letter to the *Launceston Examiner*, and said that Hampton should beware lest 'the Macquarie-street convict hulk may be wrecked by the imprudence of his subaltern'. The Macquarie Street convict hulk was the Convict Department, where Balfe had been until recently a deputy assistant comptroller.

Denison believed O'Donohoe had now violated the instruction not to criticise the administration, and by edict withdrew his ticket-of-leave yet again. Well-armed by now with Irish transportation statutes and certificates, the authorities sent O'Donohoe to the Cascades probation station for six months. This seemed to be an experience which aged and unsettled him to an extent noticed by all his friends. A month after his arrest, at a meeting of the Legislative Council all the anti-transportation members passed a motion calling on the queen to rescind the Order in Council that designated Van Diemen's Land as a penal colony. This helped Bishop Willson to be successful in intercessions to Denison on O'Donohoe's behalf, and O'Donohoe was released on 2 November after serving three months. But, not wanting him to make use of the gap between paroles which had allowed MacManus to escape with honour, the superintendent at the Cascades told him that he would be released only if he gave the normal guarantee. With no spiritual resources left, O'Donohoe signed his name to the parole. Reaching Launceston four days later, he went to see a friend whom he designated as GD – surely the businessman George Deas who had helped MacManus and Meagher escape. GD was shocked to see how shrunken O'Donohoe was and how lined his face. He argued that O'Donohoe could not last long under a regime of gratuitous imprisonments. He was after all the Young Irelander whom Denison could most punish with least local and international comment. He was thus, said his friend, 'absolved from the moral and honourable responsibility' of the parole. GD travelled to Melbourne to arrange a passage from there.

It was not until December that another friend of O'Donohoe's, Mr O'N of Sydney, arrived and told him that the escape had been arranged. In his room in Launceston, O'Donohoe changed into a sailor's jacket and walked with Mr O'N 'at a quick pace to the Y Y Steamer' (the *Yarra Yarra*). O'N concealed O'Donohoe in a succession of hiding-places – a cabin, a platform in the engine room, and then in early morning in a stove. O'Donohoe 'just fitted in to it like a monster pie in an oven'. But it was decided by a ship's officer that O'Donohoe would suffocate. As Mr O'N and the officer attempted to find another hiding-place for O'Donohoe, news came that the police had arrived on the pier. 'It was the 9th December, my friend D had his arrangements made in Melbourne for my reception and shipment from thence.' But the police were already searching the ship, and O'Donohoe crept down the gangplank and back to Deas's house.

The *Yarra Yarra* returned to Launceston on 17 December. With the help of O'N and GD, O'Donohoe boarded two days later, was concealed, and travelled without any drama the next day to Melbourne. Here he was greeted and helped by a Tipperary man named John O'Shanassy, owner of a fast-expanding drapery business in Elizabeth Street, and an admirer of O'Connell, whose portrait hung on the wall of his house. O'Donohoe later related that O'Shanassy and two others had organised a place for him on a vessel going from Port Phillip to a 'Spanish Colony' – perhaps the Philippines. But the cowardly captain reneged, keeping the £190 supplied by O'Donohoe's supporters. Trembling and weeping, O'Donohoe travelled 90 miles back through the bush towards Melbourne, living on brackish coastal water.

Now, for lack of a ship in Melbourne, O'Donohoe had to be sent to Sydney. In that port, also gold-frenzied, he remained in hiding for several weeks in the splendid Macquarie Street house of a shipowner named McNamara. The vessel O'Donohoe ultimately travelled on from Sydney on 8 February 1853, *Oberon*, was cleared by Sydney customs for the South Seas. In reality it was bound for San Francisco. The most hapless of the Young Irelanders was, in a sense, free.

The home government now abolished transportation to VDL, though transports already loaded were permitted to leave Britain, and the multitude of prisoners still serving sentences were left to complete them. The last ship of all to arrive in Van Diemen's Land was the *St Vincent* from Spithead in May 1853. Gold, as a Home Office official wrote to Denison, had ensured that 'transportation would soon be shorn of its terrors'. But Western Australia, great in mass, small in population, some 2,000 miles removed from the gold enthusiasm, had since 1850 accepted convicts and meant to continue.

At the end of April, in Tahiti, O'Donohoe was able to board the American ship *Otranto* for San Francisco. When on 23 June the *Otranto* entered the Golden Gate, the exile was enthusiastically greeted, and a group of Irishmen, flush from gold and trade, presented the captain with a bonus of $1,000. O'Donohoe was in good health and better spirits from the sea journey. But despite the presence of MacManus, now considering a move from shipping agency to ranching, he intended to travel on to New York, where it would be easier for his wife to join him from Ireland. Departing California, and crossing Central America, he arrived in New York at the height of the New York summer.

Irish-American support would ensure that he would never suffer extreme want, but people would find him too awkward an object for the brand of adulation which came Meagher's way. And there was inevitable concern over his parole. The New York Irish lined up to give him the worst kind of tribute they could have offered, drinks in the saloons of Lower Manhattan and Brooklyn. What damage Denison had not done him, Irish kindness was finishing. As winter came on and year's end approached, he took up residence in Hamilton Street, Brooklyn.

So three Young Irelanders – MacManus, Meagher, O'Donohoe – had now vanished from VDL, and there were plans for further escapes. In mid-January 1853, Mitchel visited Hobart Town and went first to St Mary's Hospital, 'where I found St Kevin in his laboratory'. O'Doherty drew Mitchel into a private room, asking him to guess who had come to Van Diemen's Land. It was Meagher's boyhood friend, Pat Smyth. Mitchel asked if Smyth had been caught and transported. 'No, my boy: commissioned by the Irish Directory in New York to procure the escape of one or more of us.' This was the secret body that had already tried to free O'Brien. Smyth, posing as a correspondent of the *New York Tribune*, was on his way south on a day coach from Launceston. He was to meet O'Brien and O'Doherty at Bridgewater, ten miles outside Hobart, that evening.

Since the 1848 uprising, Pat 'Nicaragua' Smyth had made a living editing a paper in Pittsburgh and agitating in the New York *Sun* for an American railroad to span Nicaragua, from which he took his American nickname. Meagher had been privy to the Irish Directory's decision to finance him. Indeed, the previous September Meagher had written to the Launceston merchant George Deas, telling him that Smyth was 'one of the dearest, oldest and most intimate and trusted friends I have had', but pleading, 'for Heaven's sake, take care O'Donohue doesn't see him – all will be botched if he does'.

Now Mitchel and O'Doherty – illicitly in O'Doherty's case – travelled up to Bridgewater and met O'Brien. When the Launceston coach was delayed they spent their time discussing surrender of parole. Given that O'Brien's sentence was for life, Mitchel 'earnestly pressed on him that he should first avail himself of Smyth's services'. O'Brien cited a number of arguments why he would not escape. He had had his chance at Maria Island. He hoped that without making any submission he might yet be set free, and then return to Ireland, which, should he escape, would be closed to him for ever. Mitchel argued they should all escape together and proposed a plan, 'by which we should get ourselves placed under arrest in one spot, and in circumstances that would make a rescue easy'.

The hour got so late that O'Brien and O'Doherty had to return to their registered lodgings. Mitchel was at liberty to remain and half an hour after the others had left the coach arrived. Mitchel had not had a lot to do with Smyth in Dublin and did not at first recognise the tall man in boots and an American-style cape. 'Is your name Smyth?' Mitchel asked at last. Smyth thought him a detective. 'I hastened to undeceive him, for he looked strongly tempted to shoot me, and bolt.' Their conversation began in earnest once they had moved to a private room. They resolved to see O'Brien the following day at Elwin's Hotel.

Arriving the next day in New Norfolk, they found O'Brien engaged in his correspondence. The personable and amusing Smyth tried to talk O'Brien round, but without success. So Smyth rode on to Bothwell with Mitchel to survey that region and its police strength. Mitchel wrote, 'He walked coolly into the police office, and into the magistrate's room, surveyed that gentleman a moment, and his police clerk sitting at his desk – then crossed the hall, strolled into the Chief Constable's office; made reconnaissance of its exact situation, of the muskets ranged in their rack, of the handcuffs.' Smyth came to a very American conclusion: 'three or four men, or at least half a dozen, with Colt revolvers, might sack the township, and carry off the police magistrate. A great man is Mr Colt – one of the greatest minds in our country.'

This settled, Nicaragua Smyth went off to Melbourne to negotiate for a ship. At this stage, John Martin intended to avail himself of the same escape, since Mitchel and he lived in the same district. Jenny declared herself willing to follow on to San Francisco: 'My wife does not shrink from all this risk and inconvenience.' It was an awful time for Jenny, however. She gave birth to a daughter, and was seriously ill for a month. As for the child, 'Her papa won't have her baptised till she reaches Christendom,' Jenny explained. It was probably a relief to her that by February nothing had been heard from Smyth. Mitchel still made plans.

While Mitchel awaited his day of escape, the noble-browed Yankee President-elect General Franklin Pierce sent his Irish orderly from the Mexican War, Sergeant O'Neill, down to Boston to invite the young orator Meagher to visit Pierce's house in Concord, New Hampshire. When Meagher did so, the President-elect asked him to attend the inauguration. And further glory was almost tediously available. Arriving by steamboat to lecture in the mill town of Fall River, Massachusetts, Meagher was greeted by a 32-gun salute and cheered by thousands from the shore, many of them Irish factory hands. Turning southwards, he was welcomed in Philadelphia and in Washington with similar fervour, augmented by the news that he had generously left behind $100 for two French political exiles. In Philadelphia, he was greeted by a militia unit named the Meagher Guard, who sported dark, loose pantaloons with a stripe of gold lace. Meagher cancelled one of his Philadelphia engagements, however, to attend a secret meeting between President-elect Pierce and John Mitchel's mother. We do not know if Franklin Pierce – off the record – was let into the news that Pat Smyth was already in Van Diemen's Land. When Meagher was approached by the press to comment on the meeting, 'he gallantly told them he would never abuse any intimacy he might enjoy with the President'.

Meagher – not yet even a citizen – arrived in Washington on 27 February 1853 for the Inauguration due to be held on 4 March, and spent part of the rest of the afternoon with Franklin Pierce in Willard's Hotel. The following day, accompanied by General Shields, Senator from Illinois, and young Captain Key, grandson of the author of the American anthem, he visited the Capitol and both houses of Congress. In the Senate he was introduced to practically every Senator and every significant Congressman. General Cass, the Honorable Pierre Soule, William H. Seward, General Sam Houston, Douglas of Illinois, Mason of Virginia: all lined up for a word. The elderly General Cass was a classic case of the reason Yankee blue-bloods found common cause with an Irish felon. Governor of Michigan territory after the War of 1812, in which he had been ashamed to see his commanding officer surrender Detroit to the British, he had found relations with the Canadian authorities difficult, resenting the Royal Navy's searches of American vessels on the Great Lakes, and British enlistment of the Black Hawks against the Americans. Secretary of War under President Jackson, Democrat presidential candidate defeated by Zachary Taylor in 1848, Cass served now as Senator for Ohio.

General Shields, who introduced Meagher's lecture at Caruso's Saloon on the night of 8 March, was an Irish-American phenomenon. A Mexican War hero, he had represented in the Senate at various times two states – Minnesota as well as Illinois.

Meagher continued on from Washington to South Carolina, Georgia, Alabama and Louisiana. He fell from grace again back in New York, this time speaking for the benefit of the New York Volunteers at Metropolitan Hall. 'Had the Catholic clergy, as a body, taken another course – had they gone out as the Sicilian priests went out . . . had they lifted up the cross in front of the insurgent ranks, there would have been a different story written.' Again he was denounced in Catholic papers and from pulpits. The *Irish American* defended him, but he was damned by the *Freeman's Journal* of New York, whose editor, James McMaster, still considered Meagher one of the chief assassins of O'Connell.

Out with the Church, he was still fashionable in town, and Miss Ferguson of 42nd Street composed the *T. F. Meagher Polka*. It was performed for Meagher by the composer at Niblo's Theater, a renowned New York music-hall. Indeed, as he neared his thirtieth birthday, he was being absorbed by American issues, and when the Meagher Club and the

Meagher Guards of Boston asked him to come to town in August for his birthday celebrations, he spoke chiefly of what he had learned in the South. With its hearty welcomes, casual grace and capacity to gloss over its sins with stylish, pseudo-rustic irony, the South beguiled and influenced most visitors from the outer world, not least Meagher. He argued that America was, North and South, the same fraternal nation: 'amongst all who look up with loyalty to that unviolated and inviolable flag – symbol of this confraternity – everywhere I've found that freedom of thought, freedom of speech, freedom of discussion are rights solemnly declared in the instruments under which these various states are moulded.' He had slotted into the characteristic New York Democrat position, which combined repugnance for slavery with the belief that its abolition was not worth breaking the Union over.

Patrick O'Donohoe was invited up from Brooklyn to take part in the celebrations that night. He insisted, while drunk, on making a speech. He seemed to imply tipsily that he was as worthy of honour as Meagher, had sacrificed all, yet was wilfully ignored. He was silenced by an officer of the Meagher Guards. The *Pilot*, to punish Meagher for his recent anti-clerical speech, published O'Donohoe's statements that Meagher was ungrateful and disloyal, and this may have finally destroyed what had once been, in prison and convict ship, a devoted friendship. And the sad truth was that O'Donohoe was beyond employment now. Back in Brooklyn, he was maintained on a sort of alcoholic's pension, awaiting the accumulation of funds to bring his family to New York.

Not until February 1853 did Catherine Meagher the Tasmanian set out to travel to Ireland from Hobart in the *Wellington*. Arrived in Waterford in the company of her father-in-law in late June, she was astonished to be greeted on the pier by a crowd of 20,000 people as well as the incumbent mayor and corporation. The mayor acclaimed her sharing 'the happiness of the Exile's home'. But Catherine was the exile now. She made an unaffected response. 'I can only claim the merit of that affection with which I was contented to be the companion of his solitude, whilst I aspired to join in the happier life which he now enjoys.'

In July Catherine was brought to the United States by the elder Meagher, whom Meagher himself had not seen since 1848. In humid Manhattan, Thomas Francis faced the challenge of adapting his marriage to this version of the new world under his father's gentle but exacting eye. The couple who had lived in a shack at Lake Sorell lived now in the Metropolitan Hotel, a shining venue for what the Irish world considered joyous reunion. But Lucy wrote to Smith O'Brien after Catherine had been in New York a little, 'It is said they do not suit. His fault, I am told.'

*

In Van Diemen's Land, Mitchel did not hear from Smyth again until the day after St Patrick's Day, mid-March 1853. In code, Smyth's letter declared that he had made up his party for the diggings, and all was going well. He further said that he would meet the rest of his party of diggers at the Bendigo Creek – Bendigo being here a codeword for Lake Sorell. Martin and Mitchel rode up to the lake a week later and found Nicaragua Smyth in the company of young John Connell. The brigantine *Waterlily*, owned by Mr McNamara of Sydney, was to come to Hobart, and on its return voyage would collect them from Spring Bay on Tasmania's east coast. Mitchel and Martin prepared to say goodbye to Jenny and the children. As Mitchel wrote on 9 April, 'Knox and I . . . are to present ourselves on Monday, in the police station, withdraw our parole, and offer ourselves to be taken into custody. Nicaragua brings with him five friends, all armed, as good lookers-on.' Nicaragua had also delivered a relay of fresh horses for them to the half-way point, and they were to be on the beach at Spring Bay ready to embark by dawn.

But the next journal entry some days later declared 'our plot blown to the moon!' Smyth heard from a source that the entire scheme was known to the governor – the ship involved, the place of embarkation, the signal which was to be used. The *Waterlily* had been allowed out of Hobart Town without examination, and simultaneously police reinforcements had arrived in Bothwell. The Martin–Mitchel rescue party dispersed – Smyth and young Connell started for Spring Bay to warn off the ship.

On 12 April, Mitchel received a further message at Nant Cottage: Smyth had been arrested under suspicion of being Mitchel. He was put into the watch-house at Spring Bay, and claimed that from the windows he could see *Waterlily* in the bay with the signal light shining at her masthead. Fortunately the Chief Constable at Richmond certified he was not Mitchel. But he had caught a bad chill and now lay very ill in the house of a friend in Hobart.

Mitchel rode down to Hobart to see how Nicaragua was, and found him ill but convalescent, and engaged in a sickbed flirtation with an Irish businessman's daughter named Jenny O'Regan. It was not until early June that Smyth was able to ride up again to Nant Cottage, and by then Martin had decided that it was too difficult to get two men away. A ship was leaving Hobart on the night of 8 June, and if Mitchel could withdraw his parole and he and Smyth reach the Derwent estuary after dark, the agents had agreed to place Mitchel on board. To help their chances of getting out of the police station in Bothwell on the day, Nicaragua began 'judiciously bribing' local police. On the morning of the planned day of parole-surrender, 8 June, the town was still full of police – some camped opposite the police barracks. Young James Mitchel rode off to Hobart to ask the shipping agents if they could hold the ship a further day, for Smyth and Mitchel would have to wait to visit Magistrate Davis the next day. Smyth spent the extra time in a room in an inn, meeting with and bribing further police to ensure that there would not be more than an ordinary guard on the town.

The account of Mitchel's dash on 9 June was written by the man himself for a world audience with a taste for stylishly managed escapades. That morning, Martin and Mitchel's eldest boy, John, began the walk from Nant Cottage to Bothwell, to be in place to hold the horses at the police office door when Mitchel and Nicaragua were inside. 'Before we had ridden a quarter of a mile from the house, we met James (boy number two), coming at a gallop from Hobart Town. He handed me a note from the shipping agents. Ship gone.' But they both wanted to get on with the process and, continuing to town, Mitchel and Smyth overtook a Mr Russell, who chatted to Mitchel about the price 'for certain grass-fed wethers which I had sold a few days before'. In the main street, Nicaragua and Mitchel saw that at the police barracks, on a little hill, ten constables were engaged in some sort of drill. Dismounting and giving their horses to young John Mitchel and Martin, Mitchel and Smyth entered the station and found Mr Davis sitting in the courtroom, with the police clerk beside him. 'Mr Davis,' I said, 'here is a copy of a note which I have just despatched to the Governor; I have thought it necessary to give you a copy.' The note, dated 8 June 1853, told the Lieutenant-Governor that Mitchel hereby resigned the ticket-of-leave and withdrew his parole.

Davis took the note, and he and his clerk both seemed discomposed. Mitchel repeated: 'the purport of that note . . . It resigns the thing called *ticket-of-leave* and revokes my promise.' Despite the presence of police in an adjoining room. Davis still made no move, and did not call the guard from outside the courtroom door. ' "Now, good morning, sir," I said, putting on my hat. The hand of Nicaragua was playing with the handle of the revolver in his coat . . . The moment I said "Good morning" Mr Davis shouted, "No – no! Stay here! Rainsford! Constables!" '

But Smyth and Mitchel were moving. At the little gate leading out of the court into the street they expected to find an armed constable, but he was holding two police horses as they passed him, and they jumped into the saddles of their own horses, still held by Martin and John Mitchel the younger. Mitchel naturally depicted the pursuit as something of a farce. 'Grinning residents of Bothwell on the pavement . . . who, being commanded to stop us in the Queen's name, aggravated the grin into a laugh; some small boys at the corner, staring at our horses as they galloped by, and offering "Three to one on the whiteun". This was my last impression of Bothwell on the banks of the Tasmanian Clyde.' Nicaragua himself now separated from Mitchel and rode to Nant Cottage to tell Jenny that all was well thus far. He would then catch the coach to Launceston.

A mile into the bush, Mitchel met 'my good friend J—— H——, son of a worthy English settler of those parts' who knew Tasmania very well. JH and Mitchel faced an awful 130-mile ride through wild, high country to Westbury, but, 'with the load of that foul ticket-of-leave fairly shaken off', Mitchel was ready to go. Ascending the tiers, Mitchel and JH encountered a frozen marsh, the horses skittering over the surface. They heard the barking of the dogs of Meagher's former neighbour, and so gave the lake a wide berth, passing down its western side, an area rarely travelled even in modern times. That night they camped in a 'dismal bivouac', tied their horses to a honeysuckle tree, 'picked the least polygonal stones to sit upon', and lit their pipes. They slept a few minutes at a time, awoken by the scorching of their knees from the fire, 'while our spinal marrow was frozen into a solid icicle'.

They changed horses at last at the remote homestead of a settler named Grover, 'a well-affected Tasmanian native', and before dusk that second day of escape Grover's son and Mitchel rode into the yard of a large and handsome house which still stands – Westfield, near Westbury. It belonged to an English settler named Wood, whom Mitchel would call Field in his journal. Mitchel stayed a night with Mr Wood. Since there was a police post within 100 yards of Wood's gate, though, it was decided to move the escaper the following morning to the attic of a farmhouse 6 miles away, which belonged to an Irishman named Burke. The attic was reached by a movable wooden ladder which is still displayed on St Patrick's Day in Westbury. Here he experienced the full flower of colonial hospitality. By day Mitchel read books and went out only at night, armed. For a feverish fellow, he dealt with delay well. But again it seemed nothing would ever proceed with ease for Mitchel, whether it was love, revolution, transportation, or escape. It was the middle of June before news from Nicaragua reached Mitchel at Burke's farm, the proposal being a dash from Westbury to one of Mr McNamara's ships, a brigantine named *Don Juan*. In five days' time it would put into Emu Bay, 80 miles north-west, and four flooded rivers away from Westbury.

Smyth's and Mitchel's Launceston friend (George Deas) sent a coastal smack with a message to Emu Bay, asking *Don Juan* to come eastwards again, to Badger Head, closer to Mitchel. He would still have to cross a most dangerous river, the Meander, and in the furious weather the ship might not be able to lie off a solitary beach for long. In any case, Mitchel's undaunted party of settlers started off from Burke's farm at night in a freezing downpour to make the rendezvous. Barny O'Keefe, 'an intelligent, well-informed man, who emigrated hither, after Lord Howarden's great extermination of tenantry in Tipperary', was in the escort. So were the Burke brothers, Mr Field and his brother, and two others. Mr Field cheered Mitchel on by telling him that if the ship was missed he could wait the winter out at a very remote station amongst the mountains of north-west Tasmania.

The Mitchel party rode into the dark valley of the Meander, and struggled across to O'Keefe's farmhouse on the far side. The flood 'dashed up on our horses' shoulders'. They found O'Keefe's wife and family asleep, but soon a roaring fire blazed and beefsteaks hissed. At O'Keefe's hearth that night, the Field brothers, native Tasmanians and of English stock, sat smoking and fraternally nodding as O'Keefe recounted 'the black story of the clearing of his village in Tipperary'. Mounted up in the morning, the party reached the beach at Badger Head by way of innumerable sand marshes. No sail at all was in sight, and by dark Mitchel's party were out of food and hope. They escorted Mitchel 9 miles along the coast, to the ramshackle house of a lively Cockney ex-convict named Miller, which lay opposite the tiny hamlet of Port Sorell. Miller and his wife, natural rebels against authority, entered with delight into the business of concealing Mitchel. From their residence the next morning, Mitchel could observe by telescope the streets of Port Sorell and the constables, 'sauntering about with their belts and jingling handcuffs'. At Miller's hut Mitchel would see in the month of July, smoking with his host.

It was a relief when on 5 July the Burke brothers appeared amongst the coastal marshlands, come to fetch Mitchel to Launceston. Deas had negotiated a passage to Melbourne on a steamer, and Mitchel said goodbye to the disappointed Millers, who had been busy hatching their own playful plans for getting Mitchel away from Port Sorell. But a wealth of melodramatic misses and near-misses still had to be endured. The Burkes supplied him with a cassock and large black hat belonging to Father Hogan of Westbury. A foursquare Presbyterian in Papist cloth, he waited in Launceston as the captain of the chosen vessel complained that with the present level of the police scrutiny he could not take Mitchel on his ship near Launceston: it would have to happen well out in the mouth of the Tamar. Utterly exhausted, Mitchel was put in the bottom of the boat that night. For the last section of this long haul, one of the Barretts who had helped Meagher was in charge, and left him ashore opposite George Town, at the very mouth of the river, together with a Hobart merchant named Connellan. Barrett then rowed across to the village itself

The affray at Widow McCormack's house on Boulagh Common, 29 July 1848 (p. 164).

Smith O'Brien and Widow McCormack greet the besieged police.

O'Brien conveyed back to prison after being sentenced to death, 9 October 1848.

O'Brien in the dock, Clonmel.

William Smith O'Brien (seated), with elegant Thomas Francis Meagher, the Governor of Kilmainham gaol and guard, autumn 1848.

Clonmel Courthouse. Here Young Ireland was condemned to death.

Swift, off Table Mountain, South Africa, September 1849. On this ship the four State prisoners were carried into exile.

The mountains behind Hobart, with a distant view of the Derwent and the city, 1840s.

Sir William Denison, a strong will at war with skilful Smith O'Brien.

The firm but not entirely honourable Dr Hampton, Comptroller-General of Convicts in Van Diemen's Land, and later Governor of Western Australia.

Darlington Penal Station, Maria Island, after the convict era. 'To find the gaol in one of the loveliest spots formed by the hand of nature … creates a revulsion of feeling which I cannot describe,' wrote O'Brien.

The human railway, Tasman Peninsula (p. 231).

The mastiffs of Eaglehawk Neck, which connects the Tasman Peninsula to the body of Van Diemen's Land.

Dismal and lovely Port Arthur, Van Diemen's Land.

Smith O'Brien's cottage, Port Arthur.

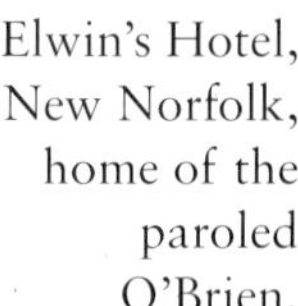

Elwin's Hotel, New Norfolk, home of the paroled O'Brien.

Bennie's Irish highwayman father, Brian Bennett.

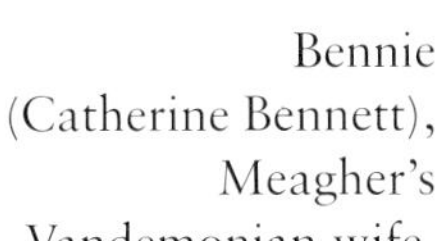

Bennie (Catherine Bennett), Meagher's Vandemonian wife.

John Mitchel's sketch of Meagher's home, Lake Sorell, with the not-quite-to-scale *Speranza* near the pier.

Nicaragua Smyth (P. J. Smyth), schoolfriend of Meagher, gallant rescuer of Mitchel. From a watercolour by Edward Hayes, 1854.

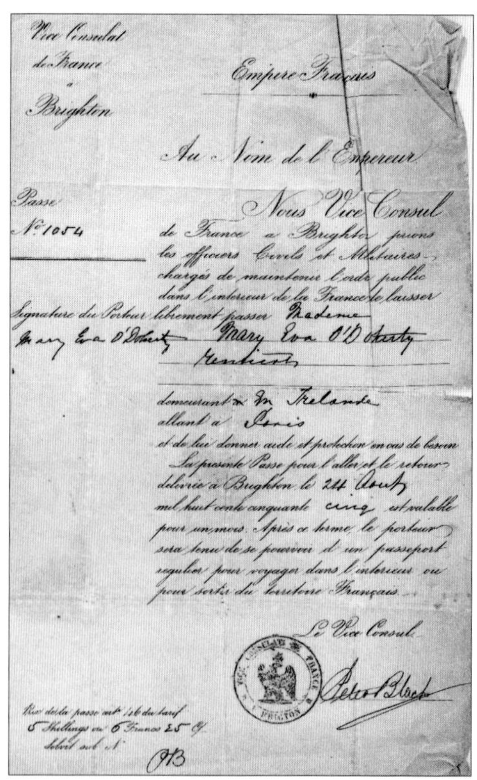

Vice Consulat de France à Brighton

Empire Français

Au Nom de l'Empereur

Passe N°. 1054

Nous Vice Consul de France à Brighton prions les officiers Civils et Militaires chargés de maintenir l'ordre public dans l'intérieur de la France de laisser librement passer Madame Mary Eva O'Doherty

Signature du Porteur: Mary Eva O'Doherty

demeurant en Irlande
allant à Paris
et de lui donner aide et protection en cas de besoin

La présente Passe pour l'aller et le retour délivrée à Brighton le 24 Août mil huit cent cinquante cinq est valable pour un mois. Après ce terme, le porteur sera tenu de se pourvoir d'un passeport régulier pour voyager dans l'intérieur ou pour sortir du territoire Français.

Le Vice Consul

Peter Black

Prix de la passe art. 126 du tarif
5 Shillings ou 6 Francs 25 C.
Débit sub N.

Eva of the *Nation*. Her passport to travel to Paris with her husband, Kevin Izod O'Doherty, 1855.

to make the required report of his movements to the police magistrate. He had scarcely set off than Mitchel and Connellan saw the black funnel of the steamer come around a wooded promontory, making for the open sea. Half an hour passed, and Barrett's boat was now returning from George Town, four men rowing with 'desperate energy'. Though Mitchel jumped aboard with Connellan, the steamer made smoke, hooted, pulled away and vanished. Rain and gales accompanied Mitchel's party all the miserable way back to Launceston. Mitchel, wearing the priest's weeds, was put ashore a mile from town and walked to the house of Father Butler. At a meeting with Connellan and Deas later in the day, it was agreed that the north side of the island of Tasmania had now become 'too hot to hold me'. All the riding, counter-riding, drenchings, kindnesses of farmers and grandees, all the chuckling ingenuity of Miller and the muscular oarsmanship of the Barrett boatmen had to be written off.

Father Butler hid a saddened but grateful Mitchel in the belfry of the church in Launceston, while Connellan booked two places in the mail coach to Hobart for the following night. At the right time, Father Butler helped a hopeful, wry Mitchel dress again as a priest, supposedly a Father Blake, and rode with him out of Launceston to wait for the coach at Franklin village. On the way they approached a turnpike gate. 'Here,' said Father Butler, 'you can test your disguise.' Clergymen were privileged to pass the toll-gates free. The keeper opened the gate without question.

As soon as the coach arrived in Franklin's one street, Mitchel climbed in. Besides the already seated Connellan, there were two other passengers, one an acquaintance of Mitchel's 'who would certainly have known me, had I been less effectually disguised'. He was Mr MacDowell, formerly Attorney-General. MacDowell tried to draw Mitchel into conversation on church matters, but Father Blake was shy. In the small hours, the coach changed horses at Green Ponds, where two policemen inspected the passengers. Under his cassock, Mitchel kept hold of a pistol supplied him by Smyth.

On a clear morning at Bridgewater, north of Hobart, the angular Father Blake dismounted the coach and went into the hotel. MacDowell remarked, 'Your Reverend friend, Connellan, does not carry any luggage.' Mitchel did not rest but spent the day hiking along the Derwent in his priest's cassock, and then caught the evening coach into Hobart as it came by. Six miles short of Hobart Town, 'Kevin O'Doherty climbed into the coach, and sat down directly in front of me, looking straight in my face.' Apparently Saint Kevin did not recognise him. Indeed, when Mitchel turned up at Connellan's house in Collins Street, and the door was opened by Pat Smyth, Mitchel introduced himself as Father Blake and walked through into the parlour before breaking down in laughter: 'I saw now that my disguise might carry me through a birthday ball at Government House.' Nicaragua and Mitchel left Connellan's house at separate times and walked by different routes to the house of Mr Manning, McNamara's shipping agent in Hobart Town.

Manning suggested the one option left: Mitchel should simply depart on the *Emma*, the regular passenger brig running to Melbourne. Nicaragua would return to Bothwell, to assist in the winding-up of Mitchel's affairs at Nant Cottage, the sale of stock, etc., so that Jenny Mitchel and her family could sail on the *Emma* also. The Mitchel family, however, would be able to board *Emma* legally at the wharf. Mitchel himself was to board 3 or 4 miles downriver, to preserve a disguise and avoid Jenny and the children. On the night itself, 18 July, on boarding the *Emma* without any trouble at all downriver, Mitchel took on the persona of a Mr Wright. Receiving him on board, the captain observed, 'You're almost too late, Mr Wright,' and then brought him down to the cabin and introduced him to all the other passengers, including Mr Pat Smyth of New York. On deck Mr Wright could see handsome Jenny Mitchel sitting on the poop deck with the children in the moonlight, nursing the youngest girl, Isabelle. When young Willie followed him about the deck, Mitchel barked, 'Aren't you Mrs Mitchel's little boy?' Willie fled.

By the evening of the next day, Mitchel saw the peaks of the Bay of Fires vanish down the horizon: 'Adieu, then, beauteous island, full of sorrow and gnashing of teeth – Island of fragrant forests, and bright rivers, and fair women! Island of chains and scourges, and blind, brutal rage and passion!'

But still it was not over. When *Emma* entered Sydney Harbour and while the police were still aboard, the captain provided his own cutter to take Mr Wright ashore and directly to McNamara's house, where the son of the McNamara family was in residence. There Mr Wright took a further identity, Mr Warren. Warren 'drove out this evening in his [McNamara's] carriage . . . assuredly, Warren has never seen so lovely a bay as this of Sydney, except Lough Swilley, in Donegal'.

Mitchel had leisure now to marvel at all the men who had assisted him. He wrote to Mrs Williams, the young widow of Ratho, 'My list of efficient assistants in the business includes Englishmen, Irishmen, Scotsmen, Welshmen, and *a man from Berwick-upon-Tweed*.' It was agreed that Mitchel would go ahead on an English bark, *Orkney Lass*, bound for Honolulu with only one vacant berth. The family could come on with Nicaragua in the ship *Julia Ann*, due from Melbourne. When in late July Mr Warren boarded the *Orkney Lass*, the captain was lamenting that his sailors had deserted to dig gold. Waiting for the crew to be re-gathered,

Warren had time to visit Mrs Jenny Mitchel and her six children in Woolloomooloo, a semi-respectable harbourside suburb where she had taken rooms. With the captain and a French gentleman, Mitchel 'went insanely to an evening party, and after that repaired with my friends to an oyster tavern – greatly to the surprise and alarm of my friend James MacNamara'. At length, its crew all back, *Orkney Lass* endured a last search of the ship at the heads, where the surging Pacific entered Port Jackson, and sailed out of Sydney Harbour on the morning of 2 August.

Orkney Lass's first call was to be Tahiti, and when after nearly a month the splendid mountains of Tahiti and Moorea were sighted, liberated Mr Warren luxuriated in the splendour of the place and in the beauty of the men and women. But Mitchel was disappointed that just as *Orkney Lass* was ready to depart for Hawaii on 12 September, a dead calm settled in. Off the reef the next day the American bark *Julia Ann* appeared, the vessel Smyth, Jenny and her family had planned to take. Her railings were crowded with passengers, and one of her boats was lowered and entered Papeete. 'And while it was still a mile off I recognised one of my own boys sitting in the bow, and Nicaragua beside him. They have come for me.' By seven o'clock that evening he had set foot on the deck of an American ship 'and took off my hat in homage to the Stars and Stripes. Here, then, Mr Blake, Mr MacNamara, Mr Wright, and Mr Warren, have all become once more plain John Mitchel . . . my "Jail Journal" ends, and "Out-of-Jail Journal" begins.'

16

The Skeleton at the Feast

> I mean to make use of the freedom granted to me as a citizen of America to help and to stimulate the movement of European Democracy, and especially of Irish Independence.
>
> John Mitchel, New York, 1853

Sir William Denison was unwilling to move with severity on the three remaining Young Irelanders, for Mitchel's escape had again concentrated the attention of the world upon him. John Martin, a sad relict of Mitchel's great escapade, had lost a great deal – companionship, a household, genial employment. For the sake of liquidity, he took employment working as a tutor to the children of the Jackson family at Ross. Though he wrote to O'Doherty that he had begun 'to convince myself that it is *pride* that irritated and almost disgusted me at first', he had the same problem with tutoring the rough companionable Jacksons as O'Brien had had with the Brock boys.

O'Doherty had at last left Hobart and was serving as surgeon in the little community of Port Cygnet (population 100) south of Hobart. He survived off grudging bank drafts from his brothers in Ireland, who were still holding tight to his inheritance. At Elwin's, a restive O'Brien tried to occupy himself by drafting a possible Tasmanian constitution. It was a wise document, suggesting an elected governorship and a Senate and House of Assembly, but it retained allegiance to the monarchy while limiting the vote to occupants of buildings worth £5 per annum, or a rural freehold or leasehold worth £100. Serving convicts (among whom Martin, O'Doherty and himself were numbered) were not eligible.

He was still locked in a struggle over the education of his son Edward. Late in 1853, O'Brien heard from Edward himself that he wished to attend an English university. 'This is the first time I have asked you to consider *my* choice in any matter,' the young man wrote pointedly. O'Brien was enraged. To enable his family to remain an Irish family he had denied himself the company of his wife and of his beloved heir in Van Diemen's Land. But now the plan seemed to be to make the boy a second-class Englishman. O'Brien told Lucy that if Edward went to an English university it would be '*Against my wishes, not under sanction of my conscience*'. His battle to ensure his eldest son grew up with an Irish mind was interrupted by unaffected letters from the younger children for whom politics and culture were not yet an issue. Charles Murrough, the youngest, wrote, 'I am growing rather tall from the hugging I get every morning when I go into Mumma's bed . . . I hope the Queen will let you go because I want to see you and I want to tell you many things.'

But O'Brien foresaw only the remotest chance of his being able to take Charles Murrough on his knee and answer those questions.

The Mitchels' ship, *Julia Ann*, entered the 'Gate of Gold', San Francisco, on 3 October 1853. Enjoying the compliment of a dinner attended by Governor Downey, an Irishman, and by the mayor of San Francisco, Mitchel declared: 'I have commenced in your state my novitiate in order to become an American citizen.' But New York was Mitchel's objective. His mother, his brother and sisters were in Brooklyn. New York lay on the same ocean as Ireland, and Mitchel had not given up hope of some intrusion into Ireland. But, 'I must tell you we were nearly tempted to remain there,' adaptable Jenny confessed.

They spent a week with an apparently happy MacManus at San Jose, where he was ranching, and penetrated the forested Santa Cruz Gap on horseback. For the first time since his imprisonment, Mitchel experienced the scent of pine trees. He left no comment on any problems 30-year-old MacManus might have been facing with business, with liquor and loneliness. After nearly a month in California, Pat Smyth, Mitchel, Jenny and the children boarded the steamship *Cortez* to start their journey to New York by the trans-Nicaragua route. 'The papers will have told you of the magnificent reception he met with here,' wrote a former surgeon from Van Diemen's Land to the young widow of Ratho, Mrs Williams. '. . . The German residents serenaded him the night before he left, and every man's heart beats stronger and all felt happy to find that another "true man" had escaped from the clutches of the English Government and that miserable devil Sir William Denison.' Jenny had been sad to leave San Fastopolis, and Dr Nuttall had seen her on the deck of *Cortez* with tears coursing down her cheeks.

The Mitchels and Pat Smyth disembarked on the Nicaragua/Costa Rica coast and boarded mules to massive Lake Nicaragua, which they crossed by steamer. The baby Isabelle became very ill and Jenny feared losing her, but the fever abated. They travelled on down the San Juan River by boat – Mitchel and his sons walking enthusiastically through brilliant forests around the rapids – and on the Atlantic side took another steamer north to Greytown or San Juan del Norte on the Mosquito Coast, and then yet another on to Cuba. From Havana, where Nicaragua Smyth took the Mitchel boys to the theatre, they sailed on the appositely named *Prometheus* and, in the last days of November, entered the outer harbour of New York through the Verazzano Narrows. Mitchel was impressed by the bulk of New York, but also by Brooklyn, and the way Jersey City on one shore echoed Williamsburg on the other. 'A constellation of cities! – a ganglion of human life!'

Mitchel's younger brother William and Thomas Francis Meagher were first aboard the *Prometheus*, and the excitement at Mitchel's arrival managed if anything to outrival that which had attended Meagher's. The *New York Times* announced it with a total of five front-page headlines: 'ARRIVAL OF JOHN MITCHEL – HIS ENTHUSIASTIC RECEPTION – MITCHEL'S SOJOURN IN BROOKLYN – SALVOS OF ARTILLERY – SERENADE IN BROOKLYN.' The Mitchels were conveyed by ferry and carriage to the corner of Hicks and Degraw Streets, the Brooklyn house rented by Mrs Mitchel senior, where, in the afternoon, John Blake Dillon, Michael Doheny and other Young Irelanders came visiting. From Brooklyn Heights, the Napper Tandy Light Artillery discharged thirty-one guns across the East River, a salute reserved for heads of state. This was designed to confirm Mitchel as president of the unachieved Irish republic, the status that the Irish diaspora had given him as Young Ireland's militant and first transported victim. As the salvoes died, an approaching band playing 'Garryowen' was heard. The Irish militias of New York and New Jersey had mustered on the corner of Chrystie and Delancy Streets, Manhattan, and were invading Brooklyn. Amongst them were the Mitchel Guards of the 9th New York, the Meagher Cadets, Jackson Guards, Emmet Guards, Sarsfield Guards, Irish Rifles, Irish Fusiliers, Meagher Republican Grenadiers and the Mitchel Guards of Jersey City. 'Union Street is quickly filled up with ranked men, glittering bayonets and waving banners.' Mitchel went to the windows, and that was the start of five hours' civic mayhem as he received deputations, made speeches, reviewed military companies 'defiling through the hall'. The Mitchel boys loved it all.

The furore continued for days. 'For the first week,' Jenny wrote, 'we did not get to our beds before two or three in the morning.' One day that week, the mayor of Brooklyn collected Mitchel for a triumphal procession through the streets, followed by a civic reception. Beautiful women threw bouquets from balconies. 'Good God! What is all this for?' he asked Dillon. 'What value am I to give for it?' Going to Manhattan, Mitchel encountered the Fulton Street markets, 'a thoroughly disgraceful and squalid mass of shanties'. But across from the splendid Astor House, he was honoured at City Hall, where he joyfully made his first notable American mistake. During his reception, he declared that he accepted American honours of this kind 'expressly as an insult to the British Government'. A friendly journalist took Mitchel aside and told him not to speak in those terms. These people did not mean any affront to the British government; 'they mean to pay you a passing tribute of respect'. He restrained himself and fell back on being impressed by the way New York and its environs operated as an absorber of immigrants. In the few days since he arrived many thousands of Irish men and women had been emptied out of immigrant ships. 'They are not to be seen crowding the streets and making mobs . . . they get railroad cars on the very evening of their arrival, and are whirled away to where loving friends are awaiting them on the banks of the Wabash, or hard by some bright lake of Michigan; or else they get immediate occupation in the city itself.'

Escape celebrations were still rolling the week before Christmas, when a huge dinner was held in Mitchel's honour at the Broadway Theater. A speech was expected of Meagher, as it was of Horace Greeley, the lawyers Richard O'Gorman and John Blake Dillon, and others. As 600 diners sat in the stalls, and 600 ladies and their attendants watched from a balcony, while Bloomfield's Brass Band from Governor's Island provided the music, Mitchel told the crowd: 'The Monarchical East casts me out – the Republican West welcomes and embraces me. One slave the less in Europe – one free man more, America, to Thee!' He confessed unwisely that he might use the United States chiefly as a base for Ireland's liberation. 'I am a professional revolutionist now, an adventurer, a seditious propagandist.' The irony which attended this statement was that he would so swiftly and painfully become involved in American politics.

Jenny found Brooklyn's winter hard, but Mitchel was full of plans. On 7 January 1854, from premises at 3 Spruce Street, New York, he began publishing a newspaper, the *Irish Citizen*, to appear every Saturday. The newspaper's prospectus stated that the 'principal Conductors', himself and Meagher, were Irish by birth, had 'endured years of penal exile at the hands of the British government' and were now 'refugees on American soil . . . They refuse to believe that prostrate and broken as the Irish nation is now, the cause of Irish independence is utterly lost.'

Meagher may have put some initiating money into the journal but was only nominally associated with it, and distanced himself more and more from it with the passage of time. When, on an early-blooming revolutionary impulse, Mitchel went to see Baron Stockl, the Russian ambassador, in Georgetown Heights, DC, he left the paper in the care not of Meagher, but of McClenehan and Savage, his two Young Irelander journalists.

Baron Stockl met the famed escaper with much warmth and said he was a 'constant reader' of the *Citizen*. Mitchel raised the possibility of Russia enabling the Irish to open a second front against Britain, 'if some material aid could be only furnished to them to make a beginning'. Baron Stockl asked how Russia could stretch a hand to Ireland when the British fleet had bottled up the Baltic in the north and the Black Sea in the south. With this rebuff 'ended my tentative effort to make the Crimean War available for our Irish purposes'. The war Mitchel did fight was against the anti-Papist, anti-Irish Know-Nothings. The Protestant Association of New York held a procession in Newark, which led to a riot in which a Catholic was killed. The *Citizen* wrote, 'Newark, it seems, has no adequate police force . . . Out of an armed mob who sack a church in open noonday not one has been arrested.' Mitchel mistakenly believed these sectarian forces were as one with the forces of abolition. 'Whether all this meant Know-Nothing or Abolition fury, it signifies little now to enquire and determine.' He began to publish his classic *Jail Journal* in instalments in the *Citizen* on 14 January of the new year.

But Mitchel and the *Citizen* took on targets who hurt them more proximately than abolitionists and the Know-Nothings. He poked fun at the Irish-Catholic idea that the causes of Hungary, Italian and Sicilian revolution were red republicanism, and the cause of Ireland somehow holier than, and thus separate from, the others. Concerning the Italians, he argued that 'there is no occasion why the Bishop of Rome should also be the Prince of Rome. And perhaps he would be more a Bishop if he were less a Prince.' As Mitchel wrote later: 'Archbishop Hughes came out and scathed us in the newspapers.'

Did that other Young Ireland newspaperman, the ailing O'Donohoe, read the opening instalment of the *Jail Journal*? He could not have read the second, for the day it appeared, a witheringly cold Saturday, 28 January, the former editor of Van Diemen's Land's *Irish Exile* perished in Brooklyn at 42 Hamilton Street. In dreadful weather two days before, he had caught the ferry to Manhattan to attempt to board the ship waiting in the harbour on which his wife, daughter and brother had travelled from Ireland. In that weather, no boatman would take him out. On the next afternoon, a Saturday, O'Donohoe's brother visited the *Citizen* office to ask for his address, but was treated with suspicion, as if he were a British agent. Before he discovered his brother's correct location, O'Donohoe had died. The death certificate nominated diarrhoea as the immediate cause, but melancholy, alcoholism, Denison and irregular diet had all had a hand. At the inquest his landlords, the Henrys, and their housekeeper all said the journey to the dock on the Friday before had much weakened him. The housekeeper told the Brooklyn coroner that the deceased had drunk brandy bought for him by the Henrys, but did not drink in the last three days of his life. The *Irish American* wrote a fair assessment: 'Through nervous irritability and a mind shattered by suffering, producing jealousy and mistrust of all who came within his reach, O'Donohoe had become estranged from those who, under other circumstances, would have been his fast and ardent supporters.'

Mitchel himself wrote in the *Citizen*, 'If that excitable disposition, stung by insolent injustice, ever hurried him into error, we lay his errors as we lay his blood, at the door of the liberal and ameliorative statesmen of England.' Although John Mitchel was not listed amongst those who attended the funeral in Brooklyn, leading *émigré* Young Irelanders were the pall-bearers, including Michael Doheny and John O'Mahony. These men founded a fund for the support of Mrs O'Donohoe, but it was not well subscribed.

A further instance of Young Ireland alienation, this time transoceanic, arose when Charles Gavan Duffy bravely published the early excerpts of Mitchel's *Jail Journal* in the *Nation*, but became offended that Mitchel called him 'unfortunate' for having produced at his trial '*evidence of character*', and for having tried 'to evade the responsibility of some of the prosecuted articles, by proving they were not written by himself'. Duffy responded with exceptional fury. Ingrate Mitchel had not escaped Van Diemen's Land with honour, said Duffy, and his friends in America hung their heads in shame over his withdrawal of parole. Duffy now published an open letter in the *Nation* of 29 April 1854, calling on Meagher to stand aside from Mitchel, and so to avoid accusations that Meagher too was a radical anti-clerical. Meagher replied that he would not communicate with Duffy at all until the slur against Mitchel was retracted.

Quite apart from Duffy and the question of escape and anti-papal bias, Mitchel *was* becoming a scandal on a secular American level. He published such material as a pro-slavery letter from Mr Scoville, former secretary to John Calhoun. 'If the South are forced to a separation to save ourselves, grass will grow in the streets of New York. The slave states are the producing states.' By the early spring of 1854, the *Citizen* was in full cry too against Harriet Beecher Stowe's recent *Uncle Tom's Cabin*, depicting it as a weapon used by abolitionists in alliance with 'the British oligarchy' to create a split between North and South. Irish seamstresses and navvies were in greatest need of liberation, Mitchel argued, whereas Christian slavery redeemed the slave from African darkness. He conducted a notorious correspondence with the Reverend Henry Ward Beecher, Harriet Beecher Stowe's brother, a celebrated New York pulpit orator. Mitchel saw Beecher as the dominating influence over Harriet, and *Uncle Tom's Cabin* and the more recent Stowe work, *A Key to Uncle Tom's Cabin*, as virtually Beecher's voice. Mitchel was, however, forced to confess, as circulation dropped, that his slavery doctrine was 'the subject of much surprise and general rebuke'. In his spring and summer of defiance, he greeted with glee and republished all the vituperative headlines against him: 'The immortal hero of two months ago reads now that he is an "imposter" (*Hartford Republican*), that he is a "suicide" (*New York Tribune*) and a "hideous lag" (*Independent*).'

'Do not be alarmed for me,' Jenny Mitchel told her girlhood friend Miss Thompson. '. . . I am not likely to become – no – nothing would induce me to become the mistress of a slave household . . . My objection to Slavery is the injury it does to the white masters.'

As the North closed down on Mitchel, the South opened. He received overtures from the mayor and council of the city of Richmond, Virginia. He expatiated on architecture to the *Journal Constitution*, and took up an invitation to give the commencement address at the University of Virginia in June 1854. He loved the sociability of Virginians, and the landscape of Albemarle County 'blooming like some great pleasure ground'.

That spring Nicaragua Smyth had been preparing a new expedition to liberate Smith O'Brien. Nicaragua had a personal reason to return to Australia. Before he had made his exit from VDL with Jenny Mitchel, he had left a message with Kevin O'Doherty asking Jenny O'Regan, the Hobart woman he had fallen in love with during his illness, to signal acceptance of a marriage proposal he had sent her by writing to him care of the law offices of Dillon & O'Gorman in New York city. Apparently Miss O'Regan's positive response had now arrived.

In the meantime Isaac Butt, Irish MP, had planned to ask Home Secretary Lord Palmerston in the House on 22 February whether, given the fall of Russell's Whig government, O'Brien could now be pardoned. Butt was late getting to question time in the House, and a colleague asked the question. Palmerston's reply was that though other prisoners had violated their word of honour, 'Mr Smith O'Brien himself, whatever might have been his faults and guilt, has acted like a gentleman' and should be rewarded by clemency from the Crown. O'Brien was conditionally pardoned, and could live anywhere outside Britain. No confession of regret was required of him.

In the House that evening, Butt made a plea that the pardon be also extended to John Martin and Kevin O'Doherty. He cited as a reason the readiness with which the Irish were recruiting for the war against Russia in the Crimea. These were terms of pleading Mitchel despised, but they worked. The news of O'Brien's pardon reached Dromoland Castle on Friday 24 February: two huge bonfires were built, houses illuminated.

By early March Palmerston announced that the pardons would also be granted to Martin, O'Doherty and three English Chartists, Frost, Williams and Jones. Palmerston's offer of conditional pardon hung in the air, as Smyth doubled the Cape of Good Hope and headed across the Indian

Ocean. O'Brien had heard rumours of pardon but believed Palmerston would make repentance an essential condition, and since O'Brien could have none of that, he believed himself under permanent capture. He was still agitated and suddenly homeless as well. In March 1854 Mr Elwin had sold his hotel and there was a 'consequent breaking up of the establishment'. Father Dunne of Richmond offered O'Brien the chance to live rent-free in the Catholic Presbytery, an offer proud O'Brien was uneasy in accepting.

The previous autumn, 1853, the California Steamship Company had offered Meagher a free passage to San Francisco, and this presented him with the possible release from the awkward intimacy of his life with Catherine and Thomas Meagher senior. Meagher argued he must take it to generate income from a speaking tour, and as he was about to start on his journey west, it was decided that Catherine would return to Ireland with Meagher senior. Her health, and even the balance of her spirit, were uncertain. Neither man thought it advisable she be in a hotel room on her own in such a challenging city, and Catherine wistfully agreed. Jenny Mitchel, who found Catherine potentially tragic, wrote, 'Thus, the girl who had come half way around the world to join her husband had been able to stay with him only four short months.' After an early Christmas dinner and exchange of presents at the Metropolitan, Catherine would sail the Atlantic in some comfort but in midwinter. She left no account of feelings of confusion or rejection, but she had had one triumph – she had conceived a child of the susceptible Meagher. A new child might enable a new claim on his affection.

Meagher landed at San Juan del Norte, where Mitchel had been lately, and embarked on a 7-year phase of enchantment with Central America. He travelled by mule up the jungle terraces and, pitching down volcanic inclines on a mule's back, he became a disciple of Manifest Destiny. Since this section of Central America was the best route between the American east and the west, it was at once obvious to him that the United States had special interests here, and that they should be pursued.

In early 1854, he spoke at the San Francisco Music-Hall, and in Oakland, and took oratory into the lovely mountain country and to desert towns such as Sacramento. But at the bottom of each evening's adulation lay the Catherine impasse. Back in New York that spring, he received news of the birth of a son, Thomas Francis Meagher III, in Ireland. Catherine had intentions, when she had her strength back and the baby was of a satisfactory age, to return to New York. The uneasy marriage had been converted into a family again. But soon further and horrifying information arrived. Weakened by the birth, on 9 May Catherine had died of typhus, the evil Famine fever, at the age of twenty-two years. Her body was taken from the Meagher house on 'the Mall' and, followed by a sizeable crowd, was buried in the Meagher family vault at Faithlegg churchyard some 8 miles outside Waterford. Meagher's father and various doting women relatives and servants tended the child. An uneasy compact was struck – the child would be raised in Waterford, educated at Clongowes, and perhaps in some years' time he could join his father in New York.

Meagher became an edgy presence in the Manhattan streets. A mixture of guilt and grief made him vulnerable. He had a brutal confrontation with James McMaster, editor of the *Freeman's Journal*, the clerically obedient Catholic paper of New York. An article in McMaster's *Freeman's Journal* accused him of dishonour in the breaking of his parole. Meagher went to McMaster's office to demand a withdrawal, but did not get one. According to the *New York Times*, he lay in wait for McMaster at his residence in East Sixth Street, and when McMaster appeared, took out a riding whip and 'struck him severely and repeatedly'. McMaster drew and fired his revolver and grazed Meagher's forehead and eyebrow, leaving his face burned from the powder flash. A policeman arrived and both men were charged at the watch-house and bound over by a magistrate for the sum of $500 each. Meagher tried at summer's height to recover from loss, guilty deliverance and shame, on the shore of Long Island Sound.

Returned from the South, Mitchel found the *Citizen* office stifling. So was Brooklyn. The Mitchels went holidaying with John Blake Dillon and his wife at Stonington, a Berkshire Hills watering place for New Yorkers. Mitchel wrote to Miss Thompson, an admirer of the North, 'We live . . . in a huge hotel with public table, the guests almost all the descendants of the Pilgrim Fathers, with a righteous horror of the South . . . On the whole, I like Virginia much better than this region; and if I had only "a good plantation" there – but I will shock you.' Simultaneously, he and Jenny, like O'Mahony, remained furiously disgruntled by the lack of action by Irish groups as Britain became further enmeshed in what looked like a scandalous and expensive war in the Crimea. 'What are they about in Ireland?' Jenny would ask Miss Thompson. 'Are they all dead or asleep or mad?' Mitchel, she said, was outraged that Meagher and Dillon, the latter about to return to Ireland under an amnesty, were not consumed with urgency.

The conditional pardons of the Young Irelanders and Chartists put O'Doherty and Martin in a much better position than O'Brien: they could return home when their ten years' treason-felony sentences had expired, Martin's in August 1858, O'Doherty's in October the same year. Martin had decided in protest, however, not to return to Ireland until it achieved independence. O'Brien, though, was apparently to be, of necessity, an eternal exile.

Nicaragua Smyth arrived in Melbourne before the pardons. He held £1,650 belonging to the Irish Directory of New York, and he used it to encourage the Irish of the boom city of Melbourne to plan resonant festivities. A welcoming committee having been set up, Smyth moved to Hobart Town to establish a similar committee. But on their own initiative, the citizens of Launceston were already at work. There was an unlucky delay: on the steamer *Queen of the South* only twenty-eight bags of newspapers could be found. But at last the crew discovered the dispatch bag. Denison announced the State pardons on 26 June. With the pardons came Sir George Grey's orders to Denison himself; despite his bad repute with settler progressives, he was to become governor of New South Wales.

O'Brien wrote to Lucy for once like a man resurrected. 'I need not tell you I am in excellent spirits.' A splendid dinner was held in the Old Bush Inn in New Norfolk under the chairmanship of his friend Captain Fenton. Smith O'Brien had won the struggle with Denison, and Fenton and the other anti-transportationists were waving Denison off also, so the conviviality of the evening was compounded. Mr William Carter, now mayor of the city, chaired the Hobart Town dinner, and the future premier of Tasmania, Richard Dry, the one in Launceston. At each occasion O'Brien declared that with increasing self-rule Tasmania had a government they could respect, and that this was a poignant contrast to the relationship between the Irish and their government.

The Melbourne committee, led by Repealer Mr O'Shanassy, who had helped ill-starred Patrick O'Donohoe escape, resolved unanimously that for Mr O'Brien's visit, a gold vase of not less than 100 ounces of £7-per-ounce fine gold, should be manufactured and displayed at the Paris Exhibition before being sent off to Ireland to honour O'Brien's freedom. O'Doherty and Martin would each receive a purse of 200 gold sovereigns.

The three freed prisoners left on the *Ariel* for Port Phillip. 'My progress has throughout been a complete ovation,' O'Brien told Lucy while visiting Geelong near Melbourne. He was living up to the duty of the released prisoner to be exultant. On the eve of his departure, at the Criterion Hotel in Collins Street in the golden city of Melbourne, the most formal of the Australian mainland dinners was held. The Criterion was a hotel favoured by American and Irish miners whose republican politics had generally been reinforced by experience on the Californian and Nevada goldfields.

These men ensured that as O'Brien, O'Doherty and Martin were led into the concert room where the banquet was laid, 'They were received with several salvos of vocal and manual artillery, and had great difficulty in even reaching the platform.' O'Brien declared to the guests that he regretted that the pardon did not permit him to return to Ireland – he would live in Brussels. However, he argued, he was not pleading for a full pardon. Since his role in the 1848 uprising was that of a patriot, not of a criminal, he had no reason to plead.

O'Doherty summoned up for the diners the ghosts of the Famine fever: 'Piled together in the fever sheds, happily unconscious, in their wild delirium, of the horrors of their condition.' At first sight strangely, given the yearning which had characterised his sentiments towards Eva, O'Doherty intended to go for a time to the goldfields in this newly proclaimed state of Victoria, referred to in the days of Hugh Larkin's overlanding as the Port Phillip area. Perhaps Saint Kevin saw a chance to acquire quick capital preparatory to marriage, and was urged along by Irish and American miners at the Criterion. Perhaps he feared meeting as a woman the ardent child he had known in Richmond prison. His travelling companion to the fields was Nicaragua Smyth, who had spent so much of the Directory's money on Australian events that he was nervous and wanted to supplement the funds.

Smith O'Brien and John Martin left Melbourne on 26 July 1854, travelling together as far as Ceylon. O'Brien wrote to Lucy from Point de Gable, as many Europeans called Galle in Sri Lanka, to tell her he intended to visit Madras and see her brother William, a Light Cavalry officer. This would delay him one month, he explained, but he was not likely to have a chance to make such a visit again. Was Ireland's greatest hero procrastinating too? He was certainly anxious about leading an exiled life in Brussels, and about how he would support himself. He sent on gifts to Dromoland with a fellow passenger, a colonial-made man who was returning to Ireland from Australia. The good companion John Martin said goodbye in Colombo too and took a ship for Aden, Suez and Cairo. He travelled by open cart across the desert and sailed from Alexandria to Marseilles. From a hotel-pension at 38 rue du Faubourg Saint-Honoré in Paris, just before Christmas, he wrote to Eva Kelly wondering 'if propitious winds and waves shall have brought to you in real bodily presence a certain tall brown-faced friend of ours – the happy dog!' In fact, Eva must have known by now that O'Doherty was not to be in Europe by Christmas. For his own part, Martin intended to spend Christmas at the house of an ageing Irish expatriate, and then to move to a less fashionable pension across the river in the Latin Quarter at 26 rue Lacépède. Both the address in rue du Faubourg Saint-Honoré and the one in not-so-fashionable rue Lacépède would become the two favourite residences of released and escaped Young Irelanders in Paris.

The visit to Lucy's soldier brother over, O'Brien set out nervously for the reunion in Brussels. By 21 November, when he was visiting Martin in Paris, every hour revived his fever about income, and he hectored Lucy. 'I wish you *most decidedly not* to bring a governess with you.' Brussels was now only a train ride removed, and he was there by 25 November, at the Hôtel de la Régence in the Boulevard Waterloo, an establishment recommended to him by Lucy.

He had now received with ill humour the news that under the family trust arrangement drawn up in 1848, their income from Cahirmoyle would be £500. The Hôtel de la Régence could not keep him, her, their four children and a maid for less than £2 *per diem*, that is, over £700 per year. At last he found a hotel that would take them for £170. He told Lucy he would not go to meet her at Antwerp in case he missed her and incurred the additional expense for nothing!

The reunion took place joyously, and the eldest son Edward, now approaching twenty years of age, showed affection and manly respect for his father. Lucy and Grace applied themselves with pragmatic energy to making a home for William. Christmas was celebrated in that wilfully joyous spirit. His daughter Charlotte, nine years old at the time of this reunion with a father she had last seen at three, would write of him that 'those very qualities which raised his public life were a difficulty in his private'.

In November 1854, as O'Brien moved towards reunion with his family, the discredit of bereaved Meagher's street battle with McMaster would be partially redeemed. He was travelling in the first-class section of the Great Western Railroad outside Detroit when his train collided with an eastbound express. In the splintered carriages forty-seven people were killed, and Meagher was reported to have hauled dead and wounded out of the tangle of steel and shredded panelling. Some of his valour may have derived from the fact that he had by now met and fallen in love with a New York woman of a much more exalted family than Catherine Bennett's. Elizabeth Townsend was a sweet-tempered young woman in her mid- to late twenties. In an age of early marriages, she was considered a late developer, and had established that sort of warm and mutually reliant relationship with her parents, people of wide connections and pleasant disposition, which was often then seen as a prelude to old-maidhood. Her father, Peter Townsend, had a Fifth Avenue residence and was chief of his family company, the New York-based Sterling Ironworks.

Elizabeth herself was a frank, jolly, not unambitious young woman, and her features even in old age would radiate a handsome optimism. Meagher described her as 'in the bloom, and pride, and the genial glorious dawn of womanhood – stationed in the highest social rank, in a community the wealthiest in the world – the oldest unmarried daughter of a family, affluent in its circumstances, and by long descendent residence in this country.'

Her sister Alice had already married the sort of man Peter Townsend would have expected as a son-in-law: Samuel Mitchell Barlow, Democrat, partner in the powerful New York law firm of Bowdoin, Larocque & Barlow, specialising in railroad work. Barlow had strong connections with the New York Democratic Party machine of Tammany Hall, and could walk into the Congress in Washington like a man entering his own club. His interests in and directorships of a number of railroads gave him great influence either side of the Mason–Dixon line, and great usefulness to his father-in-law. Barlow could be asked to call in on New York Congressman Dan Sickles and discuss progress on a new bill in Congress 'for repeal of law posted last session', which threw the navy's steel contracts open to foreign tenderers. But Peter Townsend would also ask Barlow, when he was travelling in England in the mid-1850s, to chase up a sample steel shipment sent to London and intended to impress British arms manufacturers and shipbuilders.

By comparison with Samuel Barlow, Meagher was a bolt from the blue. We do not know where and when Elizabeth and he first met, but by Christmas 1854 he was writing from the Metropolitan Hotel, New York, to 'My Dear, Dear, Miss Townsend'. In this same letter he gave a proper place in his history to poor Catherine. 'Banished to an island in the South Pacific – 16,000 miles from home . . . I grew sad and sick of life. In the darkest hour of that sick life, a solitary star shone down upon me, making bright and beautiful the desolate waters of the mournful wild lake on the shore of which I lived. In that wilderness I met her who has left me the poor child, for whom, as yet, I have no home.' But now, he told Elizabeth Townsend, her own 'great goodness, and nobler nature' forced him to retire, 'as from a Sacrament, with a steadier, wiser, purer purpose. Thus instructed, and thus improved, do I feel myself to be ever since I made known to you my love . . . I was fully sensible that in claiming the honor to be your husband, I should have to meet no slight contradictions and rebuke. For, I have no fortune – at least, nothing that I know of. I never ask my father a single question on the subject.'

He had found in Elizabeth a great companion from beyond the Irish world. So impeccable were her Yankee bloodlines that her ancestor Peter Townsend, founder of the Sterling Ironworks, had undertaken in 1777 the biggest contract ever to that time given to colonial ironworks – to forge for the Continental Congress a massive 750-link chain to be stretched across the Hudson at West Point to prevent the British navy from controlling the river.

In the Irish world, St Patrick's Day of 1855 demonstrated to Libby Townsend that Tom Meagher was still the American favourite Mitchel had so quickly ceased to be. Fifth Avenue was choked with snow for the procession, and there were fears of Orange counter-demonstrations. But at the St Patrick's Night banquet Meagher's splendid response to the toast was greeted with awe and cheers. 'There is a skeleton at this feast,' he declared of ravaged Ireland. Some did not perceive the corpse, he said. But he saw clearly 'the shroud and the sealed lips and the cold hands'.

At Ballarat, a goldfield in Victoria, Peter Lalor, healthy emigrant brother of the late, spinally crippled James Fintan Lalor, inflammatory journalist, was heavily engaged in miners' politics. James had died in 1849, a few days after his attempt to capture a police barracks at Cappaquin, Tipperary. Two of his siblings, Peter and Richard, were by then already settled in Melbourne. Peter mined first at Bendigo in 1853, and then at Ballarat. Each digger on the fields, including of course Kevin O'Doherty and Pat Smyth, was required to pay a licence fee of £3 a month for a surface stake scarcely bigger than a man could lie in. Miners were therefore paying massively more than other landholders, yet had no vote. The Ballarat Reform League, founded in November 1854, demanded that property qualifications for voters and members of Victoria's Legislative Assembly be abolished, along with miners' licence fees. A new flag of white Southern Cross on a blue ground was flown at a Reform League meeting at Bakery Hill near Ballarat where the 27-year-old Peter Lalor addressed a crowd of 10,000, calling for volunteers to resist 'digger hunts', police brutality against miners who did not happen to have their licences on them. Hundreds of volunteers came forward. Kevin O'Doherty and Pat Smyth were certainly involved in these questions but were not closely engaged in this Australian rebellion. They were busy in Bendigo, the other great field, where Smyth was losing money in a 'diggin' speculation'.

Lalor inducted his men with United Irishman solemnity. The volunteers knelt down, 'and with heads uncovered, and hands raised to heaven, they solemnly swore at all hazards to defend their rights and liberties'. On the night before British troops from Melbourne and a police detachment attacked, the password at the stockade the miners built – the Eureka Stockade – was 'Vinegar Hill'. Certainly there were many Irish amongst the rebel miners, but also Americans, Canadians, English Chartists and an

Italian nationalist, Raffaelo Carbone, who left a famous account. 'We were betrayed and taken by surprise,' wrote Peter Lalor later, in summary of the fight-cum-massacre at Eureka, in which many soldiers and, according to some modern research, perhaps as many as sixty miners were killed, and the event would remain central to Australian nationalist mythology. But though Lalor lost an arm there, the institutions of the new country after the Eureka Stockade fight proved more flexible than did those of Ireland after Ballingarry. Juries would not convict the thirteen leaders arrested. Universal male suffrage was promptly introduced and amongst those elected to the Legislature of Victoria less than a year after the uprising was Peter Lalor, ultimately to serve as Cabinet minister and three times Speaker of the House.

Without profit to boast of, Nicaragua Smyth returned to Hobart and married Jane Anne O'Regan on 8 February 1855. Smyth and his bride would set out for America later in the year. O'Doherty himself made arrangements to travel discreetly and illegally to Britain with Captain McDonnell of the *James Baines*, an American wool clipper which had just arrived in Melbourne after a record run from Liverpool of sixty-three days. When the *Baines* departed in March 1855, Kevin assumed the name of a Dr Alfred Carr of Ballarat, who was believed to have given false evidence in an inquiry into the deaths of two miners. He was able to slip back into Ireland to try to collect his modest inheritance, have his reunion with Eva, and plan the marriage to which they were committed by love, published verse, their meeting in prison and the fame of their being parted by exile. The Sub-Inspector of Police at Galway advised Dublin Castle in early July 1855 that 'it was whispered abroad that a strange gentleman was staying with the Kelly family'. With Eva's parents' support, Kevin was able to travel to Dublin with them and their daughter, and then by steamer to Liverpool. On 23 August 1855 they were married at Moorfields Chapel in the presence of Eva's father and Kevin's jovial Uncle George from Paris. The new couple travelled on to Paris then. Charles Gavan Duffy wrote to Kevin, 'A man going to marry his first love and to live in Paris has nothing to desire in the world.' But for Saint Kevin and Eva, Paris was shared exile, enriched by the friendship and good humour of John Martin and of Uncle George. Before long they were living in the Latin Quarter in the same pension as Martin. A second ceremony was eventually conducted at the British Consul's office, to give their children civil legitimacy. Young Eva was already pregnant with their first child. Kevin studied for seven months in Paris at L'Hôpital la Pitié and the Paris School of Anatomy, while in the pension in the rue Lacépède the middle-aged bachelor John Martin was Eva's companion in the dreary winter days. 'Of all the friends I have known,' she would write to him later, 'none has been more genuinely or delicately kind than yourself.' Kevin decided it would be too severe on his wife to have her give birth in Paris. Together, they caught a packet to England, then a train to Liverpool, and sneaked on to the steamer to Dublin.

A week later at O'Doherty's mother's house at Monkstown, a son, William, was born. They had been in hiding there about two weeks in all when an unconditional pardon of O'Brien, O'Doherty and Martin was announced, allowing them to live openly in Ireland. Mother and baby returned to Eva's country, Killeen in East Galway, and O'Doherty took rooms in Dublin near the Royal College of Surgeons to prepare for his final examination.

His old Vandemonian friend Mitchel had by now become a devoted Southerner! There had been a number of reasons for throwing over the *Citizen* and leaving New York. Jenny had complained of Mitchel's eye problems in letters to Ireland and blamed it on New York's guttering gaslight supply. His uncertain vision was itself, however, a metaphor for the difficulties he had brought on himself after a year in New York. If it was a journalist's job to offend the powerful, he had been a success. He had now determined, he said, 'to seek retirement somewhere far away in the wooded mountains of the interior; give up the *Citizen* bodily to John M'Clenahan'. At the end of that last 'polar winter', in the spring of 1855, he found himself and his household on board the steamer *Nashville*, bound for Charleston, 'from whence we were to penetrate the interior as far as the shady valleys of East Tennessee'. For reasons of education Johnny, the eldest boy, stayed with his uncle William in New York, and attended engineering lectures at Columbia. Having been no further south than Virginia, Mitchel was dementedly committing the rest of his family to a deeper South still. 'I have never seen Knoxville, and did not know one human being in Knoxville': still, Jenny took a considerable delight in escaping Brooklyn's comfortless winters, and harboured a hope that this might be the shift to make her husband finally content.

From Charleston the Mitchels made their way by railway to Loudon on the banks of the Tennessee River. They completed the journey to Knoxville on rutted country roads in a conveyance called a carry-all. Knoxville, with two or three 'decent streets, but not paved or lighted by gas', was on a steep hill rising from the surging Holston River. 'Like every other town in the US, it has a mighty future, and occupies itself much in contemplation of that good time.' On the morning of his arrival in Knoxville, in the rooms he had taken at the Coleman House, Mitchel was called upon by William G. Swan, the mayor of the town, and a number of other gentlemen. Swan was six years younger than Mitchel when he welcomed the Irish hero to town. Investments in the coming railroad and proposed gaslight supply had made him already wealthy; a conservative on the institution of slavery, who yet possessed no slaves himself and harboured no prejudices against the Irish, he was the beau ideal of a Southern gentleman as far as Mitchel could see. Together they would grow old in their grievous cause.

Mitchel was disgusted to find that Know-Nothingism had reached even East Tennessee, where one citizen told him that the vaults of Knoxville's first Catholic church were obviously to store gunpowder for use by the Jesuits when they came to abolish liberties and set up the Inquisition. The *Knoxville Whig* was 'a furious Know-Nothing organ', edited by a Methodist preacher named Brownlow 'who once preached with pistols and a Bowie-knife on the Bible before him'.

From the Coleman House, the family moved to lodgings at the house of a Knoxville lady. 'I tell you, dear Mary,' Jenny wrote, 'I am sick and tired of this changing . . . Of all our household goods we brought only our piano and linen.' The piano was for Minnie, who was expected to keep practising. The family were visited by some very pleasant Tennessean citizens. Amongst their friends were members of a persecuted Swiss Protestant sect fled from the canton of Vaud, led by a vigorous prophet named Dr Esperandieu, whom both Jenny and Mitchel, despite their mistrust of religious zealotry, found most pleasant company. One of Mitchel's most enduring friends, however, was the personable Knoxville circuit district attorney, Mr William G. McAdoo. McAdoo was in the strange position of having inherited some slaves, yet believing in the preservation of the Union even at the expense of abolition. One day he took Mitchel up 35 miles into the blue, vapour-shrouded ridges in the foothills of that lovely stretch of Alleghenies now called the Great Smoky Mountains. This was remote but lovely country, intensely green in the valley bottoms, which local people called coves. The forests were abundant in timber and game; the locals were tough Scots-Irish whose forebears had driven the Cherokees out in the eighteenth century and had barely wandered since. Through a rocky, forested gorge, McAdoo and Mitchel entered an exquisite valley or cove named Tuckaleechee, at the present town of Townsend in Blount County. The brawling Little River rushed through Tuckaleechee, and above it splendid escarpments rose. Mitchel returned to Knoxville enthused. The cove was remote from politics, abolition and urban fretfulness. Like many turbulent men, he saw the world's frenzy as the cause of his own feverishness, and believed that all he needed for redemption was a pastorale. Jenny listened dutifully, but she had doubts. 'When we do get a place, it may be twenty miles from a neighbour, and the truth is I think that Mr M will tire of that before I do.' Jenny also suspected that with herself and the children safely settled, Mitchel might start for Ireland any day, appear amongst his fellow countrymen and call on them to seize the chance of an Irish republic.

On 1 April 1855, Mitchel and his second son James started on foot for Tuckaleechee Cove to look for likely farms, and found a 133¼-acre mountain farm on the Little River. A two-room log cabin was located on the mountain slope – as Mitchel would have liked it to be; of all the houses in the Cove, it was closest to the clouds and thunder. Though Swan, McAdoo and other friends tried to dissuade him, he bought this farm. The deed, registered on 8 May, had an informality to it: 'Beginning at a stake on the bank of Little River corner to Frederick Rushes' Survey thence with the Same south fifty three West forty chain to a Hickory . . .' The price was $1,550.

Tennessee was far from Meagher's desires. New York held what he sought. He had been studying law with Judge Robert Emmet, and was encouraged by Court of Common Pleas Judge Charles Daly, a good friend of the Barlows and the Townsends. As a result of these connections, Meagher was admitted to the New York Bar in September 1855. He hoped to achieve the same glittering American careers as had Barlow and Daly, and thus be a valid husband to Elizabeth Townsend. As he was a foreigner – he could not yet legally take citizenship – his admission required a special order of the Supreme Court of the State of New York, but these matters were arranged through the Democrat connections of O'Gorman and others.

And in the midst of the outlay of these energies he persuaded Peter Townsend that he was a proper husband. Neither the canon law nor the Townsends wanted a full-scale St Patrick's Cathedral wedding. Meagher enthusiastically exchanged marriage vows with Elizabeth on 14 November 1855, in a small ceremony at the residence of Archbishop Hughes in Madison Avenue. Elizabeth, possibly to save her father's old Yankee feelings, had not yet turned Catholic – she would after a few years become a devout one. The *New York Times* noted the union in a sneering way, claiming Peter Townsend had disinherited his daughter. This was an absurd statement, not least because of the fondness of Mr Townsend for his children and grandchildren, abundantly apparent in his letters to the Barlows and his comments on Elizabeth. In any case, it suited all parties for the couple to move almost at once into the Townsend house on Fifth Avenue with Peter and Mrs Townsend, a move not usual in cases of disinheritance.

Meagher wrote to O'Brien of his 'noble and beautiful American wife . . . so intelligent, so cultivated, so generous, so gentle and unaffected'. He had made a partnership with a lawyer named Campbell, and they rented an office in Ann Street, near City Hall, the courts, and Tammany haunts. To supplement his earnings, he needed to continue to lecture. He had a crowd of 5,000 people in the Music-Hall, Boston; 3,000 at the Tabernacle at New York. He did not plan to be always on a train, however, orating his way around the country.

In East Tennessee, Mitchel was astonished to hear that his old colleague, and now enemy, Gavan Duffy had gone voluntarily to the Australian colonies; even though they were by now transformed by gold and by new institutions, he found it difficult to comprehend that a man who had struggled so vigorously through many trials to escape transportation to Australia was now so thoroughly severing all his connections to go there of his own choice. Yet Ireland itself seemed dormant. No one expected much of parliamentary activity, not least Gavan Duffy, Member of Parliament himself. The failure of the Tenant Rights Association and the Irish Party in Parliament, Duffy told Martin, was due to Archbishop Cullen, who suspected Duffy of being anti-clerical, and was willing to use his spiritual authority to frustrate him. 'I have laboured till my health broke down,' Duffy told O'Brien. 'I have neglected my family and lived only for the Irish cause, and at every point I have found myself thwarted.' He asked the newly freed O'Brien and others who had experienced the Australian colonies for advice on eastern Australia generally, now that it possessed representative government and had cast off convictism. Despite dust and flies, he was told the climate was vigorous and books could be had just as in London and Dublin. In March 1855 Duffy had published a report in the *Nation* of an Australian Declaration of Independence; there was a sense of a glorious future. In a few years, the colony of Victoria, Duffy believed, would grow to a population of a million. 'And a million men and women of more than ordinary courage and vigour.' Between elections he extricated himself from Parliament by one of the accepted formulae – taking the meaningless office of Stewardship of the Chiltern Hundreds. He wrote a famous farewell in the *Nation* before turning the paper over to younger men. 'The Irish Party is reduced to a handful . . . prelates of the Irish Church throng the ranks of our opponents, priest is arrayed against priest, and parish against parish . . . Till all this be changed, there seems to be no more hope for the Irish Cause than for a corpse on the dissecting table.' It was an image which in the future would be angrily quoted back to him by members of new revolutionary groups.

On 5 November 1855, the 39-year-old Duffy, his ten years younger wife, Susan, his 7-year-old daughter and his two sons sailed from Liverpool.

In Hugh Larkin's Australia, to which Duffy was on his way, the poorer Irish free settler often made friends with former felons of similar background. And so the Larkins of Goulburn became friendly with a free settler, Cornelius Sheahan, a native of the area of Mallow in North Cork, and his wife Mary. Cornelius and Mary Sheahan arrived in Sydney in 1854 with their four children, helped by Mary Sheahan's sister Margaret, who had married an Irish farmer near Goulburn and who had sent home £20 towards the cost of the Sheahan family's passage to Australia. Cornelius went to work on his brother-in-law John Lawrence's property, and it was through one of the potential points of contact – buying farm hardware, attending Mass, or in the pub – that he met Larkin. Cornelius had been through the Famine; Hugh through transportation. Between them they understood the entire dialectic of oppression. Mary Shields-Larkin was pregnant at the time this association between Larkin and Sheahan began. The Larkin children spoke to Sheahan's children with the newest of English-language accents, the long, laconic, sometimes whimsically elliptical accent of Australians. The eldest Larkin, Thomas, born in servitude, was now aged ten years. Goulburn-born Anne was six and John a little more than four, having been born in 1850. Cornelius Sheahan and his family were amongst those available to take care of these three Larkin children, when in the Australian spring of 1854, late October, Mary came to term and called the midwife to her home in Grafton Street.

After frightful labour, before the eyes of a bewildered midwife, the 36-year-old ex-clothes thief died: her heart stopped on All Saints Day, 1 November 1854. The son she gave birth to survived, and was christened Hugh after his father, an Australian version of the other and earlier Hugh Larkin now nearing manhood in East Galway. As if to point up the futilities of life, the body of an unwanted infant had been found that day in Mulwaree Ponds.

Hugh Larkin the Ribbonman, it would appear, felt the bereavement fiercely. He had resources he would never have had in Galway – he could afford to advertise his grief and the first listing under death notices in the 6 November *Goulburn Herald* read: 'At her residence, Grafton-street, Goulburn, Mary, the wife of Hugh Larkin, after a short illness, leaving three children to mourn her loss.' (The 'three' was a typographical error.) Settlers and former convicts rode in from the bush to drink with Hugh, console him, and remark on the tranquillity in the face of the little thief from Limerick. She was buried at Mortis Street cemetery by a young Irish priest.

Larkin found himself alone in this the largest town he had ever lived in. Its new golden allure permitted it the pretensions of a boom town in the midlands of England, and his own material fortunes, modest in Australian terms, were considerable enough. Well or ill, he continued to operate his chandler's shop and had a monument built over Mary's grave which declared that she had died 'in Travail of her Seventh Child'. So Hugh knew of the lost child Bridget. In case Mary should be mixed up with some other Shields, the stone mentioned, as the graves of relatively affluent deceased convicts always did, the name of her ship: 'per *Whitby*'. It declared accurately too that Hugh, four Australian sons and a daughter bewailed her death, and since Hugh and Mary had between them only four surviving children, it must have been Michael O'Flynn who was included in the count.

The death of Hugh Larkin seemed inherent in the death of his convict wife. By 1857, when Hugh had been three years a widower, the New South Wales Constitution had been finalised, a colonial legislature was in place in Australia and a wide male franchise had been introduced. There was still a property qualification for voters – to be owner of £100 in property value or £10 a year rent – a scale Larkin was perhaps able to meet, given the way property values had boomed since the discovery of gold. Within a year, all property basis for the vote would give way to universal male suffrage. The old Chartist option of secret ballot was about to be introduced in Victoria and then New South Wales. So Hugh was that Chartist dream: a common man on the verge of exercising his franchise. A society which when Hugh arrived on *Parmelia* had been a penal experiment was now clearly a social experiment.

Despite the best efforts of republicans such as Dan Deniehy, New South Wales, dependent upon British capital investment, and rendered psychologically dependent by its huge distance from the British Isles, remained loyal to the Crown. The scale of inequities which had provoked rebellion in America and Ireland, however, did not operate in the former penal colonies of Australia. There was not the same pressing basis as elsewhere for wide republican agitation, although Hugh and Cornelius Sheahan, listening to brilliant Dan Deniehy, representing the County of Argyle as an 'extreme Liberal' in the Legislative Assembly of New South Wales, would have felt the attraction of the republican proposition.

Only for the native peoples was there no advance; the gold craze and the need of beef and mutton to feed it eroded further their hold on the earth. Brodribb began to run herds and flocks on the Murrumbidgee hundreds of miles to the west of Monaro, near the present town of

Deniliquin. The Ngarigo who had gone in the spring into the upper Monaro for Bogong moths were encouraged by mission and government hand-outs of tea, flour and tobacco to go into sedentary reservations either down the escarpment on the coast south of Sydney or in scrubby land south-west of Goulburn. Some males served as police blacktrackers or ill-paid horsemen on pastoral land, and some females as servants. Grief, malnourishment, European disease and alcoholism were the marks of their communities.

The white community also had notable struggles with alcohol. Dan Deniehy, member for Argyle, had wrestled and embraced that demon, as did that humbler Irish-Australian Hugh Larkin, who had drunk absconders' moonshine, the solace of the exile, in the remotest Monaro. Over time, Hugh fell into dark ravings, and in 1857, to protect himself and his children, he was hospitalised. The Sheahans and the Goulburn priests nodded sadly over him and his children. The eldest of them, Tom, was now thirteen and already a reliable and muscular blacksmith's apprentice.

It was considered a remarkable era, the one in which Hugh went raging downwards. A Sydney-to-London telegraph was now proposed. Yet another goldfield was opening up at Oban Creek. A search for the lost Arctic explorer and former governor of Van Diemen's Land, Sir John Franklin, was under way. Over all this hugeness and energy the queen seemed the immutable and undying high priestess. 'The Queen is now thirty-eight years of age,' said the *Sydney Morning Herald*, as Hugh fought demons in hospital in the week leading up to the celebration of her birthday. 'She has worn her crown for more than half her life.'

A notice appeared in the *Goulburn Herald* for Saturday 23 May 1857, the rather festive Saturday of the Queen's Birthday weekend.

Effects of Intemperance – Yesterday week a man named Hugh Larkin, who for many years had kept 'a Chandler's Shop' in Grafton Street, was conveyed to the hospital, labouring under the effects of excessive intemperance. It is stated that, during the two previous days, he had consumed as much as two gallons of rum. It was found necessary to put him under restraint, and up to the time of his death, which took place on Thursday morning, he continued to rave in a frightful manner.

So, in his last days, he reattained the fury he had unleashed at the Seymours' door a quarter of a century before. The cosmic argument he had with himself as he lay dying would have included the old quarrel at Somerset House, the violent arrest, Esther Larkin and his Irish sons, and their too well-imagined hunger. Spike Island was part of his cyclical dispute with God, as was *Parmelia*, the journey to Monaro, the withering bush loneliness, quarrels with Aborigines and with absconders, Mary Shields arriving full of defensive charm at Coolringdon, and the brisk clarity of the Australian Alps over which Brodribb drove livestock in the Monaro drought seasons. 'Two or three days before he died he managed to escape from the hospital,' the *Goulburn Herald* said of Hugh, 'and, with nothing but his shirt on, rushed to the nearest public house for a glass of brandy.' His death certificate said that his date of death was 22 May, and cause of death was *delirium tremens*. He was forty-seven years of age. 'The unfortunate man's wife died from a similar cause about two years ago. They have left several children, we believe, wholly unprovided for.'

It seems that these last two ideas – Mary's death from alcoholism and the unprovided-for children – have a Dickensian and moralistic neatness which appealed to a developing rectitude in New South Wales but which were not matched by reality. Mary may have had a taste for liquor, but it is not likely that while fatally giving birth to a child, she had much heart for it. Nor did any of the Larkin children grow up with a sense of having been left unprovided for.

Hugh, like Mary, was buried in Mortis Street cemetery, but no monument marks his burial place; if there was one, it has long since crumbled. The Sheahan family and others subsumed the Larkin children. Cornelius was Hugh's executor and advertised a sale of his merchandise in the *Goulburn Herald* of Saturday 23 May, to take place the following Wednesday, 'The whole of the Stock-in-Trade, Comprising Groceries, Provisions, &C. Terms – Cash.' Hugh may have had liabilities, but he had been provident enough to authorise executors.

Hugh and Mary had managed to set in place an indomitable progeny for which the *Goulburn Herald* gave them little credit. Thomas Larkin, the first child of Shields and Larkin, would marry a Welsh captain's daughter, Harriet Jones, and settle in Gundaroo near Canberra in 1884, where he was a blacksmith and mail contractor. He died with an excellent reputation in 1921. The last of his seven children, born in Harriet Jones's late forties, was my mother-in-law.

John Larkin, born in Goulburn in 1850, perished as a youngish man of thirty-seven years. When his body was railed to Goulburn from his farm in the spring of 1887, the *Goulburn Herald* advised his friends to meet the train carrying his coffin at Goulburn station. Annie Larkin, the girl born in Goulburn in the wake of her parents' marriage, would marry Cornelius Sheahan's son John in 1866. Annie Larkin-Sheahan worked with her husband, blacksmithing on cattle stations near Wilcannia in the far west of New South Wales, and bore seven children. After John Sheahan died of a respiratory illness, she remarried, had three more children, and lived till 1926. The last child of the felon marriage, the Australian Hugh, would flourish, and though he would die in his parents' town, Goulburn, he would not do so until 1949 – outliving his mother by close on a century.

By the time of Hugh the Ribbonman's death at the age of forty-seven years, his East Galway sons, Patrick and Hugh, were twenty-six years and twenty-four respectively. Patrick had herded for the Seymours when they left Somerset House, scene of his father's outrage, and settled at nearby Grove Hill. He married a woman named Eileen Martin and had at least six children, none of whom emigrated. In adolescence Hugh worked a small piece of land near Eyrecourt, but then moved to Killimor. He came to own a pub and a timber mill. The legend is that Patrick Larkin became a Fenian sympathiser and was politically engaged, particularly in the Land Wars of the late 1870s and early 1880s, and that his brother, rather like Edward O'Brien in relationship to William Smith O'Brien, provided a home for his now middle-aged mother, and eschewed radical politics. The blood of both sons is well represented in the areas of Laurencetown, Eyrecourt and Killimor.

For Esther Larkin, widowed first by transportation and then by Hugh's death, there is no record of death. We could surmise she perished some time in the late 1850s, before registration of deaths became compulsory in Ireland, although the requirement to register deaths was often ignored by the anti-authoritarian Irish even after 1860. She lies un-united in one or other of the little rural cemeteries folded into the groins of grazing land around East Galway, probably in Clonfert.

The Australian grandchildren of Hugh Larkin and Mary Shields either were not told their grandparents' story or, out of a sense of propriety, did not repeat it. The faint shame which hung over the meeting and marriage marked, by the standards of booming Australia, a scandal best forgotten. It was when the Irish government made their gift of a database on Irish convicts to the Commonwealth of Australia that Esther Larkin's plaintive appeal appeared on a screen at the National Library in Canberra and set off a search through the convict records for the sometimes indefinite, sometimes precise, outline of these lost Irish souls.

BOOK II

17
Young Ireland and the Isms of Yankeedom

> A Revolutionist under a Monarchy, I am a Conservative under a Republic. This sentiment I boldly utter on behalf of thousands of Irish immigrants, invested with and aspiring to the sovereignty of American citizenship.
>
> Thomas Francis Meagher, to the Democratic Party of Massachusetts, Boston, 1 December 1856

Irish eviction numbers were falling in the year of Hugh Larkin's death. Between 1849 and 1851, nearly 45,000 families had been evicted, close on a quarter of a million people. By comparison, though the psychological weight of the idea of eviction was still powerful in the Irish mind, 913 families faced eviction in 1857, and 795 in 1858. There was a subtle complex of reasons: more advanced farming methods used by landlords; the fact that the land had – by the standards of twenty years before – already been depopulated. People were also less likely now to divide up family land to the point where farming became unfeasible, and that meant younger sons emigrated rather than founded vulnerable Irish farming families.

The numbers of Ribbon-style outrages of the kind for which Hugh was sent to Australia had also declined by the late 1850s. Outrages reported in 1847 were just under 20,000. By comparison, in 1858 there were a little under 3,500.

But though Ireland had settled, it had settled not like a creature confirmed and comforted, but like one exhausted and deprived of options. The brute fact was that famine and other forces had by 1851 reduced the population from a probable eight and a half million to six and a half million. The Irish population was in a free fall unique in Europe, one that would not be arrested until the present day. The supposedly lucky eldest son waited to tend his parents and inherit the farm entire and viable. Thus he helped create a sense which endured till modern times: that Ireland was becoming a land of the solitary and the aged, pared to the limit.

'Maguire was faithful unto the death,' wrote Patrick Kavanagh in his poem of 1942, 'The Great Hunger':

> He stayed with his mother till she died
> At the age of ninety-one.

She stayed too long
Wife and mother in one
When she died
The knuckle bones were cutting
The skin of her son's backside
And he was sixty-five.

*

After an edgy winter with her husband William in their hotel in Brussels, and some travels during the summer of 1855 in Germany, Lucy O'Brien and most of the children, together with their patient Aunt Grace, went back home to Ireland. O'Brien and his son Edward began in the autumn a journey to southern Europe. Over the coming winter the Crimean War would near a successful close for Britain, and 150 members of the Commons petitioned Lord Palmerston, now Prime Minister, for a full pardon for O'Brien and his associates. So too did a large proportion of the Canadian legislature. From Athens on 17 March 1856, O'Brien – nursing a foot injury from an ill-fitting boot – remarked to Lucy that a full pardon would be very convenient. Waiting for the next session of Parliament, he and Edward travelled on, in mutual respect but without a meeting of minds.

On 9 May 1856, in answer to a question from the floor, Palmerston announced that the queen would reward the unexampled loyalty of her dominions by granting a full pardon for the State prisoners, excepting 'those unhappy men who had broken all the ties of honour and fled from their place of banishment'. O'Brien was with Edward in rural and mountainous northern Greece when he heard the news. Kevin O'Doherty was illegally at his mother's house at Monkstown, where Eva had given birth, and now needed to return incognito to Paris to conclude his studies and then make a legal re-entry to Britain. John Martin heard the news in Paris, but, according to his vow, stayed in place.

In absolute freedom at last, O'Brien faced economic dependence, which would never cease to wear at him. He was worried even about the gold cup the Melbourne people had given him and through an influential cousin he tried to arrange to have the cup 'admitted free of duty'. Yet as he crossed from France he was now and then overtaken by simple happiness. 'How different are the sensations with which an exile returns to his country from those with which he left it!' Bonfires marked his path through Limerick at the height of the summer of 1856. Once back in the house at Cahirmoyle, though he no longer managed the estate, he would frequently surrender to his own delight. During one of Lucy's absences, he wrote exuberantly to her: 'The tone of your short note is more in harmony with my feelings than the singing of birds on a May morning, the chant of a Cathedral, the airs of an opera and even than the melody of an old Irish ballad.'

He was asked at once to stand for the seat of Tipperary, but decided, with his usual fixity of intent, not to re-enter Parliament with its unsatisfactory outfalls and dubious frenzies. 'In 1843, after having attended Parliament with continuous assiduity, I arrived at the conclusion that my time would have been much more usefully occupied if I had remained in Ireland.' In mid-September, to the disgruntlement of his family, a procession of 10,000 men, women and children crowded up the drive of Cahirmoyle to beg him to assume the position of Irish leader, whether in the House or in some other form. O'Brien came out to tell them that he had no political or revolutionary aims, though in 1848, when 'this country was reduced by misgovernment to a condition more abject than any that it had known . . . I thought, and I still think, that resistance was justifiable'.

By contrast, at Dromoland and at Cahirmoyle, his family tried to pretend that 1848 had not occurred. His daughter Lucy harboured a primal fear for him and, if he said anything political, would run crying from the room. Edward would soon inherit the control of Cahirmoyle from the hands of the family trust and, though filial, he had in all their chats in the streets of Florence or the ruins of Athens resisted his father's politics. Shorn of domestic power, O'Brien would in part occupy himself by addressing occasional letters to Ireland and the Irish people. He urged the Irish not to boast of their willingness to die for Ireland – they had failed to take the chance to do so in 1848. He noted that during the Irish Famine, £8,000,000 had been loaned for relief in a gesture of what some considered 'unparalleled generosity'. But in 1855, 'An addition of £30,000,000 was made to the ordinary war estimates of the United Kingdom with scarcely a murmur of dissension.' This amount would have been sufficient in the Famine not only to save the lives 'of the myriads' but to render the Famine period 'an era of unprecedented improvement'.

The New York attorney Thomas Francis Meagher heard the news of the full pardon of O'Brien, Martin and O'Doherty, but without any self-regret for having escaped. Answering American demands and affections, he was disappointed that over the winter of 1855–6 he had attracted to his premises at 20 Anne Street only a scatter of minor court briefs; he had begun to toy with the next obvious Irish option – to found a weekly newspaper, the *Irish News*, from the same building as his law offices. The *New York Herald*, generally kind to Meagher, said: 'With the warnings he has before him – especially the pregnant example of John Mitchel who ran through an unexampled popularity in six months, all for the want of a little common sense – Mr Meagher ought not to fail.'

Meagher told Elizabeth and the Townsends that he wanted not only to be a Democrat voice (an objective of which all the Townsends approved), but also to speak for that army of Irish who had not done themselves a great favour by emigrating. A quarter of New York City's population of 800,000 were Irish-born, and this figure did not include the American-born children of immigrant Irish. They were the city's poorest quarter. They lived without running water or sewage systems, and frequently with their economic buffer of a pig, in wooden tenements around the Five Ways, where Worth, Baxter and Park Streets met, north-east of City Hall. In the Sixth Ward in 1854, one in seventeen persons had died. But downtown on the Eastside, in the tenements named Sweeney's Shambles in the Fourth Ward, over the 2-year period from 1854, one of every five adults died, and throughout the 1850s that remained the average death-rate of Irish families in Manhattan. So too over in Brooklyn, where a similarly disease-prone Irishtown was situated. Attending Sunday Mass at the nearby Fifth Avenue Jesuit Church of St Ignatius, Meagher and Libby took for granted the coughing paroxysms of devout Irish. Archbishop Hughes called tuberculosis 'the natural death of Irish emigrants'.

Many families and clans were shattered by the slum environment, and its challenges to body and soul, and so, on top of other griefs, the Irish were seen in disproportionate numbers in all the city's almshouses, shelters, hospitals and asylums, and also amongst the 50,000 or more prostitutes of New York. These were the American domestic issues Meagher intended to address in his newspaper. He meant, for example, to attack such institutions as the Brooklyn navy yard for refusing, on grounds of racial and religious prejudice, to employ Irish.

In foreign policy, Meagher aligned the *Irish News* with the phenomenon called 'American filibustering' – American incursions into Central America – and he particularly admired William Walker, a lawyer, newspaperman and adventurer in his late twenties, who had led an expedition of volunteers from San Francisco to luscious Nicaragua in May 1855, to free it from Costa Rican rule and establish American settlements. Had not California itself been seized and liberated in the same way? Walker's expedition was financed by the magnates Cornelius K. Garrison and Charles Morgan, who hoped to take away from Cornelius Vanderbilt the control of the staging operations across the isthmus. But Walker himself had nobler and more romantic ends – democracy, settlement, destiny and renown – and so did the American volunteers who made up his ranks. The American press observed with intense interest the success of Walker's tough forces in Nicaragua as they won a number of early victories, seized the capital, Managua, and established a national government. The United States and President Franklin Pierce gave recognition to Walker's government in May 1856, and to his assumption of the presidency of Nicaragua in July.

Meagher, his friends and in-laws believed that if America did not occupy the region, passage of Americans from the east to the west coast of the United States could be regulated by the dismal powers of the old world. The *Irish News* asked whether America would consent to pay the toll for crossing the isthmus, arrived at by the same Parliament whose Stamp Act had been cut to pieces by American patriots in 1775 'and flung in the foolish face of King George'. The British had already claimed San Juan del Norte on the Atlantic coast of Nicaragua and had been prepared to outflank the United States by occupying the whole of Central America; and now the hero Walker had forestalled that. Tom Meagher was excited by the example of a young man who could bend a hemisphere to serve purposes so dear to his own heart. He called the invader Walker 'a brave soldier of republicanism . . . Nicaragua shall be free! The Democracy of America increased.'

Some officials, however, felt Walker should be discouraged from single-handedly forcing American policy. Colonel Farbins, Walker's 'Director of Colonization' in New York, was arrested by a Federal marshal for violating the Neutrality Act of 1818. Meagher saw the hand of Cornelius Vanderbilt in this, and was happy to be appointed a member of the legal team to defend the colonel before Special Commissioner Morell in New York.

This was a notable case, a good chance for Meagher, and he intended to make a mark. In early February 1857, at the Commissioners' Court downtown, the hearing began. It would run until late February. Meagher, taking like a terrier to this issue, seemed to have a political as well as a forensic motive. He may have wanted something greater than merely winning this case: he may have wished to force his old friend, the about-to-retire President Pierce, to declare America frankly and fully in favour of settling the isthmus and making it US territory!

With typical daring, he asked Robert Fuller, one of the complainants, whether President Pierce had any interest in the Mosquito Grant, land on the east coast of Nicaragua. Fuller denied it. But Meagher held a letter Colonel Farbins had given him, carrying the frank of the President, and written by the presidential secretary, Sydney Webster, 'reporting a peculiar interest in Nicaraguan lands and colonization'. If the White House tacitly approved of the Nicaraguan endeavour, why should Farbins be blamed for acting on the signals he received from that august direction? If the written proof he, Tom Meagher, held in his hand were not admitted in evidence, then he would permit it to appear in print. McKeon, the district attorney representing the government, telegraphed the Attorney-General in Washington for instructions.

Attorney-General Cushing, perhaps expecting that Meagher would ultimately suppress the letter, telegraphed back that the President did not have any interest in the production or non-production of any of the letters. An abashed Meagher had now ethically to choose his client over the President, and indeed as an American non-citizen patriot to make clear that the Democrat government had a quite proper sympathy for Walker. If he consulted his brother-in-law Barlow, which is very likely, Barlow too held a similar opinion. Meagher therefore produced in court the White House correspondence with Farbins and, when the prosecution denied that the transfer had been effected, presented an attorney-executed deed of transfer of lands in Central America from Farbins to Sydney Webster and his brother. The hearing closed with some embarrassment for the White House, for if President Pierce looked with favour on expeditions like Walker's he could not say so for fear of international opinion. Zealous Commissioner Morell committed the case to the grand jury, but it went no further.

Farbins was free, but President Walker did not fare quite as well. A coalition of Central American States, led by Costa Rica and financed in part by Vanderbilt, invaded Nicaragua, captured Managua and drove Walker to the Atlantic coast, where he sought asylum with the US Navy in May 1857.

The *Irish News*'s first presidential election in 1856 saw the rise of a new coalition named the Republican Party. Under the banner 'Free soil, free speech and Fremont', John C. Fremont, Californian military hero and western explorer, was its presidential nominee. James Buchanan, the ageing former American minister to the court of St James, was the Democratic candidate, and the fact that his father had been a Donegal man attracted Irish support. Buchanan had also guaranteed the South that he believed there were no constitutional grounds for abolition. The *Irish News* applauded Buchanan and his policy of Popular Sovereignty which made the acceptance or rejection of slavery a matter for the people of each new state. Above all, the *News* supported Buchanan's intention to open up American citizenship to newly arriving Irish, a policy which would convert Irish immigrants to the United States *legally* into an instant and huge electoral army.

Buchanan was successful, and though he failed to carry New York State he won New York City, in which Barlow and the rowdiest Irish carter from the Sixth Ward both believed that, for the sake of the Union, the

South should not be interfered with. Meagher's characteristically Democrat feelings about the South had been reinforced by a new visit there in Libby's pleasant company. Meagher expressed his impressions of this visit with fresh vigour in his series 'Glimpses of the South', in the *Irish News*. As for Southerners, they had 'no penchant for isms'. This was perhaps a swipe at abolitionism. But unlike Mitchel, Meagher did not defend slavery; merely his freedom to like the South despite slavery. 'It would be well if America could get rid of slavery. But we can't, in our time, and should therefore confine our efforts to alleviating the evils that accompany it.'

The question Meagher was least keen to address, that of his parole, had annoyingly arisen again in the last days of 1856. The controversy grew from a quarrel with Henry Raymond, editor of the *New York Times* and Republican lieutenant-governor of New York. Raymond's editorial 'Poltroonery' made fun of Irish immigrants and servant girls, and Meagher attacked it in the *Irish News*. In vengefully re-examining Meagher's account of his escape, the *New York Times* judged that Meagher's own account admitted 'that friends were collected, horses procured, routes selected, and all the arrangements for an escape made, under the protection of the parole; and that their execution was all that was postponed until after its surrender'. According to Meagher's argument, said the *New York Times*, 'he informs the magistrate that his parole will cease *twenty-four hours* after he receives this notice; and that if he attempts in consequence of it to arrest him, it will terminate *instantly*. This sounds very much like an Irish *bull*.' Raymond's attack must have marred the jollity of the Meaghers at New Year 1857, and tightened the features of Libby, ever a zealous partisan of her talented husband.

But Meagher had the prospect of achieving citizenship – it would come in May 1857 – and early in the year asked President-elect Buchanan for a diplomatic appointment in South or Central America. He was fascinated by the region and may have seen himself as a potential champion of Buchanan's expansionist policies. Despite the *News*, 'privately speaking, I am in rather sad want of a position, with some emolument attached to it'. Meagher cited Quito, New Granada, Guatemala, Havana, Rio de Janeiro as suitable. Waiting for the President's inauguration, he wrote to O'Brien: 'My disinclination to "place-hunting" no longer exists . . . The same feelings which induced me to regard such gifts with contempt and enmity in Ireland, operate in the contrary direction here. I would rejoice and feel proud in serving the American Republic.' Friends from Tammany Hall, Horatio Seymour, former governor of New York, and Amasa Parker, Democrat candidate for that post in the last campaign, wrote supporting letters. Other referees indicated the width of the connections Meagher had made. The historian George Bancroft, Democrat Senator Stephen A. Douglas and Congressman Daniel Sickles of New York, a personal and, some said, pandering friend of the President, were also in favour of the candidate. But perhaps Meagher's very enthusiasm for the Nicuraguan excursions caused Buchanan to note on the margin of Meagher's letter that it would be 'incompatible with the National interest' to give the Irish exile a diplomatic position.

'Imagine a most lovely valley, five miles long,' John Mitchel had written to Miss Thompson from the farm in Tuckaleechee Cove he took up in 1855, 'varying in breadth from a quarter of a mile to a mile and a half, and lying among parallel folds of the Alleghenies . . . Now, young lady, at the very head of the above mentioned valley . . . I have pitched my tent or wigwam.' He had horses, cows and 'a multitude of pigs'. An orchard of apple trees and peaches varied the diet. He told his sister Mrs Matilda Dixon in the north of Ireland, 'in quitting New York, I have emancipated myself from much *blatherumskite*'.

James, in early adolescence, and Willy, barely more than twelve, took to the mountains like naturals. Mitchel left the two boys on the farm while he went to fetch Jenny and the girls, 'and by Tuesday last, when we came up to our habitation, James had a quarter of venison for us'. For sixteen months or more the Mitchels would live at Tuckaleechee, Jenny Mitchel and her youngest daughter Isabelle disliking the isolation of the place. Bothwell had boasted of livelier company. Mitchel engaged his hearty sons, however, in country rambles and long rides, sheltering in farmers' houses and dining on bacon and cornbread. But while on his farm he worked hard. James and his father milked the cows twice daily, which Mitchel found 'a task of much labor and sweat', fed horses, raised new fences. As winter came on he built extensions. A tree that he was chopping fell the wrong way and altered the shape of his nose for good, but he bore the injury like an agricultural badge of honour. He wrote patronisingly yet affectionately about visiting neighbours. One asked him, 'Was it true as we have heard, that the water of the sea is all salted?' Mitchel began experiencing the effect upon the mind of being without congenial society. 'In this respect Tuckaleechee was worse than VDL.' By December 1855 too, he needed to supplement the poor income from his farming, and ironically declared, 'I am coming down from my mountains in the winter like the wolves, and with the same object – prey.' Leaving his family in the care of James, he undertook a new lecture tour.

Occasional newspaper clippings carried the distant thunder of Mitchel's themes this year – an attack in equal measure on Britain's imperial methods in India and on American Know-Nothingism. His lecturing done, he was able to visit New York again, and his mother, his son John, his brother. They knew that he liked to dance, so they organised a party. 'I remember one large dancing-party we had on New Year's night (1856 I think), at which Mr and Mrs Meagher were present.'

From New York he returned home by rail from Charleston via Atlanta to a Knoxville newly self-important from its rail connection with the world. To make up for his absence, with some of his lecture earnings he bought Jenny a well-trained saddle mare and a side-saddle. He was appalled now to see that Know-Nothingism had made advances not only in Knoxville but in Tuckaleechee Cove itself. At a political meeting at Snyder's Store, the Whig candidate 'horrified the Cove people by his picture of a bloody conspiracy organized by the Pope and Jesuits to take away from free and enlightened Americans the liberty they had acquired by their revolution'.

The dull routine of the farm set in again and, as summer came on, Mitchel made up his mind to give up farming and to bring his family down to Knoxville at the end of the growing season. In preparation for moving back to the town, he had acquired in March 1856, from a certain Mrs Isabella French for the sum of $527.34, a town site on First Creek, 'near the first bridge of the Tennessee and Virginia Rail Road'. Because Mitchel had not yet sold his farm in the Cove, the deal was financed by William G. Swan.

Mitchel began to build his house amongst tall oak, walnut and cedars fifteen minutes' walk from town. Knoxville now had 5,000 souls and three newspapers. Yet he sensed he would not last there either. 'I will make no permanent home in Knoxville,' he punned, 'nor perhaps anywhere till I arrive at *Nox-ville* and *Erebus-ville* – if even there. Jenny might as well be married to a Tartar of the Orient or to a Bedouin Arab.' The farm in the Cove did not sell until the following May. As often when sophisticates went temporarily rural, he took $50 less than he had paid for it.

By the late summer of 1857, he had become predictably restless, and advertised his new home for sale. But he knew Jenny 'would be well content to stay here, as we really have a pretty place, and the climate is lovely'. Mr McAdoo, one day to become professor of English and History at the University of Tennessee, helped by offering Mitchel a law partnership, and though Mitchel politely declined he also amused himself by borrowing and reading McAdoo's copies of *The Times* of London, *Blackwood's Magazine*, the *Edinburgh Review*, *Quarterly Review* and *Westminster Review*. It was William G. Swan who, to Jenny's relief, offered her husband the focus he sought, proposing a new weekly paper to uphold the views Swan shared with Mitchel; the writing to be done by Mitchel, the business by Swan. Mitchel described the journal as 'an organ of the extreme Southern sentiment', one of its aims being 'to advocate earnestly the re-opening of the African slave trade in the interest both of blacks and whites'.

So the Mitchels held on to their house and the first number of the *Southern Citizen* appeared in October 1857, to be published weekly for a subscription of $2 yearly. Though it was not monetarily successful, Swan was willing to bear the cost, and it enjoyed an influential circulation and attracted attention both North and South. The ironies inherent in Mitchel arguing the slavery case so ardently were accentuated by the fact that he intended never to own any slaves, that no one in the poor white enclave of Tuckaleechee Cove had owned slaves, and that they were rare in Knoxville itself. As a political bloc East Tennessee had favoured the abolition of the slave trade. Mitchel sent his friend Father Kenyon, now a parish priest in Tipperary, a prospectus for the proposed paper, and in the fall got a scandalised reply. 'Actively to promote the system for its own sake would be something monstrous,' said the priest. Mitchel defended himself. 'All my behavior from November '45 down to this November '57 seems to myself to be consistent, to be of one piece.' He told Miss Thompson, 'I consider negro slavery the best state of existence for the negro, and the best for his master; and if negro slavery in itself be good, then the taking of negroes out of their brutal slavery in Africa and promoting them to a humane and reasonable slavery here is also good.'

There are not many extant copies of the *Southern Citizen*, but those which exist show his devotion to the causes he had embraced in his past, most especially to slavery and the upholding and praising of Southern society. The paper received wide support from advertisers, sufficient to show that a significant part of the community found its editorial policy appetising. Advertisers included the agents for Conger's Turbine Water Wheel; the wholesale grocers C. Powell & Company; Thomas W. Skelly, Principal, Floyd City Collegiate Institute; Nashville Sash, Blind and Door Factory; Henshaw's Furniture Dealers and Undertakers; T. C. Champe, Modern Tailors. In the 4 February 1858 edition, amidst notices of the sale of a thousand peach trees and testimonials for Camphor Wash Mixture, is found the following chilling notice: 'SALE OF NEGROES – ON THE FIRST Monday in February Next I will offer for sale, in Knoxville, six valuable NEGROES, one third cash and balance in six and twelve months. The same may be purchased private. J. I. Dixon.'

That winter, Mitchel stayed at home in Knoxville and attacked abolitionist fervour in the new state of Kansas. 'If the rascals who infest that country, and are constantly trying to hatch up trouble, would kill each other occasionally, that would give some variety and afford relief, but they are too prudent for all that.' Even in reviewing *Missionary Travels and Researches in South Africa* by David Livingstone, Mitchel pursued his hardline Southern position: the benefit to Africans of American slavery: 'Lander has already told us of the Fellatah having killed a number of their slaves when food was scarce.' Southern slaveholders never devoured their slaves!

He was of course in the meantime all for the incursions of Nicaragua. When the US frigate *Susquehanna* arrested Walker's associate Colonel Anderson, Mitchel objected to the military hubris of that. Mitchel's spectrum of political furies, his scalding prose, the uncongenial political climate of East Tennessee, and the recession which had hit in 1857 and deepened in 1858, guaranteed a merely average performance for the *Southern Citizen*, and caused Swan and Mitchel to consider moving it to Washington, to attract subscriptions as a national newspaper.

In the new, spiritually vacant Ireland he was now permited to inhabit, Kevin O'Doherty saw his two brothers as typical of the national poverty of soul. They had no enthusiasm at all for his or Eva's principles and continued to tie up much of what was rightfully his in a family trust. Eva wrote to her mentor John Martin in June 1857 giving a dismal picture of family dissent between a sick Kevin and his brothers, William and John. 'Wm is still persisting in the course he first adopted – the irritation this man is causing him, I know, is one cause of his being ill . . . John I scarcely blame for he is passive – a mere tool in his brother's hands – the women are small and spiteful.' Martin, in reply to his friend Kevin, expressed sorrow that 'To be sure in Ireland you will meet very often with instances of flunkeyism and a moral shabbiness'.

That summer, Kevin O'Doherty passed the examination his long medical service in Van Diemen's Land had equipped him for and became a Fellow of the Royal College of Surgeons. He practised medicine at 18 Hume Street, was a surgeon to St Vincent's Hospital and lectured in anatomy and physiology at Ledwich Medical School. He also became a licentiate of the College of Physicians and acquired a diploma in obstetrics. But he remained short of money, and deplored the stunned, impotent, supine spirit of post-Famine Ireland.

Eva's problems were to do with the dour reality of domestic life, and the normal but chronic gynaecological ills of the time. In August 1858, she confessed to John Martin, 'I have had many tormenting troubles of the mean and earthy sort which, by the way, more acutely try a body strongly inclined to live in the moon apart from such influences, than even the sable woes of tragedy.' She had given birth to a second son, Edward, and would be delivered of a third, Vincent, the following year. She had been offered a literary career of a sort, however, and was excited about it. 'Lietch Ritchie, Messrs Chambers' literary hack, wrote to me and seems to have rather a good opinion of my powers . . . Mr Ritchie says that after a little time I may expect to be paid one pound per page.'

Through his work as a surgeon at St Vincent's Hospital Kevin got to know the Reverend Dr James Quinn, president of the St Laurence O'Toole Seminary in Harcourt Street. Quinn was something of a pioneer, having recruited Sisters of Mercy to nurse in the Crimea, and was a director of the Mater Misericordiae Hospital. The autocratic cast which would mar his later life was not as apparent yet, and Kevin was grateful to find amongst a clergy that treated him with wariness such a thorough friend. The friendship took root at a time when O'Doherty had written to Meagher asking advice about New York. After consulting experts, Meagher advised his old dining partner from the bridge over the Blackwater against trying to establish himself in New York relatively late in life.

In April 1859, Dr Quinn was appointed Bishop of Queensland. This huge region, formerly the northern section of New South Wales, was administered from Brisbane. After some research into the Australian medical market, Saint Kevin approached the Black Ball line, owners of the *James Baines* on which he had travelled illegally years before. The company agreed to employ him as surgeon on board one of their handsome Australia-bound ships, the *Ocean Chief*. Dr and Mrs O'Doherty were saloon passengers, as were their children, William, Edward and Vincent, and their servant Edith Mills. Eva, Ireland's muse, was five months pregnant, and taking her children out of the Ireland which had once been personified for her by Kevin.

After a longer than normal passage of eighty-nine days, the family landed in Melbourne, and Eva gave birth to a fourth son, Kevin, in November 1860 in Geelong. She stayed with Melbourne friends – the Duffys and the Callans were happy to have in their houses the lustrous Eva of the *Nation* – while Dr O'Doherty went on to Sydney, and by the New Year of 1861 opened consulting rooms at 27 Botany Street.

In this her early Australian period, between January and November 1861, Eva contributed more than forty poems to the pages of the Sydney *Freeman's Journal*. She spoke to homesick Irish immigrants in such lines as 'A Flight across the Sea':

O Ireland of that springtime fairest!
O Ireland of the murmuring streams!

> ... Across that waste of waters shining,
> The exile flees to thee again!

However trite, these verses were a call to that part of her soul which Eva had left in Ireland. Though Australia was – as she wrote – of the 'Glorious future's rosy dawning', it seemed that the move had been more Saint Kevin's concept than Eva's. In a public sense he would deal with it well. She would be for ever the exile.

Meagher would prove to be more of a dilettante newspaperman than Mitchel: he did not devote to the *Irish News* the time or volume of copy which John Mitchel did to the *Southern Citizen*. He had nonetheless employed a reliable young editor, an Irishman named James Roche, who kept the paper consistent and entertaining. Meagher meanwhile lectured widely and still had at least the hope of the law. The deposed Nicaraguan President William Walker arrived in New York towards the end of 1857 and was soon taken into custody by a US marshal for violating the Neutrality Act. The filibuster's legal team was led by Malcolm Campbell, Meagher's legal partner, and included Meagher.

Mrs Elizabeth Meagher did not accompany her husband to Washington for the trial – she had recently left to visit her father-in-law in Waterford. By now she must have suspected that for whatever reason she and Meagher would be childless, and the elder Meagher retained care of his grandson, both in the name of the child's education and of his own fondness.

In Libby's absence, Meagher was pleased by the trip down to the capital, where support for Walker was effortlessly brought into play. In the *Southern Citizen*, Mitchel reported with approval the defence of Walker in the House by Alexander Stephens of Georgia. 'Nicaragua had no sovereignty,' said Stephens. 'The only elected President by popular vote was William Walker; the only legitimate sovereign of that country was William Walker.' To Meagher's disappointment – for he needed opportunities to shine in court – the United States Attorney-General ordered that charges be dropped. The freed Walker thanked his counsel and went south to Mobile to launch another expedition from there. But further Walker attempts to reclaim Nicaragua would end first in arrest by the United States Navy and ultimately, in September 1860, in his execution by hanging when he rashly landed in British Honduras.

Given the lack of activity in his legal practice, Meagher declared he needed new material for the lecture circuit. He wrote downtown from the Townsends' house to Roche on 5 March 1858 saying that he would leave for Costa Rica the next day and would be gone for three months. The intention to visit Costa Rica seemed to emerge suddenly and be apparently random. 'I visit Central America – Costa Rica especially – for the purpose of ascertaining the true condition of things there,' he informed Roche. 'I need not tell you I have no political object – none whatever – in visiting Central America.' People nevertheless began to suspect he might be gathering information for government and business purposes. He carried a letter with him from Samuel Molina, the Costa Rican minister in Washington, and travelled with Ramon Páez, a former student of Clongowes, son of the Venezuelan rebel against Spanish rule, Antonio Páez. His old comrade in the South, John Mitchel, published in the *Southern Citizen* of 18 March 1858 a report that Meagher had denied his mission to Central America was political. His intentions were literary and his companion, Ramon Páez, 'botanist, geologist, artist', was to provide the graphics and expert advice.

The best way to Costa Rica was through Nicaragua, where travel was helped by the fact that one could steam across massive Lake Nicaragua, and then down the Pacific coast to Punta Arenas, Costa Rica. Once there, Meagher and Páez headed east by mule, ascending the volcanic mountains of the Cordillera Central, and so reached the delightful capital, San José, where Meagher began writing of his experience with typical brio. Their letters of introduction to the President, the Bishop of San José, and other notables 'obtained an unmolested passage for our luggage. It was on the road, miles behind us, jolting and smashing along in the rear of two ponderous bullocks; but whenever it arrived, the commandant at the Goreta in the pleasantest accents assured us the formality of an inspection would be dispensed with. It was due to literature and science, he said . . . Moreover it was due to the son of the illustrious General Páez.'

In San José he attended the presidential ball in a good suit. Páez's drawing of the ball at President Mora's palace is superbly atmospheric, conveying a sense of the sweat beneath the dazzling uniforms. In the midst of the company stands M. Felix Belly, a Frenchman, who had been given a 99-year canal concession by Costa Rica and Nicaragua. Accompanied by a huge French mercenary in zouave uniform, a man who had hired himself out to Costa Rica to fight Walker's filibusters in Nicaragua, Belly was a figure of subtlety and old-world malice. Meagher sniffed a possible intrusion by the French, and sent back to the *Irish News* an article entitled 'Casus Belly', advocating war if necessary to keep the French out of Central America.

Meagher found an Irish doctor in the capital's hospital, a Dr Hogan, who had amongst his patients two Costa Rican soldiers wounded in battle against the filibusters at Lake Nicaragua. Opposite them lay three of Walker's men suffering acutely from ulcers. One of these told Meagher he was from New York. Another was a boy soldier from Quebec, of Irish parents, who had joined the filibusters in the hope of receiving land as a colonist: 'he would not be eighteen until June, and yet he had been in every battle the filibusters had fought, from the burning of Granada to the last attempt of the Allies against Rivas'. Meagher would later advertise in New York papers for the parents to come to Costa Rica and fetch their boy, but no one appeared.

On the way to the Atlantic coast through Cartago he ascended the volcanic slopes of Irazu and looked down into its awful cauldron. Now successive ridges had to be crossed, thickly set with thorny forest. Meagher was unable on the steeper parts to travel on muleback but had to scramble on all fours. Whatever his purpose, to enrich a lecture or provide a magazine article, to inform American capital or American policy, it would be churlish to deny the rigorous, boyish effort Meagher put into this Central American adventure.

From the Pacific coast at Boca del Toro, Don Ramon Páez sailed for Venezuela, where his father had been reinstalled as President, while Meagher went by coastal steamer to San Juan del Norte and boarded the US sloop-of-war *Jamestown* as guest of the captain. He wrote to his friend Judge Charles P. Daly in New York that, viable as the trans-isthmus railroad might be, he thought Costa Rica was not a suitable place for immigration.

Meagher's lecture tour on Costa Rica did not stimulate as much interest as he had hoped. He gave up plans to write a book on the subject, and instead prepared three long magazine articles, 'Holidays in Costa Rica', for publication in *Harper's*. He wrote a large part of them, as Christmas 1858 approached, while with Libby in Charleston, a popular winter retreat for Southerners.

That magnificent Australian gold cup was a heartache to O'Brien still. 'It is wholly unsuited for Cahirmoyle, or rather our home,' O'Brien told Mitchel, '. . . I consider it to be a national memorial . . . and wish therefore to reserve it for public inspection.' But O'Brien could not evade paying duty on it, a distressing £130 and 6 shillings.

As well as hearing from ageing Young Ireland in this way, Mitchel encountered – in his last days in Knoxville – the new Irish revolutionary phenomenon. About two weeks before the Mitchels moved to Washington, a balding, slight though muscular Irishman appeared at their house in

Knoxville. His name was James Stephens. Mitchel knew that as a youth Stephens had 'turned out with Smith O'Brien in 1848 with his pike in good repair'. After escaping, disguised as a maid, to France in 1848, Stephens had belonged to socialist cells in Paris. He was now visiting all the Young Ireland heroes, asking both for money and moral support for a new endeavour to liberate Ireland through a body he led and had named the Irish Republican Brotherhood. He had had an indifferent reaction from William Smith O'Brien in Cahirmoyle, where he had not fully approved of the tenant housing the O'Briens provided on the estate. Meagher in New York had been lukewarm. Mitchel gave Stephens $50 and certain introductions, but would not publicly declare for his cause.

After Stephens was gone, Jenny braced herself for the *Southern Citizen*'s move to Washington, making her sixth home in as many years. The Mitchels found a large, pleasant family home on Capitol Hill, not unlike the one they had just sold in Knoxville. They found Washington turbulent, acrimonious and demanding, and in a letter written to his friend the widow Mrs Williams in Tasmania on 1 May 1859 Mitchel confessed to dwelling fondly, and 'almost with a species of perverse regret, upon memories and associations of Bothwell'. Casting his net widely, however, in the pages of the *Citizen* Mitchel published a series of letters explaining the history of the Young Ireland Movement, which would later be collected and published in book form, entitled *The Last Conquest of Ireland*.

A few months after the Mitchels moved to Washington, Smith O'Brien, to enormous popular enthusiasm, arrived in America, landing in New York on 25 February 1859, as a snowstorm raged, having journeyed from Galway with his servant Dan. He was warmly greeted by Meagher, bronzed from recent adventures in Costa Rica. Perhaps in Van Diemen's Land there might have seemed to be some parity of power between Denison and O'Brien, but in the larger world the disparity between the petty official and the ordained great soul was evident. And though at Cahirmoyle he might be a guest at his own table, he was welcome at the finest American tables.

He still possessed a political nose and was soon in Washington visiting the Mitchels. When it was known at the Capitol that O'Brien was at the Mitchels', great numbers of both houses flocked to see him. The Senate was about to adjourn, and a number of Southern senators invited O'Brien to visit their estates and plantations. Mitchel confided to O'Brien that in the view of the *Southern Citizen*, many people 'don't wonder that the British Government found it necessary to get rid of me'. O'Brien wrote to Lucy of the Mitchel couple: 'She is really a charming person and though neither you nor I agree with the political views of Mr Mitchel there are few persons more beloved by his private friends and family than this formidable monster.'

Mitchel took O'Brien to visit Richmond, Virginia's – and perhaps the South's – self-possessed capital. In the South too O'Brien was so celebrated that the only chance he got to write to Lucy was aboard riverboats. He visited the plantation homes of Senator Hammond of South Carolina, and of the leading Congressmen Toombs and Alexander Stephens of Georgia. On Hammond's estate, he attended an impressive Negro service. 'All these arrangements seem very patriarchal and very different from the picture conceived by the imaginations of those who read anti-slavery works . . . Nonetheless I am not converted in the subject of slavery . . . I cannot understand why the natural virtues which they possess should be extinguished by freedom.'

On the steamer *Mississippi*, he met a number of filibusters, determined to capture Cuba. The open sewers of New Orleans made him wonder why cholera did not occur every day of the week, but he was pleased to find there many Irish connections. He visited the plantation of Mr Maunsell White, originally of Limerick, and in the office of the *Delta* newspaper he met a cousin of Maurice Lenahan, editor of the *Limerick Reporter*. Moving up the Mississippi to Memphis, he commented that the saloon of the *Nebraska* was nearly 200 feet long. 'The living is similar to that provided by a first-class hotel.'

North, in Chicago, he found that 8,000 people lined up to shake hands with him. He was in Portland, Maine, in mid-May when the Irish elections were on, and told his daughter Lucy that he was delighted to be out of Ireland, 'lest in a moment of weakness I might be tempted to accept the offer of a Seat in Parliament'. Receptions in Portland and Toronto put a close to his first and last American adventure.

O'Brien's march of glory through the United States was overshadowed for Meagher by a murder in Washington involving people he knew well. Philip Barton Key, grandson of Francis Scott Key, the author of the American anthem, was involved in a love affair with Teresa Baglioli Sickles. The daughter of a renowned Italian musician, Teresa was the wife of Congressman Dan Sickles, a Nassau Street lawyer and a powerful Tammany figure to whom the Townsend family had frequent recourse. Having served in the London embassy under Buchanan, who was now President of the United States, Sickles had a firm friend in the White House. Gossips claimed that the President himself had had an affair with Teresa, condoned by her husband.

One Sunday that spring of 1859, the smitten Key, US district attorney for Washington, was seen by Congressman Sickles to be in the street outside the Sickles residence in Lafayette Square, spying through opera glasses and signalling to Mrs Teresa Sickles as she stood at a window. At the time, Congressman Sickles was entertaining as guest Congressman Dan Butterfield. Outraged, he confronted his wife and then, accompanied by his friend Butterfield, left the house, caught up with a retreating Key in nearby Madison Street near the entrance of a club for eminent Washingtonians, took out a revolver and shot him twice, in the liver and the thigh. As Key pleaded with him, witnesses, including Butterfield, stopped Sickles from delivering a *coup de grâce* to Key's head. The dying lover was carried bleeding into the Club House.

A White House page took news of the killing straight across Pennsylvania Avenue to President 'Old Buck' Buchanan. Buchanan immediately moved the page out of Washington, to prevent his giving evidence against Sickles. Meanwhile Sickles surrendered himself and the revolver to the Attorney-General and was put in the District of Columbia gaol.

Many leaders of Irish America flocked to Sickles. He was a splendid Democrat, a friend to the Irish in Tammany, and a friend to the Irish cause. It is hard to believe, given the sensitivity of the case and the closeness of Sickles to Buchanan, that the President was not informally consulted on the matter of Sickles's legal team. Amongst the 8-man legal phalanx assembled to defend Sickles were Buchanan's friend Edwin Stanton, soon to be rewarded with the post of Attorney-General; Irishman James Topham Brady of New York, for jurisprudence; and Tom Meagher, for his lustre and oratory. Only Key's successor as district attorney, and one assistant DA, were to appear for the prosecution.

The most famous murder case of the era began in the Criminal Court for the District of Columbia on 4 April, with Republicans hoping to see Democrat wickedness exposed. Sickles's case was helped by a signed confession of adultery which he had extorted from his wife before he left the house to kill Key. The production of Key's blood-encrusted underclothing in court by the coroner was the prosecution's riposte. But a counter-sensation was created by a note Sickles had received before the killing, now produced by the defence, warning Sickles that Key had rented a house on 15th Street from a black man 'for no other purpose than to meet your wife Mrs Sickles . . . With these few hints I leave the rest for you to imagine.'

Comments would be made on the delicacy of the prosecution in not cataloguing Sickles's own infidelities, and many saw in this the influence of the President. So Sickles's legal team got their client through to the closing arguments with his character, and the President's, unstained. Key himself, said Brady, was responsible for his death by continuing to hang around the Sickles house and not providing a 'cooling time'. Brady then read into the record robust arguments which, he said, had been prepared by his learned fellow counsel Tom Meagher against a guilty verdict. 'Do this, do it if you can, and then, having consigned the prisoner to the scaffold, return to your homes, and there, within those endangered sanctuaries, following your ignoble verdict, set to and teach your imperilled wives a lesson in the vulgar arithmetic of a compromising morality.' After a 19-day trial, the verdict of not guilty came back within seventy minutes.

The Irish had shown their power to save their allies in the Democrat compact. But Meagher hoped again that his participation in a famous trial would ensure new success. During the trial indeed, a formal notice of Meagher's sale of the *News* to one Richard Lalor was posted, which cleared the decks for legal clients. But people did not see him as a practical lawyer. So 1859 proved a disappointing year. He had still not found a career in the Townsend–Barlow sense. He wrote to O'Brien in Ireland: 'Perhaps I've lost too much faith . . . I've ceased to be a participator in historic motions. I've become an impassive spectator.' But at the breakfast table one morning in late 1859 he was energised by news of a supposedly spectacular gold rush in Central America, centred in the province of Chiriqui far to the south of Meagher's previous trip with Páez. Chiriqui lies in what is now Panama but was then part of a greater Costa Rica, and ultimately of New Granada, or Colombia. The source of the gold was in fact suspect – gold trinkets dug out of the graves of Indians. But it revived the question of the best place to build a trans-isthmus railroad.

About this time a formidable New York couple, the Dalys, known to the Townsends and the Meaghers, introduced Meagher socially to Ambrose Thompson, a young entrepreneur and shipbuilder from Philadelphia. Meagher thought Thompson had Yankee initiative, and Thompson intrigued him by mentioning that he had an option to build a railroad across Chiriqui. He had also read Meagher's Costa Rica articles with admiration. Might Mr Meagher do a reconnaissance of Chiriqui, then act on Thompson's behalf in approaching the President of Costa Rica and tying up the rights? Meagher's soul breathed anew at the concept. He had got on very well with the Costa Ricans, even if they had defeated his old friend Walker. Meagher would take Libby with him – to stay in lovely San José while he did his transit of Chiriqui. He thanked Mrs Maria Lydig Daly for arranging the introduction and for 'having enabled me to step into a new field of life . . . My noble American wife will thank you too.'

The Dalys were habitual associates of the Meaghers. Maria Lydig Daly herself came, like Elizabeth Meagher, from an old New York family; Dutch-German by descent, she was Irish not by blood but by marriage to Judge Charles Patrick Daly, an Irish farmer's son, in 1856. At thirty-nine, seven years older than Meagher, Daly had the hunger for scholarship which marked many Irish immigrants, and was considered an eminent Shakespearean scholar. Columbia University would award him a doctorate in Law in 1860, and he taught at Columbia Law School. He served on the Court of Common Pleas from his twenty-eighth to his seventieth year, and was the Chief Justice of that court, the highest in the New York area, from 1859 onwards. A Tammany man and, like Barlow, a supporter and friend of George B. McClellan, former soldier, businessman and Democrat, he possessed unexpected enthusiasms – an intense fellow feeling for Jewish emigrants, for example. He had written *A History of the Jews in North America*, and was a member of the committee which founded the New York Jewish Orphans' Home.

Maria Lydig not only married one Irish jurist herself but successfully married off her younger sister Catherine to James Topham Brady. Thus did poor Irish immigrant boys advance to the centre of American life. Maria and her husband had an excellent home at 84 Clinton Place above Canal Street, provided by Maria's father and beyond all Daly's boyhood expectations. Like her husband, Maria Daly was a hearty Democrat, and referred to Abraham Lincoln, both as he emerged and as he assumed the presidency, as 'Uncle Ape' and 'King Log'.

From 1859 until the end of his life Meagher would remain a friend of the Dalys, though the coming American conflict would render the relationship ambiguous.

The State Department asked Meagher this time to carry documents to Costa Rica to the newly placed American delegation. He sailed with an enthusiastic Libby on the *Northern Light*, and crossed again by way of massive Lake Nicaragua from San Juan del Norte to Punta Arenas, described by Meagher as the Newport of Costa Rica, and by cart to San José.

Libby was gratified to see that her personable husband had obviously made a social impact with the Costa Rican Cabinet on his last trip. Meagher had liked them in return, particularly what he saw as their democratic, egalitarian style. The President, Juan Mora, this time took the Meaghers into his palace. Meagher began, both informally and formally, the work of persuading Senor Mora, a tough-minded man who had led the army of Central American allies against the filibusters, to settle favourably the dispute over rights between Ambrose Thompson's Chiriqui Improvement Company and the Panama Railroad Company. Not that Mora's power on the matter was absolute – Costa Rica was a self-governing state of the federation of New Granada, whose federal capital was at far-off Bogotá, Colombia. But on 6 May that year, Juan Mora's government made out exclusive, conditional rights to Ambrose Thompson for construction of a railroad across the territory of Chiriqui between Bocas del Toro on the Atlantic and Punta Mala on the Pacific. One of the conditions was that the United States Navy would advance payments for the use of the ports at either end of the line.

Both these points were on land which was also claimed by the New Granadan state of Panama. So Meagher and Mora had talks with federal New Granadan representatives in San José, and the result was that Ambrose Thompson's Chiriqui Improvement Company would later have its charter ratified both by the Pennsylvania legislature and by the Colombian Parliament. The charter gave Thompson proprietary right to 'a body of land on the Isthmus of Chiriqui, in the United States of Colombia, extending from the Atlantic to the Pacific', including the right to deliver mail and introduce colonists.

More than two months later, on 13 July 1860, the Meagher–Thompson Grant of cross-isthmus rights was approved by Congress. Congress of course did not have sovereignty over the isthmus, but its recognition and commitments reflected Meagher's successful dealings with Mora, and served to warn off other American interests. An exultant Meagher now left Libby as a guest of the President and went off to reconnoitre Chiriqui. Taking ship in Punta Arenas, he brought the same literary enthusiasm to describing the aged schooner, *Fruta Dorada*, in which he travelled south some 200 miles to Boca Chica, as he had ten years earlier to describing the *Swift*. The *Fruta* was 'porous all over . . . Cockroaches, spiders, three or five scorpions . . . had the principal cabin to themselves.' The other passenger was a Mexican war veteran, a retired colonel of the Indiana militia who narrated 'how he tore his way through miles of *cacti* to the bastions of Chapultepec'. The volcano of Chiriqui overhung their coastal passage to Boca Chica. 'And there – in the midst of oranges and *mangos*, the fragrance of which was borne on the fresh breeze of the Pedrigal far out to sea – was a swarm of huts, with the shy Naiads of the river gliding in and out of them in their white *chemisettes*.'

From the port the party, including the captain and the colonel of militia, travelled in a *bungo* through wonderful forests up the river to the city of David. There, at the Hotel Francesa, which had been built for a battalion of gold seekers but was now empty, they cooled themselves with drafts of '*benicarlo* and lemonade'. Ahead still lay the omnipresent volcano and its forested ranges, but to the south, in the direction of Panama City, were great cattle pastures.

The journey across to Bocas del Toro on the Atlantic side was taken no more than four or five times a year. It required competent guides, and three such Indian guides led the way now on foot, bearing large *javas* or wickerwork baskets. Travelling with Meagher and the others from *Fruta* was Don Carlos Wagner, a German settler making for Baquete, about half-way across the isthmus, and a likeable Scot, Wagner's brother-in-law, Mr William Campbell. Ransacked Indian graves lay on either side of their road.

As they marched higher, the winds from the ice-clad slopes of Chiriqui volcano froze them. Half-way across, at the final ascent to the cordillera, the party halved – Wagner, Campbell, the Indiana colonel and the French captain making tearful goodbyes to Meagher and the Indian guides. Emerging from forests, Meagher and the Indians entered the piercing cold of Chiriqui's lava beds and were grateful to begin a descent down rugged slopes towards the Atlantic side. Meagher praised Chiriqui for its volcanic fertility, 'its inter-tropical grains, fruits, vegetables and esculent roots in marvellous abundance. The sugar is the best on the coast.'

Meagher's article on Chiriqui in *Harper's* sometimes has a boosting character. 'Perfectly free from swamps – the writer having crossed from sea to sea without once wetting the sole of his shoe except, indeed, when he had to ford the rivers – not a dollar would have to be sunk, at any point, in the construction of an artificial foundation.' He considered Bocas del Toro splendid. 'The railroad once built, ships of the largest size can ride broadside on to the wharves.'

But was there too much of the literary man in Meagher? He saw the Central American scene romantically, in too humane and textured a way to be able to look at it as the true Yankee entrepreneur should – as raw asset.

As Meagher reconnoitred for Thompson's and his own glory, Mitchel's paper went out of business. After two years of publication, the *Southern Citizen* ceased publication in the summer of 1859. Closing his office, Mitchel had come to one of those lightning decisions. He would leave Washington and go to France. 'There is an Anglo-French war in the air,' said Mitchel. 'When will it come down in bodily form to the earth?' He intended to support himself and his family by supplying material to American and Irish journals, including the *Irish American*. Jenny was relieved to hear that she should not pack up and move yet. He would test things out first.

He was in Paris by the end of August 1859, but the Anglo-French war he hoped for never took 'bodily form'. A couple of months' residence, and discussions with the Foreign Ministry, proved that, and all at once he desired to be back in Washington with his wife and family. Even John Martin was gone from Paris, having returned to Ireland in 1858 as guardian of his seven nieces and nephews – his sister-in-law and brother having died of fever. Martin was courting Mitchel's sister Henty, a further bond between the two old friends, but an eventuality which would keep him permanently in Ireland. It was drear January of a new year, 1860, when Mitchel wrote to John Blake Dillon, who had returned to Ireland under amnesty, in disgust at the peace accord the French and English had made: 'The entente cordiale, though it is false and treacherous on both sides, is for the present in full credit.'

Jenny was pleased to see him back in Washington. But American events conspired against her. The coming split in the Democrat vote between Stephen A. Douglas and Breckinridge of Kentucky delighted Mitchel, and was the mechanism he had urged in the *Southern Citizen* as a means to ensure radical Republican success, the election of Lincoln, and the separation of the long-suffering South from the undeserving Union. Mitchel and the family distracted themselves from the question of what this all might mean to young men such as their sons James and John by meeting up in New York and going on a trip to New Rochelle. Not liking it, the family removed to David's Island in Long Island Sound. Even when it came to a summer bathe Mitchel could not simply settle, and in the spirit of his restlessness was discussing with Jenny a more concerted return to Paris, *en famille*, there to make a living as a foreign correspondent. He had established a range of press contacts – the family of a friend, Senator Rhett of South Carolina, were involved in the newspaper business in Charleston and would publish whatever he sent. Thinking that Mitchel was sick of acrid American politics and was proposing a long-term residence in Paris, Jenny became enthusiastic. She could visit Ireland easily from there. And though she would have to leave her two eldest sons behind in the United States, her daughters and her youngest son Willy would get a good French education. 'What hurried me at the last, if you must know,' Mitchel wrote to his sister Mary, 'was that I found my particular ship, the *Mercury*, was in port and to sail for Havre on a certain day. They brought over all our packages, just as they had been made up in Washington, piano and all, in their packing cases.'

They settled in rue de l'Est in Paris, but life was monotonous, with the same small circle who had entertained John Martin now emerging to greet Jenny. Willy attended a day school, and a governess came three times a week to teach two of the girls. His beloved eldest daughter, Henrietta, attended the convent of Sacré Coeur, and soon he would have to vouchsafe the information to Miss Thompson and his disapproving mother that she had been for some time 'a devout Catholic. She has become extremely intimate with the ladies of the Sacré Coeur – a splendid convent here.'

*

In Costa Rica, Elizabeth Meagher still remained in the temperate capital, but Meagher went briefly back to New York to report, 13 pounds lighter and tanned. He became involved in correspondence with Buchanan's Secretary of State, his old friend General Cass, over expenses incurred on the journey. But the prospects of massive rewards remained. 'He has shown that Irishmen can succeed as well as other people,' said the *Irish News*. The US Navy, which would benefit by acquiring ports, intended to expend a then prodigious $300,000 as a down payment to the Costa Ricans on Thompson's grant, and to put in another $700,000 when Thompson got utterly undisputed title to the grant. But now the Senate refused to ratify the deal, and in a few late summer days Thompson and – more significantly – Meagher were stripped of their Chiriqui prospects. 'I'll return to Costa Rica,' Meagher wrote desolately, 'without the $300,000 which was to be deposited as a guarantee of the fulfilment of the contract.' By mid-October, after further discussions with Thompson and government officials, he was back in Costa Rica to report the sad news to Libby, and to try but fail to extract from the local federal representative of the New Granadan government any recommendation he and Mora could have taken to Bogotá.

Meagher, desperate for Yankee-style success, applied now to the Costa Rican government for an exclusive right of extracting Indian rubber. But since the Senate had prevented the planned payment of $300,000 from the navy, his standing was not as pristine as before. The Meaghers and the US minister in San José were savagely disappointed that all their negotiations had produced so little. Late in the year, Tom Meagher and Libby said goodbye to Mora, left San José, went to Nicaragua and home. Rugged souls, they must have dreaded facing relatives and friends with news of their failed enterprise. To add to their disappointments and concern, the Republican Lincoln had just been elected President. Uneasy at heart, they sailed in the *North Star* through bright seas towards New York.

18

Ireland and the Bloody Arena

> I saw a Private of a Wisconsin regiment stumbling along with a feather bed across his shoulders . . . a counterpane wrapped about him – a curious piece of needlework, gaudy enough to please a Carib prince and sufficiently heavy for a winter's night in Nova Scotia.
>
> *The Last Days of the Sixty-Ninth in Virginia*,
> Thomas Francis Meagher, Captain,
> Company K ('Irish Zouaves'), New York, 1861

On 25 January 1861, Meagher and Libby landed with their tropical complexions in a snowy New York, in a United States already beginning to disintegrate, and heard under freezing skies the news of the death of Meagher's fellow Vandemonian exile, Terence Bellew MacManus. His passing in San Francisco was of particular resonance for Meagher: MacManus had died the death of a disappointed rebel who had failed to find a place for himself in America.

Back in his father-in-law's house at 129 Fifth Avenue, the death of gentle MacManus added to the wistfulness and lack of triumph of his own season. But this personal loss was augmented by the nation's civic fear that the abolitionists' tool, Abraham Lincoln, might destroy the United States. Libby and Meagher had missed the frenetic presidential elections, but the *Irish News*, Meagher's old paper, had been solidly Democrat behind Senator Douglas, whose vote the rival Southern Democrat candidate Breckinridge split. And now, even as, in reaction to Lincoln's election, Southern states began to secede, Meagher saw his brother-in-law Barlow exercising all his powers to resolve the crisis. Barlow's solution was earnest but improbable: the Federal government should take a suit in the Supreme Court against all states, slave and free, to show cause for their behaviour. Barlow had both civic and material reasons to keep the peace. Serving on the boards of such north–south-running railroads as the Ohio & Mississippi, of which his amusing friend George B. McClellan was president, he saw any possible conflict as an unspeakable catastrophe.

The mayor of New York, Fernando Wood, a Southern sympathiser who had broken with Tammany and founded an alternative Democrat faction named Mozart Hall, argued that rather than go to war the city should now declare itself a city republic, independent of the United States.

New York was the great cotton-handling port of America, and its merchants had a unique affection for and tolerance of the South. Congressman Dan Sickles doubted any New Yorker would cross the city line to wage war against the Southern states.

But Meagher could see that traditional New York affection for the South was being tried. By the close of January six states had seceded, and Southern clients began to refuse to pay their bills to the Sterling Iron Works and New York-based railroads until payment could be made in Confederate currency. Some – including, it seemed, Peter Townsend – began to think that a brief show of military strength *could* settle that issue.

In late February, Lincoln visited New York and held a successful levee four blocks from the Townsend residence at Moses Grinnell's Fifth Avenue house. Meagher saw the avenue fill up with hostile working men, notably but not totally the Irish, fearful for their prospects of employment if millions of freed slaves were turned out on to the labour market. Meagher, perhaps worn out by travel and disappointment, might at another time have appeared on the steps and addressed them. But he did not yet know what to suggest to himself, let alone to them. He remained watchful.

At last in March, to the contempt of old Yankee Democrats, Lincoln *was* inaugurated. That month a planned long-distance Fenian transfer of the body of MacManus from San Francisco to Ireland generated a series of invitations to Meagher to deliver lectures eulogising MacManus throughout New England. 'Fenian' had been a term which derived from lean, intense John O'Mahony. After being with O'Brien at Ballingarry, O'Mahony had lived for the greater part of a decade in Paris, making his way in the world as French translator of Dickens's *Martin Chuzzlewit* and as teacher of Irish at the Irish College. Moved to America, he attached to the membership of the new Irish republican movement founded in New York in 1858 the name 'Fenian Brotherhood', from the ancient *Fianna*, Finn MacCool's warriors, seven score and ten samurai-like leaders. The Fenian Brotherhood spread rapidly throughout the United States.

On St Patrick's Day 1858, another Ballingarry fugitive, James Stephens, once O'Mahony's fellow Parisian exile but now returned home on amnesty, established the Irish Republican Brotherhood in Dublin. The title 'Fenian' would be extended to Stephens's men and women as well, even though the Fenian movements in Ireland and the United States were separate structures. Though the *Fianna* had been defenders of Ireland's boundaries, their nineteenth-century incarnations intended to free Ireland by physical force, and now the new movement sought to enlist the ghost of

Terence MacManus. San Francisco Fenians intended to exhume his remains, seal them in lead and take them on pilgrimage.

Back in New York after his speaking tour, Meagher apologised to Judge Daly for some small unrecorded lapse of manners. 'Return good for evil – Drop down to Irving Hall, Wednesday evening next, April 3rd, if you've nothing pleasanter or more profitable to do . . . I want you to know who MacManus was.' On the night, to massive applause, he introduced the audience to his late fellow prisoner: 'there he is, dashing through the multifarious business of his, at the rate of one million and a half pounds sterling a year – radiant, hearty, full of pluck, teeming with brain, and having a proud, dutiful, chivalrous thought for Ireland all the while'.

The eve of the great American conflict found little D'Arcy McGee in a condition he would, earlier in the decade, have felt contempt for. In the mid-1850s, he had begun to fancy Canada and praise that huge British dominion for the capacity of its massive spaces to accommodate Irish immigrants. The Canadian provinces were 'not necessarily miserable and uninhabitable because the British flag flies at Quebec . . . That flag, without futile landlordism, without a national debt, without a state church, is shorn of its worst terrors.' Whereas the squalor of American slums and the seductions of Tammany Hall politics weakened the faith and moral fibre of the Irish. And exiled Irishmen like Doheny, said McGee, who schemed to use the American government as a weapon against Britain, served only to fuel Know-Nothing hate. The last time lawyer Michael Doheny had met D'Arcy in the streets of New York, punches had been thrown.

By 1856, McGee had taken to depression and drink and was a near-bankrupt. He was married to an Irish-American, Ann McCaffrey, and had two small girls about whose future security he was worried. He wrote to the Bishop of Canada, Bishop Charbonnel in Toronto, to ask his patronage, and Charbonnel was probably behind the invitation extended in 1857 by the Irish Catholic community of Montreal for McGee to found there a level-headed Irish paper, the *New Era*, in competition with the other narrower, anti-Protestant Catholic newspaper, the *True Witness*. Of Montreal's 70,000 persons, somewhere between a quarter and a third were Irish, and to that community McGee brought his restless energy. Supporters provided him with a good house in St Antoine Street. One who knew him at that time, approaching thirty years of age, said of him, 'He was short and stubby. His face was homely and not much marked by shaggy hair and whiskers: it was redeemed from ugliness only by its remarkable expressiveness.'

Almost immediately he accepted the invitation of the St Patrick's Society to stand as the Irish Catholic candidate from Montreal in the general election of 1857, and was elected an independent to the Parliament which met sometimes in Toronto, sometimes in Ottawa. He had a definite Montreal Irish mandate: to achieve the right of Catholics to establish their own non-state schools, and to defend from reform the system by which less populated French Lower Canada returned the same number of representatives as the more populated and British Upper Canada.

But once in Parliament, he began voting for electoral reform with a new friend, the progressive Orangeman George Brown, editor of the *Toronto Globe*. The equal number of seats from each province, he argued, ultimately produced nothing but deadlock. Montreal Irish accused him of treachery, but to prevent the swamping of the Irish in Anglo-Protestant Canada West McGee organised efficient Irish political committees, based on the St Patrick's Society of each region, to direct votes of the entire Irish community to sympathetic candidates.

In Toronto, McGee became a Catholic hero when on St Patrick's Day 1858 at O'Donoghue's National Hotel, where he was speaking, he was attacked by an Orange crowd. The ground floor of the hotel was wrecked and the subsequent parade disrupted. But after the incident, he argued that St Patrick's Day parades should be suspended by law for a 3-year period. This made him a pluralist champion, but he lost popularity with Catholics, particularly since he did not ask for legislation suspending the Orange processions of 12 July.

The riot in which his miniscule body had been endangered led to the establishment in Toronto of the Hibernian Benevolent Society under the chairmanship of an Esplanade Street tavern-keeper, Michael Murphy. Murphy was a healthy, determined young man, of the kind normally found at the head of Ribbon societies. He would become Head Centre of the Canadian Fenian Brotherhood. And in 1860, Bishop Charbonnel, who had been so friendly to McGee, was replaced by an Irishman, Bishop Lynch, another ardent Irish nationalist. It aggrieved Lynch that in Parliament McGee stuck with a diffuse liberal alliance of politicians, the Reformers led by John Sandfield Macdonald, against the Tories led by John Alexander Macdonald. But what bound the Orangeman Brown and the Catholic McGee was a vision of immigration, with settlement of the plains and the remoter west, and a belief in the wisdom of confederation of all the Canadian provinces. In some splendid speeches to the Canadian Parliament and amongst the public, McGee was holding out to Canadians the poetic and political necessity of a federal Canada, and, in Lynch's and Murphy's eyes, ignoring the Irish question.

'I see in the not remote distance one great nationality,' said McGee, 'bound, like the shield of Achilles, by the blue rim of ocean. I see it quartered into many communities, each disposing of its internal affairs, but all bound together by free institutions, free intercourse, free commerce.' And now confederation for Canada seemed to become a more urgent matter of self-protection as the prospect grew of large armies taking the field in the United States.

Fort Sumter in Charleston, South Carolina, was fired upon on 14 April 1861. Lieutenant John Mitchel of the 1st South Carolina Artillery commanded one of the heavy batteries at Secessionist-held Fort Johnson, and so Mitchel's blood was represented in that first exchange of fire so fatal to America's young. Lincoln's refusal to withdraw Federal troops from the forts in Charleston harbour had almost guaranteed that they would be fired on, but Meagher and other shocked New Yorkers for once did not blame him. In conciliators such as Meagher, there were now unexpected feelings of outrage. Digesting the news, most New York Democrats were in fact transformed over days into *Union Democrats*. Archbishop Hughes had, before studying for the priesthood, worked as a slave overseer in Maryland, but was now vocal for preserving the Union, and so were Mayor Wood, Dan Sickles and the *New York Herald* of Irishman Bennett.

Nonetheless when Lincoln called for 75,000 volunteers that April, Meagher was not tempted to rush at once to the headquarters in Prince Street of the 69th New York Militia. With his brother-in-law Samuel Barlow, he probably hoped for a quick military settlement. In a season in which there was much petulance, he had a brief quarrel with his father-in-law, telling him, 'You cannot call eight millions of white freemen *rebels*, Sir; – you may call them *revolutionists* if you will.' Peter Townsend was distressed and disoriented, though the Sterling Ironworks would ultimately and naturally do well from the coming conflict.

In his office in Ann Street, now sharing office space with the new Fenian organisation, Meagher was at first dubious about the war. But he confided in a friend, Michael Cavanagh, a former Young Irelander, Fenian and scholarly light of the Ossianic Society, a group devoted to the preservation of the Irish language, that he believed he should fight for the maintenance of the republic which had given him asylum. Soldiers, he said, would perform a double service, American *and* Irish. 'I hold it that if only one in ten come back when this war is over, the military experience gained by that one will be of more service in the fight for Ireland's freedom than would be that of the entire ten as they are now.' Meagher thought that in speaking of one in ten potential survivors he was talking in exaggerations. The realities of America's imminent war had yet to convert hyperbole into fact.

Meagher did not view his decision to fight as an approach to a new career. Aside from motives of idealism, however, he had now a way of re-establishing his civil credit and of escaping the role of spectator. Three thousand Irishmen (D'Arcy McGee's brother James amongst them) had in the two and a half weeks after Sumter offered themselves for the 69th New York Militia led by the young fire chief, Colonel Michael Corcoran. The 69th and Corcoran had already achieved glory in the eyes of the New York Irish, since the colonel had refused a command to parade the regiment in honour of the Prince of Wales on his visit to New York the year before. But Corcoran could accept only a thousand men, with the officers and the band making in all 1,130 men.

Meagher went over to the 69th's headquarters in their Prince Street office and saw Corcoran, and on 17 April, three days after the firing on Fort Sumter, placed in the *New York Daily Tribune* the following advertisement: 'One hundred young Irishmen – healthy, intelligent and active – are wanted to form a company of Irish Zouaves – under the command of Thomas Francis Meagher to be attached to the 69th Regiment, NYSM.' Applications were to be made at 36 Beekman Street between 10.00 a.m. and 5.00 p.m. The cost of ornate uniforms for the members of Meagher's company was to be met by the committee of influential Irishmen who supported the 69th.

A huge crowd lined Broadway on 4 May to see the first detachment of the 69th march to embark for Washington, 5,000 spectators crowding outside the headquarters in narrow Prince Street itself. Watched by Meagher, who was still raising his own company, the regiment had at first to force its way uptown to broader Great Jones Street and form up there. Having managed to advance to the Battery, the companies departed, well-liquored by generous friends, on the steamer *James Adjer*. Judge Charles Daly, on leave from the Court of Common Pleas, marched with the 69th as a civilian, and would do a few weeks' stint of sentry duty guarding the ramparts of Arlington Heights, under the regiment's green battle flag which had been presented by Mrs Daly.

The influx of recruits for Meagher's company was quick. The same night of the 69th's departure, the new Zouave company held a meeting to elect officers, in this case in militia Captain Phelan's saloon at the corner of 10th Street and Broadway. It was a mere formality that Meagher would be elected captain.

Libby Meagher may have had ephemeral reservations about her husband, a man of more than thirty-five years, recently bent on Central

American glory, so martially committing himself. But he seemed for now to have a saving awareness that he knew too little to hold high rank. At the time he placed the *Tribune* advertisement he had already been offered command of a regiment and refused it for lack of experience. He had also refused to join the Scott Life Guards as its adjutant. Soldier or not, he did want his hundred men. To his oratorical mind the figure had both completeness and intimacy.

By mid-May the 69th, as yet with no Meagher Zouaves, were in place across the Potomac at Arlington Heights in a muddy encampment named Fort Corcoran. The *Irish American* proudly reported: 'That even the veteran General Scott was impressed by the physique and morale of the 69th is shown by his assigning them the post of honour (and of danger) in advance of the Federal position and detailing ten out of the forty-three West Point Cadets in Washington to assist in perfecting them in military tactics.' It would not be until early June that Meagher's green company was ordered off to join the rest of the 69th here. The hundred splendidly attired men made an enthusiastic short New York progress from Beekman Street to the pier, led by Meagher and Libby riding side by side. Aboard the steamer, the Union's fresh-minted captain kissed his Libby farewell. Joining the rest of the regiment after a few days' pitching at sea, and a train trip from Baltimore, the Meagher Zouaves were put straight to work in their exotic uniforms to raise the great muddy ramparts of Fort Corcoran. Air was humid, rations and pay were irregular. Corcoran told Daly, now returned to New York, that at the 4 July celebrations on the ramparts 'one man facetiously remarked to Captain T. F. Meagher that he would place his dinner on exhibition in Barnum's Museum'. Similar complaints arose along the line as the intense sun of Virginia drained all the sweetness out of dressing as soldiers. But Meagher was discovering what would soon become obvious to others – he had a pronounced taste for the bivouac.

In early July, the end of the three months' term for which most of the 69th had joined was in sight. Already the Irish support groups in New York were planning a reception for the return of the 69th. But the War Department had made it clear that the three months undertaken by Lincoln's volunteers dated not from the time of their enlistment but from the time the regiment was mustered into service. Since the muster date of the 69th was technically 9 May, they would have to serve at least until 9 August. When the news came from General McDowell's headquarters, men resented its legalism, and Corcoran asked the renowned orator Meagher to address and calm the regiment. The *Irish American* said that

Captain Meagher's speech featured jokes about how the Union commissary should have issued them parasols for the blistering Virginian sun.

The men's spirits rose when in mid-July they were told that knapsacks, chests and trunks had to be packed and labelled to be stored in Alexandria. Each soldier was given sixty rounds of buck-and-ball cartridge, and field rations were issued. Meagher wrote to Barlow: 'Hundreds were sending to their wives and families through Father O'Brien, their beloved chaplain, the greater portion of their two months pay, which they had just received.' He estimated that a total of $25,000 was sent to New York by the regiment. Delay followed, but on 15 July the regiment was paraded and Corcoran read the special orders for moving off the following morning. Throughout the camp that evening, Meagher heard 'snatches of songs – mostly those that Davis wrote for us'. At first light the regiment marched out in the direction of Fairfax, Virginia. The leading company were the engineers in their reddish-grey flannel blouses – they needed to cut down roadblocks the Rebels laid in their path. Behind them came four elderly fifers and ten drummer boys, the youngest of whom was eight years old, followed by the regimental staff – Colonel Corcoran, Lieutenant-Colonel James Haggarty, a former carpenter, and Captain (Acting Major) Tom Meagher, wearing a conventional uniform as Corcoran's aide for the campaign. In northern Virginia's smiling farmlands 'Garryowen' was the most recurrent tune, and became the regiment's musical trademark.

They advanced as part of Colonel Sherman's brigade. Colonel William Tecumseh Sherman, whom Meagher called 'a rude and inveterate martinet', an obscure, red-headed, acting brigadier-general, West Point graduate and former commandant of a Louisiana military institute, was the same man who in 1864 would march through the South. But even a man of such potential repute could not manage the civilian soldiers. Meagher and others recorded that the relationship between privates and officers was so democratic or lax that men in the ranks did not hesitate to pull out of line and pick blackberries.

At Vienna, in fields to the west of that village, the 69th mounted fences to advance across fields on a mass of 1,000 to 1,500 Confederates, drawn up to protect that flank of the Confederate army. Meagher, Haggarty and Corcoran simply rode ahead of them pointing the way with their swords. Ayer's Irish battery rattled up and fired canister and grapeshot shells into the woods just behind Vienna. The rebels withdrew from their well-established earthworks before the Irish got close, and this success for the 69th made war seem healthier than the accidental nature of civilian life.

After Vienna, the advance continued with an ease which would leave the men unprepared when the real war began. 'At 12.00,' wrote Meagher, 'the Green Flag was planted on the deserted ramparts of the Confederates at Germantown, the Stars and Stripes were lifted opposite to it at a distance of fifteen paces, and between the two beautiful and inspiring symbols, the Sixty-Ninth passed in triumph, hats and caps waving on bayonet points.' Beyond, they were innocently appalled to see their first burning farmhouse, a sight associated for most of them with oppression or famine.

After their first serious hike of the war, the 69th New York of Sherman's brigade passed through Centreville on 18 July. By noon that day, the Confederate General Beauregard had organised his troops in a line behind a shallow stream called Bull Run ('run' being the local equivalent of creek). Ahead of Sherman's brigade and its 69th New York, a Union brigade under the command of a veteran officer called Israel 'Dick' Richardson crossed at Blackburn's Ford and advanced up the green summery hill to throw themselves against the Confederate regiments drawn up on top. Meagher was astonished by the way the 69th so calmly ate their hard tack and canned beef even while the racket of artillery showed that Richardson had run into the Confederates.

It was four o'clock before Sherman's brigade was ordered down towards the ford to relieve Richardson. Corcoran, his deputy Haggarty and Meagher turned in their saddles to encourage the men. On the way down, they encountered several of the 12th New York Volunteers 'hurrying from the bloody arena . . . some of them dragging dead or bleeding comrades along with them'. The confusion of Union and Confederate uniforms at this stage of the war has been frequently canvassed by historians. As the Union regiment named the 13th Rochester retreated, the 69th New York mistook them for Confederates, and Meagher and Haggarty had to go along the line striking the men's bayonets upward with their swords. The disliked Sherman rode up and told Corcoran to make the 69th lie down for cover in some woods near the ford. Officers dismounted, but made a point of standing upright during the bombardment. Meagher, apparently with a kind of exaltation, waited through the bombardment, which struck shells deep into the earth and threw soil wide, 'knocking over the Wisconsin men who were drawn up in line across the road'. Occasionally, Colonel Sherman would ride up, giving way to 'a private and exclusive snarl'. The engagement at Blackburn's Ford came to nothing, however. General McDowell saw that the Irish were uselessly exposed in sparse foliage and ordered their withdrawal up the road to the 'dingy, aged, miserable little handful of houses' which was Centreville.

Meagher cried out whimsical exhortations to the men as they left unaesthetic Centreville again on the afternoon of 20 July. After some miles the 69th struck into fields a little to the east of the Warrenton turnpike, stacked their arms and bivouacked for the night, but with a pervasive sense that tomorrow would be *the* day. Father Cass, brother of an officer in an Irish militia regiment from Massachusetts, came across and heard confessions. Meagher, savouring the absolute moment, made his confession to a priest at the foot of a bare tree over which 'the boys had erected a green awning'.

Corcoran was aware that despite the Celtic mythology invoked by expressive Captain Meagher, the large, modern battle about to occur would be the first one in history to involve a railroad as a target, in this case the railroad at Manassas Junction, where the Richmond line joined the one from the Shenandoah Valley. If that were achieved, the road to Richmond would be opened, the war concluded. And perhaps by autumn most of the 69th would be engaged in the liberation of Ireland.

The soldiers were roused in the small hours and by 3.30 in the morning were on the turnpike making for the north bank of Bull Run. In early light they were deployed in a field near the stone bridge that spanned the run. In General McDowell's mind they were part of the force that was to hold in place the Confederate centre, across the stone bridge, while other Union troops crossed by a ford, Sudley Springs, far to the west and began a flanking movement. The withering Virginia day set in, and little happened until ten o'clock, so that in their field Corcoran, Haggarty and Meagher could enjoy a soldiers' breakfast of hardtack, bacon and coffee. They could all see, beyond Bull Run, the hill which must be taken, with its brow and clumps of trees, and at mid-morning a Rebel regiment was sighted withdrawing in a hurry from its position and rushing westward at the double. To the 69th, this meant the Union flanking movement from the west was in play. The men were anxious to be launched at the diminished ranks on the far side of the stream, but it was noon before Sherman got the order, and his brigade, with the 69th ahead, waded across Bull Run. On the far side they climbed up a steep, protective bluff, and formed ranks at the top of that, facing the gradual top of the hill. Here Meagher enjoyed for the last time the idea that war was an innocent pursuit. Forming up in their shoulder-to-shoulder infantry lines, the 69th saw enemy soldiers falling back to join the main body amidst clumps of trees and around a white dwelling, soon to be famous as the Henry House. Lieutenant-Colonel Haggarty noticed a Confederate straggler, raised his sword and galloped to cut the man down. The straggler turned, raised his gun, and blew Haggarty's head off. The 69th uttered a scream of rage, and directed an entire volley at the straggler. Immediately Confederates up the slope ahead of them opened fire, killing two of the 69th instantly. Sherman came up berating the regiment for their disorganised fire, and told them to hold off until the Union flanking column actually appeared from Sudley Springs. Haggarty's body was retrieved and carried back to the regimental ambulance.

In a short while, the awaited troops were seen advancing along low hilltops from the west. Confederate field guns, however, dug in around the Henry House, began tearing sections of the Union line apart, and Sherman's regiments were ordered to capture them. Meagher watched the 2nd Wisconsin go up the slope first. They still wore grey uniforms, and would believe after their two attempts to take the field guns that they had attracted the fire of their own side. Sherman next ordered the 79th New York forward. They found the enemy well protected by small copses of pine trees, and carried their dying colonel back with them. Stripped to their shirt sleeves because of the heat, and many of them shoeless, the 69th was now ordered in. They ran in with what Meagher called a banshee shriek, and cries of *Erin Go Bragh!* (Ireland Forever!). Nearing the top of the hill, said an observer, Meagher turned in his saddle and yelled to them, 'Come on boys, here's your chance at last!'

The boys Meagher called on, political and economic exiles, now came under the fire of field guns capable of causing mass death and injury as never imagined by any of these civilians from New York, and of infantry massed in the clumps of trees around the Henry House. Near Corcoran and Meagher in that first charge, the colour-bearer, with intense and irrelevant determination, refused to lower and wrap the green flag and was immediately shot through the heart. Colonel Corcoran recognised the new reality. 'Lower that flag. It's drawing their fire.' Another Irishman, however, ran forward to take the thing, but was killed before he could raise it. After more brave folly, Mrs Daly's green banner was riddled. Corcoran called his men back down the hill to re-gather their lines and try again. Irish dead and wounded were strewn about the brow of the hill with the bodies of other New Yorkers and Wisconsin men.

The 69th were ordered back three times, and went confidently by all accounts. Around the clumps of trees there was close combat. Meagher wrote with some justice, 'We beat their men – their batteries beat us. That is the story of the day.' While coming down the hill on one of these retreats, Meagher felt a huge wave of air and iron, as a canister shell tore his horse to bloody sections. He was thrown to the ground and concussed. From what was recounted of Meagher's rescue by other officers, and Meagher's detailed, published account, it seems this happened on the final, most confused retreat. A trooper of the 2nd US Dragoons, who had been a student of the Jesuits at St Francis Xavier College around the corner from Peter Townsend's house in Fifth Avenue, was himself in final retreat when he saw the renowned orator and neighbour of the Jesuits spreadeagled on the hillside. According to the young man he leaned over, seized the dazed Meagher by the back of the collar and helped him into the saddle. All around, the Union army was either in retreat or breaking up. Corcoran himself believed Meagher had been killed on the retreat downhill. In trying to cover the Union withdrawal near the ford below the fatal hill, Corcoran was captured by the Rebels, along with two officers and nine men. On the north bank of Bull Run, Sherman was discussing a renewal of the attack with his staff when the ranks around him thinned and the rush to Washington began.

The trooper had brought Captain Meagher to the Washington side of the run and revived him. Bugles were blowing retreat, and a horseless Meagher joined in what began as an orderly withdrawal in a group of Fire Zouaves (raised from New York fire companies), walking at first, then hitching a ride on the 69th's artillery wagon, which jolted him along to Cub Run. The retreating army were ambushed by Confederate Black Horse Cavalry, who in a flurry of fire killed one of the horses, the wagon itself capsizing in the water. Until this point, said Meagher, fragments of regiments had been coolly and steadily retreating, 'when all of a sudden down came commissariat wagons, ambulances, hospital couch, artillery forges and every description of vehicle, dashing and smashing each other, and with one fearful wreck blocking up the river'. Ayer's Union battery rode up and went into action quickly, throwing canisters into the Confederate cavalry. Otherwise, said Meagher, there would have been an utter slaughter.

On foot near Centreville later that evening, Meagher met up with Dr Smith, a regimental surgeon, and found an organised fragment of the 69th, but at Sherman's order they kept marching too, since rumour said the Centreville position was already outflanked anyhow. At three o'clock on the morning of 22 July, they dragged themselves back into Fort Corcoran, part of the Washington defences. Although exhaustion and unease of soul marked their arrival, Meagher, in emphatic mood, told the men they had done so well that he intended to write an account of their actions, so that the 69th should be exempted from the opprobrium that would certainly attach to other units.

An early rumour to reach New York, that Meagher was a casualty, was soon corrected. Acerbic Maria Lydig Daly had doubted the news anyhow: 'I think he will be heard from. He is a mixture of apparent bravado and much prudence, if his face does not belie him.' The next day the *Daily*

Tribune carried a story about Captain Meagher, copied from *The Times* of London's journalist, William Howard Russell, Crimean War correspondent. As quoted in the *Tribune*, Russell had Meagher proclaiming loudly that the Confederacy 'ought to be recognised tomorrow; they have beaten us handsomely, and are entitled to it'. Fortunately, the idea that Meagher, suffering concussion, a measure of sunstroke and battle fatigue, was still running and shouting over his shoulder at Centreville defied not only Meagher's honour but also all physical credibility. Meagher's fellow officers of the 69th wrote angrily to the *Tribune* and *The Times*, attesting Meagher's valour in three charges against the Confederate position. The *Tribune* of 25 July denied the Russell report of its own volition and wrote that later testimony showed that Meagher 'bore himself with distinguished gallantry'. Russell's later pro-Southern memoirs mentioned the outraged officers' letter, which, he said, claimed Meagher went into action 'mounted on a magnificent charger and waving a green silk flag embroidered with a golden harp in the face of the enemy'. Such a description, said Russell, should cause Meagher more embarrassment than anything he, Russell, had written.

O'Brien was watching these developments in America with a passionate concern. He had 'never heard any satisfactory answer . . . to the question – "Would you wish to be a slave yourself?" ' But he also discouraged the involvement of the Irish young in the American war and in Fenianism at home. By the time Tom Meagher found himself in a brutal conflict on the hill above Bull Run, O'Brien had assumed even more markedly the role of Ireland's ambulatory conscience, its wandering secular pontiff. He stayed aloof from Parliament, but had proposed an unofficial Irish council, meeting in Dublin, to place moral pressure for reform on the British government. This plan was considered unworldly by politicians and contemptible by James Stephens and his Fenians.

As for life at home, the broad O'Brien family was not a happy one any more. O'Brien's formidable mother had died in 1856. His brother, Sir Lucius, about to acquire the title Lord Inchiquin through the death of a childless uncle, had lost his wife and married a turbulent second one, Louisa, a widow twenty years younger than he. On 13 June 1861, Lucy, who balanced the relationship between Sir Lucius and William, and between William and his reserved, distantly affectionate son Edward, died in her mid-fifties after a brief illness. She was taken to her grave by a weeping husband and mourning children with the massive *caoine* – keening – appropriate to a chieftain's wife. In John Martin's perception, O'Brien was never the same afterwards: 'his spirits had become bad and his fine person spoiled by fatness – a pale unwholesome fatness'. O'Brien began travelling even more energetically because he was 'depressed by the sorrows of a domestic calamity – the greatest that I could sustain – and at the same time I have been so harassed by anxiety connected with my property'. He left Cahirmoyle, and made his Irish home in a house near the sea, in Killiney, near Dublin, where his loyal and politically engaged daughters Lucy and Charlotte stayed with him. He attempted to retrieve 'my property' from the family trust, but Sir Lucius refused to arrange the transfer. O'Brien wrote of Lucius's conduct that 'After the death of my dear wife' he 'having been both treacherous and unfeeling I have resolved never to speak to him again'. But in the end Smith O'Brien was able to achieve a settlement through the Court of Chancery by which his son Edward acquired the entire property and paid his father an annual £2,000.

The Mitchels in Paris had also been watching American developments. In May 1861, a month after the war between the North and South began, they left the semi-squalor of rue de l'Est to go and live in Choisy-le-Roi, a leafier western suburb of Paris. Mitchel had heard that his two elder sons were now 'soldiering in one form or another'. James, Jenny's mainstay in Tuckaleechee, was serving in the Montgomery Guard, a fine company of the 1st Virginia Volunteers, and for the moment, following the bombardment of Fort Sumter, John was training with heavy artillery in Richmond.

Mitchel's income these days derived from his writings for the *Irish American* of New York, the *Charleston Mercury* and the Dublin *Irishman*. 'I wonder', he reflected in the *Irishman*, 'whether the working people of New York are beginning to think it would have been better to go on as they began with that abolition treason – namely, by hurling it down, mobbing it, pelting it with cabbage stalks to the devil.' In Choisy, though, Mitchel found it hard to gauge the intensity with which people like Meagher were reacting to Fort Sumter. It had been a dazzling and sedating spring, and fifteen minutes from Paris on the Orléans line the Mitchels had the house to themselves. Willy, a born naturalist, collected beetles along the shores of the Seine but had also attended some classes at the Sorbonne. And then in July 1861, before the first great battle of Bull Run demonstrated the potential scope of the war, the family had the excitement of a visit from bereaved Smith O'Brien. He came to them on his way to inspect one of the splendid French army camps. Drinking tea in Mitchel's garden, O'Brien argued with his friend over the abiding Irish expectation that, if England and France entered the American War, Ireland had anything to gain from the France of Louis Napoleon.

When it was time for Mitchel to see O'Brien off on his further intended travels to Italy, Austria and Hungary, he and his son Willy went with their friends to the railway station and the last words of O'Brien were: 'As for your southern Confederacy, you will hear of the collapse of *that* in a few days.' Mitchel took O'Brien's reflection in good humour. 'Farewell, then, royal heart! – The best and noblest Irishman of our generation, and for this reason alone, sentenced to be hanged, drawn and quartered!'

The Mitchels' increased concern for their sons emerged in a letter John wrote to his sister, Matilda. 'At present we are anxiously looking out for some intelligence of James. He is on more dangerous ground than John for the present . . . and the first serious fighting will be on the Potomac.'

Back in Fort Corcoran after the demoralising experience at Bull Run, the 3-month volunteers clamoured to leave the army. Sherman mustered his pre-war regulars to guard the camp and to fire on anyone who tried to decamp or to attack government equipment. Even so, he had reported to the War Department that, of his three regiments, 'I have the Irish Sixty-Ninth New York, which will fight.' The opinion was shared by others. The *Tribune* of 2 August quoted a Southern correspondent as saying that though the 69th might be made up of 'sprawling drunken vagabonds' from the low groggeries of New York, 'they fought like tigers'. There was recurrent mention of the 'Bloody Sixty-Ninth' in Northern papers. It was noted that they had lost in total close to 200 men, of whom nearly a hundred were missing, presumed to be prisoners.

Three days after the battle, Sherman's brigade and the 69th were visited by Abe Lincoln and Secretary of State Seward. 'We'd heard you'd got over the big scare', Lincoln told Sherman, 'and we thought we'd come over and see the boys.' Abe himself spoke to the 69th and praised its devotion. Democrats to a man, they were charmed. 'He said that Bull Run had been a misfortune but not a disgrace, and brighter days were sure to come.' When the men raised an Irish howl of approval, Abe said, 'I confess I rather like it myself, but Colonel Sherman here says it's not military, and I guess we had better defer to his opinion.'

It became apparent that the Confederates were too depleted to make an attack on the capital. The 69th was therefore boarded on trains with other 90-day men and travelled in picnic mood to Baltimore to take ship home. The final New York parade of the 69th, up Broadway from the Battery, drew what the newspapers called the biggest crowd ever seen in New York. The 7th New York provided an escort of honour, and Irish societies lined the pavement all the way along Broadway. The men looked like veterans – their flagpole now a trimmed branch cut in Virginia; many of them lacked coats. Drawn up at their armoury on Essex Street, they were dismissed with instructions to return on Monday and be mustered out of the militia.

The *New York Daily Tribune* pushed the candidacy of Meagher for the colonelcy of any new regiment which might be based on the disbanded militia corps, and it was apparent to Libby that her husband had found a new vocation. As Meagher would later say, life was simpler in the field. And Libby was now as enthusiastic as she had been about the Costa Rica adventure. Over dinners at Maison D'Oree in Union Square, which Meagher said 'beats Delmonico's to Ancient Nick', the officers of the disbanded 69th wanted to induce the men to sign up for a longer term of service. A circular headed *Erin Go Bragh* urged the Irish of New York to avenge Lieutenant-Colonel Haggarty, and 'to rescue Corcoran if living, or avenge him if dead'.

The charming but exacting Maria Daly was happy to report the glowing accounts of Meagher's valour she received from a chaplain, Father O'Rourke. 'Meagher behaved very gallantly when the ensign who bore the green flag was killed. He seized it, and calling to his men, "Remember Fontenoy", charged and carried the battery, not seeing that his horse was shot until he fell from him.' Mrs Daly would find it easier to believe such gallantry of Meagher while he still held the modest rank of captain. She was a Yankee competing with another Yankee, Mrs Meagher, for madonna-ship of an Irish regiment. Her sense of proprietary right over the 69th was clear. 'My flag, which I gave to the 69th, was lost, the ensign dropped it in his retreat, and as he escaped unhurt has not dared to show his face.'

Although Mrs Daly would accuse him of it, in the months after Bull Run Meagher did not seem quite as frantic as many other public figures for high rank. Some of the 69th's officers joined other regiments, getting up a step or two as veterans of the big battle. Yet Meagher refused the colonelcy of an Irish-American regiment from Rhode Island, as well as of New York's 3rd Regiment of Irish Volunteers. 'I have no ambition to increase the catalog of blunderers and impostors.' General Fremont in Missouri, soon to be engaged in bloody combat there, had telegraphed through an offer to him to serve as aide-de-camp with colonel's rank. He declined this too. The uncharitable view was that Meagher saw the value of remaining in an all-Irish group in New York where his influence was strongest. But he could have as easily used that influence in the 3rd New York Regiment, soon to be the 63rd, or from a vantage point in Fremont's staff.

19
Faugh-a-Ballagh

Raise that green flag proudly, let it wave on high.
'Liberty and Union' be your battle cry;
'Faugh-a-Ballagh' shout from your centre to your flanks,
And carry death and terror wild into the foeman's ranks.

Song composed 'by an Irishman',
69th New York fund-raiser, New York, 1861

In the late summer of 1861, Meagher was engaged with the concept of raising an entire Irish brigade from New York, Philadelphia and Boston. The very name, 'Irish Brigade', resonated. After the lost battles of the Boyne in 1690 and Aughrim, East Galway, in 1691, and the disastrous Treaty of Limerick, also in 1691, brigades of Irish exiles and their descendants, nicknamed 'the Wild Geese', served in the French army. The motto of the Irish Brigade of the French army was Faugh-a-Ballagh, Irish for 'Clear the Way', and the brigade had most famously fought against the British army in 1745, at the Battle of Fontenoy, a Belgium hamlet where the Duke of Cumberland's forces were decimated. Of all expatriate victories, Fontenoy in particular had entered a mythology hard-pressed for Irish victories. And now Meagher, his Fenian friend Lieutenant-Colonel Robert Nugent of the 69th, Judge Daly, Michael Cavanagh and others were developing the idea of a new Irish brigade for defence of this most worthy system, this imperilled republic.

Judge Daly and Meagher had been writing to General James Shields, a remarkable Tyrone man Meagher had first met at the time of Franklin Pierce's inauguration. Shields had achieved American repute as a brigade commander in the Mexican War, but his experience then gave him reason to be wary now of the idea of an Irish brigade. During the conflict in Mexico, Irish Catholic troops in the army had been so brutalised by Know-Nothing officers, and had so disbelieved in their cause, that they defected to the Mexicans, forming a San Patricio Brigade of the Mexican army. Shields knew better than most how fragile was the standing of the Irish soldier with the officer corps who would run this new war. His passion lately had been for attracting Irish immigrants westwards, to save them from the stews of the eastern cities. He led Irish city-dwellers to Minnesota, where such hamlets as Shieldsville, Erin, Montgomery and Kilkenny would represent his efforts. These days he had business in California, owned a ranch in Durango province in Mexico, and wished to attract Irish immigration both to Durango and Mazatlan. In San Francisco, he felt 'at such a distance from the seat and centre of the excitement'.

Quite apart from his political and military lustre, Shields knew the President well. He had once challenged Lincoln to a duel in Springfield, Illinois, over an article which had satirised Shields as a questionable state auditor. The article had been written by Mary Todd, later to become Lincoln's wife. When asked by Shields's seconds to choose weapons, Lincoln had whimsically nominated broadswords at 7 feet. Rancour broke down in laughter, and Shields and Lincoln had remained friendly thereafter, which, Judge Daly believed, would be a great help to any Irish brigade.

For the New York Irish leadership, it was a matter of waiting for Shields to come east and receive his envisaged command. Richard O'Gorman and Daly had already written to Washington urging that he be confirmed a brigadier-general, and Meagher seemed as concerned to produce this result as anyone. From his law offices at 41 Ann Street he wrote to Judge Daly on 23 August, 'Run in, my good fellow, for an hour, I want to see you in relation to General Shields. Some enemies of his are at work to get a revocation of his appointment as Brigadier-General.' The problem was a small group of New York Republicans. Shields was confirmed a brigadier-general on 31 August. Meanwhile, Meagher's repute, bright with the public and with the officers of the proposed brigade, was helped by the fact that the Meagher Guards of Charleston had changed their name to the Emerald Light Guards, and the same city's Hibernian Benevolent Society had expelled him.

Shields was in fact waiting for a more spacious military offer directly from the federal government. He was chagrined that aged General Winfield Scott at the Department of War seemed to have so forgotten his Mexican exploits. While everyone waited, Judge Daly believed that Meagher should go forth to the recruiting platforms with the rank of colonel. Daly seemed to envisage Meagher as an elevated recruiting sergeant holding ornamental rank. After some urging, even – it seems – from Robert Nugent, who was a veteran officer of the 69th Militia, Meagher accepted the acting colonelcy of the reorganising 69th New York State Volunteers, in place of Corcoran who was a prisoner in Libby prison, Richmond. Meagher's agreement to this glittering rank was a reversal of his earlier stance on the 63rd, and though Libby was delighted, Mrs Daly would snipe at him for it. The Assistant Secretary of War, however, made it clear in recognising Meagher's commission as colonel that its continuance would be dependent upon his performance as a recruiter. Washington and

Governor Morgan of New York had authorised eighty persons in New York State alone to raise commands, offering to each the prize of the *official* rank of colonel if the time limit of thirty days could be met.

Meagher had no such problem, though. The recruiting process for an Irish brigade began in earnest at the end of August, in a pleasure ground named Jones's Wood on the upper Eastside. The newly envisaged 69th held a picnic to raise money for the benefit of the widows and orphans of men killed at Bull Run. The press reported, reliably or not, that an extraordinary crowd of 100,000 people paid 25 cents each to attend. Meagher and Libby were handsomely present and at the end of the day Meagher rose to the platform. His audience was either ambiguous about Lincoln or hostile to him. But Meagher told them that the question of what party the President belonged to had become an irrelevance: 'The moment he took the oath from Chief Justice Taney to support the Constitution of the United States, that moment the platform disappeared from view, and we beheld nothing but the Constitution.' Defeat of the Union would encourage the evil designs of European royalty and knaves, 'to whom this great commonwealth . . . has been, until within the past few weeks, a source of envy, vexation, alarm and discomfiture'. Meagher was still a staunch Democrat; but the national interest overrode the interest of Democrat factions and machines – Tammany Wig Wam, Mozart Hall, or the Pewter Mug.

This bright, evocative Sunday helped fix in place the idea that Irish and Union interests were identical. The offer to raise an Irish brigade had, according to the *Daily Tribune*, been accepted with great satisfaction by President Lincoln. The civilian committee of the brigade, of which Daly and James Topham Brady were effective members, financed a recruiting station located in a vacant store at 596 Broadway near the Metropolitan Hotel, and Irishmen from all over the city enrolled in such numbers as allowed Nugent and Michael Cavanagh to select only the better specimens. Of all foreign-born New Yorkers in 1861, 87 per cent were Irish, and a range of recent immigrants as well as New Yorkers of Irish origin presented themselves. Most were labourers, navvies, railroad-track-layers, hod-carriers, cabmen, streetcar-drivers, waiters from Delmonico's, barkeepers. There were some enlistees from the New York Bar – indeed, the energetic Judge Daly had a Bar committee to provide equipment and comforts to lawyers now going to war. Schoolteachers, academics and journalists such as Cavanagh also enlisted. A company of 150 trained militia from the 23rd Illinois came to New York by rail and enrolled *en masse*. All the brigade surgeons were Irish-born. Chaplains came from Jesuit Fordham and from Notre Dame in Indiana.

One of the new arrivals in America was Lieutenant John Gosson, a gentleman horse lover from Swords in County Dublin. He was a characteristic Wild Goose: had served in the Austrian army, campaigned in Syria and most recently held a commission in the 7th Hungarian Hussars. Captain William H. Hogan of the brigade artillery was a New York newspaperman who had started the war as captain of a coastguard gunboat. Hogan took command of the already formed Napper Tandy Light Artillery of Brooklyn. There were also veterans from the British army who had served in India and the Crimea. Others had campaigned with Meagher's younger brother Harry in the Papal Irish Brigade, some as recently as at Spoleto and Ancona, the two papal cities that had been lost to Italian forces the summer before. They had tales of appallingly ill-trained papal officers.

During September's mid-recruiting, MacManus's body arrived in New York in its lead-lined coffin and under the care of two San Francisco Fenians. An obsequies committee was put in place to organise the body's New York stay, and the three members were John O'Mahony, Colonel Meagher and Colonel of Militia Michael Doheny, himself a devout Fenian but in less than good health. On the committee's behalf, Meagher was pleased to go up Madison Avenue to Archbishop Hughes's residence to suggest that the remains of his friend be admitted to St Patrick's Cathedral for a Requiem Mass. After all, Meagher pointed out, Hughes came from the same town as MacManus: Temo, in County Fermanagh. The body would lie at first in a militia armoury and then, Meagher suggested, be taken to St Patrick's in solemn procession. Hughes agreed, even though he was wary of Fenianism. MacManus was a Young Ireland hero, and Young Irelanders – Meagher, O'Gorman, Doheny – were powerful figures in the archbishop's flock. The Mass was celebrated in St Patrick's on 18 September, and the archbishop acknowledged the holiness of MacManus's sacrifice, 'upholding the right of an oppressed people to struggle for their liberation'. Libby Meagher, if she wondered at the company the accidents of marriage had brought her into, was still fascinated both by the Irish question and by the solemnities of Catholicism.

After the Mass, thousands accompanied MacManus's coffin downtown to the steamer *Glasgow*. The Catholic hierarchy of Ireland were for the most part determined not to admit to their churches the body that a secret, oath-bound society was using for its own purpose. In Cork, Meagher read, MacManus lay in state at a chapel under the jurisdiction of the Carmelite Order. In late October, it was accompanied by a crowd, estimated by some at 300,000, through the streets of Cork to the railway station. The American delegation had been enlarged by Doheny, Meagher's friend and fellow recruit Michael Cavanagh, and John O'Mahony. On its way to Dublin, wherever the train paused, solemn crowds, rosary beads in hand, stood hatless to pay their respects.

Since Archbishop Cullen had flatly refused to admit the body to the pro-cathedral of Dublin, it lay until 10 November in the Lecture Hall of the Mechanics' Institute. As thousands visited it, the question revived as to who owned poor MacManus's bones. At the Shelbourne Hotel, Terence's sister met the American delegation in a reception room, but some of the non-Fenian men of '48, James Cantwell, Father Kenyon, and John Martin who had shared the same exile as MacManus, were there too. They wanted to argue Miss MacManus out of letting the Fenians manage the remains.

The veterans of Young Ireland were considered to have been unduly chastened by their '48 adventures and were looked upon by Fenians as laggards now. Miss MacManus told them that the men who had disinterred her brother in San Francisco, and brought the remains 'such a great distance with much labor and expense, were the only ones entitled'. At a meeting of the Irish obsequies committee, Kenyon and Martin made another failed attempt to retrieve MacManus, and Smith O'Brien might have involved himself if he had not been on his bereavement travels in Europe. The young Fenian medical student John O'Leary remarked that his brethren were not always kind to the living Young Irelanders. They were all welcomed, however, in view of their past sufferings and friendship with MacManus, as honoured guests to the funeral.

On the day of the interment, the Metropolitan Police 'abdicated their functions', said O'Leary, and left the control of the crowd entirely to the Fenian organisation. The coffin was carried atop an enormous funeral car, with the American delegation behind. The celebrant, who had recited the *De Profundis* as the coffin left the Mechanics' Institute, was the Fenian priest Patrick Lavelle. Waiting to greet and join the procession, crowds had begun to assemble in Abbey Street as early as nine o'clock in the morning, in cheerless weather of 'true November character'. They fell in following the bier, behind the two bands playing the Dead March, the ceremonial harper on his own spectacular carriage, the Dublin committee and the pall bearers. The funeral cortège crossed to the south side of the Liffey at the Essex Bridge to enable sites sacred to the national cause to be visited. 'At the Bank of Ireland and along the College railings,' the *Freeman's Journal* reported, 'large crowds were assembled, who fell in and swelled the procession as it proceeded through Sackville Street.' A further multitude were in place at Glasnevin in North Dublin when the bier arrived at 6.00 p.m. In a brief, impromptu funeral oration, Father Lavelle told the crowd, 'The demonstration this day in the streets of Dublin will not be lost on the oppressor.' He was 'here to pronounce that in Terence Bellew MacManus there died one of the bravest and best of Ireland's sons'. In guttering torchlight, an oration crafted by James Stephens was delivered by Captain Smith, the San Francisco Fenian. 'We have raised him from the grave, and with feelings that no King has ever won – could ever command – have borne him over a continent and two seas – the greatest space over which the dust of man has ever been carried by the faith, love and power of his kind.'

Next day, the establishment *Irish Times* piously regretted the event, not least since a cutting wind and sleet 'must have tried the frame of the humble artisan'. What was significant, however, was the power of the event on Fenian recruitment. The ornate monument erected above MacManus's tomb implies to this day a line of succession between him and the Fenian leadership. And one outfall of the Fenian funeral was that relatively few Irishmen would cross the Atlantic specifically to join the Union army. The Irish Republican Brotherhood, in other words Fenianism, provided them with sufficient militancy and hope right at home.

By the time of MacManus's burial Meagher had been to Boston to address a public meeting at the Boston Music-Hall at which Governor John Andrew occupied the chair. Meagher referred to the period during the nativist frenzy when Irish militia regiments had been disbanded by the Massachusetts authorities. 'This, too, I know – that every Irishman this side of Mason and Dixon's line is with me. If there is one who is not, let him take the next Galway steamer and go home.' He was credited with having raised two regiments in Massachusetts – the Irish 28th and Yankee 29th Massachusetts.

In Philadelphia, Meagher sought to enlist a regiment of infantry and one of dragoons. As he spoke, a Southern sympathiser rose in the audience to derail him with a question about his treatment of 'the Irish girl who aided him in making his escape from Australia'. Meagher hated to be dragged from fresh and glorious fervour back to melancholy Van Diemen's Land and its moral squalor. In fact he would succeed in raising the Irish (and, in part, German) 116th Pennsylvania. But though it was dangerous for local officials dependent upon the support of the Irish community to oppose him too actively, neither Governor Curtin of Pennsylvania nor Governor Andrew of Massachusetts wanted their citizen volunteers subsumed in a brigade headquartered in New York. Each state had its quotas to fill, and Philadelphia had already lost a lot of the Irish Americans to the California Brigade.

The next place of recruiting was back in New York. 'Dined with Meaghers,' wrote Mrs Daly for 6 October, 'and went then to hear his recruiting oration. The oration was full of point, full of sarcasm and of wholesome truths . . . I like people who commit themselves.' Her alienation set in again, though, when Meagher criticised those old members of the 69th Militia who did not re-enlist. Had Corcoran still commanded, she argued, the 69th would have re-enlisted as a group: 'but in Meagher they do not place such reliance. A countryman said of him a few days ago that God Almighty had just made him to step off a scaffold with a big speech in his mouth.'

But it was with the support of all other brigade officers that Colonel Meagher was confirmed as acting brigade commander on 21 October. The assigned camp of the Irish regiments of infantry and artillery was at Fort Schuyler, a fortress on the end of a peninsula in the Bronx. On Sundays wives and families came out either by carriage or by ferry. So did members of the various civilian committees of the brigade, or of its subcommittees for Finance, Equipment, Relief, Collections, etc. These men included Archbishop Hughes, the Young Ireland and now Fenian newspaperman John Savage, Richard O'Gorman with his Tammany connections, Daniel Devlin, a Manhattan merchant, James Topham Brady and his brother-in-law Judge Daly. On 4 November the Dalys drove with Libby to visit, and were greeted on arrival by bands playing Irish airs. The men had decorated their blue caps with green cockades and the officers wore green plumes on their hats.

The Meaghers and the Dalys dined with the officers that day, and Meagher was frank about his ambitions. Mrs Daly wrote, 'He is tempted to try for Brigadiership, and his wife will urge him on. She seems to be very fond of a soldier's life and told me that she might join the brigade when it is ordered off.' A week later, with Shields's continuing failure to appear, there was a large meeting of the Irish leadership at the Dalys' house in Clinton Street on the question of what should happen to the command of the brigade. The Meaghers went out with the Dalys afterwards. 'In the carriage,' wrote Mrs Daly of Tom Meagher, 'I saw him exchange a very equivocal glance with his wife when the dear, *innocent*, frank judge told him his mind on the subject.' Meagher told Libby he would not accept field command of the brigade. ' "No, Lizzie," said he, "no, I certainly will not. You may look as cross as you please." '

Captain Lyons, who had as a boy visited Meagher in his cell at Clonmel, was an officer at Fort Schuyler, and saw the brigade's officers put great pressure on Meagher to accept the command. Washington was about to allot an American-born officer, but a delegation from the brigade went to Washington by train to petition the Secretary of War and the President to appoint Meagher.

By mid-November, the troops were having such a good time at Fort Schuyler with visits and picnic days that Meagher wrote to the Secretary of War suggesting the brigade be transferred away from New York. The Department of War telegraphed back to Meagher: 'Get your command ready for marching orders. We shall have quarters for you at Harrisburg in a few days.' On 18 November 1861, the entire brigade travelled into Manhattan by ferry to see the 69th New York, commanded by Robert Nugent, leave for Washington. Outside Archbishop Hughes's residence in Madison Avenue (the archbishop himself was in Ireland, encouraging Irish youth to enlist in the Union army), the regiments were presented with their battle flags. Smiling and dimpled Elizabeth Meagher had the honour of presenting to the premier regiment of the brigade, the 69th, the flag she herself had embroidered. On the green base were harps and sunbursts, and the motto *No Retreat.* The regiments soon to follow – the 63rd New York, the 88th New York, the 2nd Battalion, New York Volunteer Artillery – were also presented with flags by members of the Women's Committee. It was in the ranks of the 88th that the survivors of Meagher's Zouave Company were found, so the regiment had chosen to call itself 'Mrs Meagher's Own'. 'These colours', said Judge Daly, after referring to the actions of the eighteenth-century Irish Brigade at Ramillies, the ramparts of Fontenoy, the gates of Cremona, 'are a gift of fair women to brave men.'

By mid-December the assembled brigade found themselves not in Harrisburg but near Washington, as part of General Sumner's division at Camp California, a muddy fortified position about 2 miles from Alexandria. General Edwin Vose Sumner, sixty-five years old, nicknamed 'Bull' and a veteran of the Mexican war and of the 1st Dragoons' Indian engagements, was admired by ordinary soldiers, even if General McClellan, the darling of the Union army, thought that 'nature had limited his capacity to a very narrow extent'. That hopeful early winter, the Irish Brigade revelled in the possibility of war breaking out between the United States and Great Britain. A US ship had stopped a Royal Mail steamer, the *Trent*, in the Atlantic and taken from it the Confederate Commissioners to England and France, Mason and Slidell. There were protests from Whitehall, but the Union did not budge, considering Britain to favour the Rebels. Meagher told his men that if war did break out, 'We'll let the Yankees and the Germans handle the Confederates, and we'll take care of the English.' Lincoln authorised the return of the imprisoned commissioners, however, and the crisis passed.

On Christmas Eve 1861, in the constant downpour of northern Virginia, the Irish built a canopy of brush over a huge fire beside which men could recline and listen to musicians such as Johnny Flaherty, Bostonian fiddler of only fourteen years of age. His father accompanied him on the pipes. The brigade's coloured servants slapped their hands on their knees and went 'capering and whirling around'. Songs that were sung that night included 'Home Sweet Home', 'Fontenoy', 'The Green above the Red'. The Fordham Jesuit Father Ouillet and Father Dillon of Notre Dame celebrated Midnight Mass.

By now General Shields had arrived in New York and was offered the command of a division in the army of Nathaniel P. Banks in the Shenandoah Valley. (He would soon enough be outmanoeuvred by a young Rebel general named Stonewall Jackson.) But before departing New York, he had told a number of influential people that Meagher was the right person to lead the Irish Brigade. To Mrs Daly's chagrin, some New York Democrats had been urging Lincoln to grant Meagher a brigadier-general's commission. There is no evidence that Meagher instigated this lobbying, but he hardly discouraged it. The Senate was due to confirm a number of men to the rank of general in early February, and amongst the nominees were George Meade, Lew Wallace (author-to-be of *Ben Hur*), Winfield Scott Hancock, all of whom were or had been professional soldiers, and Meagher, whose training consisted of inspecting Irish militia regiments in the 1850s, and the chaotic experience of Bull Run. On 3 February 1862, the Senate ratified Meagher's general's star. He rode up from the lines at Camp California, across the river to Washington to celebrate at Willard's Hotel with some of his officers, and ultimately accepted his glittering rank by military telegram. 'I have the honor to acknowledge the receipt of my commission of Brigadier General of Volunteers, and hereby signify my acceptance of the same. My age is thirty-seven years, was born in Ireland and residence when appointed was the City of New York.'

Only three days later, Colonel Michael Corcoran was exchanged for Confederate prisoners and returned to New York to drink whiskey punch with the Dalys. But Meagher was serenely and confidently in place at the head of the brigade, and, as spring approached, on 3 March, Elizabeth Meagher joyously visited his camp and sent her mother, Mrs Peter Townsend, 129 Fifth Avenue, New York, a simple message: 'Safe here – all right.'

In keeping with Little Mac, their flamboyant commander General McClellan, thirty-five years old and showing a Napoleonic flair in camp, the Irish Brigade and their general developed a reputation for high colour. As Meagher got his headquarters *properly* organised, he slept in a tent with a boarded floor, his bed covered with a buffalo robe. Visiting generals could drink whiskey from the famed escapee's portable kegs, and admire the skin of a Central American tiger shot in Costa Rica. Captain David Conyngham would describe the slightly portly general at his baize-covered table in fairly florid terms: 'There is a grandeur and stateliness and a sense of intellect and power about him, that makes you almost think you are looking upon one of the old Irish princes of medieval times.' Father Corby, the 88th's chaplain from Notre Dame, would also write that the general possessed a superior intellect, had had a liberal education, was a fine classical writer and a born orator. He was brave as a lion, but not above 'going to confession from time to time, especially before battles'.

Under steely skies, the brigade, with the rest of Sumner's division, were ordered out of Camp California to advance into Virginia. The Virginian countryside, parched last July, was now a freezing morass. The brigade camped near Warneton Junction in a comfortless wood of dark, bare pines. Meagher, muffled in a blue cloak, reported making his way at night amongst poor fellows who had eaten their standard meal of compacted twists of vegetables, soluble in hot water, and now lay with their toes to the sky and knapsacks and coffee kettles under their heads. 'They might as well have drowned us at once!' he heard one soldier say. His brigade headquarters consisted of a few dozen stakes planted in the bog to form a circle, the spaces in between interlaced with branches and twigs, and the whole surmounted by his tent. 'A basket of noble dimension', he called it.

That March of 1862 there existed a naïve anxiety in the ranks of the three regiments that the war would end before their timbre could be proven. Grant had captured Fort Donelson on the Mississippi; Tennessee and Florida had fallen. Union armies had landed along the coasts of the Carolinas. In the cockpit of Virginia, the Confederates pulled back towards the Rappahannock, half-way to Richmond. The Irish Brigade's advance, watched by sullen Southerners, had involved a brief exchange of fire along the road to Warrenton, and an interesting find. On 31 March 1862, the War Department sent to Senator Ben Wade, chairman of the Joint Committee for Conduct of the War, 'a certain carpet bag of papers, said to have been found at Manassas by General Meagher'.

Without having had to fight a battle yet, Bull Sumner was elevated by Mr Stanton, the new Secretary of War, to command of the Second Corps. The Irish Brigade found themselves part of this under their new divisional commander, Israel 'Dick' Richardson, who had led the Union attack at Bull Run. An easygoing fellow of sixty, he was as anxious to campaign as any 19-year-old. Though he was a West Pointer, his raffish style was admired by the Irish. Under him Meagher's brigade advanced, by the easy stages McClellan preferred, to the north bank of the Rappahannock River, well beyond fated Bull Run. Its drummers and pipers, some of them children, played them into camp with 'Patrick's Day'. Richmond and the end of the war were not much more than 60 miles off. For the moment Meagher enjoyed the martial immanence of his new life. 'We are under orders to hold ourselves in readiness to march at an hour's notice,' he proudly told Barlow, 'and consequently, we are all in a hurry and flurry and tempers getting into trim to be off. You can easily picture the predicament I am in – orderlies from Divisional Headquarters riding up every ten minutes with circulars, special orders, and every sort of urgent epistolary missive – and the Brigadier sending them back with satisfactory acknowledgments.'

20
The Chickahominy Steeplechase

> But the dawn revealed it all. Here was a Georgian – a tall, stout-limbed, broad-shouldered fellow, lying on his face; his head half buried in the mud . . . nearer to us, close to a burned stump, lay one of our own artillerymen; his bold handsome face streaked with sweat and the smoke of battle; his right leg torn off by a shell above the knee.
>
> Captain Lyons, the Irish Brigade,
> Fair Oaks, Virginia

The only problem with the advance of McClellan's army towards Richmond was that it got further and further from Washington. This made the capital nervous about the activities of Stonewall Jackson on the far side of the Blue Ridge Mountains, in the Shenandoah Valley. McClellan, who always desired to occupy ground other than that which he presently held, was able now to get approval to engage his Army of the Potomac in a massive flanking movement. It would involve transporting it by steamer down the Virginia coast to the Peninsula, a spit of broad land between the York and James Rivers. On it the east–west roads led to Richmond. If the Union army turned up there, Stonewall would have to desist from threatening Washington.

Meagher's Irish Brigade marched back to Alexandria to embark on transports for the Peninsula. Meagher found it a rough voyage down Chesapeake Bay, and the transports lay pitching for five days off Fortress Monroe, at the tip of the Peninsula, waiting for the landing order. Wading ashore in icy water, the men found themselves ordered into camp on the low, wooded shore beside Oliver Howard's brigade of Richardson's division, and General Howard ordered his men to share their already constructed huts, their firesides and rations. Less than 70 miles up the Peninsula, on the James River, lay Richmond. But the difference between this position and their earlier one on the Rappahannock was that they were now to the south-east of Richmond.

When Meagher's brigade marched up from the beach towards the old British defences of Yorktown, it broke up along boggy country roads. Only 200 men arrived with Meagher in their allotted camp in front of the entrenched Confederates of Yorktown, where he set up his headquarters in an abandoned shanty. He certainly thought of Ireland now, walking up and down in some anxiety. 'Great God, the Irish Brigade will be brought into action at daybreak, and the work of a Brigade will be expected from them, while I have scarcely two hundred men. Are these the men I expected in some future time to free Ireland with?'

But since McClellan remained cautious, there was time for the rest of the men to arrive. Amongst the turpentine trees and dwarf cedars of the low, scrubby, malarial Peninsula, the Irish were put to accustomed work, digging roads, mortar emplacements and redoubts. Meagher liked his surroundings: 'we are in camp in the middle of the tall Virginia woods, in the midst of peach and apple blossoms, and under a gentle sky, waiting for our turn to *walk in*'. The support committee of the 63rd New York had by now sent a circus tent, which was erected in camp to serve as the brigade chapel. On May Day it was decked with flowers, as up the corduroy roads from the transports McClellan manoeuvred such a quantity of guns that Confederate General Magruder would abandon the Yorktown lines on 3 May. The Irish rested as a battle was fought for Williamsburg. Richmond was now 50 miles off, and on the Peninsula Meagher's Irish had not suffered a casualty! They went to the unnecessary trouble of feeling inglorious.

Boarded now on transports on the York River, they steamed along the swampy northern shores of the Peninsula, along the broad reaches of the York and then into the serpentine Pamunkey River north of Richmond. They were unloaded at a pier named Cumberland Landing. From their new, painlessly achieved camp, Richmond lay only 20 miles to the south-west, and was inevitably theirs. One problem of terrain, however, was that inland from them, down uncertain and boggy roads, the swampy main artery of the Chickahominy River cut the Peninsula in two, and with its profuse networks of tributaries separated them from the Rebel capital.

In their new depot, a Chickahominy steeplechase was organised by Meagher and his fellow officers for 31 May. There would be a Gaelic football game early in the day, followed by a series of horse races, then amateur theatricals. A racetrack had been prepared, hurdles had been erected and water jumps energetically dug. Entries, purses and prizes were decided on by the officers. General Meagher put up as a prize the skin of a tiger he had shot in Costa Rica. Captain Jack Gosson, a brigade favourite for his spacious gestures, had run up a jockey's suit for himself out of flame-red curtain material, a general's jacket turned inside-out, and a smoking cap 'bedizened with beads and gold fringes'.

The race meeting began with Generals French and Richardson in the judges' stand. Amongst the entries were Lieutenant-Colonel Kelly's bay gelding Faugh-a-Ballagh, with Katie Darling, Mourne Boy, Molly, Tipperary Joe and others supplying the field. By mid-afternoon the

Chickahominy Steeplechase had been run and won, and a mule race to be ridden by the brigade drummer boys was being marshalled. Just then the entire crowd, from generals to neophyte privates, heard a huge firing of artillery from the far side of the Chickahominy and looked simultaneously south. What they were hearing was the opening of a battle at Fair Oaks, a Confederate attempt to break McClellan's army in two. The struggle that was beginning now would within a month consume a great part of this audience.

Orders from McClellan by way of Bull Sumner arrived almost at once, and Richardson and French descended from their judges' stand and mounted their horses. Sumner's corps had been asked to perform an enormous manoeuvre. From their place at the right or northern end of the Union army, they were to move south-east down the confusing system of country lanes, where any movement was masked by monotonous forests, cross the Chickahominy River and end up on the left flank of the Union army, where they could conveniently and unexpectedly be thrown into the battle. Meagher, his officers and men accepted this as a reasonable demand. They marched for the rest of that day and almost all night, until in the small hours, wearing their pup tent halves, the brigade crossed the Chickahominy in darkness and downpour by the Grapevine Bridge. The water of the river washed over this rickety apparatus, so Meagher walked his horse Dolly across amongst men wading wet to the knees. Before dawn they arrived at the lethal zone, where General Sedgwick's Union division had stopped the Confederates the previous dusk. It was littered with broken caissons, disembowelled horses, corpses, howling wounded, and the yellow lanterns of surgeons searching for the latter pricked the blackness. 'The weary men of the Brigade lay down to rest', Captain Lyons would always remember, 'upon the drenched and torn ground, in the midst of the havoc of the day, hardly conscious of the ghastly companions who slept amongst them.'

As dawn broke, a tree stump marked the headquarters of the Irish Brigade. A stirring Meagher started a conversation at five in the morning with a wounded young Irishman, a Confederate from South Carolina, 'whom I found propped up against a mouldy, old tree, disabled by a musket shot in the side, and manfully suppressing the expression of his pain'. In mid-discussion, a massive volley came from the direction of the Richmond & York River railroad, which ran all the way to Richmond, 500 paces away, on the edge of deep woods. The little depot named Fair Oaks station, from which the battle would take its name (it was also called Seven Pines), lay a short way along the railroad to Meagher's right. Beyond the rails stood 'a vicious swamp', which offered both cover and means of retreat to the Rebels. The day before, the Rebels had surprised General Casey on the far side of the railroad and destroyed the hopeful young men of his division. Generals Sedgwick and Kearny had stopped the Rebel advance in the very field of trampled-down corn where the 69th and 88th New York now stood. 'Richmond was at most four miles distance from the colours of the Sixty-Ninth New York Volunteers, the right of the Brigade,' wrote Lyons, and one of the older soldiers had climbed a pine tree close to the rail and seen the dome of the Confederate Capitol flashing through the smoke. In front of the railway, according to General Richardson's orders, the Irish Brigade hastily formed two lines in a wide cornfield which 'had been thoroughly trampled out of sight'. Rebel musket fire continued to pour upon them out of tall woods beyond the rail track. Meagher had the 69th and 88th New York drawn up facing the enemy, and kept back the 63rd with the assigned artillery. The enemy they confronted as they talked to each other and loaded and cocked their weapons intended to drive Richardson's division away from the railroad and back into the Chickahominy, as much morass as river.

A few minutes after the volley interrupted Meagher's conversation with the wounded young Confederate, Richardson sent Howard's brigade across the railroad, and on into the woods and swamp against a brigade of Georgians. 'French's Brigade followed. Our turn came next.' As the Confederates, having mangled Oliver Howard's brigade and shattered Howard's arm as well with a musket round, formed up in the woods and charged French's men, forcing a retreat, an externally calm, internally frantic General Sumner rode along the Irish line. 'Boys, I am your General. I know the Irish Brigade will not retreat. I stake my position on you.'

The Rebels were coming on, raging over the line. Meagher and the Irish Brigade behaved with exemplary solidity – crucially so for the hopes of the Union. If they had been crumpled by the assault, one flank of Sumner's corps could have been turned, and a confused retreat across the Chickahominy swamps would have been the result, with the Union army split in two. Meagher rode up and down the line resonantly encouraging his men. His groom kept near him, and as firing began was shot through the legs.

The Irish volleys broke up the Rebel assault. In pursuit, the 69th rushed the railroad and, reaching it, deployed into line of battle on the track. The 88th New York now went forward beyond the rails and centred itself around a log-built cottage and various outbuildings – 'Property of a lethargic German with pink eyes and yellow hair,' said Meagher, ever the littérateur. Meagher told the 69th and 88th to re-form, and then at his word the brigade advanced again, yelling in Irish. A battered little barn near the railway became the regimental hospital. Father Corby moved amongst the dying laid out on damp straw.

The Irish Brigade's charge into the woods and the swamp caused on an important scale a flight by the Rebels, and cost the Irish only thirty-nine men. One of the privates who died at Fair Oaks, however, stood for all the shifts and passions of the world's Irish soldiery – Michael Herbert, the first man killed in the brigade. He had served in the British army in India during the Sepoy Mutiny, in which Indian soldiers rose against their British officers (a concept which was about to be tried by Irish Fenians). In 1860, like Meagher's brother, Herbert served in Italy with the Papal Brigade. He had not been long in New York when he enlisted in the 69th New York. Rural poverty, Catholic zeal and national fervour had determined his soldiering career, which now ended in steamy Virginia.

Fair Oaks was a disaster for the Rebels. They lost 8,000 men and failed to split McClellan's line. Later, a South Carolinian who was in Richmond that day would tell Meagher that the fragments of Joe Johnston's Confederate army had run in panic through the streets of the capital. Meanwhile, savouring Sumner's applause and the trust and enthusiasm of his brigade, General Meagher made camp beyond the railroad on the ground gained that day. As the dead were buried, he exuberantly named the place Camp Victory. He was the sort of man for whom occasional fear, not inwardly countenanced, could in any case be quickly amended by the right gesture of bravery, or by sipping a little whiskey. Currier and Ives would rush out a print of him, mounted ahead of his men, for sale to America's Irish. Any whisper of improper behaviour which attached to the Irish at Bull Run had been erased. To his Irish prospects were added the chances of the civic honours that awaited American heroes; they made the tidewater a landscape of illimitable possibility.

A Spanish general named Prim came with US General Heintzelman that week to Camp Victory to review Meagher's men. Little Mac also rode up, sat with Meagher before his tent and gave a message to be relayed to the men. 'Officers and men of the Brigade! It is my pleasing duty to announce to you that General McClellan has desired me to express to you the gratification he feels at your steady valour and conduct at the battle of Fair Oaks, June 1st.' For Irish surgeon Thomas Ellis, the reality was not as splendid. He would soon be back at White House on the Pamunkey, cutting blood-stiffened uniforms from the wounded. 'In many instances maggots were creeping out of their festering wounds.'

Meagher and other members of the Union army had suffered obliquely an imponderable loss: the Confederate general Joe Johnston, watching the action at Fair Oaks from a position near the railway line, had been wounded in the shoulder and chest. He might have lost Richmond had he gone on commanding, but the command was now passed to Robert E. Lee, who had the capacity to save the capital, lengthen the war and interminably delay action on Ireland.

After exaltation came static tedium. The Irish spent three weeks at Camp Victory behind zigzag breastworks of huge logs, and heard reveille and retreat sounded in the Rebel lines as 'loudly and as spiritedly' as in the Irish Brigade's. At mid-June, they were relieved and ordered back to rest near Fair Oaks station. Their supplies came up, a speakeasy appeared, and the chapel tent. Meagher's Irish Brigade was reinforced by the 29th Massachusetts, commanded by Colonel Ebenezer Pierce, a man of old Yankee stock. The taciturn New Englanders of Pierce's regiment got even for Meagher's parade orations by plundering a Meagher whiskey cellarette aboard one of the wagons. Meagher could claim here, however, that his use of whiskey was medicinal. The surgeons were issuing it to the men as a remedy against malaria, but under the influence of a chaplain, Father Dillon, many had taken the temperance oath, which some of them, to challenge the caricature of the Irish dipsomaniac, adhered to despite any health risk. Father Corby said that the *Adeste Fideles* was frequently heard as the brigade musicians accompanied an abstaining malaria victim along the camp's gritty white roads to his grave amongst turpentine trees.

Stonewall Jackson was now on his way from the Shenandoah to reinforce Richmond. Meagher, however, expressed anger at the 'grand policy'. Republican Washington, Meagher complained, detained a splendid army – McDowell's – along the Potomac and in the Shenandoah, 'which would have been of great service in the Peninsula'. Stonewall's approach activated McClellan to make another defensive decision: despite the risks and complications, he believed he must move his base from White House on the Pamunkey River, all the way south across the Peninsula and down to the James River, a distance of more than 30 miles. He would bring his entire army south of the Chickahominy. This massive movement across the Peninsula now began. The thousands of wagons and troops vacating the north side of the Chickahominy were screened by the troops of Generals Porter and McCall. On 25 June, the Irish Brigade, a little south of the river near Fair Oaks, had been in reserve and heard a renewal of fighting to the west, on their side of the river. But the next day, as they watched the masses of relocating Union men and wagons pass them, they heard the Confederates attacking the screening forces of Fitz John Porter, up on the river's north side, near Mechanicsville. This assault converted what was to have been a manoeuvre into a frantic retreat, and made inevitable a frenzied week – a string of brutal encounters known for ever after as *the* Seven Days – during which both armies fought by daylight, and then marched and took up new positions by night. For Lee the objective was the destruction of McClellan's army and a peace settlement. For McClellan, and thus for Meagher's Irish, it was survival.

Porter's forces on the north side gave way and retreated overnight east, beyond a village named Gaines's Mill. Sumner now was asked to send two of his brigades across to the north side to support Porter. French's and Meagher's were ordered out. They crossed the Chickahominy in melancholy late afternoon light, amongst scrubby forests which limited what Meagher could see of the battle going on to the north-east.

It was a little after 7.00 p.m. in the evening when Lee ordered the entire Confederate line forward against Porter's men. Meagher's eloquent report gave something of the flavour of his own brigade's advance into the chaos beyond the Chickahominy. 'The head of the column had just appeared on the opposite side when an immense cloud of dust through which teams and horsemen hastily broke indicated something more than a repulse to our arms. These teams were followed by crowds of fugitive stragglers on foot whose cry was that "they had been cut to pieces".' The Confederates were near, Meagher was told by Bull Sumner, and he and General French were ordered to line their men up, French to the left, the Irish on the right, along a road covering the two most crucial bridges, Alexander's and the Grapevine. French's lines of men had to their left the Chickahominy. Meagher's had to their right a morass named Elder's Swamp. There was potential for a great tragedy in the triangle of earth they occupied. Two regiments each from French's and Meagher's brigades were ordered by Bull Sumner to march forward up a gently sloping, cleared hill ahead, wheel to the right, and reinforce the regular army brigade of General George Sykes on whom the storm was breaking. In his official dispatch, Meagher proudly recorded this movement. His men advanced through the 'broken masses of the Union forces that had been engaged all day' and across a clearing which housed the main hospital of the Union army, crowded with retreating Union forces. 'My brigade reached the summit of this hill in two lines of battle . . . and having reached it, despite of the cavalry, and artillery, and infantry that were breaking through them, preserved an unwavering and undaunted front.' General Fitz John Porter, riding up, greeted Meagher and told him to hold. So the Irish lines stood close-packed, and returned an awful fire.

Captain Conyngham wrote that had the Rebels 'succeeded in breaking through our lines . . . McClellan could not have saved his army'.

The image of Meagher at Gaines's Mill proffered by some historians is not entirely flattering: one modern historian claims that General Meagher 'led his Irish brigade with the courage found in a bottle, galloped about drunkenly, trying to rally everyone he saw'. One of French's men, James Miller, wrote that he saw Meagher ride into a group of walking wounded and single one man out: 'He struck him over the head with his sword, knocking him down, then galloped on.' Rumours of Meagher's tipsiness – tinged with anti-Irish bias or not, and coloured by the rigorous temperance of some soldiers and officers – would pursue him throughout the war. They were always uncritically believed, for officers knew Meagher to have no aversion to a drink. But random reports should in justice be put against the fact that none of Meagher's Irish Brigade ever offered such an unflattering picture of Meagher. Father Corby, the chaplain, admitted in his memoirs that, 'especially when no fighting was going on', Meagher's 'convivial spirit would lead him too far'. But Corby insisted that this was only on convivial occasions, not during battles, that love of sport and joviality caused Meagher to drink, and his bouts were 'few and far between'. Would it be possible for a habitually and dangerously drunken general to retain his junior and senior officers' regard? No one else reported less than glowingly that evening of his brigade's performance. Colonel Estevan of the Confederate cavalry said, 'A Federal Brigade commanded by Meagher, consisting chiefly of Irishmen, offered the most heroic resistance. After a severe struggle, our men gave way (beyond Gaines's Mill), and retired in great disorder.'

Meagher and his staff sheltered under trees as rain began, and watched the Union army troop past them all night. In the final hours of dark, Meagher's men and French's were the last to cross from the north of the Chickahominy and climb up the river bank on to a low plateau where the exhausted Union army was collapsing behind roughly thrown-up fortifications. Captain Conyngham observed that the two mighty armies slept within a mile of each other.

Next morning, after a few hours' sleep disturbed by Pickett's fire, Meagher was told to guard the Union rear as the army withdrew south-east through White Oak Swamp. This order must also throw doubt on the idea that his courage came entirely from the bottle. In air full of explosions, Meagher drew up the 88th New York, Mrs Meagher's Own, behind fences by the road which led south to White Oak Swamp and Malvern Hill, with the Union army behind him slipping south to their base on the James. As he rode along the lines of his men, a number of officers, including Captain Hogan of that regiment, asked him to dismount, since his uniform and his grey horse Dolly made him a target. 'If I'm killed,' he said, 'I would rather be killed riding this horse than lying down.' Father Corby admitted in his memoirs, however, that on the Peninsula the more flamboyant officers of the brigade did make brilliant targets. They possessed 'great Austrian knots of gold on their shoulders, besides numerous other ornamentations in gold, which glistened in the Virginia sun enough to dazzle one'. In future campaigns, they learned to dress more plainly.

When ordered to retreat, the brigade now had to pass through their old Fair Oaks camp, which the engineers were putting to the torch. Father Corby saw the chapel tent go up and thought it more replaceable than his books and manuscripts inside.

On Sunday morning, 29 June, they encamped in fields and the edges of woods just a little south of that same Richmond & York River railroad where they had fought at the start of the month, and close to the small rail village of Savage's Station. It was not till 4.00 p.m. that the Rebel artillery started pounding at Sumner's men in their clearings in front of the village. Mysteriously, Meagher was not in official command that day; he had been placed under 24-hour open arrest on the retreat through Fair Oaks the evening before. There is no record of the arrest in Meagher's War Department file. Could it have been tipsiness, or the result of a civilian gaucherie that Bull Sumner or General Richardson found temporarily offensive? No charges resulted, and Meagher, at Nugent's side, took up official control after twenty-four hours and wrote the brigade dispatch. 'It gives me the heartiest satisfaction to bear witness to the able and intrepid manner with which Colonel Nugent fulfilled the duties which devolved upon him during my arrest.'

At Savage's Station, when General Sumner himself commanded the brigade forward, Captain Conyngham recorded, 'About four thousand went off at once with a roar which might have drowned the musketry.' Sumner and the arrested Meagher, side by side and friendly, were delighted to see Mrs Meagher's Own, the 88th New York, drive off the men of a Virginia battery and their supporting infantry, haul two guns away, spike them with broken-off lengths of bayonet, and chop the carriages to pieces with engineers' axes. As Dr Ellis wrote: 'night came on and put an end to the carnage'. The two armies stood basically where they had that morning. Meagher's brigade, wavering with fatigue, held their section of line as the bulk of the army was again withdrawing south, along the roads through White Oak Swamp. Surgeon Ellis had to do what he could for the wounded and say goodbye to them. Father Ouillet and a new chaplain, named Scully, volunteered to stay with them. It was midnight before the Irish themselves were ordered to fall back urgently. Many had left their rations behind when they charged, and could not now retrieve them. The enemy was continually around their flanks, firing at them from the woods, racing them towards the higher ground just beyond the swamp.

In daylight, the Irish Brigade were halted around a farm belonging to a Mr Nelson. They knew they would fight another battle that humid afternoon. Yet Meagher, like many of the others, seemed suited by temperament to the light-headed, febrile utterness of the moment. As Cuchulainn, the Irish warrior-hero of the Ulster cycle, was transformed by process of battle, undergoing a so-called *battle-rage* which turned him into another and more terrible being, so Meagher – whatever Mrs Daly thought – seemed to let battle transform him, and reward him somehow with its frenzy.

Thus, when General Lee pursued that very afternoon a strategy to destroy McClellan's Army of the Potomac, Stonewall Jackson attacking from the north while Lee attacked along the roads from the west, a lack of orchestration permitted Meagher's Irish, with apparent enthusiasm, first to be used against Jackson to the north, and then later in the evening to be marched down the Long Bridge Road towards the village of Glendale to take on a Confederate brigade of A. P. Hill.

Lieutenant Turner remembered that after stemming the initial assault by Jackson, the Irish Brigade were ordered to line up to protect Hazzard's battery. Meagher ordered the men to lie down on their arms. Turner wrote:

> A round shot ricochets, strikes with a dull, heavy sound the body of a fine brave fellow in the front rank, and bounds over him. He is stone dead; the two men on each side of him, touching him as they lay, rise up, lift the stiff corpse, lay it under a tree in the rear, cover his face with his blanket, come back to the old place, lie down on the same old fatal spot . . . A hundred thousand of these Celts would – but no matter: What is speculation here?

Turner also related how 'poor, brave Captain O'Donoghoe' of the 88th New York reacted calmly when a cannon ball buried itself into the ground 6 inches from him, making 'a hole deep enough and wide enough to put an infant into'. Lieutenant Emmet, grand-nephew of the martyr Emmet, suggested to O'Donoghoe that he ought to sit now where the shot had landed, since two shots never struck in the same place. The captain did not move, however. 'It was just as well; he had another day's life, for immediately another ball plunges into the same spot.'

When Jackson's corps were 'pressing us badly' at five in the afternoon that day, the US gunboats *Galena*, *Aroostook* and *Jacob Bell* opened up from Turkey Bend on the James River to the south with shot and shell from their immense rifled guns. After eight o'clock in the evening, the Irish, having stood up and fought off an assault by Jackson's men on Hazzard's guns, were ordered to march in quick time 2 miles west towards the Glendale crossroads and Lee. General Sumner observed them clatter up the road and roared at them, 'Boys, you're going to save another day!' They were lined up along the north–south-running Quaker Road to resist the charge of A. P. Hill's last reserves, the brigade of Confederate General Anderson. Here there was a sharp short contest. One Union officer wrote, 'The enemy ceased firing. We give tremendous cheers. They send us a terrible volley which we return. Both parties give three cheers and the day's work is done.'

And so another dazed night retreat began. Bull Sumner, riding along the line of withdrawal, told Meagher he believed the Second Corps had won the battle for McClellan, and should have been allowed to remain in place. But withdrawal from a held battlefield seemed to be standard with the Army of the Potomac.

Inland from the safety of Harrison's Landing, an open, farmed slope named Malvern Hill rose uninterrupted between two creeks. The Rebels would need to use the road which ran up Malvern Hill if they wanted a last chance to race to the James River and cut the Union army off. During the night, Meagher's men stumbled up and over Malvern Hill and fell into position beside Meagher's friend Sickles and his brigade. Meagher was able to eat beef and drink coffee with Richardson and Sumner, older men who nonetheless matched him for strange wakefulness. Other men fell profoundly asleep on that last hill before the river.

At six o'clock in the morning of 1 July, the last of the seven days of that intense campaign, Meagher and his men, if not already awake, were roused and put into position amongst cannon on the south side of the hill. Meagher, wild with sudden rage, rode across the lines of his advancing men to upbraid the colonel of the 63rd New York, Colonel Phelan, the saloon owner from downtown Manhattan in whose premises Meagher had first been elected a captain, for dilatoriness in going forward to protect one of the artillery batteries. 'Give me your sword, sir! You are a disgrace to the Irish Brigade. I place you under arrest, sir.' But Meagher and Phelan, fatigued and half-crazed, quickly seemed to forget the confrontation.

After the action began, at three o'clock in the afternoon in this case, the Irish Brigade were able to rest on that blind side of the hill. Indifferent to what could not be seen, though it could certainly be heard, some of the Irish had found and slaughtered sheep. They were cooking the meat and were just about to eat, when, over the crest, Fitz John Porter's desperately pressed brigade saw fresh Rebels massing to their front. Meagher was at the time seated chatting at the headquarters of General Sumner, when Sumner got a message and ordered him to take his four regiments forward. Sickles's brigade was similarly ordered up. Abandoning the lamb supper in the Irish camp, doomed Captain O'Donoghoe told Lieutenant Emmet, 'I think some of the twenty-five who engaged supper will not be on hand when it is ready.'

Cresting the hill a little after six, Meagher and his men met the remnants of the 9th Massachusetts carrying their dying colonel, Cass, to the rear. A staff captain witnessed this encounter. 'As they recognised a fellow countryman,' Captain Auchmuty wrote, 'they gave a yell that drowned the noise of the guns.' Further along, Meagher encountered McClellan and his staff. Little Mac had spent a large part of the day on the *Galena* in the river, a fact which would be used against him in a later presidential campaign, but he had landed at 3.30, and was now in place. Hats were doffed. Meagher and his men did not glimpse the terror behind McClellan's neat features and judicious frown. Brigadier-General Butterfield, who had been with Sickles the day he shot Key and was now on Little Mac's highly Democrat staff, grabbed the distinctive green flag of the leading regiment of the brigade. He 'exhibited the ardour of a general who was personally interested in its honour, and thereby renewed and re-excited the spirit of the advance'.

Over the top of the hill, the brigade, the 69th leading, was then sent forward against a wood on the left where the Rebels were concealed. Surgeon Thomas Ellis was impressed that Meagher was riding at the head of his troops and ordering them to fling everything off, including their jackets, and go into battle in shirt sleeves. A rifle ball grazed Meagher's hand. 'Coming in contact with the enemy,' Meagher wrote in his battle report, 'the Sixty-ninth poured in an oblique fire upon them with a rapid precision and an incessant vigor.' They repeated the process of advancing and firing, again and again. Their smoothbore muskets had become hot and powder-clogged when the 88th took the front line, and the 69th 'coolly and steadily' moved out by the flank. Then the 69th moved up again when the 88th exhausted its ammunition. Meagher declared in his report that it was 'simple justice' to praise their composure and steadiness 'under an unremitting fire of some hours'.

Sergeant Haggarty, brother of Lieutenant-Colonel Haggarty killed at Bull Run, was amongst the brigade's dead that evening. Captain O'Donoghoe of Bantry, County Cork, twenty-two years old, took his death wound in these exchanges at Malvern. Lieutenant Temple Emmet was wounded. In a last attempt to break the Union position, Irishmen of

General Semmes's 10th Louisiana struggled hand to hand with Irishmen of the 69th New York. Near a Union battery far up the Quaker Road, the farm road which ran through the battlefield, a very tall Louisiana Irishman fell in cross-fire and marked the furthest advance for the Confederacy that day. His motivation – to chastise Lincoln and then to liberate Ireland – had got him to the top of that incline above the James before dispatching him into the void.

The losses of Lee at Malvern Hill were so severe that many Union generals, including one-armed Irish-American General Phil Kearny, wanted McClellan to counter-attack. Kearny said of the plan for withdrawal to Harrison's Landing: 'Such an order can only be prompted by cowardice or treason.' But McClellan was committed. After two hours' rest amongst the dying on Malvern Hill, the Irish Brigade marched numbly through the dark hours. The Fenian Major Michael Cavanagh met on the slope behind him a Confederate Irishman named Arthur Scanlon who had known Meagher before the war and who was now lying with an apparently fatal wound. Scanlon asked Cavanagh to remember him to a young woman they both knew in New York, and gave him a locket and a photograph to return to her.

It rained ferociously, units lost each other, officers lost their men. But the Confederates, who had sacrificed 5,600 men the evening before, were incapable of taking advantage. In early morning, Meagher watched his men collapse inside the half-built ramparts of the new federal base at Harrison's Landing on the James. They had no tents, few clothes, little equipment, but the river below was full of supply boats. Their morale was high, said Conyngham. 'The retreat, for retreat it was, was ably conducted in the face of vastly superior numbers of men, brave and desperate as ourselves.' The 'vastly superior numbers' of the other army was one of the false articles of faith for McClellan supporters.

That morning the brigade was paid, and money travelled to New York and Ireland. Back on Malvern Hill, indifferent to personal finances, the wounded Lieutenant John H. Donovan of the 69th, shot in the right eye, regained consciousness and had an argument with Rebel Generals Hill and Magruder, who, riding up the slope, called on wounded officers to surrender their swords and revolvers. Lieutenant Frank Hackett of the Irish Brigade had sat in vigil on Malvern Hill with his brother's body all night, and buried him shallowly at dawn before being amongst the last to leave. Creeping down the road to Harrison's Landing also was the wounded colour-bearer of the 29th Massachusetts, the colours of his regiment wrapped blood-soaked around his body.

In new underwear and clothing, eating fresh beef and bread, most of the Irish Brigade looked refreshed. But General Bull Sumner seemed aged and exhausted. Meagher showed Sumner the battle flag of the 69th riddled by Confederate rifle shots. 'That is a *holy* flag, General,' said Meagher, but Sumner – in less than martial mood – did not respond. It was not yet Meagher's turn to think of futility. The Union deaths were to him still more sacred than obscene. The 69th New York had certainly made its contributions to the holy dead and noble maimed. It had been reduced from 750 men at Fair Oaks to 295 at the end of Malvern Hill. The 88th and the 63rd had lost more than 500 men between them. Meagher now made an ambitious but also tribal proposal to the Adjutant-General to put all the Irish regiments in the Union army under his command. No doubt his request was praised in the brigade officers' mess tents, but it served only to annoy the War Department: the organisation of troops on ethnic lines was now considered 'unwise and inexpedient'.

'I'm finally cheated by the *Irishman*,' John Mitchel had complained in a letter from Paris that year to his sister Matilda, beginning to suspect that his association with the South made him unfashionable. Along with occasional Union blockade-delayed payment from the *Charleston Mercury* office had been news of his son James having a hard time but surviving Bull Run and other engagements. But after visiting newspapers in Paris, particularly the *Constitutionnel* and its remarkable woman editor Marie Martin, Mitchel brought back a new sense that the Union would not easily yield. Now in Choisy-le-Roi in the summer of 1862, he and Jenny waited fretfully for reports from the Peninsula, and began to consider that at least one of them should be in the Confederacy with the boys. The best way home, said Southerners he spoke to in Paris, was to evade the Union blockade by going to the North and then passing through the lines. If he chose to penetrate the South, Jenny and Isabelle should go with Father Kenyon to Ireland, and the two other daughters – Henrietta and Minnie – would stay in Paris at Sacré Coeur.

As mentioned earlier, Henrietta had in early 1861 converted to Catholicism, as her sister Isabelle would at a later date. The scrupulous Mother Superior showed Mitchel the archbishop's directive that the nuns must avoid 'conversion by *surprise*', but 'I instantly wrote the required consent. For this acquiescence I was most earnestly blamed by some of my connections.' The nuns of Sacré Coeur were now Henty's real home, and Minnie was also attracted by the Order's mystique. Whereas Willy wanted to be with James in the 1st Virginia.

'So there is another break-up of our household,' said Mitchel, blaming circumstance. '. . . Two trembling and saying their prayers in Ireland; two passing anxious hours in the Paris convent; two in camp and garrison beyond the Atlantic; and two making ready to penetrate the Yankee blockade in disguise, and by way of New York.'

21

Woefully Cut Up

> If Irishmen had not long ago established for themselves a reputation for fighting, with a consummate address and a superlative ability; if it had not long ago been accepted, as a gospel truth, that Galway beats Bannagher, Bannagher beats the devil; and if the boys of the Irish Brigade had not, with an untoward innocence, shown themselves, the first chance they had, as trustworthy as their blessed old sires . . . the Irish Brigade would not have had any more fighting to do than anyone else.
>
> General Thomas Francis Meagher,
> New York, 1862

In July 1862, Meagher got permission to return with wounded, pale Lieutenant Temple Emmet to New York to recruit. General Dan Sickles travelled with Meagher for the same purpose – recruiting for his Excelsior Brigade. They were shocked to find that after their friend McClellan had performed that great manoeuvre of shifting his base, the *New York Times* implied McClellan and other Democrats in the army might be fighting the war with less than a full heart. Though it probably made no dent on the joy of reunion with Libby, the Republican press was labelling as Copperheads, from the venomous snake of that name, those who feared that emancipation of slaves would flood the labour market. That is, it was insulting the Irish proletariat from which Meagher now sought to recruit. On top of that, the huge casualty lists from the Peninsula were themselves a drag on enlistments.

When Meagher addressed a rally at the 7th Regiment Armory over Tompkins Market in Lower Manhattan, 5,000 people crowded into the drill hall to hear him, but not all of them were admirers. A Celtic voice in the audience shouted, 'Why don't the Black Republicans fight?' There was for the first time a certain tone of war-weariness in Meagher's speech. 'We don't need any more officers. We have enough of them in the Army of the Potomac, and more than enough, if we are to judge the shoals in which they are coming down the James River.' He was challenged by a question about whether he sought personal glory by overworking the Irish Brigade. He denied that the Irish Brigade had been worked harder than anyone else: the brigade had done no more marching than French's brigade, and no more picket-and-trench duty than the brigades of Caldwell and

Sickles; 'nor was it more exposed to the unhealthiness of the climate – to the dampness, to the miasma, to the drenching rain, or the deadening sun of the foul lowlands in front of Richmond – than any other brigade along the line'. Even in answering his critics Meagher was forced into a far from flattering picture of the environment awaiting recruits, and was left to argue that it was the Celtic spirit itself which was the cause of so many Irish casualties. 'Heroic old Sumner', Meagher argued, 'would otherwise not have asked so often, "Are the green flags ready?" '

Over the next two months there were only 250 new recruits for the brigade. The prisoner-exchanged Corcoran, more clearly a Fenian than Meagher, was able to enlist five regiments, largely of Fenians, in the Corcoran Legion, while the lustrous battle record of the Irish Brigade was good enough to draw a mere company. And even commerce was war-weary; both Meagher and Dan Sickles appealed with little success to a group of New York businessmen to provide enlistment bounties.

It was while the recruitments were underway that Lieutenant Temple Emmet died at the age of twenty-six years at his father's house in Astoria, Long Island, joining his great-uncle Robert Emmet in the heroic shades. According to Conyngham, it was typhoid remittent fever, 'the relapsing fever', a killer during the Famine, which finally took the young man's weakened life. Lieutenant Emmet's New York funeral raised the question of whether America was more fatal than Dublin Castle for the descendants of Irish heroes.

By midsummer, a disappointed Lincoln had already decided that McClellan's army was to be pulled out of the James and returned north. For now that Lee had penned up the army in Harrison's Landing, Jackson was again sweeping north up the Shenandoah. A Union cavalry general named Pope, despised by McClellan men, was to have overall command when the army was concentrated again in northern Virginia. McClellan would be subordinate to him, and this was seen as another 'Black Republican' plot.

Meagher returned from New York to the James by navy steamer to supervise the evacuation. As the brigade withdrew, moving down the Peninsula past the Yorktown defences, the Irish found the ground they traversed now in ruins. Shells of ruined houses and burned villages filled them with melancholy. Some felt as if they had somehow been trapped into reproducing the same evicting effects as the British army in Ireland. Conyngham was appalled to find emaciated child corpses waiting by the road in cots for passing soldiers to bury, the parents being too famished to do that work themselves. 'It reminded me of the famine years in Ireland.'

While much of McClellan's withdrawn army was still on steamers, Lee and Jackson struck at Pope at Bull Run and Manassas Junction and humiliated him. The Irish Brigade arrived in Washington and had fires going in their old bivouac at Fort Corcoran when they were ordered out to the old 69th's haunts at Centreville to cover Pope's withdrawal. They found his retreating men so debased by their thrashing that the Peninsula veterans taunted them as they passed. Meagher heard with delight that McClellan was back in command. Little Mac ordered Meagher to stay fairly close to Washington. 'If he moves,' McClellan told the War Department, '. . . it leaves us without any reliable groups in or near Washington.'

Again the Confederate threat to the capital failed to present, and so the Irish Brigade effortlessly advanced as they had before through desolated northern Virginia towards Fredericksburg on the Rappahannock. An officer wrote home, 'The Confederates occupy the same lines they did last winter.' But did they? Though Rebel pickets were active along the river, Lee had now sidestepped from Fredericksburg and the approaches to Washington. Meagher woke one morning in his tent by the river to find that Lee's men had gone from the defences ahead. They had joined with Stonewall's army and were making a vast flanking movement into western Maryland: an invasion of the North. Urgent if not panic-stricken orders came to Sumner, Richardson and Meagher; to stay where they were would be useless, they were to move across country from northern Virginia towards South Mountain in Maryland, where General Hooker was trying to come to terms with the advancing Rebel flank.

The Irish Brigade crossed the Potomac to Georgetown, and marched by pleasant stages through Seneca Mills and Hyatt's Town. By nightfall on 13 September, they had covered 50 miles in easy marches, those who had grown up in rural Ireland enjoying the sights of soil-rich Maryland with its friendly people and plush farms. In a field full of haystacks near the orderly town of Frederick, they were bivouacked comfortably. In a similar field nearby, under a tree, two soldiers from Indiana would find an authentic copy of Lee's orders wrapped around two cigars, and McClellan received thereby all the information he needed to destroy Lee. But he feared the document had been planted to mislead him.

Sumner's men were held in reserve on the long ascent up South Mountain. Then they were moved up through Hooker's exhausted men and sent in pursuit of the Rebels. Richardson's division became the lead division of Sumner's corps on the roads of western Maryland, and Meagher's the lead brigade, marching in good weather through broad Turner's Gap and then turning south-east down red dust lanes into western Maryland's well-ordered countryside, the landscape of the Jeffersonian dream.

The troops now heard with some anger that Union Colonel Miles had disgracefully surrendered Harper's Ferry to Jackson. This meant that Jackson *would* be moving in to join Lee somewhere ahead, amongst these lovely orchards and fields of grain. Meagher's report declared with a little awe that on the afternoon of 15 September, as the brigade neared the western limits of Maryland formed by the bend of the Potomac, and stood on slightly high ground north-east of the village of Sharpsburg, 'the enemy was discovered in full force, drawn up in a line of battle on the heights near Sharpsburg'.

All that stood between Meagher and the Confederates was the creek named Antietam. By its banks, the brigade made camp that afternoon. One look at the map showed how penned in Lee was, with the Potomac behind and Antietam Creek ahead. Meagher sat chatting before his tent with acting colonel Patrick Kelly of the 88th, Jack Gosson, Captain McGee (D'Arcy McGee's brother), Colonel Robert Nugent of the 69th, the surgeons Ellis and Reynolds, and the nationalist poet and newly promoted Captain James Turner, aide-de-camp to Meagher and a chronicler of the brigade. A few miles to the south-west of where now Meagher sat expatiating stood the occupied town of Sharpsburg with its one modest church spire. He probably did not guess that John Mitchel's son James was there, with the 1st Virginia. Dimly discerned, perhaps, on the Hagerstown pike north of town stood the plain chapel of a pacifist sect, the Dunkards or Dunkers, who eschewed all decoration, including steeples. The rest of Sumner's corps arrived during that afternoon, to be joined to the north during the evening and night by Hooker's and Mansfield's corps.

The next day, 16 September, was restful in the camp by the creek, no one aware that they were on the eve of the greatest American slaughter. Many officers sniffed the chance that if a Confederate rout occurred in the farmlands in front of town, Lee's army could be destroyed trying to cross the Potomac back to Virginia. At four in the afternoon, Hooker's men were ordered to cross Antietam Creek at the upper ford, above the site where Richardson and the Irish Brigade were camped, and attack the Rebel left in some woods. The Irish casually listened to the exchange of fire over there. Of the Irish New Yorkers who had just caught up from Washington, 120 young recruits had been told they would be employed on provost duty the next day. They sent a delegation to General Meagher and insisted on participating in the battle. Meanwhile, over the creek, Hooker had caused the Confederates to retreat a little southwards towards Sharpsburg, over fields owned by the pacifist Dunkards. The Union bridgehead made by Hooker on the Rebel side of the creek allowed another Union corps, Mansfield's, to cross that night too and camp in a screen of woods. Sumner, Richardson and Meagher remained where they were, in rustic composure.

Waterford-born surgeon Lawrence Reynolds of the 63rd New York was poet laureate to the Irish Brigade and 'Center' of the Potomac Fenian circle, the secretary being Captain John Rorty from the regular artillery. In the field, pending the end of the war, Fenian meetings were largely social. Dr Reynolds would make a boilerful of a punch of condensed milk, hot water, nutmeg and whiskey. He had composed a history of the Irish Brigade in rhymed verse, and he would read that; or else there would be singing of ballads. It seemed that nearly all the officers of Meagher's 'original and famous Irish Brigade' were Fenians by late 1862. John H. Gleeson, for example, a Tipperary man and former member of the Papal Foreign Legion, who would ultimately become colonel of the 63rd New York, was a particularly ardent member. Many of the leaders of the American Fenians were serving in the army, including John O'Mahony, who had raised the O'Mahony Guards, the 1st Regiment of the Phoenix Brigade. He and his Fenians had been marched off to guard Confederate prisoners at Elmira, New York. The esteemed Michael Doheny, Young Irelander *and* Fenian, recently returned from the MacManus funeral, had died in New York in April 1862, but there were many to replace him. Members were not restricted to such Irish units from New York as the Corcoran Legion. In Milford, Massachusetts, out of a 'circle' of 115 members, 80 would enlist in the Union army under their Center, Major Peard. Two thirds of the 9th Massachusetts Infantry were active Fenians. There were Fenians of varying degrees of conviction in the Confederate armies, and especially in their seven distinct companies of Irish, which included Company E of the 2nd Tennessee, a company in the 6th Alabama, and another one recruited at Augusta, Georgia.

American Fenianism was directed for the moment towards the War between the States, and the flow of donations from America to Stephens of the Irish Republican Brotherhood in Ireland was poor. 'It would pain you to hear all that is said about the American branch,' the Irish Fenian leader Stephens wrote to O'Mahony. 'It would also pain you to see how my friends here received the announcement of a money order of £10.' Stephens's focus reduced the events that Fenian soldiers in the Union and Confederate armies were now enduring to an intermediate stage in the preparation for an Irish republic. For Irishmen fighting battles in Virginia and Maryland, however, the American quarrel was becoming the issue in itself.

At length Stephens sent his lieutenant, a 40-year-old former Young

Irelander, the quiet Thomas Clarke Luby, to look into American Fenian affairs and to replace O'Mahony if necessary. With O'Mahony as guide, Luby made a visit to Corcoran's Legion in the field at Suffolk, Virginia, where the Union army had established a bridgehead. When operations began there, wrote Luby, 'Corcoran was most anxious to get John O'Mahony out of harm's way . . . It speaks highly of Corcoran's patriotism that at such a time he managed to get the officers together for our purposes.' But again Luby defined 'Corcoran's patriotism' entirely in Irish terms.

The tragedy was of course that, in the legion alone, twenty-four Fenian officers would be killed or wounded, mainly in the bloody campaigns of 1864. The Douglas Brigade of Illinois suffered broad losses of its Fenian officers and men, and hundreds perished in Meagher's brigade.

In a thinning fog the next dawn, the Irish were eating their breakfasts of bacon when across the creek the rage of firing began. Hooker's men were advancing down the Hagerstown pike towards Sharpsburg, attacking the North Woods. By 7.30 in the morning, they were supported by Mansfield's corps. The Irish were experienced enough to drink their coffee and wait their turn. Bull Sumner sent Sedgwick's division splashing over the creek. The Confederates seemed for a while to be giving way, and abandoned the Hagerstown pike into town, but only to come back ravening and resupplied to form up again around a spinney called the East Woods. They caught Sedgwick in open fields, and by hectic fire deprived him of 2,300 of his men in fifteen minutes. Bull Sumner sent McClellan a message: 'Things look blue . . . Our troops are giving way.'

At nine o'clock Richardson's division, including the Irish Brigade, its three New York regiments and the 29th Massachusetts, were told it was their turn to cross the Antietam. Meagher rode, but the cool water reached to the hips of the men crossing on foot. When they got to the other side, they sheltered under an escarpment, and like picnickers emptied their shoes and wrung out their socks. Then they checked their rifles. They came up over the high bank into the well-farmed fields of the Dunkards, people named Poffenberger, Piper, Mumma and, perhaps sinisterly, Roulette. Many of the fields had recently been ploughed, though there were pastures, crops of trampled corn, and a scattering of orchards. Meagher dismounted and walked amongst his men telling them to strip to their cartridge belts and shirt sleeves.

The colonels and Meagher remounted their horses, as did Father Corby, who gave the men a general absolution of their sins. At first the brigade was protected from the awful artillery fire by shallow dips in the terrain.

But they were quickly subject to musket fire coming from Confederates behind one of Mr Roulette's snake fences on a ridge. Meagher's orders were that he should take his men 150 yards beyond that ridge and capture a bend in an east–west sunken road ahead. He told a hasty gathering of his officers that the men were first to rush the snake fence and tear it down. The Irish, he would proudly relate, did this in the face of 'a galling fire'. The brigade now straightened its lines again. Corby dismounted to attend to the already fallen. All this calm behaviour was characteristic of the futile splendour and awfulness of the day. Meagher rode along the ranks of his men, yelling, 'Boys, raise the colours and follow me!' He was leading his men against the same soldiers the Irish Brigade had fought recently near the Charles City crossroads on the Peninsula – General Anderson's North Carolinians. They lay in the sunken road – or, as it would hereafter be known, *the* Sunken Road – which shielded the approaches to Sharpsburg. The division of Meagher's friend General French, already on the edge of these farmlands and under heavy fire, cheered the Irish as they marched up to the left and filled a dangerous vacancy in the line, only 50 yards from the Confederates.

As they had moved down to occupy this gap, a thunderclap of gunfire greeted them, 'in volume the greatest yet delivered from the Sunken Road', said one of the brigade's officers. Meagher's men crowded in with French's and poured an awful fire against the bend. Meagher would report, 'I permitted them to deliver their fire for six volleys, and then personally ordered them to charge upon the Rebel columns.'

In these first few minutes of combat, pouring in fire from the ridge and then charging the lane with bayonets, the 63rd and 69th New York may have lost as many as 60 per cent of their number. The Irish colour-bearers fell so often in the attacks on the Sunken Road that McClellan, watching through a telescope, presumed that the Irish were either being cut to pieces or running. 'The day is lost, General,' an aide cried out to McClellan. 'The Irish fly!' When Captain McGee bent to pick up the colours from the ground, the staff was instantaneously cut in two by a bullet. For three hours the Irish Brigade was the centre of five frontal attacks on the Sunken Road, some Irish reaching the road and wrestling with Rebels on a shifting floor of dead and wounded. And then there was bitter defence against Rebel attempts to rise up out of the lane and sever the Army of the Potomac in two in Roulette's fields. Like French's men, Meagher could do very little in the end but withdraw to their low ridge, hug the ground and try to return fire. Officers gathered cartridges from the boxes of the dead and wounded, filling their pockets and hats with them, and bringing them to the infantrymen.

Amongst the dead left lying as the brigade ultimately withdrew this short distance was Captain John Kavanagh, of the 63rd New York, who had been shot dead at the head of his company near the Sunken Road. A piece of shell had smashed the drum of one of the boys of the band and then fatally entered his body. The 19-year-old Tom Connors of County Down died leaving no family in America to mourn him, so that his officer, Bernard O'Neill, had the awful task of interpreting these events to Connors's parents in Ireland. Colonel Patrick Kelly, shot through the jaw, was still in place with his 88th New York.

At some stage in these operations – no one is specific in timing the incident – Meagher's horse was shot from under him. Meagher fell to the ground concussed, and was carried off the battlefield. The *New York Tribune* claimed that Meagher had been 'struck in the breast by a shell', but that he had recovered consciousness. In a few papers he was reported as having been killed. A more malign rumour was harder to defuse. Colonel Strother of McClellan's headquarters staff, who was some miles away, wrote, 'Meagher was not killed as reported, but drunk, and fell from his horse.' This seems to have been an unfounded rumour. Many of the men who were near Meagher were temperance Irishmen; Corby, Lyons and Conyngham, all present, reported that his horse was simply killed beneath him. Lieutenant Mackie of Meagher's staff was killed by the same shell that unhorsed Meagher. Not one of the general officers who witnessed his behaviour that day made any reference to drunkenness in their reports. The annotation which, some years later, Union Brigadier-General Jacob Cox made in the margin of his personal copy of McClellan's *Own Story*, reads: 'Commonly reported drunk.' But General Cox was in no better position to comment reliably on Meagher's behaviour than Strother, since he was waiting miles away near the southern end of the battlefield, above what is now called the Burnside Bridge leading to Sharpsburg. However, Meagher was enough of a toper for the accusation, once uttered, to be accepted as credible by many, especially those who were far from the incident. As for his repute with his own men, it lingers in the belief that he was responsible for the 69th's lethal regimental cocktail, which lived on in that regiment to the Second World War and beyond – one part Irish whiskey and two parts champagne.

About the same time as Meagher's fall, General Richardson was preparing for a general advance along the line, when a Rebel case-shot exploded nearby and felled him. It was a fatal wound, and he was carried off the field. Sumner called for the young former regular soldier Brigadier-General Hancock, to take over Richardson's division. Hancock galloped along the lines held by the Second Corps to report for duty. Arriving behind the Irish, he told them to hold. Until he gave this sensible order, they had crazily thought they would be attacking the road again.

The casualties from Meagher's four regiments were 540 men. Of the 120 newcomers who had refused safe provost duty, 75 were either killed or wounded. It was one o'clock. Meagher had by now been carried to the rear concussed, and the brigade withdrawal which General McClellan would praise in his report was conducted by Colonel Bourke of the 63rd New York:

The Irish Brigade sustained its well-earned reputation. After suffering terribly in officers and men, and strewing the ground with their enemies as they drove them back, their ammunition nearly expended, and their commander, General Meagher, disabled by a fall from his horse, shot under him, this Brigade was ordered to give place to General Caldwell's brigade, which advanced to a short distance in its rear. The lines were passed by the Irish Brigade breaking by company to the rear, and General Caldwell's by company to the front, as steady as on drill.

Bull Sumner would mention Meagher in dispatches as one of those general officers he thanked for 'their zeal and devotion'. Some time later, visiting wounded Colonel Barlow in New York, Mrs Daly declared, 'Barlow gave a fine description of the fighting of the Irish Brigade and said that Meagher rode before his troops during *fire*.'

During the afternoon, hundreds of wounded of the brigade had to be carried to a large straw stack on the Roulette farm which answered for a hospital. Union troops at the Burnside Bridge, a mile and a half south of the place where the Irish Brigade had suffered their losses, began an assault late in the day which took them into the streets of Sharpsburg. A Confederate counter-attack drove them back to the outskirts at dusk. But the battle was certainly, in spite of the carnage, a Union victory.

That night the brigade rested amongst the maimed in the fields, half a mile behind General Hancock's front line at the Sunken Road. In darkness pricked by the lanterns of surgeons and chaplains lay the day's 25,000 casualties. By next morning Meagher was recovered and was back with his troops, who retrieved their knapsacks and breakfasted amongst shattered trees. An order to renew the attack was expected. But perhaps even to Meagher's surprise McClellan did not try to exploit the good ground he held, to bring into play his 34,000 fresh troops, and drive Lee into the Potomac. For failing to act, Washington would judge him harshly.

Meagher was called on by General Hancock to speak with Confederate General Roger Pryor, a Virginian about his own age, former Congressman and newspaper editor, who appeared from the direction of Sharpsburg in front of the Sunken Road under a flag of truce. Hancock may have thought that to deal with the political Pryor the political Meagher would serve best. Pryor suggested a pause in hostilities to allow the burial of the Rebel dead who lay with Hancock's dead around the bend in the lane. Though considerations of decomposition and respect were urgent – Hancock had himself needed to chase away Union plunderers from the Sunken Road dead – the dealings were tragically abortive. Like McClellan, Hancock was edgy, concerned about the possible renewal of the mayhem. He ordered Meagher to seek proof from Pryor that the truce was sanctioned by Lee. Pryor admitted he had no such authority; the idea had arisen out of discussions between pickets of the opposing forces. When another truce flag appeared that afternoon, Meagher was sent again to meet the bearer, 'who proved to be a lieutenant-colonel in the Rebel service'. The day went by without either commander, McClellan or Lee, seeking an official truce.

All night the Union troops heard the groan and rumble of wagons, and next morning the Rebels were gone. The brigade advanced to occupy the vacated lines and the burial of dead men and horses began. Many Irishmen now burst into tears when untangling the corpses of Rebels of sixteen years from those of grandfathers. Meagher found his partial release in letter-writing, and his letter to Libby was that of a man undaunted:

> It was an awful battle. Fancy a deafening storm of artillery and musketry raging along a line of over two miles in length, and when at last it subsided, the glorious Stars and Stripes flying triumphantly three miles beyond where the Rebel colors had been planted in defence. The poor little Brigade was woefully cut up – I have not more than 750 in Camp today – the best of my officers too, killed.

If there was a muted sense of triumph in the fields around Sharpsburg, in Washington there was a jubilation the battle-shocked troops could hardly have imagined. Captain Gosson was in Washington a week after Antietam, in a capital frenetically celebrating the Union victory. While in a theatre box listening to the songstress Mrs Wood singing the 'Bold Soldier Boys', he saw an elderly gentleman in the box below with a bouquet of flowers in his hands. He drew his sword, dragged the flowers out of the man's hands and delivered them by swordpoint at Mrs Wood's feet. As far as Washington was concerned, grace had re-entered the war.

As arranged, Jenny and Isabelle Mitchel were by late summer 1862 back with Father Kenyon in Tipperary's soothing hill country and planning a visit to Newry to see Mitchel's sister Matilda. For Jenny it was her first time home since she joined John in Van Diemen's Land, but she missed Willy, who had won his argument about participating in the war. Confederate prospects seemed good: Lee's army having rebuffed McClellan's mighty host on the Peninsula, one Confederate outflanking of Washington would bring a settlement. Would Willy have even finished his training before that happened?

Mitchel learned that the Hamburg Line took French passengers in a small steamer to England from Le Havre, and put them directly on board the line's flagship *Belorussia* at Southampton without their having to land. However, when the little French steamer arrived with Mitchel and Willy aboard in Southampton Water, the *Belorussia* had not yet arrived. Mitchel found himself illegally ashore in England. 'Walking through Southampton we saw a newspaper placard announcing the second battle of Manassas (Second Bull Run), and the supposed defeat of the Rebels. This was of course a Northern dispatch, and the English we spoke to said Northern dispatches were to be treated with a grain of salt.' At last the *Belorussia* left port, and by 23 September docked in New York.

John Mitchel and his Rebel son booked into a Broadway hotel: 'many absurd-looking officers, with plumes in their hats, were stamping round in the reading room and office, expounding to civilians on some startling newspaper army reports'. These reports concerned a battle in western Maryland at a place named Antietam, where, though his father did not know it, James Mitchel and the 1st Virginia had had a harsh time. This would turn out to be a crucial Union victory, but amidst Northern propaganda Mitchel had no means of knowing that either. He and Willy reached Washington by way of Baltimore. Here he ran the risk of identification, and so put up at an obscure hotel and sent a message to a young pro-Confederate lawyer of his acquaintance. The lawyer turned up in a funk. 'Why are you here? . . . This place is peopled with spies.'

Mitchel eventually made his arrangements through Southern contacts. John and Willy were to cross the Potomac well to the south of Washington, beyond Camp Springs, where the river broadened, turned south-east, and was not guarded by pickets nor by as many gunboats. Travelling out of Washington, they met up with two Confederate officers who had been to Maryland on some secret mission, and ultimately the four of them approached the farmhouse of an old man who had got others into the South. The Mitchels were to undertake their adventure in a party of eleven, including the Confederate officers. Amongst those waiting in the farmhouse were two Hassidic Jews, with bales of goods they hoped to sell in Virginia, and a man dressed in blue Yankee cloth, supplier to

Confederate sutlers, who had an Irish accent and seemed to recognise Mitchel. The mixed but colourful party left the farm after midnight, but the vessel the old man had sent them to was in awful repair and not large enough for everyone and their goods.

All the next day they waited at and around the house as Union gunboats inspected the shore through binoculars. After dusk, the farmer brought out a second boat from its hiding place and it was hauled down on to the beach. Now, between both boats, there was room for all. Mitchel and his son felt unsafe crossing in the dark, and indeed the other boat with the traders and their goods aboard was almost immediately intercepted by Union sailors. 'Two men jumped on board the little boat, drove it ashore, rolled out the Israelites' goods, stove the boat with an axe.' In Mitchel's boat the Confederate officers decided that the patrols were too thick. They rowed back to the Northern shore, hid the skiff and lost themselves in the woods until the next night. The Irishman in blue garb had been intercepted in the first boat, and by the time Mitchel, Willy and the Confederate officers secretly landed, he had turned informer, leading a party of twenty Union soldiers and sailors up to the farmhouse. The soldiers broke in, smashed trunks and cupboards, and demanded information on all who had been sheltering there.

It rained all night in the woods, and the Mitchels and their two Confederate officers could not light a fire. The next day, the Confederates bought a better skiff from a fisherman. It was still small for the party, but the night was calm and the river perfectly smooth. Though lights of gunboats could be seen out in the river, the crossing was almost routine. On the far side, still in Union-held territory, they travelled uneventfully in a spring wagon well to the south-east of the main bodies of troops. They did not encounter Union troops at all, and arrived by afternoon at the little depot at Milford on the Richmond & Fredericksburg line. There they simply waited for a train to the Confederate capital.

So Mitchel and Willy came to wartime Richmond, a self-possessed, proudly surviving city set on escarpments above the James. It was frenetic, full of brave, determined women, and pale-faced soldiers with injuries from which there would be no recovery. The Mitchels stayed first at the home of an old Washington friend, Mr John Dooley, a journalist. Dooley, a former major in the 1st Virginia, had been invalided out, but still had two sons in that regiment in which James Mitchel was also serving, by now as a captain.

Willy Mitchel enlisted immediately and desired to be posted to the same renowned regiment. Mitchel himself seemed calm about the choice. Perhaps he did not yet understand how suddenly regiments could be consumed. His host's son Private John Dooley certainly knew: he and

James Mitchel had stood on Cemetery Hill outside Sharpsburg at 4.00 p.m. on the afternoon of the battle and seen their companies torn apart by Union guns from beyond the Antietam. The advancing Union infantry poured in such fire that day that, of some 450 Virginians, barely half remained to retreat through the streets of Sharpsburg. Not that individual gallantry had been borne away. 'I was afraid of being struck in the back,' John Dooley wrote, 'and I frequently turned half around in running, so as to avoid if possible so disgraceful a wound.' A long-legged captain, possibly James, ran backwards for the same purpose, and Dooley kept pace with him.

Mitchel called on President Jefferson Davis at the neo-classical Confederate White House. Though he found he was not considered fit for service in the field, there was an instant offer of employment for him. He took over editorship of one of Richmond's two most important dailies, the pro-administration *Richmond Daily Enquirer*. The *Enquirer* was a broadsheet, published by Tyler, Wise and Allegre from a Greek revival building in Richmond. Despite the withdrawal of Lee's army from the North after Antietam in September, the paper was still in fine editorial fettle by early October, when Mitchel took over the editorship. One of its functions was to provide communication across the lines of war: 'Wiesbaden – I am indeed sorry to learn you have been so ill but glad that you are quite recovered . . . Answer through *New York Daily News*.' But the chief vocation of the *Enquirer*, apart from support of Jefferson Davis, was wrath against the invasive North, an emotion into which Mitchel entered readily. 'The North is like a desperado who throws himself into an abyss in order to draw his adversary down . . . it has lost its liberty – we will preserve ours. Its peoples are subjects – ours shall continue citizens and freemen.' He wrote off Lincoln's Emancipation Proclamation after Antietam as the ploy of a US President desirous of ultimate re-election. Mitchel must nonetheless have flinched at the casualty lists from battlefields, and from Chimborazo Hospital south of 31st Street.

After Lee's army departed western Maryland, what was left of the Irish Brigade and of Hancock's division marched over the Potomac to Harper's Ferry, and to wooded Bolivar Heights, above the steep-streeted, burned-out little town where the Shenandoah met the Potomac. Here on 1 October they were visited by President Lincoln, accompanied on horseback by McClellan. The President was grateful to an army which had enabled him to issue an Emancipation Proclamation, but some of the working-class Irish in the ranks were probably dubious about it.

Libby Meagher came down from New York to visit her husband in a very sociable camp, marked by dinners under canvas, and horse-races. She admired the mountainous scenery and on Sunday was proud to ride to Mass with him at the head of the regiment. Father Corby described her as 'a woman of marked character and possessing more than an ordinary degree of refinement and excellent virtues. She was a devout convert to the Catholic Church.' Her husband's survival merely amplified her faith in prayer's power. But she must now perhaps have seen with concern some signs of fatigue and shock in him, and heard him cry out in his sleep for loss and terror.

A new regiment, the 116th Pennsylvania under Colonel Dennis Heenan, was assigned to the Irish organisation. They raised the numbers back up to 1,700. Private William McCarter, Irish-born, a tanner by trade, a stammerer by his own confession, was a member of the regiment and brought a fresh eye to the war and to General Meagher, describing him as younger than he actually was – about thirty-five years old, said McCarter, 5 feet 8 or 10 inches, 'stout build, and had a clear high-colored complexion'. He noticed that these days Meagher, although uniformed in camp in the full dress of his rank, dressed as a private soldier in battle. 'In thorough military skill and in courage and bravery on the battlefield, he was second to none in the army of the Potomac,' McCarter wrote later. McCarter also later claimed that 'In kindness and thoughtfulness for his men he was the shining light and bright star of the whole Union Army'. McCarter had seen Meagher take sick or wounded soldiers into his tent in cold weather.

Summoned to Meagher's tent now because the general wanted to use him to copy orders, the highly literate McCarter found the general in fatigue dress, stretched out on a wooden bench covered with brown army blankets. His feet were propped up against an empty cracker box.

On a small, plain wooden table there were a few books, maps and a field glass. In another part of his tent stood a large empty box covered with an India-rubber blanket and holding three canteens. Nearby was a bright tin bucket full of clear spring water with a tin cup attached by a string. Along one of the sides of the tent were placed three or four camp stools and a writing desk . . . These articles constituted the entire furniture of General Meagher's tent on Bolivar Heights, Harper's Ferry, Virginia.

McCarter recounted in the most intense detail, since it was his first experience of war, a small battle to which other officers of Meagher's – Cavanagh, Conyngham, Turner, Lyons – devoted barely any attention. On 16 October, almost a month after Antietam, Meagher was ordered to march his brigade next morning to Charlestown, 6 or 7 miles south-west, to drive off a force of Confederates, said to number 3,000, sitting on the Union army's flank. Departing through Harper's Ferry, the troops sang 'John Brown's Body', for this was the town where Brown had made his final abolitionist gesture, and Charlestown was the site of his execution. The singing of an abolitionist song by largely Irish soldiers indicated that emancipation had achieved validity in the brigade. McCarter thought the Irish still an impressive body of men, with the 69th New York leading, then the brigade band, the 4th New York Artillery of six guns, the Pennsylvanians, then the 29th Massachusetts, the 63rd, the 88th and finally the ambulances.

Near a ridge about three quarters of a mile from Charlestown, Meagher's veteran skirmishers, approaching the town, were met by massed fire from Rebels occupying upper rooms and roofs, and so halted. McCarter saw Meagher consulting with his staff. All regiments except for the 116th Pennsylvania, which was left to protect the artillery, were to charge the town. The brigade's guns, 50 yards ahead of McCarter, were firing spherical case-shot into the streets ahead.

McCarter admired Meagher's management of the scene. A signalman with a flag was positioned on a limb of a high tree commanding a view of Charlestown: 'he kept General Meagher, who was constantly patrolling the ground on horseback between the signal station and his troops, fully informed of the movements of the rebel force within the town and on its outskirts'. At last, on Meagher's command 'Attention, forward, double quick, march', the 116th descended the hill. McCarter saw the long line of grey coats emerge from the edge of the town break without a shot being fired, and withdraw through the streets to vanish into fields and hills beyond. Amid 'the deafening yells and cheers of the remaining portion of the brigade', General Meagher rode into town at the head of the 69th New York.

McCarter was horrified, however, to find in one of the houses a young woman whose only child had been killed, while looking from an upstairs window, by a Union shell. Soldiers stood guiltily around a melodeon on top of which lay 'a sweet little girl, some seven or eight years old, cold and stiff and dead'. Her face was intact, but blood soaked the white quilt which covered her. 'A young colored woman was cutting the long brown curls from the child's head and perfectly saturating them with her tears.'

The rest of Hancock's division now followed the brigade as they marched south down the valley, where they stayed on the alert for two weeks against an attack by Jeb Stuart and Stonewall Jackson. In camp, 'we were entertained by General Meagher. He gave a short speech, politely informing us that we were now the advance of our entire division.' But on 2 November, having assessed Hancock's strength, the enemy was gone. So the brigade marched back to camp on Bolivar Heights, where the 28th Massachusetts, a very Irish regiment, was added into the brigade. Thus Meagher briefly commanded six regiments. These events should have reinforced faith, but Meagher was beginning to experience a crisis of belief.

Sent back into Virginia, the Irish found it sometimes amusing yet fundamentally dispiriting to be seen as occupying forces, rather than liberators. In Warrenton, Virginia, as the Irish Brigade marched through, McCarter experienced the blazing resentment of Rebel women – 'a shower of missiles, including stones, brick bats, chunks of firewood, bottles, shoemaker hammers, and pieces of coal. They were all thrown at us by the hands of these fair Virginia damsels, aimed from windows.'

The gradual movements of McClellan's army as a whole gave the Confederates plenty of time to reposition themselves in front of Richmond. As early as 5 November, Lincoln authorised General Halleck to relieve over-cautious McClellan of the command of the Army of the Potomac. A Washington general, riding through a snowstorm, gave the news to McClellan himself two days later. An order of 9 November called on troops to assemble at 6.00 a.m. the next day to greet and bid farewell to General McClellan, and in passing it on to his officers Meagher declared that no other brigade in the entire army would feel the general's departure more intensely. To Barlow he wrote:

> The sentiment of an army of 100,000 men is that a gross injustice has been done McClellan . . . Were it not for the Brigade I wouldn't serve a moment longer in the army. As I brought them out, I feel bound in heart to bring them back . . . Ah, if the gentlemen of the White House could have seen what I saw this morning – could they have heard the cheers of those 100,000 Soldiers which rent the air and deadened the artillery itself.

McClellan's dismissal generated far more heat than the Emancipation Proclamation. Emancipation had not moved Irish officers to offer their resignations, as they now did in numbers to Meagher over McClellan's dismissal. Meagher and the rest of them talked each other around, however, and awaited events. With any luck, the year's campaigning was coming to a close. The day after McClellan left, in the brigade camp at Stafford Hills behind Falmouth snow began to fall.

Ambrose Burnside, a man who had been hours late committing the Union left wing at Antietam, now commanded the Army of the Potomac. For the moment, he took the Yankee 29th Massachusetts away from the Irish, reducing Meagher's brigade to five regiments, which was still more than normal. At eight o'clock in the evening of 11 November, according to McCarter, Burnside met with other general officers in Meagher's tent, and Private McCarter became a copier with a vengeance – forty-two plain copies of General Burnside's immediate orders were to be produced. When half of the orders were done, the rest of the copying was postponed until morning, since an officers' party was to be held. McCarter was put on sentry duty outside the tent, where after some hours he saw the results of Meagher's going on a binge. The young Pennsylvanian sentry's post was close to one of the huge bonfires which dotted the camp. Late at night, he saw the general open his tent flap and perceived that if Meagher let go of the pole he would be pitched into the huge fire. Other officers still inside did not seem to be aware of Meagher's danger. And now he released his hold. 'He ran or rather plunged forward towards the fire.' McCarter used the side of his bayonet to stop Meagher's body pitching into the flames. The musket itself then fell into the fire and accidentally discharged. A senior general, now running with other officers from the tent, helped pick up Meagher and told him, 'General, you owe your life to that man.' The next morning, when he went to Meagher's tent to copy further orders, he found 'a beautiful new musket with bayonet was there'. Significantly, McCarter said Meagher seemed to feel deeply mortified by the incident. 'To his honor and credit, I never saw General Meagher intoxicated again.'

Sumner had been put in overall command of what was called the Right Grand Division, and his Second Corps, of which the Irish Brigade was part, was put under the command of General Darius Couch. Hancock remained at division and Meagher at brigade, sharing reminiscences of many mutual Democrat friends as autumn advanced. From their position on Stafford Hills the brigade could look across the Rappahannock to the well-made town of Fredericksburg. Sumner sent an officer across on 17 November to demand its surrender. The Rebels refused and, on the escarpment called Marye's Heights behind the town, began digging redoubts. Ambrose Burnside took no action. Sumner argued with Burnside to let him cross the river, occupy the entire town and try for the heights while they were still lightly defended. He had in fact sent Meagher's Irish across already, but Burnside countermanded that order. McCarter later wrote, 'I am of the opinion and I am not alone in it that General Burnside, not withstanding his alleged unprepared condition . . . committed the saddest blunder of his whole military career.' This decision led everyone to presume that Burnside would do nothing until the spring. A blizzard came and the men were happy to begin building log huts, roofing them with canvas, covering their walls with pictures from the illustrated papers. In the first week of December drill was suspended, confirming that the year's campaigning was over.

Since the season now seemed lulled, Meagher sent the brigade colours north, in the care of Captain James McGee, for presentation to the civilian committee in New York. A banquet was in fact held to receive these tokens of Celtic valour, and a number of officers home on sick leave attended. Heavily bandaged Colonel Patrick Kelly was asked to speak, but McGee had to explain that the colonel's jaw had been smashed.

The committee meant to bring down to the winter camp new battle flags. Meagher, ever an enthusiastic arranger of banquets, was actively preparing to receive them. The men of the brigade began refurbishing a theatre in the Union-held outskirts of the town, reachable by boat across the Rappahannock. Turning it into a banquet hall, they decorated it with boughs for a feast to be held on 13 December. In the meantime, Meagher showed Surgeon Ellis a full-blown ulcer which had developed near one of his knee-joints. As for the men, said Private McCarter, they 'anticipated spending what many of them termed "a gay and happy winter in Dixie's little land" but alas, poor fellows, hundreds never left the place'. For on 9 December, orders were sent, which Meagher's renowned copyist McCarter had to write out, and it became apparent to him that an attack on the Rebel lines above Fredericksburg was in fact planned. On 10 December, each man was furnished with three days' cooked rations and eighty rounds, and that night Union engineers, on Burnside's belated orders, began pushing pontoon-bridge segments out across the Rappahannock towards the town of Fredericksburg. Watching these preparations, a young Irish soldier of the 88th New York turned to his chaplain, Father William Corby, and said, 'Father, are they going to lead us over in front of those guns which we have seen them placing unhindered for the past three weeks?' Corby said, 'Don't trouble yourselves; your Generals know better than that.'

At Hancock's urging, Meagher sent a telegraph to the Irish Brigade Recruiting Office, 596 Broadway. 'Every officer in this brigade in or about New York will instantly rejoin his command.' It seemed that every general, including Joe Hooker, was advising Ambrose Burnside against an attack on the Confederate positions. But as Father Corby confessed, 'To our great surprise, the poor soldier was right. On December 12, we were ordered to move.' Before leaving his tent, Meagher locked up his possessions in a chest and gave the key to McCarter. 'If my fate is to fall, hand it over to General Hancock.' McCarter was discontented at being left and was later able to talk his way into crossing the river and catching up with the brigade.

Helped by a morning mist, the Irish Brigade crossed the pontoons to

Fredericksburg. Under Union pressure of numbers the Confederates gradually withdrew from the centre of the town, leaving a city in which the remaining civilians stayed in their cellars. Meagher broadly forbade looting, but it was nonetheless widespread. Men dressed up in plundered clothing and were grateful to find a supply of whiskey. There were also warehouses full of tobacco and barges laden with it. McCarter found a small bakery and some barrels of flour in its cellar. Everyone had resigned himself to dying the next day, on the defences above the town, and during the afternoon officers had to drive away undertakers' clerks who approached men and guaranteed shipment of bodies back to the North on good terms. Now some drank, some went to confession; many did both. They studiously wrote their names on slips of paper for pinning to the backs of their jackets.

Meagher, sleep interrupted by his leg ulcer, was never to record what he thought during this bitter night. The whimsical pen which had silent the nuances of transportation and Costa Rican travel was silent. He talked with Hancock, who like other generals had tried to dissuade Burnside. A philosophic lassitude combined with flaring hope tempered his blood. In the morning, summoned by bugles and pipers, the brigade emerged from houses, took up parade rest formation in the riverfront section of town, and at 9.30, in residual mist, they moved up to a street that ran east–west in the centre of the city; here they formed in line of battle. Meagher, on horseback for now to relieve his ulcerated leg, gave a brief speech to each regiment. Sergeant William McClelland published an account in the *Irish American* of what General Meagher said to the 88th New York. The general's eyes filled with tears. 'Soldiers – This is my wife's own regiment, "her own dear 88th," she calls it, and I know, and have confidence, that with that dear woman's smile upon you . . . this day you will strike a deadly blow to those wicked traitors who are now but a few hundred yards from you . . .' But just in case they might be confused with some other, less distinguished brigade, Meagher 'sent to our officers the bunches of boxwood requesting them to present in his name a green sprig to each man in the ranks'. To an extent this was another gesture, but also a means of marking those who were killed as Irish.

A few days before, Mitchel and his journalist friend John Dooley started from Richmond to visit the camps outside the town of Fredericksburg and see their sons. Arriving at the railhead near Guiney's Station south of the town, Mitchel and Dooley walked to Marye's Heights above Fredericksburg and found their boys sitting at a campfire with comrades, and on the morning of 13 December Mitchel and Willy ate a breakfast of corn and hardtack with the Richmond Howitzers, who were commanded by an Irishman, Ned McCarthy.

From where he chatted with Willy that morning, Mitchel, the journalist Dooley and Dooley's son, indeed the entire Confederate army on Marye's Heights, could see 'the gathering hosts of the Yankees filling up the plain', and he admired 'their order and celerity'. He found that the location where he was sitting, close to Confederate artillery, began to attract Federal fire. Mitchel was now no more than a mile and a half from his Vandemonian colleague Meagher. Yet everybody agreed that Burnside would not fight that day. So Mitchel bade both Willy and his officer brother James goodbye, and he and Mr Dooley left the camp. As they neared the railhead they heard the huge and sudden rage of the battle.

In Fredericksburg, on the side of the street the 116th Pennsylvania faced, a cotton factory was on fire. McCarter feared that it might fall on him. 'Here and there Negro women were seen rushing out of half demolished houses, frequently with young children in their arms or crying and clinging to their skirts, perfectly frantic with fright.' A parson and his wife emerged, demanding that they should be allowed safe passage across the river to seek compensation.

As the brigade went into motion, they had to enter streets running north–south and subject to terrible fire. Up ahead, McCarter saw Meagher at the head of the column, waving his glittering sword. A shell entered the calf of McCarter's left leg. Artillery smoke added to the mist as they crossed the small millstream between the town and the heights. The planks of the wooden bridge were gone, and only the stringers were intact. Beyond was a slight indentation in the terrain where the Irish dumped their haversacks and blankets. Meagher told them, on General Hancock's instruction, to fix bayonets. A prisoner of war had told Hancock that the Irish bayonet charges at the Sunken Road at Antietam had been decisive. A Pennsylvanian at McCarter's side, who would be killed within seconds, remarked, 'That's the thing to fetch the sons of bitches.'

The slope of Marye's Heights was 150 yards off. When French's men went off uphill in broad day, the Irish were able to watch them swept away and obliterated by musketry and canister and grape. Regiments with whom the Irish had socialised in Camp California were reduced by half in seconds, then, on bravely moving in to fill the gaps, were halved again, and finally fell to the ground to take any cover they could. Meagher now received Hancock's expected order to take the brigade forward. With his severe but secret leg ulcer, Meagher had dismounted, for it was not the terrain for equine gallantry. As ever, the Irish went forward at their *de rigueur* rush, trying to prove their worth to nativist America. They crossed a ruined cornfield to the first fence, rushed to the second and were now struggling past French's maimed men, 50 yards below the stone wall and the Rebels. This was as far as any human on the Union side got. Thomas F. Galwey, a scholarly young Irish veteran of Antietam and an officer of an Ohio regiment in French's division, hugging the ground with the remnants of his company, wrote:

The Irish Brigade . . . comes out from the city in glorious file, their green sunbursts waving . . . every man has a sprig of green in his cap, and a half-laughing, half-murderous look in their eyes. They passed just to our left, poor fellows, poor, glorious fellows, shaking goodbye to us with their hats! They reach a point within a stone's throw of the stone wall. No farther. They try to go beyond, but are slaughtered.

He saw them lying in line by 'that terrible stone wall'.

Lee would have reason to be more than pleased. The Union lost 13,000 men, the same as at Antietam, but Lee only 4,000. Pickett's Virginian division had repulsed the Irish Brigade, and Pickett, under whom James and Willy Mitchel served, wrote to his wife, 'Your soldier's heart almost stood still as he watched those sons of Erin . . . My darling, we forgot they were fighting us, and cheer after cheer at their fearlessness went up all along our lines.' The mild Captain Conyngham of the Irish Brigade had a harsher verdict: 'It was not a battle – it was a wholesale slaughter of human beings – sacrificed to the blind ambition and incapacity of some parties.' 'As for the brigade,' wrote another of its officers, 'may the Lord pity and protect the widows and orphans of nearly all those belonging to it. It will be a sad, sad Christmas by many an Irish hearthstone in New York, Pennsylvania and Massachusetts.'

Meagher, said Surgeon Reynolds, had concealed his ulcer from General Winfield Scott Hancock. After the fatal, first and only attack failed, he sent an orderly to fetch his horse, and limped down the hill a little way to meet them coming back. General Hancock rode up and ordered him to withdraw the remains of the brigade back into Fredericksburg. Survivors huddled in the streets as the dressing-stations filled up. Meagher gathered what was left of his staff. Fortunately the night was mild for the season and Private McCarter, wounded in hand and leg, tried to walk down the hill into town. He collapsed with loss of blood and a raging fever, but was found by a sergeant of his regiment. He would on recovery write of Meagher: 'As a benefactor and friend, the men of the Irish Brigade who fought their way by his side up the mouths of whole batteries of Rebel cannons at Fredericksburg will never forget him.'

Now not even Meagher could convince himself that today a terrible beauty had been born. But he maintained a good front. In Fredericksburg, in the theatre the brigade had decorated, the banquet for the presentation of the new colours went ahead. The sutlers' wagons came up over the pontoon bridge with whiskey and champagne, tables and banners. Many officers were not present, they were out in the dark, trying to retrieve wounded. The guests from New York attended, and the corps commander Darius Couch. Meagher told the civilian visitors of the committee that he wanted them to take the flags back to New York and save them until the brigade could be rebuilt. An orderly amused the company by bearing in a salver covered with a napkin. Removing the napkin he displayed a cannon ball. General Hancock, unaccustomed to wakes, secretly wondered how the Irish could follow such a slaughter with a feast. But what Meagher took to the banquet was less a gaiety than a manic heart. He had begun darkly to consider that the Irish Brigade had to this point been expressing a debt to the Union. Now – in his mind – the debt column was overtopped and the Union needed to express its debt to the Irish Brigade. 'Of the 2,200 men I led into action the day before,' he would write the next morning, '218 now appeared on that ground that morning.' Hancock saw three Irishmen standing alone. 'Close up with your company,' he ordered them. 'General, we are our company,' one of them replied.

Sundered by loss and divided by oceans of gore, the Irish of the divided states were still poignantly united in hope for Ireland. Dennis J. Downing, a Union captain, Cork-born, schoolfriend of the most famous Cork Fenian, O'Donovan Rossa, claimed that on the night after the Battle of Fredericksburg, socialising at a campfire, he began singing the ballad 'Ireland Boys Hurrah'. It was a marching song of O'Donovan Rossa's radical Phoenix national and literary clubs in Cork, paramilitary groups of young men who had been heavily pursued by the police and were now merged with James Stephens's Irish Republican Brotherhood. The chorus spread from Irish voice to Irish voice 6 miles along the river, and then was echoed by Irishmen in the Confederate lines on the further bank.

A medical certificate, written by Surgeon Reynolds two days after the battle, certified that Meagher was suffering from a ' "Furunculous Abscess" of the left knee, which quite disables him for active duty in the field'. It must have been clear to him in that icy camp that he might now with profit abandon his Irish base, given that the brigade was so decimated. There seemed to be nothing in his purely military record to suggest he could not have been promoted to command of division or corps. He would have arrived at far better decisions than Burnside did at Fredericksburg. Fellow brigadier-generals such as French, Sickles and Howard either had been or soon would be promoted. But Meagher chose to remain with his Irish.

He left camp three days before Christmas, accompanying, as a telegram to Major Horgan's sister in New York indicated, the body of that officer to the foot of Sixth Street, Washington, at noon on Monday 22 December. On Christmas Eve in wistful New York City, Meagher spent the day at his desk at the Broadway headquarters of the Irish Brigade, writing letters to the families of dead officers. Soon he would be at home in Fifth Avenue, at Libby's side, chatting with Peter Townsend and Barlow, and feeling the dislocation from civilian reality all veterans of that awful year experienced.

In early January 1863, Judge Daly met a colonel who, wrote Mrs Daly, 'said that Hancock and Meagher were the only ones who persevered at Fredericksburg'.

22

Let Me Have Idaho

> It has long since occurred to me, that in compliment for his [Meagher's] valuable services, and those of the Irish soldiers generally, it would be fitting acknowledgment on the part of our Government, to select some desirable portion of our territories and call it New Ireland, of which no doubt General Meagher would in due time be elected Governor.
>
> William West, US consul, Dublin, to Secretary Seward, November 1863

To mark the New Year, on 2 January 1863, John Mitchel, editor of the *Richmond Enquirer*, remarked that 'the air was parted brightly'. Union General Rosecrans had been defeated in the west, Fredericksburg had been a disaster for the Union. 'It was felt to be a happy augury for the new year.' But the notices the *Enquirer* published for conscripts from the counties of Middlesex, King and Queen, Essex, King William, Buckingham and Fluvanna, seemed to indicate the Confederacy had become desperately man-hungry.

Of course, Mitchel kept his readers informed on how the British and Irish press saw the war. The *Nation* in Dublin, wrote Mitchel, 'cautions the Irish against enlisting in Lincoln's army. Whilst the other, the *Irishman*, terms us rebels, and traitors, engaged in destroying the "best government the world ever saw".' John Martin was quoted: 'All true Irish Nationalists are not partisans of the North in this war.' Mitchel commented, 'Let Mr Martin, however, and all just and generous Irishmen take comfort in the fact . . . that there are more Irish in the army of the Confederate States (in proportion to the population) than in that of Lincoln's. It is true, they flaunt no green banners nor *Sunbursts*, nor shout *Fontenoy!* Nor *Remember Limerick!* They are content to fight simply as Virginians, or as Georgians.'

Early in the new year, Mitchel joined the Ambulance Committee, a volunteer civilian ambulance service. It gave him a sense of serving his sons, about whom he held tormenting fears. James, now a staff captain, was with the army at Fredericksburg. John served in the much-bombarded and blockaded fortifications of Charleston, but Willy had been sent with his regiment away from the cockpit in Virginia to North Carolina. During a few days' leave in Richmond, Willy's exposure to a warm house and a dry bed gave him a severe cold. 'Since then he has returned to bivouacking in the snow, and is as well as ever.'

'For me, I am doing the principal writing of the Richmond *Enquirer*,' wrote Mitchel to Miss Thompson, 'which is *supposed* to be in the confidence of the Government. Prices in Richmond are so severe, from four and a half dollars per pound of coffee to $75 to $100 per month for rent, that it's impossible for Jenny to come over.'

Home on his sick leave, a partially refreshed, lame Meagher commenced a press campaign to get his brigade back to New York for rebuilding. This tactic would not endear him to the War Department. But the *Irish American* supported him: 'If the Brigade were not so markedly and distinctively *Irish*, they would not have been treated with the positive injustice and neglect to which they have been exposed.'

A Requiem Mass was said at St Patrick's Cathedral for the repose of the souls of the numerous dead. General and Mrs Elizabeth Meagher attended. In an age when there was no acknowledgement of what would later be called war neuroses, Libby was the one who knew how shaken her husband was. Rossini's beautiful *Cujus Animam* was sung, but was it enough to mute the screams of falling soldiers? Later, a number of officers went wistfully to Delmonico's for 'refreshments'.

Charles C. Halpine wrote:

> Then in silence we brimmed our glasses,
> As we rose up – JUST ELEVEN,
> And bowed as we drank to the loved and the dead
> Who had made us THIRTY-SEVEN.

Meagher, called on to speak, remarked percipiently that the battlefield had done more to cement the Union than anything else. He offered an ambiguous toast: 'The Stars and Stripes', but also: 'The heroism of both armies'. He congratulated the Irish for doing their duty to the adopted land, when they had not said a word to bring on that crisis! The *New York Times* of 17 January 1863 said that Meagher then remarked with a laugh, 'I shall never be a major-general after this.'

His leg had not healed, and he stayed on in the Townsend residence. There was no rush; spring was remote. On 30 January 1863, Halleck, general-in-chief, with little time for individualists such as Meagher, sent a directive to the Adjutant-General to 'enquire of Brig. General Meagher by what authority he is absent from his command'. Four days later, Meagher wrote to notify the Adjutant-General that 'the afflicted part still continuing so sore as to incapacitate from active duty', he was enclosing further certificates furnished by Dr William F. Edgar, USA. He promised that he would report in person on Wednesday 11 February at the War Department.

He would not in fact return to Washington until 14 February, and was automatically charged for being late. He appeared before a military commission at Falmouth, Virginia, headed by an old friend, one-armed Major-General Howard. The commission at once accepted his explanations. Part of the delay had been due to the fact that, while in Washington, he had waited on President Lincoln and made a personal request for the brigade to be relieved. The President had received General Meagher in a levee *en masse*, perhaps an answer in itself, but took the trouble to cross the room and shake hands with him. On General Meagher's return to his headquarters, the men surrounded him and cheered enthusiastically as he told them that he was looking forward to the day, 'if any reliance could be placed on the promises of those in power', that he would have the 'gratification of leading them back to their repose, to the less exacting duties that their gallantry, their enthusiasm, their lofty and single courage had so deservedly won and so richly earned'.

General Meagher sat down in his tent to write what were for him momentous letters to Secretary of War Edwin Stanton. 'Sir – I have the honour to request that three regiments of the Brigade I command may be temporarily relieved from duty in the field.'

He detailed their present strength:

On duty including pioneers, drummers etc. . . . 340
On extra and daily duty . . . 132
Sick and wounded . . . 59

No history, however vividly and powerfully written, could do more than these plain and stern statistics in attestation of the cordial loyalty and devotion unto death of this Brigade.

General Hancock agreed with Meagher that if older brigades should be given furlough, every man on leave would serve as an unofficial recruiter. There was little risk either in resting veteran regiments during the winter and spring. But Hooker, the new commander, returned Meagher's letter to him. 'A Commanding General cannot entertain the proposition for the temporary withdrawal of the Irish Brigade from the Army, without positive assurances that it will be immediately replaced by an equal body of troops.' A second letter from Meagher asked for permission to 'proceed to Washington for three or four days . . . the undersigned respectfully submits that his proceeding to Washington on the matter in question, will enable him to secure the cooperation of influential and active friends'. In

Washington General Halleck, who hated generals with 'influential and active friends' in Congress, simply wrote on the application: 'Not approved'.

The late winter camp itself helped restore what was a muscular soul. Meagher certainly brought all his usual gusto to St Patrick's Day. He strolled through the camp in the garb, kindly brought down from New York by Libby, of the Irish gentry – tall white beaver hat, blue swallow-tail coat with brass buttons, white buckskin breeches and black topboots. First, Mass was said in a brush-and-log church, with Meagher as lay master of ceremonies. Lunch was prepared in a marquee. Generals Hooker and Sickles were there for the planned racing, with Generals Sedgwick and Butterfield. At the improvised racecourse, Meagher saw soldiers standing and sitting under the ramshackle grandstand. He pointed his whip. 'Stand from under! If that stage gives way, you will be crushed by four tons of Major-Generals.'

With Libby beside him, Meagher was utterly his old self, acting as Clerk of the Course. Ten thousand troops watched as three heats were run for the final of the Grand Irish Brigade Steeplechase, with a purse of $500. The winner was Captain Jack Gosson, riding Meagher's grey hunter Jack Hindon. There were foot races too, casting weights, a soaped pig chase, and a contest of Irish reels, jigs and hornpipes.

But sourness invaded the day. On 24 March 1863, Meagher felt bound to write a letter of apology for offence caused undeliberately to one of his favourite officers, Captain James O'Beirne, on the night of the feast day:

> You must kindly and generously ascribe the circumstances to the excitement of the day . . . and to the additional fact that at the moment at which it appears this affront to you was offered, I was somewhat bested and irritated by what I considered to be a dereliction of duty on the part of two or three officers who had undertaken to prolong the entertainments of the day but failed for no sufficient cause to do so.

In April Meagher was permitted leave to go up to New York to address a crowd about a new onset of hunger in Ireland. A series of droughts and floods in the west of Ireland had ruined crops of wheat and oats. Blight had returned to part of the potato crop. In some places peat fields were drowned, so that people had no warmth. The already accursed peninsula of Belmullet and Erris Head in Mayo suffered worst. Relief efforts saved people from a revisiting of 1847, but increased evictions brought aggrieved young Irishmen into the Fenian movements in Ireland and the USA. It was 20 April before Meagher telegraphed from Willard's Hotel, a block from the White House, to General Hancock. 'I report to you tomorrow. I am a day behind my time but have Dr Clymer's certificate that it was impossible for me to move. He wanted me to remain here one week longer – but under present circumstances I must be with you and with the Brigade.' A dinner he had in Falmouth on 26 April with his old friend General Butterfield confirmed some suspicions. Generals Hooker and Butterfield had devised a huge flanking movement to end the war. Hooker would order three corps to slip away from their position opposite Fredericksburg and make a secret march north-east 30 miles upriver, to appear on Lee's flank and destroy him.

Two mornings later Hancock's division left their camp intact in the pre-dawn and set out cross-country in this great wheeling motion. Miles up the river Meagher's men crossed the Rappahannock's United States Ford, where they sent out pickets. There was no enemy as they entered the tangle of forest known as the Wilderness, south of the river. They noticed with delight that the woods were full of deer. At Scott's Mills, a few miles north of a hamlet named Chancellorsville, Meagher occupied and loopholed the mill and offices.

A number of Union divisions remained in front of Fredericksburg, and when they lunged across the river against the town on 30 April, Lee withdrew. After a screaming assault Marye's Heights were abandoned by the Confederates. Amongst the Rebel wounded was Mitchel's son, James, now an officer in General Gordon's staff, struck in the chest by a shell splinter.

By that time, off to the north-west, Hooker's main Union army's lines ran in a dogleg from Wilderness Tavern to Chancellorsville in the middle, where the large Chancellor house provided his headquarters, and north to the river. Lee did not yet realise that the movement had occurred, and the diminished Irish Brigade believed that this was the decisive manoeuvre which would justify all losses. About midday, Meagher heard Rebels clash with Union positions a few miles to the east. This was Hooker's chance to advance his superior hosts on Lee, but he had a rush of timidity and drew his men back into the woods around Chancellorsville. The Irish at Scott's Mills were all at once in defence.

The Irish worked on their defences all through Saturday 2 May, and in the late afternoon heard a furious hubbub not to their east but to their west. They did not know that Stonewall Jackson had led his men in a typically huge encircling march which would put him west of Hooker's army. Jackson's corps now came on down the road towards Chancellorsville and Scott's Mill. The Irish knew they were coming by the birds and animals which took flight out of the forest all around. A deer leapt the abatis and ran through the Irish lines like an omen. General Meagher had to throw a line across the Chancellorsville road and into the woods in order to intercept General Howard's panic-stricken fugitives, who had seen their comrades killed while drinking coffee. Some of them were persuaded to join the Irish line.

Early the next morning, 3 May, Meagher received orders to take the brigade down the dirt road towards the Chancellor house. 'As we marched through the columns that lay in the way, we were loudly and repeatedly cheered,' a gratified Meagher wrote. The position they were ordered to take up was a few paces to the rear of the Chancellor house clearing, where Hooker had only one battery of six guns in place, the 5th Maine. Meagher understood now that the great strategy had failed. From unseen positions in the thick woods ahead, thirty Rebel field-pieces opened on the 5th Maine and the Irish Brigade, and, as Meagher would later report, his men were for the next two and a half hours exposed to 'a most galling fire'. Conyngham observed that Meagher was active along the lines, and 'a shell burst which killed four of the Irish Brigade occurred in a spot he had just left'. Within twenty minutes five of the Union caissons had blown up, and all the battery's horses were killed or wounded. Only one gun, commanded by a corporal, was still in action. Meagher ordered the 116th Pennsylvania, under fire, to drag away into the woods the remaining guns.

Stationed on the porch of the Chancellor house, Father Corby saw a cannon ball strike the pillar against which General Hooker was leaning, hurling him to the ground. Another ball immediately cut in two a soldier who was slaking his thirst at the well in front of the house. Surgeons had set up a table of planks near the house and the Irish lines, and a ball landed on a patient undergoing surgery. Corby recorded with horror that the surgeons were paralysed with shock, and the patient was obliterated. The Chancellor house itself now took fire, as did the forest around it, and Captain Conyngham found this melancholy because of the numbers of wounded sheltering in both. Hancock came to Meagher and informed him that Hooker had now departed, dazed. A retreat of the Union army northwards towards the United States Ford had been ordered, and Meagher was to command the divisional rearguard.

Meagher held the position along the road out of Chancellorsville for the entirety of Sunday night and Monday morning. He wrote: 'For the two days and nights intervening between this disastrous morning and that of the 6th May the Irish Brigade, along with the other brigades of Hancock's division, was right in front of the new line of defence, and held their ground . . . most nobly.' In between snatched sleep on a pup tent half, and exchanges of fire, he was kept busy absorbing stragglers and commiserating with passing wounded. Tuesday was a rainy day, with scattered exchanges of firing and everyone stupefied by exhaustion, and that night the Irish again lay down in puddles in their damp blankets before being told around midnight to withdraw down a new trail recently cut through the forest. According to Meagher, the 88th were the last regiment in the Federal army to retreat, protecting the shrinking U-shaped defensive formation of Hooker's multitude as it withdrew to the Rappahannock River.

Conyngham was shocked on the withdrawal to encounter rural Virginian families who were starving.

On 8 May Meagher, back in the dispiriting camp at Falmouth from which they had marched out a week before to end the war, felt bound by earlier warnings he had given the War Department. His letter of resignation would be a gesture which he expected, with too much confidence, to act as a stimulant to the government. Addressed to the Assistant Adjutant-General, it represented

> my resignation as Brigadier General commanding what was once known as the Irish Brigade. That Brigade no longer exists. The assault on the enemy's works on 13th December last reduced it to something less than a minimum regiment of infantry. For several weeks it remained in this exhausted condition. Brave fellows from the convalescent camp and from sick beds at home gradually reinforced this handful of devoted men . . . These facts I represented as clearly and forcibly as it was in my power to do, in a memorial to the Secretary of War.

Meagher confessed with unmilitary frankness that 'the depression caused by the ungenerous and inconsiderate treatment of a gallant remnant of a brigade which had never once failed to do its duty most liberally and heroically, almost unfitted me to remain in command'. Yet he had tried to be true to those that had been true to him, even though 'feeling that it was to a sacrifice rather than to a victory that we were going. I accompanied them and led them through all the operations required of them at Scott's Mills and Chancellorsville beyond the Rappahannock.' But to remain in the companionship and in charge of such men would be 'to perpetuate a public deception, in which the hard-won honours of good soldiers, and in them the military reputation of a brave old race, would inevitably be involved and compromised'. In tendering his resignation, however, he was not withdrawing his services, which belonged to the Union.

A week later, the War Department, unmoved by his eloquence, sent him a terse two-line answer. 'Sir – Your resignation has been accepted by the President of the United States, to take effect this day.' Meagher said goodbye to his brigade on the evening of 19 May. His command consisted of a mere 400 men formed in a square to listen to his last speech. The band of the 14th Connecticut played. Meagher told his men, 'The graves of many hundreds of brave and devoted soldiers, who went down to death with all the radiance and enthusiasm of the noblest chivalry, are so many guarantees and pledges that, as long as there remains one officer or soldier of the Irish Brigade, so long shall there be found for him, for his family and little ones, if any there be, a devoted friend in Thomas Francis Meagher.'

He shook hands with the entire remaining brigade, and then turned what was left of the brigade over to Colonel Patrick Kelly. The officers presented him with a combined farewell address. 'We regard you, General, as the originator of the Irish Brigade in the service of the United States . . . In resigning the command of the remnant of the Brigade, and going back to private life in obedience to the truest dictates of honour and conscience, rest assured, General, that you take with you the confidence and affection of every man in our regiments.'

When Meagher returned to New York, the mayor, Republican George Opdyke, called to offer him the hospitality of the city. In a formal address, the mayor declared that Meagher had given the nation 'three of the most potent instruments – the eloquence of your voice, the force of your pen, and the power of your sword'. Meagher was reassured enough to think he would not long be idle.

As early as 18 May 1863, Mitchel reported in the *Enquirer* that Meagher had resigned his commission because 'he *cannot recruit his brigade* . . . This fact . . . proves to us what we have believed before, that the Irish of the Federal States are entirely sick of the war.' There was some truth to that, but some wishful thinking too, as there was when the *Enquirer* held out hope to its increasingly distressed readership that the 3-year servicemen of Lincoln's army, 300,000 strong, would be free to go home the next month, and 'the war must collapse and die out'.

Sometime in May, Mitchel discovered that during the renewed struggle for Marye's Heights, his second son, James, had been seriously wounded. James was to be sent to Richmond for recuperation. But a further grief descended almost at once. A Confederate officer of Irish origins entered the *Enquirer* newsroom one day with a copy of the Dublin *Freeman's Journal*. It carried a paragraph announcing that Henrietta Mitchel – adored Henty – had died at her convent school in Paris. She had perished – Mitchel consoled himself – without violence, and amongst the nuns she loved. Her burial in the Montparnesse cemetery was attended by her young sister Minnie, also a student at the Sacré Coeur convent. Jenny and Isabelle Mitchel's grief can be imagined, but Mitchel in Richmond was oddly comforted by the presence of other Southern parents who had endured the same acute losses.

During Lee's midsummer advance into the North, Mitchel spent time training with the Ambulance Committee on the banks of the Chickahominy, to which Lee would be able to ship his wounded from a conquered Philadelphia. Editorially, Mitchel had urged the advancing Confederates not to be fussy about property. 'Would it not do a man's heart good to get one glimpse of the fat burghers, and highly bedizened ladies of Philadelphia at the moment when the first brigade of Mississippians marched down South Street!' He was pleased just the same to have one son, John, safe behind redoubts in Charleston, a captain of artillery. John had found garrison duty tedious, however, and had earlier in the year led a company of snipers in capturing the *Isaac P. Smith*, a Union gunboat. Mitchel reported to John that 'Everybody speaks highly of James, and, like you, he gets every luck except promotion.' James, mended, had rejoined General Gordon's brigade for the invasion of the North, and with the rest of the Confederate forces he would descend on the massing Union army at the Pennsylvanian town named Gettysburg. Willy's 1st Virginia of Pickett's division was on its way there as well.

Later Mitchel would write with pride to John at Fort Sumter that Willy had been ill in Staunton, Virginia, and had needed to catch up with his regiment, and his friend Captain John Dooley, whom he loved like an older brother, at Chambersburg, Pennsylvania, a few days before the battle. To do so, he walked 130 miles in six days. Captain James Mitchel would come safely through the three days of Gettysburg. But on the third day a desperate Lee chose to throw in General Pickett's Virginians on a long, crazed attack across open ground towards the Union forces on Cemetery Ridge. The Confederate line lay on Seminary Ridge, about a mile to the west, and young Willy Mitchel was amongst Pickett's men who formed up in the woods below and then came yelling forth. According to John Dooley, Willy died 200 yards from the stone fence behind which the Union army was lined out, which meant that he got further than most but not as far as a few demented souls. Mitchel wrote, 'Those who were in that advance lay where they fell; his remains were never identified.' The minuscule Irish Brigade was at Gettysburg, and left behind a quartermaster, Captain Haverty, to look for Willy's body. There was a report that it had been buried with a note attached: 'Private Mitchel, son of Irish patriot'.

The hope that Willy would simply turn up, staggering back into the South, or writing from a prisoner-of-war pen, lingered on. Confirmation of Willy's death came from an eye-witness. 'So poor Will finished his first and last campaign,' wrote Mitchel to John. The family would treasure a little knapsack of entomological memoranda and drawings which had been left in the woods near Seminary Ridge and was now returned to them.

The South set about protecting themselves from awareness of the full import of the fact Philadelphia had not been captured and Lee had withdrawn from Gettysburg and as part of this process Mitchel promoted in his editorials the idea that if shirkers in the Confederacy had been at Gettysburg the Union line might have broken. And: 'If any short-sighted Confederates, of weak knees and pallid livers, have been deluding themselves with the idea that in case of subjugation by our enemy, the worst that could happen to us would be merely to go back into the Union *as it was* with the Constitution *as it is* etc, it is time for them to awake from that dream.'

On 31 August, more than seven weeks after the battle, he was still publishing Gettysburg casualty lists.

Early in that same summer, Meagher had relaxed with Libby at the Long Island house of Mr Dan Devlin, Donegal immigrant and pioneer of ready-to-wear men's clothing. But nearly eighteen months of frustration awaited him. Of necessity he and Libby still chiefly lived in her father's house, and he was restless. In June, the month of Lee's new advance in the north, Meagher wrote to President Lincoln a futile letter offering to raise 3,000 Irish troops. His political supporters helped his military legitimacy by presenting him with the first Kearny Cross, named for Phil Kearny, killed at Chantilly the previous autumn. Mayor Opdyke, in a letter to Mr Lincoln on 8 July 1863, reminded the President that Meagher was popular with the Irish 'not only in the field but in the forum'.

At Gettysburg, Meagher knew, his friend and former client Sickles had commanded a corps, albeit leading out of alignment with the rest of the Union army on Cemetery Ridge, creating a dangerous salient through whose gaps the Confederate forces rushed and came close to destroying the Union army. Still waiting, Meagher went to Washington and wrote from Willard's Hotel on 13 July to Secretary of War Stanton. 'I have now to request permission to withdraw my letter of resignation and beg to renew the offer of my services to the Government.' But by evil chance, the New York draft riots, blamed on the Irish, began the same day, and spoiled any attractiveness Meagher might have held for the Department of War.

Conscription of men for the army was brought to New York through a military draft which had begun at the Ninth District draft office, Third Avenue and 47th Street, on Saturday 11 July. Under the supervision of the Acting Provost Marshal, a numbered wheel was turned and names corresponding to the numbers were thereby conscripted. The Provost Marshal on the premises was Meagher's close friend, Colonel Robert Nugent of the Brigade, convalescing from a Fredericksburg wound.

On Sunday the draft office was closed, but on the Monday a workers' protest meeting was held in Central Park. Brief as it was, there was much talk about the recent use of black labour to break waterfront strikes. The Black Joke Engine Company Number 33 marched from the meeting to Nugent's draft office, invaded it and smashed the draft wheel. Someone set fire to the building. Neighbouring houses began to burn. Factories closed and workers and artisans flooded into the streets, where railtracks were pulled up and telegraph poles felled. Some notable Peace Democrats, nicknamed Copperheads, emerged from their homes and offices to address the crowds, assuring them of their right to resist the draft. One party of rioters made a friendly visit to General McClellan's house in East 33rd Street, as if for his blessing. Others moved downtown to burn Robert Nugent's house to the ground. A week after the riots, Nugent's broken sword of honour would be found in the hands of an Irish child on the upper East Side.

At the Colored Orphan Asylum at Fifth Avenue between 43rd and 44th Streets, there were cries of 'Burn the niggers' nest'. Firemen trying to put out the blaze had their hoses axed. Orphans were rescued and taken to refuge in the firehouse of the Twentieth Precinct, and fed and protected by local priests for the duration of the riot. As similar attacks on brothels showed, race was not the only matter at hand. Over a number of days the rioters attacked the houses of known Republicans and unjust employers – the same thing in the minds of New York's poorly paid. Grain elevators, which had replaced many grain-handling jobs, were also set alight.

The same Monday, Irish Colonel Henry O'Brien of the 11th New York used a howitzer to clear a crowd in Second Avenue. A woman and her child were killed. That night his house was burned. When he visited the ashes of his residence, he was beaten to death by a mob, and his naked and savaged body dragged through the streets. Many owners of plundered houses blamed these attacks on the inflammatory speeches of anti-war Copperheads, Governor Seymour, Fernando Wood, former mayor, and Clement Vallandigham. Editors of the *Daily News* declared that they had warned America of the consequences of the draft: black people were reaping the results of abolitionist excess. When mobs passed the *News* office they cheered it. In Varick Street a black man was hanged; on Fifth Avenue three blacks were hanged. Brooks Brothers was looted, and Lord & Taylor employees were armed to defend their store at the corner of Grand and Christie Streets.

Governor Seymour issued a proclamation declaring the city and county in a state of insurrection. Secretary of War Stanton was able to send Mayor Opdyke five regiments. On Wednesday morning, too, the *Herald* carried a letter from Archbishop Hughes pleading for peace, and calling a public meeting outside his residence on Friday. Just when Meagher returned to New York that week is uncertain, but he knew that some of the rioters had advanced against armed military formations and attacked the US flag, while others had offered three cheers for Confederate President Jeff Davis! From these his own people, how could he now raise a warrior legion?

The riot ended savagely. As a house-to-house, tenement-to-tenement battle began between 22nd and 31st Streets, where a large number of the 6,000 Federal troops were concentrated, Irish women exhorted their husbands to 'die at home'. Many people jumped to their deaths from roofs. With a death toll hard to establish, the riots withered. Solid citizens complained that the rioters had not been punished because the courts 'are all in the hands of the Irish'.

Justly or otherwise, the Irish took the blame for what was a proletarian riot. The draft would be a failure, producing only 50,000 conscripts instead of the 250,000 hoped for. Back in New York, Meagher complained of the Copperhead behaviour of Vallandigham, who 'after aiding in the equipment of volunteers, and fanning the martial fire twirled or sneaked about to the rear'. But many resented this attack on a Democrat darling. The *Irish American* began to depict Meagher as in his heart a Lincoln man – in their view, the worst you could say of a person.

Not least because the riots were seen as specifically Irish, Meagher had to tolerate further months of inaction. He was reduced to taking a fall vacation in the mountains of Orange County, New York, and when asked to stand as godfather to gallant Major O'Beirne's new baby, said that he was consoled by 'the approval and friendship of intelligent minds and sound chivalrous hearts . . . The fact is, I hate being out of the field. Military life is my true life – It is, perhaps, the only honest, generous, noble life we can lead.'

John Mitchel set out that fall to seek family comfort by riding north-west towards the Rappahannock to visit James at General Gordon's headquarters. As he sat down to converse around the campfire with James and General Gordon, an assault by General Meade 'ruined the occasion'. Two Confederate brigades to the west were overpowered, but the line was for the moment shortened and held.

As a result of his discussions, Mitchel wrote to his daughter Minnie on 22 October 1863 that James was willing to try for a furlough so that he could go to fetch his mother and sisters. But it was obviously the women's idea, and he tried to dissuade them. 'You would have to come by way of Wilmington, in a blockade-running steamer, which is dreadfully expensive . . . This is by no means a comfortable or desirable place for a family.' In the event, James failed to get the furlough, which, Mitchel hoped, put an end to the matter. For in the last months of 1863, he was losing faith; he was moving away from supporting President Davis in the *Enquirer* towards the more critical mode of the *Richmond Examiner*, which condemned Davis for his support of Generals Bragg, Pemberton and Hood, whom Mitchel considered to be in the process of losing the war in the western arena. He also believed Davis too soft in retaliating for Federal outrages against Southern homes.

The owner of the *Richmond Examiner*, a dandified fire-eater named John M. Daniel, had satirised Jefferson Davis's polite instructions in this matter by reporting that during Lee's campaign in the North in 1863, while Virginia howled with devastation, three railroad ties had been pulled loose on the line between Washington and Baltimore. Mitchel now found he had a lot in common with small, viperous, tubercular Daniel.

O'Mahony had, only a few days before the New York riots, inducted Meagher into the Fenian Brotherhood at its offices in Ann Street. 'I, Thomas Francis Meagher, solemnly pledge my sacred word of honor as a truthful and honest man that I will labor with earnest zeal for the liberation of Ireland from the yoke of England and for the establishment of a free and independent government on Irish soil.' Two factors would deliver him from obeying the letter of the pledge. One was the increasing disfavour of the Fenians with the Catholic Church. The other was the ultimate factional split of the Fenians in America. For the moment, however, General Meagher was a plum catch, whom O'Mahony asked to represent New York at the Fenian convention in Chicago in the coming November.

To evade attending the convention, Meagher wired O'Mahony that he was 'on call' to the War Department. In fact, he had been invited to visit the Army of the Potomac, and particularly Brigadier-General Michael Corcoran. Before departing for Virginia, Meagher wrote a defence of the Union for the Dublin newspaper the *Irishman*. It was in a way a response to O'Brien, who, in a public lecture, asked, 'If Poland or Hungary could declare their independence, why shouldn't the South?' He pointed even to the Irishmen that Meagher had led up the hill at Fredericksburg: 'the manpower which would be needed for the liberation of Ireland?' As reward, he said, the Union had treated Meagher shabbily. 'Earnestly do I warn all those who are about to emigrate from Ireland against taking any part in the disastrous contention.'

Corcoran's Irish Legion would never be as hard-used as Meagher's men, and had not suffered casualties on the same scale. They were encamped that December at Fairfax Court House, and Meagher spent a number of days there, attending concerts, and being honoured by serenaders and bands. On 22 December, he had to return to Washington and then entrain to New York for Christmas with Libby. Corcoran insisted on riding the 17 or so miles to Washington with him. On the way back, riding one horse, leading another, he fell from his mount on to the icy road and suffered a head injury. When found by his staff, he was dying. There was rumour about his sobriety at the time of his accident, but his death certificate said he had died of a stroke. Meagher, still in Washington, received the news of the death and sent a telegram to Daly on 23 December. 'By this you have learned our gentle, gallant, noble friend – Colonel of the old 69th – General of the Irish Legion – is dead . . . It is a black Christmas with us.'

The same day he was told that the War Department had at last cancelled his resignation. But although he was again an active member of the Union army, no command came. It was unlikely that Meagher, the reluctant Fenian, would become commander of the thoroughly Fenian Corcoran's Legion. The *Irish American* took exception to what they saw as pro-Lincoln bias in his funeral oration for Corcoran at the Cooper Institute in New York. General Hancock himself would have been more than happy to have Meagher in his corps, but he told James Topham Brady, Meagher's friend, Charles Daly's brother-in-law, that 'the War Department seems to regard the Irish general as a communicable disease, something which ought to be isolated for the protection of other members of the organisation'.

During the opening campaign of 1864, Mitchel worked for the Ambulance Corps at Guiney's Station, but kept up correspondence with his two remaining sons. Major John Mitchel was a popular and respected figure in Charleston, commuting between the lively city and the harbour forts where he served with the 1st South Carolina Artillery. In the summer of Willy's death he had narrowly escaped death or capture himself when Fort Morris was overrun, and Fort Sumter, where he now served, was subject to constant Union bombardment. In Charleston he had made important friends, especially the Rhett family, whose patriarch, former Senator Robert Barnwell Rhett, had been a Southern champion in Washington. His son Robert Rhett junior, editor of the *Charleston Mercury*, had employed John Mitchel the elder. But Claudine Rhett, 17-year-old daughter of the former Senator, was in 1863 Major Mitchel's closest attachment.

The preoccupied Mitchel men did not realize that Jenny and her two remaining daughters were determined to join Mitchel and the boys, and live or die together. Kenyon and Martin advised Jenny, now in her early forties, against undertaking the perilous journey, but perhaps she wanted to be reassured by John Mitchel's towering certitude should news of other deaths reach her. Advised by Confederate contacts, Jenny and her two daughters went to Falmouth in Cornwall, where the blockade-running steamer *Vesta* was moored. As *Vesta* loaded a cargo of boots, hams, tea and coffee, the Mitchel women took cabins aboard.

It was a pleasant trip as far as Bermuda, but nearing the coast of North Carolina they were chased and fired upon by a flotilla which Jenny claimed was made up of some eight or ten Federal ships of war. Over several hours, as the Mitchel women waited below in the main cabin, the chase continued, and *Vesta* finally skittered round Cape Fear and into the Cape Fear River. Legs of bacon destined for the Confederate commissary were used to fuel the boilers. No sooner was *Vesta* bottled up in the Cape Fear River channel than the captain decided to run her aground, landed the passengers in coastal scrub with their small luggage and set fire to the vessel.

The women spent the night on the beach, but at last a wagon was found, and Mrs Mitchel and the two girls were carried 'half dead' into the town of Smith. After resting in that unadorned place, they caught a steamer to Wilmington, North Carolina, where Jenny Mitchel at last telegraphed her husband. She had proved again her remarkable mettle. Jenny and her daughters were able to catch a train by way of Goldsboro to Richmond, a tedious journey of over 200 miles. Mitchel wrote: 'No more destitute refugees ever came to Richmond, even in those days of *refugeeing*, than my wife and two little girls.'

Jenny found that by now Mitchel had adjusted his employment to his politics and had moved to the *Richmond Examiner*, whose editor was his friend, short, dapper, tubercular John Daniel. In quicksilver temperament, impulsiveness and lack of tact, Daniel, former US representative in Sardinia, was a soul-mate of Mitchel's. As a rabid Southern nationalist, early in the war he had sought 'an honourable scar', and had achieved one in the right arm at Mechanicsville. Now he expressed his preference by favouring Walker's dictionary over the Yankee Webster's, and maintained in the *Examiner* spellings such as 'musick', 'dyspeptick', 'politick'. But by the summer of 1864, he had lost faith in the government's will to pursue the war, lost faith in the generals, and was advocating a negotiated peace.

Mitchel had abandoned his support of Davis in June, and came to the *Examiner* as Daniel's editor. 'I am quite sensible that there is one vice in this Confederacy,' Mitchel wrote for his new paper:

one weak spot in its harness; one taint in its heart – namely, that the poorer people – the mean whites – have not the same interest in the contest which wealthy planters have. They cannot, indeed, bear the thought of being, what they call, whipped; and have fought well these three years, still hoping that the Northerns will tire of their many defeats and humiliations . . . Now they begin to see that the North is growing stronger every day, while *they* are growing weaker.

Mitchel had moved his family into a house on Fifth Street, Richmond, at the corner of Cary Street. Despite the critical demeanour of the *Examiner*, Jefferson Davis still considered him a friend and welcomed the newcomers, Jenny Mitchel and her daughters, into the Confederate White House. Gentlewomen trying to break into Richmond at such a questionable time were a novelty and an omen of hope. Mrs Mary Pegrim Anderson, wife of General Anderson, also entertained Jenny and the girls. Mrs Anderson was an admirer of Mitchel's, and applauded him for behaving very well when several English officers and journalists had visited her. He conversed 'apparently utterly unconscious of anything at all unpleasant. The Englishmen, on the contrary, were very ill at ease.'

Throughout most of the stalemated summer, as the war in Virginia returned to the country it had been fought over in 1862, the opposing armies occupied trenches in front of Petersburg. John Mitchel was on duty around Richmond with the Ambulance Committee. The city that summer was continually distracted by the Dead March being played as an officer was borne to the cemetery through the 'bowery streets'. For part of the time, James Mitchel was serving with Gordon in dangerous lines in the vicinity of Petersburg where his father could visit him. That struggle had developed into a pounding attrition, whose brand of trench warfare would be seen again half a century later, in the First World War. But then James was moved up into the Shenandoah Valley with the rest of Early's division to fight Hunter, and afterwards Sheridan, in a more conventional war of movement.

In June, to Mitchel's great pride, Major John Mitchel junior was put in command of Fort Sumter. On 20 July 1864, while Daniel and Mitchel were working in the *Examiner* office, a telegram arrived from Major-General Sam Jones, commander of the Department of South Carolina. 'Your gallant and accomplished son fell mortally wounded by the fragment of a shell about 1pm today, whilst in the faithful performance of his duty as commanding officer of Fort Sumter.' Mitchel took his hat, excused himself, and walked for 2 miles before being able to enter his house and face his wife and two daughters.

In the eleventh month of a bombardment during which the Union lobbed 43,000 shells into Sumter, Major Mitchel had mounted a parapet to persuade a sentry to do a better job of reporting the fall of Sumter's shells on Union positions at Morris Island. A mortar exploded in the air above him, lodging a fatal metal fragment in his chest and killing him almost at once. He was given a splendid military burial at the beautiful Magnolia cemetery, Charleston, with the cadets of the Citadel providing the honour guard. Claudine Rhett would keep Major Mitchel's memory green, publishing articles on him and visiting his grave every anniversary. Ultimately a committee would erect a monument, with surrounds which were a stone model of Fort Sumter.

If Mrs Jenny Mitchel ever threw up her hands in inexpressible pain at the life Mitchel had led herself and her children, we have no record of it. Mitchel himself had reached the conclusion that Jenny and the girls and he had suffered enough. He harried officials in the administration, presenting himself to Clement C. Clay, a confidant of Davis's, a former US Senator for Alabama and Confederate negotiator with the British and Canadians, and to others. He was thus able to arrange that his remaining son, James Mitchel, be now removed from the front to the staff of General Kemper, garrison commander of Richmond. Mitchel himself set out from Richmond on the Shenandoah Railroad to deliver the redeeming order to his son.

The *Examiner* meantime remained the leading critic of the manner in which the Atlanta campaign had gone. 'Those fights lost us Atlanta, and the smallness of our loss in killed and wounded proves that, by generalship alone, the enemy got possession of the city . . . The fact is, while Hood thought the bulk of the Yankee army was in his front at Atlanta, it was twenty miles in his rear, on the Macon Road. We hope he will be on the lookout for a repetition of the movement.' The situation in Georgia gave Mitchel and Daniel some small, delusional comfort. 'Our army, from all we can hear, is safe and in good condition. Sherman's army is *not* safe.'

Mitchel's former fellow prisoner Smith O'Brien was remote from the decline of the Confederacy. Still Ireland's Visitor-in-Chief, he had been in Hungary again and taken up the cause of the imprisoned Hungarian nationalist Count Teleki. In Warsaw he visited a notable Wild Goose cousin, a reactionary commander of the Tsar's troops in Poland, used to exiling and imprisoning Polish activists. These excursions profoundly tired him, but were necessary to a man for whom the concept of 'home' had grown ambiguous. His last general comment on the Irish situation, written, as were earlier such commentaries, in the form of a long letter, was thus marked by wistfulness. He grieved that the liberal Protestantism for which he had stood before 1848 no longer had a presence in a highly sectarian Ireland.

He was visiting Wales when he became very sick. In an earlier letter to his daughter Charlotte, he had complained that he was in low spirits and suffering from 'a terrible oppression of an asthmatic kind'. After refusing to call a doctor, on 18 June 1864 he died in the Penrhyn Arms Hotel at Bangor of what may have been a pneumonic heart attack, combined with complications of the liver. The *Freeman's Journal* of 20 June said that his liver disease had caused loss of appetite, depression and 'general break up of a frame naturally robust'. He was sixty-one.

The family would have preferred that the return of the body to Dublin be a private affair, and not a pretext for a national demonstration. But before dawn on the fifth day after his death, crowds greeted the ship, as did the Lord Mayor of Dublin and John Martin and Pat Smyth, now returned to Ireland. *The Times* is believed to have underestimated the crowd, putting it at 2,000, 'among whom there could not have been more than a dozen persons of respectable exterior'. The *Nation* put the assembly at 20,000 and said that as the procession passed the place where Robert Emmet was executed, men removed their hats and the pace slackened; the family would have abhorred the drawing of a connection between Smith O'Brien and Emmet. At 6.00 a.m. the coffin was placed on the train west to Limerick. The burial at Rathronan churchyard near Cahirmoyle was more sedate, presided over by two of Lucy's clergymen brothers. *The Times* of 21 June signed off on O'Brien for the moment: 'He was certainly one of the weakest, as we would fain hope he was the last, of agitators, but he was also one of the most humane and honest.' John Martin mourned him most sincerely at a meeting of the Irish National League. 'I confess that when I heard that Smith O'Brien was no more, I looked around the land, asking myself almost in despair whence and from what quarter was there likely to rise another O'Brien.'

O'Brien's friend Meagher was at the time of the great man's burial pleading with the War Department for the usual allowances made to army officers. He could not have been helped by the fact that a presidential contest was in progress, that McClellan was standing for the Democrats against Lincoln, that Samuel Barlow was Little Mac's campaign director, and that he himself acted as occasional window-dressing on McClellan's platforms. In September, at last, orders came for him to travel to Nashville, Tennessee, taking rail to Pittsburgh, and then travelling by steamers on the Ohio and Cumberland Rivers. He was to report from Nashville by telegram to Major-General William T. Sherman, who would give him an assignment.

Meagher had recently angered some by arguing that Irish immigrants were under-represented in the Union army. 'Towards the great bulk of Irishmen in the country,' he had stated, 'I frankly confess to an utter disregard, if not thorough contempt.' To be a Democrat of the Peace variety, he said, was to be a partisan in a 'selfish and conscienceless faction' which would cripple the national power. While Meagher was on the Ohio River, the *Irish American* wrote: 'Between him and the people who loved and trusted him once he has opened a gulf he can never bridge over.'

Upon Meagher's arrival that autumn in Nashville, a city on the south bank of the Cumberland River which had been captured by the Union more than two years before, he was asked by the installed Union governor to speak in the House of Representatives. This speech was copied to Northern papers and created further resentment. Though he praised the Democrat parliamentary candidate, his friend and former commander George B. McClellan, for the sake of the coming victory over rebellion he was obviously in favour of Lincoln's re-election.

Sherman, away to the south-east on his march to the sea, now delayed issuing Meagher orders. He derided Meagher as 'Mozart Hall', a nickname derived from a faction of the New York Democrat party – ironically, one associated with a desire for a peace settlement. At last General James B. Steedman in Nashville got a signal from General George Thomas in Chattanooga – 'assign him to the command of the convalescents of Fifteenth and Seventeenth Corps'. The convalescents were fellows who had already seen too much. But ordered south to Chattanooga, Meagher and his command did well at the job of guarding 70 miles of track of the Chattanooga & Knoxville Railroad to the north-east, as well as the Chattanooga & Atlanta as far south as the Union army's control extended. Meagher moved his brigades by rail and deployed them in depots along both lines with what General Steedman considered great efficiency.

Having done this guard duty for a little more than a month, Meagher was then put in command of the military district of Etowah in Tennessee, temporarily replacing Major-General Steedman himself as an acting major-general. His headquarters were at Chattanooga, and his command area ran north-east again, parallel with the mountains of eastern Tennessee – country well known to John Mitchel. Meagher had a force of 12,000 infantry, 200 guns and three regiments of cavalry. To his west, Confederate General Hood was pushing up towards Nashville with plans to go on into Kentucky, a last attempt to draw Sherman off from his rampage towards the sea. Meagher and his men were in considerable peril of being cut off from Nashville. In addition, as Meagher's former officer from the Irish Brigade, Lyons, would record, Etowah was overrun with guerrillas 'with whom he sometimes dealt with the full severity of martial law'; the War Department records no communications on the matter from Meagher, so we are left to wonder what Lyons meant by this.

But on Christmas Eve 1864, General Thomas at Nashville drove off Hood's Confederate army. The victory was greatly celebrated by the troops in Chattanooga. An officer wrote: 'We had numerous reunions amongst the officers and wound up with another great dinner party at General Meagher's at which he shone brilliantly with his Irish wit and humour.'

Steedman returned to Chattanooga in the new year, and Meagher was told that a great part of his convalescent Provisional Division of the Army of Tennessee would soon be travelling to Savannah to link with Sherman's forces. Before Meagher departed, Steedman wrote enthusiastically to him. 'I beg leave to express to you my profound regret that the fortunes of war call you from this Department.' He praised him for 'your splendid success in protecting the railroad and telegraph to Knoxville and Dalton, the steamboat transportation on the Tennessee River, the public property exposed to capture by the enemy's cavalry, and the harmony and good order maintained by you throughout the district'. Meagher was to take his troops to Nashville and embark them on the steamboats which would ship them up the Cumberland, and then eastwards along the Ohio, all the way to Pittsburgh. After some days on river boats, Meagher reached Pittsburgh, but in the meantime General Grant had expressed concern about the arrangement. 'If Meagher's command stops in New York it is feared many will desert.' Halleck ordered Meagher to bring his command to Washington instead of New York. Meagher's telegraph in reply explained that his division of 6,000 or 7,000 men were still scattered along the river, delayed on their way by ice on the Ohio. The War Department was alarmed to read the opinion of the editor of the *Cincinnati Commercial* that the troops were ill-treated and badly managed, 'shamefully deserted by drunken officers, etc. etc.' Secretary of War Stanton telegraphed Meagher for names of recalcitrant officers. But Meagher answered, enclosing letters from his Assistant Quartermaster, his Provost Marshal, and Colonel Roughton, one of his brigade commanders. Vehemently denying the accusations, all mentioned the frozen Ohio and scarcity of rail transportation.

Halleck, in Washington and in no position to know what was happening on the Ohio, signalled Grant concerning Meagher's men: 'They are in utter confusion, and he seems to be ignorant of what troops he has and where they are.' When the division had at last all arrived in Washington, the men were entrained for Annapolis, where they joined their transports. Meagher took over one of the waiting steamers in Chesapeake Bay. A transport officer, Major Scott, had an argument with him over the fact that, as Scott complained, 'he has selected a steamer for his headquarters, and directed her to be kept empty until certain troops arrive'. Halleck supported Scott: the ship should be loaded and dispatched as fast as troops arrived. On the evening of 5 February Scott delivered orders to General Meagher on board the *Ariel*, to the effect that Meagher was to deliver his command to General Palmer at New Bern, North Carolina. Scott signed off the papers: 'Copy furnished to Capt Flagg A Q M 8.30pm his Commander (Genl Meagher) being too drunk to understand anything.' While it is credible that General Meagher may have been too drunk to understand, we only have the word of one transport officer, who needed an excuse to explain transport delays. But again, Meagher's drinking was public and copious enough to shock some and to put a tool into the hands of his enemies.

By 13 February nearly all Meagher's men had arrived at Beaufort, North Carolina, and an as yet unreplaced Meagher reported with his command to General Palmer at New Bern, the large Federal garrison on the estuary of the Neuse River, amidst coastal lowlands and turpentine forests. Palmer, yet another of the West Pointers who had little time for the Irishman, described Meagher's command as 'but a mob of men in uniform'. If so, Meagher bore the blame. Had Meagher lost control, said Grant, 'it will afford a favourable pretext for doing what the service would have lost nothing by having done long ago – dismissing him'.

Six days passed before Grant signalled Halleck, 'Has General Meagher been dismissed?' The response came the same day: 'The President has not acted on Meagher. The Secretary of War thinks you had better order General Schofield to relieve and send him home.' And Schofield did it, apparently very tactfully. For steaming home from New Bern, Meagher was under the impression that he had performed the movement of his troops competently, and he clearly did not feel in any sense culpable. But he was once again faced with all the problems of 1860–1: What to do? How to make a mark? As the war wound down, he toyed with the idea of writing a biography of General Bull Sumner. In April 1865, as he still cast about him, the war ended and then, on 14 April, Lincoln was assassinated. Meagher travelled to Washington in mid-April to take part in the Honour Guard of general officers for the lying-in-state, under the Capitol dome, of a President he had served, whatever General Halleck thought, very thoroughly.

The *Richmond Examiner* was nearing the close of its war too. Everyone in Richmond seemed thin, and, like most citizens, Jenny and John could afford only the plainest and sparsest of meals. Little Daniel, proprietor of the *Examiner*, was sinking under poor diet and over-exertion, but Mitchel was still vigorous. Mrs Anderson wrote: 'When his own heart was almost broken by the deaths in battle of his two sons . . . he never stopped to bewail his afflictions, but with the Ambulance Corps in the field, or in the hospitals at home, did all he could to soothe and relieve the suffering.'

On 27 February, the *Examiner* had dissented from President Jefferson Davis's speech in the Confederate Congress, which had contained the sentiment: 'If the campaign against Richmond had resulted in success instead of failure; if we had been compelled to evacuate Richmond as well as Atlanta, the Confederacy would have remained as erect and defiant as ever.' The *Examiner* attacked 'this fatal error . . . The evacuation of Richmond would be to the loss of all respect and authority towards the Confederate Government, the disintegration of the army, and the abandonment of the scheme of an independent Southern Confederation.' Fatal errors abounded. General Lee was urging that the slaves be conscripted to Southern military service, and Mitchel went so far as to raise the blasphemous doubt as to whether Lee was 'a "good Southerner"; that is, whether he is thoroughly satisfied of the justice and beneficence of negro slavery'. As late as 24 March, he was holding out desperate hope not of British but of French intervention, quoting the French *Courrier du Dimanche*: 'We must not deceive ourselves. War with the United States is inevitable.' It was the presence of the French Emperor Maximilian in Mexico which made this delusion popular for a few days. But Grant was extending his trenches towards the capital. Lee made an attempt to split the line in two by attacking Union Fort Steedman in front of Petersburg, but the Union forts either side of Steedman ferociously held. Twenty-four hours later, U. S. Grant got his men around the southern end of the Confederate trench line. It became obvious not only that Petersburg would fall but that Richmond would need to be evacuated. In Richmond in the last days of March and in early April, men and women seemed in a trance, but not Mitchel. The *Examiner* continued to come out with a determined and almost manic air of normality. As the Confederate garrison prepared to burn the warehouses and depots on 2 April, Mitchel attended the hasty burial of his friend Daniel, who had perished of pneumonia. The eccentric newspaperman's death coincided with Richmond's last full day as a capital; he would have liked that. Mitchel faithfully produced the last wartime edition of the *Examiner*, for which he wrote the obituary of its proprietor, as Jenny yet again packed up in Cary Street. The Mitchels, carrying a few bags, evacuated Richmond on 3 April 1865, travelling with Kemper's command, including Colonel James Mitchel, south-west across the James River. Richmond was no longer serviced by the Richmond & Danville Railroad, and John and Jenny had 14 miles to walk before they reached the Confederate railhead.

A fire from the destruction of military equipment would spread throughout the city. The *Examiner* building was destroyed. On the evening of 4 April, the blazing city was occupied by Federals, and Abe Lincoln, in the last ten days of his life, came down from City Point, where he had been waiting, inspected the ruins, and sat at Jefferson Davis's desk in the Confederate White House. Grant's great army headed off Lee's retreat on 8 April, at the hamlet named Appomattox near the Richmond to Danville Railroad. The surrender would occur the next day. Having come to Danville on one of the last trains from the Confederate railhead, John and Jenny were living in a room in the crowded town. Here they heard of Lincoln's assassination and feared it would key up the extreme party in the North. Travelling with a 'deeply distressed and humiliated' Colonel James Mitchel and a few other Confederate officers, John and Jenny peaceably made their way back through Halifax County to Richmond. Mitchel's rose-tinted Confederate money was useless. 'The green is far above the red now,' he wrote in reference to Davis's ballad. But the Mitchel house remarkably still stood amidst ruins, and having settled his family there, Mitchel got straight on the train to New York, an apparently daring advance. But he had a plan: to persuade the North to resume normal relations with the South. It was as if he had expected to return to the Southern-leaning city of pre-war. But thousands of New Yorkers were dead at Rebel hands, and Meagher thought his old friend crazy to return to this city and to pursue a virulent line on all the North's plans. The display of Lincoln's body, brought across to New York from Jersey City by ferry and thence in a hearse to City Hall, where it lay in state, had not enlivened affection for the South. 'I fear,' Mitchel told a friend, 'if they once erect a gallows, it will have many victims.'

On 3 June, Mitchel was offered and took on the editorship of the *Daily News*, 'a staunch Southern newspaper which has opposed the war from the beginning'. Its premises had been saved by the draft rioters and, like only one other New York paper, had failed to fly the flag on the day peace was announced. His mother had returned in bad health from Brooklyn to her Irish home, Dromalane House, and now, to be close to work, Mitchel moved to a boarding house in Manhattan. But he had none of the humility of the vanquished. 'Of course I set myself at once to tell the truth concerning the Southern cause, to explode and expose the villainy of affecting to consider Jefferson Davis as a criminal and our Confederacy as a penitentiary offence.' He was soon in familiar strife. The *New York Times* and the *Evening Post* were 'continually raging and warring against me'.

In early June an order was made out and signed by General Grant for Mitchel's arrest. General Dix, garrison commander of New York, did his best to avoid enforcing it and even sent Mitchel futile warnings. In the end he activated the warrant, designating the place of imprisonment as Fortress Monroe, on the humid, miasmic tip of the Peninsula. Mitchel was in the *Daily News* office on 14 June, about to write a letter to his wife and children to join him in New York, when an artillery officer appeared, backed by a number of army and peace officers. Mitchel was loaded into a carriage, inside which the officer and a detective travelled with him as the wagon galloped off to the Battery. It took three days for Mitchel's steamer to make the journey. He had time to reflect, 'I suppose that I am the only person who has ever been a prisoner-of-state to the British and the American government one after the other. It is true the English Government took care to have a special Act of Parliament passed for my incarceration; but our Yankees disdain in these days to make any pretence of law at all.'

While he was in Fortress Monroe, Mrs Mary Mitchel died at Dromalane, the house they had all occupied when John was a boy.

Meagher's friend Major O'Beirne was now Special Aide to the new President, Andrew Johnson. Meagher had spoken with O'Beirne at the White House before meeting with the new President the very morning after Lincoln's assassination. With a Union Democrat for President now, Meagher was hopeful of something developing. But in conformity with General Orders number 79, on 12 May 1865 he wrote tendering the resignation of his commission, as all generals of volunteers were required to do. A card from the White House said the resignation was accepted by the President, but then a document in the National Archives reads, 'It is ordered by the President that the Communication from the War Department accepting the resignation of Brigadier General Meagher be forthwith cancelled, and that his commission as Brevet Major General be forthwith made out.' The question of whether Meagher could or could not consider himself a brevet major-general was one which would confuse friends and enemies alike.

On 20 June, he wrote an insouciant and fateful letter to his friend Major O'Beirne. First he asked 'to have my Brevet as Major General'. He could not 'help writing to you and beg you will see the President, and request him, in my name, to have it made out as soon as possible – indeed without another day's delay'. He referred to the imprisonment of Mitchel. 'If in one striking case, an Irishman is being punished for his bad conduct towards his country – in another equally striking at least, let an appropriate recognition be made of good conduct and devotion . . . Let me have the delightful satisfaction of wearing my two stars on 4th July and showing that the Government is true to Irishmen who are true to it.'

He then mentioned that he had just seen in that morning's *Tribune* that the governorship of Idaho Territory was vacant. 'Entreat the President to let me have it, and all will be forthwith right and glorious with me. Urge this at once.'

'*Let me have Idaho*,' he finally wrote boldly across the folded letter. As energetically as he sought a post, his enthusiasm for the West was not artificial. With Libby he had attended a lecture at the Cooper Institute by James Fiske, frontiersman. Fiske, evoking improbable mountains and illimitable high plains, was to lead an expedition to Montana in the coming summer. In those wholesome spaces, Meagher began to argue, the Irish could remake themselves! It is worth wondering what the widows and bereaved families of the Irish Brigade made of his new passion for the West. No officer of the brigade ever complained about it. The war had been so much longer and bloodier than anyone's imagining that any further deployment of the remnants of the old brigade was preposterous.

These remnants he led down Fifth Avenue on 4 July, wearing not his uniform but civilian clothing. At last, at the summer residence of Daniel Devlin, the ready-to-wear king, in Manhattanville, Long Island, he received the telegraph he and Libby both wanted. The President wondered whether he might accept the Military Secretaryship of Montana, a post equivalent to territorial minister of defence. Though one historian of the region would claim that two other men had already refused the offer, Meagher telegraphed Colonel William A. Browning, the presidential aide. 'Thanks to the President for the complimentary and friendly remembrance. I accept the Secretaryship of Montana. Shall proceed at once to Bannack City and Virginia City.'

He heard from O'Beirne that a young territorial governor named Edgerton was waiting in Montana for an excuse to leave the year-old territory, and Meagher's arrival would be the pretext. Meagher would therefore become not only Military Secretary of Montana but its acting governor. Late in the season, Captain Lyons saw Meagher with Libby at the Townsend house in East 23rd Street. The general sat at his desk, holding a letter he had just received, enclosing a photograph, from his son Thomas Francis in Waterford. Lyons thought the 10-year-old lad in it looked splendid, and he later remarked matter-of-factly, 'Of course, Meagher had never looked upon his face.'

A mystery lies in that 'Of course'. One wonders why a man who during the war could have been killed in one of a dozen battles did not seek to have his son brought over to the United States. Perhaps he did not wish to interrupt the boy's education. Perhaps he had an unspoken fear of confronting this new face of his guilty relationship with Catherine. About the same time Lyons said goodbye, Meagher wrote to his father an undated letter which reads dutifully, like an adult version of what a child might write from school, saying that he hoped that Montana would be a splendid enterprise and that it might enable him 'to pay you a visit in France next summer'.

Fortress Monroe, where Jefferson Davis and John Mitchel were now located, was an item of American Gothic; moat-encircled, its walls, though only 30 feet high, 95 feet thick. Within this sinister solidity, Mitchel was kept in a small, grim, whitewashed and vaulted room lit by a casemate. Low in the wall was a barred opening, which the prisoner could talk through. He had an iron bedstead and a little deal table. He was warned that he could not meet with his fellow prisoners, Mr Davis, captured in Georgia after the end of the war, and Mr Clement C. Clay, Davis's adviser. He could not have books, and was served, directly on to an unscrubbed table, with a lump of bread and a piece of cold pork.

Visited by the commandant, General Miles, the prisoner Mitchel complained that he was not informed ahead of time that he would be allowed no exercise and no books. Miles explained that these conditions were regulated by the War Department. In seeping damp, Mitchel sat up at night heaving with asthma, and the prison surgeon, Dr Craven, reported to the War Department that the Confederate newspaperman could not live long unless he was supplied with better food. From mid-August, he was allowed exercise and books and newspapers. The meals improved, and were served on a plate. Once he was permitted to face Mr Davis silently in the yard, and shake hands with him.

Mitchel spent four and a half months in prison before the combined pressure of Irish-American Democrats, Peace and Union both, and of the potent post-war Fenian movement, brought his release. On his last morning at Monroe, 30 October, before leaving, he was allowed to visit Mr Davis for a few moments, and speak to him, bent over, 'through the bars'. Mitchel wrote to Mrs Varina Davis, who was not permitted to visit her husband, that Davis was 'in morning deshabille . . . But I assure you, when he dresses to go out he looks well, steps as firmly and holds his head as high as he ever did on Capitol Square.'

On release, he was four days short of his fiftieth birthday, but in no way finished with his career as a lightning rod. He returned home to Richmond briefly to see Jenny and his children in their unmarred house, and then took train yet again to New York. Jenny noticed that he was heroically unchastened, and in New York he discussed with Richard O'Gorman and other New York attorneys the option of suing the government for permitting a violation of Habeas Corpus at his arrest. The lawyers wisely advised him to leave this matter alone.

*

Meagher was determined to get to Montana before winter, but he was to travel without a military escort. Libby would come in the following spring. His twentieth-century biographer reliably states that General Meagher's route was by rail to Atchison, Kansas, and after he declined a departing serenade offered by the local Fenians, from there on the overland coach. He chose the irksome, bruising coach because, though the Missouri was full, it could take a river steamer forty days or more to reach Fort Benton, which was still nearly 200 miles' ride from the seat of government, Virginia City. Apparently, on 6 September, he reached Denver and was given a reception; and a similar reception awaited him amongst the Irish mining community of Salt Lake City. He suffered from atrophy of the muscles, though the splendid mountains and vast openness of the country diverted him. From Salt Lake he turned due north, through little Mormon settlements like Ogden, to raw Pocatello in Idaho and so into Montana. In a telegram to Seward, he indicated that travel was slow and uncertain, due to Indian troubles. It took seventeen days from Salt Lake to reach Bannack City, Montana, and cost $600.

Arriving in Bannack City's clapboard main street, he was met by Montana's young Ivy League governor, Sidney Edgerton, all packed to depart. Edgerton shook hands, passed over a valise of territorial papers and left by the same coach Meagher had arrived in. Meagher rode with some of the territorial staff on over difficult Badger Pass and the Ruby Range to reach Virginia City, a township held in a bowl of mountains on which the snow did not fully melt in summer.

Since all this seems accurately to describe the route Meagher took to Montana, we are left wondering about an article he would write under the *nom de plume* of Colonel Cornelius O'Keefe, a circumstantial account of a journey from Oregon into Montana. This would be published posthumously in *Harper's* and was certainly specific. Meagher/O'Keefe described reaching Portland by steamer, taking a coach to Walla Walla, and travelling up the Columbia into what is now southern Manitoba in Canada. Then down the Pend d'Oreille River and the north fork of the Clark, through northern Idaho, and so into the valleys of Montana on the western side of the Rockies.

The article described Pend d'Oreille City, Idaho Territory, in intense detail – 'standing on a picturesque slope', with 'its store, billiards saloon, hotel and half a dozen private residences'. So that if Meagher did not visit it on the way into Montana, he must have spent time there on his territorial rides. From Cabinet Landing, Meagher had O'Keefe travelling with a Flathead half-breed and a former army quartermaster down the Clark fork towards the Flathead Reservation at St Ignatius, founded by

Father de Smet and run by the Jesuits. On the trail, O'Keefe claimed to have met Kootenais, Pend d'Oreilles and Flatheads, who 'boasted joyously that they'd never stained their hand with the blood of the Pale Faces'. Meagher/O'Keefe and his quartermaster and Flathead guide encountered in the town of Plains the first sight of a phenomenon which would be a plague to Governor Meagher. Vigilantes had strung up a man.

O'Keefe, crossing the Jocko, came to the Jesuit-run Flathead Indian Reservation. Ahead, suddenly, the enormous wall of the Rockies rose. The narrator claimed that the priests 'have done more to reconcile the Indians to our government and progress than all the agents, superintendents, traders and interpreters that ever drew pay from Pennsylvania Avenue'. Significantly, he saw the plush Flathead Reservation with its 12,000 souls as 'an extravagant franchise' which should be made available to white settlers. The Indians 'virtually do not hold, and most certainly do not turn to advantage, one-sixteenth of it'. The former defender of the rights of Irish peasants and tenants felt little sympathy for the idea that the Flathead might have uses for their remaining land.

The narrative of Colonel O'Keefe, which was intended to be continued in further issues of *Harper's*, came to a close here. But whichever way Meagher got to Virginia City, in October 1865 he was commendably seated at the modest gubernatorial desk in his upstairs office in Virginia City, as the glacial winter began to penetrate the canyons, and he wrote with something close to accuracy to his former officer and now newspaperman Lyons, of 'my being *Acting Governor* of the richest territory of the *Union*. I want you, like a good fellow, to have this announced in the *Herald*.'

23

Glorio, Glorio, to the Bold Fenian Men

> It is worthy of observation with what regular gradations sedition and treason have been declining in respectability and prestige ever since 1798 – then noblemen were the traitors – O'Connell had many men of some position associated with him . . . Phoenixism and Ribbonism were lower still. But Fenianism is even lower than Phoenixism.
>
> S. L. Anderson's report to Lord Naas

By the time Fort Sumter was fired on in the spring of 1861, the population of Ireland had dropped by death and emigration to less than six million, on the way down to the figure of 5,200,000 that would be counted in the census of 1881. In the altered landscape, there were only a third as many 1–5-acre farms as there had been in 1841. Throughout the 1850s, Munster's population, already lowered by the Famine, dropped by a further one in five, and much of that loss was through the great harbour of migration at Cobh, renamed Queenstown in 1849 for some seventy years. Ulster's population fell by a further one in twenty, and this was again on top of a 16 per cent decline during the Famine.

Throughout the early 1860s there were enough young Irishmen who believed the inequities which created these losses must be addressed in Ireland itself, not through some oblique struggle under heroic Meagher and Corcoran in Virginia. Typical was a Fenian named John Kenealy, who had grown up in dairy-cattle country near Newmarket in north-west Cork. As Kenealy admitted later in life, the Irish Fenian movement 'knew the disruption of the Union would strengthen England, make her hold on Ireland stronger, and check liberty in the world over'. But the most direct duty was the forcible creation of a just republic in Ireland, not the saving of a threatened one in the Americas.

Kenealy's background was similar to that of much of the Fenian leadership, who often came from the class that typically generated members of the Catholic clergy. He was the second son of a dairy farmer, James Kenealy. A Kenealy clan of six families were thickly settled in cabins and farmhouses on a townland called Glenlara, 950 acres in extent, 460 acres of which they rented conjointly from the Earl of Cork, as their forebears had been doing since 1603. As well as the potato gardens, everyone kept dairy cattle, which they could graze on the slopes of the nearby Mullaghareirk Mountains.

Many of Kenealy's relatives had garrulous tendencies, liked drink and ballads, could be easily disabled by melancholy, were notorious faction-fighters at fairs such as Mallow in Cork and Listowel in Kerry, to which they took their butter for sale. They esteemed themselves also as hurlers and footballers. John Kenealy, however, possessed a restrained cast of mind. He had been less than ten years old when the blight manifested itself in 1845. Though North Cork was not the unspeakable catastrophe that West Cork was, by late 1846 there were already private soup kitchens in Kanturk, the local Poor Law union for Kenealy's family. By 1847 nearly all small farms of less than 2 acres had lost their cows and pigs. That summer, in the baronies of Duhallow and Fermoy, 10,000 were employed on the public works at an average wage of 10 pence per day, and though John Kenealy is sparing in his recollections of childhood, members of his larger family were probably amongst them. In the Kanturk district in 1847–8, forty out of every hundred people were receiving Poor Law relief. In 1848–9, the time of greatest need for North Cork, as it was for Esther Larkin in East Galway, the number rose close to six out of every ten. If 10-year-old Kenealy was not one of them, he knew plenty of their number, and observed their shame. Once the Gregory or Quarter-Acre Clause came into operation in the summer of 1847, those women whose husbands were still at home trying to hold the land were turned away from the Mallow workhouses by many Poor Law guardians. Destitute tenants had to give up everything first, and their cabins were knocked down once they were admitted to the workhouses. Perhaps the guardians of the neighbouring Kanturk Poor Law union were more merciful – the relief figures would suggest it – but the countryside was rife with instances of smallholders willing to perish rather than give up soil on which they had expended lime from the quarries along the Listowel road, kelp brought in by cart or man-hauled from the Kerry coast, years of care and love.

These were powerless people; even a slightly better-off farmer like James Kenealy lacked leverage. A Fenian called John Denieffe described a visit he had made at that time to Kenmare in Kerry, an area not far from Kenealy's home ground, and the gothic tyranny exercised by Lord Lansdowne and his agent. 'If anyone should go to a wake, no matter how great a friend, or near the relative, you must first get the agent's consent. Tenants were not permitted to marry without his sanction.' This brand of overlordship was not unknown in the landscape of Kenealy's childhood.

At fourteen or fifteen years of age, John would have heard his father and turbulent uncles raging against the failures of the Tenant Rights Movement, which had held out the hope of secure tenure, rent arbitration and compensation for any improvement on the rented land, particularly to farming tenants like James and Hannah Kenealy. John Sadleir, a leader of the movement elected to the Commons, had formed a Tipperary joint-stock bank, set up to buy back large estates for small tenants, and tens of thousands of Munster small farmers had invested in it. Bought off by Lord Aberdeen in 1853 with the Cabinet post of Lord of the Treasury, Sadleir also embezzled £1,250,000, threatening James Kenealy with ruin and bringing it to others. So John Kenealy learned at an early age that constitutional stratagems were always brought down by corruption.

In Newmarket's National school, he no doubt participated in the sort of political catechism witnesses reported having heard recited by classes in republican areas of Ireland.

Master: For what crime was John Mitchel sent to Bermuda by the Saxon government?

Boys: For his love of Ireland; and for his noble and brave attempt to save her from starvation, degradation, misery and slavery.

Master: When John Mitchel comes back to Ireland, what will he do?

Boys: He will make Ireland a nation once again.

Kenealy was one of those Irish autodidacts not utterly uncommon amongst marginally prosperous farmers' sons. He went to Cork City in late adolescence and escaped for ever the drudgery of farming which befell his elder brother Daniel, by finding work in the fabric and clothing business at a company named the Queen's Old Castle, or Fitzgibbon's. By the age of twenty years John had somehow met the Fenian chief, James Stephens. One of the factors which attracted him to Fenianism, said Kenealy, was Stephens's motto, *Silent Action*: 'he would not tolerate any member going on the public platform to talk politics'. This embargo suited Kenealy, who had observed that Ireland was to its own ruin a land of cheap talk.

As for the delicate-framed, balding Stephens, he had learned his radicalism in Paris, after escaping Ballingary, as a member of the International Workingmen's Association of which Karl Marx was also an enthusiastic member. Yet there was an intermittent and strange conservatism in him. He would at one stage propose Marshal MacMahon, the French general of Irish origins, as a possible king of Ireland. He advocated presidencies for life for the Irish Republic, and would not be averse to envisaging one for himself. Stephens and his lieutenant Thomas Clarke Luby, a man then in his mid-thirties, had crossed from France to England in 1856 with the strategy of liberating Ireland by means of republican revolution in England itself. Though they found much discontent in the industrial cities, Britain, victorious in the Crimea, was in an expansive state of hope and self-confidence. Stephens now applied himself more directly to Ireland. He had some modest savings from his years of teaching English in Paris, and he and Luby began a 3,000-mile walking reconnaissance of Ireland, a long march from which he derived the nickname 'the Wandering Hawk', *An Seabhac Siubhalach*, or *Shooks*. He had visited veterans of the '48 uprising, including Smith O'Brien at Cahirmoyle. Some of the '48 leaders introduced him to local Ribbonmen, who were seeking a national structure, an indication in itself that Ribbon crimes such as the one committed by Hugh Larkin had a dimension of politics. On his wanderings he proved susceptible to fairly innocent but high-blown romantic attachments to young women. But, above all, he assessed how a decade had changed Ireland. Few of the bourgeoisie and nobility, so prominent in Young Ireland, were any longer in favour of achieving a republic by physical force. There were few equivalents to Meagher, Thomas Davis, Kevin O'Doherty, and certainly there was no Smith O'Brien. But the young men of the lower classes, he found, the clerks, artisans, schoolteachers, Irishmen serving in the British army, were ready for a new republican enterprise.

Stephens had been promised that substantial money for a new body would come from the United States. He did in time receive $400 from a New York group named the Emmet Monument Association, of which Michael Doheny was a founder, and so initiated in 1858 the oath-bound Irish Revolutionary Brotherhood, soon to be renamed the Irish Republican Brotherhood (IRB), or – popularly – the Fenians. The American Fenians were content with a pledge, but in Ireland an oath was needed which competed with the oath of loyalty to the queen, taken by all holders of public office.

In 1860 John Kenealy had participated in a remarkable test of the intentions of the British government. Lord John Russell defended in the British Parliament the right of the Italian people to choose their own form of government. Kenealy and other young men set up a petition for an Irish plebiscite and manned tables outside parish churches on Sundays. In the end, with over a million signatures, it was taken to England and ignored by government. 'But it afforded a great opportunity of bringing men together publicly without attracting the attention of the Government, and it enabled active workers to recruit and spread the work of the organization.'

Kenealy's elevation to the post of lace purchaser for the Queen's Old Castle made him a suitable Fenian. Stephens used commercial travellers to carry coded instructions for Fenian circles in Ireland, Scotland and England. His trips were to Dublin, Nottingham, Manchester, Liverpool, London, and regional towns. He often conscientiously travelled by train at night to make up time spent with members of the Irish Republican

Brotherhood amongst the Irish of England and Scotland. Within Ireland, the early carefully planned meetings of the relatively small, secure IRB were held in National reading-rooms in the principal towns and cities. In Cork itself, Kenealy lived in employees' dormitories, sharing rooms with a friend, and this domestic closeness favoured political talk and the cautious spread of Fenianism.

Only two persons were to be present when the Irish Republican Brotherhood oath was administered. A Bible was never used, because its bulk precluded it. Catholic and Protestant generally swore on a small pocket-size prayer book. But Kenealy was concerned that growing recruitment brought in its train an amount of sloppiness. By the last year of the war in America, the IRB had spread to almost every town and hamlet in Ireland, and the caution which went into early enlistments became impossible. Nonetheless the brotherhood remained organised for security in divisions, or 'circles'. The commanding officer of a circle was known as A, a rank equivalent to colonel. Each A had nine Bs or captains, and each B, nine Cs or sergeants. Finally, each C had nine Ds. The use of *nines* was based on the significance of the number in the mythology of the *Fianna*.

The growth of the organisation demanded the appointment of officers to arrange details and preserve discipline nationally. Kenealy's rank was that of a staff level A working for Stephens. 'In Cork City,' the Fenian John Devoy would later write, 'the chief organiser all looked up to was John Kenealy . . . Although the system of County Centers did not exist in the old Organization, John Kenealy practically exercised all the functions of that office for Cork County. He was an even-tempered man with a judicial mind and fine judgement, and was highly respected by everybody.'

Because of police surveillance and British garrisons, urban opportunities for the military training of Fenians were limited. Yet citified Fenians nonetheless tended to believe themselves the core of the movement. Young John O'Leary, a bourgeois Fenian, warned that 1848 showed peasants did not make good revolutionaries, and it would be better to recruit Orangemen than Ribbonmen. Michael Davitt, a clever young man from Mayo, was aware that there was a divide between rural and city Fenians. Local land struggles of the sort which normally concerned Ribbonmen were more important to rural Fenians than the dream of a republic. Davitt would later say with a little contempt for Fenian priorities that landlords enjoyed a decade of peace while the Fenians were educating 'peasantry and working class in the principles of Wolfe Tone and Emmet . . . This, perhaps, accounts for the fact that from the year 1858 to that of 1870, these same landlords succeeded in evicting close upon fifteen thousand families from homes and holdings.'

*

The majority of Fenians, with such notable exceptions as John O'Leary and Thomas Clarke Luby, were Catholics. But they were not great admirers of Dr Cullen, Catholic Archbishop of Dublin. In 1864, Cullen became a founding patron of the National Association, designed to attract young men away from radical Fenianism. Kenealy complained that Dublin Castle was happy to see the constitutional agitators at work in the National Association. 'The British Government simply enjoyed these harmless vapourings, and the vanity of the professional patriot was tickled.'

In the meantime, Cullen wanted Fenians denied the sacraments. The meaning of a papal document dealing with secret societies, *Quo Graviora*, issued by the Vatican in 1826, figured prominently in all arguments on whether priests could give absolution in the confessional to Fenian youths. There were two Dominicans 'and a Spartan Vincentian' (a priest of the Vincentian Order) to whom Cork Fenians could turn for confession and absolution. Dr Keane, Bishop of Cloyne, also offered the consciences of the Fenians some assistance; Kenealy described him as 'the most patriotic bishop in Ireland at that time'. However the Church thought of Fenians, John O'Leary, who came from the Protestant professional and land-owning class, found meeting a number of Cork Fenians a spiritually exhilarating experience. He met Kenealy, 'to be well known to me afterwards in Portland' (that is, Portland prison on England's south coast). The Cork Fenians 'afforded me a fair example of the manner of young men I was to meet otherwise afterwards'.

O'Leary – later to be immortalised in W. B. Yeats's dismal refrain on 1913: 'Romantic Ireland's dead and gone,/ It's with O'Leary in the grave' – was himself Cork-born. He had attended the newly opened Queen's College, Cork, and had inherited a modest share of a large property. By the time of his father's death in 1849, he was a veteran of two insurrections, that of the Young Irelanders at Ballingarry in 1848, and an ill-starred attack by Fintan Lalor's men on a police barracks in the autumn of 1849. A professional medical student, he spent thirteen years attending lectures in Cork, Galway, Dublin, London and Paris. His beloved brother Arthur had died of tuberculosis in 1861, and during his mourning he took to Fenianism, and his sister Ellen began writing Fenian verse.

Because Fenians were lambasted by what Kenealy called 'the regular press', James Stephens started a newspaper of his own. On 28 November 1863, the first issue of the *Irish People* appeared. It had a remarkable staff. John O'Leary was editor. The highly accomplished literary men Thomas Clarke Luby and Charles J. Kickham were the chief writers, and the former West Cork grocer O'Donovan Rossa was manager. From the start one of the *Irish People*'s particular targets was 'felon-setters', those –

clerics or not – who betrayed, by deliberate indiscretion or condemnations from pulpits, the names and opinions of certain Fenians. O'Leary also published the names of those who harried newsagents out of stocking the *Irish People*. 'A friend has just informed me that he heard from the agent here that after this week he should discontinue selling your paper,' wrote a correspondent to the *Irish People*. 'For this kindness you are indebted to the parish priest, the Rev. John Fitzpatrick, formerly Parish Priest of Skibbereen, over which he presided in the famine years with what benefit to himself is well-known.' When a West Cork Fenian named Con Keane was temporarily arrested, Father Collins was burned in effigy in Skibbereen. Though some priests praised the *Irish People* – 'I have been a constant reader . . . and I solemnly assert that I have never read in it a single sentence that . . . was opposed either to sound doctrine or morality' – others warned that the employers of those who read or possessed the paper would be informed and asked to dismiss the men or women in question. The paper itself condemned 'another kind of priest . . . who in the Confessional gives it as penance to refrain from reading the *Irish People*, and even from entering a shop where it is sold'.

Charles Kickham, who wrote most of the anti-clerical, anti-Cullen material for the *Irish People*, on the grounds that he could get away with it when a Protestant such as Luby could not, was a self-taught man whose sight and hearing had been impaired by an accidental explosion of gunpowder he was playing with when he was thirteen. He was hard on all clerical denunciations of the movement. 'We notice that Bishop Duggan (of Chicago), by way of proving that he was right in denouncing the Fenians, told his flock that the society had been denounced by Dr Cullen; while Dr Cullen, by way of strengthening his case against the devoted Fenians, told his flock that they were denounced by Bishop Duggan.' 'Hunger and despair', Kickham wrote in one article, 'sit by the poor man's hearth . . . What must be the feelings of this man's heart when he thinks that the dignitaries of his church, who know not wanton nakedness themselves, are the allies of his tyrant?' Cardinal Cullen struck back against the *Irish People* with what Kickham called 'a furlong or two of Pastoral'. But many former Young Irelanders, including John Martin and Pat Smyth, members of the National Association, approved of the cardinal's cannonade against the Fenians.

As with Gavan Duffy's *Nation*, poetry was considered by the *Irish People* to be both a humanising and a political tool, and as with the *Nation*, women poets were the stars. Amongst the contributors was the teenage Miss Fanny Parnell, and O'Leary's sister Ellen. Miss Irwin of Clonakilty, who, fresh from convent school, was to become Mrs O'Donovan Rossa, also wrote well and, like Eva earlier, saw her beloved as an incarnation of the revolution:

O, but my love is fair to see!
And Erin his fairness is all to thee
Strong with a lion's strength is he,
And gentle with doveling's gentle is he,
My love and thine, oh, Erin.

Eva of the *Nation*, now living in the remote Australian colony of Queensland with her surgeon husband, Kevin Izod O'Doherty, also sent a verse:

Oh! Ye dead, – ye well beloved dead!
Great souls, fond hearts, that were once linked with mine,
Across the gulf that yawns between us dread,
I fling the longings that invite a sign
  – a faint, faint shadow of your presence.

But though women were welcomed as the poetic strain of the *Irish People*, their role as defined by Luby was limited. 'The influence of woman appears in its grandest form, when a true and noble housewife endeavours to sustain and cheer, in the dark hour of trial and discouragement, the hopes and faith of her husband.'

In 1863, 'Shooks', the Brotherhood's Captain James Stephens, a man nearing forty years of age, married a charming young woman named Miss Hopper. Unlike other Fenians, Kenealy would not leave behind any written opinion. But some bitterly criticised him and O'Leary said that some Fenians felt he had married beneath him, 'Miss Hopper being the daughter of a tailor in a small way of business. Most of the men were furious democrats in theory, but not without a certain leaven of that aristocratic feeling which, I think, lies . . . in the breasts of most Irishmen.'

Under the name of Mr Herbert, Stephens rented Fairfield House in Sandymount, the Dublin seaside suburb. In the end, the marriage did not seem to alienate either the Irish provinces or the Americans as much as did Stephens's increasingly dictatorial manner. Though he sometimes chastised them, many of the American Fenian Brotherhood were doing all they could to supply the men at home in Ireland with the sinews of war. At a Fenian fair in Chicago in the summer of 1863, organised by an as yet informal Fenian Sisterhood, an auction of Wolfe Tone and Emmet memorabilia was held to feed the Irish organisation. The San Francisco Fenians contributed a full gold brick and a few silver ones to the IRB.

During his own journey to the United States and the Union army, Stephens said, 'In the small town of Peoria, $1455 was subscribed by some fifty or sixty men I met there at a single meeting . . . Quincy, where all are poor men, $505 were subscribed.' The irregularly paid 90th Illinois contributed $507. Stephens's air would always be that he had, by right of Ireland's exclusive and eminent grievances, the final authority over all Fenian sums raised in the new world, and some would challenge that.

Though William West, the American consul, was issuing free tickets to young Irishmen willing to join the Union army, Fenians in Ireland were not tempted. Kenealy drilled with his men in glens outside Cork City, depending on former British army NCOs for guidance. Rifles were only occasionally seen, sometimes an old pike, more commonly staves. Fenian rolls recognised the fact that a particular man possessed a rifle or pistol by placing an inverted V beside his name; a horizontal stroke denoted a pike; and a zero indicated that the IRB man in question had no weapons at all. Now, with the end of the American Civil War in the spring of 1865, Stephens raised the expectation that the Irish Republican Brotherhood would be able to take to the field in Ireland in the fall of that year.

John O'Mahony sent two American envoys, grandly named 'plenipotentiaries', to Ireland to report on the state of readiness. The first envoy was an Illinois politician, P. W. Dunne of Peoria, who wanted the Fenians in America and Ireland either to take immediate action or to disband. The other member of the mission was the editor of the *Irish American*, P. J. Meehan. Meehan carried documents – including a letter of introduction from John O'Mahony, addressed to 'James Stephens, CEIRB' (chief executive, IRB), a comprehensive table of organisation of the IRB including the names of centres and As, and a draft for £500 ($2,000). All Meehan's papers carried the address of the then New York headquarters of the Fenian Brotherhood, 22 Dwayne Street. O'Donovan Rossa himself, manager of the *Irish People*, was on the same ship as the envoys, returning to Ireland after a visit to New York:

> Going into the Cove of Cork, I told Mr Meehan that . . . it should be well for him to give those papers he had to his sister, or to Mrs Dunne, who accompanied us. He told me that they were all right, that he had them sewed up between the soles of one of his carpet slippers . . . Pursuant to the caution given him, and to his own promptings, he thought it better not to have those papers in any pocket of his, he fastened them with a pin inside the waistband of his drawers.The upshot was that on landing in Kingstown, Meehan lost his

table of organisation document in the lavatories at Kings Bridge railway station, in the train into Dublin, or else at Westland Row station in Dublin.

Dunne and Meehan rushed into Denieffe's tailor's shop in the city and reported the loss. Denieffe and Meehan went to Westland Row station, questioned the old man on the luggage wagon and searched the coach. The Meehan documents had in fact already been found near the Kingstown railway station by a messenger boy, who turned them over to a woman in the telegraph department. She in turn took them to a local police inspector. These papers, O'Mahony said, 'put the bloodhounds on the track of the Irish Revolutionary leaders'. They gave conclusive proof of the connection between the US Fenian Brotherhood and the IRB, and provided a comprehensive table of organisation. Stephens also believed that 'the loss of these documents was the immediate occasion of the arrests in Ireland'. Kenealy remembered that, in Denieffe's upper room, 'There was a private meeting held where the matter was discussed, and where it was proposed to do away with Meehan, but Stephens would not allow it without full proof'. Some believed Meehan had jettisoned the documents out of fear.

Kenealy had already met the envoys when their ship first put into Cobh, and had not been impressed. Before leaving Cobh, Dunne had told him that the Fenian Brotherhood would land 30,000 men. Kenealy said he 'had been for a little while accustomed to American exaggeration, so I gave the matter no thought'.

The Fenians hoped that the government, if indeed they now had Meehan's lost papers, would not take any action on them until after the general election in a few months' time. Lord Palmerston's Liberals would surely desire to avoid outraging the Irish population until then. Meanwhile, the Fenians expected to be under considerable surveillance, though even they would have been astounded by the extent of what was reported to Dublin Castle or Whitehall, by police, agents and the public. 'My Lord,' wrote a concerned loyalist in Cork, 'will you send troops and protect women and children if you do not care for the men of this place. A very bad and seditious house is in a street from the Mall close to Parliament Bridge. Surely you do not want an Indian mutiny or a Cawnpore tragedy.' An agent named Thomas Saunders told the Metropolitan Police that he had attended a Fenian drill in a public house in Newburgh Street, Dublin. Then he had gone to Bride Street, where thirty or fifty Fenians were assembled in a hall. Some drilled with rifles, others sparred, others trained with swords and some played cards.

A Constable Meagher from Roscommon told the superintendent of the Metropolitan Police: 'From what I could learn from several persons both in Athlone and here I fear that the subordinates of the Midland Great Western Railway are all more or less "Fenians" or sympathisers with the movement.' A characteristic report from Mitchelstown, Cork, shows how intimately observed a society Ireland was:

A number of strangers on a two-horse car from Fermoy visited this town and put up at Miss Jane Russell's Public House, amongst who were three men of the 4th Dragoons from Fermoy in uniform with a few in civilian clothing supposed to be Officer's servants – the only persons of the party I could learn the names of are a Mr Edward Sheehan of Fermoy and John Casey (*The Galtee Boy* in the *Irish People* newspaper) . . . they intended to hold a meeting on the Galtee Mountains, but got some hint of the police being there on the lookout in plainclothes.

Patrick Phelan, second head constable, likewise reported how he drank in Cork City with an American who told him that

he was the first to receive the late General Corcoran in his arms, after his fall from his horse, which killed him. He bestowed more praises on Corcoran than Napoleon ever deserved . . . This man is about 26 years of age, five feet nine inches in height. Black hair . . . He is of most respectable appearance and gentlemanly conduct and demeanour, dressed in a black frockcoat, light tweed trousers, and vest, a massive gold chain to his watch.

Even in America Fenians were subject to surveillance. Sub-Inspector Doyle spent two years there, working with the very effective British consul in New York, Archibald. And from the Continent, the British consul at Saint-Nazaire warned the Secretary of State for Foreign Affairs that a British steamer, the *Collima*, of Glasgow, had entered Saint-Nazaire three times in August and September and shipped 13,000 shells to Liverpool from the foundry of M. Voucy, who had supplied shells to the Confederacy during the American Civil War. Amongst this welter of disturbing news, however, a reassuring report *did* reach Dublin Castle on the matter of the supposedly secret papal decree issued to Irish and American bishops that *Fenianos non esse inquietandos* ('Fenians are not to be disturbed'). An agent reported that his investigations showed that such a decree had never been published by the Vatican, and was merely a sectarian rumour.

More crucially for the future of the Fenians, in Dublin Superintendent Ryan of the Metropolitan Police had in place an extremely handy informer, Pierce Nagle, a worker at the *Irish People*. Nagle reported that Hugh Brophy, a building contractor and intimate of Stephens, was importing rifles from Sheffield.

*

Kenealy made his last buying trip for the Queen's Old Castle in early September 1865. Coming back to Dublin from England, he was met at the boat and told that 'the Captain wanted to see him'. Kenealy travelled out to Stephens's house in Sandymount, where Stephens, now a little portly, handed him a telegram from Cork. It read, 'Tell John not to return the same way.'

After thinking a moment, Stephens cried, 'Why this refers to John who went to New York a couple of weeks ago,' a courier to O'Mahony. Stephens now gave Kenealy 'final instructions' – they included orders to appoint deputy As who would keep rank-and-file Fenians ready for the coming revolt. Stephens's last words to Kenealy were: 'There will be great changes before we meet again, if indeed we ever do.'

Two nights later, wrote Kenealy, 'The *Irish People* was seized, Luby, O'Leary, Rossa and others were arrested in Dublin, and the same night Brian Dillon, John Lynch, myself and two or three others were arrested in Cork.' By the time Meehan stepped on board a steamer for Philadelphia, to attend the Fenian Brotherhood Convention of Philadelphia, the leadership of the IRB was already in prison. These arrests signalled the onset of a catastrophic period of reckless Fenian endeavour and failure, yet of gestures potent enough to set the tone of Anglo-Irish discourse for the remainder of the nineteenth and twentieth centuries.

Kenealy gave a highly detailed account of his last two days as a free man in Cork. 'When I returned I gave the other centers the information, and each one called a meeting of his Bs and told them they were to elect one, in case of necessity, to take the place of the Center. Fearing that these might be arrested also, we had three to fill the places as the others were removed.' The night before the arrests, J. J. Geary, a Fenian publican, thirty years of age, frequently mentioned in police reports, asked Kenealy not to sleep in the Mill Street dormitory accommodation the Queen's Old Castle provided for its staff, 'as I would most certainly be arrested . . . But for several reasons I would not change.' One reason was that Stephens had told his As (staff officers) not to go into hiding. Kenealy reflected later, 'With the same prospects . . . though I have tasted something of British prisons, I would do the same now.'

On the evening of 15 September 1865, Kenealy left his office with another employee of the Queen's Old Castle, James Barrett, and attended to the last of the Fenian visits Stephens had asked of him. He and Barrett caught the local train from Cork City to Queenstown (Cobh) and met a party of senior Cobh Fenians in the upper room of a hotel. Returned to the city by train, and on their way to their dormitory, Kenealy and his friend went into a corner 'cigar divan', or smoking pub, to have some cheese and porter. The proprietor of the pub, a liberal Orangeman from the north of Ireland, took him aside and said, 'Don't go to your room tonight – let James go; but you go and sleep with some one of your friends tonight.'

Kenealy and Barrett went back briefly to Kenealy's room; his roommate, Scanlon, another buyer, was absent in England. Again, Kenealy did not feel justified in fleeing or going into hiding. Leaving him, Barrett exchanged 'a rather sad good-night', and went to his own room on a higher floor. At two in the morning, Kenealy's room was all at once filled by armed police led by Mr O'Neill, Chief Constable of Cork. Asked for the key of a trunk in the corner, Kenealy told a sergeant that that trunk belonged to Mr Scanlon. He pointed to Scanlon's own trunk and claimed it as his own. Kenealy's real trunk contained a gift from John O'Mahony, 'a very fine revolver'.

Sympathetic Head Constable O'Neill told a policeman who tried to handcuff Kenealy to desist, remarked that it was raining a little and that the prisoner had 'better put on an overcoat'. Kenealy told the senior policeman that it was upstairs in a friend's room. The Head Constable said, 'Go and get it, Mr Kenealy.' Kenealy went to the fourth floor, knocked on James Barrett's door, asked him for his overcoat, handed him the key of his (Kenealy's) trunk, and asked him to extract the revolver as soon as the police took him away. That arranged, Kenealy went back downstairs in Barrett's coat. On reaching the street, the Head Constable asked Kenealy quietly if he had any papers or documents he did not wish to be seen. 'If I had he would destroy them.' Kenealy did find a sample home-made Fenian cartridge in his pocket, and dropped it on the pavement in the dark. 'It is only fair', Kenealy would write long after, 'to say that many of the police have good hearts.'

Now conducted through the columned gateway and under the portcullis of the county gaol of Cork, on his way along a corridor he passed cells from which newly arrested Cork Fenians, John Lynch and Brian Dillon, called out to him. At daylight the prisoners were taken to the square in front of the gaol and arranged in single file, a policeman standing by each one. On either side of this party, there was a long file armed with rifles. 'Among those marching with the rifles, I noticed two or three glancing slyly in our direction. One, I knew well, did on occasion act as drill master – and not one of them gave information.' The prisoners were then taken a little way through the streets to the city gaol near the court and locked in separate cells.

The police had raided overnight a blacksmith's shop in Cork kept by a man named Heggarty, who had fled to England to escape arrest. They discovered on the hearthstone a recess in the ground, 'wherein were two

The Famine remnant: natives of Donegal photographed in the 1870s.

The stock of Irish convicts:
Tom Larkin, born in the Monaro in 1844 of Hugh Larkin and Mary Shields, photographed with his daughter, Minnie Mae Larkin, Sydney, *c.* 1920.

Eviction: THE JUSTIFYING MEMORY

Planning the operation.

Moving in: a man shelters against the wall and behind the baulk, in expectation of thrown boiling water from the *vanithee*, the woman of the house.

The ram breaches the wall.

Smith O'Brien's statue:
the first nationalist monument raised by the Dublin Corporation.

Captain Thomas Francis Meagher,
K Company, 69th New York State Militia, in Zouave's uniform, 1861.

Corcoran directs 'The Gallant Charge of the "69th"' on the rebel batteries at the Battle of Bull Run, 21 July 1861.

General Meagher at the Battle of Fair Oaks, 1 June 1862. 'The bayonet charge of the Irish Brigade, at this battle, was the most stubborn, sanguinary and bloody of modern times.'

The Battle of Fredericksburg, 13 December 1862.
'This battle shows with what undaunted courage the lion-hearted Army of the Potomac always meets its foes.'

The Army of the Potomac marching through the 'wilderness' near Chancellorsville, 2 May 1863. Sketched by Edwin Forbes.

Kevin Izod O'Doherty:
Eva's beloved, at mid-life.

The Fenian headquarters move
uptown to Union Square, New York.

The Fenian and Land War class. Dunlavin, County Wicklow.

The court martial of a Fenian soldier.

Cork Fenians, including John Kenealy, moved into the county gaol to guarantee a rural jury (p. 428).

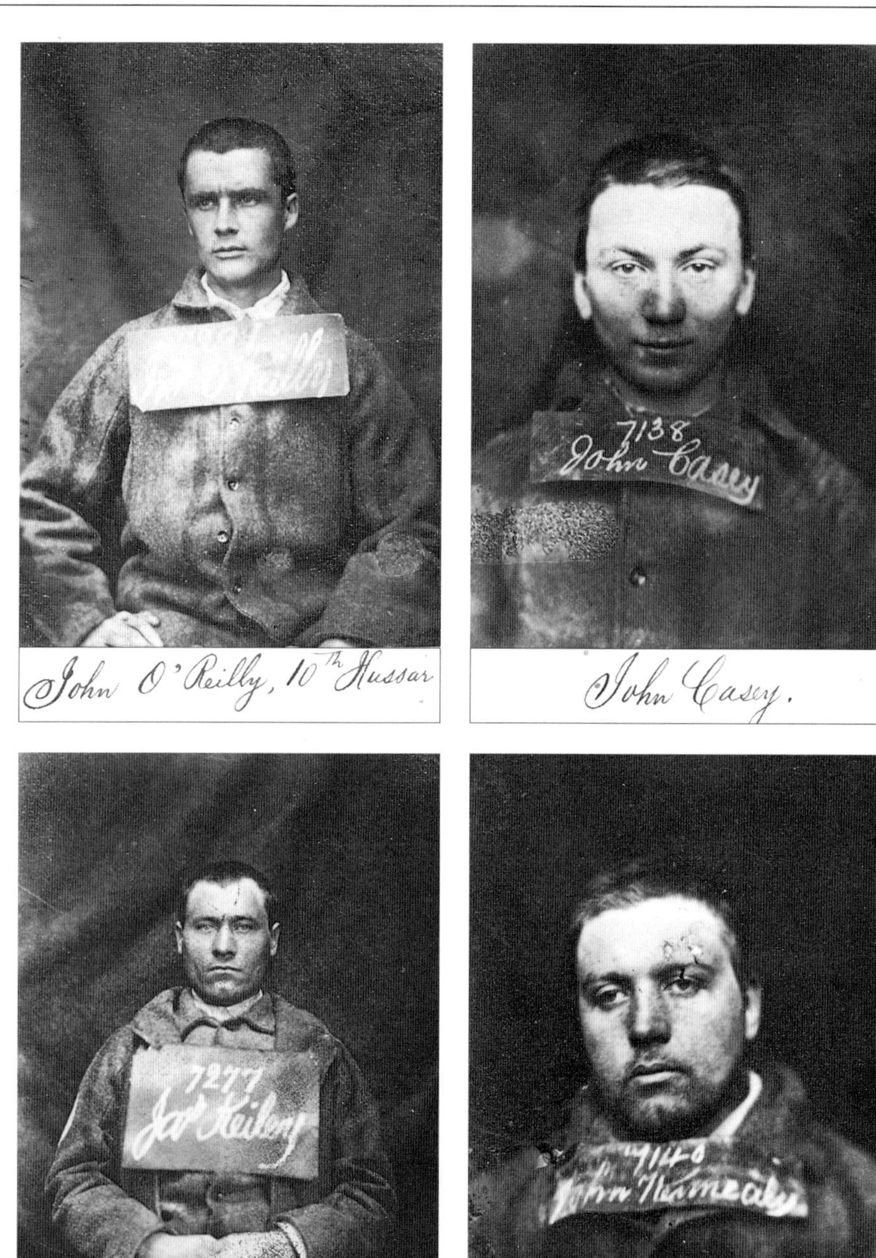

Mugshots:
(*Clockwise*) John Boyle O'Reilly, unabashed; bright-eyed John Casey; wary John Kenealy; James Keilley, the man they left behind.

pikes and a ring-locked bayonet . . . The barb-pointed, horizontal spike across one of the pikes is intended to catch the bridles of cavalry.' Heggarty would later testify that these pikes had been commissioned by John Kenealy.

The mass of Fenians were still free. Small, intense John Devoy was at work as the new Chief Organiser for the British army. Devoy thus first met Boyle O'Reilly in October 1865, a meeting between two men who would ultimately have enormous impact on the Irish abroad. For the moment, both men were under some pressure – there was a warrant out for Devoy's arrest. But they were exultant as well, expecting the transmuting word from Stephens.

O'Reilly's regiment was stationed at Ireland Bridge Barracks, now Collins Barracks, on the western outskirts of Dublin, and Devoy was taken there by a young Fenian veterinary surgeon. Admitted by Fenian sentries, they were led then to where the 10th Hussars were quartered in tents in one of the enormous barrack squares which characterised garrisoned Ireland. O'Reilly was cinching his saddle to get ready to ride to Dublin Castle with a dispatch from General Rose, commander of British forces in Ireland. Devoy remembered O'Reilly as an exceptional soldier, handsome, muscular, intelligent, with penetrating dark eyes. Though only twenty years old he was a very active Fenian sub-recruiter in an army in which more than thirty out of every hundred soldiers were Irish. Rather like American troops in Vietnam who wore the peace sign on their helmets, O'Reilly had embroidered Fenian devices on the underside of his saddlecloth and in the lining of his military overcoat. From that time to the following February, when they would be arrested, Devoy saw O'Reilly nearly every day, encouraging him to widen his organisation into other regiments.

A special commission was appointed in December by Dublin Castle to try the Fenians in Dublin and Cork. In the intervening three months, the spirit of the prisoners remained excellent. Many warders carried information from one cell to another, and from the outside to the inside. What was most stimulating was news of the skilful rescue from Richmond prison of the Captain, James Stephens, in late November. On 11 November Stephens had been tracked by police to his home at Sandymount, where he lived under an assumed name, and arrested. The plan for his rescue, devised by John Devoy and Captain Thomas J. Kelly, an American military man then in Ireland, was communicated to the prisoner by a medical orderly named John Breslin, who also passed on to Devoy a soap imprint of the key to Stephens's cell block. On the night of 24 November, Breslin opened Stephens's cell, gave him the forged key, and directed him out of his block to the wall, beyond which Kelly and Devoy awaited him.

He was taken to a secure house, and the Fenian leadership, particularly the American soldiers, urged him to raise the rebellion. 'Stephens plainly did not want to fight,' wrote Denieffe, '... in fact, I concluded then and there that Stephens's work was done, and his usefulness ended on that night of November 26, 1865.' A Miss Butler, a couturier, helped shelter Stephens during his months at large. When she came under suspicion of the police, she lost the patronage, said Denieffe, of society, 'including the respectable *loyal* Shoneens'.

The men in prison lacked the information that left Denieffe and the American officers so disillusioned. They also knew nothing of a dangerous split which had occurred in the American Fenian Brotherhood. The American Fenian Senate, voted into place to ensure more democracy in the movement, had authorised the issue of Irish Republic Bonds, which Irish Americans could buy now and redeem after an Irish republic was established. The issue was to be made under the authority of a Fenian bond agent named Patrick Keenan. But Keenan resigned, and without the Senate's approval, O'Mahony told the printing company to engrave his own signature on the bonds. An aspect of the dispute was that O'Mahony's salary as president was $2,000, and as bond agent he was entitled to an extra $1,200 a year. O'Mahony accused the Senate of being an illegal assembly. But led by the Manhattan dry-goods merchant William Roberts, the Senate dismissed him from office for calumnies against Stephens, the chief executive of the Irish Republic, and against the Senate and membership of the Fenian Brotherhood.

O'Mahony still had supporters, and they retained the new Fenian Brotherhood headquarters in the Moffatt Mansion in Union Square and barred entry to the Senate and its supporters. General Thomas W. Sweeny, who had lost his right arm in the Mexican War and who had also served in the Civil War, gave legitimacy to the Senate wing by becoming Roberts's War Secretary. So, O'Mahony summoned his own Fenian Congress in New York and invited the schismatics of the Senate to appear. General Sweeny did so, to make a futile appeal for unity. Meagher – in Montana – must have been pleased to have evaded the bitterness of this split, and the blandishments both sides might have held out to him.

By the end of January, while Irish Fenians began to fill up the gaols of Ireland and England, Sweeny and Roberts were on the road, visiting every large centre of Irish population in the United States. The general's plan was a departure from O'Mahony's. It was to 'make a warlike demonstration on Ireland by way of Canada'. General Sweeny 'declared his willingness to submit that plan to any six general officers of the American

Army, and if any of the six decided against its feasibility, then he was willing to adopt any other calculated to bring about the independence of his native land'.

Whatever the mixture of nobility, faction and venality in the movement, American Fenianism had begun to look sufficiently farcical for the late Mr Lincoln's favourite humorist, Artemus Ward, to raise an easy laugh from it. 'The Finians', went one of his sketches, 'conveened in our town the other night, and took steps toord freein Ireland.' The meeting described in Ward's sketch was of course attended by an amusing gaggle of non-Irish politicians who wanted to be voted in on the Democrat ticket for county clerk and dog-catcher. 'There's two parties – O'Mahonys and Mc O'Roberts. One thinks the best way is to go over to Canady and establish an Irish republic there, kindly permittin' the Canadians to pay the expenses of that sweet Boon; and the other wants to sail direck for Dublin Bay . . . But there's one pint on which both sides agree – that's the Funs.' Funds. Both sides actively sought them.

The special commission appointed by Dublin Castle to judge the Fenians in Dublin and Cork was headed by Solicitor-General William Keogh, of the betrayers of the Tenant Rights Movement, and J. D. Fitzgerald – both Catholics. 'To the outside world, especially the countries in sympathy with Ireland,' wrote Kenealy, 'this might have seemed fair on the part of the Government.' But Kenealy and the others knew that Billy Keogh had a few years before sent brothers named McCormack to the scaffold in Tipperary, 'when it was well known they were innocent of the crime charged'. The government charged the Fenians with Treason-Felony, under the same statute which had been rushed through Parliament in two days for the purpose of convicting John Mitchel in 1848. In Green Street courthouse in Dublin, the approaches blocked off by dragoons at either end of what was a narrow thoroughfare, Thomas Clarke Luby was the first to be placed on trial before Judges Keogh and Fitzgerald. He was defended, as the Young Irelanders had been, by Isaac Butt, QC.

It was through Luby that the government tried to establish the conspiracy: if they got him, they got the rest. Prosecution was made easier by documents seized in the *People* office, including 'Manuscripts Selected by reason of their Seditious Tendency'. One anonymous manuscript seized conveys their general character:

> We're slaves my boys and slaves we'll be
> Till maddened by our chains
> We'll raise the flag of liberty
> And muster on the plains

And sweep the Saxon from our shore
As once we did the Dane . . .

Luby was found guilty and sentenced to twenty years' penal servitude. John O'Leary got the same. 'I am a working man,' he declared, 'and if a man is found guilty of high treason, earning his honest livelihood in his own country, I just put it forward as a sample, and as a proof to those that are to come after me to live in this country.' For Charles Kickham, the hearing-impaired editorial writer for the *Irish People*, the charge was read 'through an acoustic instrument', and he was found guilty. O'Donovan Rossa, the fire-eating Cork man, was brought forward, made an 8-hour speech in defence of the Fenian position, and was given a life sentence. John Boyle O'Reilly served with the detachment of hussars who guarded the courtroom in Green Street for the trial of O'Donovan Rossa.

The first batch of Dublin Fenians having now been dealt with, the judges took the train to Cork. As in Dublin, the outskirts of the city were patrolled by cavalry, and field-guns rolled into town. The Cork men were transferred from the city to the county gaol again. This enabled the court to empanel a county jury of landowners.

Kenealy saw his friends sent out of their cells one by one, and marched through a passageway into the nearby county court. John Lynch, Brian Dillon (a polite young man with whose family Kenealy sometimes took tea), Charles Underwood O'Connell and Tom Duggan were all convicted and sentenced to ten years' penal servitude. A few others received 5- or 7-year sentences. Rumours reached Kenealy in his cell as he awaited his own turn that 'some persons were using influence to keep my trial back and allow me out on bail with two or three others who were not brought to trial'. Even friendly warders told him the government feared acquittal in his case, since there was little documentary evidence to prove that he had proposed that the Crown should be deprived of its sovereignty over Ireland.

Christmas, marked for Kenealy by small gifts from his family in Glenlara, passed less pleasantly and in greater silence than had been the rule for O'Brien, Meagher and the other Young Irelanders in Richmond seventeen years before. The first day of the new year of 1866 brought a quick end to the rumours Kenealy might be released. On 1 January, he came through the tunnel and rose up the steps to the dock to stand trial. There were two chief witnesses against him – Pierce Nagle, a copy-reader of the *Irish People* who had been used against other accused men in Dublin and Cork, and a man named Warner. In the course of his own Fenian initiation, Warner, a former soldier, testified, he had learned the passwords and signs. One of the passwords was 'Speed', and 'the sign given by placing the thumb on the back of the hand . . . Geary's public house was the place of resort for Fenians, and if a stranger was there the way he would ascertain whether or not he was a brother was to ask him if he was a "Speed".' Warner admitted to the defence that he had himself sworn in fifty Fenians between late 1864 and July 1865, but that, he said, was merely to give himself good entrée into the Fenian organisation. He had made a pretence of taking the Fenian oath and becoming a Catholic just to expose the Fenians! He had already testified in Dillon's trial that he had seen Kenealy chair a Fenian meeting at Geary's pub-grocery.

The next day Nagle the informer appeared. He had by now been required to repeat information many times and to face the contempt of defence lawyers and the accused. Now, edgy, he asked Kenealy's junior counsel, Dowse, 'Do you think that I am a dog, that you speak to me in this manner?' 'Oh, no,' said Dowse, 'God forbid I should compare you to such a faithful animal.' 'Well,' retorted Nagle, 'there are some decent men I have not identified, but now I won't spare one of them.' Nagle identified Kenealy as being in the habit of visiting the *Irish People* office on his journeys through Dublin.

A letter was presented by the prosecution, written by Brian Dillon to O'Donovan Rossa and declaring that 'John K' would meet Stephens at the Italian Hotel, Cork. When Stephens had visited Cork in April 1865, the prosecution claimed, Kenealy was in a group greeting him and Mrs Stephens at Mrs Thompson's boarding-house, Myrtle Hill Terrace. Mrs Thompson, the Myrtle Hill boarding-house keeper, could not, when called to the stand, swear that Kenealy was at her place – 'He is changed since I saw him. He is stouter.'

Timothy Heggarty, the Cork blacksmith, who had been caught in England, deposed that he made a sample pike for 3 shillings and 6 pence for Kenealy to take to Dublin. Butt told Heggarty, 'You didn't say so in your initial evidence after your English arrest, but only on the boat home.' But the prosecution also depended on two letters of Kenealy's – one to Luby and the other to Rossa. The letter to Rossa thanked him for a pair of opera glasses, and the prosecution wrongly argued that opera glasses were code for arms. The court called the cashier of the Queen's Old Castle to identify the writing, but since there was no signature, the cashier would not say that the handwriting was Kenealy's. 'Even Judge Fitzgerald took a hand by threatening him with imprisonment for contempt if he did not make some more definite answers . . . The cashier's name was Alex O'Leary, and when Habeas Corpus was suspended in 1866, he was punished with 18 months in prison.'

Next the court put in the stand Mr Fitzgibbon himself, the proprietor of the Queen's Old Castle, a man who had promoted the young Kenealy to his senior buying post. According to the *Cork Examiner*, he identified Kenealy's handwriting. But according to Kenealy himself, Fitzgibbon loyally indicated that he too could not swear to it. The Attorney-General asked, 'Is it possible, Mr Fitzgibbon, that you cannot recognize the handwriting of a young man on whose demands you have paid out thousands of pounds?'

'I never paid attention to his writing. I looked only at the signature . . . These letters are only signed *John*.'

Mr Butt was about to address the jury when the court ordered a recess of half an hour, and Kenealy was taken down to the holding cell under the court. One of the defence lawyers visited him and said that the court had offered to release him if he pleaded guilty. They wanted to wrap up the session. Given that two reputable men had refused to identify Kenealy's writing, a guilty plea with a suspended sentence might be the best the commission could hope for.

Kenealy refused: 'almost every crime on the calendar, including capital traitors to our country, was charged in the indictment. That was too much to swallow – we could not plead guilty.' The judges, Keogh and Fitzgerald, were obviously disappointed to get this answer. They 'both stared at me when returning to their seats'. In his summing-up, Butt declared that the jury had at the bar 'a young man who had hitherto occupied a respectable position and borne a good character, and on whose honourable exertions others were dependent'. Kenealy's Glenlara family, which included five younger brothers and sisters as well as the older brother Daniel, were clearly not prosperous, if they had ever been, and were happy to receive remittances from Cork. The guilt of the prisoner, said Butt, 'can only be established by very refined criticism, putting together a word here and there, denoting an act done at one time with an act done at another time of trifling importance'. Butt questioned whether Kenealy was even in Cork at the time Stephens was in the city. As to Kenealy's visits to the *Irish People*, Luby was a scholar. Of course Kenealy would want to visit him. At the times Kenealy called in, the newspaper was being distributed legally through Her Majesty's mails.

There was no quick verdict: 'when the jury was out a couple of hours, rumours were circulated that there was a disagreement'. The young prisoner could see many hopeful faces around the crowded courtroom. While the jury was still out, two American officers were also brought into the dock area to await the fixing of bonds – they were to be released on bail on the condition that they left the British Isles. Some of these men would in fact simply alter their base of operations to England. 'We talked to each other freely, and one of the gentlemen assured me that even if I were guilty, my imprisonment would not last long. The Fenians would take Canada, in some incredibly short time, and would, of course, demand our release.' Obviously Kenealy had by now heard the idea of an invasion of Canada. He observed aloud that, 'After they take Canada, they will go to New Zealand and help the Maoris. Ireland can wait.' One of the Americans told Kenealy, 'I don't blame you for feeling badly, but my presence here shows what I wanted.' Their bonds fixed, after a warm handshake the Americans left.

The jury returned and the foreman told the bench that there was a disagreement, and that one juror did not believe a word of the evidence. 'Then Judge Fitzgerald said he could not conceive how an intelligent jury could have any difficulty in arriving at a verdict. It was plain that the ambiguous expressions used in the letters could have only one meaning, and he continued to impress on the jury that it was their duty to convict.' The jury returned soon after and not surprisingly found Kenealy guilty on all counts. Asked if he had anything to say before sentencing, he declared, 'I am sure, from the charge of Your Lordship, the jury could find no other verdict than has been found. The verdict against me has been found by the means by which political convictions have been always obtained in this country.' Justice Fitzgerald told Kenealy the verdict was fair. 'When you say you have been convicted by perjured and corrupted evidence . . . you seem entirely to ignore that there were, under your own hand, three letters which to every reasoning mind carried the inference that you were a party to this conspiracy.' He confessed to a reluctance to treat Kenealy harshly, but, 'You at least should have understood the folly and criminality of a course which had it been for twenty-four hours temporarily successful, the probability is that this very city in which we are administering justice would have been first in ruin and bloodshed.'

He was sentenced to ten years.

The Cork Fenians were brought up to the capital in trains with barred and painted windows, and put in Mountjoy prison. Here they were photographed – becoming pioneers of the mug shot, each holding across his chest a board that was hung by string around his neck, on which his name and number were written in chalk. In his mug shot Kenealy looked perhaps more lost than he was. Even so, no one here was happy. The cells in Mountjoy were 10 feet by 7 and contained a water closet, table, stool and a hammock-bed 'made like a coffin'. Each prisoner was handed 1 pound's weight of oakum to be picked during the first day of imprisonment.

O'Donovan Rossa, Luby, O'Leary and others had already arrived in England, and had been marched through Yuletide streets into Pentonville prison near Euston station in London. That name, Pentonville, was a penal byword, designed to reduce physical contact, conversation and other stimulation between prisoners and the outside world. Roofless cells were supervised by felt-slippered wardens patrolling on catwalks above. The prisoners were not to move about their cells by day, but were to sit picking oakum. In the spirit of a penal system which favoured dull rather than sharp sounds, a wooden clacker was used to signal exercise and lock-up times. The diet was designed to remove all the excitement of variety. Bread, 4 ounces of meat and 1 pound of potatoes, and 1 pint of porridge was the daily menu. In every cell, Rossa tells us, craving for food was intense. The Catholics began by refusing meat on Fridays, but even a strong man such as Rossa soon repented of that.

On the first working day, as the prisoners were marched out, John O'Leary whispered to Rossa, 'This is hell.' ' "Yes," said I, "hell." ' Even at the weekly bath, barriers of sheet-iron were erected down the middle of the washing trough to prevent conversation. Exercise was taken in a large yard in what was called 'the coach-wheel'. 'It had fifty spokes, and on every spoke was a wall ten feet high. Between every two of these walls one of us was confined.' O'Donovan Rossa took to throwing a small piece of slate he had found in his cell over the barrier of the coach-wheel with a few words written on it. Once he got the slate back with return greetings from a fellow prisoner.

Rossa was also able to mutter to someone in the straight line of prisoners during Mass in the chapel, 'Where is Stephens? Are they going to have a fight? How many of ye came?' He learned that Stephens had escaped, and that the men kneeling behind included Kickham, Brophy, the newly arrived Kenealy, and an Irish American, William Roantree. In the exercise yard the following week he happened to be in the compartment next to Kenealy, who threw him a message written on slate. 'When I had gotten the latest news they had brought from Ireland, our "telegraphs" focused on our cold and hunger.' John Lynch, a Cork associate of Kenealy's, whispered to Rossa one morning, 'Rossa, the cold is killing me.' Indeed Lynch would be sent to Woking hospital and within a few months was dead.

One morning at six o'clock, the twenty-four accumulated Fenians arrested in '65, including John Kenealy, were taken from their Pentonville cells, connected by chains, and transported by van through London streets to a railway station. They arrived by train at Portland station, on the south coast of England, and were loaded into vans which took them through the town to Portland prison on its coastal heights. It was another penitentiary on the Pentonville model, inside whose gates the politicals were lodged in basement cells which had not been occupied before, each cell 7 by 3½ feet. The walls between cells were of corrugated iron.

Fenian prisoners were put to work in the wash-house – O'Donovan Rossa congratulated himself on having seized the job of working the water pump. Next they were required to work in the Portland quarry, in a valley 300 yards from the main prison. Here, on great stone benches in a large pit, in isolation from other prisoners, they worked with chisel and mallet at blocks or 'nobblers' of building stone. Occasionally they pushed the blocks on the trolleyway, or were set to clean the privies in the punishment cells.

O'Donovan Rossa's wife was at last due to visit. Among his fellow prisoners was Martin Carey, an East Galway Fenian, who had a hand injured in a quarry accident; coming from Eyrecourt, Carey would certainly in childhood have heard the tragic tale of Hugh Larkin. He asked permission to talk to Mrs O'Donovan so that she could take a message to his ailing mother. Permission was refused, and the visit itself was tyrannically supervised. 'I went back to work with a heart heavier than ever,' said Rossa. Soon after, Moore, a Dublin Fenian pike-maker and his next-door cellmate, heard from the governor of the prison that Rossa had been writing to Mrs Moore. Even the prisoners held a secret court of inquiry, during which O'Donovan was required to explain himself. He had written, he told them, not to Moore's young wife Kate but to his mother, Mrs Mary Moore, and had made a notation in the corner of the envelope, 'For Mrs O'D'. Outraged at the suggestion of improper behaviour, O'Donovan Rossa achieved an interview with the governor and accused him of having mischievously misinformed Moore. For this frankness he was thrown into a darkened cell. He insisted on reporting the governor's malice to the director of prisons, but every time the director visited Portland, Rossa was conveniently found guilty of some misdemeanour and locked in disciplinary cells. Indeed a warder named Jones had companionably warned a group of Fenians in the quarry that, as the director of prisons was about to visit, he had been ordered to report seven or eight of them for misdemeanours. The following day, on cue, Luby, Kenealy, Keane, O'Connor and O'Donovan Rossa were charged with having illicitly taken a blanket from their cots to wrap around their bodies under their clothing.

In the spring of 1866, O' Donovan Rossa was sent back to London, to Millbank prison. The Fenians he left in Portland were still confident. What was of comfort to Kenealy and other sentenced Fenians was that the structure was still intact. The Captain was out there somewhere. Many Fenians were still at work.

If Kenealy was representative of civilian Fenians, John Boyle O'Reilly, whose career was remarkable, was characteristic of Fenians within the

British army. O'Reilly had been born on 28 June 1844 in the tower of Dowth Castle, which served as a National school. This was an area of Druidic burial tumuli, such as the now famous Newgrange, heroic mounds which bespoke Beltane Night, the pagan Night of Blackness before St Patrick's arrival. But for O'Reilly's father, William David O'Reilly, a reader of the *Nation*, Beltane Night still prevailed in ill-governed Ireland. The kingly hill of Tara, consecrated by a lost Croppy battle during the 1798 uprising and site of a monster meeting, was within a walk of O'Reilly's birthplace. The Boyne, river of national loss for some, of rational triumph for others, ran sweetly to the north.

John Boyle was the second of three sons and had five sisters. His parents had the resources to be bookish, to subscribe to the *Nation* and to write and admire verse. A later friend of O'Reilly's claimed the boy was a thoroughly accomplished writer by the age of twelve. By 1855, at the age of eleven, O'Reilly was capable enough to join the staff of the Drogheda *Argus* as an indentured print-monkey, copyboy and writer. He had replaced his elder brother Will, whose health had not stood up to the work, but for whom the *Argus* had paid a £50 premium to the family. When John Boyle O'Reilly was fifteen, the proprietor of the *Argus* died, and the family suggested O'Reilly go across the Irish Sea to Preston, Lancashire.

O'Reilly worked in Preston for four years at the local newspaper, the *Guardian*, living with his uncle James and aunt Cissy in Deepdale Road, and serving as an NCO in the local militia, the 11th Lancashire Volunteer Rifles. Although admirers would suggest that this early service had a subversive intent, there is no evidence.

He was nineteen when in March 1863 his father wrote asking him to come back home and find work on an Irish paper. His mother was missing him. O'Reilly at nineteen years was the sort of yearning young man who tried to combine in one body the athlete, the poet and the rebel. Yet he did not join an Irish paper. For whatever reason, he joined the elite 10th Hussars, the Prince of Wales' Own. It has been suggested that his was a seditious enlistment. It may equally at first have meant a lack of journalistic opportunity. In any case, he was certainly a Fenian soon thereafter, even as he transformed himself into a distinguished member of Troop D, and became the regimental boxing champion.

Such elegant regiments as the 10th Hussars were targets for the Fenian recruiters, such as eccentric Patrick or Pagan O'Leary, an ex-seminarian and Mexican War veteran, who believed literally in Tír na n-Og, the Land of the Ever Young, inhabited by all the heroes of Ireland. When Pagan was arrested, an equally vivid figure, William Roantree, a handsome, 2-revolver-packing veteran of General Walker's filibustering, and later of the US Navy, took over. He recruited amongst garrisons from Dublin to Cork, Waterford to Derry. At a word from the Captain, Stephens, these men, carrying their arms with them, would desert the British army and join the civil Fenians in an unstoppable rebellion.

But Roantree, himself a victim of Meehan's loss of documents, was arrested in September 1865. He was replaced by a young man named John Devoy, for whom there was a warrant out at the time of his first meeting with Trooper O'Reilly. Indeed Devoy had something of a headquarters in Clare Lane, in Peter Curran's public house, not far from Dublin's Merrion Square. These were seriously managed premises – there was a stress on sobriety amongst Fenians, and Devoy tried to create an ethos of temperance. At Curran's in early 1866, when some Fenian trials had already been concluded, Devoy introduced O'Reilly and others to a recently arrived, stylish, mustachioed man named John McCafferty, who had been a Confederate cavalry officer with Morgan's raiders in the Civil War. McCafferty had at one stage taken a detachment of his men behind Union lines, captured an ammunition dump, loaded it on barges and brought his booty down the Mississippi raked by fire from Federal batteries. He argued from his Civil War experience that swords were ornamental, but revolvers counted. McCafferty dismissed the skill of Fenian Martin Hogan, a renowned swordsman of the 5th Dragoon Guards, who had with one cleave of his sabre cut in two an iron bar.

In good humour, the Irish argued for the sword or the revolver, while awaiting the all-clarifying signal from Stephens, still in hiding in Dublin. No one doubted that within weeks or at most months Stephens would walk through Dublin as the President of the Irish Republic. But they needed orders soon. John Devoy was already hiding twenty men of the 87th Regiment who had come to Ireland on Christmas leave from Portsmouth, and soldiers were every day walking away from the army to hide and await the imminent uprising. A sergeant of engineers named O'Brien, home on leave from Woolwich, put in front of Devoy a radical plan for blowing up Woolwich Arsenal. Stephens rejected with abhorrence the proposition of bringing terror to England. But the concept had been released into the air.

John Boyle O'Reilly, ready for the signal, had divided his enlistees into two Fenian troops, and acquired the key of an unused postern gate, through which he could take his squad on a moment's notice out of barracks to join a revolution. 'The signal never came,' Devoy complained, 'and all his and other men's risks and sacrifices were thrown away through incompetent and nerveless leadership.'

O'Reilly was looking out of the barrack windows of Ireland Bridge, Dublin, on the afternoon of 12 February 1866 when he saw one of his fellow conspirators arrested and led to the guardhouse. He went through the soldierly motions, but was himself put under arrest within forty-eight hours. As he was led across the barrack yard, his commanding officer, Colonel Valentine Baker, met him, shook his fist in his face, and said: 'Damn you, O'Reilly, you've ruined the finest regiment in the service!'

O'Reilly and other Fenian soldiers were placed in Arbor Hill military prison on Dublin's north side. O'Reilly claimed to have been put through a session of threats and blows from a muscular provost sergeant named Dellworth. But the expectation of imminent uprising sustained him. Others have confessed, O'Reilly was told, so why can't you? How do you think we knew to arrest you? As he was taken back to his cell, the old warden, a retired soldier, murmured, 'You better do as he says, O'Reilly. And damn ye, I'd like to choke you with my own hands if you do.'

Devoy was arrested in Pillsworth's public house in James's Street on 22 February 1866. In severe anguish, some soldiers now yielded information. The risk of mass execution for treason or, in other cases, desertion, was a prospect likely to panic men with wives and young children. O'Reilly's fellow prisoners in grey Arbor Hill included Colour Sergeant Charles McCarthy, Privates Patrick Keating and James Wilson of the 5th Dragoon Guards, Private Michael Harrington of the 61st Foot, and Sergeant Thomas Darragh of the 2nd Queen's: veteran soldiers with distinguished martial careers. Thomas Darragh was a veteran near to middle age, a Fenian, a Protestant, and also a member of the Delgany Orange Lodge. In the 2nd Queen's he had spent from 1844 to 1859 in various forts in South Africa, and had then gone with his regiment to Hong Kong before being shipped back to Dublin. Avuncular Michael Harrington had fought in nearly every action of the Punjab campaign of 1848, winning a medal and two clasps for bravery. When the Indian mutiny broke out in 1857 the 61st was stationed at Cawnpore, focus of the mutiny by Indian soldiers. Harrington distinguished himself in the desperate fighting that followed, and once the rebellious Indian sepoys were crushed he was decorated again. By the time of his arrest he had nearly twenty years' service. The prisoner James Wilson had served for seven years in the Bombay Artillery and travelled at various times in America, India and Syria. He had re-enlisted in the 5th Dragoon Guards, and was sworn into the IRB in 1864.

The leader of them all, James Stephens, remained in hiding until March 1866, when with the help of Fenian port officials he escaped with his wife to France. Miss Ellen O'Leary, sister to the already sentenced John O'Leary, was in Paris to greet him, and she later told Denieffe that although she herself sent money to assist the prisoners, 'No financial assistance came from Stephens . . . and according to Eddie O'Leary, John

O'Leary's younger brother, who was in Paris at the time, it required two cabs to take their baggage to the hotel.'

Rainy spring came to Arbor Hill's dismal yards, yet still, each day, the military Fenians who had kept faith expected to hear the onset of rebellion beyond the walls. On 27 June 1866, however, the day before his twenty-second birthday, with nothing having developed, O'Reilly's trial began in the mess room of the 85th Regiment at the Royal Barracks. The charge against him was that he had come to a knowledge of the intended mutiny of Her Majesty's forces in Ireland and had failed to give information on the 'said intended mutiny' to his commanding officer. The president of the 15-officer court martial was the colonel of the 5th Dragoon Guards, and the prosecutor Captain Whelan of the 8th Regiment. O'Reilly was advised by counsel, Mr O'Loghlen, to plead not guilty. The first witness against him, Lance-Corporal Fitzgerald of his own 10th Hussars, reported on a Fenian conversation between Devoy, O'Reilly and himself in Pillsworth's public house. The second witness was a less willing one, Private McDonald of the 10th Hussars. McDonald bravely denied there had been any Fenian conversations at Pillsworth's. He was so careful not to remember anything that the president of the court, Colonel Sawyer, was moved to remark, 'Public houses must be mortal slow places according to your account.'

The next witness, Private Denny, gave more conventional evidence, including that, at Hoey's in Bridgeport Street, O'Reilly had tried to swear him into the Fenians. O'Reilly believed Sergeant Dellworth had got to Denny and turned him with threats of violence. It was more than possible, after the Irish evasions and gallantries of earlier soldier witnesses, that counsel for O'Reilly could pass off all Denny's evidence as circumstantial. But Private Patrick Foley of the 5th Dragoon Guards, the man Devoy would mention as the only thoroughgoing betrayer, now appeared. Foley said that at Barkley's public house O'Reilly's conversation had been directly on electing a president when Ireland became a free republic. At two other pubs, he had heard explicit Fenian utterances from Trooper O'Reilly. 'I reported to my colonel in February the subject of the conversation,' said Foley. On cross-examination, Foley admitted, 'I took the Fenian oath. I did not call God to witness.'

The president of the court stressed to his panel of officers that 'although you may feel very great suspicion of the prisoner's guilt yet if you're not satisfied that the charge is proved . . . no amount of suspicion will justify conviction'. The court was then cleared, and the result not known until officially promulgated at the Horse Guards in London. On 9 July 1866, formal sentence of death was passed on some of the military prisoners – McCarthy, Keating, Darragh, Chambers – but not yet O'Reilly. Some days passed again before O'Reilly was taken before the reconvened court and his death sentence was read to him. This was a serious business, to confront execution at the age of twenty-two, with summer well advanced and no sign of deliverance. He faced it with an exceptional maturity. It was soulless routine which sapped his spirit, rather than such arresting and absolute possibilities as execution.

The same day, O'Reilly was told the sentence had been commuted to life imprisonment. In all, sixteen military Fenians had been condemned to death and had their sentences commuted to life imprisonment. A number of others received lighter sentences. Seven of the men sentenced to death, however, had deserted their posts, walking away in uniform and bearing their arms. These were to have the letter 'D' dug with an awl into the flesh above their hearts, and the wound treated with indelible ink so that it would always blackly declare their desertion.

A penal eternity lay ahead of O'Reilly, a young man bursting with imagery, political passion, restless energy, and the usual hormones. It was possible to be an imprisoned poet, but, given no paper, he was reduced to scratching lines of verse on the wall with a piece of slate. At least one compelling military rite interrupted the tedium. On the afternoon of Monday 3 September, in the parade square of the Royal Barracks, Dublin, in the presence of the 5th Dragoon Guards, the 92nd Highlanders, and three other infantry units – a complement of at least 3,500 men – O'Reilly and other Fenian soldiers were paraded bareheaded. The 'Rogue's March' was played as the Fenians made their transit of infamy across the square. In the middle of the drill ground, each was halted to listen to the reading of his sentence, to be stripped of his military uniform, reduced to his underwear, and ordered to pick up convict clothing which lay on the ground. The drums played a bare, dull, condemnatory tattoo as the prisoners were escorted off the square under guard to be driven to Mountjoy prison on the north side of town by the Royal Canal. Many years later, one of the informers, probably Foley, approached in Boston a man he had betrayed, the prosperous and rescued O'Reilly, and confessed that his life had become intolerable; he pleaded for money, and was given an amount on condition that he remove himself from Boston. But such powerful gestures were beyond imagining at the moment.

The stay at Mountjoy was brief. The administration did not want these men in Ireland. Chained to a friend, Corporal Chambers, O'Reilly was, like civilian Fenians, shipped across the Irish Sea by steamer. Put on a train with barred and painted windows, he was taken to Euston station in London, and then marched along Euston Road, where the locals had become accustomed to seeing chained convicts proceeding eastwards to Pentonville prison. Later O'Reilly and other Fenian soldiers were transferred to another London prison, Millbank, on the site where the Tate Gallery now stands. Here they found some of the civilian Fenians, and much emotional energy was spent on trying to make contact under a regime of silence and isolation. O'Reilly was able to extract a nail from his three-plank bed, and used it to write poetry. One morning an unknown benefactor threw a copy of the *Imitation of Christ*, the mystical work by Thomas à Kempis, through the iron bars of the door. It was the sort of unpietistic, graphic, absolutist work which appealed to O'Reilly.

Then, in early winter 1866, he was taken from his cell, chained to other Fenians, marched through the streets and transferred in the usual barred railway carriage to Devon. Here his string of men were herded up a bleak road into the renowned and dreaded high moors prison at Dartmoor, comfortless above its various drainage works. The Fenians found themselves in a special section, in cells made entirely of iron, 7 feet long by 4 wide. Ventilation came from a 2-inch hole at the bottom of the door. Prisoners were generally employed by day in a huge project to drain the moor below the prison by building trenches in the glutinous soil. It was damp, awful work, and over it all lay the Sisyphean reality that the moor was undrainable. In some of their drain-digging the prisoners encountered remains identified by warders as those of American prisoners captured during the War of 1812, and of French Napoleonic prisoners-of-war. According to his biographer, O'Reilly, with Chambers and McCarthy, erected a small plaque to the memory of the French and Americans who died in Dartmoor prison from 1811 to 1816.

When the drainage work flooded, prisoners worked in the bone shed, a large ill-ventilated hall full of animal material. Men were required to pound the bones and adhering tissue into dust or jelly. Bean porridge was the Dartmoor staple, O'Reilly later recorded, and boiled salted beef, with rye coffee the bitter morning drink. Like other convicts, O'Reilly devoured mudcake-weed roots in the drainage ditches. Occasionally, too, he ate tallow.

24
Re-Making Montana; Violating Canada

The governor is next.

Note attached to the corpse of James Daniels,
Helena, Montana, 1866

While in Ireland a new and more numerous generation of political prisoners were facing trial, the acting governor of Montana, now close to middle age, was absorbed by Montanan and American questions.

When Thomas Francis Meagher had first come to Virginia City, the resident federal judges and other lawyers and worthies had visited him early and persuaded him that under the Organic Act which had created Montana Territory he lacked the power to call the territorial legislature, which had dissolved itself under Edgerton. He did not want to act *ultra vires* – a sure way of being censured or summoned back to Washington. But he felt it a pity, for he was aware that Montana, which had been a Republican demesne, was through increases in population turning Democrat. In September 1865, just as he was arriving, a federal election had taken place to send a member for Montana Territory to Washington, and a Democrat Union veteran named Colonel McLean had defeated the machine of the young Republican war veteran Wilbur Fiske Sanders.

Though Libby would not be arriving until the spring, the general enjoyed a sociable Christmas season in freezing Virginia City and then in Helena, Montana's largest town, visited by way of a succession of high passes. There citizens including Andrew O'Connell, the territory's Fenian centre, made continual demands for a legislature to pass laws on commercial matters, to settle legislative questions of land and mining rights, to enable the appointment of territorial officials in townships that had been instantaneously created by random gold discoveries. A legislature was also needed to do away with the undue rewards voted by Edgerton's earlier legislature to the federal judges, to take the regulation of law and order away from the vigilantes of the Vigilance Committee, who imposed summary punishment both on miscreants and opponents, and if necessary to vote to raise militias for the protection of settlers. In early 1866, Meagher explained to a Helena crowd that when he had first come to the territory he had fallen into the hands of a bad adviser who had told him he lacked power to convene a territorial parliament. Now he advised President Johnson that he intended not only calling the legislature together in the spring of 1866, but also calling a convention, from which he was confident a popular application to be admitted to the Union as a state would emerge. To Secretary of State Seward he wrote: 'On more maturely considering the powers vested in me by the Organic Act and the laws of the territory, I came to the conclusion that a Legislature did legally and constitutionally exist here, and that it was legally and constitutionally within the scope of my prerogatives to summon it into action.'

Meagher was roundly accused by the Montana old guard, amongst whom Federal Judge Munson and young Wilbur Fiske Sanders were notable, of changing his stripes and becoming a 'Missourian kind of Democrat'. The reference to 'Missourian' Democrats arose from the fact that a considerable phalanx of General Sterling Price's Confederate army had retreated into Montana after their failed invasion of the state of Missouri. They were heavily Democrat, frequently willing to crow that Price's had been the only Confederate army not to surrender. Wilbur Fiske Sanders's implication was that Meagher quickly saw the political base these secession-tainted Democrats would provide for him, and that this was what caused him to call the legislature. The charge would be repeated, fairly uncritically, even by historians. Meagher sympathisers in Montana claim that it is no accident that Wilbur Fiske Sanders was eventually founder of the Montana Historical Society, since it was crucial from early 1866 that Meagher be written off as the crassest of political opportunists, at dalliance with secessionists, a reckless violator of the Organic Act, a tyrannical opponent of the public will, and a man in all of whose decisions strong liquor took too substantial a part. Meagher's call for a territorial convention was attributed by Sanders entirely to his desire to become a future Senator from Montana. But to be Senator from Montana, albeit a Republican one, was precisely the ambition which possessed Sanders himself. In fact, in Meagher's calling of a territorial convention, a case could be made for his statesmanship. He saw that statehood would obviously serve as a device to deliver Montana from the narrow power of the Vigilance Committee. Public and personal considerations coincided in Meagher's motivations.

By early 1866, too, he must have been well acquainted with, and personally appalled by, the shameful history of Governor Edgerton. Edgerton had, as citizens complained to Meagher, made it possible for the Republicans to have a majority in the original territorial legislature by devising an oath which depicted Democrats as betrayers of the Union. At the very first Montana federal election in September 1864, after its separation from Idaho, Sidney Edgerton had denounced the Democrats in the name of his nephew, Republican candidate for Congress, Sanders. He called a Democrat meeting a 'disloyal demonstration', even though many of the men he attacked had served in the Union army. Some elected representatives had not been willing to take it. When Democrat Colonel McLean won, Edgerton withheld his certificate of election, arguing that there were 2,500 votes still to come in from soldiers at Fort Union, an outpost near the present town of Three Forks. Sanders had already packed his bags for Washington when two honourable Republican elders pressured Edgerton to issue the election certificate to McLean.

Because Hell's Gate Canyon was still frozen and the delegates to the territorial convention from Missoula Canyon would not be able to reach the capital, Meagher's convention would not meet until 26 March 1866. But for whatever reason, the climate did not delay the earlier election and gathering of the legislature, or, as it was called, Montana's House of Representatives. This new, heavily Democrat legislature met in some rented upstairs rooms in Virginia City on 5 March, and the *Montana Democrat* described the scene: 'In front of the House of Representatives Chambers, a band of music commenced playing National Airs and thirteen rounds were fired, and then the Stars and Stripes were raised on the legislative halls.'

Not all citizens were delighted. The acting governor knew of the frenzy of letter-writing to Washington from angered parties in Montana. Did Meagher ever ironically compare his situation to that of Governor Denison of Van Diemen's Land – a remotely placed administrator, trying to make representations to the central authority before others fatally undermined him? Meagher's enemies in Washington had even accused him of being involved in the Fenian military threats towards Canada, developing in the east about this time; and Meagher had to write to Secretary of State Seward and the President assuring them both that these reports were absurd.

The degree of vituperation against him is seen from the letter of a Republican, William Chumasero, to Senator Lyman Trumbull. When Meagher came to Montana, said Chumasero, 'on his first arrival in Virginia City he became intoxicated and remained so for a number of days in his room polluting his bed and person in the most indecent and disgusting manner . . . In Virginia, it is publicly stated in the streets that the Executive Office was the place of rendezvous for the vilest prostitutes.' Chumasero also claimed that the legislature had been convened in rooms above whiskey shops rented at an inflated price from the governor's supporters. Paper was supplied to the legislature 'at $50 per ream from a Democrat stationer'. Whatever can be said of Meagher's drinking or his taste in Virginia City prostitutes, a good part of this graphic list of crimes was hearsay. For none of the territorial newspapers bitterly opposed to Meagher gave any hints of such seraglio extravagance, and none accused him of having overpaid to rent the assembly rooms, as they would have been pleased to do had Chumasero's stories been true.

The Republican officials of the territory correctly feared that the legislature would repeal the Extra-Compensational Law which gave federal judges $2,500 per annum each from the territorial funds, and rewarded other officials to scale. When they did so, many officials, including Judge Munson, became deadly enemies of Meagher. By St Patrick's Day 1866, with the legislature in session, Meagher was thoroughly back in line with his Irish Democrat constituency, denouncing the radical Republicans and the Vigilance Committee, and attacking the proposition that Irish American loyalty to the United States was vitiated by an attachment to Ireland. He told a crowd in Virginia City, 'It's out upon the bastard Americanism [great cheering] that spews this imputation in the face of the gallant race whose blood, shed in torrents for its inviolability and its glory, has imparted a brighter crimson to the Stripes, and made the Stars of that triumphant flag irradiate with a keener reverence.' His position would be one of 'knowing no Republican, no Democrat, no Rebel, no Missourian, in the discharge of his duties'. In calling the statehood convention later that month, he was recognising that 'the war was over, and he, for one, would not plant thorns in the graves where the olive had taken root'.

The first sitting of the legislature held, Meagher was left with a clearer budgetary base and a set of administrative acts. In the next Congressional election that year, Sanders was again heavily defeated by McLean, and the defeat was seen by the populace as a vote of confidence in the work of Meagher's legislature. But before the legislature had even finished sitting, Judge Munson, the territory's senior federal judge, made ominous remarks about his right to decide on the validity of the legislature's acts. As early as 8 March, Meagher had written a blast at Munson, and perhaps unwisely let it be published in the *Montana Democrat*: 'I do not and shall not, hold myself in the least accountable to you for my official acts.'

In a decision published in June, Munson declared Meagher's legislature and all its legislation illegal. Meagher wrote to Seward asking that Judge Munson and his colleague Judge Hosmer be removed from the territory, or at least that he be empowered to assign them to areas in Montana still inhabited only by buffalo and Indians. 'Let the judges read Blackstone to the Aborigines!' he urged.

Meagher certainly had a taste for this huge territory, and wanted a Montanan future. If Edgerton resigned, he told the President, he himself would be anxious to be appointed chief executive of Montana. 'Nothing delights me so much as being on horseback,' he told Johnson, expressing a taste which would sometimes become jaded by Montana's massive distances, 'and taking long, rough and adventurous journeys.'

A picture of Meagher in his hopeful Montanan phase emerges from a Belgian Jesuit, Francis Xavier Kuppens, twenty-seven years old at the time of his first meeting with the acting governor. In the early winter of 1865, when Meagher was making north for his first visit to Fort Benton, the general's small party found Kuppens's tented camp along the Missouri north of Helena. Kuppens was attached to St Peter's, a new mission to the Blackfoot tribe, and was manning one of St Peter's tented outstations. He found the Blackfoot on the east of the Rockies less biddable than the Flathead on the west, and was pleased to see Meagher and his party.

As a Montana blizzard set in outside, the general chatted about his Jesuit education in Clongowes and Stonyhurst. The mercury went down to minus forty that night, and Meagher's party of five slept on a tent floor rendered comfortable by a number of pine boughs. They were all stuck there for two days, during which Kuppens got an eloquent summary of the history of the Young Ireland movement, and tales of Tasmanian imprisonment and of the Army of the Potomac both. When the blizzard stopped, Meagher rode on towards Great Falls and over the central plateau, coming for the first time to the red bluffs of Fort Benton on the Missouri, one of the great depots of American migration west.

Ultimately, in the spring of 1866, the Jesuits decided to abandon St Peter's. But Kuppens was pursued by a special messenger from General Meagher. If the US military authorities could be shown the well-established buildings of St Peter's, they might be encouraged to place a garrison there, to guard the road from Virginia City to Fort Benton. Meagher asked Kuppens to come with him and meet up with the officers of a small detachment, which was presently being towed up the Missouri to Fort Benton in flat-bottomed barges. In an environment where even Jesuits were cowboys, Kuppens set to work breaking in a bronco, and then on this newly tamed horse chased after Meagher, catching up with him on the high plains some 40 miles south of Benton. The near-waterless stretch from Sun River to Fort Benton, Kuppens found, was made very pleasant 'by the inexhaustible supply of anecdotes of the General'. Meagher was disappointed on reaching Benton, however, to find no soldiers had arrived. Their barges, too large for the pre-thaw river, had got them only as far as the mouth of the Judith, some 70 miles east.

Meagher and his party rushed aboard a steamer which was attempting to make a fast turn-around for St Louis. Kuppens remembered that some of the black deckhands considered him bad luck and referred to him as 'Sky Pilot Jonas', a view which became fulfilled when, under the high red bluffs of the Missouri, the steamer stuck on a sandbar. Crew and passengers worked all night carrying cargo ashore to lighten ship. But the tide did not lift it – in fact, they saw with frustration that the spring melt from the mountains was actually cutting a new channel to their right. The general and the four remaining members of his party gave their commiserations to the captain, waded their horses ashore, and headed overland to the Judith River, guiding themselves by the lines of the Bears Paw Mountains and the Judith Range.

Meagher and his four companions suffered from thirst in the wide-open plains of eastern Montana, depending on murky water from the centre of a buffalo wallow. Meagher himself was thrown from his horse in a ravine full of alkaline mud and rode on covered with a 'yellowish-whitish' substance which permeated every fibre of clothing, every pore of skin. At last they saw the tents of the new fort on the Judith River. An Irish sentry looked up into Meagher's alkali-covered face and said in whimsical prophecy, 'Begorrah, sir, you look *two* governors!' – the living one, and the coming ghost. Lieutenant Hogan, a Fenian officer of the garrison, knew Meagher from the Army of the Potomac, and a prime frontier banquet was planned for that evening.

Ultimately, the army was persuaded to rent the buildings of St Peter's Mission from the Jesuits. Thus Meagher achieved both an army garrison for the territory, and the continuing presence of priests to serve a growing Irish community. Meagher desired the Irish not so much as souls, however, but rather as Democrat voters and citizens of the potential state.

Later, with institutions of civil power in place, the Montana Vigilantes, a semi-secret, law-enforcing fraternity, which had strong connections with the Republican gentry of Montana, were happy to use such historians as 'Professor' Dimsdale, a Montanan newspaperman, to produce a graphic account of the rough equity but ultimate probity of their actions. They would apply themselves in particular to proving their case against one James Daniels, the defendant in a murder trial in which the acting governor was involved.

Daniels had been charged with having knifed a man named Andrew Gaitley – according to many accounts, an honest citizen – during a game of whiskey poker in the winter of 1865–6 in a saloon in Helena. According to the Vigilante side of the tale, repeated not only in Professor Dimsdale's book but in a number of territorial histories, at the time of the killing the Vigilance Committee was aware that Daniels had a bad record and had already killed a man in Colusa, California. But though its members knew the victim Gaitley – goes the tale – the Vigilance Committee forbore to give Daniels justice: it agreed to let Judge Munson try the case. Despite Munson's associations with the Vigilance Committee, the trial did not find Daniels guilty of murder. As a result of Munson's advice to the jury, a verdict of manslaughter was found, and Daniels was given a 3-year sentence.

Then, after a petition from a number of Daniels's business and other associates, Meagher pardoned the man. The proclamation pardoning James B. Daniels does not read like an act of drunken recklessness, as it was later depicted, but rather as a reasonable exercise of executive power. Basic to the matter, said Meagher's proclamation, was 'the petition of numerous good citizens of the County of Edgerton, where said conviction occurred, including several jurymen, who, by their verdict, contributed to the aforesaid conviction'. The petition was signed by thirty leading Montana businessmen of the new kind, who resented the old Vigilante–Republican axis. It argued 'that the circumstances under which the aforesaid offence was committed were most provoking on the part of the deceased or the parties in conflict, and, to a great extent, justifiable on the part of the said Daniels'. On this basis Meagher charged the sheriff of Madison County immediately to release Daniels.

Judge Munson insisted that the pardon be rescinded. Meagher refused. According to the Vigilante version, Daniels returned to Helena to attack those who had given evidence against him. A decent populace was so angered that they hanged him at the Dry Gulch on the outskirts of Helena appointed for these purposes, and pinned to the dead man's coat a notice: 'The governor is next'.

On 31 March 1866, to justify the hanging, the *Post*, edited by Dimsdale, gave James Daniels a fictional background. He had lately been pardoned out of the California state prison by Governor Lowe, after conviction for manslaughter, as – said the *Post* – all the readers of the *Sacramento Union* knew! For good measure the *Post* claimed that the wife of Gaitley had died of a broken heart. Munson and the *Post* could not, however, explain why, if Daniels was such a desperate man, his funeral was well attended by a large and respectful crowd, 'the largest audience ever gathered in this territory', and why at the grave an eloquent citizen delivered a speech against the 'secret midnight conclave'. Afterwards, the crowd expressed their outrage against Vigilantism further in what the *Democrat* described as a large protest meeting. Even a self-confessed Vigilante named Langford would later argue that Daniels's killing had been an unwarranted execution carried out by 'certain irresponsible' Vigilantes.

In the previous autumn of 1865, John Mitchel had been released from Fortress Monroe, and on arrival in New York was at once aware not only that the Fenian organisation had become extensive, but that President Andrew Johnson, in conversation with a Fenian deputation, had used language that led them to think 'that the United States government may really contemplate the policy of permitting, or at least conniving, at any enterprise the Irish-Americans may undertake'. In that enthusiastic season, before the split between William Roberts and John O'Mahony, Mitchel joined the American Fenians. 'In short,' he wrote, 'if this gallant game is to be set afoot, I must have a share in it.' O'Mahony, knowing that Mitchel needed activity, devised a safe and effective role for him: he could go to Paris, where he could act as Fenian agent 'for the safe transmission of funds to Ireland – a thing which had been attended with much loss through the intervention of the enemy's Government'. But Mitchel was empowered to be a legate too, to pursue 'diplomatic relations with the French government, or any other public or private parties on the European continent, that may be found useful to the Fenian movement'.

Less than two weeks after his release from prison, therefore, he had told Jenny with that heightened excitement she might by now have learned to dread, that he was to be stationed in France, where she and their daughters could soon join him. He was not long in a comfortable pension in rue du Rocher before he began to doubt the exaggerated claims of Irish readiness for an uprising. Brave, honest but credulous men, sent from Dublin or Liverpool, entered Mitchel's lodgings and told 'wonderful stories of the masses of men that were coming from America, and how General Sheridan was coming to lead them'.

When the escapee Stephens arrived in Paris in March 1866, hope revived a little for Mitchel, though he suspected the roseate view Stephens gave him of Irish military possibilities: 'Our strength exceeds 200,000 sworn men in Ireland alone . . . Of these 200,000, at least 50,000 are thoroughly trained men, a fair proportion being veterans . . . Rely on these figures, and then say if we can do nothing till France or America goes to war with England.' Mitchel confessed to Jenny's old friend Miss Thompson, 'I begin to have some misgivings re: the Chief Executive of the Republic.' On 17 February he had received by express from New York a large package of 'Bonds of the Irish Republic', the ones that had caused the Fenian schism, and a letter asking him to sell them in France. In the light of the American split, Mitchel saw this suggestion as fatuous. The French authorities, at peace with Whitehall, were likely to arrest him for so much as advertising bonds whose purpose was hostile to a friendly nation.

When his money ran short, and he left his lodgings at rue du Rocher to go to the cranky and familiar old pension in the rue Lacépède, three British spies moved with him, settling into a wine shop across the road.

But these *mouchards* were themselves watched by the outraged younger inhabitants of the pension. A number of young men wanted to go over the street and beat up the agents on Mitchel's behalf, but Mitchel crossed to the wine shop, introduced himself to the three gentlemen, and told them he had needed to restrain a husky youth named Bonnerie from attacking them. This caused the three, or so he claimed, to abandon their post. Mitchel believed the men to be agents of Lord Cowley, the British ambassador, and he took his complaint against them to an admirer, the private secretary of the Emperor Napoleon III, Monsieur Piétri. Piétri made it pleasantly clear that the French appreciated his 'reserve', and that their tolerance of him and his movements was based on a continuation of that reserve. In fact all his contacts with Piétri and other figures in the administration convinced him that 'It is quite out of the question to open any kind of negotiation with the Emperor or his Ministers. While France is at peace with England, they would not even listen.'

In America, the Civil War survivor Colonel James Mitchel was about to be married to a young woman of a powerful Bronx political family named the Purroys. Having fought the North for so many bitter years, James was going to re-enter it by marriage – although the Purroys were characteristic Tammany Democrats who had retained a peculiarly New York sympathy for Southerners. Mitchel did not leave Paris for the wedding, but the event caused him to consider what America signified for him. 'How happens it, that though I have lived so long in America, and have met many good people there, I can never think of any Americans as touching me very closely?' And yet he had left two dead sons there, and sought the company of Southern families in Paris, the Bayers and the Connollys.

Though Montana abutted remoter Canada, Meagher found himself fortunately and distantly placed when it came to any of Fenianism's proposed adventures against the Canadian border. There nonetheless existed a tradition of American forays into Canada. Apart from American attempts in the Revolutionary War and the War of 1812, the republican ideal of delivering Canada from the British was pursued throughout the 1830s and 1840s by officially unendorsed bodies such as the Hunters, organisations made up of Americans who lived along the Canadian border and who considered Canada as the 'Texas of the North', ripe for liberation. The Hunters' 80,000 sympathisers were generally temperance, abolitionist and anti-Catholic, but some immigrant Irish Ribbonmen joined them. During the Canadian uprisings which began in 1837, Americans from the Hunters' Lodges in upstate New York and Vermont infiltrated Canada. These American 'brigands' were tried – generally by the same courts martial as the Anglo-Canadian rebels of

Upper Canada and the *patriotes* of Lower. Some were shipped to Australia with the Canadian rebels, whose ultimate presence in New South Wales is marked by Canada Bay on the broad Parramatta River.

In 1842, angered by perceived damage to American commerce from the actions of British banks, the Hunters planned raids along the Canadian frontier as acts of disobedience against the Neutrality Act, and against the Webster–Ashburton Treaty, which recognised the eastern border between Canada and the United States. America's pursuit of Manifest Destiny, however, was in the 1840s–1850s directed more to the south, against Mexico, than towards the north. Even so, at the height of the Irish Famine in 1848, Lord Elgin, the Canadian Governor-General, detected signs of American-style republicanism in Canada. Papineau, the Quebecois leader, was angry enough about the impact of the repeal of the Corn Laws on French Canadian farmers to talk about French Canada as 'la Petite Louisiana du Nord'. Elgin also complained that he was nervous about his ministers: four were Irish-born and disgruntled about the Famine and its impact on Canada, one had Irish parents, four were French Canadians, and only three were of English or Scots background.

Popular enthusiasm for invading Canada revived with the onset of the Civil War. American grievances against the British were increased by the number of Southerners, including paid agents of the Confederacy, who were harboured on Canadian soil; Clement C. Clay, Mitchel's friend, for example, and the wealthy former Secretary of the Interior, Jacob Thompson. In Canadian cities, especially in St Catherine's near Niagara, they met with Peace Democrats from the States, subsidised Peace Democrat journalists, financed the seizure of a Union gunboat on Lake Erie, rescued Confederate prisoners from Johnson Island off the Ohio coast and from a camp in Lake Michigan, and sent volunteer arson squads into the North. On the afternoon of 19 October 1864, a group of twenty-one Confederate raiders crossed the unguarded border into the United States and robbed three banks in St Albans, Vermont, of over $200,000. The *Chicago Tribune*, like other papers, called upon the American government 'to march a sufficient body of troops to Montreal, Quebec, or any other place where the St Albans pillagers may have taken refuge'.

To D'Arcy McGee, who had been until recently President of the Council in John Sandfield Macdonald's reformist Canadian Cabinet, these bellicose noises from the United States were a potent reason for a Canadian Confederation. But since some of McGee's Irish constituency would have welcomed an invasion, McGee lost the ability to deliver the Irish vote of Montreal *en bloc*. Dumped by his leader, McGee was forced to run in his old ward, St Anne's, Montreal, with two Conservatives. Elected, he moved up the hill to a house provided by his new allies and became

Conservative Minister for Immigration under Alexander Macdonald. Nearly everything McGee did in office was motivated by the fear of American invasion. Confederate, McGee warned the provinces, or be infiltrated one at a time!

For it was obvious now that amongst American Fenians, General Sweeny's idea of a Canadian invasion was attracting young veterans of the Civil War. Some of those who stayed with O'Mahony were anxious to win back the mass of Fenians, and were themselves discontented with the lack of action in Ireland. One such man was O'Mahony's treasurer, a St Louis Fenian named B. Doran Killian, who had campaigned hard for Mitchel's release from Fortress Monroe. He argued at a meeting in New York on St Patrick's Day 1866 that the O'Mahony wing of Fenianism should retrieve credibility by occupying Campobello Island, claimed by both Great Britain and the United States, close to the coastlines of Maine and of New Brunswick. A Campobello stronghold could serve as a base for the dispatch of Fenian troops to Ireland and for privateers to attack British shipping. Killian had bought a small Confederate ship at a government sale and wanted to deploy it.

James Stephens, President of the Irish Republic and resident of a Paris hotel, was already on his way to New York in the *China* to attempt to restore peace between the two factions, and knew nothing of the hastily conceived and embraced Campobello Island scheme. O'Mahony Fenians, veterans of the war, began to gather on the north coast of Maine at Eastport and Calais about 9 April. The Toronto Fenian Michael Murphy, innkeeper and enemy of McGee, was dragged off a train in Cornwall, Ontario, along with several of his followers, while *en route* to join Killian. Bishop Thomas Connolly of New Brunswick felt bound to write a letter to Lieutenant-Governor Arthur Gordon assuring him that the Irish Catholics of the Canadian provinces knew they would gain nothing from annexation by the USA except 'increased taxation, diminished income, decided fall in the social scale and the scathing contempt of their new rulers'.

Killian's Fenian steamer *Ocean Spray*, manned by navy veterans, was in place by 14 April, but spotted a British man-of-war patrolling off the border. Some armed Irishmen from *Ocean Spray* captured the British flag on Indian Island. At Calais, Maine, an exchange of fire developed between Fenians and British soldiers from St Stephens, New Brunswick. US citizens joined with the Fenians in the fight and drove the redcoats back over the bridge to Canada. There were to be no other Fenian triumphs. The US government was reacting slowly to Britain's anger, but decided at last to prevent an international incident by sending three ships north. The 'Border Scare' ended on 19 April, with the arrival of Union General Meade in Eastport. The next day 200 disappointed Fenians, their arms confiscated by details of the United States army, departed the invasion scene aboard the steamer *New Brunswick*. 'Hundreds of fine young fellows', said the *Tribune*, 'left their homes, threw up their situations, gave up everything to join, heart and soul, in this movement, and it was truly a melancholy sight to see them leave by the boat.'

The Campobello Island enterprise was a disaster for O'Mahony and made Fenianism a laughing-stock in the press. But in early June, other and more serious rumours of Canadian invasion began to be heard, this time to do with the Roberts wing of the movement. There were straws in the wind: a 1,000-stand of Fenian arms was seized by Federal marshals at St Albans, Vermont; 500 unarmed Fenians had already been noted to have left Fitchburg depot in Boston to take part in a Fenian invasion via Buffalo; a thousand Irishmen – bound for California – interrupted their journey to present themselves at Buffalo for the invasion. One-armed Fenian General Thomas Sweeny, War Secretary of the Roberts wing, who had commanded a Union division in Sherman's campaign against Atlanta, had developed a grand strategy against Canada, involving four simultaneous onslaughts, in the early days of June 1866. On the extreme left a small feinting force was to start from Chicago, land ultimately at Goderich on Lake Huron, and so draw off thousands of British regulars and Canadian militiamen from the Niagara and Vermont borders. A second feinting movement of 5,000 men was to cross Lake Erie and threaten London and Stratford, astride the road to Toronto. Meanwhile, on Sweeny's inner-right wing at Buffalo, Fenians were to be towed across the Niagara River to attack the Niagara Peninsula and the crucial Welland Canal; and a massive outer-right wing was to follow the old route through Vermont, as used by the Americans in the Revolutionary War, and seize Montreal and Quebec. If this were done quickly, the United States would recognise it as a *fait accompli* and give the Fenians official belligerent status. General Sweeny composed an *Address to the People of British Canada*: 'We come among you as foes of British rule in Ireland . . . We have no issue with the people of these provinces . . . Our weapons are for the oppressors of Ireland.'

An invasion anthem had been written:

> We are the Fenian Brotherhood, skilled in the arts of war,
> And we're going to fight for Ireland, the land that we adore,
> Many battles we have won, along with the boys in blue,
> And we'll go and capture Canada for we've nothing else to do.

In reality, only one of Sweeny's four attacks was properly developed –

the one across the Niagara River from Buffalo. This Buffalo assault was led by a brave young man in his early thirties, red-haired John O'Neill. O'Neill had been commissioned during the Civil War, and had campaigned with the 15th US Colored Infantry and the 7th Michigan Cavalry. He was created a Fenian brigadier-general by Roberts, and would show himself, unlike others holding that title, a more than competent field officer. His job was to take a Fenian brigade across the river from Buffalo and attack the Niagara Peninsula, an objective so near that from its shore the lights of Buffalo could be seen.

O'Neill and his fellow invaders were towed by tugs at night across the Niagara to a point near Fort Erie on the Canadian side, and landed in the pre-dawn of 1 June 1866. O'Neill sent one of his battalions west along the railway towards Port Colborne, on the Lake Erie shore and at the mouth of the Welland Canal. These Irishmen overran the small detachment of Canadian militia in Fort Erie. Canadian prisoners taken by the Fenians at Fort Erie were aware they had been dealt with by a professional force.

O'Neill's main Fenian body marched north along the river to Frenchman's Creek, where they built breastworks of fence rails. Though popular Canadian history depicted O'Neill's men as drunken excursionists, in fact they applied all the skills of campaigning acquired in the Civil War. Small parties went out seizing horses. Others cut down all telegraph wires. Looting was proscribed. O'Neill threatened to shoot one of his men who confiscated a woollen shawl from an inn.

A Fenian head centre back in Buffalo told the press that between 2,000 and 3,000 men had crossed into Canada and were 'very active'. Although O'Neill's force was in fact an under-strength brigade of barely more than 1,000, potential reinforcements were numerous: 5,000 other Fenians under the command of a veteran named Sherwin were ready to cross. But there would soon be logistical problems. The anti-Fenian mayor of Buffalo had ensured that the cross-Niagara ferry stayed on the Canadian side and could therefore not be of use in ferrying Fenians. Although President Johnson had not yet enforced the Neutrality Act, the USS *Michigan* and *Harrison* patrolled the river under orders to prevent crossings if possible. General Grant, not as tolerant of Fenianism as his President, was on his way to Buffalo.

A British regular, Colonel Peacocke of the 16th Regiment of Foot, was in command on the Niagara front. De-training with men of the Royal Artillery and members of two infantry regiments at St Catherine's, 25 or so miles north of O'Neill's landing place, he travelled by rail and road southwards, past the Suspension Bridge to the United States. His plan was to move diagonally across the peninsula for an ultimate link-up with the militia regiments from Fort Colborne, in the western lower corner of the peninsula. The place he chose for the rendezvous between his redcoats and the militia was the village of Stevensville, which lay in a landscape of gentle farmland and fringes of forest. From there he intended to drive the Fenians back into the toe of the peninsula at Fort Erie and destroy them.

But the senior officer in Port Colborne, Lieutenant-Colonel Dennis, a Canadian surveyor, had already left the town at four o'clock that morning in an armed tug to go to Fort Erie. His next-in-command, Alfred Booker, an English merchant from Hamilton, Ontario, left in charge of some 900 men, received a telegram from Colonel Peacocke directing him to meet up at Stevensville that morning. Booker decided to take the railway about 10 miles east as far as the village of Ridgeway, and it was claimed that by the time his men de-trained at Ridgeway that morning they were well liquored. O'Neill's scouts heard them forming up in the rustic stillness to shouts, laughter and bugle calls. Booker's Canadians set off up Ridge Road, named for a long limestone ridge running parallel to it. Along this ridge Fenian skirmishers formed up and then descended to the crossroads ahead of Booker's column. The Canadians, as O'Neill expected, lined out enthusiastically and rushed them. The Fenian skirmishers retreated, tempting the Canadians on to the next intersection. Here, and on the ridge, the main force of Fenians waited in the cover of woods.

Intense firing now came from both parties, and though Booker's men soon ran short of ammunition – supplies had not yet been unloaded from the train – his regiments began to put pressure on the Fenians along the crossroads. Booker, however, saw some horsemen on the ridge: they were probably either Canadian onlookers or Fenian scouts, but they caused him to order his 13th Regiment to form into a traditional British infantry square. On both sides of the road, the bugle calls dragged Canadian militiamen back from their assault and into the square. When Booker realised there was no massed Fenian cavalry on the ridge, he gave the order to create a line again. But as the men tried to do so, they were hit by heavy Fenian fire and began to retreat. The Highland Company and the University Rifles, far out on the right, found out too late that the withdrawal had been ordered. The University Rifles withdrew across the front of the Fenians, and suffered many losses. The Fenians came on down either side of the road, maintaining a hard fire, and chased the brave rearguard a quarter of a mile beyond Ridgeway.

It was about nine o'clock in the morning, and O'Neill was told by his scouts that there was a greater force of 1,200 regulars behind him. He decided to call the pursuit off. In the next hour or so, the Fenians had efficiently quartered out with farmers the battle's wounded of both sides, and appointed two doctors to tend them. The Canadian volunteers had suffered from fifteen to twenty dead. The Irish dead were few but included an Ed Scully from Cincinnati, and a Union veteran named James Geraghty. The Canadians would ultimately return to exhume their dead buried by O'Neill's men. According to the *Hamilton Times*, one of the Fenian dead was later retrieved in mistake for a militiaman of the Queen's Own Rifles, and was buried with full honours in Toronto, his coffin draped with the banner of the Orange Lodge.

Alfred Booker, exonerated by a later military enquiry, would be hounded by the Canadian press for the ineptitude at Ridgeway. Meantime, the far from speedy Colonel Peacocke made his men rest in the fields north of Stevensville. Here at mid-afternoon he got the news from Ridgeway. He advanced warily south, expecting ambush. There had indeed been a second tragedy for the Canadians. Canadian Colonel Dennis, with more than seventy artillerymen and sailors, had landed near Fort Erie and taken receipt of Fenians captured by local farmers. Dennis, who would be tried for and acquitted of cowardice, headed now by road back to Fort Colborne, to receive further information, and the men he had abandoned were soon joined by parties of rattled militia turning up at Fort Erie with news that the Fenians were coming in full force from the west. The Fenians marched into town, and Canadians took cover behind piles of cordwood and fences and in the house of the postmaster, from which they inflicted heavy losses upon the Fenians. One Fenian was killed by a bayonet thrust received while he tried to enter the postmaster's clapboard house. Colonel O'Bailey, one of the Fenian leaders commanding a party who were attacking the tug, with its little force of fifteen artillerymen, was shot through the body while riding at the head of his men. 'He was the only Fenian officer of rank wounded in the raid,' said Major Denison of the Canadian militia, who wished to counter wild stories about mass graves filled with Fenian dead.

Outside Fort Erie, Peacocke's men camped rough for the night. But O'Neill had not received reinforcements. When 700 Fenians tried to cross from Buffalo to Fort Erie in a scow, they were arrested by the USS *Michigan*. O'Neill withdrew all his forces in excellent order and good spirits towards Fort Erie. One of his battalions – Starr's – pulled up the track of the Grand Truck Railway as they went. Canadian householders who saw some of them pass later reported O'Neill's men to have been in exuberant mood. But O'Neill got reports that night that more and more British and Canadian regiments, including artillery, had arrived from Hamilton. He sent a message via one man in a small boat across to Buffalo that he needed the main force now. The Fenian command in Buffalo told him that for transport reasons only one full-strength regiment could be crossed. O'Neill refused the offer as inadequate. But, he said, in his innocence of the fact that his would be the only true invasion, if the western feints and the other eastern invasion from Vermont had begun, he was willing to sacrifice his command to tie down substantial British forces. In fact, Fenian General Lynch watched his men sitting in open scows along the shores of Lake Erie near Cleveland waiting for transportation promised by General Tevis, who would later be found guilty of cowardice by a Fenian court martial.

General Grant, passing through Buffalo, ordered General Meade to ensure no more Fenians crossed into Canada. On the morning of 3 June, with Peacocke's regulars and militia closing on them, O'Neill's men destroyed their ammunition dumps, and returned to the United States. Thirty of their pickets were captured by the Anglo-Canadians. The US army intercepted the vast majority of O'Neill's Fenians as they recrossed the Niagara in small craft. They were all taken aboard the USS *Michigan*, and would be demoralised only when they discovered that General Sweeny was not marching on Toronto. But as O'Neill said, 'Our people are glad they didn't fall into the hands of the Canadians.'

Fenians from Chicago now turned up in Buffalo 1,200 strong but could not cross. They told anyone they met, including sympathetic US soldiers, 'We will have the place yet.' On 6 and 7 June, General Spear's Fenians crossed the Vermont border briefly and raised the green flag at Pigeon Hill. Spear had little more than $20 in his pocket, so his men had to plunder, in contrast to the good behaviour of O'Neill's men. A strong force of British and militia drove them back over the border by 8 June, and by then President Johnson, too late to appease the British and too early to satisfy Fenian opinion, had sent troops to shut the Vermont border. At the Philadelphia Conference of the Fenian Brotherhood, Stephens denounced the raids. He did not approve 'any breach of the Neutrality Laws by which this country might be compromised, and the cause of Ireland ruined past redemption'.

The *New York Tribune* remarked, 'The most suggestive fact of the movement is that it required the presence of Grant in Buffalo and Meade at Eastport. To be defeated by these two warriors is a significant, if not an unusual, compliment and may be considered the chief glory of the Fenian campaign.' But in fact the chief glory of the Fenian campaign may have been that it made apparent to Canadians the urgent need for confederation.

D'Arcy McGee declared, 'This filibustering is murder, not war.' He thought no mercy should be shown to either American or Canadian Fenians. But he did not want death penalties, since executions would rally American support again behind Fenianism. As, in October 1866, the

Canadians began trying Fenians held in Toronto and Sweetsburg, in New York State the *Rochester Union* remarked, 'The execution of the first man now under arrest in Canada for Fenianism will be the signal for a movement here that will wrest Canada from the men who now control it, and make it part of the American Union.'

Fenian captives who were American citizens were charged not with treason, but with having feloniously entered Canada and having been found in arms against Her Majesty. One Fenian colonel claimed to have been in the area purely as a journalist for the *Louisville Courier*. John McMahon, a priest from Anderson, Indiana, declared he had been on his way to Montreal to collect a small legacy left by his brother when the Fenians forced him to act as their chaplain. He had administered last rites to combatants. In late October, he was sentenced to death with six others.

As New Yorkers discussed lynching the British consul, Secretary of State Seward wrote to Sir Frederick Bruce, British ambassador in Washington, asking him to intercede. Seven men, including McMahon and Lynch, were due to hang on 13 December, but twenty-six had been acquitted, taken to the Suspension Bridge on the Niagara River, and given $5 to get home. The executions were ultimately commuted to twenty years' penal servitude. William Roberts of the Senate wing wrote an apparently barbaric letter to one prisoner. It fell into the hands of the *Toronto Globe*. 'I regret to tell you that you are not going to be hanged. So great a crime upon a non-combatant like yourself would make every Irishman in America a Fenian.'

Thirty more Fenian prisoners, captured either in Fort Erie or on the Vermont border, and tried in Sweetsburg, Quebec and Toronto, were found guilty. All were pardoned by the summer of 1872 and returned home to the USA, except Thomas Maxwell, a young man in his early twenties, who had died in prison on Christmas Eve 1869.

The Fenian raid helped Mitchel in his post in Paris finally lose faith. He resigned as financial officer of the Irish Republican Brotherhood on 22 June, and told Stephens, 'I need assign no reason further than I have now lost all hope of being enabled to communicate with the French government and that I do not think it right to continue, with a considerable salary, to merely receive and pay over sums of money.'

A visit by John Martin, his brother-in-law by his marriage to Mitchel's sister Henty, and frail old Father Kenyon, cheered him briefly. Martin's association with the National League, an organisation despised by Mitchel, did nothing to dampen the old friendship. Former Confederate General Beauregard also visited Mitchel, discussed the diminished South, but made him think all the more of America. He visited the grave of his daughter Henrietta at Montparnasse cemetery and placed there a large pot of laurustinus; and then he packed: 'one cannot live forever astride upon the Atlantic Ocean'. He carried with him the manuscript of his *History of Ireland from the Treaty of Limerick*, a revised and newly edited version of a history he had written for Duffy years before. His plan had been to write in a composed and neutral style, but the tone was scathing.

O'Mahony welcomed him back to New York, but Mitchel was fed up with the Fenians. 'I do not wish your branch of the organisation, or that of Mr Roberts, to use my name in any manner whatsoever.' He began to argue, as he would never have done once, that the Fenian Brotherhood, given 'the *interium in interio* they propose to create in the US', was inconsistent with the members' duties as US citizens.

He found that his three remaining children were flourishing. His daughter Minnie had married a former Confederate Colonel Page, and Isabelle married a Dr Sloane and converted, like her late sister Henrietta, to Catholicism. Mitchel and Jenny took a house in the Bronx, near Fordham Universty, and Mitchel recommenced publication of the *Irish Citizen*. It would run only briefly, until July 1867, and was strongly Democratic, opposing in particular President Grant. But his *Letters on Fenianism* were so critical of the movement as seriously to injure circulation amongst the Irish. He had not lost the old gift to offend both sides of an argument.

Fenianism was still alive in Montana. From the small army outpost on the Judith, where he had greeted Governor Meagher, Lieutenant Martin E. Hogan of the 13th US Infantry ran a lively and typical correspondence with the Fenian centre for Montana, the Union war veteran Andrew O'Connell, who lived in Helena and Blackfoot City and was a close friend of the Meaghers. Hogan's was a typical US Fenian's record. At the war's commencement, he had enlisted as an 18-year-old in a cavalry unit from Terre Haute, Indiana. Commissioned in the field for retrieving General Rosecrans's flag at Carnifax Ferry in 1861, he was ultimately promoted to captain. Captured in 1864, he served eleven months in Andersonville prison, from which he escaped, to become ultimately a witness against the commandant, Henry Wirz, condemned to death for crimes against humanity.

On a silken Montana night, by lamplight, with the pickets out to guard against the Blackfoot and the Sioux, Hogan wrote to Mr O'Connell about an Irish matter, a meeting with James Stephens at the Metropolitan Hotel in New York. 'He spoke very hopefully and with unmistakable confidence of the future of Ireland.' Hogan looked forward to Fenians being permitted an unimpeded invasion of Canada. 'I shall make it my business to be somewhere in that vicinity with a squadron of Irish Cavalry. This is an inclination of a lot of Irishmen in the army.'

But the hope of leading Fenian cavalry into Canada was thwarted by the follies of 1866. Later, from St Peter's Mission, in accommodation leased by the army from the Jesuits, Lieutenant Hogan had time to inform O'Connell that he had been to the city of Helena to establish a mail route between that place and the mouth of the Judith, and that while in Helena he had met John Kingsley, Centre of the Brian Boru circle of the Fenian Brotherhood. Here was a soldier heavily involved in the Union's affairs, maintaining a parallel existence as a committed Fenian. Nor did he see Fenianism as detracting from his duty to the United States. One reinforced the other. 'I've often told brother officers that when that event took place, I would bid the mess goodbye. They laugh and don't believe me.' But: 'America has been kind to me. As proof of the impartial kindness, she has in a few short years placed me, a Stranger on her Shores, while yet a boy, in a position that, if duty called me to England, England's Queen would receive me as her equal or not at all.' Irish affairs would in the end fail to give him the pretext to leave his post, and in 1873, he was still creeping up the seniority pole towards his captaincy in Fort Randall, Dakota Territory.

In Washington in the summer of 1866, a new governor had in fact been appointed to officially replace Edgerton. He was Green Clay Smith, a well-connected Kentuckian in his early thirties. He had fought as a Union officer in the Civil War but was not an automatic member of the old Montana clique. Of course, appointment was easy, but reaching Montana was tough. So Meagher would be Montana Territory's chief executive until Green Clay Smith could arrive, which would not be until early October 1866. Having then met and liked Meagher, within a few weeks he would apply for five months' leave to visit Washington on business. At that stage Meagher himself – who had served in the territory a year – had decided to resign his military secretaryship. He might have wanted to meet with his father and son in France, as he had mentioned in a letter to Waterford the previous summer. He seemed also to have commercial plans, and to be planning to stand for Congress in the elections of 1868. But Clay Smith urged Meagher to stay on, and sent a telegraph to the President asking him not to accept Meagher's resignation. Meagher approved of Green Clay Smith, described him as 'a genial, light-hearted, high-minded young fellow', and so agreed.

Early in the New Year of 1867, Smith departed for the East on a steamer from Fort Benton, and once more Meagher was what even he had now begun to call himself, 'the Acting One'.

Elizabeth Meagher had arrived in Montana, and for the Meaghers the summer of 1866 was a blessed and hopeful season. From the executive offices in Virginia City Meagher was able to write to Samuel M. Barlow about 'a truly delightful excursion of fully three months through the Western portion of our territory' from which 'Lib and I returned last week'. It was a country of bracing air, august mountains, wonderful camp-sites by huge lakes. But it was true that his political enemies, the Radical Republicans as he called them, diminished the peerless territory Libby and he rode through. 'Every day intensifies my hatred of the Radicals – I see them here face to face, in such colours as I fail to perceive them in the greater crowds of the Eastern cities. So fiercely do I detest them, I am often on the brink of wishing that the South had won the day in the field.' But he was delighted to recount the result of the latest legislature election: 'thirty ... staunch Union Democrats to three emasculated disunion Radicals'.

Like other friends, and indeed enemies, Barlow surmised Meagher had his eye on the Senate. Meagher's answer could be considered coy. 'I'd infinitely prefer, any day,' he told a number of correspondents including Barlow, 'to have a splendid yacht, a box at the opera, and a four-in-hand, than have a seat for six years in the Senate.' Perhaps he thought he might, through Montana's mineral wealth and numerous Democrats, achieve both. When, in early July 1866, the territorial Democrat convention urged him to accept the nomination to Congress, he had 'obstinately' declined, 'not being rich enough as yet to support the grand responsibilities of position'.

The work of the 'Radicals' of the territory had been to send to Washington a lobby group, of which Wilbur F. Sanders was a member, and over the coming winter to persuade Congress to nullify the laws of Meagher's two 1866 legislatures; in March 1867, on motions of Congressman Ashley of Ohio and Senator Ben Wade, a congressional Act to this effect would be vengefully passed. A commentator in Montana wrote: 'Certain Republican office holders smilingly marched up to the crib and drew their back pay under the law they had thus revivified.'

Republicans and the Blackfoot were the Acting One's grief. From the eastern side of the Rockies, Meagher received in the summer of 1866 many representations about unregulated bands of young Blackfoot who had left the reservations and attacked travellers and remotely placed settlers. He began asking General Sherman, commanding the Department of the Missouri, for a larger garrison. He had, he said, just ridden up to Fort Benton, and the country along the way between Virginia City in the south of Montana Territory and Fort Benton in the central north had plenty of forage to support cavalry. He asked Sherman to send at least 850 men, and to make Montana a separate military district. Sherman answered from St Louis: 'Were I to grant one/tenth part of the calls on me from Montana to Texas, I would have to call for 100,000 men, whereas I doubt if I should expect to have 10,000 men in all. You ask for a Regiment of Cavalry. I have only the 2nd for Montana, Dakota, Nebraska, Colorado, Kansas, and New Mexico.'

Meagher's quarrel was not with the Blackfoot elders and chiefs, who had already made their accommodation with the government for good and ill. In the spring of 1866, Meagher had officiated in Fort Benton at the concluding phases of an uneasy and long-disputed treaty between the Federal government and the Blackfoot, including Bloods and Piegans. The *Post* recorded that 'the Red delegates' seated themselves before the blanket-covered seats which had been laid before them, and faced Gade Upson, the Indian Agent, General Meagher in his role as Superintendent of Indian Affairs, and US Judge Lyman Munson as legal counsel to the government. The Blackfoot elders had been persuaded by the offer of annual payments, by pressure of settlers and fear of horse soldiers, to cede a massive area of lands northwards and eastwards of Virginia City and Helena. These included all land along the Teton River near Fort Benton, along the Marias, and along the Missouri River as far as the Milk River. That is, they consented to limit themselves to the area now identified as the Fort Peck Indian Reservation in eastern Montana. In the spirit of the day, the *Montana Democrat* declared: 'So we concluded a treaty in the highest degree advantageous to the whites: which gave over to us all that vast extent of country (embracing between two and three hundred thousand square miles) in which is situated our largest towns – Helena, Virginia City, Bannack.'

A few days after the treaty with the Blackfoot, a large party of young tribesmen stole horses from a rancher and killed a herder. A war party of Bloods killed two white men on the Musselshell River and rode unabashedly into Fort Benton with horses, saddles and arms. Two white prospectors setting out from Fort Benton were killed by a Blackfoot party in the Bears Paw Mountains 50 miles downriver from Benton. On top of that, four men who left the mouth of the Judith River to come to Fort Benton vanished utterly. At a newly opened Fenian Library in Deerlodge County near Helena in late 1866, Meagher made a speech that eloquently showed how Irish Americans saw no parallel between Irish dispossession and the crisis for the tribes. 'The rascalities in crimes, robberies and murders, with which the liberality of the United States was repaid, might well be cited with condemnation of the costly and wasteful policy with which it was believed in Washington the Indians could be tamed and subsidised.'

In the winter of 1866–7 Virginia City hunched down in its high canyon amidst rumours that in the spring Red Cloud intended to lead some 4,000 Sioux, Cheyenne and Arapahoe into the Gallatin Valley to the east of the capital and clear the white settlers away. These bands were themselves refugees from the encroachment of the railroad further south, but they caused considerable fear throughout the territory. Meagher would later be accused of orchestrating this fear, but it could be argued that the locals did not need orchestration. John Bozeman, for example, a resident of the Gallatin Valley, wrote to Meagher asking for protection. Meagher telegraphed General Grant that immediate action was necessary. Until regular troops could be brought up the Yellowstone, 'We earnestly entreat permission from the War Department to raise a force of 1,000.' Grant, in the process of dealing with Fenian border activity, noted on the back of Meagher's telegram, 'The citizens of Montana ought to have some organization to defend themselves . . . and if the services rendered by them warrant it, they should afterward look to Congress for compensation.'

When news came from the Gallatin Valley late in the winter that John Bozeman had been killed by a party of Blackfoot Indians, the *Helena Herald*'s headlines shouted: 'THE PANIC AMONG THE GALLATIN SETTLERS! . . . THEIR APPEAL TO GOVERNOR MEAGHER AND THE PEOPLE OF THE TERRITORY! PROMPT AND FRIENDLY RESPONSE BY THE GOVERNOR AND MINUTE MEN CALLED FOR TO MEET THE EMERGENCY!' The sense of desperation felt by the Sioux, the Cheyenne, the Blackfoot and the Crow at the shrinkage of their traditional ground and their food resources has been well documented. Meagher was facing a land war, although he did not interpret it in those terms. On 8 February 1867 the distracting news came to him from eastern Montana that three officers and ninety men, part of the garrison of Fort Phil Kearny in the Dakota Territory, had been surrounded by a party of 2,000 Sioux and Cheyenne Indians and slaughtered. Green Clay Smith himself telegraphed Sherman asking him for a battery of mountain howitzers, a request which Sherman dismissed. Clay Smith urged Meagher to preserve his present friendly relations with the Crow Indians in the Big Horn area, near present-day Billings, who could serve as a buffer between the Sioux and the settlers near Virginia City.

Immediately after the military massacre, Meagher called for 600 volunteers for three months' service in the Gallatin Valley and on the Yellowstone River, in the south central area of Montana. So immediate did the need seem to the whites of the territory, panicked or otherwise, that one of Meagher's virulent enemies, Henry Blake of the *Montana Post*, volunteered to lead the new military force. The volunteer force mustered in Helena and Virginia City. Like the Fenian army, it possessed plenty of officers, but also a rank and file, and it was kept together, billeted and fed at territory expense, although Meagher hoped the federal government would take up that load.

Sherman wrote to Secretary of War Stanton: 'Meagher, in Montana, is a stampeder.' Sherman was supported in this view by the new Indian Agent in Montana, Chapman: 'Acting-Governor Meagher's Indian War in Montana is the biggest humbug of the age, got up to advance his political interest, and to enable a lot of businessmen who surround and hang on to him to make a big raid on the United States treasury.' But Meagher's friends in business did not see a grand and instant bonanza in an Indian War. Any bills would be paid late by a distant Congress and pared down by Congressional vote. And having singularly denounced Meagher, General Sherman said that the other governors of the western territories were not much better. Governor Alexander C. Hunt of Colorado had also informed Sherman and the Secretary of War that his state was about to be overrun. Sherman told Secretary of War Stanton that he had spoken to Governor Green Clay Smith on his way back east through St Louis. 'He understands with me that the grant to them of 2,500 muskets, dispatched by one of the first boats up the Missouri, was all the people asked to enable them to defend themselves.' That musket shipment would in fact serve as a tragic catalyst.

As Meagher had been hoping, authority did come through to Virginia City from Sherman acknowledging that Washington would permit a battalion of 800 men for two months' campaigning to be funded by the United States. Sherman instructed Meagher to be careful to use this force purely for 'self-protection'. Major Lewis, a Union veteran and quartermaster for Meagher's militia, showed the Sherman telegram to recalcitrant merchants in Virginia City, Bannock and Helena. Meagher issued vouchers to various Montana suppliers, who bumped up prices to cover the uncertainty about whether the vouchers would ever be honoured.

Soon Meagher had his militia in place at Camp Elizabeth Meagher, near one of the principal passes leading over the Madison Range into the Gallatin. A rumour reached Washington that Meagher had sent his volunteers out saying that they could keep Indian property they captured – robes, decorative and ritual items, horses, rifles. The east was watching, sometimes in judgement, sometimes in whimsy. The *New York Herald* of 31 May 1867 wrote almost benevolently, 'If anyone can carry it to a successful issue, he is as good at a palaver as at a fight, and his eloquence is just of the character to suit the Indians. He will quiet them by talking their heads off – a much less costly and more humane process than that of exterminating them.'

The spring threat of 1867 would not develop. Between April and June 1867, the volunteers did not come in contact with any Indians but were occupied principally in patrol duty. Not that all of them were available for such work at once. Meagher's complaint about his militia – 'I am Commander-in-Chief, not of an invincible, but of an invisible militia' – was uttered in a number of letters, and remained for a time the Acting One's favourite joke. The militia numbered at any time no more than 200 men, with the task of keeping open lines of communication from Fort Benton to Helena and Virginia City. As well, they had the east–west task of keeping the road open between Butte and Bozeman.

It was already early summer 1867 when Meagher wrote to Sam Barlow saying that he had been away 'posting our volunteers 200 miles from here, against the Indians. Governor Smith has not yet relieved me . . . On his arrival I shall be free – and right glad it will make me to be so for I am downright sick of serving the *Gvt* in a civil capacity.' He had already asked for Barlow's help concerning a Major Vielé, who wished to acquire mining crushers, for work on various promising quartz leads around Helena. 'I am perfectly satisfied that any interest you might purchase in it would prove splendidly productive – I am, myself, largely interested in it and have no doubt that my share will be a little fortune in itself.' He sent his affection to Barlow's two children, whom in earlier letters he had called 'the Mysteries' but whom now he dubbed the 'Birds of Paradise'.

The militia, of similar mind to their leader, began to fade away in late spring 1867, in part because in their patrols they had come across likely gold-panning sites they wanted to test out during the summer.

Meagher was aware that his old friend from VDL, the physician Kevin Izod O'Doherty, with whom he had satirically dined half-way across the stone bridge at the penal settlement of Tunbridge, was back in Australia. The O'Dohertys had moved with their children to the new northern Australian state of Queensland at the beginning of 1862, at the same time as the Irish Brigade was manoeuvring towards its first bloody Virginian confrontations. Perhaps Saint Kevin and Eva would not have gone north to the raw colony of Queensland but for their Dublin friend Bishop Quinn, first bishop of the region, but when they did they settled not in the capital, Brisbane, but rather in what some would call a backwater, the inland town and former convict outstation named Ipswich, with a population of 3,500. O'Doherty was only the fourteenth physician to be officially registered as a medical practitioner in Queensland. Since he was well enough qualified to open a surgery anywhere, one modern writer suggests that his purpose in going to Ipswich may have been to keep an eye on an enemy of Bishop Quinn's, Father McGinty, the parish priest. McGinty was a turbulent priest, used to operating until now far beyond the reach of fussy bishops, and now the newcomer, Bishop Quinn, was in contest with him over what share of McGinty's revenues now belonged to the diocese. If Meagher had the Republicans and the Vigilance Committee, O'Doherty had the duty of forging a liaison between peppery McGinty and an old friend, Quinn, liberal as a young priest, now growing autocratic as a bishop.

Saint Kevin became honorary surgeon at the Ipswich hospital, where a number of his procedures were praised in print in the *North Australian*. One of these was a breast cancer operation, in which the woman's breast was removed but the cancer apparently cured. A second was an operation on the septicaemic ankle of an 8-year-old girl named Anne Kelly, which saved her from an amputation. In another case, the treatment of a diamond snake bite, the bitten man was struck across the back with a whip to stop his sliding into coma! These were the bush applications O'Doherty pursued in the days when Fenianism was a-forming and the Confederacy and the Union were locked in bloody attrition.

Eva, living in a rough wooden house in a sub-tropic torpor of dazzling light and fierce summers, was dislocated from the source of her verse. She gave birth to two babies, a boy and a girl, in 1862 and 1864 respectively, and lost both of them in the first year of life. The infant death-rate was high in the hastily erected, ill-drained, sweltering towns of Queensland. Perhaps Kevin's later reputation as a public health champion derived from the grief of these losses. In 1865, with his medical renown enhanced, the O'Dohertys moved to Brisbane. Kevin had civic tendencies, and in a town of 13,000, many of whom lived in what the *Brisbane Courier* described as 'paltry humpies' with fly-blown sanitary arrangements, he was soon elected a visiting surgeon by the subscribers of the Brisbane hospital, at a time when the premises were a former convict hospital. Almost at once plans for a new hospital were announced, as if to break the link with the penal origins of the Moreton Bay region with which Dr O'Doherty was not totally unacquainted. Perhaps old ticket-of-leave men recognised the good doctor in the street as the former segregated State prisoner of their ship, the *Elphinstone*.

His rooms were in Edwards Street, Brisbane, and on the basis of consultations there and at the nearby Brisbane hospital O'Doherty became esteemed as one of Brisbane's two leading surgeons. He was considered such a good after-dinner speaker that despite his rebel youth he was elected surgeon to the Brisbane Volunteer Rifle Corps, and had no problem doing what Eva avoided: drinking the Loyal Toast. Like

D'Arcy McGee in Canada, living under happier institutions than those of Ireland, he did not intend to violate the civic pieties. He donned morning dress and top hat each year to attend levees in honour of the queen's birthday given by a succession of governors. Eva expended energy on running efficient stalls at fund-raising fêtes for hospitals and schools, but she was a stall-holder with a difference – she was *au fait* with Irish and Fenian politics, since she received occasional briefings by mail from John Martin. She liked the women of Queensland but felt a certain nullity and fear in them. They seemed distanced from their own sources of culture and unsure of their place on the map.

In 1867, as Meagher rode to Fort Benton to collect his consignment of muskets, the Irish community urged O'Doherty to stand for election for the Queensland Legislative Assembly as a candidate for North Brisbane. In one of his four campaign speeches, he said:

> A generation ago when I was a young man with hot blood in me, I was mistaken enough as some supposed, to risk my life and lose my liberty in an attempt to secure civil and religious liberty for my native country . . . I had seen the effect of civil and religious liberty in Australia, and I determined to come out and settle amongst you. It is not likely that I came out with the desire to impose fetters, the existence of which compelled me to leave my own country.

On election day, Saint Kevin was called out of town on a medical visit, and while returning asked a passer-by how the voting had gone. The man announced, in Ulster brogue, 'Bad enough, that bloody papist O'Doherty got in.' As a representative in the Queensland Parliament, O'Doherty took an anti-pastoralist line – unlock the land and bring in the immigrants! From diagnosing wives who had unknowingly contracted syphilis from their husbands, he proposed compulsory medical examination of prostitutes. He was launched too on what would become a long campaign for the reform of the archaic and abusive Woogaroo asylum, in which the expatriate Irish were notably represented, exiles from softer air and more ambiguous suns.

The O'Dohertys, especially Saint Kevin, appeared to be tranquil souls. The former felon had found a political system which he believed had room for him, and noble-hearted Eva, with no outlet for her voice, supported him in his doctoring and his political career. She had time to write only intermittently to her confidant Martin, but received from him reliable news of old friends. Pat Smyth, for example, was living in Normandy with his Tasmanian wife and children – letters of his had been found amongst the materials seized at the raid on the *Irish People* in 1865, and, though not active in the movement, he feared arrest. 'A queer, solitary, suspicious, nervous grey-headed man, he is become. Such are the results of our unhappy Irish politics.' Martin's picture of the new Ireland must indeed have reconciled Eva somewhat to Queensland. 'God help the poor Fenians,' he said, 'who are now breaking stones in the jails of England or pining in the jails of Ireland.'

In June 1867, Meagher, expecting the muskets Sherman had promised, undertook a journey from the gubernatorial seat in Virginia City to Fort Benton, 200 or so miles in hot weather. He had half a dozen of his officers for escort. The arrival of arms, this first token of federal favour, would have, he knew, a large impact upon future militia recruiting.

Mrs Meagher accompanied her husband as far as Helena and kissed him farewell. For Meagher himself, the leg from Helena to Benton was the least appealing of his excursions. The refreshing splendour of the mountain country slowly vanished behind the riders, and the way ahead lay across a bare, rolling, high plain, monotonous, hot and featuring, by courtesy of the spring rains and the wallowing of buffalo, sumps of black mud sometimes miles across. Fort Benton figured in the governor's and in America's plans; it was as far as steamers from St Louis could beat their way upstream on the Missouri. And from Benton, the Mullen Trail ran west to Idaho, Washington and Oregon. On the south bank of its deep green river, and set amongst cottonwoods beneath brilliant red bluffs, Benton featured at the western end of the town a substantial log fort and then, strung out along the bank, the traders, taverns and victuallers of the new West.

One modern historian describes Meagher as riding forward to Benton through his 'last few dipsomaniacal days on earth'. There was a rumour of a carouse in Sun River along the way. But there is no evidence at all that Meagher was drinking dispsomaniacally as he approached Fort Benton, and plenty of evidence that he was not. That such accusations should have still been mouthed by respectable commentators a hundred years after Meagher's death is a tribute to the manner in which the Vigilante version of Meagher's life and death was sold to posterity.

Meagher's party had had to make a series of long detours to circumvent mud holes and buffalo wallows, and he was ill as much from bad water as plenteous whiskey by the time he came over the last rise, saw Fort Benton, and rode down into it on 1 July, the last day of his life. Some witnesses say that as he travelled up the main street, Meagher heard a man cry emphatically, 'There he goes!' He interpreted it as a death threat. Some attributed his reaction to tiredness, or perhaps to alcoholic delusion. If *delirium tremens* could be proved to posterity, then his death could be more credibly depicted as the culminating tipsy accident of his career.

Visiting the three steamers in the river, the general was disappointed to find that none of them had brought the rifles. So he went by invitation into I. G. Baker's one-storey storehouse and residence to rest. Baker would do so well trading with travellers to the West and buying skins from trappers that his little split-log store would generate a large corporation and a St Louis bank. He later told a journalist: 'General Meagher stopped a couple of days in Sun River on his way to Benton, and I believe he got on a bender there, but I met him at the wharf when he arrived in Fort Benton and took him to my house. I am prepared to swear that he was stone sober.' He kindly gave Meagher some blackberry wine to ease his stomach and bowels, and after a time the governor got up and rode along the river bank west to visit the fort. He came back more distressed still.

There is overall to Meagher's last day, as related by those who had reasons for enmity towards him an expectation that in accepting their version of what befell him we should not only discount what Baker and others tell us but also ignore all we already know about his character; in particular his characteristic boldness. The governor was a man until that day patently not easy to scare, a man who had stood fast both in government and in some of the most ferocious battles of the Civil War. Was all his concern that long June day credibly to be written off to paranoia, gastritis and alcoholism? Was it not half-way credible that he had received at the fort, as Baker surmised, a further concrete notification of death?

G. A. Thompson, one of three steamers along the bank, had taken more than three months to get up the Missouri from St Louis to Benton, and had had to unload twice during the trip to clear sandbars. Johnny Doran, Irish master of this vessel, went ashore looking for the governor and found him reading a newspaper in the back of Baker's store. The Irish-born Doran was ecstatic to meet Meagher of the Sword in this remote port. Decades later, on 8 June 1913, his account of Meagher's last afternoon would appear in the *New York Sun*. According to the aged Doran, the depressed state of Thomas Francis Meagher's health was due to a 6-day dysentery attack. Similarly, according to Doran, Meagher was disappointed that the arms had not arrived. He intended to press on to Camp Cook on the Judith in hope of finding them stored there. 'He also spoke in the most tender and affectionate terms of his wife, residing at Helena, saying that in their mountain home they were as happy as two thrushes in a bush.' Seeing that Meagher was genuinely concerned for his safety,

Doran invited him to use one of the staterooms on the *Thompson*, and so get a good night's rest. Doran's steamer was moored between two others, the *Guidon* and *Amelia Poe*.

Doran and Meagher strolled through the town that afternoon – Meagher feeling safe in the open, amongst witnesses. They were invited to participate on 'several occasions' of normally full-blooded Western hospitality, but Doran said that in each instance Meagher politely refused. 'Thus, in walking and talking, we spent the afternoon and, toward evening, wended our way to the boat to take tea.' The two of them sat on chairs by the guard rails of the boat, lit their cigars and commenced reading. Doran had loaned the general a book, *The Collegians* by Gerald Griffin, a great favourite amongst Irish Americans. 'He seemed to peruse it with great attention for half an hour, when suddenly, closing it, he turned to me, and said very excitedly, "Johnny, they threatened my life in that town!" ' It was then he asked Doran for a revolver. The sun went down and after a light supper Doran showed Meagher to a stateroom, reassured him that the door could be opened only from the inside, and left him a revolver. Doran intended to return later in the night to occupy the lower berth.

'Now the lock on the door leading into the cabin was very defective,' said Doran, 'but I did not mind it much, as I intended to return without delay. I had been on the lower deck but a short time when I heard a splash in the dark waters below.' Doran said he heard two groans, the first very short, 'the last prolonged and of a most heart-rending description'. He and the sentry rushed to the paddle-wheel and lowered themselves hip-deep into the water, looking in darkness for the man overboard while others threw out ropes and boards. Nothing was found. 'The river below is dotted with innumerable small islands of different and various areas, the activity of hostile Indians preventing us from exploring the ones furthest down; and no doubt the body of the gallant but unfortunate General was washed ashore on one of them.'

I. G. Baker recounted, 'About nine o'clock the dock watchman came into my room, where I was sitting by the window and said he'd just seen a man fall off the boat, and disappear under the keel of another boat. He seemed to be vomiting and lost his balance, the watchman said.'

The drunken accident version would become the standard version in Montana, though many disbelieved it. If Meagher was as terrified as reported, would he have got up, opened his own stateroom door, and wandered to the stern? So far was Meagher from being either sick or drunk, he was clear-headed enough to write to friends before retiring. Richard O'Gorman, New York lawyer, would receive a letter addressed to him from the cabin that evening in Meagher's decisive, spiky hand.

Certainly, a bout of sickness could have driven him out, but it would have needed to be very desperate and very sudden.

Meagher's army friend William Lyons, now a New York journalist, mentioned, accurately or not, that the guard rails in front of Meagher's door had been accidentally broken. Lyons wrote: 'there was a coil of rope on the verge of the deck, over which he stumbled, throwing him off balance, and while grasping vainly for the guard – which was not there – he fell into the dark, rushing river'. But Lyons was writing at second hand, in New York. No one in Benton, neither Baker nor Doran, mentioned the missing guard rails. Distance from the site muted the suspicion of Meagher's friends, and no one in New York seemed to voice the same suspicions as a modern commentator on Meagher, Chris Stephens, that the death was the work of 'the twelve organisers of the Vigilantes, eleven of whom were freemasons who had dealings as well with British Pinkerton men'. This scenario, especially the Pinkerton men, is impossible to prove. But the credibility of Vigilante involvement remains. Other historians and a number of Montana newspapers have raised over the last 130 years or more the possibility that Meagher, summoned to Washington in disgrace, committed suicide. 'All lies,' says I. G. Baker. 'He was not bound for Washington, but for the mouth of the Judith . . . He was not in low spirits.'

A grieving Libby rode up over the harsh, dusty, boggy plain to visit the site. It seemed that she accepted her husband's death as an awful accident, in the face of stated evidence that it may well indeed have been. She arranged extensive patrols of the Missouri downriver, but when the fall came without her husband's body being found, she returned to New York. There she lived a widow for the next forty years.

Meagher's death, accidental or planned, brought no immediate success to the Republican cause. Wilbur Fiske Sanders stood again for Congress but was defeated by James N. Cavanaugh, Democrat. And only one Republican was elected to the next territorial legislature. These routs were seen as endorsements by the people of Montana of Meagher's policies. And though Sanders would claim in the *Helena Herald* and elsewhere to have been the best of friends and neighbours to Meagher, Meagher had early told Secretary of State Seward that Sanders was the 'most vicious of my enemies, an unrelenting and unscrupulous extremist'.

The Helena battalion of Governor Meagher's little militia was engaged in a brief summer campaign against the Indians, while far away at St Francis Xavier's Church on 16th Street, New York, on Wednesday 14 July, a solemn Requiem Mass was celebrated, organised by the officers of the brigade. Cherubini's Requiem was performed, and survivors of the Irish Brigade, though not in uniform, each wore a sprig of box tree, their badge since that brutal day at Fredericksburg. The officers of the Irish Brigade were still not sure about Meagher's rank. One of them wrote to the War Department about it, but there is no reply on record.

To the other potential causes of Meagher's death – Vigilantes, accident-cum-*delirium tremens*, suicide – must be added the remote possibility of an unauthorised Fenian assassination. Could the Fenians have been disgruntled by Meagher's lack of enthusiasm for their plans to invade either Ireland or Canada? It is improbable that either wing of the Fenian Brotherhood sanctioned such an attack, but Meagher's very abstention from the Canada campaign, his embracing of Montana, may have appeared to a fanatic as treachery. The idea that Fenians at any official level resented Meagher runs counter to his friendship with Andrew O'Connell, Head Centre of Montana. Meagher shared business interests with O'Connell, and had written to him earlier in the year about a patent for some processing, drilling, or crushing machine: 'Walch's patent, I should say, is safe – hurrah! . . . The fewer people knowing anything about this now, the better.' For the nearly four decades of Elizabeth Meagher's widowhood O'Connell would be her Montana friend and supporter, supervising the financial interests – shares in mineral leases – which the Meaghers had acquired during their brief, intense history in Montana. In 1902 Elizabeth Meagher had left New York and come to reside in a cottage in Rye, New York, which 'I've bought and named after the old house of the O'Meaghers in Tipperary. I came to end my days here, but the city of NY is taxing my small income so heavily that I do not know if I can stand it.' She asked O'Connell, still her helper, if he could sell for her a one-third share of a Helena gold-mine.

As Libby aged, it became fashionable amongst some to look upon the career of the Acting One as an aberration. He and Montana were temperamentally ill-matched, argued the writer Joaquin Miller. 'The impetuous Meagher, true to his race and record, set Montana on fire in less time than it takes to write his strange life and long deeds of endeavor and achievements.' He had 'no comprehension at all of the Montanese'. If so, it is hard to understand why his equestrian statue stands so dominantly today before the front door of the Montana legislature. Perhaps it was only an influential minority of Montanese that he did not comprehend. For in the last two years of Libby's life, she was consoled, though too aged to attend, by the gala on 4 July 1905, when what seemed like a majority of the state turned out in front of the Montana State House in Helena under a bright sky to see the Stars and Stripes removed from Meagher's huge statue. So her husband had won the battle of symbolism.

But the mystery of his death also made it inevitable that she had to bear sensational press reports, and even a travelling freak show that purported to display his remains. Photographs of a 'Petrified Man' appeared in New York papers in 1899: the remains of an ossified man had been found below Fort Benton by a farmer and hauled by wagon to Yellowstone, where the curiosity was sold for $2,500 to a Mr Arthur Miles, who then exhibited it at fairs, claiming it to be the body of General Meagher, petrified through freakish physical causes but retaining in the middle of the forehead a bullet hole. For the better part of twenty years the exhibit would be shown at fairs in the United States and, as an ultimate irony, was shipped to Australia, a supposed second transportation, and made the rounds of agricultural shows in New South Wales.

This was itself a populist sign that the question of who or what killed Meagher had never quite receded, and in heavily Irish Butte, Montana, the proposition that he was killed by Vigilantes is still widely accepted. In June 1913, some years after Libby's own death, a pioneer named Pat Millar, alias Frank Diamond, on the verge of expiring in Kalispell, Montana, confessed to having murdered Meagher on behalf of the Vigilantes for a pay-out of $8,000. Recovering, Diamond recanted the story. Immediately one Dave Mack, in Montana since 1865, said that Pat Millar's statement was true – he had heard Millar and others tell the story many times. Meagher had been taken from the boat at Fort Benton by a party of ten Vigilantes, executed and secretly buried. 'Meagher had ample warning,' Mack related. 'When Daniels was hanged there was sent the Governor a piece of the rope, about six inches long, by the Pony Express accompanied by this message: "It don't take a bigger rope to hang the Governor of Montana than it does to hang a horse thief or a murderer." '

Leaders of society vouched for David Mack's reliability. The son of Wilbur Fiske Sanders rushed into print to claim wrongly that the depredations of the Vigilantes had ceased years before Meagher's death. Meagher was a significant ghost in Montana, and remains so to this day.

25
Fenians Transported

> Now, sir, perhaps no one in this Colony knows better than I do the daring audacity – disregard of life (own or of others) of American ruffians. I had experience of them previous to my leaving Peru . . . Two or three of them as leaders *could*, before the *Hougoumont* discharged her surplus stores, have full possession of her, and sail away with such of our wives and daughters that they are pleased to select.
>
> Captain Charles Manning,
> Western Australian Volunteers, December 1867

For the Fenians imprisoned in Britain, 1867 had been a long wait. Some of them heard by whispers or messages on slips of paper that in July 1866 James Stephens had told audiences in the United States that an army would be fighting on Irish soil before the new year. Stephens had replaced O'Mahony as chief executive of the US Fenian Brotherhood with just that result in mind, yet he grasped at excuses for delay. Attacked by the American Fenians, he hysterically offered to go back to Ireland immediately to 'get hanged' and prove he was no coward. But he would not go back to Ireland, as it turned out, for another thirty years.

After seven months as chief of what used to be called the O'Mahony wing, when the new year of 1867 arrived he declared the uprising impossible. He was deposed and replaced as chief executive of the Irish Republic by Colonel Tom Kelly, an officer determined to make things happen. Kelly's colonelcy was of the Fenian variety, but he had fought with the 10th Ohio during the Civil War and achieved the rank of captain. He crossed to Ireland as soon as the Civil War ended and had been one of the organisers of Stephens's escape. Escaping himself back to New York, in January 1867 Kelly volunteered with other former Union officers to cross the Atlantic yet again and initiate the rebellion. Kelly, the renowned McCafferty and Captain Ricard O'Sullivan Burke, formerly of the 15th New York, travelled to England, which they saw as one of their theatres of war. Kelly appointed to overall military command of the Fenians a French soldier he had known and admired as a brevet brigadier-general in the Union army, Gustave Paul Cluseret. Cluseret's command would be called – to utter a name which would ultimately mean many things to many people – the Irish Republican Army.

The first sign of apparent hope for Fenian prisoners came in February

1867, when the Confederate raider McCafferty decided, without discussion with Cluseret or Kelly, to attack Chester Castle, an arms depot in the north of England. Numerous Fenians from Ireland and from the British north participated. The munitions were to be rushed to Holyhead and so to Dublin on the mail boat. When they arrived, the entire Fenian movement in Ireland was to rise!

A little after one o'clock on the day of the proposed raid, 11 February, McCafferty learned that the authorities had been alerted. Chester Castle had been fortified and Guards detachments were on their way from London. McCafferty managed to call off the escapade in time to save some arrests, but throughout the next day many young Fenians were detained as they landed at Dundalk and Dublin.

Though an American officer, after inspecting Fenian preparations in Ireland, advised Kelly and Cluseret in their lodgings in London that there was not the least chance of Fenians holding the field for a day, Kelly was determined to strike on 5 March. He believed there were 14,000 men ready in Dublin and 20,000 in Cork. The Fenian 'General' Godfrey Massey, a former corporal in the British army, was sent to Ireland by Kelly to inform the Irish Fenians of the date for the uprising. With him travelled a former member of the Irish Brigade, now turned British informer, a man named Corydon. Massey was arrested on Limerick railway station as he arrived to lead the Limerick Fenians. Nonetheless, in early March, Fenians in Dublin, Drogheda, Cork, Tipperary, Clare and Limerick assembled in locations on the edge of cities and marched against the institutions of government, particularly against police barracks.

There were successful attacks on two police barracks near Dublin, Stepaside and Glencullen. But an armed force of police opened fire on the Fenians who assembled at Tallaght, south of Dublin. Similarly forty police equipped with Lee Enfield rifles dispersed a barely armed body of perhaps 1,000 Fenians in the Potato Market in Drogheda. In Limerick the police at Kilmallock held off a determined Fenian attack led by a man in a green uniform and green slouch hat. In Cork 2,000 men led by the former Union captain of infantry Michael O'Brien captured the police barracks at Ballyknockane, tore up the Great Southern and Great Western railway lines, and cut the telegraph. Another group raided the coastguard station at Knockadoon. But without an Irish headquarters through which Cluseret's concerted orders could be conveyed, there was no chance of any further coherent action. Soon flying columns of troops and police were scouring the south-west and west of Ireland breaking up parties of Fenians, on whom snow was now falling. The last, sharp action was fought in Kilclooney Wood in Tipperary, where the Fenians were surrounded. From Dublin on 12 March, Colonel Thomas Kelly wrote bitterly to America, ' "Little Baldy" [Stephens] has finally given up the ghost and acknowledged that if he came to Ireland the people would be certain to make short work of him. The rascal is in Paris, taking his ease with his wife, while the destiny of Ireland is in the balance . . . We now begin to realise fully the madness of McCafferty's attack at Chester.' Now, 'It is war to the knife. *Only send us the knife.*'

In fact a Fenian privateer was on its way, the *Erin's Hope*, a brigantine of 138 tons which had been confiscated by New York Customs and which somehow the O'Mahony wing acquired. When it sailed from New York that month, it carried in the hold approximately 5,000 modern breech-loading and repeating rifles and 1,500,000 rounds of ammunition. But it was ultimately unable to find anyone in the shattered Fenian movement to take, store and distribute those arms. In June, off Waterford, twenty-eight Irish Fenians landed from the *Erin's Hope* and were all arrested within a day. All of this must have been grievous intelligence for Fenians in prisons across the south of England.

On Dartmoor in the spring of 1867, John Boyle O'Reilly – having heard distant rumours of Fenian disaster – waited for a day when the prison gun which signalled incoming fog would be fired. When it happened the warders hastily gathered the men, since fog gave opportunities for escape. As prisoners were assembled, O'Reilly remained huddled against the wall of a deep drain. Climbing out at night, he walked towards the sea with a plan to reach Dartmouth or some other port and escape by ship. He found it appalling out on the moor and, after a second drenched night, was very nearly pleased to be tracked down by warders and bloodhounds.

More depressing Fenian news would reach him. On 11 September 1867, Colonel Kelly was arrested in a doorway in Manchester, in company with a Captain Deasy, who had fought in the Cork uprising the previous March. A week later a prison van taking Kelly and Deasy from the police court to prison passed under a Manchester railway arch, where it was ambushed by thirty Fenians. Inside the van with the two Fenian prisoners and other non-political criminals was a police sergeant, Brett, who refused to surrender. A Fenian fired his revolver through a ventilator and the bullet fatally wounded Sergeant Brett. A female prisoner in the van took the keys from the dying sergeant and passed them through the ventilator to the Fenians outside. Kelly and Deasy were taken out, led over a wall and across the railway line. They were never to be recaptured and would reach America.

But five young Irishmen – none of them the man who had fired on Brett – were arrested and charged with murder. One, an Irish soldier serving in the Royal Marines, was obviously falsely arrested, and though sentenced to death – a result which said little for the objectivity of the court – was pardoned. Another condemned man, an American named Condon, would ultimately be saved at the insistence of Secretary of State Seward. American Captain Michael O'Brien, lately an officer of the Union army, had been sentenced to death along with William Allen and Philip Larkin. All three made the eloquent statements before sentencing which in this century of revolutionary failure came to stand as a kind of victory in themselves. On a foggy day in November, O'Brien, Larkin and Allen were executed, the first two suffering greatly through the incompetence of the executioner. The three became at once the Manchester Martyrs, revered and made the subject of monuments from Canada to New Zealand. Even the constitutionalists such as John Martin attended and spoke at the funeral of the martyrs, their bodies having been brought back to Ireland for burial near MacManus and O'Connell in Glasnevin.

An Irish-American war veteran, Ricard O'Sullivan Burke, was now in charge of Fenian responses in England. He was less than thirty years old at the time he found himself the commander of a dwindling enterprise. Well-travelled, he had served in the Chilean cavalry, and spoke Spanish. As an engineering officer, he performed well on the Peninsula in 1862, and by war's end had become a very young brevet colonel. He took perhaps too much hope from the Irish demographics of England; there were by now 600,000 Irish-born, and hundreds of thousands of first-generation English who had Irish parents. But though there was much Fenian sympathy, it did not translate into massed Fenian action.

Friedrich Engels seemed to understand the distinction better than the Fenians. His mistress was an Irishwoman and his home in Manchester a centre of Fenian activity, and even decorated in Fenian colours of green and black. Though he was critical of the activities of the IRB, speaking of their 'braggart, aimless propaganda through action', he and Marx both had resolutions of support for the Manchester Martyrs passed in the International Workingmen's Association and the more middle-class Reform League. Marx wrote, 'I sought in every way to provoke this manifestation of the English workers in support of Fenianism.' But in the end he decided it was hopeless: 'England possesses a working class divided into two hostile camps, English proletarians, and Irish proletarians. The ordinary English worker hates the Irish worker as a competitor.'

Ricard O'Sullivan Burke could do little more than hide until arrested in London in December 1867. He was put in Clerkenwell prison in east London, where other Fenians including Mayo's Michael Davitt were being held. Now Clerkenwell became a malign location for the relationship between Britons and Irish; a group of Fenians anxious to release Captain Burke set a barrel of gunpowder alight against the wall of the prison. In the surrounding working-class suburb the result was tragic. At the church of St James, Clerkenwell, can be found the memorial plaque to the 'victims of the terrible outrage which occurred in this parish on Friday, December 13 1867. Perpetrated by certain misguided and wicked persons, who, being members of the so-called FENIAN CONSPIRACY . . . placed a barrel of powder against the northern wall of the prison and, firing the same, suddenly rendered the immediate locality a mass of ruins.' Fifteen people of the neighbourhood including two children were killed instantly or died of their injuries.

Though the main, failed purpose was to rescue a Fenian leader, Clerkenwell set the pattern of Irish terror in London, and of a wilful English judicial incompetence. Michael Barrett, a young Ulster Fenian who had actually been in Glasgow at the time of Clerkenwell, served as a target of convenience, and like the Manchester three was found guilty on the most shaky evidence. On 26 May 1868, he was the last man to be publicly executed in England. Nearly 2,000 local people collected outside Newgate gaol at 11.00 p.m. for the execution, singing 'Rule Britannia', 'Champagne Charlie' and 'Oh, my, I've Got to Die'. As if to imply that Manchester, Clerkenwell and Barrett had established the nature of the discourse between Ireland and England, more than a century later, in 1973, a car bomb exploded beside the Old Bailey on the spot where Michael Barrett had died.

In Millbank prison, O'Donovan Rossa, who had spent much time on punishment, sometimes in the 'black cell', from which all light was excluded, sometimes with his hands manacled for weeks so that he had to eat his skilly by lowering his head to the bowl, was visited by the governor. 'I've come to learn if you'll volunteer to go to the penal settlements of Western Australia.'

Rossa replied, 'But I'll do no volunteering.'

'The government won't send you otherwise.'

'Then I'll remain. I prefer to receive their tortures here than in the wilds of Western Australia.'

Ultimately Rossa would be sent to the military prison at Chatham, where many of the American officers were kept. Here, their excessive punishments would help produce the committee of inquiry known as the Devon Commission.

But the Fenians in Dartmoor were to be shipped, willy-nilly. Including the much-reduced John Boyle O'Reilly, they were marched out of that awful door and had their last dim glimpse of the Farm, the huge, foul drainage system below the prison. They were chained together for their journey with a 'bright, strong chain', and rode to the railway station.

Reaching Portland by rail late at night, they moved through a near-empty world to the prison. Here by lamplight they surrendered their Dartmoor clothes and stood about naked for some hours. 'To the prison officials this seemed highly amusing,' said O'Reilly, 'but to me . . . the point of the joke was rather obscure.'

Re-clothed and sent out to exercise next day, they found themselves with a party of twenty other Fenians. Many were surprised to see how the Dartmoor regime had weakened athletic O'Reilly. All were aware by now that a ship named *Hougoumont* already stood off Portland with London prisoners in its hold, and though O'Reilly and the others did not know it some friends from the London prisons, notably Millbank, were aboard. Now, on 6 October, chained at wrist, ankle and to each other, twenty men to each gang, the Fenians being kept separate from other prisoners, they were marched a short distance to the little harbour steamer which was meant to take them out to the transport. On the wharf waited a young woman who threw herself weeping against the shoulder of the Dublin Fenian Patrick Dunne. Before the 'merciless officials' removed her, O'Reilly saw Dunne, whose hands were tethered, lower his head to kiss the woman, his sister. The 22-year-old Dunne had been given a sentence of twenty years, which his sister must have thought the equivalent of life.

Seated in chains on the steamer, they were taken out to board the *Hougoumont*, and climbed up a stairway to a deck lined with what O'Reilly called soldiers, but what were probably the 50 veterans of the Pensioner Guard, recruited for service in Western Australia. Chains were now knocked off convicts' ankles and wrists, and the Dartmoor and Portland Fenians were ordered below into the dim Hades of the convict deck. As they descended into a space whose sides were entirely made up of massive iron bars, 'the prisoners within clutched the bars and looked eagerly through, hoping, perhaps, to see a familiar face . . . As we stood thus, a tall gaunt man pushed his way through the criminal crowd to the door.' It was O'Reilly's friend Patrick Keating, a man of nearly forty years, a soldier from the 5th Dragoon Guards. As they were admitted to the teeming, rowdy prison deck, Keating led them aft, 'to a door leading amidships from the criminal part of the ship'. That door was unlocked by someone. And: 'we were with our friends – our brothers. Great God!'

Denis Cashman of Waterford, a 25-year-old married clerk of genteel manners, had been sentenced to seven years as a Fenian. While picking coir fibres in Millbank prison in London, he had heard that he was to be transported to Australia, and so separated from his young wife Kate and his two children. Moved out 'chained to a foxy animal, who growled like a bear if I diverged a jot from my course', he had been delighted that on the little steamer which took him up the Thames the silent system by which he had lived in prison for the past nine months was over. His meeting with O'Reilly on *Hougoumont* now was the beginning of a kindly lifetime association on two continents. Cashman had moral strength and would play an almost immediate role in soothing O'Reilly's desperation.

The ship *Hougoumont* was 875 tons, less than 60 yards in length, only 34 feet broad at main-deck level; and into that cramped equation the master William Cozens would need to fit and maintain 280 male convicts, amongst them 63 Fenians. *Hougoumont*'s passage would end the transportation to Australia of British convicts which had begun with the little ships of Captain Phillip's First Fleet in 1788. Perhaps there was an inherent neatness in the fact that Irish politicals, present on so many of the convict ships, should be represented so emphatically upon *Hougoumont*.

As the ship loaded its last felons at Portland, not everyone in the geographically huge, sparsely populated colony of Western Australia was delighted to be receiving these newcomers. A Western Australian farmer, William Burges, who happened to be visiting London at the time, sent back an alarming letter which was published in the Western Australian press. A gentleman at the Colonial Office told Burges 'he regretted their having been sent'. There was fear the Americans would raid Western Australia. 'They had attempted to rescue Smith O'Brien from Van Diemen's Land and they would surely attempt to rescue those men by bombarding Fremantle, knocking down the prison walls and letting six thousand ruffians loose.'

The governor of Western Australia was the same Dr John Stephen Hampton who had tussled with O'Brien in Van Diemen's Land. Hampton had suffered since those days: in 1857 a court of inquiry found he had engaged in corrupt practices in running the Van Diemen's Land convict department – he had gone off to Canada on half-pay, and under a shadow, and many considered he had been lucky to be offered the governorship of Western Australia in 1862. To his administration of Western Australia he brought the same toughness as he had shown in Van Diemen's Land, interfering very much in convict matters. The Howard League, a famed prison reform movement in London, had already condemned the prison system in Western Australia for its physical and mental cruelty. Now Hampton received from Downing Street, in a dispatch dated 17 October 1867, the official yet offhand news that Fenians were aboard *Hougoumont*: 'Some of the Fenian prisoners to the number of —— should be included.' The Whitehall clerks did not get around to inking in what number Hampton should expect. But Hampton was an enemy of colonial panic. His own Crown Solicitor, George Leake, warned citizens about Fenian privateers. 'A vessel merely armed with one long 18 pounder might with shells lay Fremantle in ashes in a few hours.' The commander of the

Fremantle company of the Western Australian Volunteers, Captain Charles Manning, warned Hampton that Western Australia was 'a community where the Irish element largely prevails, and where about three fifths of the military at my disposal are Irishmen'. Just before Christmas 1867, with *Hougoumont* still at sea, Commodore Lambert of the British naval station in Sydney told Hampton he would send him HMS *Brisk*, a corvette of sixteen guns, to protect Fremantle. Two companies of the 14th Regiment were being sent from Tasmania, though the troops from Tasmania would quickly be withdrawn again. And HMS *Brisk*, despite its promising name, failed to reach Fremantle before the Fenians did.

Even before *Hougoumont* sailed, O'Reilly observed everything, for it was his intention to seize the ship. He would, of course, need to deal with the Pensioner Guards. Many had wives and children aboard. Also aboard were four assistant warders and their families. But O'Reilly sought a near-bloodless coup, which would leave these women and children, and indeed his fellow convicts, unharmed.

On 12 October, the wind shifted to make departure from Portland possible. The first morning at sea was Sunday and the Fenians were permitted on deck at 6.00 a.m., when a service was conducted without the help of the seasick young chaplain, Father Delany. The officiator was instead the Cork Fenian youngster John Sarsfield Casey. Casey, whose penetrating eyes shine from his mug shot in a manner which might have confirmed all the bad opinions people had of Fenians, was in fact a noble-hearted, virginal young man. He bore the nickname 'The Galtee Boy', because of his exposure in the *Irish People* of the landlord of Galtee, County Cork.

O'Reilly and the sixteen other soldier Fenians had developed a greater edge of despair because they lived on the crowded, brutalising main prison deck. Here sleeping space was limited, and seventy hammocks were needed as well as bunks. But some of the Pensioner Guard had served in the same regiments as the Fenians and treated them gently. O'Reilly, notable in any company, easefully charming, was ultimately allowed to sling his hammock permanently in the area occupied by the civilian Fenians. He rushed to the company of Denis Cashman and another civilian Fenian whose friendship he cherished, John Flood. Flood, now in his early thirties, had been involved in the Chester Castle raid and in the armed affray at Tallaght in March 1867.

Towards the non-political offenders on the prison deck, Fenian attitudes were ambiguous. The politicals saw themselves as a separate caste. 'Of course,' wrote Cashman proudly, 'we did not associate or scarcely speak to the unfortunates, although I believe a portion of them had been *very respectable* and well educated.'

Decades later, Cashman would acknowledge O'Reilly's plans to take over the ship. 'A number of us secretly consulted and decided to try the experiment, provided we could get the greater part of our associates to determinedly enter the project.' Cashman says O'Reilly would have attempted it like 'a thunder-clap' and that, had the seizure succeeded, they could have counted on Flood, a first-class navigator. The concept was put to the Fenian prisoners, but the family men with short sentences were dubious. After all, a successful mutiny would not allow a return to Ireland, where their families waited. There was also the problem of what to do with the 200 criminal convicts. If *Hougoumont* sailed into New York, would America want to take the non-Fenians?

Bad weather over, the Fenians organised their concert parties, with Cashman president of the revels. He tried to involve the tormented O'Reilly too, without much success at first, but concert parties operated as a distraction from O'Reilly's perilous scheme. The performing Fenians included Cashman and Joseph Noonan (singing duets together), John Flood, and the comic turns of John Sheehan, an older Limerick Fenian, the *card* of every concert. John Edward Kelly, an Irish American captured at Kilclooney Wood, was popular for his recital of 'Gertrude of Wyoming'. Word-weighing John Kenealy stepped forward to recite 'To Be or Not to Be', a Shakespearian soliloquy not irrelevant to O'Reilly, and Davis's poem about the old Irish Brigade at Fontenoy. Every concert was concluded by the singing of 'Let Erin Remember'.

Depressed, O'Reilly did not participate in the first two concerts. He had not yet committed himself to the voyage and the duty of performance poet. But one night he did sign up, reciting one of his own works, 'The Old School Clock', which would become a popular recitative poem, though it was once withdrawn from the copybooks of the Irish National School Board because of its Fenian origins. He also performed 'Uncle Ned's Tale', a narrative verse about an old dragoon, which O'Reilly would much later publish for the diversion of his audience in the United States, along with its sequel, 'How the Flag Was Saved'.

> A truer, braver soldier ne'er for king and country bled.
> His wanderings are forever o'er. God rest thee, Uncle Ned.

O'Reilly's fellow Fenians hooted and applauded, validated by O'Reilly's easy literary talent. Even ship's officers came to hear O'Reilly do his own material.

Towards the end of October the *Hougoumont* was off the Cape Verde Islands. The classes given by this or that scholarly convict were suspended, Cashman recounted, until the ship again reached the temperate zone. 'The air was foul smelling and oppressive,' John Boyle O'Reilly would later write in his novel *Moondyne*. 'The deck above them was blazing hot. The pitch dropped from the seams and burned their flesh as it fell.' Yet *Hougoumont* does not seem to have been a markedly brutal ship – Surgeon Smith, RN, allowed juries of peers to try misdemeanours. Only one Fenian ended up in the punishment cell, and that was the quiet but stubborn William Foley, formerly of the 5th Dragoon Guards, who had concealed a rope. A number of non-political prisoners were also condemned to irons. 'It was awful to hear the unfortunate with the chains clanking everywhere they went,' wrote Cashman. Two – neither of them Fenians – were flogged, the first one receiving forty lashes and being cheered by the convicts at the end of his stoically endured punishment. Throughout the ritual Cashman averted his eyes.

One convict died, a man named Corcoran. Cashman wrote, 'I saw the poor fellow smoking on a hatch a few days since.' Corcorcan was committed to the sea by Father Delany, and a choir Delany had trained sang the *Miserere* and a *Te Deum*. Corcoran had the honour to be the last transportee of all to die aboard ship in this extraordinary phase of British penal transportation to Australia.

By late November, back in colder air, Cashman saw the wind tear the sails to shreds. It had by now, however, been decided by the committee of Fenians that they would produce a handwritten newspaper and literary magazine, and that it would be called the *Wild Goose*. Father Bernard Delany had agreed to provide the paper. The journal's title-page was intricately ornamented by Cashman with shamrocks and ivy wreaths, designs which must have taken days to produce and which were therefore welcome therapy. The journal subtitled itself, in Cashman's script, *A Collection of Ocean Waifs*. Flood was editor, John Boyle O'Reilly sub-editor.

John Edward Kelly, a former Bostonian captured at Kilclooney Wood, contributed to one of the weekly editions of the *Wild Goose* an ironic piece called 'Australia':

This great continent in the south, having been discovered by some Dutch skipper and his crew, somewhere between the 1st and 19th Century of the Christian era, was in consequence taken possession by the Government of Great Britain . . . That magnanimous government in the kindly exuberance of their feelings, have placed a large portion of that immense tract of country at our disposal, generously defraying all expenses incurred on our way to it.

Many of the humorous pieces were contributed by Kelly, who in a character named 'Paddy from Cork' went in for a little of the Irish-mockery to which he himself might have objected had he seen it in the British press. 'Yez is able to write pothry and purty stories wid anny one – I don't care who's his father – this side o' the Galtees.'

Joseph Noonan, who would much later come into bad odour with some of his fellow prisoners, described for his readers the events surrounding his first arrest in Kerry, his escape to England, his subsequent escape from the window of a speeding train, his return to Tralee, his final arrest. O'Reilly signed his work 'Boyne'; Kelly was 'Kappa' or 'Laoi' (the Irish for K); and Father Delany 'Beta' or 'Delta'. Thomas Duggan, a 45-year-old school-master from Cork, who would live into his nineties in Western Australia, signed himself 'Mushra', and handwrote for the *Wild Goose*, under Cashman's flourishing title design, a weekly prose serial named 'Queen Cliodna and the Flower of Erin'. Flood wrote under the title 'Binn Eider', after his birthplace north of Dublin. Each completed, hand-produced and handwritten edition of the *Wild Goose* was marked: 'Printed and published at the office, No. 6 Mess, Intermediate Cabin, Ship *Hougue-ment*. Ed. John Flood, and J. B. O'Reilly, and J. E. K., registered for transmission abroad.' O'Reilly consistently misspelled the name of the convict transport in exactly the way he would, years later, when writing his novel.

Seven weekly issues were released on Saturdays throughout the remainder of the voyage, and Captain Cozens and the mates asked for copies of the Christmas special. The entire ship's log regarding latitude and longitude for the previous week was published in each edition – a result of co-operation between the quarterdeck and convict deck. Captain Cozens was tolerant of the satiric nationalism of the *Wild Goose*, and permitted O'Reilly to move fully out of the main convict section to join his fellow editors in No. 6 Mess. The editors were also given certain extra luxuries, such as a delicious meat loaf, and the privilege to stay on deck till 7.30 p.m. for the duration of the voyage. It was good for the soul to enjoy the deck after it had been cleared for the evening. 'I had a splendid walk and chat with Jack [Flood] and John [O'Reilly],' said Cashman of one such dusk promenade.

The *Wild Goose* proved to be O'Reilly's light in darkness. He would later remember the eagerness with which men waited below for himself or Flood to read the articles to them. 'Amid the dim glare of the lamp the men, at night, would group strangely on extemporised seats. The yellow light fell down on the dark forms, throwing a ghastly glare on the pale faces of the men, as they listened with blazing eyes to Davis's *Fontenoy* or *The Clansman's Wild Address to Shane's Head.*'

Christmas was marked by a meal of 'plum-duff and salt horse', two glasses of wine for each man, a stroll on the deck, and then the descent below to listen to O'Reilly read the Christmas edition of the *Wild Goose*. The day had not been marked by any Mass, for the ship was too unsteady. But Flood's farewell editorial was like a secular version of *Ite Missa Est*, the dismissal at the end of Mass. 'Hearts are beating for you from which time and space cannot separate you. Prove worthy of their interest in you, and for the rest – Courage, and trust in God. Adieu.' Bad weather continued. On New Year's Eve the ship was struck by a tremendous wave which overturned the skilly pots and scalded convicts working as mess prefects.

Cashman was excited as the *Hougoumont* neared Western Australia. He believed that his 7-year sentence might yield an early ticket-of-leave, and enable him to bring out 'my dearest K and dear boys with me, wherever I may pitch my tent, as quickly as I possibly can'. O'Reilly also found the first sighting of Western Australia's shore momentous: 'From morning light they leant on the rail, looking away over the smooth sea to where the land was yellow with heat above the unseen continent . . . The shore of Western Australia is quite low, and the first sight of land are tall mahogany trees in the bush.' It had taken *Hougoumont* eighty-nine days to make the passage.

At noon they passed within a stone's throw of Rottnest Island, offshore from the port of Fremantle, where naked black men worked in the sand, the island being a place of punishment for refractory natives. Soon the inshore waters and beaches and the town itself were seen:

> The green shoal-water, the soft air, with a yellowish warmth, the pure white sand of the beach, and the dark green of the unbroken forest beyond, made a scene almost like fairyland . . . But there was a stern reminder of reality in the little town of Fremantle that lay between the forest and the sea . . . in the centre of the houses, spread out like a gigantic star-fish, was a vast stone prison.

Governor Hampton of Western Australia came aboard with an official party and the water police. The governor in *Moondyne*, no doubt modelled on Hampton, 'wore a blue tunic, with epaulettes like a naval officer, white trousers, and a cocked hat'. A *Fremantle Herald* reporter found out from the captain that the Fenians had behaved well during the journey. The town of Fremantle itself was in a state of great excitement, and divided between those who sympathised with the Fenians and those who expected the worst. To ease the perpetually stated fears of coastal Fremantle's loyalists, Governor Hampton had moved his residence for the time being from the capital Perth, some 10 miles up the broad reaches of the Swan River, to the Fenian-threatened port of Fremantle on the sea. He reported to the Secretary for the Colonies, the Duke of Buckingham: 'The public anxiety gradually diminished and ultimately almost wholly ceased when it became known on the 9th January that the conduct of the Fenian convicts during the voyage from England had been good in every respect.'

26

The Fenians of the Desert Coast

> Western Australia is the Cinderella of the South. She had no gold like her sisters. To her was given the servile and unhappy portion. The dreams of British society were poured upon her soul. The robber and the man-slayer were sent thither. Her territory was marked off with a *Red Line.*
>
> John Boyle O'Reilly, *Moondyne*

> Boyle, poor Boyle, cried and cried in desperation for help.
>
> James Maguire, settler, Western Australia

The Fenians were landed with the other prisoners by way of barge on the sultry morning of 10 January 1868. Patrick Walle, a Drogheda labourer who wrote stylishly, described the houses of the town of Fremantle as constructed 'of all white sandstone, nothing is seen but white'. Marching in early light through this pale-stoned, glittering landscape, on a coastline whose winter rains of less than 20 inches produced huge, hardy native forests but whose hinterland was, simply stated, a million square miles of desert, the prisoners entered through the main gate into an immense, high-walled and sandy parade ground, and so on in through a further gate which led to the cells. They were bathed and shaved, and their particulars were recorded. Clothing was issued – according to Walle: 'A suit of Drogheda linen, ornamented with a red stripe and black bands, typical of the rank we hold in the colony, to wit – convicts.'

In most cases, the Fenians had already served in British prisons the first stage of imprisonment – six months' solitary confinement. John Kenealy, beginning the third year of his sentence, was relieved to find that the authorities seemed to be aware of these technicalities. The Fenian prisoners were told they would now be admitted to a probationary stage, at the end of which they would be given their tickets-of-leave. Men with five-year sentences were now within a year of that. Their prospects were so utterly different from those of the soldier Fenians, who might receive a ticket-of-leave but would never be permitted to leave Western Australia.

The *Hougoumont* convicts, entering a felon population of 3,000, were given two days' rest in prison cells and then put to work stone-breaking and making roads on the outskirts of Fremantle. Hampton, despite his inglorious reputation, put the civilian Fenians into their own work parties. 'As their conduct on board the ship and their demeanour on landing had been so satisfactory, I considered it desirable to order the civilians to be separated from the ordinary criminal class.' But this degree of indulgence did not apply where the 'particularly aggravated nature of the treason' military Fenians had committed was concerned.

Assistant Warder William Howard, an officious and small-minded fellow, and the more lenient Charles McGarry, both of whom had been amongst the new warders shipped along with the Pensioner Guards on *Hougoumont*, had been given a gang of twenty civilian Fenians each to take into the bush to work. Howard's group marched south of the little port of Fremantle to a camp on the Clarence Road, 4 miles outside town. McGarry's party marched north-east to a road camp at West Guildford, between Perth and Fremantle. Patrick Walle, who lived and worked in the party commanded by the more exacting Howard, described the camp as consisting of 'four miserable tiny huts and a tent'. There were constant visitations of bugs and mosquitoes. Though the heat was intense amongst the giant trees of Western Australia, there was the comfort of being near the surf, and swimming at day's end. Kenealy, prisoner 9795, was fortunate to be in McGarry's road party, which also included the teenager John Sarsfield Casey, and 23-year-old Eugene Geary of Cork, whom Kenealy had known at home. George Connolly, a Dubliner in his early forties, described in a letter to his wife the situation in which he and the others found themselves: 'To lie upon we have each got a hammock, but neither sheets, beds or pillows, and at night our only visitors are fleas and mosquitoes . . . Our work here is quarrying and blasting stones under almost a tropical sun.'

Some military Fenians might have become labourers in the blinding, sweltering quarries, where local Aborigines sometimes sat to watch the phenomenon of slaving white men. But most of them were dispersed in road gangs, where they endured what they considered the indignity of being chained, sometimes by day and night both, to British thieves. Father Lynch, the new Fremantle gaol chaplain, had been persuaded by Father Delany to have the vulnerable O'Reilly assigned to him as an assistant in the library, and six Fenians in all remained at Fremantle prison. As well as O'Reilly, John Flood and Denis Cashman worked as clerks. O'Reilly's services to Father Lynch were suitably diverse and engaging. He attended to the office work, kept the chapel clean, organised choir practice four times a week, acted as school monitor and helped prisoners write their letters home. All this was much better than the horrors of incarceration as he had experienced them in Dartmoor. His friend Cashman admitted, 'Prison discipline is by no means as strict as it is in England'; they were adequately fed and issued with pipes and tobacco.

*

After four weeks working for Father Lynch in Fremantle, O'Reilly was ordered to report to a vessel in Fremantle Harbour, and 'deliver the articles named in this bill of lading; read it!' On the way to the pier, O'Reilly read the bill and saw that it called for the delivery in good order and condition of three articles – one convict, Number 9843, one bag, one hammock or bed – down the coast to the port of Bunbury. O'Reilly travelled unchained. Chains were seen here more as a matter of punishment and behaviour control; generally the penal system in Western Australia operated on the principle that there was nowhere to escape to.

The officer in charge of the gang to which O'Reilly was assigned by the authorities at the Bunbury depot was a compassionate fellow, a man in his early forties, Deputy Warder Henry Woodman, who employed O'Reilly as a clerk and constable. Constables wore a red stripe on their sleeves as their badge of office. O'Reilly's assumption of this post under the regime of the reasonable Woodman does not seem to have created any enmity amongst his fellow prisoners. Working on the road gang, O'Reilly found himself amongst some of the oldest and tallest of forests on the Australian mainland, and therefore on earth. He felt an enthusiasm for the full-blooded yet spiritually unappeasing Australian landscape. Certainly, it seemed to have left a pronounced mark on his imagination, and he would write some of his best verse about it:

> Here the aisle
> Moonlit and deep of reaching Gothic arms,
> Realm for towering gums, mahogany, and palm,
> And odourless jam and sandal; there the growth
> Of arm-long velvet leaves grown hoar in calm
> – In calm unbroken since their luscious youth.
> How can I show you all the silent birds with
> Strange metallic blinking on the wing?
> Or how tell half their sadness in cold words –
> The poor dumb lutes, the birds that never sing?

Soon after their arrival in Western Australia, an event occurred on the other side of the continent, in the populous, hopeful and pleasant port city of Sydney, which would bring opprobrium upon the Fenians but also on the Irish throughout the British Empire. The queen's younger son, Prince Alfred, the first of royal blood ever to visit Australia, had come to greet his mother's Australian subjects. A royal charity picnic open to the public was arranged, to be held at the pleasure grounds at Clontarf in Sydney harbour, a place which carried a name resonant in Irish history as the place of Brian Boru's final victory and death. The picnic was attended by a huge crowd, amongst them a solitary and self-declared Fenian named

Henry O'Farrell. He was a 'ruined seminarian', in his mid-thirties, and he harboured equally passionate feelings against the Church, particularly the Archdiocese of Melbourne, as he did against the British Empire. The Archdiocese had employed his brother as their lawyer but left him dangling in a scandal over creditors. O'Farrell himself had recently been released from the nursing home where he underwent treatment for delirium tremens. He carried with him on the harbour ferry to Clontarf on 12 March 1868 two loaded revolvers, a Smith & Wesson and a Colt. Hidden in an enthusiastic crowd, O'Farrell, as the prince passed, fired point-blank, striking him in the back. When a government official stepped between the prince and O'Farrell, the self-appointed assassin hesitated to fire a second time. The delayed shot went wide as he was grabbed from behind. 'I'm a Fenian – God Save Ireland!' yelled O'Farrell.

Lord Belmore, the urbane, personable governor of New South Wales, an Anglo-Irishman and lord of grand Castle Coole in Fermanagh, was near the prince to see Fenian evil apparently manifest itself on, of all colonial turfs, his own! The bullet had entered to the right of the prince's spine and lodged in the flesh on that side of the chest. The prince – it was reported – sought no anaesthetic when having it removed. A young, robust man, he made a good recovery.

O'Farrell claimed when arrested that the Fenian organisation had allotted him the task of assassinating the queen's son. On the eve of his execution in Darlinghurst gaol, Sydney, in late April, he withdrew the statement about a conspiracy, and said he had acted alone. Lord Belmore himself – who did not wish a witch-hunt – said that his own opinion, 'although it is not shared by my leading advisers', was that 'the balance of probabilities was in favour of the truth of his dying statement'. But loyalists from New South Wales to British Columbia were only too willing to believe O'Farrell, and to paint all Irish Catholic immigrants in O'Farrell's colours. Worse, demagogues such as Sir Henry Parkes, Attorney-General of New South Wales, saw votes and new popularity in promoting the idea that O'Farrell was a visible sign of a pervasive, fanatic network amongst Irish Australians. Even in the bush, on his farm at Gundaroo, south of Goulburn, Tom Larkin, blacksmith and Royal Mail carrier, child of Irish Ribbonman convict Hugh Larkin, felt the force of sectarian suspicion.

The New South Wales Colonial Secretary's papers for the time indicate the level of hysteria. Attorney-General Parkes was so anxious to prove a conspiracy that he allowed a prisoner named Charles Miller, a convicted confidence man who had shared a cell with O'Farrell, to be released from Darlinghurst gaol to begin an investigation into Fenian cells in the towns throughout the bush. Every communication between agent Miller and the

Inspector-General of Police dealt not with hard intelligence but with money. From the Albion Hotel in the gold-mining town of Grenfell came an urgent telegram: 'Not sufficient funds for Bathurst – please send more money'. Miller continued to swan his way from country hotel to country hotel, buying drinks and implying by letter that he was closing in on Fenian cadres.

A further index of the frenzy was that even a primitive Methodist journalist named Boggis, of the *Newcastle Chronicle*, was under investigation for saying at a camp meeting that Prince Alfred was 'a Sabbath breaker, a gambler, and, if report speaks true, a drunkard'. A Detective McGlone of Berrima was investigated for opinions expressed at Shalvey's Hotel, where he was reported to have said that if a poor man with five children were killed no one would pay this much account.

Questions were asked in the New South Wales legislature about even the humblest of Irish labourers: the intended St Patrick's Day demonstration of certain persons styled 'Fenians' on No. 5 contract of the Great Western Railway Works. In fact, the police reported, 'Persons did collect, but were easily dissuaded from marching.' An Irish employee of a baker named Mr McBurnie, delivering bread in Edgecliff, an eastern suburb of Sydney, was reported to have said that the prince was a rare boy for the girls, but if he took away a wife of his he would cut him and pickle him in salad oil. A taxi driver named Stoneman, proprietor of Sydney cab No. 148, said he had driven an Irishman named Laing to Homebush, west of Sydney, that Laing had confabulated with a number of other Irishmen there, and had then got back into the cab and told Stoneman the prince would be shot.

Belmore was appalled by this sectarian fever, but Parkes relished it.

The tide of feeling against the Irish in Australia and elsewhere was probably accentuated too by events in Canada, where the Canadian politician D'Arcy McGee paid an exorbitant price. In the list of his anti-Fenian sins was included not only his refusal to call for mercy for the captured Fenians of 1866, but also a speech made in Wexford, his birthplace, when he went in 1865 to represent Canada as Minister of Agriculture and Immigration at the Dublin International Exhibition. The speech he gave, entitled 'Twenty Years' Experience of Irish Life in America', encouraged Canadian immigration and attacked Fenian threats against Canada. The Americans might share with the Irish a certain hostility for Britain, he said, but that did not mean they accepted the Irish as social equals, the way Canada did. 'For if wages in North America were higher, life was shorter.' McGee called his republicanism of 1848 an 'honest folly which had nothing in common with the Punch and Judy

Jacobinism of the Fenians'. The speech, belittling '48, offended even former Young Irelanders. In North America it bred Fenian hostility.

With the invasion of 1866 repulsed, and Canadian confederation accomplished in 1867, Prime Minister John A. Macdonald had to pay off various Irish supporters from the maritime provinces of Canada, and D'Arcy McGee lost his Cabinet position. He decided to contest the seat of Prescott, near Ottawa, as candidate for the new Ontario Provincial Assembly. By winning Prescott, in which there were 900 Catholics out of a total of 2,000 voters, McGee could make the point that his influence was not dependent on the Irish; that he had a pluralist value.

McGee simultaneously stood for the new federal seat of Montreal West. A Fenian sympathiser, the lawyer Bernard Devlin, who had ten years before invited McGee to come to Montreal, opposed him in Montreal West's three wards – Saint-Antoine, largely Protestant; Saint-Lawrence, French-Canadian; and Saint-Anne's, Irish. Taking the lead of the *Irish Canadian*, Devlin and his supporters denounced McGee as 'the Goulah of Griffintown' – Griffintown being the Saint-Anne's ward location of McGee's offices, and 'Goulah' being a reference to Goulah Sullivan, who had betrayed O'Donovan Rossa's Phoenix Society in 1858. The Montreal Fenians denounced McGee as equal with Corydon the informer, and Massey the vacillator. This rhetoric was meant to hurt him politically. It might also have encouraged physical harm.

Fatally, McGee declared he had strangled Fenianism and would not be annoyed by its carcass. Walking to his committee rooms in Griffintown, he was pelted with stones thrown by pro-Fenian Irish, and soon found it impossible to hold a public meeting. He left for Prescott, arranging to have his exposé of Fenianism published in the *Montreal Gazette* in his absence. His articles spoke of a number of railway police who had refused to take the loyalty oath during the Fenian invasion. He asserted that the Fenians had gained influence in the St Patrick's Society of Montreal, of which Devlin was president. He named names.

McGee was defeated in the polling at Prescott, but he won Montreal West itself by a slight majority, though he ran behind Devlin in the Irish Saint-Anne's ward. When the victory was announced, Devlin's supporters attacked McGee's committee rooms. It was a little over ten years since his life had been endangered by Toronto Orangemen. Now he was at risk from his own. He told the Canadian House of Commons that the suspension of Habeas Corpus, which had been in operation since the invasion of the previous year, should remain in force because of Fenian influence in the St Patrick's Society. Here was McGee wielding one of the traditional weapons of oppression in Ireland against his own people in Canada!

McGee was in Ottawa, representing Montreal West, for most of that glacial winter of 1867–8, the same period during which the *Hougoumont* men were at sea and then settling into their Western Australian regime. After considerable research by at least one Fenian assassin, McGee was followed to his lodgings at Mrs Trotter's in Sparks Street, Ottawa, in the early hours of 7 April 1868, after a late-night sitting of the Canadian House of Commons. It was barely a month after O'Farrell shot the prince in Sydney and a week before McGee's forty-fourth birthday. According to the police, an Irishman named Whelan lay in wait, and, moving up as McGee paused to open the door, 'had come behind and shot him through the back of the neck, the ball passing out through his mouth and carrying away some of his teeth'. McGee died almost at once. John A. Macdonald was immediately informed, and McGee's body was still lying in Sparks Street in a sea of blood when the Prime Minister arrived and knelt beside him. A half-smoked cigar lay by McGee's hand, and a hat newly bought to celebrate the opening of Parliament. Macdonald sent a telegram to McGee's parish priest in Montreal, who broke the news to Mrs Ann McGee at home in St Catherine Street at four in the morning. McGee's 10-year-old daughter, Peggy, had just received a letter from her father: 'Mamma sent me all your kind messages and kisses, which I have counted up, and find that you owe me in all 220. Remember that.' Macdonald considered McGee's assassination a tragedy. The man was 'just at the beginning of his usefulness' as 'the most eloquent prophet of Confederation against all those, particularly the Nova Scotians, who opposed it'. McGee was a fallen soldier who 'deserved well of Canada and her people'. In fact, McGee's last speech in the late-night debate on 6 April had been in support of Dr Tupper, a Nova Scotian confederationist.

McGee's state funeral was a massive affair. The man convicted and executed for the murder, Patrick James Whelan, was a tailor by trade, who had served in the British army for nine years. His employment as regimental tailor in Toronto, Kingston and Quebec, all garrison towns, suggests that he may have tried to recruit Fenian sympathies from amongst Irish soldiers. During the election campaign of 1867, he worked as a scrutineer for Devlin. It is not known whether he was even a member of the Fenian Brotherhood, but, when arrested for assassinating McGee, he had in his possession a badge of the Toronto Hibernian Society and a copy of P. J. Meehan's Fenian New York paper, the *Irish American*.

There were no witnesses to McGee's shooting, but Whelan was depicted as having followed McGee over some time: though married to a Montreal boarding-house keeper, he was in Prescott during McGee's campaign there, returned to Montreal when McGee returned, and then began work as a waiter in Ottawa when McGee took his seat in Parliament. On 1

January 1868, Whelan, giving his name as Smith, had gone to McGee's Montreal house and warned him that an attempt would be made to burn it down. Finally, Whelan had been in and out of the Parliamentary gallery, watching McGee the night of the assassination, and possessed a pistol of the calibre that had killed McGee. His defence counsel, Orange Grand Master John H. Cameron, argued that the circumstantial evidence was consistent with both guilt and innocence. After the trial and on the eve of his execution, Whelan signed a statement that he had been present at the killing but had not fired the shot. This was consistent with the recent opinion of ballistic experts that the bullet which killed McGee did not come from a box of cartridges Whelan was carrying.

From the attack on Prince Alfred, and perhaps from that on McGee, which confirmed the idea of Fenianism's worldwide malice, there was fallout in Western Australia. The soldier Fenian Martin Hogan, working at the quarry in Perth in a mixed gang, responded to a particular warder's maligning of the Irish by walking off the job. But Hogan was not given the justice he expected from the resident magistrate; he was sentenced to six months' hard labour in separate confinement, which was as bad as anything meted out by Pentonville or Millbank – hard labour, a bread and water diet, strict silence, and confinement at night in a cell without bedding, or, if with bedding, then without clothing.

Hogan, former dragoon, would in the end serve three months of this bitter regime, darkly occupying his thoughts, before the medical superintendent recommended he be removed because of peril to his health. He was transferred to a work party at Champion Bay.

And perhaps there was a fallout for O'Reilly too. The Chief Warder of the Bunbury area, to whom Warder Woodman sent him with messages, accused him of dallying between the road camp and Bunbury. The penalty would be to receive no mail for six months. This was a refined psychological torment – O'Reilly was to carry letters to other prisoners but to be given none for himself. During the penalty period, he was shown a black-bordered letter and told, 'You will receive it in six months.' When O'Reilly did receive it, it broke news of the death of his mother, Eliza Boyle O'Reilly. These gestures of petty yet absolute tyranny seemed to influence the prisoner's morale as severely as no doubt they were meant to.

In Western Australia the rainy season coincided with winter – June, July and August. Inadequate road camp structures, whether in the Perth–Fremantle area or further south in Bunbury, were incapable of keeping moisture out, and the scant bedding could not combat damp and cold. For the middle-aged and consumptive Fullam brothers, Luke and Lawrence, former Drogheda shoemakers, the winter at McGarry's West Guildford camp near Fremantle was most dangerous. But the majority of prisoners found the habitual pettiness of the system the most disabling. Thomas Duggan, a Cork schoolmaster, who had written under the name 'Mushra' for the *Wild Goose*, and 20-year-old Maurice Fitzgibbon, were charged with being absent from Warder McGarry's Fenian work party. Duggan claimed that they had gone mushroom-picking in a field 400 yards from their camp and been ambushed by four policemen. The police kept them for two days in a lock-up until a magistrate returned them to their party. Warder McGarry had his merit allowance suspended for 'allowing the convicts at West Guildford to ramble about the bush and do as they like'.

Almost routinely, a great number of letters the Fenians wrote and received during their prison term were confiscated for containing 'improper matter', particularly reflections on Irish politics. The otherwise 'well-behaved' John Kenealy had the most letters suppressed – one outward and four inward from family and friends in Ireland, particularly from his brothers Daniel and Nicholas. Thomas Fogarty, who had a brother living in Portland, Maine, was not given the political letter his brother had written him. Michael Moore, the Dublin pike-maker, was 'to be informed that unwillingness to deprive him of a letter from his wife is the reason for which alone he is permitted to receive a letter containing such objectionable material'.

Young John Casey, the Galtee Boy, got into a strange imbroglio over a letter. Expecting to get his ticket-of-leave at the end of October 1868, and having no resources for freedom, he wrote a pleading letter, without permission, to the Catholic Bishop of Adelaide. Somehow the mail was not delivered, and was returned to Fremantle as a dead letter. Casey was sentenced to three months' hard labour. A gentle young man of literary tendencies, he was horrified at being locked up with the hard cases of the chain gang. Kneeling to pray on his first night, he was assaulted with a shower of books and caps. 'One fellow beside me commenced singing a highly immoral song; a second recounted with pride numerous exploits of ravishing unfortunate girls in London, and robbing through their agency, their masters' houses.' Casey was delighted when the Comptroller-General altered his sentence to one month's solitary in Fremantle.

Despite these minor infringements, Henry Wakeford, the new Comptroller-General of Convicts, suggested to Hampton that the Fenians receive tickets-of-leave earlier on account of generally good behaviour. Only Martin Hogan, the former soldier who had walked away from his work party, was excluded from this provision. Hampton wrote to the Home Secretary in Whitehall in terms which would have amazed the late Smith O'Brien, suggesting it might be politic to give the Fenians early tickets-of-leave, 'when they have completed half the regulated time for granting such indulgence to convicts generally'.

This was his near-to-last viceregal act – he left the colony in November 1868, going home to England with a sick wife and in less than good health himself. During a 6-year term as governor, he had quarrelled badly with the settlers, but managed to avoid contests of will with Fenians. His temporary successor, a 60-year-old military veteran, Colonel John Bruce, would quickly be embroiled in such a contest.

The conflict arose from the behaviour of Assistant Warder Howard, who had received orders to move his Fenians north to West Guildford, only 5 miles from McGarry's Fenian group. Howard's prisoners were already enraged by what they saw as police harassment of the recently released boy-Fenian Casey. On receiving his ticket-of-leave, Casey, taking a job as Catholic schoolteacher at the town of York, was arrested at 10.15 p.m. on Christmas night for violating his curfew by enjoying the hospitality of the house of a gentleman in York, 'situated within pistol-shot of my lodgings'. Though the case was ultimately dismissed, it left bad feeling.

Amongst Casey's friends in Howard's camp, passive disobedience had by now become the mode. Howard faced not only his Fenians, but a wife who took up their cause, as they did hers. They were appalled for Mrs Howard's sake when Howard was visited in his camp by a prostitute, and now Mrs Howard herself publicly accused her husband of excessive cruelty to her and his prisoners both. Full-blown mutiny broke out on 1 February 1869, when Howard charged one of his Fenian work party, David Cummins, with 'idleness and insolence', and another, the pike-maker Moore, with insubordination. Hugh Brophy, former Dublin centre and intimate of James Stephens, was convict constable in Howard's party, the same post O'Reilly occupied far to the south in Bunbury, and when instructed to march Cummins and Moore to Perth to face charges, he refused. Instead, with Moore, he made his way to Perth to register his grievances. The Superintendent in Perth ordered that all those refusing to obey Howard's orders be arrested. By the time that was done only one remaining Fenian, the young cook Thomas Cullinane of Ballymacoda, Cork, was left. He refused to remain alone, and ensured that he too would be marched away.

On the day the mutiny got out of hand at Howard's camp, the royal yacht *Galatea* arrived with the convalescent Prince Alfred aboard. His visit to such a small colony, one full of supposedly disaffected Irish, was in many ways an act of valour. There was a grand reception by the remaining troops of the 14th Regiment, and the Volunteer Corps. Then, escorted by Colonel Bruce and Wakeford, Prince Alfred toured the

Fremantle penal establishment. It is quite possible that Comptroller Wakeford communicated news of the Fenian disturbance at Guildford to the prince or his attachés, to reinforce that the party should beware. The prince then went to attend a cricket match between colonials and the *Galatea*'s crew. On Friday night, 4 February, a characteristically warm Western Australian evening, he was guest of honour at a Government House ball in Perth. Next day he hoped to see some pelicans, but a contrary wind on the river made that impossible.

On the Sunday morning, on Bruce's advice, the prince left by the back entrance of Government House and was conducted to the Perth jetty where the launch of the *Galatea* awaited him. The *Fremantle Herald* claimed that the prince had visibly been in a nervous state throughout his stay. The previous arrival of Brophy and his companion, come to Perth to complain of the conduct of Howard, the mutinous state of the rest of the party now under arrest, and the fact that twenty ticket-of-leave Fenians were around Perth and Fremantle, 'caused, as his friends assert, great fears in the mind of the Acting Governor which in an evil hour led him to advise the prince to hasten his departure'.

As the prince left, the rebellious two dozen or more Fenians in Perth prison were now given an ultimatum to go back to their old work party or be punished, and when they refused were ordered to a variety of gangs. But they refused to work with any party except the Fenian group of Warder McGarry. Ultimately, they were all returned to Fremantle at Wakeford's order to be put in solitary confinement until they cracked, which they had no intention of doing.

These men were playing with skill the game of passive political defiance, and Acting Governor Bruce saw the potential scope of the rebellion. What if the concept of communal action spread to the entire Fenian, or even the entire convict, population? Bruce and Wakeford agreed amongst each other that as a first step Warder Howard should be replaced at West Guildford by another officer. The Fenians had managed in one month, without planning, to drive the son of Queen Victoria out of Western Australia (Bruce was not to know that many of the prisoners would have found an attack on the prince's person morally indefensible), and to win their moral victory over Her Majesty's humbler servant Warder Howard. In the negotiations to get the Fenians back to their camp and their labour, they were told informally for the first time by Wakeford that there was world pressure for pardons, and it might be nullified if they persisted with these disturbances.

The *Fremantle Herald* had itself stimulated the souls of the Fenians in their scattered work gangs by publishing a letter about possible free pardons for thirty-nine of them. There was a basis for the rumour in the Liberal Gladstone's victory over Disraeli's Tories in the elections of December 1868. Gladstone had declared his mandate was to bring peace to Ireland by making concessions.

Down the coast, at a place called Koagulup in the bush near Bunbury, O'Reilly was attached still to the work gang of Warder Henry Woodman. He had by Christmas heard the rumours of pardons, but knew that he and other soldier Fenians were unlikely to be included. His life sentence, in the light of possible release of others, sang to his nihilism. So did the hopelessness of a new affection. His round of visits on Woodman's behalf in Bunbury each week had included the taking of messages from the encampment to the Woodman house. There he very early met and was kindly treated by Mrs Woodman and Jessie, the warder's daughter. O'Reilly's biographer friend Roche, out of sensitivity to O'Reilly's later American family, claimed that the good-looking Fenian passively 'attracted the ardent attention of a young girl, daughter of a warder'. His quality of bruised desperation made a number of men and women, including generous Jessie, feel they must help this noble lad. A small vellum-bound notebook found in 1989 in Western Australia, bearing O'Reilly's name, and manuscript copies of some of his poems, includes piquant little notes in his own peculiar shorthand on this romance. 'I wish she was not so fond of kissing,' reads one notation, but then, 'I am in love up to my ears . . . it would take a saint to give her up.' In his novel *Moondyne*, O'Reilly would depict secret meetings in the bush between a noble character named Alice Walmsley and a young man named Will Sheridan. 'Their sympathy was so deep and unutterable that it verged on the bounds of pain.' But the love between O'Reilly and Jessie was hopeless, since they could not marry until O'Reilly got his ticket-of-leave, and that was still eight years in the future.

The counsellor to whom he now turned, O'Reilly later said, was a priest. The Reverend Patrick McCabe, an Irishman then in his thirties, rode from one convict camp to another, and one evening lay down in a blanket under the trees near the Koagulup camp of Woodman's gang. O'Reilly approached McCabe and confessed his schemes for escape. McCabe said, 'It is an excellent way to commit suicide.' McCabe knew that escape was nearly always destructive in one way or another; a choice between dying of exposure or thirst in the interior, or trying to get away on the heavily policed shipping of the Western Australian coast. The recapture of absconders was undertaken by the Pensioner Guards, by prison officers, mounted police and Aboriginal native trackers. The only convicts who had managed to escape the colony had been ticket-of-leave holders who had been able to earn money to pay bribes. So certain were the authorities of recovering convicts that they had abandoned the practice of running up a red flag on the mast at Fremantle gaol and firing an alarm cannon whenever a prisoner escaped.

McCabe could tell that the balance of O'Reilly's unusually febrile mind was at stake, and that some stratagem of relief had to be found. He said, 'Don't think of that again. Let me think out a plan for you. You'll hear from me before long.' It appears though that two days later, O'Reilly attempted suicide. Sub-Inspector William Timperley of Bunbury police records in his interview diary for 27 December 1868 that he had while leaving town overtaken a surgeon, Dr Lovegrove, 'accompanied as far as Woodman's camp where the probation constable named Riley, one of the late head centres of Fenianism, had attempted suicide by cutting the veins of his left arm'. He had been found by a fellow prisoner, 'when in a faint from loss of blood'. This was clearly O'Reilly he wrote of, since the only other Fenian of that name, James Reilly, was more than a hundred miles to the north in Fremantle.

There were rumours Jessie was pregnant by O'Reilly, and that O'Reilly's moral despair and the impossibility of marriage had driven him to the act. But no inquiry was made into O'Reilly's suicide attempt. If there had been one, it might have raised the issue of O'Reilly's association with Jessie, an outcome Jessie's father, Woodman, would not have wanted. As for O'Reilly's attack on himself, intense shame, remorse and helplessness must have worked on him to drive him to an option which, in his theology, committed him to hellfire.

As for the rumoured pregnancy, there might have been a miscarriage, since researchers have found no child carrying the names Woodman, O'Reilly or Pickersgill – the name of the farmer Jessie soon after married – in the birth records for 1868–9. Is *Moondyne* the key to what happened to O'Reilly's and Jessie's child? The hero is guilt-stricken when the heroine Alice gives birth to the stillborn child. 'And Allie's white face will haunt him, even in sleep, with her dead child in her arms. Oh God help poor Allie tonight! God comfort the poor little lassie!' This stillborn and unbaptised child might itself have been the trigger for O'Reilly's damning himself by picking up a knife.

Since Father McCabe had not seen anyone make good a convict escape, he was now engaged in planning a unique and perilous event. An impetuous plan would ruin his own position in Western Australia but would destroy what was left of Boyle O'Reilly. James Maguire, a young Irish settler to whom McCabe turned for help, would remember later that, 'Boyle, poor Boyle, cried and cried in desperation for help.' Maguire was a farmer from a place named Dardanup, inland from Bunbury. Thirty-four years old, he was a justice of the peace and chairman of the Dardanup Road Board. His brother was the Dardanup postmaster.

As O'Reilly, on an errand to Bunbury in the new year of 1869, crossed the Bunbury racecourse, he heard a *coo-ee!* from the edge of the bush, and saw a sturdy man, axe on shoulder, emerge from scrub. It was Maguire, who had been given a contract to clear some land. He said to O'Reilly, 'I'm a friend of Father Mac's', and as proof of *bona fides*, he handed over a card bearing the handwriting of McCabe. It was expected, Maguire said, that a number of American whalers would touch at Bunbury in February. Maguire pledged, 'You'll be a free man in February, as sure as my name is Maguire.' But O'Reilly was suspicious of such bluster.

In the ferocious Western Australian summer, O'Reilly dealt badly with the anguish of delay. But while the prince was visiting Perth and Fremantle in February 1869, a woodcutter friend of Maguire's met O'Reilly on the edge of the convict camp and casually stated that three American whaling barks had arrived at Bunbury. For O'Reilly, amongst huge forests of gum and jarrah, native mahogany trees, and beneath that massive, blazing sky, the anticipation of any resolution to his suffering, welcome escape or welcome death, was an itch in the blood. At Spencer's Hotel in Bunbury, Father McCabe had met and, for a small sum, made an agreement with Captain Anthony Baker, commander of the Yankee barque *Vigilant*. Baker would take O'Reilly aboard if O'Reilly met up with the ship outside Australian waters. Captain Baker would cruise *Vigilant* up and down the coast north of Bunbury for three days and keep a lookout for the escapee. At the Koagulup camp, on the appointed night for Maguire to aid O'Reilly's escape, 18 February 1869, the prisoner wrote a letter to his father, telling him that he had hopes now of a getaway to the United States. The eve-of-escape letter must have been given to Jessie or Maguire for posting, for it was published two months later in Irish newspapers.

At seven o'clock that evening Woodman made his rounds and looked in at all the convicts in their slab timber huts. He would declare that he saw O'Reilly sitting in his bark hovel. Soon after Woodman passed, a convict visited O'Reilly to borrow some tobacco, and remained chatting a little while. Alone again, at eight o'clock, O'Reilly changed into the clothes and boots a supporter – apparently Jessie – had got for him, put out his light, and headed off for the rendezvous in the bush. He had a great advantage in his civilian-style footwear, since convict boots had a broad-arrow pattern of nails in the sole to make it easy for trackers to find any absconder. A few hundred yards into the bush he found he was being followed by a convict sawyer. Whoever it was, he acted with nobility. 'Are you off?' the man asked. 'I knew you meant it. I saw you talking to

Maguire a month ago, and I knew it all.' O'Reilly was expecting to be urged or threatened to let the sawyer join in, but instead the man held out his hand and said, 'God speed you. I'll put them on the wrong scent tomorrow.'

Near an abandoned convict station on the Vasse Road, O'Reilly was to lie in the bush until he heard someone approach whistling the first bars of 'Patrick's Day'. Half an hour passed before Maguire and two friends rode up, leading a horse for O'Reilly. The party was made up of Maguire's cousin and a man O'Reilly later called M——. This discretion was from regard for the man's situation in Western Australia. After some hours' ride north-east, they reached the Collie River and a long inlet, the Leschenault Estuary, stretching north, protected from the Indian Ocean by a long, low coastal strip of land where M—— worked. John Boyle O'Reilly and his party met up with three more friends waiting near Bunbury. These new men were 'Mickie Mackie', a shoemaker from Bunbury, and Mark Lyons, both Irishmen. The third was an English ticket-of-leave man and former burglar named Joseph Buswell, whose fishing boat would now be used. The old British lag Buswell had in his day been one of those demons of the convict deck to whom the Fenians had felt superior. The party dragged the boat through the mud to reach the water. M—— refused to get aboard – he had promised his wife not to go in the boat. Maguire's cousin yelled, 'All right, go home to your wife!', which O'Reilly thought rather harsh treatment for a man who had already taken risks for the sake of someone he did not know.

Once out of the lagoon, creeping past Bunbury through the relatively narrow heads of the port into the Indian Ocean, they bent vigorously to the oars in open sea. At sunrise only the tops of the sandhills of Mowenup could be seen by O'Reilly, and the boat lay off them waiting for the *Vigilant* to put out from Bunbury. But by early afternoon, *Vigilant* had not appeared, and did not seem to be putting out at all that day. Ravenous and extremely thirsty, O'Reilly's party ran the boat ashore through strong surf, pulling it up high on an enormous length of beach.

Maguire, O'Reilly and the others wandered for hours through the dry swamps searching for water, even films of moisture beneath the bark of paperbark trees. Mark Lyons eventually located a slab hut where his brother-in-law, Jackson, lived remotely, overseeing a herd of water buffalo. Maguire thought it too dangerous to take O'Reilly to Jackson's, so the party left him in a screen of paperbarks, where he dealt with his thirst by eating a raw possum he had dragged from a hollow tree. He made a bed for himself in the sand dunes out of the boughs of the snake-, ant-, and centipede-repelling peppermint tree. Next morning his party of abetters was back, and at about one o'clock one of them who had been in the dunes on lookout with a telescope came running down the beach with news of having sighted *Vigilant*. The Buswell fishing boat was run out immediately through the surf, and O'Reilly and the party rowed to intercept the whaler. Maguire fixed a white shirt on top of the oar, and the entire party, O'Reilly included, roared and shouted. But the *Vigilant*, though obviously on search, passed them by, disappearing into haze.

O'Reilly's disappointment as they landed him that night was of course savage, but Maguire decided to introduce the charming escapee to Mr and Mrs Jackson. Before Maguire left, he took trouble to reassure devastated O'Reilly that missing *Vigilant* was not the end. He guaranteed to be back within a week with new arrangements. This seemed to constitute a promise in which O'Reilly put childlike trust. The escapee's three Irish companions and the Englishman Buswell now put out in the surf again and rowed back to Bunbury, leaving O'Reilly in the limbo of the dunes.

As Maguire found out back in Bunbury, *Vigilant* had been a day late in coming up the coast because a convict named Thompson had absconded from Bunbury the same night as O'Reilly's escape. He had been spotted by the daughter of Principal Warden Woodrow walking through town after curfew, and so the water police descended on *Vigilant*. The whaler was so crowded with whale-oil casks, lumber and provisions that Sub-Inspector Timperley complained to Captain Baker that one of his warders, who had crawled into narrow spaces to probe for escapees with a wire prong, was not able to crawl out again. Thompson was not discovered aboard, but, as Timperley returned to his office, 'I received a report that No. 9843 John O'Reilly had absconded from the Vasse road party . . . I may also state that this same prisoner attempted suicide on the 27th of December last by cutting the veins in his arm.' By then *Vigilant* was clearing the harbour under full sail, and Woodrow and Timperley believed O'Reilly to be aboard.

When next day Timperley spoke to Woodman, O'Reilly's warder at Koagulup, Woodman said he had spoken to O'Reilly at ten-thirty or so, warning him as night watchman to keep a lookout on a bushfire that was burning close to the camp. In saying so, Woodman was either lying or mistaken. And if lying, was he doing it to save O'Reilly or to be quit of his potentially tragic love for Jessie? In any case, Timperley reasoned that if Woodman was right, O'Reilly would have been unable to get to *Vigilant* before it sailed. He had the sand dunes around Bunbury searched, and found not O'Reilly but Thompson. He also boarded two other Yankee whalers in port, *Gazelle* and *Classic*, to offer them each £5 in reward for catching O'Reilly on board. As for local people, 'I am . . . certain', he warned, 'that many would assist a Fenian who would not stir hand or foot for an ordinary prisoner of the Crown.' Superintendent Hare of Perth, a

Galway Orangeman enraged at Fenian escape, would become dissatisfied with Timperley's contradictory bulletins to headquarters, particularly a new one suggesting that O'Reilly *must* have got away on the *Vigilant*, and asked petulantly, 'Is any horse missing in the neighbourhood, for O'Reilly was a cavalry soldier?' Perhaps, pleaded Timperley, O'Reilly was boarded on *Vigilant* after the whaler left by Joseph Buswell, who had been under suspicion of similar attempts in the past. All this argument and multiplicity of searches helped O'Reilly.

O'Reilly, tormented by the possibility that the *Vigilant* might still be making inshore searches, had, about 21 February, found an old dory half buried in sand. He dug it free, re-floated it, and rowed out at dusk to try to encounter the whaler. Seeing nothing, he returned to shore, killed some possums and kangaroo rats in the dunes and skinned them, and in early light took again to sea with the meat wrapped in a cloth and towed behind him in the water. All day he searched, hoping the northerly current would sweep him within view of the lingering whale ship. He suffered a great deal from the sun, and the possum and kangaroo-rat meat was taken by sharks. In the afternoon he did sight a ship, almost certainly *Vigilant*, but again it tacked away. Later, in America, O'Reilly accepted Captain Baker's explanation that neither Buswell's larger fishing boat nor the dory had been seen by lookouts. The fact that Baker was still looking for him on 21 February was in itself testimony to the trouble this Yankee whaler would take to fulfil his arrangement. Baker's thoroughness was in part explained by the bitter memories Massachusetts whalers retained of British-built Confederate raiders. Added to this was the New England passion for liberty, a value second only to Scripture in moral authority. It had found concrete expression in the abolition movement, and Baker tried to give it moral expression on the Western Australian coast.

O'Reilly remained at sea that night, sleeping in the bottom of his dory, and returned exhausted to shore the next day. As a recluse of the dunes and the peppermint groves, he was now underpinned by the tenuous mercy of wild colonials and old lags. But he was cheered by the arrival by boat of Maguire, Mickie Mackie, and the previously much-abused M——. Maguire brought a letter from Father McCabe, whose certitude – McCabe asked O'Reilly to remember him when he was long escaped and safe – revived O'Reilly. McCabe told him that a new arrangement had been made with a Captain David R. Gifford of the barque *Gazelle* of New Bedford, Massachusetts, due to sail from Bunbury the next day, and willing to take O'Reilly on board. Gifford had agreed to take O'Reilly only as far as Java, and Father McCabe had paid him £10 for that. It would become apparent that the money was not paramount.

By storm lantern in Jackson's hut, Maguire now broke to O'Reilly the less welcome news. A 'local ticket-of-leave man', Thomas Henderson, alias Martin Bowman or Beaumont, had somehow already heard of the escape attempt. Years later O'Reilly would surmise that the unwitting link who gave Henderson the news was Jackson's young son, Matthew. Henderson was a volatile quantity, but his ticket-of-leave explained how he could visit Bunbury to blackmail McCabe and at the same time be local to the Belvedere area.

The next morning, 27 February, O'Reilly said goodbye to the Jacksons, who had kept faith with him through their reflex hatred of authority as it existed in the penal colony. At first light Maguire's crew of four or five, with O'Reilly and Henderson/Bowman, rowed out through the surf to intercept the path of *Gazelle*. O'Reilly must have felt mounting disappointment as afternoon came without a sighting. It was towards evening that they saw the whaler, and this time there were no near misses. *Gazelle* hailed them, specifically using O'Reilly's name.

Buswell's boat pulled alongside *Gazelle*, and after O'Reilly climbed up on to the outboard shelf where whale-oil casks were lashed, he was helped over the gunnels by a young Yankee officer, the third mate, Henry C. Hathaway, who would become a lifelong friend. Now O'Reilly was welcomed aboard by Captain Gifford. He was told he would be given accommodation aft. Martin Henderson was given quarters in the foc'sle with the crew. While O'Reilly was still shaking hands with Captain Gifford and the officers of *Gazelle*, Maguire stood up in his rowboat and called, 'God bless you; don't forget us, and don't mention our names until you know it's all over.' Seeing these men distanced now by water, about to row back to their colonial existence, their Australian futures, O'Reilly wept.

Hathaway, the young third mate, became O'Reilly's closest friend aboard *Gazelle*. O'Reilly impressed him by not being content to be a mere passenger. When a whale was sighted off the north-west coast of Australia, he petitioned Gifford to be allowed to go hunting it in Hathaway's whaleboat. O'Reilly seemed to cherish the encounter more for its literary potential than its whale oil, as, getting in close, Hathaway himself launched the lance. So recently a felon, O'Reilly was now placing himself at the heart of the quintessential Yankee rite of valour. It was an omen for the sort of American he would become.

The whale dragged Hathaway's boat and then turned, striking it with its flukes – according to Hathaway, 'knocking her to atoms'. The crew jumped into the sea, taking oars for buoyancy. The whale swam away, dragging its harpoon, its trail of blood and a fragment of the bow of the boat with it. Clustered at the shattered stern, the men sighted O'Reilly floating face-down. Hathaway clung to the stove-in boat's side with one hand, reached for O'Reilly's hair with the other and pulled him upright. Froth was running from nostrils and mouth as Hathaway used a form of artificial respiration: 'punching him to revive him'. O'Reilly and the others lay on the wreckage a long time before they were picked up by the fourth mate. The escapee suffered such severe concussion and head pains that he asked why they had bothered to rescue him. Later in life, though, on the sometimes too solid earth, faced with furious Irish factionalism, O'Reilly would write a great deal, including one of his famous recitative poems, *The Amber Whale*, praised by poets like Whittier and popular arbiters such as Horace Greeley, about this journey of escape, the simple apolitical elements of friendship and physical daring. The poem dealt with a whaling legend heard aboard *Gazelle*, a tale reminiscent of Melville's *Moby Dick*: the accursed, abnormal whale and demented men, tethered together by the rope and the lance, going to hell together. ' "It's just fifteen years, shipmates," said old Mat, ending his tale; "And I often pray that I'll never see another Amber Whale." '

The *Gazelle* did not in fact drop O'Reilly in Java. His presence was welcome in the cabin, and the charm and narrative ability which had enchanted Jessie Woodman was at work on those whale hunters.

Ultimately, need of fresh water forced *Gazelle* into Rodriguez Island, a British possession in the Indian Ocean near Mauritius. Gifford must have thought the risk acceptable. Perhaps he wanted some way to unload Henderson too. Just before sunset on the day of *Gazelle*'s arrival in the harbour, the resident magistrate of the island and a party of police came aboard. The magistrate asked Hathaway, as officer of the deck, whether, amongst other escapees including Henderson/Bowman, a man named John Boyle O'Reilly was on board. Hathaway asked for descriptions. Uttering a story he and Gifford had worked on together before putting into harbour, Hathaway said that a man named Brown, survivor of a shipwreck, resembled the description of O'Reilly, but he had died two months before in the Sunda Strait. The magistrate demanded that the crew be lined up on deck, and according to O'Reilly's biographer Roche, it was during this muster that a young sailor who had been persecuted by Henderson/Bowman in the forecastle gave away his tormentor's identity. O'Reilly himself would never forget Bowman, including him by name in his later novel, depicting him as 'satisfied with his own depravity, and convinced that everyone was as vile as he'.

Gifford, ashore at the time, felt threatened by the magistrate's actions and feared that O'Reilly would now be identified and that the British might confiscate *Gazelle*. Nor did O'Reilly seem to behave with the coolness he'd shown during the magistrate's visit. He had got hold of a pistol somehow, and told Hathaway that he was determined to shoot it out with the British authorities. In dealings with other humans O'Reilly was a moderate and sympathetic man; but he contemplated only extreme resolutions for himself. A more practical stratagem was devised, said Hathaway, an arrangement to which, apparently, not even Captain Gifford was party. Hathaway would engage the night watch in conversation while O'Reilly walked out across the darker reaches of the deck to the gunnels with a grindstone and his hat, drop both of them overboard, then run down the cabin companionway and hide himself in the small locker behind it. Hathaway had taken care already to tell the watch to look out for O'Reilly, because he had earlier tried to kill himself in Western Australia. The splash of the grindstone coincided with this warning. One of the suggestible young sailors claimed to have glimpsed O'Reilly's face before it sank beneath the water. The crew searched the harbour for hours, only O'Reilly's hat being found. Hathaway was still on deck to greet the second mate as he climbed back aboard, and leaned out over the side with tears in his eyes. 'He's gone, poor fellow! Here's his hat.'

O'Reilly remained hidden overnight while his wet hat lay on the hatchway for presentation to the police. In the early morning, the police boat arrived with the magistrate and Henderson/Bowman, who was now willing to identify O'Reilly in return for a deal. Gifford broke to the magistrate the news of the man lost overboard, and the grief on all faces was no doubt convincing. That evening *Gazelle* set to sea with official blessing. As the ship cleared the harbour, Hathaway went below and, hauling away the companionway steps which had been pushed up against the locker, found O'Reilly lying in the cramped space in a tortured heap. 'I can see his face right before me now, white as chalk, eyes as black as night.' Hathaway helped him extricate himself. 'Now,' said Hathaway, 'go and shake hands with the captain.' When O'Reilly came up the companionway, Gifford wasted little time on speculation about phantoms, understanding at once the subterfuge. Hathaway said the skipper 'burst out crying, just like a baby'. Frederick Hussey, former first mate on the *Gazelle*, would when himself a captain express his belief that the magistrate was 'not so badly fooled as we thought'. His wife was Irish, and he had advised Gifford not to keep the flag at half-mast, since it would only lead to an insistence by the Rodriguez police authorities that the harbour be dragged.

The next landfall for *Gazelle* would need to be one of the British islands in the mid-Atlantic, St Helena for example. Captain Gifford knew O'Reilly would be at risk from talkativeness amongst his fellow sailors.

But off the Cape of Good Hope *Gazelle* encountered the bark *Sapphire* of Boston, on its way to Liverpool from Bombay, and commanded by a Captain Seiders. A seaman named John Soule had deserted from *Gazelle*, and O'Reilly took Soule's name and papers aboard *Sapphire*. Seiders, however, having been told O'Reilly's true name and history, gave him a room in the cabin section, and treated him with every kindness. The escapee carried with him £20 Gifford had advanced him, which would again suggest that the £10 deal he had done with McCabe had not been his chief motivation in aiding the escape. O'Reilly had argued with Gifford, 'I may never reach America; I may never be able to repay you.' To which the Yankee whaler stylishly replied, 'If you never reach America, I shall be very sorry for you; if you are never able to repay me, I shall not be much the poorer.'

Four years later, O'Reilly's first book of verse would bear a dedication to Captain David Gifford of the whaling bark *Gazelle* of New Bedford. But just in case Gifford wanted to go whaling again, O'Reilly would maintain the fiction that the *Gazelle* had stumbled on O'Reilly. 'It pleased God that my boat was seen from the masthead of the *Gazelle*, commanded by Captain Gifford, who picked me up and treated me with all kindness during a seven months' whaling cruise.'

O'Reilly's transshipping to *Sapphire* left a sense of vacancy aboard *Gazelle*, where the escapee had been for five months. Hathaway wrote a touching letter to O'Reilly dated 29 July 1869, the very day O'Reilly left the whaler: 'Dear old fellow: I am now seated at the old donkey, where we've sat side by side for the last five months, more or less, and have been reading over some of your pieces of poetry, and it makes me lonesome.' As if this voyage were indelibly marked by O'Reilly, Hathaway would eventually give his *Gazelle* journal to him.

On board *Sapphire*, O'Reilly made friends with a sympathetic English gentleman named Bailey, who undertook to help him secure passage for America after *Sapphire* reached Liverpool in October. Landed in the great port he had not seen since his career as a young journalist, O'Reilly lodged in a house organised for him by Captain Seiders. He toyed with the idea of visiting the town of Preston, some 30 miles north, and the aunt with whom he had lived in his adolescence, but decided this was too dangerous. He liked in later days, however, to relate how he and the Englishman Bailey engaged in a long conversation with a Liverpool policeman about directions.

Captain Seiders and Bailey organised passage for O'Reilly aboard the Yankee ship *Bombay* of Bath, Maine, whose captain lacked a third mate and now made room for O'Reilly to fulfil that role. Two days out of

Liverpool on *Bombay*, O'Reilly saw the Antrim coast passing by beneath dappled clouds. 'Ireland was there, under the sun; but under the dark cloud also,' he would later tell an audience in Boston. He would never see that or any other Irish coastline again. On 23 November 1869, a little more than two years from the date of his taking passage on the *Hougoumont*, he arrived at Philadelphia. Ever the tender of celebratory verses, O'Reilly wrote a poem for *Bombay*'s captain.

May you bear your master always as through perils past away:
And whatever sea you sail upon – God speed you old *Bombay*.

Despite the stake Gifford had loaned him, he may have looked ashore at the city's golden domes with some anxiety. What could be made of this sprawling republic? Would he be lost here, as the Young Ireland escapee MacManus had been, finding validation only as a corpse?

In the Atlantic a few days before O'Reilly arrived in Philadelphia, Hathaway had written to him of both friendship and Yankee attitudes to political prisoners. 'I hope the time is not far hence when some of your old friends from Australia will be with you, enjoying freedom instead of bondage . . . God bless them! and may the time soon arrive when they will have a helping hand to assist them in escaping. There goes eight bells.' Apparently Hathaway and O'Reilly had daydreamed of a mass escape of Fenians by whaler, an expensive and intricate project which would take six more years and other engaged souls to arrange.

The day after O'Reilly's arrival, an excited Philadelphia Fenian delegation came on board and took him ashore. When he recounted his adventures, they found them too difficult to credit, which for a moment left him chagrined. But they treated him handsomely, even though the Fenian movement in Philadelphia was in some decline following the disasters of Canada and Ireland. O'Reilly insisted on being taken almost at once to the United States District Court to apply for naturalisation. He may have done so on legal advice: citizenship would seal his escape. But neither Meagher nor Mitchel had had at the time of their escapes citizenship immediately available to them, and had not suffered the remotest risk of being returned. Perhaps it was that an instant and ardent commitment to America suited his thoroughgoing character. Two years later, speaking at an International Music Festival in Boston, he argued that the newcomer owed a duty of citizenship to America. 'He resigns his prejudices on the threshold of the Temple of Liberty. They are melted down in the great crucible of public opinion.'

The Philadelphia Irish then put him on the train up to New York to face a full reception and to give his first American lecture, the mechanism by which Australian escapees had traditionally stood up for Ireland and themselves in that great city of the Americas. Accommodated in a hotel on Broadway, he received visits and suggestions of public receptions from the rival Fenian factions, the so-called O'Mahony wing, led now by Meagher's old friend John Savage, and the Senate or Roberts wing. He had a sense of people competing for his blessing and for ownership. Given the way Irish prisoners had been kept waiting for the uprising as factions formed, money had been squandered and Canada invaded, he was angered. He associated for a time with John Savage's moderate wing of the Fenian Brotherhood and enlisted in a newly formed Legion of St Patrick, becoming nominally the adjutant to the First Battalion. And when he lectured on his escape at the Cooper Institute before Christmas 1869, it was with John Savage in the chair.

In congratulatory chat after the lecture, it became apparent that everyone expected him to settle in New York, as had Thomas Francis Meagher and other Young Ireland escapees. Horace Greeley, who had published *The Amber Whale*, offered him a job on the *Tribune*. But there were pressing invitations to Boston. Dr Robert Joyce, a Boston literary man and physician, took a warm interest in O'Reilly as a poet. After the escapee arrived in Boston on reconnaissance, Patrick A. Collins, son of impoverished immigrants, now a 24-year-old State Congressman with a law degree from Harvard, quickly became a friend of O'Reilly's. Thomas Manning, wealthy Irish Bostonian, gave him lodging, and Collins and Joyce set out to get O'Reilly a job with the British-based Inman Steamship Company. Sadly, the Irishman who ran the Boston office received orders that O'Reilly be sacked. An eminent Irishman, Patrick Donahoe, forty years a Boston newspaperman, offered him the job of reporter at the *Pilot*, the journal of the Boston Irish community.

O'Reilly adjusted to the life of an asylum-seeking political prisoner with great ease and much more civic grace than John Mitchel. Few other than the most factional Irish were unimpressed by O'Reilly, and he began making friends amongst Old Boston as well as amongst the Irish of the North and South End. In January 1870 he gave a public lecture, 'England's Political Prisoners', in the Boston Music-Hall, the first of a number of pleas for his fellow prisoners in Australia. Hathaway and Gifford, having brought the *Gazelle* safely and profitably to port, sat on the stage and heard him praise them. According to witnesses, people delighted in the nobility of O'Reilly's face and expression, the brightness of his eye, and his rich, browned complexion. He was asked to repeat the lecture in Salem, Lawrence, Providence and elsewhere.

The Boston Irish *were* grateful to him for his sufferings; that Ireland would be delivered by Christ-like suffering as much as by battles won was a concept the Irish took for granted. As Irish hero, he had the right gestures of nobility. A Ladies' Committee in Ireland, where his escape had been well chronicled, sent him £10 to help him set up. O'Reilly returned it with a letter. 'There are many in Ireland – many who suffered from the loss of their bread-winners in the old cause – they want it; let them have it.' Leaving Mr Thomas Manning's house, he took good lodgings in Staniford Street, Charlestown, and wrote to his aunt in Preston that he worked for magazines, reported for the *Pilot*, drilled the Irish Legion, and gave lectures. He was ecstatic to be so busy.

27

Fenians at Large

And what have the liberated Fenians done to deserve an ovation where Royal blood was so recently spilt?

Sydney Morning Herald, 16 October 1869

In the second week of May 1869 a dispatch from Gladstone's Secretary of State for the Colonies, Earl Granville, arrived on Governor Bruce's desk in Perth. It granted 'a Remission to Thomas Cullinane or Bowler and the other prisoners named in the accompanying Warrant under the Royal Sign Manual'. Significantly, recognising their political status, Earl Granville said the pardoned prisoners did not belong 'to the Criminal Class', had no opportunity in Western Australia to repeat political offences of which they have been guilty, and would be less of a peril to public order 'than any ordinary offender who receives a pardon'.

In all, thirty-four were conditionally pardoned. But there was inconsistency: James Kearney and George Connolly from McGarry's party, with unblemished records, both serving 7-year sentences, were not on the list, whereas John Kenealy, far higher in the Fenian organisation, serving a 10-year sentence, was given a free pardon, as also was the Dubliner Hugh Brophy, Warder Howard's rebellious convict constable. All the members of Howard's party except John Edward Kelly, Bostonian and contributor to the *Wild Goose*, were pardoned. A delighted Denis Cashman was released, but not the editor of the *Wild Goose*, John Flood, serving fifteen years. The illogicalities of the list were more a matter of clerical incompetence than malice, and to some of the Fenians not named that must have seemed crueller than design. The pardon in particular tormented the minds of those whom the Duke of Cambridge, commander of the British army, would not permit to be released. These were men such as Hogan, Cranston, Hassett, serving life sentences as former British soldiers.

For the thirty-four pardoned men in Western Australia, freedom descended like a thunderclap. The men were simply brought to Fremantle and allowed to walk out of the convict establishment into the streets. They lacked the finances, however, to do it in any meaningful way. In Dublin and Cork, huge dinners marked the announcement of the amnesty, and money was slated to be sent from Ireland. But on the spot, and at the time, the Western Australian convicts would have welcomed a fragment of what was raised at those events. Two of the pardoned, Hugh Brophy and

Joseph Noonan, had been in the construction industry in Ireland, and now applied for and were democratically granted a contract to build a bridge over the Swan River. Noonan and Brophy employed a number of the others on the Swan River project. Through a Fremantle priest, Father Gibney, John Kenealy was offered a job in Champion Bay managing a general store. But the pardoned men wanted to leave the colony as a group and pointed out to Kenealy that, in case assistance soon came, he would in Champion Bay be too far off to communicate with swiftly. So Kenealy joined the rest of the corps of freed men in the bridge construction camp, 'and I am to be provided with a gun or a dog to hunt possums, or do anything I desire, and live with them awaiting developments'. Only a day or so later, two letters arrived, one from an Irishman named Fearon in Melbourne, one from Adelaide, offering help to the pardoned men, who now decided that Kenealy should go to the eastern colonies of Australia to collect and raise money to help the men move.

Kenealy had personal friends in the dry-goods business in Melbourne and the hinterland of Victoria. He also had returned to him on release a family watch which had somehow been shipped from Portland prison aboard *Hougoumont*, and undertook to sell it to pay his fare to Melbourne. 'Our circumstances got noised around,' Kenealy later recounted, 'and three or four good Irish girls, one of them a cousin of young Allen of the Manchester Martyrs, immediately came to our rescue and insisted that I should keep my watch.' Patrick Maloney, 'a good Clare man', accommodated a number of Fenians free of charge in his Perth pub. He loaned Kenealy £25 for expenses.

Leaving Perth on the mail coach on 25 June 1869, Kenealy travelled down to Albany to meet the mail steamer from England on her way to Melbourne. Somewhere between Perth and Bunbury, he was trying to fall asleep at night on the hard seat of the halted coach when he heard a knock on the door. It was Sergeant Darragh, a Fenian soldier, a Protestant, once a veteran of the 2nd Queen's. Kenealy was delighted to be escorted to a warm hammock. In the morning, Darragh served his freed compatriot 'a prime kangaroo steak'. Kenealy would never forget that favour, nor Darragh's predicament.

His Western Australian passport said that he was a liberated convict, and he knew that South Australia and Victoria had legislation prohibiting convicts from any penal settlement from entering until three years after being released. Would he be permitted to land in Melbourne? In Albany, Father Delany, former chaplain of the *Hougoumont*, was the pastor, and insisted that Kenealy take £5 from him, and argued emphatically that Kenealy travel first class on the steamer, since that might help him slip past the scrutiny of the Melbourne police. And so Kenealy, having travelled to Western Australia in the convict quarters of a transport, now went east aboard the steamer *Geelong* in first class, making friends with a genial old Scotsman and his wife who had made their final visit to Scotland and were going home to New South Wales. The old Scot advised that Kenealy – if allowed to land – should stay at the Duke of Rothsay Hotel in Elizabeth Street. 'It was one of the most exclusive and expensive in the city, *but* it would have a good effect.' It cannot have been unpleasant to have everyone he met urging him towards the best of everything.

When the steamer put into immense Port Phillip Bay, detectives from ashore walked amongst them crying, 'Anyone from Western Australia?' Kenealy recognised an Irish accent, so handed this man his pass. The detective argued that he could not land, but seemed reassured when Kenealy said he would stay at the Duke of Rothsay. After landing then at Port Melbourne and booking into his hotel, Kenealy went late at night to the house of James Fearon of Nicholson Street, knocked on the door and was admitted by Fearon's adolescent son. Then, 'a middle aged man trying to divest himself of night clothes and get into some others as quickly as possible, came downstairs, pale and trembling with nervous excitement, rushed at me, pulled me into a drawing room or parlour, got everybody, from wife to baby, out of bed, to come and take a look at me'.

Even though it was midnight, they hurried off to the house of Edward Dillon, who had the dual distinction of being a senior executive of the Union Bank and of having a brother, Brian, Kenealy's Cork friend, still serving a prison sentence in England. There were huge embracings, and then Dillon roused from their beds, to meet the midnight hero, the three Dillon children, Tone, Emmett and Fitzgerald. Kenealy was delighted to see that the Irish could prosper in Melbourne as they had, and his new friends further cheered him with news that a Released Irish State Prisoners Fund had been started in Sydney and that a Melbourne committee was put together by the editor-owner of the Melbourne *Advocate*, Australian-born Samuel Winter. Money came to the committee even from New Zealand, addressed in care of such prominent Victorian politicians as Charles Gavan Duffy and John O'Shanassy.

The next day's papers carried the news of his arrival. 'Amongst the distinguished visitors from the *Geelong* was Mr John Kenealy, one of the lately released Fenian prisoners. We would wish to know the destiny and destination of this gentleman.' But though some collectors found that the Irish prosperous classes were dubious about helping the Fenians, one collector writing that many Irish believed 'that the surest and quietest way to social equality with their English friends' was to eschew Irish causes, when Kenealy met Sam Winter, the *Advocate* editor, on his first morning in Melbourne, all he was aware of was enthusiasm. Many Irish on the gold-fields of Victoria and New South Wales had sent substantial amounts to the fund – a miner from Grenfell in New South Wales donated £5 under the name 'Vinegar Hill'. Winter, child of an English father and Irish mother who had both come to Melbourne by assisted passage in 1841, called a public meeting that very night. At it, Kenealy explained the debts the released Fenians had already accumulated, told of amounts owing to the Fremantle publican Maloney and Father Delany, and the general want of his fellow Fenians. The meeting agreed that £250 would be sent at once both to settle debts and enable the freed prisoners to travel eastwards. Since there was no telegraph between Melbourne and Western Australia, the bank draft for £250 had to be remitted by ship. Sending it off, Kenealy suggested that after paying Maloney and paying other debts, the departing prisoners might buy Mrs Maloney some valuable article for her kindness.

One of his visits in Melbourne was to the home in the suburb of Hawthorn of Charles Gavan Duffy, Young Ireland hero, who in 1855 had decided to become a free emigrant to Australia. Kenealy, like other young Fenians, held against him his famed parting aphorism which had likened the Irish cause to a corpse on the dissecting table. Kenealy admitted that 'several of us were not quite in love with Duffy'. But meeting him at home, Kenealy felt at once 'a sense of his own littleness' compared with the former editor and proprietor of the *Nation*. Duffy surprised Kenealy, and would have certainly surprised the *Argus*, by speaking highly of the Fenians. When he asked Kenealy about Ireland, Kenealy said, 'She is not dead yet.' Duffy assured Kenealy that 'he had been misquoted and misunderstood'. He generously poured a fine colonial claret for Kenealy.

The Melbourne *Argus* began drawing to the attention of the authorities Victoria's Influx of Criminals Prevention Act. But the government was unwilling to make a martyr out of Kenealy by expelling or imprisoning him. In the hiatus, Kenealy and Winter spoke at a meeting called on the gold-fields of Ballarat, and there were pledges for £1,000 by the people of that wealthy mining community. Altogether the pledged amounts from the Victorian and New South Wales funds would be £5,000, which in modern terms was probably the equivalent of $1,000,000, and gave the prisoners a basis on which to make serious decisions. To raise this amount, Kenealy spent his time 'visiting friends not only in Melbourne and Ballarat but in Castlemaine, Kyneton and other towns'.

In Ballarat, Kenealy had met 'one or two old Cork chums', who offered to raise £2,000 to set him up in the dry-goods business in a corner store in a building on the gold-fields. Kenealy said he could not accept. He was there as a representative of his comrades, not to scout opportunities. And the Influx of Criminals Prevention Act also hung over all business proposals. Kenealy was interviewed while in Ballarat by Captain Frederick Standish, the Chief Commissioner of Police, and asked to state definitely to Standish how much more time he needed to complete his Victorian business. But when Kenealy's determined belief in his political status prevented him from fixing a date, Standish announced that his instructions were to order the arrest of the Fenian. He desired to know where Kenealy could be found at twelve o'clock that day. Kenealy said he would be in the library of St Patrick's Hill, Ballarat. Before the appointed hour, accompanied by Winter and others, he was in place. An inspector of police came in amongst the bookshelves and made the arrest. Conveyed to court, however, the prisoner was released on £1,000 put up by Winter and a Ballarat businessman.

Captain McMahon, an Irishman, police commissioner of Victoria in the 1850s, reminded the Chief Secretary of Victoria that he had permitted the entry of several conditionally pardoned Young Irelanders from Tasmania, including Smith O'Brien, to whom he did not believe the terms of the act applied. But Kenealy still had to face a panel of thirteen magistrates in a packed court in Melbourne on 10 August. Nearly forty years later, in Los Angeles, the dying Kenealy wrote a little airily but truthfully: 'I had not the remotest intention of remaining in Australia and did not care at all whether I was expelled or not, but I saw my countrymen were excited, and I owed them a debt of gratitude.' The Irish community in Victoria certainly saw the case as a chance of winning ground. But the case was lost, and Kenealy and his supporters had to deposit a sum of £1,000, which would be forfeit if he did not leave the colony within seven days.

Kenealy's supporters, however, wanted to appeal to the Supreme Court. 'Irish blood was up.' Duffy himself showed Kenealy letters and petitions from the local Irish. 'From these messages here,' Duffy told Kenealy, 'you can see that our countrymen are very excited, and I fear if you leave them now . . . they might think you ungrateful.'

The appeal was at last heard in the august Supreme Court, before the Chief Justice of Victoria, Redmond Barry, an impressive Cork-born jurist, socially engaged, a powerful Orange sympathiser, unlikely – as Kenealy seems to have known well enough – to stretch the law for a Cork Fenian. Kenealy's defence counsel argued that the act had been improperly enforced in Kenealy's case, that since it was passed a new, more liberal constitution had come into being in Victoria. Chief Justice Redmond Barry rejected the argument. By an irony, the court decision was seen by some as proof of the independence of Victoria from the imperial will of Westminster. The imperial authorities had placed no condition upon

Kenealy and the other Fenians other than that they should not return to the United Kingdom for the residual term of their sentences. The colonial parliament of its own authority had placed this extra inhibition on their movements!

Kenealy had served to the full local Victorian-Irish purposes. Departing for King George's Sound and the port of Albany, he carried an immediate £950 to be distributed equally amongst the pardoned Fenians. On top of that, tickets would be provided free of charge to any who wanted to leave Western Australia and to go by steamer to New South Wales, since that colony had no explicit law restricting the entry of former convicts. For his own journey back to Western Australia, his Melbourne friends had bought a ticket under the name of O'Sullivan, the latter his mother's maiden name. Just the same, several detectives were on the wharf to see him off, 'one of whom I knew when we were boys together learning the dry goods business in Cork'. When his steamer *Rangatira* docked in Adelaide, Kenealy was met by a detective who told him that if he landed the police would be obliged to arrest him and he would be fined £500. The master of the vessel, Captain MacLean, overheard this and told the detective warmly that 'his ship was no prison, and I was at liberty to do as I pleased'.

The captain went off to argue the case with the governor, and got back at ten o'clock that night very excited, 'and in the most classical sailor language' declared no one had power to make his ship a prison. Calling a steward, he instructed him that all the refreshments of the ship were to be available to Kenealy and Kenealy's guests. One of the latter was a dear friend of Kenealy's, Tim Lonergan, whom Kenealy had sworn into the IRB. Lonergan had sought Stephens's permission to emigrate and take over his uncle's extensive dry-goods business. The next morning, as *Rangatira* was about to depart, the new governor of Western Australia, Mr Weld, came on board. He treated Kenealy with great courtesy and asked him a considerable number of questions about Western Australia.

Twenty-five of the State prisoners, having received the initial money sent by Kenealy, decided to travel from Perth for Albany in King George's Sound, and meet Kenealy on his return. The departure on Sunday 11 September was quite ceremonial, a parade of horsemen and women, followed by a horse-drawn bus containing the departing exiles. 'The whole company', wrote Casey, the Galtee Boy, 'reached a wayside inn some 20 miles from Perth, where an excellent dinner had been prepared.' Mounted police travelled with them on their journey to King George's Sound, to stop them fraternising with convict parties. Despite this, the group somehow managed to converse with and bid 'a sorrowful adieu to the cheerful, and much persecuted, victims of English court martials'.

Their journey through the 'immense heaths' and 'hopeless barrenness' of the road to Albany took ten days. The little port itself had a population of just 500 persons, one of them the agent of the P&O Company, whom they immediately visited. He told them a letter had arrived from the Colonial Secretary of Victoria instructing him that any captain who conveyed them to Melbourne would subject himself to a fine of £100. There was a chance, though, that the captain of the *Rangatira* would take them to Sydney. If the captain would not do so on his own initiative, the awful alternative was to return to Perth near-penniless.

They saw the white funnel of the *Rangatira*, and its ornate figurehead of a Maori chief, approaching. It was captained by the spiky Captain MacLean, and on the deck was Kenealy, 'his pleasant countenance beaming with delight and good humour, as he conveys the joyful intelligence that the *Rangatira* will convey us to Sydney'. Kenealy sought out Father Delany and repaid the £5, and the whole pardoned company of Fenians, who had planned to spend the night in a roofless barn, went to Albany's one hotel. So the party boarded the *Rangatira* on 21 September, and one hour later in bewildered elation were on their way along a shoreline of desert cliffs to Sydney via Adelaide and Melbourne. They made Adelaide the following Sunday and anchored opposite what Casey describes as 'the little village of Glenelg'. A detective boarded and demanded their papers, which they refused to give since they had no intention of landing in South Australia. When the steamer touched the wharf, men and women streamed aboard, some of them weeping. For the four days they were in Adelaide the ship was guarded by policemen, 'no doubt with the intention of arresting us should we dare to pollute the immaculate South Australia with our unhallowed footsteps'.

Newspapers picked up in Adelaide indicated that the Victorian government had so yielded to public opinion as to permit the approaching Fenians to land. But 'in consequence of the barbarous treatment Mr Kenealy received on his first visit', the group determined not to disembark there, much as they wanted to thank the people who had subscribed to the Melbourne committee. And so similar scenes as those in Adelaide occurred in Port Melbourne. Crowds formed at the gangplank, and a nervous police force persuaded Captain MacLean to leave port earlier than intended. For from the crowds on the wharf cheers would break out, including some for O'Donovan Rossa, not amongst the amnesty list of Gladstone's government and now serving in his fourth prison, Pentonville. 'Hats, caps and handkerchiefs were waving in dozens. Green streamers encircling the swanlike necks of Erin's fair and lovely daughters fluttered on the breeze.' The authorities came aboard and told MacLean that he would have to cast off for Sydney during that night. On the next day, Sunday, some thousands of people assembled on the quay from all parts of the colony of Victoria, only to find that the *Rangatira* had departed.

By now most of the prisoners had decided to embark either for Ireland or the United States, so they would be in Sydney for only a week or two. But in squally rain, the welcome was prodigious, a crowd gathering to meet the ship as it put into Circular Quay in Sydney Cove. A Sydney committee made up of four Irishmen, including the editor of the Sydney-based *Freeman's Journal*, was there too, and so were hostile presences, what Casey called 'several notorious ultra-montanes', by which he probably meant members of the Orange Lodge. The prisoners marched to five carriages, which were waiting to take them to their hotel (according to Casey, the Swiss Hotel) in North George Street. For days the press of people outside was so great 'that it was utterly impossible to have one moment to ourselves'. Some travelled 300 miles or more from the bush to point out the Fenians to children 'as a pattern for their future conduct'.

Now, without apparently consulting the Fenians, the editor of the *Freeman's Journal*, Richard O'Sullivan, the radical of the reception committee, persuaded some of his fellows to proclaim a grand welcoming picnic for Tuesday 19 October at Clontarf, the same picnic area at which Henry O'Farrell had shot Prince Alfred. O'Sullivan's announcement produced loyalist rage in Sydney. The proposed Clontarf picnic was, said the *Sydney Morning Herald*, 'one of those insolent outrages on public decency . . . where the apotheosis of O'Farrell was to be celebrated on the scene of his crime, and those who had lately experienced the mercy of the Queen are to participate in the orgies'.

Cashman, Kenealy and two other Fenians went by invitation to meet the Colonial Secretary, Jack Robertson, a Scot, former premier of New South Wales. Robertson, a renowned land reformer, had been president of the local branch of the Irish League in 1864–5. He politely asked the Fenians for their assistance in avoiding bloodshed. Kenealy records, 'We left assuring him we would do everything in our power to avoid trouble.' The Galtee Boy warned Richard O'Sullivan that insistence on the picnic might lead to hard treatment of Fenians still in Western Australia. But O'Sullivan was determined, and Jack Robertson in the end advised him by letter that the proposed picnic at Clontarf was prohibited, and that he hoped the committee would forgo any demonstration altogether. Robertson and Lord Belmore, governor of New South Wales, handled the Fenians and their support committee with a calmness which some of their more rabid constituency objected to. And though, in bringing about the cancellation, the Fenians themselves acted as moderators, Kenealy wrote:

'All the bigotry and anti-Irish hatred of the Orange and *Seoinín* were aroused, and it looked for a while as if there might be some senseless and useless blood letting.'

A condemnatory circular letter from the vicar-general of the archdiocese of Sydney prohibited Catholics from attending the picnic. It was read from the altars of Sydney, including St Mary's Cathedral, on the Sunday before the proposed event. Though the Fenians did not want the picnic, they did not want to hear reflections on their good faith by the vicar-general either, and tried to avoid hearing it by going to Mass at the French Marist church of St Patrick's, Church Hill. When they found that even there it was read at sermon time, they stood up as a body and quietly left.

Before the end of October, Sam Winter arrived from Melbourne for a settling up and disbursement of all relief funds. In addition to the £950 Kenealy had already taken to Western Australia, £1,500 was split up amongst the twenty-five Fenians in Sydney at the rate of £30 each, and £300 set aside for ten pardoned comrades who had remained in Western Australia. Four hundred pounds was also forwarded to Perth in care of Hugh Brophy, Joseph Noonan and Cornelius O'Mahony in trust for the soldier Fenian prisoners. Hundreds more was spent on ships tickets for the released men.

In Sydney on 21 October, the Fenians bound for San Francisco boarded the *Baringa*, a sailing ship; Kenealy was a little surprised to report that there were no steamers to California. Amongst those travelling to America was O'Reilly's friend from *Hougoumont*, Cashman, who hoped to find a career in journalism. Ten others were to return to Ireland by way of Melbourne, their terms being already expired or due to expire. These included the Galtee Boy, John Sarsfield Casey.

As the California-bound *Baringa* cleared Sydney Cove at the point where now the Opera House stands, the Fenians raised a green silk flag and exchanged three cheers with a large crowd on the wharf.

In the new year, on 27 January 1870, the Anglophobic *New York Tribune* gave the Fenians newly arrived in California the status of escapees – 'Fifteen political prisoners . . . have escaped and arrived in San Francisco.' As soon as the *Baringa* entered the Golden Gate, Captain Smith, the Fenian head centre who had accompanied MacManus's body to Ireland, was notified of the fact and sent the accustomed group of Irish worthies to escort the former prisoners around the city. Those who wished to go east, it was made clear, could comfortably do so on the Central Pacific Railroad.

In the same season in Dublin, a crowd gathering in early morning on a mere rumour to meet the Holyhead steamer *Countess of Erne* as it entered the Liffey brought to the ten home-coming Fenians the gifts of enthusiasm reserved for the deaths or resurrections of Irish heroes. 'On the quarter-deck stood the ten confessors,' said the *Irishman*. That night the Lord Lieutenant attended the pantomime at the Theatre Royal, Dublin. As the third scene of the performance began, a party of the released Fenians entered one of the private boxes. The entire audience, with the exception of a few people in the circle, rose and set up 'a deafening round of cheers which lasted for several minutes'. Casey watched, astonished, as people stood on their seats. Children were held in parents' arms. Here were bourgeois Irishmen and women who would not themselves have thought of taking the Fenian option, but who admired the sacrifices of those who had. As the cheering ceased, 'God Save Ireland' was sung, a tribute to the Manchester Martyrs, and then sung again, and three cheers were cried for O'Donovan Rossa, still in prison.

As those like Casey whose homes were in Munster returned home, the *Cork Herald* reported that a line of police with fixed bayonets outside Cork railway station could not be maintained, and the crowd swarmed the train, climbing on to the coaches. Cork City men Eugene Lombard and Morgan McSwiney went straight to their homes, which were on Coal-quay. When called on to address the crowd, the Fenians asked people to behave themselves, 'as any disturbance would only fasten the chains of the men in prison'. A connector train which took released prisoners to their homes in the country was mobbed at every station, and when John Sarsfield Casey emerged gleaming-eyed and elegant at Galtee, the whole town went into a shouting delirium.

But for the former Fenian prisoners in the United States, San Francisco proved a rigorous test. Young John Walsh wrote nostalgically to John Boyle O'Reilly on the other side of the country about good times he had enjoyed in Sydney. 'Had we stayed in Sydney we would have all got first-class situations from the wealthy Irishmen there; but like fools, as we were, nothing would do us only to come to this place, where we are loafing about for the last six or seven weeks and can't get employment. Were it not for the money we got in Australia . . . some of us would be off soldiering for Uncle Sam.' Kenealy was launched, however – he took a job with a San Francisco Fenian dry-goods dealer named Talbot, and had ideas of starting his own business as soon as the expiration of his sentence in six years' time enabled him to make buying trips to Ireland, England and Scotland.

The pardoned Fenians who had stayed in Western Australia would live orderly and, by the standards of the time, generally satisfactory lives. Former convict constable Hugh Brophy, who was in partnership with

Noonan and had built the bridge across the Swan, became a building contractor in the Melbourne of the great boom times of the 1870s, and, living until after the First World War, died in the flu pandemic of 1919. Some of the others had shorter expectancies. Brophy's partner Noonan married the daughter of a respected Western Australian Irish family and died in Perth in 1885. Cornelius O'Mahony, a Macroom, Cork man, taught at a Catholic boys' school in Perth and in 1875 married an Irish milliner, but died in Melbourne four years later. The two oldest Fenians were Tom Duggan and Luke Fullam. Duggan, after tutoring privately for a time, became a teacher in a school near the Western Australian town of Northam and had a long life, but Luke Fullam and his brother Lawrence, both of them suffering from tuberculosis, did not long survive. They worked at their trade of shoemaking and, after Luke's death in 1870, Lawrence married an Irishwoman, but died while his son was still an infant. The brothers were buried side by side in Fremantle cemetery.

The first writing assignment which brought O'Reilly to prominence in the eastern United States was his coverage of the Fenian invasion of Canada in late May 1870. By the spring of 1870, it had become clear that yet another Fenian invasion was being planned by certain members of the Roberts wing. 'It is the fact that "experienced military men" are now found among the leaders', wrote the *New York Times* on 4 May, 'which makes it so easy to persuade Bridget and Patrick that with one dollar more the green flag may be hoisted on the Plains of Abraham, and a Fenian navy launched on the track of British commerce.'

In April, the plans had come under threat when John O'Neill, who had won the Battle of Ridgeway in 1866, and was now president of the Roberts/Senate wing, appeared 'awfully drunk' at a strategy meeting. A disgusted Senate wing voted the presidency out of existence, but a powerful breakaway group was formed to support O'Neill. O'Neill meant to go ahead with an invasion, preferably for the queen's birthday, 24 May, before the Fenian Senate could meet to take away his military authority.

He had the problem that earlier that year the Vatican had specifically outlawed the Fenian Brotherhood. There had been debate amongst priests and in the Fenian ranks as to whether the Fenian Brotherhood had been covered by the decree of the previous year, *Apostolicae Sedis*, which simply mentioned secret organisations. The British minister to the Vatican had worked very hard to persuade the Pontiff to issue a Fenian-specific decree, as a means of protecting both Canada and Britain. The new decree of January 1870 made it clear 'that the American or Irish society called Fenian is comprised among the societies forbidden and condemned in the

Constitutions of the Supreme Pontiff'. There were still subtle priestly minds in Ireland and in the United States who could find a path for sensitive Fenian youths through the minefields of Papal condemnation. Some pro-Fenian papers treated the press reports of the decree as lies. 'It is a contemptible fraud therefore,' said the *Irish People* of 12 March.

Free in conscience at barely more than thirty years old, O'Neill was still brimming with coherent schemes for supply and personnel. He had spent months successfully storing Confederate surplus arms, re-tooled in a factory in Trenton, New Jersey, in rented warehouses and barns along the Canadian border. But his security was slapdash, and his adjutant, Civil War veteran and surgeon Dr Henri LeCaron, was a long-established and competent British agent, born in southern England and really, and prosaically, named Beech.

Letters delivered to Fenian circles required officers to start their men moving towards Malone near the New York–Quebec border, and into northern Vermont during the night of Monday 23 May. Fenian officers needed to move their entire membership at individual expense, all within a space of twelve hours. Nonetheless, the enterprise was supported with a poignant enthusiasm by sundry Irish labourers and clerks, though with a lesser proportion of Civil War veterans than there had been four years earlier.

O'Reilly, dispatched as a journalist by the *Boston Pilot*, and by some means or other fully aware of the Fenian plans, was sceptical of the moral and practical value of Canadian raids. We do not know if he seized the assignment or was persuaded to take it by Donahoe, the editor-owner of the *Pilot*. But if he crossed into Canada and was caught by Canadian forces, as escapee and Fenian he would suffer doubly. He took the train from Boston to western Massachusetts, having a delighted look at rural New England, and picked up the railroad north into Vermont. As he travelled, President Ulysses S. Grant, a Republican, and not as pro-Irish as Johnson, issued a proclamation dated 24 May condemning 'sundry illegal military enterprises and expeditions on foot within the territory and jurisdiction of the United States . . . against the people and district of the dominion of Canada'.

To begin the campaign, O'Neill depended on men from Massachusetts, Rhode Island, Vermont, and northern New York. O'Neill said, 'I would have under my command in this section on Wednesday morning upwards of four thousand men.' From 1,000 to 1,500 men were in the meantime to assemble at Malone, New York.

O'Neill's plan of campaign was to enter Quebec and capture Saint-Jean-sur-Richelieu, called locally St Johns. But in St Albans, Vermont, where O'Neill and LeCaron waited on Tuesday morning, 24 May, the six o'clock train brought not 1,200 men from Massachusetts, as expected, but just twenty-five to thirty, led by a Fenian colonel named Sullivan. In lieu of the 600 men promised by Vermont and north-eastern New York, eighty to ninety were on the train. A company of sixty-five Irishmen from Burlington, Vermont, had arrived the previous evening and had already been sent north to Franklin, only 2 miles from the border. O'Neill decided not to delay. Since he expected reinforcements, he would take up a position at Franklin, and then cross the line. He also ordered the movement across the border of men assembled far to the east, at Malone, New York. To begin with fewer than 200 men seemed an act of recklessness, but he was working on the same failed supposition as Smith O'Brien at Ballingarry – that an early success would draw in more men. He claimed to have promises from prominent American military men that they would join the expedition 'once the demonstration was fairly under way'.

Beyond the town of Franklin, the nearest crossroads to the border was Hubbard's Corner. It served as a mustering point for armed Fenians. Arms and ammunition had been voluntarily hauled up from depots by Vermont citizens, 'all of whom will please accept my thanks on behalf of the brotherhood', wrote O'Neill, 'for their unpaid and untiring exertions on this and on other occasions'. O'Neill was delighted that this time the enemy had no force near the line to oppose them. He intended to make all necessary arrangements to cross over and take up a position on Eccles Hill on the Canadian side. But his Adjutant-General, LeCaron, sent to St Albans to hurry on the men who arrived on the six o'clock evening train, deliberately took his time, and overnight the border remained uncrossed and Eccles Hill unoccupied.

Within a short ride of the border, O'Neill occupied as headquarters a home which belonged to an Alvah Richard or Rykert. Here Fenian General Donnelly had turned up, telling O'Neill that the US marshal in St Albans was making moves to arrest him. He also reported that between four and five hundred men had arrived on the train the previous evening, and were now but a few hours' march from Franklin. 'In fact it turned out to be not over 230 or 240 men arrived. Sixty or seventy of that number were under Major Daniel Murphy of Connecticut. They lost their way coming to Franklin and did not arrive until five o'clock in the morning.' A handful of men under a Captain Keneally of Marlboro, Massachusetts, also arrived. Early that morning of 25 May, with these forces, O'Neill could still have simply crossed and occupied Eccles Hill, but did not do so.

O'Reilly reached the Fenian positions that morning and left a pithy and graphic account of that Wednesday morning. In Franklin, 'the solitary street filled with wagons and teams of every description, and a large crowd of men, composed principally of citizens attracted by curiosity'. He found the Fenian uniform most attractive – 'a green cavalry jacket, faced with yellow, army blue pantaloons and a blue cap with a green band'.

At 10.30 a.m. the US marshal General George P. Forster, accompanied by a number of citizens, came to the camp around Rykert's house. There were too many armed Fenians there to make an arrest feasible, so the marshal limited his discussion with O'Neill to the question of whether the Fenians would kindly keep the road open. The marshal gone, O'Neill ordered a force of 176 men moved forward at 11.30 a.m., but Colonel LeCaron, perhaps as a stratagem, rode up and informed him that the New York Fenians were close at hand and it was worth waiting. LeCaron was secretly concerned at what would happen to him if he were captured by Canadians or British who did not know of his arrangement with Her Majesty's government. It would be ridiculous to be shot or lynched as a Fenian!

Amongst these induced delays, the Canadian militia suddenly turned up on the border. They had already captured a few Fenian scouts near Cook's Corner, two miles inside Canada, and were joined by an irregular body of armed local farmers wearing red sashes, men outraged by the raid of 1866 in that area. These irregulars willingly posted themselves on Eccles Hill about 300 yards from the frontier. O'Neill acknowledged they had taken up 'a splendid position'. Fenian companies were now, too late, sent over the border and across the little bridge at the bottom of Eccles Hill. Once over they deployed skirmishers. There was a volley from the top of this escarpment, and Fenian John Row of Burlington, Vermont, shot through the heart, fell dead in the centre of the road.

O'Neill tried outflanking, ordering groups coming up from the rear to cross an open field in Vermont to the timbered hill on the Fenian left. Three of them were shot, one fatally. The Fenians wavered. John Boyle O'Reilly, unlike the reporter of the *New York Herald* who had fled, advanced with O'Neill from Rykert's house and met some men making for the rear. 'They seemed to have a very erroneous idea as to the number of the enemy,' wrote O'Reilly. Canadian fire from Snyder rifles was ending Fenianism's credit on that rustic border.

'Men of Ireland,' O'Neill told the Fenians gathered near Rykert's, above the position where General Donnelly's men at the border itself lay huddled, 'I am ashamed of you! You have acted disgracefully today.' He himself, he declared, would lead them to a new attack, but first, 'I will leave you under the charge of John Boyle O'Reilly, and will go after reinforcements and bring them back at once.' This curious appointment of O'Reilly went without further explanation, and O'Reilly himself would imply he had in no way welcomed it. Everything he wrote of the expedition after that day was disapproving of the enterprise, but on the day itself was he tempted, for the last time in his life, by the military possibilities? O'Neill obviously hoped O'Reilly's lustre as Fenian and escapee would settle the men, and also remembered from his Civil War days how men who behaved badly at the start of the battle rallied when reinforcements began to arrive. O'Neill himself intended to meet the reinforcements coming up from St Albans, but down the road he saw General Forster stationed. Fearing he would be arrested if he were on his own, he returned to ask O'Reilly, as a gentleman of the press, to accompany him, and put Major Daniel Murphy in charge for the moment. He started again with John Boyle O'Reilly, but at a crossroads General Forster emerged from a crowd surrounding a wounded Fenian soldier, shook hands with O'Neill, and said, 'I think, General, you had better get in the carriage and drive back with me.' O'Neill argued that he would not let himself be arrested and pointed to O'Reilly's presence. The marshal said that he had more armed men in the vicinity now than O'Neill. O'Neill later explained that he was carrying only his sabre, and that he knew that the Vermonters, sympathetic as they were, would back up a Federal official. He told O'Reilly to take journalistic account of the fact that he was powerless to resist. In the marshal's carriage, he was cautioned against calling out to any of his men who might be coming up to support the Fenian front. The driver, said O'Neill, lashed the horses and drove furiously through the Fenian depot where a further battalion of Irishmen had just arrived. In justice to him, it must be said that O'Neill had no reason to want to be arrested at this stage. He had taken great pains till now to avoid it; had travelled indirectly and in disguise to St Albans in the first place.

In an account O'Neill later prepared in prison, he reproduced a report written the next day by O'Reilly. 'As you ordered me, I told my command on the hill that you had been arrested. I then gave command to Major Daniel Murphy, of Bridgeport, Connecticut . . . I then went down to General Donnelly.' Donnelly was commanding the troops who had tried to cross the ground below Eccles Hill, and there was some risk in O'Reilly's reaching him. 'He was deeply affected when I told him of your arrest. He could not leave his place, determined to do so in the night. He did so last night, and is now with the main body at the stores.' This letter seemed to indicate that O'Reilly saw himself as at least a disillusioned officer of the enterprise.

On the afternoon of 25 May, the Fenians abandoned their flanking position of the timbered hill, and darkness mercifully permitted Donnelly's men to withdraw.

*

In O'Reilly's published reports in the *Pilot*, there seemed to be a distance between him and the other militant Irishmen. The recurrent term 'we saw' may have been a justifiable journalistic device, but also riveted O'Reilly in the posture of a witness, not an enthusiastic actor. O'Reilly's sympathy in his reports, as President Grant moved US army units up to the border to prevent any more Fenian assaults, was for the rank and file of Fenianism. 'The citizens here all feel for the poor fellows who are left destitute in their towns.' And if there had been any identity of intent between O'Reilly and these Fenian men, it was the last time in his life he would give room to physical force.

As operations ceased in Franklin, O'Reilly travelled by train from Burlington across to New York State, to report on the outfall of the Fenian attack at Trout River. The Fenians had crossed the border near Malone but been hit by rapid fire from well-placed Canadians behind fences and in woods at a crossroads. The situation had been rather like Ridgeway in 1866, but with the roles reversed. O'Reilly was outraged enough by the débâcle to deal harshly with the common Fenian usage of the rank of general: 'We use the word general as a mean – there might have been a colonel, and there probably *was* a field-marshal.' Fenian General John H. Gleeson, who had served three years with Meagher's 63rd New York and would later be attacked by O'Neill in his bitter report, got little credit from O'Reilly either. Gleeson was holding court at the Ferguson house near the Canadian border and expressing 'disgust'. He 'interlarded said expression with Munchausen assertions of what could be done, were things after his way of thinking, and especially of what he himself could do'. Meanwhile, many of the men O'Reilly met – 'poor disheartened fellows' straggling along the road from Malone to Trout River – burst into tears at what they called their disgrace. 'Judging from the military physique of the greater number, there can be no doubt that, with qualified officers, these men would prove that they did not merit the name they now feared – cowards.' Back in Boston by 11 June, O'Reilly speculated in the *Pilot* on the good which would have been done had the money been sent to Ireland for land purchases and for supporting schools.

In his Federal prison cell, O'Neill would have leisure to list the many reasons for failure: 'thousands of good men who were anxious to be with us, kept indulging their doubts and fears until too late to be of service . . . The Senate party had their emissaries walk all over the country, destroying the confidence of the people.' Of the $30,000 O'Neill had earlier specified as the sum needed to meet the expenses of an invasion, only $2,000 had been paid into the treasury before he left New York for the border.

'Shall another attempt be made to invade Canada?' he asked at the end of his report, 'to which I answer, no! Emphatically no!' But O'Neill did make one last abortive attempt the following year, at Pembina, Manitoba, to link up with the Metis leader Louis Riel. From that point, there was no further armed assault over a line which in modern times became one of the most stable on earth. The Fenians had in fact demonstrated to the United States that an unstable border was of no advantage to them, and that Canadians did not long by the hundreds of thousands for the benefits of American republicanism.

After 25 May 1870, O'Reilly stated his disenchantment with Fenianism in a Boston speech on the new Irish Home Government Association – the Home Rule movement which had been inaugurated at a meeting in Dublin in May 1870 to seek an Irish domestic legislature. O'Reilly himself would as a young Fenian have despised this option, for it countenanced a continuing nexus to Britain. But a pragmatist now, he saw Home Rule as an honest first step in the process of deliverance. At the same time, however, he supported the obstructionist group amongst the Irish members of the British Parliament, who set out to delay government business in the House of Commons to force Gladstone to attend to Irish reform. O'Reilly would come particularly to admire and support the emergent leader of this Irish group, a complex young squire from Wicklow, Charles Stewart Parnell.

O'Reilly had also developed almost instantly into a pluralist American. A month after the failed invasion, he damned the behaviour of his fellow countrymen in anti-Orange riots brought on by a 12 July procession in New York. Orangemen, parading with the normal flags and music, were heard to yell, 'To hell with the Pope!' and 'Croppies lie down!' ('Croppies' had been the nickname for rustic Catholic rebels in 1798.) The upshot was that 'a terrible melee' broke out, and four lives were lost. 'What are we today in the eyes of Americans? Aliens from a petty island in the Atlantic, boasting of our patriotism and fraternity, and showing at the same moment that deadly hatred.' He foresaw a time 'when America, tired out and indignant with her squabbling population, puts her foot down with a will and tells them all – Germans, French, Irish, Orange – "You have had enough now. There is only one flag to be raised in future in this country and that is the Stars and Stripes." ' Critics of John Boyle O'Reilly began to complain that he was 'sneering at the Sunburst', the symbol at the centre of the Fenian flag.

Since an Amnesty Association to campaign for the release of imprisoned Fenians had been founded in 1868 by a Dublin dry-goods merchant Fenian named John 'Amnesty' Nolan, it had achieved considerable success. Its meetings in Dublin and London were massively attended, and had been one of the factors which led to the release of the thirty-four Fremantle Fenians. The association particularly sought to have O'Donovan Rossa released, and so nominated him for election to the House of Commons, a daring stratagem which would be repeated with other political prisoners in the twentieth century. In November 1870, while still serving at Chatham prison, O'Donovan Rossa was elected member for Tipperary *in absentia*. This set off meetings of rejoicing throughout Ireland. Towards Christmas 1870, Gladstone announced that specified civilian Fenians in British prisons, and the eight remaining Western Australian civilian Fenians, were to be conditionally pardoned. Only one of the newly pardoned, James Kearney, a Cork man in his mid-twenties, stayed in Western Australia. He was in love with a local Irish immigrant woman, would marry, earn his living as an itinerant bootmaker in the bush, and die an Australian elder in 1923.

The newly pardoned included one of the editors of the *Wild Goose*, that natural newspaperman John Flood. Also amongst the pardons were those of John Edward Kelly of Cork and Boston, and Kenealy's friend Thomas Fennell, who had suffered a bullet wound in the testicles and thigh during the skirmishes of 1867. Settling in the large Irish enclave of Elmira, New York, Fennell would give certain parties advice concerning the rescue of other Fenians still serving life sentences.

Five freed men, including Flood and Goulding, used the £30 Brophy and Noonan were holding for each of them to take ship to Port Lyttelton on the South Island of New Zealand in May 1871. This was the venue of the hour, serving the Otago gold-fields, the world's latest bonanza. Adventurous settlers needed to move themselves and their luggage up the steep escarpments surrounding the port to get to the hinterland, but the Fenians were never put to that trouble, for they were arrested on landing. New Zealand had, like Victoria, passed an Introduction of Convicts Prevention Act in 1867. All five men appeared before a magistrate the next day, and were able to produce a letter from the Colonial Secretary of Western Australia stating that he was not aware of any restriction against their landing in New Zealand. The magistrate dropped charges against Goulding, who had a totally free pardon and had by now already served his time. But the prosecutor pressed that the others be returned to Western Australia as a warning to that colony. Bail was posted, to be forfeited if they did not quit the colony within fourteen days. A hundred pounds was raised by the Irishmen of Christchurch so that the Fenians were able to pay for five passages to Sydney.

In Sydney, the men found much suspicion of Fenians at all levels of society. The new British Secretary of State for the Colonies, Lord Kimberley, had sent off a coded cable warning all the Australian governors of intelligence, which he said he did not fully believe but felt it right to send, that a Fenian filibustering expedition was about to leave San Francisco to raid Melbourne, Sydney and Otago. The governor of South Australia, Sir James Fergusson, unwisely sent an *en clair*, uncoded, telegram on the subject to Lord Belmore, and so soon the word was leaked to the press by telegraph employees. Militia units started drilling in Sydney and the British Naval Squadron arranged gun practice in the Pacific Ocean outside Sydney Heads. The frenzy became more muted when in June 1871 the British consul in San Francisco finally assured Kimberley that there was no basis for the rumour.

A Fenian dinner was held in Sydney for these last released Fenians, four of whom decided to stay in New South Wales, one – Flood – to go to the new gold-fields of Queensland, three to go to San Francisco. The chair argued that there was 'more liberty, freedom and toleration (with the exception of a few persons)' in Australia than in any other country in the civilised world, and for that reason no one was more attached to it than the 'Sons of St Patrick'.

John Goulding, however, a charming young carpenter from Cahirciveen in Kerry, who had taken part in the 1867 Kerry uprising and had been sentenced to five years just in time to be put on *Hougoumont*, had been very well treated by an urbane Irish farmer, John Feehan, who owned land on the south coast of New South Wales at Gerringong. Feehan himself was of Fenian disposition, well-read – possessing his own extensive library of works on Irish history – and affluent. Gerringong itself lay in a lovely valley between steep coastal mountains and the Pacific. Goulding's contacts with Ellen, Feehan's daughter, helped him decide to take up Feehan's offer to go farming. Twelve years later, as Ellen Feehan's husband and a successful dairy farmer, he died of congestion of the lungs at the age of thirty-eight, leaving his widow and seven young children, and was buried on a headland by the Pacific. Goulding's widow, Ellen, would live till 1938, and told her grandchildren that one of the reasons her husband had become a Fenian was that, when a boy, he had been walking his dog near Kell's Cove, Kerry, when it presumed to bark at the landlord's coach. The landlord ordered his coachman to shoot the beast.

A former Fenian prisoner who would live to achieve some retribution against the penal settlement of Western Australia was Michael Cody, who went gold-seeking in the bush and then settled in Sydney as a hotel-keeper. He became organiser and fund raiser of the Fenians in New South Wales, an administrative task which only partially suited his man-of-action temperament. In Park Street, Sydney, John Flood and Edward Kelly began a newspaper under the same name as Mitchel's New York newspaper – the *Irish Citizen*. It existed largely to combat, over the course of a state election, the anti-Irish hysteria encouraged for political purposes by Sir Henry Parkes. The election over, Flood now joined the gold rush to the Palmer River gold-fields, 2,000 miles north of Sydney in tropical Cooktown in Queensland. Here, after two years' mining, this former editor of the *Wild Goose* took up the editorship of the *Cooktown Courier*. In that humid monsoonal port, closer to New Guinea than to Brisbane, he married an Irish immigrant, Susan O'Beirne from County Leitrim, and they moved south to a more temperate zone of Queensland, Flood working as a newspaper editor in the gold-mining town of Gympie, where he also became secretary of a gold-mining company. Throughout, he remained a devout editorialist for Irish land reforms, and, like O'Reilly in Boston, for Home Rule as the first step towards an independent Ireland. He died an honoured citizen in Gympie in 1909.

An old friend of Kenealy's from Cork, Con Keane, who had once found it hard to get his child baptised because the nominated godfather was a Fenian, also waited out the residue of his sentence in Queensland, working as clerk of petty sessions and mining registrar on a number of gold-fields, including Charters Towers and Cloncurry. In such places one encountered much genial Irish company and even Fenianism, but when he died in 1891 at Limestone, Queensland, he had not been reunited with his wife and two children.

O'Reilly's future as an eminent Bostonian was still a-forming in Staniford Street, Charlestown, in 1870–1. He was certainly not fully free of Western Australia, and was delighted to find out that Jessie's father, Warder Woodman, whose occurrence sheet had not shown that he had visited the camp at 10.30 p.m. as he had earlier claimed, had evaded more than a reprimand. For a time, too, he sent copies of the *Pilot* to Maguire in Dardanup, and to Father McCabe, who would ultimately leave the colony to take a parish south of Minneapolis.

Like Meagher when he had first arrived in America, O'Reilly was, nearly from the start, a busy lecturer for a range of causes – the Engineer Corps of the 9th Regiment, St Stephen's Church in Boston, Home Rule in Ireland – but he returned frequently to the question of un-amnestied soldier Fenians. There were eight civilian and fifteen military prisoners who had been excluded from the latest amnesty and were still serving sentences. Chambers, one of the military prisoners still in gaol in Britain, wrote his chain-mate O'Reilly a pathetic letter which O'Reilly read regularly from public platforms. 'It is my birthday as I write this, and I know I am turning it to the best account by writing to such a dear old friend . . . I will count the time I spend here as nothing if I could only see the factions in America and elsewhere all united in one grand organisation.'

There were of course soldier Fenians in Western Australia who were either free or about to be: Patrick Killeen of the horse artillery, for example, who would spend the rest of his life, which did not end until 1925, in Western Australia working on the outlying stations. A particularly pathetic aspect of his career was that he had applied to have his wife and children sent out to Australia, but his file in the Home Office showed that he had previously declared himself unmarried, a position which disqualified him from the privilege of reunion. Yet he was free, and a number of O'Reilly's other friends from prison were either free or close to it, with a finite term to serve. Their names did not weigh on O'Reilly as much as those of the men who, like himself, had been serving life sentences.

In the early Australian winter after O'Reilly's escape, the life-sentenced soldier Fenian Thomas Hassett, feeling the first rain fall through the roof of his hut, believed that he could not sustain yet another season in imprisonment. He decided to try a similar strategy to O'Reilly's. Hassett was a tough campaigner. He had served with the Papal Brigade in Italy, and then in the 24th Infantry. In early 1866 he had walked off sentry duty at the Royal Hospital, Kilmainham, and reported in his scarlet uniform, with knapsack, rifle and sixty rounds of ammunition, to an upstairs room in Donald Street full of other Fenian deserters. Now he was serving a life sentence and bore over his heart the loathed letter 'D'.

In June of 1870, he had cleared out from a work party, and turned up at the Fullam brothers' house in Perth, asking them to hide him. The Fullams, knowing that it meant re-imprisonment for them, tuberculosis or not, gave him the modest and wary help they could. Various ticket-of-leave Irishmen he called on suggested he go to Bunbury, where they would make arrangements to get him aboard an American whaler. He was, however, given only £1, as much as his friends could raise, to make the 130-mile journey. He knew that, held in trust by Noonan and the others against his name, was £30.

In the Bunbury district he was taken in by a poor Irish family who gave him employment and pay in kind, and he hid with them for some months. When eventually he went to town and found a whaling captain who agreed to ship him out for £30, he sent off an urgent request for his money to be sent down from Perth. It never came, and the whaling captain sailed without him. His friend James Wilson would later write to John Devoy and complain that the Relief Fund trustees, Noonan, Brophy, and O'Mahony, had been culpable in not freely advancing any money for escapes. But Noonan and Brophy had made particularly successful lives for themselves in Western Australia, which they would have forfeited if implicated in an escape.

Left frantic, Hassett smuggled himself aboard the *Southern Belle*, but surrendered to the water police as they were about to penetrate his hiding-place with their long steel probes. Having been on the loose for ten months, a highly punishable time, he was sent back to Fremantle prison and sentenced to three years' hard labour, the first six months in solitary confinement. This was his most disabling experience, from which in his way he would never revive. And it was as if in Boston O'Reilly, always recaptured in his own nightmares, shared Hassett's waking horror. O'Reilly's lifetime problems with sleeplessness had begun.

28

Home Rule and Dynamite

> I am glad you are sick of all these claptrap proceedings and *bloody England* meetings ... I wish to the Lord there wasn't so much ranting and blatherskite. I'm sick of the Irish papers.
>
> John Boyle O'Reilly to John Devoy, 1871

In January 1871, O'Reilly was delighted to hear that in a new batch of pardoned Fenians was his old friend the recruiter and Foreign Legion veteran John Devoy, along with the most hardline of Fenians, O'Donovan Rossa. Devoy and Rossa almost at once took ship and arrived in America with three other pardoned men, John McClure, a young man named Harry Mulleda, and Charles Underwood O'Connell, thus making the '*Cuba* Five', named for the steamer on which they had crossed the Atlantic. Devoy approached New York with a desire to heal all the rifts and redeem Fenianism. O'Donovan Rossa, tough, amiable, whimsical, was an unyielding revolutionary. He would be joined by his poetic wife and, working from the hotel he acquired in Lower Manhattan, would ultimately found the infamous Skirmishing Fund, a predecessor of such twentieth-century structures as Noraid, for the underwriting of acts of modern terror against Britain.

As the Cunard steamship *Cuba* was off the Battery, it was greeted with the enthusiasm so often recounted in this narrative – torches blazed and cannon boomed; city fathers and Fenian wings came out by launch and boarded the steamer. Behind the courtesies, O'Donovan Rossa discerned 'that the question of our reception had grown into a party fight'. On the dock, 'the usual hand-shaking having taken place', wrote the New York *Irish People* on 28 January 1871, the former Young Irelander and New York Superior Court Judge Richard O'Gorman welcomed the released prisoners. He praised them for their devotion to the cause of Ireland, and invited them to accept a public reception from the citizens of New York and 'the City Government'.

Devoy in his *Recollections* recalled damningly that O'Gorman took 'no part in Irish affairs since his arrival in the country and was active only in American politics'. While he was still speaking for Tammany and the Savage or O'Mahony wing of Fenianism, the Roberts/Senate group turned up by cab and tried to seduce the five. General F. F. Millen pointed to O'Gorman and told O'Donovan Rossa, 'Unlike this gentleman, I don't offer you a reception at the hands of the City Government, but I extend to you the hospitality of the United States.' A health commissioner named Mullaley asked, 'Are you the United States, sir?' General Millen said, 'No, but I desire to save the men from being a tool of the Tammany tricksters.' In an interview in the *New York Herald*, Devoy expressed disgust at the scene. 'Do they think that by dangling the dollars before us they can influence us?'

The O'Mahony or Savage wing of the Fenians, in their efforts to claim the newly released 'Fenian exiles', organised a grand parade so massive that engravings were struck for sale to Irish America. Some $22,000 was collected through a subscription raised by Tammany, and, of this, $15,000 was handed to the Fenian exiles through O'Donovan Rossa, the financial agent elected by them. The balance was used in paying the hotel bill at the Metropolitan on Broadway – the same which had once been Meagher's home. According to Devoy's memoirs, this amounted to a sumptuous $6,000, more of it run up by Tammany than by the exiles.

By May 1871, John Boyle O'Reilly was able to sense the faction-weariness in the 29-year-old John Devoy and warned him that 'the great mass of the Irish people have never belonged to any organisation for national revolution'. The disaffection of the freed men was such that the *Cuba* Five found almost welcome a fraternal visit from American Communists, proposing the impossible, an alliance between Irish revolutionaries and those who had embraced the rugged, temporal, universalist faith of Marx and Engels. At the First Communist International in London, Karl Marx had spoken with some point of 'the people of Ireland who more and more are replaced in the North by machines and in the South by sheep, although in that unhappy land even the sheep diminish in numbers, though not so rapidly as the men'. Marx had also condemned the prison treatment of O'Donovan Rossa and others. Now a delegation of the North American Central Committee of the International Workingmen's Association waited on the exiles at the Metropolitan and congratulated them on their release from prison. One of the Central Committee suggested that the Irish should not isolate themselves but join in the struggle against the common enemy.

O'Reilly was one of the nine members of a committee to welcome the *Cuba* Five to Boston, and his nomination was opposed by a Fenian who said that the released men would shoot fellows like him, renouncers of the Fenian creed. O'Reilly confessed to Devoy, 'John, I hate that infernal name – Fenianism. It has done us more harm than thoughtless men can see.' O'Reilly's committee decided not 'to inflict a *reception* on you here – but to send you instead the proceeds of a general subscription with an address'.

This was all of a piece with O'Reilly's contempt for blarney. Amongst other examples, he despised a common utterance of Irish supporters of demagogues: '*He's a friend to the Irishman* is simply an insult, and should be resented accordingly.' For the Irishmen and women O'Reilly frequently saw in Boston's rougher quarters were in fact friendless election fodder. A Cork immigrant to Boston would report being shocked on seeing the wharves and wretched tenements of East Boston, 'with ragged, hungry-looking, dirty children playing in the ash-heaps of a nearby railroad . . . Thinks I to myself: – "Is this the great country of peace and plenty there is so much talked about?" ' As late as 1890, 65 per cent of Boston's Irish-born performed the lowest of manual labour, and nearly 50 per cent of Irish-born women were servants. Early in his American career, before he had a good job, he had advised his sisters: 'I hate New York and Boston, which are all corruption and misery for poor girls.' Tuberculosis, alcoholism, mental illness, and a sense that they could not match the pace of America, were the common lot of the lower orders of Boston Irishdom, and men and women from Donegal and Mayo approached the heavy machinery of the new, proliferating Massachusetts textile mills with the tentativeness of a people who still believed in the malign influence of fairies. In Boston's North and West Ends Irish young contributed massively to the infant mortality rates. Smith O'Brien's daughter Charlotte went so far as to say of New York when she visited it in 1880 that three out of four of the children of the Irish poor died in infancy! 'It would keep you poor burying your children,' one woman told her. Charlotte's report might have been impressionistic, but she took the same picture from the slums of Boston. O'Reilly realised in 1871 that, in the circumstances under which most Irish lived in the cities of America, politicians who claimed to be 'a good friend to the Irish' were offering very little except bare toleration.

John Devoy got a job as a journalist at the *New York Herald* and started work to achieve factional peace through an Irish Confederation. O'Reilly warned Devoy the various factions had too long a history of grievance to be brought to the same table. 'Take my word for it,' O'Reilly advised his friend, on the basis of his own bitter, destructive imprisonment, and what he had seen on the Canadian border in 1870, 'the men who make the most noise now will be the first to fall through . . . The political prisoners have the confidence and affection of our people everywhere, and I am convinced that that confidence would be increased untold were they to settle down for a time, and begin a commonplace business course.' There was in any case an organisation already in existence which would ultimately give Devoy, Rossa and the other released Fenians a new home. It had been founded in July 1867 by Jerome J. Collins and a number of men from both wings of the Fenian movement, and named the Clan na Gael, the United Brotherhood, or – in the crude code used by the movement – the VC. The Clan still recognised the council of the IRB at home as the *de facto* government of Ireland, and pledged to support it.

Rossa would in the end be expelled from Clan na Gael for his championship of the Skirmishing (or, more accurately, dynamiting) Fund, but little Devoy, having joined, remained for half a century its organiser-in-chief and its celibate and daring high priest. As two old men, Devoy and Rossa would in the twentieth century, on the eve of the Easter Uprising, be reconciled at O'Donovan Rossa's deathbed, and Devoy would still, as crusty Clan head, be in place in 1920 to fall out with Eamon de Valera over diplomatic and fund-raising tactics in America.

O'Reilly and Devoy were at one in that personal appeals kept coming directly or indirectly to them from rebels still in prison in Britain and in Australia, from men who were not merely names but whom they had recruited. It may have been one of the factors which made O'Reilly an insomniac, frantic worker, as if he were living in fact for other men as well as himself. In Western Australia, Hassett's attempted escape showed the remaining seven soldier Fenians who were serving life sentences and would never be released from Western Australia that they could not depend on Noonan's committee to finance O'Reilly-style getaways. In 1871, Martin Hogan, former soldier, a man of restless energy, thirty-four years old and looking towards a limitless existence as someone less than a citizen at peace, saw in a newspaper smuggled into Fremantle gaol that amongst Fenians recently released in amnesty from British prisons was Peter Curran. In Curran's pub in Dublin, Hogan and others had undergone Fenian drilling. Hogan wrote illicitly to Curran now, using Father McCabe as his postbox, and in the hope that the letter would be given wide circulation.

Perth, Western Australia, 20th May, 1871

My Dear Friend, In order that you may recollect who it is that addresses you, you will remember the night of 17 January, 1866, some of the Fifth Dragoon Guards being in the old house in Clare Lane with John Devoy and Captain McCafferty. I am one of that unfortunate band and am now under sentence for life's penal servitude in one of the darkest corners of the earth, and as far as we can learn from any small news that chances to reach us, we appear to be forgotten, with no prospect before us but to be left in hopeless slavery to the tender mercies of the Norman wolf.

It was a letter which in its desperation made all appropriate claims and exploited all appropriate imagery. It was of course seen and indeed published by O'Reilly and by Devoy. At consecutive conventions of the growing United Brotherhood or Clan na Gael, in 1872 and 1873, Devoy spoke of the Australian prisoners and their claims upon the concern of Irish nationalists everywhere. Thomas Fennell, in his late twenties, former Western Australian prisoner settled in New York, had already suggested to Devoy the idea of buying a ship to export grain or some other commodity to Western Australia, thus using it as a self-funding vehicle of escape. In both 1872 and 1873 the Clan executive had doubted their capacity to raise the funds which would be necessary for that sort of enterprise. In modern-day terms the acquisition and setting up of a sailing vessel and cargo were roughly equivalent to the modern purchase and fitting out of a 747 jet. But the remaining Fenian prisoners were unquiet claimants upon the attention of their fellow Irish.

News of the death in Dublin, under the care of O'Reilly's two sisters, of his father William at sixty-three years of age shook him that year. His father had not had an ample pension, and he was without too many friends – it seemed he had made enemies in the National School system. But O'Reilly had been able from 1870 to remit cash to ease his father's end, and now had the means and the freedom to commemorate him publicly and honour his name in front of some of Boston's illuminati.

Kindly Jessie Woodman being now beyond O'Reilly's reach, he had begun calling on a Miss Mary Murphy of Charlestown, the child of Irish immigrants, who lived with her widowed mother Jane Murphy, *née* Smiley. Her Fermanagh immigrant father, John, had died in her childhood at less than forty years of age, but had left them with means to live with modest gentility. O'Reilly had been led to her through reading her story in a publication called the *Young Crusader*, and told the editor he would like to meet her. On 15 August 1872, when Mary was twenty-two years old, and O'Reilly twenty-eight, they were married in St Mary's, Charlestown. Mary Murphy seemed his wholesome Columbia, the cure to intolerable and even guilty memory. But she had sought an early chance to tell him that she did not want to be considered a poet or novelist; that unlike him she had no literary addiction.

The young couple moved to an elegant town house in Winthrop Street, Charlestown, and began a married life which would produce four daughters – Mollie, Eliza, Agnes and Blanid – in eight years. The daughters grew up devoted to their father – he did not bring from his imprisonment the hair-trigger irritability which had marred O'Brien's family life. Mary O'Reilly was loyal but, always allowing for four difficult births, it is true that she and her husband were never at one in mind and spirit. She did not become a grand companion in adventure, as Jenny had been to Mitchel, or Libby Townsend to Meagher. Naturally, there was a side of O'Reilly which frightened her. An indefinable condition of ill health would overtake handsome Mary in the 1880s.

Even in the first years of marriage, O'Reilly relished a poetic repute through contributing to the *Pilot* and various metropolitan papers a variety of narrative verse, including the enormously popular series called *Uncle Ned's Tales*, at least one of which he had first performed on *Hougoumont*. But catastrophes which did not at first seem to bode well for O'Reilly struck the *Pilot*. The editorial offices in Franklin Street were burned to the ground in the Great Fire of Boston on the Saturday evening of 9 November 1872. At last new quarters were taken on Corn Hill, which, within days, themselves burned to the ground. The *Pilot* then moved to Washington Street, where nine months later another fire partially damaged the premises. 'When the fire comes to Boston nowadays,' wrote O'Reilly, 'it comes looking round all the corners for its old friend the *Pilot*. It is evident that the fire has a rare appreciation of a good newspaper.' In these black events lay the seeds of O'Reilly's ultimate proprietorship of the paper. Patrick Donahoe, proprietor of the *Pilot*, lost $300,000 on his fire insurance. Boyle O'Reilly forwent wages and made financial contributions to try to save Donahoe. So soon after escaping from Australia, waking at night to the first panic of thinking himself still in Bunbury's leaky huts, it was hard for him to see himself as a potential owner.

O'Reilly had gathered a Boston salon who met in his rooms in Staniford Street. Dr Robert Dwyer Joyce was Irish, a physician and a poet, but Boston literary figures Charles E. Hurd and Edwin Percy Whipple were Old Yankees. At Young's restaurant, where members of the group would sometimes go for dinner, they encountered Emerson, an occasionally visiting Walt Whitman, or Joaquin Miller. Through literary evenings such as those hosted by Whipple, literary editor of the *Globe*, O'Reilly, who weekly commented on the struggle for the Irish vote and remained solidly Democrat, made beloved Republican friends. It may in fact have been at Whipple's that he first met Wendell and Anne Phillips, founding veterans of the abolition campaign of the 1830s, now in their sixties, and still agitating for a range of liberal Republican objectives, from labour reform to women's rights to prohibition.

Phillips gave O'Reilly *entrée* into the community of heroes of the abolition struggle. Pioneer abolitionists included William Lloyd Garrison, now in his mid-sixties, who had once visited O'Connell to discuss his abhorrence of slavery. Garrison was considered the greatest of them all. A freed slave, veteran of the Underground Railroad, wrote to Garrison from Saratoga on 22 June 1874. 'The good you have done for our Race has been penned by the recording Angel . . . a black man can now walk the streets of Saratoga without fear of being recognised by some slave holder from when he had made his escape.'

The ageing Lydia Maria Child was also a noble and impressive soul – and literary as well. Her most famous and influential book, however, was *An Appeal in Favour of the Class of Americans called Africans*. Her memories included collaring a man who was shaking his fist in Mr Phillips's face at an anti-abolition demonstration outside the Music-Hall – 'and her surprise when he tumbled down'. This formidable New Englander had volunteered to nurse John Brown when he lay wounded in Virginia. She, Garrison and Phillips thus belonged to that class of abolitionists most Irish considered extreme. They combined their abolitionism with temperance and prohibition, strictures culturally repugnant to the Irish.

O'Reilly's attitudes to black America, as they would emerge in the *Pilot* and elsewhere, were influenced by these splendid figures. He was at ease with Wendell Phillips's idea that the destiny of the coloured American, not the liberation of Ireland, was the chief agenda item for the United States. 'The day is fast coming', O'Reilly wrote of the former slave, 'when this man's claim cannot be answered by a jest or a sneer . . . this man's children and grandchildren are coming, and they are receiving the same education in the same schools as the white man's children. In all things material before God and man, *they* will feel that they are the white man's equal. They are growing above the prejudice, even before the prejudice dies.' On this he was at odds with many of his poorer constituents.

Yet when Phillips stood for the office of governor in Massachusetts, in a political alliance with another Republican, the former Union general Benjamin F. Butler – 'Beast' Butler, as the citizens of New Orleans, which he had governed during the Civil War, called him – O'Reilly would not permit himself to vote Republican, even though his filial affection for Wendell Phillips lasted a lifetime. Indeed O'Reilly obviously approved of the fact that the Democrat machine in Boston had become better organised in the mid-1870s, an objective which the Irish, with their glee for faction, were well suited to bring about. One potent Irish party boss was Patrick McGuire, and another was O'Reilly's patron and friend Patrick A. Collins. So accomplished were they at 'getting out' and keeping the Irish vote in line that in the end, in 1878, Beast Butler had to move to the Democratic party to convince the Irish to support him.

O'Reilly made much use of his splendid, panelled study in Winthrop Street. His *Songs from the Southern Seas* was published in book form in 1873. It was dedicated to 'My Dear Wife' and her 'Rare and Loving

Judgment', but also honoured Captain Gifford of *Gazelle*, who had that year died, too young, of fever on board his ship off the Seychelles. His literary reputation was, he would always consider, now made by the kindly comments of Edwin Percy Whipple, literary editor of the *Boston Daily Globe* from 1872, a short, glittering-eyed Boston guru in his early fifties when O'Reilly first met him. Whipple's two chief works, *Character and Characteristic Men* and *Literature in the Age of Elizabeth*, had given him a large place in the city's literary scene. His Sunday soirées attracted the literary figures of what was called 'the Golden Age' in Boston. As in the 1880s Boston began to lose its literary pre-eminence, so too would Whipple, but O'Reilly remained always until Whipple's death in 1886 his grateful friend. O'Reilly declared, 'You were the first distinguished literary man who recognised anything serious in my poor work; and you cannot know, because you cannot be a foreigner . . . how delightful and vitalizing it is to be recognised.' To Whipple, O'Reilly could confess how much at home he felt in Boston, despite the normal bifurcation of the Irish soul in exile. 'Now my foreign feeling exists only in your tenacious joke. I am more Bostonian than any of you . . . Truly, if I were not editor of "The Pilot" . . . you never would think me such a terrific Papist and Paddy.'

By the time the poems were published to good notices in Ireland, the United States and Australia, a new and eminent Boston literary club had come into being, with O'Reilly as a devoted member. The Papyrus Club developed from a reception given in December 1872 by the newspapermen of Boston to the visiting explorer, discoverer of David Livingstone, Henry Morton Stanley. Amongst the membership of the Papyrus were O'Reilly's Irish friends Dr Joyce and Collins, and also Francis H. Underwood, first editor of the *Atlantic Monthly*, Alexander Young and George M. Towle, historians, the artist William M. Hunt, and Thomas Bailey Aldrich, descendant of *Mayflower* people and Civil War veteran. Aldrich's most popular work, a Yankee Tom Sawyer-ish book, *The Story of a Bad Boy*, was selling superbly well in the year the escapee O'Reilly came to Boston. Aldrich would go on to be a renowned and powerful editor of the *Atlantic Monthly* throughout the 1880s. Altogether, this group was not characteristic of the company most escaped or pardoned Fenians kept, was planets removed from Warder Woodman's Koagulup camp, and was an index of how quickly O'Reilly had embraced progressive Yankeedom, and with what enthusiasm it had embraced him.

Compared with Thomas Francis Meagher, who ten years earlier beheld the Flathead Indian reservations and considered them too large, O'Reilly was appalled at the dispossession of America's indigenes. Captain Jack, chief of the Modocs of California, had surrendered to the United States army in 1873 after some bitter engagements in the lava beds on the California–Oregon border. He had earlier killed United States General Edward Canby near Lake Tule, and retired with his people to a complex of lava caves and outcrops called the Stronghold, from which he made raids, one of them obliterating a command of eighty-two men. He was forced out by lack of water, and, after his hanging, the *Pilot* protested the removal of the Modocs to inferior, harsh land over the Oregon border, where they had been made to live on a reservation with their ancestral enemy, the Klamath Indians. It was not to be wondered if they again broke out and fought to remain on their traditional grounds, said O'Reilly. These arguments were not popular in the booming, westering nation, with its theological certainty of its right of possession. O'Reilly urged his Irish readers, who were sometimes the most clamorous for vengeance, to be compassionate. 'We have too much and too old a sympathy with people badly governed, to join in this shameful cry for Modoc blood.'

But he was forgiven his independent line. The gifts of soul which had caused men to co-operate at their peril in his deliverance from Australia, kept him a popular figure with most of Irish Boston and with Boston at large. As early as the 1872 International Musical Festival, O'Reilly gave the occasional address after 23,000 voices sang the Anvil Chorus from *Il Trovatore*, a hundred Boston firemen hammering out the rhythm on as many anvils. Employing oratory akin to that of Citizen Kane, he spoke about the phenomenon of the newspaper as 'a biography of something greater than a man. It is the biography of a *Day*. It is a photograph, of twenty-four hours' length, of the mysterious river of time that is sweeping past us forever. And yet we take our year's newspapers – which contain more tales of sorrow and suffering, and joy and success, and ambition and defeat, and villainy and virtue, than the greatest book ever written – and we give them to the girl to light the fire.'

In letters to his aunt in Preston, he showed something of his private life. His late mother's picture hung in his home in Winthrop Street, 'and I have it grandly framed and hung in our parlour. My little Mollie loves to kiss it, and I can only allow her to kiss the frame for fear of injuring the picture.' Mrs Mary O'Reilly was 'getting strong again, from the birth of our *second* baby, our Eliza Boyle O'Reilly'.

It was not certain, though, that Mrs Mary O'Reilly would be fully strong again. She suffered acutely in childbirth, and would in modern times have stopped bearing any further children. To do him credit, O'Reilly – unlike less sensitive men – never spoke a negative word about her, but her ill health, post-natal and somewhat depressive, was an unspoken shadow over the household.

*

Having lost tens of thousands of dollars through the cruel succession of fires, Patrick Donahoe had at last in 1876 to sell the *Pilot*. Buyers were scarce and the only credible consortium to make an offer was one consisting of the Most Reverend Archbishop John Williams of Boston and John Boyle O'Reilly.

One wonders whether O'Reilly felt trapped by the fact that the archbishop had found three quarters of the $100,000 purchase price. The archbishop was an American, and a gentle extrovert not given to pietistic scruple. He accepted that the bulk of his flock were Irish but did not carry from childhood or youth any set ideas about Irish politics. And though O'Reilly remained a moderate in terms of what should be done in Ireland – Home Rule, not revolution – the presence of the archbishop did not lead him to mute what some saw as an idiosyncratic blend of opinion. Now, though in debt, O'Reilly was a man of genuine substance, as long as he made the paper work. He was to be its editor, and to receive an excellent salary of $5,200 a year. As editor, he would have the support of good writers, including the recently liberated Denis Cashman, his wise friend aboard *Hougoumont*, and ultimately of James Roche, who in the late 1850s had run the *Irish News* for Meagher.

There were more than the usual creditors to be paid out. A number of the Irish poor of Boston had invested small sums of money with Donahoe, who had acted as something like a banker. The total amount was $73,000, and in strict legal terms these unsecured creditors were not entitled to be repaid. But neglect of the poorer depositors would have been morally offensive to the new editor and the Archdiocese of Boston, and would as well have brought social odium. Roche claimed that within ten years all these voluntarily assumed obligations had been paid out of a newspaper which, with the twin benefits of good management and continuing immigration, grew continually in circulation.

At the age of thirty-two, an editor and a significant Bostonian, the *Atlantic Monthly* having published his verse, O'Reilly was also becoming perhaps the leading occasional poet of Massachusetts, and a noted one in America as a whole. One of his verses marked the Boston celebration of the centenary of O'Connell's birth in 1875.

> Races and sects were to him a profanity:
> Hindoo, and Negro and Celts were as one . . .

He wrote and performed a poem at the opening of the Chicago armoury of an Illinois State Guard regiment, on Meagher's doomed brigade at Fredericksburg.

Twelve hundred the column, their rent flag before them,
With Meagher at their head, they have dashed at the hill!
Their foemen are proud of the country that bore them;
But, Irish in love, they are enemies still . . .

Thousands wept. But the prisoners of Western Australia and England remained on his soul.

A few months after his failure to get endorsement for a rescue effort for the Western Australian Fenians at the 1873 Clan na Gael convention, John Devoy received a letter from the prisoner James Wilson. Wilson, like Hogan before him, listed complaints about Noonan, including Noonan's lack of care for the soldier Fenian William Foley, who had been released with a weak heart and lacked money. But then the writer moved on to crucial business: 'There are some good ports where whalers are in the habit of calling and several other towns in the interior of the country . . . There is a guard of Pensioners at Fremantle and Perth. They are about 300 strong all told . . . So you see that it would not be much risk for any vessel, whaler or otherwise, to run in on some pretence or other.'

The soldier Fenian Keating, who had clasped O'Reilly's hand on the convict deck of *Hougoumont*, died the following January in hospital in Western Australia, Wilson at his side, and was buried in a grave next to Luke and Lawrence Fullam. Now Wilson wrote a second letter, dated 15 June 1874, which became known in Clan circles as the 'Voice from the Tomb'. It detailed these Fenian deaths in a remote place. 'This is as true Holy Writ,' wrote the 35-year-old Wilson; 'most of us are beginning to show symptoms of disease, in fact we are all ailing to a greater or less extent.' Wilson was sincere in expecting death, even if as yet his chief anguish may have been mental. He had sat beside the dying Keating. He was aware of how failed escape and solitary confinement had prematurely aged the 32-year-old Thomas Hassett, and of how unsettled that former great exponent of the sabre, Martin Hogan, had been to read smuggled press of the reception of the *Cuba* Five and other groups. 'And what a death', Wilson wrote, 'is staring us in the face, the death of a felon in a British dungeon, and a grave amongst Britain's ruffians . . . it is a disgrace to have us in prison today. A little money judiciously expended would . . . release every man that is now in West Australia.' The paragraph which had the greatest impact on Devoy and members of the Clan ran, 'Now, dear friend, remember that this is a voice from the tomb . . . Think that we have been nearly 9 years in this living tomb since our first arrest, and that it is impossible for mind and body to withstand the continual strain that is upon them.'

Devoy was careful to remove all incriminating references from the segments of letters he read to the Clan na Gael Conference in Baltimore that July. The convention's sixty-one delegates, representing 5,000 members, included O'Donovan Rossa, Thomas Clarke Luby, Captain McCafferty himself, William Roantree the filibuster, and Colonel Ricard O'Sullivan Burke, whose attempted rescue from Clerkenwell prison had become an East End tragedy. All these men had served time in British prisons, and so had a basis of sympathy with Wilson. As a result of lobbying by Devoy, Roantree and others, Clan na Gael's supreme council of five recommended to the convention that a rescue of the Australian prisoners should be undertaken. It was proposed from the platform that funds be raised for an unspecified rescue project, but, before the vote was taken, delegates asked for fuller information. Under conditions of greater confidentiality, Devoy promised, he would give a fuller briefing to individuals.

All the delegates voted in favour. But Devoy wondered if the enterprise was in characteristic Irish peril from secrets shared too widely. For the broadly sketched resolution to authorise a rescue attempt had now to be printed and sent out to the eighty-six existing branches of Clan na Gael. The report would be read by the majority of the 5,000 membership in good standing. Branches which were founded after the authorisation of the rescue, as the membership rose to 7,500 men, increased the possibility that the plan would be given away. And some members questioned the authenticity of the 'Voice from the Tomb' letter. Devoy had to present the envelope with its Australian postmark to convince them. Even so, there was not a single immediate dollar available from conventional Clan na Gael funds. In its seven years of existence the Clan had collected $42,000, which according to the Clan's articles could be devoted only to insurrection in Ireland – not in Canada, and still less in Australia.

Firebrand John McCafferty had devised a somewhat cheaper but less viable scheme: to kidnap the Prince of Wales, rakish Prince Edward (the future Edward VII), and hold him as a hostage on a sailing vessel until the British government agreed to release the remaining Fenian prisoners. McCafferty had even drawn up a memorandum on the prince's favourite amusements, and sought a grant of $5,000 from the Clan. He was told that other actions would be taken.

An Australian Prisoners Rescue Committee was selected, of whom the most effective members included Devoy and James Reynolds, a very successful New Haven glass founder. Another active committeeman was Dr William Carroll, a Philadelphia surgeon, County Donegal-born, Presbyterian, who had been a Union army surgeon with the rank of major. A heroic contributor of funds was John C. Talbot, a dry-goods merchant in San Francisco, who had employed Kenealy soon after his arrival from Western Australia. Talbot was clearly a devoted organiser, who caught fire at the Baltimore convention, and on his return home informed Devoy, 'I have not been idle since I left New York.' He had got off the train on the way west, and held a meeting in Virginia City, Nevada, at which he read Wilson's letter and one of Hogan's. 'I spoke manly, yet feelingly, told them that I was there at a great personal loss to my business but that worldly considerations with me were set aside when such a *letter* was placed in my charge.'

Arrived back in San Francisco, he intended to summon and invigorate 'Ds' – that is, club leaders, from the considerable Irish community in Los Angeles, San Jose, Sacramento, Mexico City. 'John Kenealy,' wrote Talbot, 'was elected Treasurer for San Francisco. I insisted that some person should be appointed, so that a check would be placed on me. Business is business now, my dear boy.' Talbot and his lieutenant Kenealy would prove to be excellent fund-raisers in San Francisco's golden hinterland. John Kenealy had recently married May Dillon, the sister of a co-worker, and was in the process of planning a move from San Francisco by coastal steamer to the small and, but for tremors, delightful town of Los Angeles, population about 8,500. There, as soon as his original 10-year sentence had expired, allowing him to undertake buying trips to England and Ireland, he intended to go into business with his wife's brother, James Dillon. Kenealy's value to the enterprise was not only financial; like O'Reilly, he knew the routines of Western Australia. The editors of *Devoy's Post Bag*, a compilation of all Devoy's correspondence, described Kenealy as 'one of Devoy's first confidantes in the rescue plans'. Even after he moved to Los Angeles, Kenealy remained John C. Talbot's treasurer, and the Californians' effort would be so large that they would ultimately demand that one of the agents sent ahead by steamer should be nominated by them.

Even the ageing John Mitchel was asked to give a fund-raising lecture. Rossa organised the event and sent Mitchel a fee of $100, which Mitchel returned. 'When I was in Australian captivity I never could have dreamed of any possibility of escape, but for the means supplied for that purpose by our good countrymen.' Copies of Mitchel's letter were likewise circulated to Clan branches to stimulate funds.

Subscriptions to the rescue effort were slow, and it seemed the money to buy a ship would never be raised. The committee discussed that a whaler might be paid to call into Western Australia and take the men on board. O'Reilly and Devoy were in consultation, and O'Reilly suggested Devoy should get advice from Captain Henry C. Hathaway of New Bedford, formerly third mate aboard *Gazelle*, the ship which had rescued O'Reilly.

Devoy made his living at that stage as night editor of his paper, and left New York at dawn on 29 January 1875 for Boston to see O'Reilly, and then to go on to New Bedford to meet Hathaway. From the main depot in Boston, Devoy went straight to a meeting of the officers of the Celtic Club, a branch of the local Clan na Gael. The men he met were strongly against any involvement of O'Reilly. They told him that a few years before, at the request of the Archbishop of Boston, many eminent Irish – O'Reilly, Robert Dwyer Joyce, Patrick Collins and John 'Honey' Fitzgerald – had all weakened and resigned from the Clan. Devoy found that his maligned friend was working at a savage, self-punishing pace, often sleeping the night on a cot in the office and waking to write copy. Long after, the *Wexford People* quoted an O'Reilly sentiment when it greeted US President Kennedy to Ireland in 1962: 'Freedom is more than a resolution – he is not free who is free alone.' It was an aphorism which grew from his special circumstances as the only life-sentenced soldier Fenian who had got away.

Devoy spent that Monday talking to O'Reilly's journalist Denis Cashman and making notes on the Fremantle penal establishment. On Tuesday, carrying a letter of introduction written by O'Reilly, he took the train for New Bedford. This coastal town was the great centre of Yankee whaling in the nineteenth century. Amongst its whalers Herman Melville had absorbed the whaling lore he would exploit for *Moby Dick*. Though the New Bedford hillsides a little further up the river from the whaling port boasted numerous textile mills – great employers of Irish and Italian immigrants – New Bedford liked to be regarded as a city of whalers, not of satanic mills. Devoy booked into the Parker house and located Hathaway, now night captain of the New Bedford police, at the courthouse. Hathaway read O'Reilly's letter, and took Devoy to confer in a vacant room. The former whaler – 'splendid physique; handsome, honest face; quite English-looking, wears only side whiskers' – warmly entered into the project. He recommended the buying of a vessel, 'and gave solid reasons why any other course would not be safe'. Hathaway suggested that the ship, once bought, should be fitted out as a whaler, and a trustworthy captain found. If the whaling was good, the ship would pay for itself. On the other hand, if they merely paid a captain to attempt the rescue, said Hathaway, the value of two good whales would exceed by far whatever fee the Rescue Committee promised him. 'The captain would be tempted to stay out in the whale grounds near Africa and abandon the rescue.'

Devoy needed to argue this case with the committee, and began with his reliable ally, the New Haven businessman James Reynolds. On 3 February, he wrote to Reynolds, 'A ship could be bought and fitted out for $12,000, to go there direct – ostensibly on a whaling voyage – and bring them straight to San Francisco, where she could be sold for $4,000 or $5,000. By doing a little whaling or taking a cargo *all the other expenses could be cleared*.' Devoy kept at Reynolds: 'The more I see of this thing the more clear it appears to me that we can't do it *in our time* nor safely at any time, unless we buy a ship.' But he needed to accumulate $15,000 to be safe, and the Clan subscription had so far brought in only $7,000. As well, many branches of the Clan wanted to send their men ahead. O'Reilly thought this crazy. 'One man is all that is needed to go to Australia: that man should be yourself.' In the end, though some branches never subscribed, others pledged the requisite funds to buy a whaler. Yet in Devoy's own branch of the Clan in New York, a trustee held up a disbursement of $2,500. Devoy, with an active but troublesome young committee member named Goff, a future New York Supreme Court judge, arrived in New Bedford on 9 March to make a bid on a ship Hathaway had advised them was available. O'Reilly again sent excuses on the grounds that, though he wanted a ship bought, he could after all offer no useful advice. His correspondence showed that he was in active contact with Devoy, whom he trusted, and also with Hathaway. But he was either too busy or too careful to travel around the countryside with members of the Clan.

Devoy and Goff arrived too late to bid – the ship they wanted went for $6,300. Goff had to go home, but, 'I will stay here until a ship is bought,' Devoy told Reynolds. 'D1 voted $1,500 last night, and $1,000 more is required. How is that for spirit?' Hathaway had by now introduced Devoy to John T. Richardson, a New Bedford shipowner, middle-aged and of no notable Irish connection, who in turn pointed Devoy to a suitable bark named *Catalpa*. Richardson declared it a good buy.

And so John Devoy had news for Reynolds. 'We have bought a vessel and she must be paid for Saturday. The amount is $5,250, and there are some fees, pilotage to this port, ballast, etc., to be paid besides, and some of the outfit and stores already bought.' All he had in hand, however, was $4,900. Richardson proved altogether very accommodating – he advanced his own money to buy *Catalpa* and transferred the ownership to James Reynolds of the committee, on condition that Reynolds sent personal surety for repaying Richardson his advance within a month. Indeed, incoming Clan na Gael funds did redeem the note within thirty days.

After the ice thawed in the estuary of the Acushnet River, *Catalpa* was taken north along the river to a dock where she could be fitted out. To the modern eye, the ship's dimensions were modest: a mere 202 tons, 90 feet in length, 25 feet broad, with a depth of 12 feet. On her last journey she had carried a cargo of logwood from the West Indies. The centre house, where coxswain, carpenter and other leading hands bunked, and the galley stood on a little island above the open hold. Now the decking had to be extended, and a forecastle built for the crew. It was discovered too that the keelson, the beam in the keel against which the main mast rested, had rotted. It was deftly replaced by a New Bedford shipwright.

Hathaway helped Devoy with expenses by indicating items normally taken aboard a whaler which might safely be dispensed with. This was a time of furious activity for little Devoy, as he kept scuttling back and forth between New Bedford and the branches, urging them to vote more money. According to some, he lacked diplomatic skills. But he had acute problems. By mid-April, J. T. Richardson was indicating to Devoy that the vessel fit-out might well bring the total costs to $17,000. Devoy needed to meet bills as they were presented. 'I hope you will be punctual in forwarding more money as soon as possible,' he begged the Rescue Committee.

Richardson was so emotionally engaged by now that he supplied a captain too: his own son-in-law, a handsome, stocky whaler of twenty-nine years, George B. Anthony, a man – like Richardson – with absolutely no Irish background. He was married to Richardson's daughter Annie, who expected him to take a safe land job, for they had an infant named Sophie. Anthony, an excellent navigator and a natural commander, had recently come home from the sea, and himself represented the changes overtaking the whaling industry. In Pennsylvania in 1859, petroleum oil had been discovered and was replacing whale oil. It had been a good era for Anthony to tell his young, pregnant wife that he would take the offer of a suitable supervisory job in the mills. But he was anxious for a last chance to command a whaler, take a final run. Thus Richardson conspired against his own daughter, having probably himself felt an occasional impulse to give up the fragmentary, fretful life ashore for a last dose of the clarity and pure terms of whale chasing. When Devoy briefed Anthony on the scope of what the whaler was to do, Anthony became excited. There was glory and profit in it, an extra bonus, said Devoy, on top of the normal whaling profit. The *Catalpa* project was designed to be a man's last, wonderfully managed ploy, one calculated to cement in New Bedford whaling myth the title 'Captain' inseparably to Anthony's name. The young Mrs Anthony was somehow reconciled to this final voyage. The captain's share of a whaling expedition, along with the good mill wages, would ensure the Anthony family a decent affluence.

Writing to Devoy, Captain Hathaway was also excited by the inherent mischief of the enterprise, and referred to the ship as 'the Horse', and to

New Bedford as 'Charleston'. 'He will more than pay for himself this coming season on the track . . . I hope you will be punctual in sending us the fodder, as grain is on the rise here.' On 22 April, Hathaway told Reynolds that the vessel was expected to go to sea the following Thursday morning. But Mr Richardson 'wishes me to state that the amount that will be required for ship and outfits will be about $18,000'. Hathaway was apologetic that this much money was involved, but 'we have been as prudent as possible and bought everything at the lowest market price, and bought nothing but what is actually required for the voyage. Mr Devoy will be here in time to see her go, for I want him to see her as she is fitted for sea. You have a good ship.'

If Devoy ever suspected the contractors were creaming the Clan, unaccustomed as it was to the purchase and preparation of whaling vessels, he never expressed it. In fact he considered the costs reasonable. The large items of *Catalpa*'s cost, which in the end totalled $19,010, was the ship itself, $5,250; carpentry, $1,500; coppering, $1,600; beef and pork, $1,150; casks for whale oil, $1,550. On top of that there were the costs of pilotage, sail-making and cordage.

As Devoy planned his Yankee raid on Western Australia, John Mitchel was considering his own climactic invasion of Ireland. When last seen in 1867, indomitable Mitchel, repenting of Fenianism, had returned to New York and become a grandfather. He still seemed to many, despite his Confederate sins and Union chastisements, an incarnation of Irish republicanism. Yet he was somehow amused that his old friend, fellow prisoner and brother-in-law, John Martin, had renounced revolution and, in 1871, had gone to the extreme of being elected member for Meath in the House of Commons. Here Martin aligned himself with Isaac Butt's Home Rule movement. Mitchel forgave such silliness in few, but he did in Martin.

By the summer of 1872, Mitchel was forced by ill health to give up editorship of his latter-day *Irish Citizen*. He was easily exhausted now, his eyesight was poor, and though writers then thought it bad form to give a medical name to the illnesses of great men, he was likely to have suffered from the normal cardio-vascular problems of what would later be called an A-Type personality. His old friend Father Kenyon had died that year, and evil luck continued for the Mitchels. Colonel James Mitchel lost both his wife and daughter to the same fever in a week, leaving James and his young son, John Purroy Mitchel, to mourn. Admirers raised a testimonial of $10,000 to support Mitchel in his grief and old age. But in self-reliance he undertook a lecture tour in the Midwest. The lecture platform, once a stimulus, drained him. He considered the map of Ireland in his study in

Brooklyn, and yearned to go back home. In the summer of 1874 he decided to go and be damned. Surely a British government would not arrest him now, twenty years after his escape, with his sentence of fourteen years long expired? He was accompanied by his daughter Isabelle, and Dr Carroll, the Clan leader and *Catalpa* committeeman from Philadelphia.

Landed at Queenstown, and on Irish soil for the first time in twenty-six years, he urged Cork people who rushed to meet him that no one should light bonfires, and that there should be no speeches. The authorities did not arrest him. They did not want a furore, and neither, for once, did he. He journeyed up to the small family home, Dromalane near Newry, the house of his childhood. Then he visited his sister Matilda near Dromore, and so, still tired, went up to Belfast to visit old friends, and next to Dublin. He was avoiding those campaigning for Home Rule, which he called 'that helpless, driftless concern'. Home Rulers were milksops to want such a tiny objective. In Dublin, he and Isabelle stayed two weeks in lodgings, declining invitations, 'especially a most pressing invitation from A. M. Sullivan to stay at his home. I will be the guest of no Home-Ruler in Dublin, not even with John Martin.'

In Dublin he had the great joy of going to dinner at the Wildes' house, with Lady Wilde – deathless Speranza – and her husband, the renowned surgeon and author of *Aural Surgery* and *Epidemic Ophthalmia* Sir William Wilde. 'The Giantess and the Dwarf', as this odd and brilliant couple were called, had been married in 1851, after a courtship which began with Speranza's favourable review of Sir William's *The Beauties of the Boyne*. In middle life, Speranza dressed and behaved with an increasing flamboyance, and even went to Castle balls in what correct Dublin considered extravagant and garish layers of fabric. She had passed on the tendency for idiosyncratic dress to her son Oscar, who was a 20-year-old undergraduate at Oxford at the time Mitchel visited. The Speranza with whom Mitchel dined was formidable and renowned, the high priestess of literary salons in London and Dublin, certain of her bardic immortality. Neither Speranza nor Sir William saw much hope any more in Fenianism, though Speranza had contributed verse to the *Irish People*.

In Cork, Mitchel embarked for New York on the *Idaho*. As on the convict ship years before, he suffered severe asthma. Most significantly, he had been persuaded to leave behind an election address to be published if a county seat became vacant. He wanted to stand, it seemed, mainly to ridicule the system. Back in Brooklyn, he experienced a sudden and perhaps phantom increase of energy when a House of Commons vacancy occurred in Tipperary. He wrapped himself in scarves and overcoats and sailed for Cork again on 6 February 1875. His remaining son, James, travelled with him, but, worried about Jenny's health, Mitchel asked his wife to stay by the fire in Brooklyn. He would never return to America. As he panted his way up and down an icy deck, helped along by James, he was now aided in his campaign for Tipperary by a letter John Martin wrote for publication. Martin admitted that Mitchel looked on the Home Rule party 'in a spirit which seems to be neither impartial nor friendly'. Nevertheless, Martin hoped his friend would be elected for Tipperary. 'No living Irishman better deserves the highest political honour his country can bestow.' Mitchel's own, already published, election statement called for 'the sovereign independence of Ireland', the total disestablishment of the Established Church, and amnesty for remaining Fenian prisoners. Mitchel proved to be the only candidate to nominate for the seat, and he was resoundingly endorsed at the polls.

But the Tory prime minister, Disraeli, moved a resolution in the Commons that a warrant for a new writ of election be issued – Mitchel was an undischarged felon and not entitled to take his seat. A writ declaring the election invalid appeared on 20 February 1875, and 11 March was picked for the new election. From his retreat in a hotel at Sunday's Well in Cork, an exhausted Mitchel travelled by train to Tipperary with a number of the old Young Irelanders, including George Barry and Nicaragua Smyth, now a Member of Parliament himself, and Mitchel's sister Mrs Henty Martin. At Tipperary Town he made his last full-scale public speech. 'There is a man over there in London who writes novels [laughter], and he is of the opinion that he knows better who Tipperary should elect than you do.'

Returned to Cork, Mitchel could utter only a few brief sentences at the Theatre Royal. On 9 March, he began travelling home to County Down by way of Dublin with his sister Henty, his son James having had by now to return to New York. Mitchel was observed by detectives as he stayed after all at the house of Home Ruler A. M. Sullivan in Dublin. He spent polling day in bed at Dromalane House, watched by Henty, his other sister Matilda, and his brother William. Though there was now a Liberal candidate against him, he won the election, receiving more than three quarters of the vote. This time the Commons decided to let the matter be settled by the courts. After several days in bed, on St Patrick's Day Mitchel wrote a final statement: all that was possible for the Tipperary franchise or Tipperary freeholders to accomplish had been done, he said. 'Am I dying, William?' he asked his brother. 'For that would be a serious business for me.' He tried to rise up from his bed on 20 March, but fell into a coma. He died within a few minutes without pain or struggle. After all his frenetic travel and coruscating enthusiasms, he expired within feet of the room in which he had spent his boyhood. A witness said, 'His face lost the worn look it had in late years, and I thought it beautiful.' The news was telegraphed to Mrs Mitchel in America, as Mitchel was buried in the Unitarian Cemetery, High Street, Newry, outside whose gate there now stands a statue of the man, a statement of his evangelical republicanism. On the day of the funeral a gale blew, but Martin insisted on attending, was soaked and developed pneumonia. Henty put him to bed in Dromalane House. In what seemed a brand of loyal obedience to his chief, Martin himself died within the week. His death, like his transportation and noble character, was overshadowed by that of his friend, for Martin could not compete with the prophetic lightnings which had broken in life about Mitchel's head.

Jenny, still as passionate a lover of Mitchel as when he had left Dromalane House to elope with her, was soothed by many tributes. Charles Dana, newspaperman, wrote accurately in the *New York Times* that 'He not only spoke the truth at all times, but he spoke the whole truth by a kind of moral necessity. He knew no reserve and no disguise, and, we may even say, no prudence in this regard . . . his sincerity was perfect and his courage fearless.' The ex-president of the Confederacy, Jefferson Davis, sent a telegram from Tennessee: 'Together we struggled for states rights, for the supremacy of the Constitution, for community independence, and, after defeat, we are imprisoned together.'

Jenny herself would live until the last day of 1899, and her grave in Woodlawn Cemetery in the Bronx, in which her son, James Mitchel, would ultimately join her, is surmounted by a Celtic cross.

29

The Fenian Whaler

> About thirty men . . . went out in a yacht, got on board and remained there until she was well out, giving three hearty cheers with the usual *tiger* for the barque and her crew. Not a man but ourselves had the least suspicion of her mission.
>
> Devoy to Reynolds, 29 April 1875

In the stern of crowded *Catalpa*, the first mate Smith had a cabin on the port side to himself. Two rooms on the starboard side were knocked into one for use by Captain George B. Anthony. Further accommodations would need to be added for the escapees, but Anthony and Devoy knew that to build additions on deck now would have created speculation. His under-informed crew was made up of one or two Yankees, a Cape Verdean Islander, three natives of St Helena, four Malays, a number of African Americans, and finally, after much quarrel between committee members, Dennis Duggan, carpenter and Fenian representative. Duggan had attended a Dublin model school as a classmate of Devoy's, had been one of Stephen's bodyguards on the night of his escape from Richmond prison, and was a veteran of the Fenian uprising of 1867.

The committeeman Goff was angry, his nomination for this post on *Catalpa* being a man named Tom Brennan. But since a crewman generally died on the way to the Azores, or deserted upon arrival there, Captain Hathaway made the appeasing suggestion that Anthony should let Brennan travel separately and meet up with the ship in those Portuguese islands. The entire Rescue Committee accepted this solution, but Anthony insisted that his decision about taking Brennan aboard in the Azores would be final, and secretly he did not want him.

In the *Gaelic American* on 27 August 1904, Devoy explained why he had not put himself aboard. 'My disappearance would have at once indicated that I had gone to Australia and the consequent loose talk would almost certainly have ruined the chances of success. I gave up the idea very reluctantly.' As it was, despite the numbers of Clan na Gael members who had general knowledge of Devoy's intentions, British Consul Archibald of New York, a distinguished spy-master, did not receive any but the vaguest tip-offs. In *Catalpa*'s favour had been the fact that stories of Fenian raiding ships had always figured in reports from some of Archibald's thirstier informants when they were short of cash, and generally proved untrue.

An illness of Captain Anthony's mother had delayed sailing. Industrious little Devoy, still night editor of the *New York Herald*, had a hard time shuttling between New York, Boston and New Bedford to be in place for *Catalpa*'s putting to sea. But at last, on the night of 29 April, Devoy wrote to Reynolds from New Bedford with rare lyricism. 'Brennan and I have just returned from seeing the ship forty miles out to sea, eating our dinner of hard tack, salt beef and cheese aboard.' A minister of religion had also gone for the ride on *Catalpa* out past the Cuttyhunk light and asked to see the chronometer, a clock set on Greenwich time and upon whose accuracy depended the measuring of longitude. Anthony took him to the cabin and was unable to find the chronometer key. A mechanic filed an old clock key down to fit, but the chronometer would prove to be a disaster.

When, late in the afternoon, the yacht carrying friends back to shore left the *Catalpa*, Captain Anthony fell into a depression. No one else on board knew what he knew. And navigation was almost instantly a problem. Computations two days out of New Bedford showed that the vessel was in inland New York State! Anthony had to reconcile himself to never knowing his exact longitude – a visible sign of his inner uncertainty.

For the moment, *Catalpa*'s voyage, even without its unstated purpose, was typical of the commercial and physical perils of whaling in an era when no one spoke for the whale. The first small whale was taken in mid-Atlantic on 6 May. It was hauled in to the side of the vessel, and the cutting of its blubbery flesh and the boiling down in vats amidships began. Once the oil was separated out, it was poured into twenty casks which – still hot – were lashed to ledges and rails on the ship's side. Then, two weeks out, *Catalpa* reached the famed 'Western Ground' off the Azores, and two whales were killed. Here Anthony encountered a brig, the *Florence Annapolis* of Nova Scotia, forty-nine days out of Liverpool with a cargo of salt, its sails and rigging destroyed in a storm and its crew starving. Anthony supplied provisions, and put his crew, including the carpenter Duggan, to work at rigging two jury masts for the ship. The *New Bedford Standard* of 15 June 1875 carried a shipping notice which Hathaway sent Devoy in New York for comfort. 'Brig *Florence* of Annapolis N.S., with salt, arrived at St Stephen yesterday, 62 days from Liverpool . . . May 30th, barque *Catalpa*, Anthony of this port, rendered assistance.'

It was the end of June before another whale was sighted and the boats again lowered from *Catalpa*. Sam Smith, the mate, whose boat worked up close to the whale, threw a harpoon and was thrown overboard by one of the great beast's flukes, severely cutting his head on the gunnel. The crew pulled him aboard again and he crawled forward and drove a second lance into the animal, before falling unconscious. By the next day he was still very weak, but Anthony was impressed to notice that he insisted on overseeing the cutting-in process.

Catalpa cruised off the Azores throughout July without any whales being taken, and the scarcity continued into August, when the whaler *General Scott* appeared. Anthony and others went aboard her to *gam*, or converse. In mid-gam, the lookouts on each boat simultaneously spotted a whale. Both of them lowered boats, and the officers agreed that between them the whale would be *mated*. The first whale would be shared, and if either ship took a further whale before the first had been boiled, this would also be equally shared. From the whale the two ships jointly hunted, 140 barrels of whale oil made up *Catalpa*'s share. There was more gamming in early September with the barque *Draco*, a ship Anthony had sailed aboard as a young man. Such was the social solace of a young master under a solitary and exceptional burden.

On *Catalpa* in July a so-called Kanaka boat steerer had died and been buried at sea. So there was now room for Brennan.

Hardly any of the committee other than Devoy himself knew John J. Breslin, the New York journalist Devoy wanted to send ahead to Australia as agent of Clan na Gael. His chief claim to legitimacy was that, as a young Richmond gaol warder in 1865, he had been a main actor in the escape of Stephens. Breslin was not even a member of the Clan, and he bridled at the idea of being forced to join. He was a reserved and private man, and like many prospective Clan members he disliked the quasi-Masonic rituals associated with initiation. After diplomatic handling by Devoy, he joined the organisation's Hoboken chapter.

Breslin became aware as Devoy already was that nearly half of all the money collected for the rescue project was raised by California Clan na Gael. The Californian treasurer of the Clan was John Kenealy of Los Angeles, who nominated as Breslin's accomplice for the endeavour a Civil War veteran named Captain Tom Desmond. Kenealy sent Desmond, a deputy sheriff in Los Angeles, up to meet Breslin and Talbot in Sacramento, where a warm relationship formed between the New York journalist and the Westerner. Later Breslin would say in his report to the Clan: 'I now believe that if Desmond alone had been sent, the rescue would have been as successfully accomplished, and at far less cost to the organisation.'

Breslin, supported by a $100 advance from Talbot, was now forced to hang around Sacramento for four weeks waiting for funds already remitted from California to the Rescue Committee to come back from New York. At least he was able to use the time by going down to Los Angeles and quizzing John Kenealy, who liked him because he was no blowhard. Breslin was back in San Francisco by 10 September 1875, and found that the funds had now arrived at the Telegraph Office. In withdrawing the money, he needed to call on the assistance of an old Fenian, Judge M. Cooney of the California Supreme Court, who had also been an enthusiastic rescue man. Once the withdrawal was made, Breslin booked a passage for Australia in the name of James Collins, supposedly a Californian and Nevadan speculator.

On the morning of 13 September that year, Breslin in the cabin and Desmond in steerage sailed for Australia from San Francisco. Ahead of them was a month's meander across the Pacific, during which they kept separate from each other.

Catalpa sighted Flores, an island of the Azores, in mid-October, a month after the Clan agents left San Francisco. Captain Anthony landed briefly to trade for potatoes some albacore the crew had caught. At sea again, fierce weather delayed Anthony on his way south-east into the port of Horta on Fayal, the chief island of the Azores, but on arrival the crew began re-casking the whale oil, 210 barrels worth something close to $12,000, for shipment home to New Bedford. Anthony bought a new chronometer from another captain in port for $110. At the shipping agent's office he found a letter with a photograph of his daughter. What an alluring concept it was simply to whale his way home again.

As frequently happened, a number of sailors including the third mate deserted at Fayal, and three others were sick and had to be sent ashore. Anthony needed to enter into an arrangement with an agent to supply men to fill the gaps. The new men would need to be shipped to the Canaries by another vessel and smuggled aboard there, since they had no passports. But such arrangements were not abnormal ones for anarchic individualists such as whaling masters. As Anthony and Smith were busy contracting new rigging, a telegram arrived from Tom Brennan, Goff's nominee. He was on his way to Fayal, having only just missed the *Catalpa* at Flores. Anthony, despite his need for men, still wanted to avoid Brennan, believing him turbulent and likely to gossip. 'I think we have all the crew we need at present,' Anthony told his mate Smith, who did not understand the significance of Brennan anyhow. 'Mr Brennan may get lost.' The next morning as *Catalpa* cleared the port of Horta on Fayal, it passed the steamer on which Brennan was travelling into the port. Brennan himself saw the whaler, cursed it, but determined to catch up with it in Tenerife, where, according to the plan, Anthony was to purchase the lumber to build quarters for the escapees.

Long before *Catalpa* turned south for the Cape of Good Hope and passed into the Indian Ocean, a poorer whaling area, Smith would need to be told the truth. Anthony decided to unburden himself now. If Smith did not approve of the plan, he would be free to leave the ship in the Canaries. The captain related to the chronicler of *Catalpa*, Pease, the details of his recruiting of Smith in the captain's cabin one pleasant October evening two days out of Fayal. 'I want to say to you now,' Anthony told Smith, 'before we get to Tenerife, that the *Catalpa* has done about all the whaling she will do this fall.' An increasingly surprised Smith heard that they were bound for the west coast of Australia to liberate Fenian prisoners. 'This ship was bought for that purpose and fitted for that purpose, and you have been utterly deceived in the object of this journey. You have a right to be indignant.'

Anthony, though short in height, seemed an utter whaler, solid-jawed, piratically moustached, hawk-eyed, straight-backed. Smith, by contrast, was a man of chubby face, slightly balding, with a walrus moustache. But he was of rugged material. He asked Anthony a few further questions. They were not really going to the River Plate, then, in South America? No, certainly to Australia: 'God knows I need you, and I give you my word I will stand by you as never one man stood by another.' According to Anthony, Smith said then, 'Captain Anthony, I'll stick by you in this ship if she goes to hell and burns off her jib boom.'

As this conversation was taking place off the Canaries, on 15 October that year, Breslin and Desmond entered the heads of Sydney Harbour. In Sydney, their contacts were John Edward Kelly and his former partner in a small newspaper, John Flood. Kelly, having written an unsuccessful book called *Illustrious Exiles; or Military Memoirs of the Irish Race Abroad*, twenty-two biographies of Irish exiles, intended to depart for the United States soon. He would settle in the city of Boston, where he had spent his boyhood, and though O'Reilly helped him financially, his health had been shattered by imprisonment. It would be only ten years before O'Reilly would deliver an oration at a monument raised in Mount Hope Cemetery, Boston, over Kelly's grave.

But in Sydney in October 1875, Kelly was an excellent contact, and able to introduce Breslin and Desmond to a number of men in Fenian cells in Sydney. One of these, John King, a Dubliner, a former grocer and gold-prospector, had begun his own independent fund to finance a rescue of the men in Western Australia. During his seven years on gold-fields in New South Wales and in New Zealand, he had formed a rescue organisation of his own. His plan was to charter a steamer, man her with Fenians, go to Fremantle to rescue the prisoners, and seek asylum in the French settlement of New Caledonia. He was now accumulating into one central fund all that had been contributed by friends in the various Australian colonies and in New Zealand. In the meantime he worked at a quarry run by his Irish friends at Petersham, a middle-class suburb on the railway line west from Sydney. One day as he was returning to Sydney by horse-drawn bus, he noticed John Edward Kelly seated with a stranger on top of the approaching outbound bus. 'We all left the buses and sat down in the shade of a gum tree by the roadside. Then Kelly introduced me to the stranger and for the first time I had the pleasure of shaking John Breslin by the hand. He was travelling under the name of Collins.' King decided at once and without factional rancour to place all the funds he held at Breslin's disposal.

He now telegraphed one of his lieutenants, a former Fenian prisoner, and asked him to come to Sydney from Queensland, detouring to the gold-mining centres throughout New Zealand's South Island, collecting from the IRB groups there. It was particularly in Otago and on the north-west coast of New Zealand's South Island that the IRB were active, and at the end of this fund-raising between $6,000 and $7,000 in gold had been collected. Not that Tom Desmond, alias Johnson, waited for it. Desmond left for Albany via Melbourne by steamer. Breslin remained a little longer, but decided to follow Desmond, for John King offered to bring the funds on to Fremantle as soon as they arrived. In Melbourne, both Mr Collins and Mr Johnson, not acknowledging each other, took ship to Albany, and from there boarded the steamer *Georgette* for the stretch from Albany to Fremantle. They landed in penal Fremantle in mid-November, and wrongly expected that they would not have much more than two months to wait for the whaler.

Breslin and Desmond, independently of each other, rode up from Fremantle to Perth, the inland capital on the Swan River. Desmond took a modest room in Perth and got a job in a carriage factory, where the other workers inevitably called him *Yankee* Johnson. After his normal calm assessment, Breslin concluded that coastal Fremantle, where the prison was located, was a better centre for him. He returned to the port and signed in as Mr Collins at the Emerald Isle Hotel, Fremantle, whose proprietor Patrick Maloney was a former Irish policeman, a native from County Clare, who had been generous to the pardoned Fenians in 1869. Breslin/Collins found it worthwhile casually to leave a letter from Judge Cooney of the California Supreme Court on his desk for Maloney's staff to absorb. Cooney's letter described Mr Collins as a wealthy holder of mines and land in Nevada and elsewhere. A letter signed by one C. Coddington Yardley was also left lying about Breslin's room. It advised that 'as of this date, $100,000 has been deposited to your credit in the Hollanders Bank . . . The other members of the syndicate are agreed that they will allow you to be sole judge, whether to invest the funds in

Australian gold shares, timber, farm or grazing land.' The concept of such an enormous resource of capital being poured into Western Australia, a colony of a mere 50,000 people, generated a great deal of respect for Mr Collins. But despite the pretensions of wealth, frugal Breslin was later proud to relate that the real costs of his stay in Fremantle were less than those of an ordinary commercial traveller.

On board *Catalpa*, Captain Anthony, exhilarated by his first mate's fraternal support, expected to see the 12,000-feet-high peak of Tenerife's volcano straight ahead, but was appalled to find himself 60 miles off course. The new chronometer was as faulty as the old. Once in Tenerife, Anthony employed the help of the US consul so that as new crew members recruited in Fayal turned up by passenger ship and came aboard, he obligingly issued them passports.

Though Anthony himself went ashore, he dared not give the crew liberty. He spent nearly three days aboard a nearby American schooner doing comparative navigational tests. He also spent $300 in buying timber and, as it came aboard, told the crew it was to serve as spares for the boats. *Catalpa* sailed from Tenerife on 25 November, its papers saying that it was cleared for 'River Laplatte and other places'. In December, three small whales were taken in the mid-Atlantic, and then towards midnight on Christmas night the *Catalpa* crossed the equator in longitude 27. Here it would suffer two months of light breezes, which destroyed hopes of a quick transit around the Cape of Good Hope.

Mr Collins suspected there might be a potential line of contact with the prisoners through Father McCabe of Fremantle, whose Sunday Mass he had attended, the congregation half made up of convicts in yellow prison clothing. One version of how Collins met the priest was that, seeing the thin chasuble McCabe was wearing, he offered to donate a new set of altar vestments. However it was done, on O'Reilly's advice Breslin confessed his purpose to the priest.

Patrick McCabe later said that he was delighted to meet Mr Collins and to discover him to be the John Breslin who had liberated Stephens. The priest agreed to carry messages to men, and in making that offer was moving out of the limits considered appropriate for clergy by the Irish-dominated hierarchy of Australia. Western Australia, however, did not yet run to a bishop – the area was administrated from the distant archdiocese of Adelaide nearly 2,000 miles east. Uninhibited by Church authority, therefore, McCabe told Breslin that the best contact with the prisoners was Will Foley, a former soldier who had received his ticket-of-leave. A tall man – nearly 6 feet – Foley had a 'weak heart', apparently a congestive condition. But he was a joker, a favourite of the guards and warders, and so even after his release had the run of the prison. Meeting up with Foley, Breslin immediately liked him and wrote a note for him to take to James Wilson, the author of the 'Voice from the Tomb' letter.

Most of the prisoners Breslin wanted to liberate had trusty jobs, Foley told him. Hogan was a painter; Cranston was working in the storehouse. Red-haired Darragh worked as clerk and attendant to the Church of England chaplain; Hassett was a gardener in the superintendent's garden. Harrington, the oldest, now forty-eight, normally worked on the docks, and Wilson had been recently given the job – as an ex-cavalry man – of looking after His Excellency the Governor's horses for a forthcoming visit from Governor Robinson. There was another soldier Fenian, James Keilley, who also had a trusty job but who lay under a cloud with his colleagues, and we do not know if he was mentioned at this stage as potential escapee or problem. The turbulent and alcoholic Thomas Delaney of the 5th Dragoon Guards had a ticket-of-leave but was temporarily in prison for unruly behaviour, and Collins was warned for security reasons, and because Delaney's time was nearly up, against including him.

In any case, Will Foley took Breslin's letter to the stables and put it in Wilson's hand. It read: 'To James Wilson and all the rest, Greetings. Those who have not forgotten are close by . . . Destroy this for the sake of old Erin.' The tomb door was ajar.

Mr Collins himself was in the meantime given a tour of the prison by an Irish friend of the hotelier Maloney, melancholic Superintendent Joe Doonan. Breslin's plans would destroy Doonan's career, but he suspected nothing. Soon Foley was able to pass another message to Wilson which indicated that the prison had been reconnoitred. And not only the prison. As Christmas neared, the new governor, Sir William Cleaver Robinson, invited Collins to a Christmas party at Government House, Perth. Robinson was a youngish man, fourth son of a member of the Anglo-Irish gentry, born in Westmeath, and member of that corps of regularly reposted colonial administrators. His orders in the case of Western Australia were to delay the colonists' demands for self-government. He had already served as governor of Prince Edward Island, an experience which would prove crucial for all parties in weeks to come. He would go on after Western Australia to govern Singapore, South Australia, and ultimately to return to Western Australia in 1890 to administer the beginnings of a self-government he was presently resisting. Governor Robinson's guests at Government House admired his capacities as a musician – in the end he composed a comic opera which would be performed in Melbourne. Songs he was writing at this time – 'Remember Me No More', 'Imperfectus',

'Severed' – would become commercially successful later in the century, and were probably heard in early draft by Mr Collins.

In the withering heat of New Year, Father McCabe had begun to use a trap to travel round the various convict stations and depots, and he persuaded Doonan to give him Wilson as a driver; thus a meeting between Breslin/Collins and James Wilson, 38-year-old veteran of the Bombay artillery and the 5th Dragoon Guards, took place 4 miles south of Fremantle. In thick coastal bush, Breslin met the lean, sun-burned convict and told him that the plan was to get the prisoners off in the way John Boyle O'Reilly had escaped. Wilson wondered aloud how Breslin could bribe a sea captain to take half a dozen. Breslin reassured him, telling him that the Clan had bought an American whaler. Wilson could barely believe it. Breslin emphasised that everyone must be on good behaviour and have work as trusties or convict constables outside the prison walls.

Breslin had promised the fatally ill go-between, Will Foley, that he would advance the passage money for a transit home to Ireland, but asked only that Foley did not move until he was no longer required. By mid-January, with Breslin's blessing, Foley set off for Ireland and the United States. After saying goodbye to his relatives in Ireland, he would arrive in New York in mid-July that year, and the heart disease he had contracted in prison would kill him soon thereafter in St Vincent's, Staten Island.

Late in that January of 1876, Lord Carnarvon at the Colonial Office sent a warning to Governor Robinson of Western Australia about the possibility of a Fenian rescue: 'money has been collected in this country and Ireland and a scheme set on foot for the purpose of assisting the escape from Western Australia of certain Fenians (I believe Military) now in the colony'. Those 'charged with carrying out this attempt have either lately sailed for Western Australia or may do so by the mail steamer which brings this dispatch'. Lord Carnarvon, however, forbade Robinson from warning the gaol and police authorities of the colony. Robinson was to take measures, but to keep the strictest secrecy, confiding only in one or two faithful and intelligent officials. Carnarvon's communiqué did not call for the locking up or scattering of the Fenians. If it had, escape would have been rendered impossible.

Robinson consulted his superintendent of police, Captain Smith, and the Acting Comptroller-General, William Fauntleroy. Smith took responsibility for the two Fenians presently on ticket-of-leave in Champion Bay, and Fauntleroy for the eight Fenian convicts in Fremantle prison. Robinson assured Carnarvon, 'The eight who are in prison will be carefully watched by the Comptroller-General and I think I may assure your Lordship that any scheme of the nature referred to which may possibly be set on foot, will end in total failure.' Fauntleroy in turn advised Robinson that during daily work details, the Fenians would be kept scattered in various parties around the prison. To lock them up would merely prove that official suspicion existed, and this would run counter to Lord Carnarvon's command.

Carnarvon was in fact warning Western Australia about a separate Fenian rescue attempt from that involving Breslin; an attempt to be conducted by two Irish members of the IRB. Had Breslin, or even Devoy in New York, known of it, it would have filled them with fear that soon Fremantle would have an embarrassment of conspirators.

Catalpa edged its way southwards in the Atlantic, looking for the same Roaring Forties which the convict ships had always sought. When it reached a little over 41 degrees south, a gale hit from the south-south-west. Anthony had been warned that *Catalpa* was flat-bottomed and needed sail to prevent it rolling to windward and shipping water aboard. Therefore, contrary to normal maritime instincts, he kept some of his topsails up, and, though the gale began to tear them to shreds, the *Catalpa* settled well in the surges of water.

As the storm abated and the sun came out, Anthony saw a little copper-bottomed bark and could not avoid speaking to her without creating suspicion on both ships. The bark was *Platina*, commanded by an old friend of Anthony's, Captain Walker Howland, a relative of the shipwright who had restored the *Catalpa*. Four months out from home, *Platina* had a mere fifty barrels of oil, and Howland had decided to try the Seychelles and the Mozambique Channel. On deck, the whaleboat crew chatted with the crew of *Platina*, and found out clearly for the first time that they were not anywhere near the River Plate in South America, but nearer the Cape of Good Hope. One of the Portuguese sailors from *Catalpa* was, however, able to offer a reasonable explanation – they were probably bound for New Zealand, whose whaling grounds had a high repute.

The crew of *Catalpa* was consoled off South Africa by the capture in late December of four small whales. By now some of the whalemen were complaining that they should make for Ascension Island in mid-Atlantic, to revictual, for the chief diet of *Catalpa* had become 'simp', pounded hard-tack mixed with molasses. But such hardships were routine, and no crewman dared challenge Anthony. When 1876 came in, the whaler was still tacking in the South Atlantic.

Then, in mid-February, a hundred or more miles south of present-day Port Elizabeth, South Africa, a most extraordinary chance meeting occurred. A vessel named *Ocean Beauty* bore down upon *Catalpa*, and

Anthony went on board. He found the captain to be a very large, genial Englishman named Cozens, bound from Liverpool to New Zealand. During his conversations, Captain Cozens mentioned that he had once captained a convict ship to Western Australia – in 1868 in fact. It had been named *Hougoumont*. Anthony asked about the refitting facilities of Fremantle, and Captain Cozens spoke warmly of Bunbury, produced from his chart locker a map he had used aboard *Hougoumont* and gave it to Anthony.

The excitement of having such a fine chart did not, however, do much for *Catalpa*'s progress. It was 4,700 miles from Cape Town to Cape Naturaliste, south of Bunbury, Western Australia. During eleven days in February and March, *Catalpa* made only 60 miles south and 120 miles east. Then, on 10 March, the wind turned round behind them, and after five heady days the whaler raised the French isle of Saint-Paul, roughly half-way between South Africa and Western Australia. Whalers always liked to stay at this unpopulated and dramatic island, to enter its bay which was the partially submerged crater of a dead volcano. *Catalpa* paused to fish but not to land. Anthony and Smith had Bunbury on their minds.

Under some lights it might seem strange that as Wilson and the other Fenian prisoners waited tremulously in Western Australia for a whisper of deliverance, two of the strongest voices of Young Ireland were by choice living on the far more politically advanced east coast of Australia. Eva Kelly, the former girl muse of the *Nation*, lived still as a doctor's apparently unremarkable wife in Brisbane. Few seemed to know that she had written occasional verse for the Fenian *Irish People* in Dublin. The money the former prisoner Michael Cody collected in Brisbane and on the Queensland gold-fields may have included a contribution from the O'Dohertys, but Kevin O'Doherty had largely kept apart from the Fenian enthusiasm. While Eva intermittently and calmly stated her radicalism on Ireland, Saint Kevin had become an Old Ireland-style improver. He had stood again for the Queensland Parliament in 1868, and yet again in 1870, and had been returned for North Brisbane as an independent 'Town Liberal', arguing for public health – considered an eccentric concept by some – and the clipping of the exorbitant power of the large pastoralists or squatters in the hinterland. O'Doherty disliked them on a number of grounds: for their locking-up of the rich sub-tropical coastal strip and the great black-soil plains inland, which inhibited immigration; and for their misuse of labour, including indentured labourers from the Melanesian islands of the South Pacific.

In the Queensland Parliament which no longer met like a half-baked colonial council in the old convict barracks but in a new legislature building, O'Doherty had in 1866 supported the youngish Charles Lilley, a newspaperman and former soldier from Northumberland who had once served a month's confinement in a British military prison for fraternising with strikers. But O'Doherty's disenchantment with the promising Lilley set in almost immediately, when Lilley appointed two squatters to his Cabinet. Lilley fell from power, and O'Doherty's part in his downfall in 1870 was approved of by the people of North Brisbane, who returned him again. Saint Kevin also took time to maintain the status of distinguished practitioner, and Governor Denison of Van Diemen's Land, who having governed Madras was now living out his last year in Surrey, would have been astonished to hear that O'Doherty was called in to treat the fatally ill governor of Queensland, Samuel Blackall.

Eva and Saint Kevin were people who took their own marital blessedness for granted, but much had intruded between the two: verse, as much a divide as a link; imprisonment, transportation, surgical studies, colonial pursuits. One of the latter, from the start of his political career, was his campaign against the great Queensland shame of 'blackbirding' – the capture of Melanesians, particularly from the New Hebrides, and their use as indentured labour in the cotton and cane-sugar plantations of Queensland. The 'recruitment' of South Sea Islanders as 'blackbirds' was carried out with all the cunning and brutality which had earlier marked the recruitment of African slaves for the Americas. During Lilley's brief premiership, the Polynesian Labourers' Act was passed under the influence not only of some reformers but also of landowners who knew they could not get away with an unregulated flesh trade any more. O'Doherty disliked it because it legitimised the practice.

The campaign against blackbirding, rather than Fenianism's lost hopes, exercised O'Doherty. He drafted a bill of his own to abolish the trade, and was ready to present it to the house by 1871. It was a pragmatic, not an absolutist, bill – it left in place existing arrangements regarding Kanaka labour, since a repatriation provision which already existed would soon have the last of the blackbirds back at home in the New Hebrides. O'Doherty invoked as a reason for abolition the moral disrepute the trade brought with it, but also the fact that blackbirding inhibited immigration of free labourers from the British Isles. He being thus in an Australian sense an abolitionist, we can wonder what might have befallen him in America had Meagher's letter about New York medical practice been more encouraging. His bill failed, but ultimately the institution of blackbirding was abolished.

His position as Honorary Consulting Surgeon to the Hospital for Sick Children convinced him that Queensland needed new and very broad health legislation, and that some of his ideas would be opposed by the anarchic individualists who have always characterised Queensland politics. In 1872, under the spur of the arrival of smallpox-afflicted ships from Melbourne in Moreton Bay, he introduced the first Public Health Act to be passed by the Queensland Parliament. It established practices of quarantine and compulsory reporting of disease. 'Unrewarded by any higher solace than the confidence and esteem of his constituents,' said the *Courier*, O'Doherty declined to renominate for parliament in 1873. He had found it exhausting to sustain politics, a medical practice and other duties, such as his committee work on the plan to establish at Brisbane Hospital a preliminary school of medicine for young Queenslanders. He served too as a member of the Medical Board, becoming a severe judge of medical standards, submerging the memory that he had worked as an unregistered physician in Van Diemen's Land.

Irish issues would ultimately fatally reclaim him, but for the moment his aim was to eradicate colonial bigotries. In the inland town of Warwick, after an Ulster-style riot in which supporters of an Orange candidate attacked an all-too-triumphal procession of the supporters of an Irish Catholic candidate, O'Doherty and two Protestant friends founded the Hibernian Society. A similar organisation had been used in Canada as a front for the Fenians, but in Queensland it served the interests of the sort of tolerance under the Crown which D'Arcy McGee had preached. Saint Kevin's opening address as president would indeed have done credit to McGee: 'We are here, thank God, completely independent of that discord among our countrymen at home. Here the British Constitution is not an empty name.'

Indeed, at this stage of his life he seemed the blithest of the remaining Young Ireland State prisoners. He delighted in his teenage sons, shining colonial boys of handsome parents. They showed sporting ability, and drew the inexhaustible O'Doherty into the committees of rugby football teams and of the Brisbane regatta. William O'Doherty, and a youth appropriately named John Devoy, took first place in a skiff at the Brisbane regatta of 1873. The O'Dohertys' younger son Kevin would ultimately play rugby for Queensland against New South Wales. Eva's surviving daughter Gertrude was now about five years of age and the object of her father's baby-talking infatuation. 'Dearest Darling Titsum Kitsum, I send you 200000000000 million kisses . . .'

In 1875, when a few were engaged in the plans for Fremantle, the O'Dohertys were engaged with the worldwide centenary celebrations of the birth of Daniel O'Connell, whom O'Doherty had once defied. Saint Kevin and Bishop Quinn suggested that the date be celebrated by Queensland as a whole, but this line did not quite wash with the general community, identifying as it did all Irish enthusiasm with Fenianism. Since Protestant clergymen preached against the idea, the celebration of O'Connell's centenary became a purely Catholic matter. Just as the collectors of the Fenian relief fund had earlier found, O'Doherty saw that some Australian-born of Irish descent were not willing to participate even in something as innocent as the O'Connell centenary. 'They are jealous of their Australian dignity,' wrote O'Doherty, 'which they consider compromised by celebrations of men and events which have no direct connection with their native land.'

Dr O'Doherty's oration at the O'Connell commemoration in St Stephen's Cathedral was followed by the chanting of an ode composed by Eva, and reminiscent of the clarity of the lines she had written for the *Nation.*

> Led by his prophet might
> Rose ye to manhood's height,
> Flashing the sword of right,
> Forth from its sheath!

In Fremantle, the metaphorical sword of right lay at Breslin's side in the Emerald Isle Hotel, awaiting the arrival of *Catalpa* that it might be unsheathed.

As February progressed, Breslin understandably began to hang around the ship's bulletin board outside the telegraph office in Fremantle. He telegraphed Kenealy in obscure terms, saying that the Californian finances had not arrived: he would be able to play the Yankee investor only until about the first week in March. And to allay suspicion, he felt he should seem to be about to move on the business front. He hired a team of horses and drove to Guildford, York, Northam, and Perth. In Perth he managed a few minutes' quiet conversation with Desmond.

His financial situation was growing desperate when, in early March, John King, the Fenian from the Petersham quarry, arrived on *Georgette* in Fremantle carrying funds. He had somehow evaded being quarantined in Albany with the rest of his shipmates, and now signed himself into the Emerald Isle under the less than inspired soubriquet George Jones. Breslin was still away on his swing through the bush, and King told Maloney he had a personal letter for Mr Collins, from Collins's banking connections in Sydney. When Collins returned from the dusty interior, King came to his room, opened his shirt and undid a money belt. There was £800 sterling in it. King said he had been communicating with Kenealy by coded letter, and it was Kenealy's and King's considered idea that King should lend Breslin assistance in engineering the rescue and escape on *Catalpa*. Breslin was pleased at the prospect of such reliable company.

For the American Clan na Gael too, March was a difficult month. Judge Cooney got a letter from Breslin expressing anxiety over the late arrival of *Catalpa*. Cooney sent the letter on to Devoy in New York, who began to wonder if Anthony had in fact deserted the project. The ship would, however, arrive in Bunbury two days after the date on the letter which so alarmed Devoy.

In the stress of waiting, Breslin had, like O'Reilly before him, fallen in love with a local woman, and in drawing close to her had committed a rare but egregious breach of his normal caution. The young woman, Mary Tondut, was the daughter of a French immigrant and Perth winegrower, Charles Tondut. Breslin was neither a man of outrageous charm, nor a philanderer. But in March, Tondut conceived a child by him. This was no casual fling – Breslin and Tondut were contemplating marriage, and if Mary Tondut knew anything of Mr Collins's true purpose she never revealed it.

At ten o'clock on the night of 6 March, Fauntleroy, Acting Comptroller-General, asked for a private word with Superintendent Doonan on the road outside the great white prison of Fremantle. Doonan suspected Fauntleroy was seeking a means to spread responsibility should any attempt at escape succeed, and sat up afterwards writing a detailed minute on the conversation. According to it, Fauntleroy told him, 'When you visit the prison of a night, I want you to examine the exterior doors of the division and be exact about it.' Doonan thought he was entitled to know the reason why, and after argument Fauntleroy took Doonan into his confidence on Carnarvon's confidential dispatch. Doonan said that if there was any chance of a rescue, the Fenians should be kept inside the prison. Certainly Darragh should be shifted from his billet as chaplain's groom, for at the stable 'he has every opportunity of communicating with pensioners and their wives and other people'. But Fauntleroy backed away from the idea that special precautions must be taken. The Fenian prisoners were nearly all convict constables, Fauntleroy argued, and suddenly to lock them in by day would merely create suspicion.

Doonan told him that one of their warders, Booler, in whose charge two Fenians worked on the pier, held communistic views. 'Shall I shift these two from him?' But Fauntleroy said no. So Doonan would claim that, 'except the order to myself to examine the exterior doors of the division the Acting Comptroller General never issued a single verbal or otherwise order to anyone . . . consequent upon the warning'. The

Western Australian authorities seemed more concerned to obey Carnarvon's order for secrecy than to render an escape utterly impossible.

In that late summer, while his liaison with Tondut was in full flower, Breslin was driven to dream up schemes for wool-marketing, and pretended to a passion for a new mineral exploration – prophetically, since a gold rush would bring thousands into the Western Australian desert later in the century. And to add to Breslin's acute but well-hidden stress, two new Irishmen, agents of the IRB in Dublin, had arrived in town after a month's quarantine in Albany. These men were in fact in Fremantle to carry out the very conspiracy of which Carnarvon had warned Governor Robinson, and knew nothing of Breslin as he knew nothing of them. Detective Sergeant Rowe, given the job of reporting on new arrivals in Western Australia, noted that they booked into the Port Hotel, one of the other Irish establishments in Fremantle, under the names Alfred Dixon and Henry Hopkins. Dixon's true name was Denis McCarthy.

Nearly thirty years later, King would tell the readers of the *Gaelic American* the story of the testing out of the newly arrived Irishmen. He started out that evening to meet Dixon/McCarthy. Strolling up the main street and spotting him, King chatted with him and agreed to meet him for fuller discussions on the beach within the hour.

There, by the scattered light from the town behind them and with the immense Indian Ocean stretching into illimitable darkness to the west, McCarthy showed King a document which proved that he and his companion Walsh, alias Hopkins, were acting as agents of the IRB of England and Ireland. King was so convinced that, despite the lateness of the hour, he took McCarthy and Walsh back to the Emerald Isle and introduced them to Breslin. Walsh had in his possession a large sum of money collected in Ireland, about $5,000. The two Irishmen offered their services and this sum of money to Breslin. 'We declined their money but took their revolvers.' In Fremantle in that season of waiting, the accession of Denis McCarthy and John Walsh to the scheme was both logistically and emotionally welcome. It did spread the secret amongst five men plus the Fenian prisoners, but on the day of escape, if ever it should come, McCarthy could cut the telegraph wire between Fremantle and Perth, and Walsh the wire southwards between Fremantle and Bunbury. A third man would be needed to ride rearguard as the escapees headed to their rendezvous with the whaler, and King took on this job.

Breslin had already made a reconnaissance journey to Bunbury in early March – Sub-Inspector Wisby later reported him to have come down with a Mr Charles Searle, a Fremantle acquaintance, put up at the Wellington Hotel, and gone shooting along the estuary. 'Collins did ask about the whale ship *Catalpa* but it was not thought of any more at the time.' He was long gone when on 27 March *Catalpa* got its first sight of Western Australia – Geographe Bay, within which sat Bunbury. Anthony eased the *Catalpa* south into the Leschenault inlet and dropped anchor in the harbour of Bunbury as darkness came on. Wary of desertions, he went ashore with a picked crew and reported to the Customs Office. The customs officials stressed, as to all captains, that he needed to give notice before he sailed again.

He found no messages at the telegraph office, and ate a meal at Bunbury's Spencer's Hotel, where no one presented himself as co-conspirator. While he dined, Sam Smith ran up *Catalpa*'s flag upside down, a sign there had been desertions. The captain and Sam Smith had to wait smouldering in the water police office for the four deserters to be rounded up.

In Fremantle early the next morning, Breslin read the telegraphed news of *Catalpa*'s arrival on the bulletin board, went back to the Emerald Isle Hotel in an exhilarated state and took from the bottom of his bag a code he and Devoy had devised. When the telegraph office opened at nine, he sent off the neutral message. 'To Captain Anthony, Master barque *Catalpa*, Bunbury. Have you any news from New Bedford? Can you come to Fremantle? J. Collins.' Anthony also had a code, and telegraphed back: 'No news from New Bedford. Shall not come to Fremantle.' The message thus declared that no suspicion attached to *Catalpa*. Breslin booked a seat on the next day's stagecoach to Bunbury. Meanwhile, he got a note to the prisoner Wilson. 'Our friend has reached port with greetings from Old Erin,' Breslin's message read. 'He wishes you all well, and hopes you are always amenable to your warders. He hopes to see you soon.'

While waiting for the arrival of the Fremantle coach, Anthony bought meat for the ship. A wholesale butcher remarked that since Anthony was a Yankee he might be interested to know there was another Yankee in the region, a rich one named Collins. The butcher was standing beside him when the mail coach ground into Bunbury at four o'clock on Friday afternoon, and pointed out Collins. 'That's the very man . . . Come to Spencer's Hotel and I'll introduce you.'

Brought together by the butcher, it was quite natural that Anthony and Collins should dine together. Anthony told Collins that the only men he could trust were the men in his own whaleboat; already he had three other men in irons aboard ship for desertion. Breslin in return told Anthony that by reconnaissance he had chosen a beach south of Fremantle, Rockingham Beach, as the place from which the prisoners could be lifted by Anthony's whaleboat. He and Anthony should catch *Georgette*, he said, due into Bunbury the next day, and visit Fremantle and inspect the place. With the arrival of the *Georgette*, however, the escape became suddenly overstaffed. Travelling under the name Hall, the unstoppable, hulking Brennan came ashore, and hunted down Breslin at Spencer's Hotel. From that first meeting, Brennan and Breslin would never respect each other, Brennan accusing Breslin of behaving as if he owned the escape, Breslin finding Brennan a malcontent and bully. Even now, Brennan wanted to go aboard *Catalpa* straight away, which would have been noticed at once. Breslin insisted that Brennan go on to Fremantle in his own time, and board *Catalpa* only at the time of the escape.

Leaving command of the whaler in Sam Smith's hands, Captain Anthony boarded the *Georgette* with Breslin for the journey up the coast. Anthony was introduced to Captain Grady, the master, who had sailed for a long time as mate on a London/New York merchantman. Even before the ship had cleared Bunbury, Anthony was already in *Georgette*'s pilot house, chatting with Grady about the coast, courses, bearings, Australian winds and storms. Anthony even had a chance to borrow Grady's spyglass to look at long, north–south-running Garden Island, off Rockingham.

But as they arrived at Victoria Quay in Fremantle, Anthony and Breslin were appalled to see a British gunboat, HMS *Conflict*, moored at the opposite end of the quay. *Conflict* possessed two guns and a crew of thirty. With steam up, and in light wind, *Conflict* would quickly catch and sink *Catalpa*. Inquiries in Fremantle pubs indicated that *Conflict*'s men believed they would be in Perth in eight to nine days. With no option but to go on preparing, Anthony and Breslin rode down to Rockingham, timing the journey at two hours twenty minutes at most. Anthony was pleased to discover that Garden Island sheltered the long arc of Rockingham Beach from the open ocean. Devoy had wanted the boats which picked up the escapees to be procured in Australia, so as to keep 'the captain and the ship from being made amenable to international law'. But suitable boats were scarce and rental likely to cause comment, so Anthony would use his own whaleboat. If Breslin could deliver the men, Anthony himself would convey them to *Catalpa*, 12 to 16 miles out: at most a five-hour row. Anthony enthusiastically marked the chosen spot for Breslin to deliver the men with two driftwood logs he and Breslin hauled high to the edge of the sand dunes.

HMS *Conflict* for the moment made these calculations academic. There was doubt too about whether, when *Conflict* left Fremantle, it would head north to Darwin or east to Adelaide. If it headed north, it would remain on the flank of *Catalpa*'s escape route. It was agreed before Anthony returned to Bunbury and his whaler that, when *Conflict* left Fremantle, Breslin would send Anthony a telegram which would read: 'Your friend N (or S) has gone home. When do you sail?' If the gunboat headed to Adelaide (S), it would leave the seas off Western Australia clear.

Before leaving Fremantle, Captain Anthony was invited to dinner at the residence of Governor Sir William Cleaver Robinson up the Swan River in Perth. As Anthony was about to go in to dinner, a government aide put his hand on his shoulder and said brusquely, 'Excuse me, sir, but what is your name and business and what are you doing here?' Breslin, also a dinner guest, stepped up, laughing, to explain to Anthony that this was the blunt way inquiries were frequently made in Western Australia. But even when casually buying an updated map at the hydrographic office in Fremantle, Anthony was harshly questioned. He was glad to catch the mail coach at last back to the slightly less complex environs of Bunbury, a 32-hour journey over sandy roads which utterly exhausted him. Back with the ship, he passed to Sam Smith the job of calling regularly at the telegraph office in Bunbury, while he himself directed the building of additional cabins in the steerage area forward. He told the crew to keep it quiet, but that they might be taking some passengers back to the United States to supplement their profit from whaling.

On Tuesday morning, 11 April, Breslin woke up in Fremantle to find the warship *Conflict* gone from the wharf. The bulletin board showed that it had sailed for Adelaide, leaving open the escape route. Breslin sent his coded telegram and as soon as Anthony received the news he ordered his boat over the side to go ashore and seek port clearance. Customs men and water police were dispatched to the whaling bark to search her for stowaways and contraband, while Anthony sat in the Customs Office signing endless papers. A quarrel began over a barrel of caulk *Catalpa* had landed and not paid duty on. The vessel was under custody. Rowed out to *Catalpa*, Anthony found that a uniformed customs official was sitting in the cabin beside the first mate Smith, who had landed the barrel as pig feed. Dealing with this minute point took hours. By the time it was settled and *Catalpa* permitted to proceed, the day had been lost.

Anthony waited for the telegraph office to open next morning, and sent a message to Breslin. 'I sail today. Goodbye. Answer if received. Anthony.' This message, picked up at the Fremantle telegraph office, galvanised Breslin. He calculated that if Anthony left Bunbury that day, Wednesday, he would be off Rockingham Beach on Friday morning. Friday was Good Friday – government buildings would be closed, the prisoners locked up inside the prison. Breslin therefore sent off a further desperate telegraph. 'Friday being Good Friday I shall remain at Fremantle and start for York on Saturday morning. I wish you may strike oil. Collins.' Fortunately, Anthony went ashore before sailing to seek an answer to his original message. He found everyone speaking pessimistically about the weather, and predicting north-westerlies.

At five o'clock on Easter Thursday, just as the telegraph office in Fremantle was closing, Breslin was delighted to receive a reply from Anthony. 'Yours received. Did not sail today. Winds ahead and rising. Sailing in morning. Goodbye. Anthony.' The *Catalpa* would be off Rockingham on Easter Saturday morning then. Breslin now alerted Tom Desmond, care of his modest lodgings in Perth. Desmond was to set out for Fremantle on Friday night with the trap and matching team of horses he had already ordered from the livery stables in Perth. As part of his luggage he would carry guns, ammunition and clothing. Late on Thursday, someone – perhaps a pro-Fenian warder named McMahon – was able to warn the prisoners that the break would be on Saturday, appropriately enough the eve of Resurrection. Amidst all this, Breslin had the matter of the maid Mary Tondut. About to leave her, he made arrangements for her to have money to follow him to America. To what extent she was let into the plan is not known.

That night, as Breslin attempted sleep, a gale which had struck the town early in the evening now increased in force. Breslin understood that the same gale was audible to the Fenians in their cells, and wondered how in their tormented expectation another delay would sit. In Bunbury, by seven o'clock that Thursday evening, the *Catalpa* was taking the brunt of a north-westerly storm. In the middle of the night, she dragged her anchors. A sleepless Captain Anthony theorised that by deploying the main topsail and battening the fore topsail it should be possible to hold the ship stationary, which would allow the anchors to be dropped again. He ordered it, the anchors were dropped, and *Catalpa* was prevented from running aground. As Good Friday morning broke, the sun appeared, but the wind continued ferociously against him. *Catalpa* obviously could not clear Bunbury for Rockingham Beach that day. Anthony composed from Devoy's book of codes a message for such an eventuality. 'It has blown heavy. Ship dragged both anchors. Can you advance more money if needed. Will telegraph you again in the morning.'

It was afternoon on Good Friday before a whaleboat could be launched from *Catalpa* without swamping. Sam Smith went ashore to send his message to Breslin, and found the telegraph office locked. But he had over the past weeks got to know the telegraphist, Beatrice Warren, and ran to her house, knowing that the Perth and Fremantle telegraph offices, even if their doors were shut, were always staffed for government telegraphic traffic. Smith was able to persuade Beatrice to leave her home, walk through rain and gale with him, open the office and tap on her transmitter the letters FR for Fremantle. The telegraphist at the end of the line in

Fremantle took the message – that Anthony needed money because of storm damage.

Breslin received from Father McCabe that Good Friday a note which read: 'Foley says he delivered the goods and they were received in good condition.' Since William Foley had already left for Ireland, the Foley in question was probably John Foley, the former horse artilleryman still settled for the moment in Western Australia. The message meant that the men were all now ready to break away the next day, Saturday. In the hope that Christ would smile on Fenians, Breslin attended the Mass of the Presanctified on Good Friday. In the pews behind him, each involved in apparently singular worship, sat Desmond, King, Walsh, McCarthy and Brennan.

But then, leaving Mass, Breslin received the telegram Anthony had devised. There would be no *Catalpa* tomorrow. The prisoners would now have to be notified yet again of a change, and Walsh and McCarthy must be prevented from cutting the telegraph wires out of Fremantle the next day. Desmond had driven into town with a team of chestnuts drawing a wagonette. He would need to be sent back to Perth for the moment. In some anguish, Breslin went to see if Father McCabe could get a message to the prisoners, and fortuitously found Martin Hogan, a ravaged version of the young swordsman who had argued in a pub with McCafferty the virtues of the sword over the revolver. Hogan had been sent from the prison with some message to Father McCabe and had stayed on in understandable fervour to make the Stations of the Cross, a traditional Good Friday devotion. Breslin told him the news directly. The soldier Fenian, who had been honouring Christ's anguish in the Garden of Gethsemane, now displayed his own. He warned Breslin that the authorities were thinking of building a new road, which would involve the dispatch of road gangs to various far-flung parts of the bush. There might be none left in Fremantle to flee by the time the ship arrived. Breslin told Hogan that at Easter Mass he would signal if the attempt was to be made on Easter Monday by putting a finger alongside his nose, and then drawing it across his right cheek. On such flimsy gestures depended all hope.

Next morning, at the telegraph office before it closed, Breslin received the delightful confirmation: 'I shall certainly sail today. Suppose you will leave for York Monday morning. Goodbye.' Since Desmond was supposed to be largely unknown to Breslin, Breslin did not risk another telegram to him. He sent John King to Perth on horseback to let Desmond know that the *Catalpa* was definitely sailing. Breslin was also able to get a verbal message to Wilson. Strolling on the wharf, where Wilson was working late on Easter Saturday, Breslin mouthed a single word: 'Monday'.

Easter dinner on Sunday at the Emerald Isle proved hard to digest as Mr Maloney made pleasant but unknowing table talk. It was harder to digest still when, during the afternoon, Breslin saw Desmond ride into town from Perth not with his earlier splendid team but with a poorly assorted pair of nags. His fine chestnut pair had been rented to someone else. When Breslin went to hire a team that he had already reserved, he suffered a similar inconvenience. Albert's Livery had hired out the better horse of the pair to Superintendent John Stone of the water police. It had been an emergency – Stone's brother-in-law was in a critical condition in Perth hospital. The Easter Monday regatta on the Swan River at Perth had just about cleaned Albert out of horses. So the idea of a dashing conveyance of the prisoners to Rockingham Beach looked less and less likely.

30
Perth Regatta Day

So come all ye screw warders and gaolers,
Remember Perth Regatta Day;
Take care of the rest of your Fenians
Or the Yankees will steal them away.
Traditional song

At noon on Easter Day the *Catalpa* lay offshore 30 miles south-west of Rottnest lighthouse. The lighthouse itself stood 12 miles offshore from Fremantle, and the approach of vessels could be signalled to town. Anthony, preparing to go to Rockingham in his whaleboat, cautioned Smith to keep well to the south of this light, and at least 12 miles off the mainland. If the water police or a gunboat hailed *Catalpa*, Sam Smith was to tell them Anthony had gone to fetch a new anchor. If Anthony failed to return to *Catalpa* with the prisoners, Smith should take the ship on a conventional whaling voyage, and earn back its cost.

Anthony's whaleboat was now dropped over the side. The captain took ashore with him the new third mate picked up in Fayal, Sylva, together with Toby, the boat steerer; Louis, a Portuguese whaler; and Mopsy and Lombard, two Malays. As rations, the captain had aboard a bag of bread, two kegs of water and a boiled ham. His crew hoisted the leg-of-mutton sail, and the whaleboat soon made the southern end of Garden Island off Rockingham. Once there, to lessen visibility the sail was furled. They surfed breakers into the smooth waters of the sound off Rockingham. With a telescope Anthony spotted his markers ashore, and the crew landed at 8.30 on a temperate evening, ate a meal of biscuit and cold ham, drank some rum, and then stretched out in the smooth grass of the dunes.

In the prison at Fremantle, Superintendent Doonan had ordered a special Easter meal for prisoners: boiled mutton, cabbage, potatoes and carrots. Treacle was served with plum duff, and native fruits rounded off the penal banquet. Afterwards, James Wilson sat down to play cards with the others and passed round the information about the next day. The unwitting prisoner who went uninformed was James Keilley, former soldier of the 53rd Regiment of Foot, life prisoner, whom – as Breslin knew by now – the others intended to exclude from the escape. This decision was only in part due to Keilley's being strongly suspected of having, in desperation and while serving his sentence in Dartmoor and Millbank, offered information to the authorities. In Millbank, he had tried to commit suicide 'by suspending himself by a coir rope from his gas pipe – believed to be a genuine attempt'. In the personal and other descriptions of 280 prisoners received per ship *Hougoumont*, it was noticed Keilley had scars on both wrists, an indication of a further attempt at suicide. This was the level of despair which had driven Keilley to his banal and totally unrewarded treacheries. Married, with two children, he had been only twenty-one years old when sentenced in June 1866, and therefore still barely thirty at Easter 1876.

But it was not only the 10-year-old fallibilities of Keilley which excluded him from this escape. What may have counted even more was that, early in 1876, Keilley had been assigned as servant to Acting Comptroller-General Fauntleroy. He had become so friendly with the Fauntleroy family that he was permitted to remain at the residence up to nine o'clock at night, and sometimes later. It was Keilley's tendency to be cosy and appeasing with Fauntleroy which led to a vote to exclude him, and to Breslin's agreement with that vote.

On Easter morning, Anthony and his crew woke in the sand dunes of Rockingham to see activity on a nearby jetty belonging to the Rockingham Jarrah Timber Company. Anthony realised he had made a mistake in marking the beach so close to this pier, for a gang of five men were already working there, stacking a pile of timber. Anthony, with his temperamental audacity, walked up and began chatting with one of them, William Bell. He told him they were on their way to Fremantle to fetch an anchor, but Bell shook his head. He knew what the truth was: they were deserters from a ship. Anthony slid over this accusation. What worried him was that the stacked sawn timber was to be collected by *Georgette*, apparently due into Rockingham that morning.

A more neurotic man than Anthony might have concluded the enterprise was so cursed by cumulative difficulties that his responsibility to his own boat crew would justify his setting out to sea at once. Sly Bell advised Anthony to keep close in to Garden Island going out, and thus avoid the wedge of coral in mid-channel.

In the prison, reveille sounded at 5.00 a.m., followed by breakfast, parade inspection and then the assignment of prisoners to jobs. In dawn light the *Georgette* steamer stood at Victoria Quay, making lazy smoke, due to leave on her mail run. Before 5.30, the IRB man McCarthy, with a bundle tied to the end of a stick, set out from town on the Bunbury road. Inside the bundle was a pair of heavy-duty wire cutters. North of Fremantle, on the road to Perth, Walsh, similarly equipped, was on the move. The two IRB men, after carrying out their task for the escape party, were to take cover at their hotel and brazen it out. There was not room for them on *Catalpa*.

At the Emerald Isle, after the restlessness of the night, Breslin had knocked on Desmond's door, on King's and Brennan's, and roused them. Breslin knew that this was a day when all the past fatuities of the Fenian impulse could be redeemed by one splendid exploit. His party ate an early breakfast downstairs. Breslin then went out to the stable yard and was astonished to find a first-class matched pair already harnessed to a light, four-wheeled wagonette. He talked the sleepy stable-hand into renting them to him, and by 7.30 was riding south along the road to Rockingham. Brennan had already loaded the luggage of the entire rescue party – Breslin, Desmond, King, himself – into a two-wheeler, and it was racing ahead of Breslin. McCarthy and Walsh had by then returned to town, having cut the telegraph wires. They had met nobody – this was after all Easter Monday, a holiday, and many were in Perth for that day's regatta. The Fremantle Freemasons' Hall was to be opened the next day, and that gala tended to keep in town people not already in Perth.

Breslin took the Rockingham road at a casual pace in his fine wagonette. Desmond caught up with him in the inferior vehicle brought from Perth, and once they had entered bush country parked on the side of the road. Three six-shooters, three caps, three pairs of pants and half the ammunition were placed in each trap.

In Fremantle gaol, the prisoners Robert Cranston and Thomas Hassett were allowed out of the gate during the time the stores office was closed for the accountant's breakfast – a routine arrangement. They were, they told the gatekeeper Warder Lindsey, detailed to dig potatoes in the clerk of works' garden. Robert Cranston himself did not go there. Instead, he strolled down to the south jetty, where a party of convicts were quarrying and dressing stone for building up the dock. His message to Warder Booler was that the superintendent had asked for two constables, Harrington and Hogan, to accompany him to the governor's Fremantle residence in Hampton Road to move furniture. Booler, a believer in universal brotherhood, and therefore not cut out for his job, was impressed that Cranston was twirling a large key in his hand, and let the three Fenian prisoners head off in the direction of the prison. Edging past the wall, they came upon Tom Hassett and Thomas Darragh, who had left the stables, already digging potatoes in the clerk of works' garden. Darragh and Hassett shouldered their shovels and casually joined the others. Drawing level with the Fauntleroy house, the group saw Martin Hogan at work painting the walls. Hogan picked up his paint pail and joined the party.

In the shade of the tall trees, on the road to Rockingham where Breslin and Desmond waited, it was a splendid autumn morning, and Breslin watched white cockatoos scud, chattering, across a brilliant sky. Three convicts came in sight – Wilson, so often the contact during this process, Cranston, and the oldest soldier, Michael Harrington, moving freely. Breslin thought they seemed dangerously exhilarated. As he launched himself into the bed of Desmond's wagon, Harrington yelled, 'Ireland for ever!' Breslin believed the cry a little premature. With three aboard, Desmond's wagon now headed off towards Rockingham, and Breslin could see the three men aboard stripping off the hated penal cloth and hurling it into the bushes. The second squad of escapees, Darragh, Hassett and Hogan, were within sight, waving their arms and shouting too loudly. Breslin's horses were startled by the yelling, and Darragh grabbed their bridles to soothe them. 'Let go! He'll kick your head off!' Breslin shouted.

Breslin reined in the team, they settled into a trot, and the three prisoners ran behind and scrambled aboard, laughing; they grabbed at the pile of civilian clothes and began changing immediately. According to the *Perth Inquirer*, it was between the cemetery and the piggery, characteristic edge-of-town amenities, that the escapees jumped aboard their carriages and jettisoned their prison weeds. At the scatter of huts at Ten Mile Well, Breslin slowed the wagonette and the Fenian escapees composed themselves. They rolled through town, as far as they knew undetected.

At nine o'clock, John King, the Sydneysider whose job was to be rearguard, went out to mount his horse like a man going on an excursion. He rode north up High Street, seemingly on his way to Perth, then turned sharply round by the prison and headed south through Fremantle's back streets. He had in his pocket a large piece of cake he had seen in the dining-room after breakfast, and which he had commandeered in case of coming need. When, without meeting anyone, he caught up with Desmond, Breslin and their parties near the Rockingham Hotel, he was able to tell them that there was no sign that the escape had been noticed.

Brennan, with the luggage, was the first to park his trap on the edge of Rockingham Beach and see Anthony's crew. Of the party of timber workers at the wharf, only Bell was still present, and some sources say that Brennan urged Anthony and, later, Breslin to shoot him as a precaution. Behind, as the two wagons were still rolling through Rockingham, each prisoner sat with his hand on the pistol in his pocket. Tom Somers, proprietor of the hotel, asked whether *Georgette* had left Fremantle yet. 'It was still at the wharf when we left town,' said Breslin.

The last few miles were particularly sandy and, after the rain, boggy. On either side of the track grew huge eucalypts and hardwoods of the kind amongst which the prisoners had spent much of their eight Western

Australian years, and which they hoped never to see again. At last, near the dunes, the forest gave way to low brush. On the beach, observed by Bell, Anthony began to get the whaleboat ready for departure. The mast lay to hand for hoisting. In a claim credible enough in view of *Georgette*'s timetable, Anthony later said that he could see *Georgette*'s smoke approaching from the north of Garden Island even before the two traps with the prisoners aboard came racing down the last of the track. The men jumped down, slapped the rumps of Breslin's horses, which galloped madly off, tangling their traces in the undergrowth, before coming to rest and grazing. On seeing the Fenian prisoners run towards them, some of the whaleboat crew drew sheath knives. Others grabbed their oars, suspecting the newly arrived party were customs and excise men. As Anthony reassured his people, the Fenians were trying to push the boat out, managing to get it beam on to the waves. Though he had with him now men beside themselves after two hours of freedom, Anthony's authoritative voice penetrated hysteria well. He ordered everyone to board in orderly manner, and to give the rowers room; the passengers were to hunch down in the bottom. Before obeying, either Brennan or Breslin waded ashore and shoved a sovereign into Bell's hand in the hope of buying his silence.

The boat crew now pushed the load of convicts and rescuers out into the surf, vaulted aboard themselves, and began rowing. From his position in the stern, Anthony watched Bell mount one of the horses and whip it into a gallop. Anthony told his chronicler, Pease, that the boat was only half a mile offshore when the police arrived, but surely it was further, since the escape party had the better part of two hours' start. Through a telescope, Breslin saw a knot of uniformed police armed with carbines on the beach. They had a number of native trackers, wearing short coats of kangaroo skin bolted at the waist. Unalarmed, Breslin seemed to think the escape was now secure. He called for order, took from his pocket a sheet of paper and a wrapping of sealskin and read aloud the contents. 'This is to certify that I have this day released from the clemency of Her Most Gracious Majesty, Victoria, Queen of Great Britain, etc., etc., six Irishmen, condemned . . . for having been guilty of the atrocious and unpardonable crimes known to the unenlightened portion of mankind as "love of liberty" and "hatred of tyranny". For this act of "Irish assurance" my birth and my blood being my full and sufficient warranty.' He finished his proclamation with some poor verse.

> I've the honour and pleasure to bid you good-day.
> From all future acquaintance, excuse me, I pray.

Breslin rewrapped the letter in its sealskin, hacked off a small piece of one of the thwarts of the boat with a hatchet which lay in the stern and bound the packet to it. Finally he produced a small red sail, wedged it in a cleft in the bit of board, and set the whole apparatus afloat. This was a show of unusual bravado for the reserved New York journalist, who did not understand that, once they passed the tip of Garden Island, sea, wind and tide would turn against them.

Doonan later reported that it was at 9.35 a.m. that the gatekeeper Lindsey told him Hogan was missing from the Comptroller-General's quarters. He immediately sent a warder to tell the police, and then searched for the other Fenians, but found six missing in all. The prison bell began to toll madly. There was a general muster of convicts, and the names of the missing six were verified. Doonan sent an officer to wire Perth immediately, since it was thought likely the Fenian convicts would have headed in that direction, but the operator, naturally, could not get through. From the verandah of the Port Hotel, McCarthy and Walsh observed the sudden galvanising of the forces of authority – water police summoned from their homes and rushing, half-dressed, to their headquarters near the pier, parties of blacktrackers heading up the Perth road and down the Rockingham track, and the militia and Pensioner Guards who happened to be in town drummed and bugled into formation under one Major Charles Finnerty.

Doonan suspected the escapees might be hidden by a Pensioner Guard named Taafe, who had shown Fenian sympathy. The Taafe house was searched, but nothing found. Bell the timber worker came yelling into town on one of the escapee's horses at one o'clock, having made the journey in an hour and forty minutes. About the same time, Water Police Superintendent Stone returned from visiting his injured brother in Perth. He tried to telegraph to call on the gunboat *Conflict* in Albany, but found the line dead. By the time the cut telegraph wires south of Fremantle were repaired, the *Conflict* had left Albany, bound for Adelaide.

At the regatta in Perth, Breslin's prospective father-in-law, Mr Charles Tondut, was winning in both the dinghy-pulling and the sailing races with his little yacht *Frenchman*. Here, on the banks of the Swan, Governor Robinson got the news of the escape early in the afternoon. He left at once for Fremantle. By the time he arrived, Superintendent Stone of the water police had gone through copies of the telegrams transmitted in the last month. From the volume of transmissions between Collins and Anthony, it was concluded the vessel involved was *Catalpa*. At once, a water police cutter, under the command of Coxswain Mills, was ordered to search the waters southwards between Rottnest and Garden Island, to intercept the whaleboat before it reached *Catalpa*, and arrest everybody.

The conversation that afternoon between Robinson and Stone about the powers they could exercise under international law was influenced by Robinson's experience as governor of Prince Edward Island, at a time when freedom of the seas was a fiercely debated matter between Britain and the United States. Robinson knew sufficient maritime law to be able to argue, in his ultimate report to the Secretary of State in Downing Street, according to the principles laid down by the leading maritime law authority, Lord Stowell: 'All nations being equal, all have an equal right to an uninterrupted use of the unappropriated parts of the Ocean for their navigation . . . I decided that under the circumstances of the case it would be a violation of the principles of International Law to fire into her in the first instance, when beyond territorial waters, and directed the Superintendent of Police accordingly.' But the pursuit of the whaleboat containing the absconders could legally be continued beyond territorial waters.

Within an hour of arriving in Fremantle, Robinson commissioned the *Georgette*, which had returned to Fremantle in mid-afternoon, as a warship in Her Majesty's navy. Its master, Captain Grady, would now be subject to Water Police Superintendent Stone's orders. Grady protested against his ship being impressed: it was not adequately coaled for a high-seas chase, he said, and his crew were not rested. Stone asked him, 'Is a voyage to Rottnest Island such an ocean adventure?' Twenty members of the drill company of the Pensioner Guards were gathered throughout the afternoon and ordered to go aboard *Georgette* under Major Finnerty. They would be accompanied by seven armed police. With its steam engines and its sails, Robinson believed, *Georgette* should be able with ease to run down *Catalpa*, since the westerlies blowing that afternoon and into the evening would keep the whaler pretty much in place, and also make the going difficult for the whaleboat.

Soon after the commissioning of *Georgette*, Coxswain Mills returned bearing the package launched by Breslin. Amongst the Irish population of Fremantle, there was already considerable joy. An Irishman wrote home: 'I need hardly tell you that the Irish people here are in the very highest state of jubilation at the escape of the prisoners.' James Keilley might not have felt the general Irish excitement. That bitter Monday afternoon, he was already constructing a face-saving myth that the others had been unable to find him that morning. But even as the Irish of Fremantle toasted the success of the escape, Robinson was drafting his own telegraph to go out over the repaired wires to all points of the Australian colonies. 'Detain, by force if necessary, American whaling barque *Catalpa*, George

Anthony, Master. Arrest said Anthony, his officers and crew, and any passengers who may be aboard.'

By noontime that Easter Monday, *Catalpa* was 16 miles offshore on a calm sea, wearing very little sail, and maintaining an intense watch. As the afternoon advanced, though, the wind picked up and white horses appeared, which meant that the whaleboat would be harder to see. As darkness came on, Smith ordered a lookout in each topmast during the night, and lanterns lashed to all the masts as well as at the bows. 'I want her to look like a floating city,' he told his men.

After five o'clock in the afternoon, the men in the whaleboat briefly sighted *Catalpa* 4 miles away. This glimpse was curtailed by darkness. Throughout a horrible night, heavy seas dumped water on rescuers and rescued, and Hogan and Cranston were kept bailing madly. The hectic exultation of escape was gone and everyone except the oarsmen lay sodden and mute. Perhaps one or another of the escapees longed for his dry cell in Fremantle, especially when, two hours after dark, the mast snapped close to the base and everything – timber, rigging, sail, halyard – was washed overboard and threatened to drag the whaleboat down with it. Third mate Sylva grabbed a hatchet and hacked away at the shrouds and hauled the tangled mass back aboard. By ten o'clock in the evening the debris had been reconstructed into a jury mast.

In the midst of terror and discomfort, one of the prisoners was briefly cheered by the phosphorescence of the sea. But though Anthony told a prisoner he had been in far worse storms, he later confessed to suffering severe doubt. The boat was overloaded with sixteen men, and the gunnels were rarely more than 2 inches above water level. They did not know it and would not have been comforted to be told that Coxswain Mills's boat also stayed out all that awful night.

Towards Tuesday morning, though the winds moderated, the seas were still high enough to catch Anthony now and then to the level of his armpits as he knelt on the stern sheets, working the rudder. Dawn came up clear on a sea still running strongly. All the men on the whaleboat cheered to see *Catalpa* at a distance and standing in towards them. But the smoke of the newest ship of the Royal Navy, *Georgette*, was also visible to the north-east. *Georgette* was soon close enough to cause Anthony to order the sail taken down, and everyone to lie in the bottom of the whaleboat. Without sighting them on the white-capped sea, the steamer passed within half a mile, Anthony plainly seeing an officer on the bridge searching the shore of Garden Island, sure that a whaleboat with so many aboard could not have lasted the night. *Georgette*, twice the size of the whaling bark, edged up to meet *Catalpa*, and Anthony feared it would remain close to prevent his whaleboat approaching.

The dialogue between *Catalpa* and *Georgette* on their first meeting was well covered by newspapers, Australian and American, and certainly marked by the residual heat of the post-Civil War relationships between Britain and the United States. Upon being hailed, Sam Smith said that Captain Anthony had gone to Fremantle to buy an anchor. Superintendent Stone announced his intention was to come aboard and search for prisoners. In one account, Sam Smith is said to have answered, 'You try it and you'll be goddamned good and sorry . . . What the hell did we lick the pants off you damn Britishers in 1812 about? You don't own the goddamn ocean!' According to the *Fremantle Herald*, Smith's answer was milder. 'Don't know; got no instructions; but guess you better not.' Governor Robinson, in his ultimate report to Whitehall, declared the request 'was peremptorily refused by the chief officer'. Smith was seen taking a harpoon in hand to resist boarding.

Grady informed Stone at this point that *Georgette*'s coal reserves were about to run out. Confident that winds would keep *Catalpa* in place all day, Stone agreed to turn back to Fremantle. On the way back in, *Georgette* met the police cutter and told Coxswain Mills that he was to cut the whaleboat off from *Catalpa*. It was early afternoon by now, and *Georgette* swung so close across the stern of the whaleboat that Anthony and Breslin could see the Pensioner Guards on deck. *Georgette* having passed on, Anthony ordered the oars out again. At first the *Catalpa* was barely visible, but then it swung around and loomed larger. Breslin gave a red whaling flag to Wilson and ordered him to wave it. The bark broke out its topgallant sails and headed down on them all the more strongly. It was Tuesday afternoon, and Sam Smith had at last sighted them. The water police cutter was, however, seen rowing hard from the north towards *Catalpa*. All the escaped prisoners aboard the whaleboat began reloading their revolvers, replacing the wet cartridges, declaring furiously their intention to fight. Anthony himself, apparently as willing as the others to resist authority, distributed rifles to Breslin and Desmond. But he was reassured to notice that the police cutter needed to luff frequently to spill the wind from her mainsail, and that his whaleboat retained an advantage.

When the *Georgette* reached Fremantle late that afternoon, Walsh, McCarthy and Father McCabe, from their separate vantage points, were elated to see it did not have the escaped prisoners on board. Local sympathisers were rejoicing on the pier and singing 'God Save Ireland'. The *Fremantle Herald* surmised the rejoicing 'arose chiefly out of the popular impression that Fenian convicts are political prisoners, convicted and punished for offences against a Government, not against society'. Robinson declared in his report that, had the *Georgette* stayed by the *Catalpa* a few hours longer, the boat with the absconders would have been intercepted. But he did not doubt Stone's wisdom in returning to Fremantle for coal, for 'had the *Georgette* been caught in a gale of wind and under canvas the chances are she would have been lost'. Work parties of Pensioner Guards now filled the *Georgette*'s bunkers with thirty tons of coal.

At sea that afternoon, Coxswain Mills tried all seamanship to catch Anthony's whaleboat before it reached *Catalpa*. But to help Anthony's crew, Smith took *Catalpa* between the cutter and the whaleboat. From the whaleboat, Anthony was yelling, 'Hoist the ensign!' The American flag was raised to the peak where it had last flown during the earlier conversation between *Catalpa* and *Georgette*. Smith also ordered his deckhands to display muskets and lances. Mills dauntlessly increased sail and put three or four men on the sweep to hasten the cutter's progress. He got close enough to hear Smith yelling threats to sink him.

Anthony's whaleboat slammed alongside its mother ship at about 2.30 on that Tuesday afternoon. To raise it quickly out of the Indian Ocean, men aboard *Catalpa* threw the forward boat tackle to Mr Sylva and the after boat tackle to Captain Anthony. As the whaleboat was winched to its station amidships, Anthony found that he was now the only man still aboard. The prisoners and their associates were already climbing fixedly on deck, rifles and revolvers still in their hands. The boat was hoisted on the davits, and the police cutter swept across the bows of *Catalpa* to a new barrage of threats from the deck. The final distance between the two was later claimed by Smith and Anthony to have been only a hundred yards – in such an immense sea, a small space indeed. This, in the spirit of the overladen melodrama of events, may have been an underestimation: members of Coxswain Mills's crew told newspapermen they had been 400 yards too late. But that Mills was close emerges from Governor Robinson's report to London. The reasons Her Majesty's government, said Robinson, was entitled to ask the American government to take action on this matter were: '1. The Water Police saw the absconders get on board from the whale boat to the *Catalpa*. 2. The master of the *Catalpa* with his speaking trumpet in his hand, on the deck of the *Catalpa*, was recognised to be the man in charge of the whaleboat which left Rockingham . . . 3. The Coxswain of the Water Police boat saw and recognised two of the Absconders in the forepart of the *Catalpa*.' Seeing aboard the police cutter various officers they knew, the prisoners indiscreetly crowded up to the rail, waved their rifles and shouted 'salutations and farewells'. Coxswain Mills knew he could not board *Catalpa*, gave the military salute and called 'Good morning!' to Anthony.

Breslin was impressed with Smith's handling of *Catalpa* before and after the pick-up. It took Sam Smith only two minutes to hoist up the whaleboat, raise the ensign, change sail to take best advantage of the slight winds, and work *Catalpa* out to sea. Anthony embraced and complimented Smith, then called for the ship's steward and told him to put on the best dinner the ship could afford. The meal that was provided for the men redeemed that evening included canned chicken and lobster, boiled potatoes, canned fruit, tea and coffee – a meal of joy and innocence over which hung the threat of further action by *Georgette*. The rescued prisoners were all painfully grateful, but soon they would move on to other phases of feeling.

Sam Smith later told George Anthony that if he had not turned up he had determined to run *Catalpa* into Fremantle and demand Anthony's release. It was unlikely that Smith – in making this claim – was blowing hard after the fact. Earlier nightmares of American ruffians (or Portuguese or Kanaka or liberated American slaves) sacking Fremantle might have become reality.

As the escapees feasted beneath a westering Indian Ocean sun, in Fremantle *Georgette* was still coaling. Dark fell before the process was completed, and Sir William Robinson set off by carriage for his residence in Perth about 9.30 that night, having been assured the *Georgette* would be ready to go to sea by eleven o'clock. At 10.00 p.m., however, Coxswain Mills brought his cutter into Fremantle and reported having seen the convicts embark on the *Catalpa*. It was on Comptroller-General Fauntleroy's word that *Georgette* was returned to the chase. As Robinson said, 'had I been at Fremantle when the Water Police boat returned I should not have allowed the steamer to go to sea again'. All *Georgette* could hope for was to provoke *Catalpa* into firing on the British flag, thereby warranting the sinking or capture of the whaler.

The detachment of water police and Finnerty's reinforced Pensioner Guards marched on board again by ten o'clock that night. In the breasts of some of the Pensioner Guards there may have been less than a willingness to perish boarding a Yankee vessel against its will to retrieve prisoners some of them knew from the days aboard *Hougoumont*. The crew of *Georgette* were sworn into the armed forces. A 9-pounder field piece (Anthony says 12-pounder) was dragged aboard and lashed to the gangway. It was meant to have been taken on *Georgette*'s earlier expedition, but Grady had feared that in the rougher weather it would have destabilised the steamer. Powder, round shot and canister were stored beside the cannon, visible means to destroy *Catalpa*. The escapees' supporters, said the *Fremantle Herald*, observed the steamer's departure with foreboding. Those 'who were not acquainted with international law or aware of His Excellency's instructions' were justified in thinking a sea battle lay ahead.

Aboard the good republican *Catalpa* certain distinctions of status, likely in time to irk men still edgy from the release of tension, were established that evening. Breslin, Desmond and King dined with the captain, while Brennan and the rescued men ate in the crews' mess with the Fenian carpenter Duggan. Anthony gave Breslin his own cabin to rest in, lying down himself on a little 4-foot lounge, and telling Sam Smith to work offshore if the wind permitted it. Exhausted, he knew he would have to be available to stand by the helmsman a good part of that night.

The prisoners and their rescuers took willingly to their bunks, but then awoke to feel the sea tranquil and the wind slack. They seemed magnetised to Western Australia. The ship did not, as Anthony put it, move her own length during the entire night. The irony was that they needed the turbulent sort of weather which had characterised the night before. Wakeful and back on deck, dizzy with fatigue, Anthony asked one of the crew to rub his back with aromatic ointment. Then, at first light, he climbed into the main topmast with his telescope and spotted the mast of newly coaled-up *Georgette*. The steamer, approaching *Catalpa*, flew a man-of-war and vice-admiral's flag, the flag the governor was entitled to fly. Anthony, not easily awed, nonetheless saw a serious intent behind those pennants. A south-easter had come up but was too slight to give *Catalpa* much help in terms of escaping the coast. *Georgette* overhauled the whaler with ease.

The prisoners were warned over their breakfast that *Georgette* was on its way. Sad-eyed Michael Harrington, oldest of the prisoners, looked down on the remnants of perhaps his last meal. Anthony allowed the Fenian soldiers to stay armed but they were to keep utterly out of sight. From Anthony, Sam Smith, Farnham and Sylva there did not seem to be any resentment that these volatile escapees were about to drag master and crew into bloody confrontation and diplomatic outrage. According to what Anthony later told his memoirist, Pease, Sam Smith was raging up and down the companionways and across the decks in a mood of utter defiance. 'Damn him, let him sink us . . . I'll never start sheet or tack for him.' Anthony himself walked the deck telling his crew that they would be thrown into the same prison from which the men on board had been freed. Some of his whalers he armed with harpoon lances, others with cutting spades normally used for slicing whale blubber. Sam Smith supervised the

Fremantle and, distantly, its great white prison, where the Fenian prisoners were detained on their arrival in Western Australia, January 1868.

Bunbury, the Leschenault Channel and the Indian Ocean – scene of John Boyle O'Reilly's escape.

General Meagher, about the time of his appointment to Montana in 1865.

Virginia City, Montana, in 1866.
Perhaps vulnerable to Blackfoot attacks, as Meagher saw it.

The Governor's residence, abutting a stone building in Idaho Street, Virginia City.

The 'Acting One's' executive office, upper floor. Photographed in the 1870s by E. H. Train.

The other city: Helena, Montana. Photographed in the early 1870s by E. H. Train.

Elizabeth Meagher as a brave widow.

General Meagher wins the symbolism battle.
Above left: an Irish legend clothed in Old Glory, 4 July 1905.
Above right: Riding north towards Fort Benton.

The people of Sydney, ever adept at fireworks, welcome Prince Alfred's *Galatea*.

A source of anti-Irish frenzy: the shooting of Prince Alfred by demented Henry O'Farrell, at Clontarf, near Sydney, in March 1868 (p. 491).

Ireland: labourer's cottage, 1870s.

Australia: the convict-built pier, Fremantle.

America: grand parade in honour of the amnestied Fenians, including John Devoy and O'Donovan Rossa, New York City, 9 February 1871 (p. 536).

The escape of the Fenian prisoners. The melodrama of this version may have been encouraged by the inherent drama of the real escape in 1876.

Catalpa's flag. Run up to protect the whaler.

Fenian's rest: on the south coast of New South Wales lies John Goulding, beneath a Celtic cross.

Fenian's rest: Los Angeles in 1885, and the dry-goods department store of Dillon and Kenealy, the People's Store, centre left.

The Fenian as civic officer: John Kenealy, second from right, in his sixties, as City Treasury Clerk to W. H. Workman (centre), 1903.

bringing up of grindstones from below, and spare spars, all of which could be dropped on any boat which tried to near *Catalpa*. As the light strengthened, Smith ordered a harpoon gun mounted amidships, and brass explosive cartridges stacked. More a rhetorical than a genuine riposte to *Georgette*'s cannon, it at least bespoke a determination not to be boarded.

Breslin, King and Desmond had come on deck and crouched under the gunwales, each with a rifle. Everyone seemed to be weirdly elated by the closeness of a resolution, of any resolution. Breslin had confidence in Anthony. But *Georgette* was 400 tons, and what passed for a small forest of bayonets could be seen on its deck. The Pensioners were in the bows, the water police in the stern prepared to board. Captain Grady waved his hat to Captain Anthony, whom he had once entertained on the bridge of *Georgette*. Grady was concerned about the freshening wind and the sudden advantage it might bring *Catalpa*. He quickly ran up the signal instructing *Catalpa* to heave to and shorten sail. Of course Anthony did neither.

Hence Stone ordered a shot fired across *Catalpa*'s stern. The air above the Indian Ocean seemed for an instant to crack open, and Anthony said later the water from the ball flew as high as the whaler's masthead. The startled Fenians, sheltering in their mess, expected a shattering barrage. But none came. The resultant dialogue between ships is variously reported, but no version departs drastically from that recorded in the *Fremantle Herald*.

STONE: 'I demand six escaped prisoners now on board this ship – in the name of the Governor of Western Australia . . . I know the men I want are on board, for the police saw them go on board yesterday.'

ANTHONY: 'I have no prisoners on board.'

STONE: 'You have, and I see three of them.'

ANTHONY: 'I have no prisoners here: All are seamen belonging to the ship.'

The wind was now threatening to produce a collision, so *Georgette* was compelled to move away from the whaler. Said Stone: 'I will give you fifteen minutes to consider what you do.'

Georgette hung off a little and everyone waited, looking at watches. For Wilson, Darragh, Hogan and the others below, the wait cannot have been beneficial, for they were not as aware as Stone of maritime law. At the end of the wait, *Georgette* again went alongside and Stone again demanded handover of the prisoners.

ANTHONY: 'I have none on board.'

STONE: 'If you don't give them up, I will fire into you and sink you or disable you.'

ANTHONY: 'I don't care what you do, I'm on the high seas, and that flag protects me.'

But if there were escaped convicts on board, said Stone, 'your flag won't protect you in that'.

ANTHONY: 'Yes it will, or in felony either.'

STONE: 'Will you let me board your ship and see for myself?'

ANTHONY: 'You shan't board my vessel.'

STONE: 'Then your Government will be communicated with, and you must take the consequences.'

Anthony said, 'All right.' Then in silence the ships manoeuvred. Fifteen minutes' further grace expired. According to Anthony, someone called out that he had a telegram from the American government authorising the seizure of *Catalpa*. Anthony was to heave to. 'I'll blow your masts out unless you do so.' Behind the gunwales, Breslin expected a raking shot to land amongst the masts. But again it failed to come. The vessels were now 18 miles offshore, with Anthony running *Catalpa* inshore to catch the wind but trying to avoid straying into Australian waters. When *Catalpa*'s crew, to quote Pease, 'hauled up the clews on the mainsail, hauled down the head of the spanker, and let the gaff topsail run down', the officers on *Georgette* thought *Catalpa* was coming to a stop, and the steamer hove to as well. But Captain Anthony put the wheel up and the vessel swung off quickly and headed straight for the *Georgette*, causing Captain Grady to believe Anthony was trying to run *Georgette* down with his bows, which were reinforced with metal sheets for ice-cutting. Though Anthony had no such intention, as the *Catalpa* swung by, her jib boom was said to have just cleared the steamer's rigging, an incident which added to the subsequent legend.

Catalpa's sails now filled, and she headed offshore. *Georgette*, under steam and sail, followed *Catalpa* for an hour. Discipline on neither ship broke. The wind grew fresher and constantly increased, and the good news was taken down to the prisoners below as *Catalpa* began to draw ahead. Anthony could still see the military and police officers aboard *Georgette* in an animated huddle. But as *Catalpa* gained distance, Anthony brought the rescued prisoners on deck. 'Boys, take a good look at her, probably you'll never see her again.' *Georgette* peeled away about 9.30 a.m. Within his instructions, Stone could do nothing more.

Denis McCarthy, the IRB man, looking from the verandah of the Port Hotel where he and Walsh had been keeping quiet these past three days, was astonished to see *Georgette* returning to Fremantle. If she had stuck with *Catalpa*, he thought, nothing could have saved the whaler. But as the

Herald said, 'The Governor . . . was not to be led into committing a breach of international law, to ratify a feeling of resentment against the cool effrontery of the Yankee.' In his report, Robinson declared that the escape of the Fenians, anxious as he was to recover them, 'would not justify me in involving Her Majesty's Government in an undesirable discussion with the Government of the United States'. The governor dismissed with thanks the armed parties, and returned *Georgette* itself to its agents.

Keilley retired with a bitter heart to his cell that Wednesday night. But he would maintain his composure admirably. He received a purely local conditional pardon in 1878 but was never to be reunited with his family. At one stage in his old age he was reduced to living in a tent, until in 1904 a local Irish group took over his care. In 1905 he would be honoured by the visiting Irish politician William Redmond, his minor betrayals, like his friendship with Fauntleroy, forgotten. Here was a likeable, chatty Irishman whose life had been destroyed early by his association with Fenianism. He would die in Western Australia in 1918 at the age of eighty-two.

In the Indian Ocean that night after *Catalpa*'s shaking off of *Georgette*, the wind grew to a gale. By midnight on Friday the whaler was 400 miles to the south-west from the scene of its extraordinary Fremantle enterprise. As the storm ended, Captain Anthony ordered two barrels of naval clothing hauled on deck. 'Take all you care for,' he told the prisoners and their rescuers. Below decks, where new tiers of berths were built for them, they were assigned a steward.

Breslin spent those first two days of hectic travelling in writing a celebratory verse, copies of which were handed out to the prisoners.

> Right across the Indian Ocean, while the trade-wind follows fast,
> Speeds our ship with gentle motion; fear and chains behind us cast.
> Rolling home! Rolling home! Rolling home across the seas;
> Rolling home to bright Columbia; home to friends and liberty.

Farnham, second mate, would not see bright Columbia. He dropped dead of a heart attack on 8 May and was buried at sea.

Ashore, the governor had now ordered the immediate detention of the few non-life-serving Fenians who were on ticket-of-leave in the colony, even though their record was clear. James McCoy and John Shine, ticket-of-leave men, and the prisoners Keilley and Delaney, were all locked away in high-security cells. To be incarcerated, McCoy had to be fetched from the Vasse or Bunbury region of Western Australia, and, as he passed the

Emerald Isle Hotel, the hotelier, Maloney, and McCarthy were on the front verandah within sight of a police agent who reported that Maloney shouted, 'There's Jimmy McCoy come back.' McCarthy 'bent down and took off his hat as McCoy passed'. But McCarthy might have unwittingly encouraged this lock-up. He had mischievously pointed out to the agent, one McAuliffe, an American schooner lying in Fremantle Harbour, and made a teasing remark about her finishing off the rescue of Fenians.

Walsh and McCarthy were taken to the police station and heavily questioned by Detective Sergeant Thomas Rowe. Experienced in this sort of pressure, they were ultimately released for lack of evidence. They had, Rowe noted, grown 'stout' (McCarthy) and 'very stout' (Walsh) during their weeks of waiting. At last, without anything happening, the authorities were pleased when a Fenian schoolmaster, O'Callaghan, escorted them to the *Georgette* at Fremantle jetty, where a large party of Irish saw them off, amidst much joking about police panic.

Evil days lay ahead for Walsh, the elder of the two. He would later be a founding member of the extreme group named the Invincibles, of whom McCafferty was also a leading figure, and whose most notorious exploit would be the murder with long knives of the Chief Secretary for Ireland, Lord Frederick Cavendish, in Phoenix Park, Dublin, in 1882. Later in the 1880s, Walsh died in poverty in New York. The somewhat younger McCarthy, also an Invincible, was still living in Chicago in 1904.

Maloney of the Emerald Isle Hotel was also questioned heavily by the police, but he was helped by having been a former member of the Royal Irish Constabulary. Detective Sergeant Rowe later made a report, perhaps reliable, and certainly fascinating: 'Mary Tonduit [Tondut], a Roman Catholic of this Colony, late servant at the Emerald Isle Hotel, where Collins was lodged, was seduced by Collins and is now enceinte. She left this colony in the schooner *Northern Light*. Her expenses were paid by Collins through Maloney. She is to be accouched at Sydney where further arrangements are promised to be made to take her to Collins.'

Miss Tondut did travel to Sydney later in the year, took accommodation in Sussex Street, and gave birth to a child named John Joseph in December 1876. John Joseph were Breslin's first names. But perhaps she did not want to be the wife of a political activist. Or perhaps there was some salient truth Breslin had kept from her. For whatever reason, she would never go to America, though Breslin left Maloney the funds to enable her. She worked as a servant until 1880, when she married a Sydney watchmaker named Thomas.

This was Australian convictism's final escape, and it demonstrated in full the neuroses, rivalries and scapegoating which characterised officials in enclosed and remote penal colonies. All penal events were subject to ultimate judgment by an improbably distant Secretary of State, and – like O'Brien's friend Lapham – officials were dependent on their salaries to save them from falling back into the demi-respectable mass of ticket-of-leave and free settlers. Governor Robinson called a five-man panel of inquiry, whom – of course – everyone tried to influence.

Joseph Doonan's report to Fauntleroy pointed the finger at Warder Lindsey, who had, contrary to orders, passed Cranston and Hassett through the prison gate. As to Booler, the socialist warder on the pier, 'I think him very culpable.' All Booler had to do, on returning to the prison that morning, was to tell Doonan he had let Cranston, Harrington and Hogan go off to move furniture and 'steps would have been taken which would have made it impossible for the escape to take place'. So, at the lower level of command, the warders were to blame. But at the higher level, Doonan rightly or wrongly believed that as an Irish Catholic he was a convenient scapegoat, and complained to His Excellency in May that a prisoner named Hall, and Henderson, or Bowman, the man who had tried to escape with O'Reilly, had been offered inducements by the policeman Rowe to testify that they were holding stolen jewellery for Doonan. Doonan wrote of one of the Comptroller-General's decisions: 'But your Excellency need not be surprised to hear of an imprudent direction like this from an officer, who kept out of the Prison in and about his quarters one of the Fenian Convicts (9797 J. Keilly) until 9 pm and occasionally a little later.' The board of inquiry directed Fauntleroy to remove Warders Lindsey and Booler from the service. As Doonan suggested, the Fenians had been training and testing the warders for slackness for some time before the escape. Booler, married to an Irish nationalist named Honora Glynn, left the colony, apparently with a £200 subsidy said to have been paid out of Fenian funds by Patrick Maloney at the Emerald Isle Hotel, but Warder Lindsey was in the end reinstated.

Doonan, suspended, saw himself as the final Irish martyr of the Fenian escape and suffered a nervous breakdown. Invalided out of the service in September, his appeals to the Home Office and the Colonial Secretary did not save him. But Acting Comptroller Fauntleroy, charged with general incompetence, went too in the end, dismissed on a pension. It would be December 1876 before the Home Office reported to Lord Carnarvon, Colonial Secretary, on 'the question raised by the Governor whether he was right in giving orders that the American Ship *Catalpa* was not to be attacked'. According to the Home Office, he was.

As *Catalpa* was making its escape across the Indian Ocean, the Eastern Extension Australasia and China Telegraph Company told the British

Foreign Minister Lord Derby that the telegraph cable had been cut on 24 April about 45 miles from Darwin. *Catalpa* was nearly 2,000 miles removed from this area, but even Clan na Gael, when they heard of the break, considered quite wrongly that this was due to co-ordinated action by their agents.

It meant that news of the *Catalpa* rescue did not reach London until 6 June by a ship-borne dispatch from Melbourne. In May, a debate on amnesty for the remaining Fenian prisoners came on in the House of Commons. Prime Minister Disraeli opposed any further release of military Fenians, and the London correspondent of the *Irish World* complained that his expression in so doing 'was one of royal contempt towards the Irish nation, its martyrs and its advocates'.

As a cable from London announcing the escape came in on the wire at the *Pilot* office in Boston, O'Reilly felt a pulse both of delight and moral relief. He sent a telegram to John Devoy: 'Grand glory and complete success. Ireland triumphs. London despatch admits all our men safe aboard *Catalpa*. Watch your cables from abroad for more details. Erin go bragh.' O'Reilly wrote the rescue story for the *Pilot* and took the proofs in his coat pocket to New Bedford. He found Annie Anthony in the back of her house, taking in clothing from the line, with Anthony's daughter Sophie walking around her, dropping pegs in a wicker basket. The news and O'Reilly's proofs created a tremor of joy not only in Mrs Anthony but throughout America. O'Donovon Rossa, fund-raising in Omaha, saw people dancing in the streets. The other Boston newspapers stormed O'Reilly's office. Amongst them was a journalist from *The Times* of London, so O'Reilly did not give the ship's name. Somehow, the New Bedford papers concluded from their study of the shipping news that the whaler involved was *Catalpa*. One Boston paper copied this, but O'Reilly was able to persuade the others not to. He also may have been responsible for spreading the news that the ship was making across the Pacific for San Francisco, instead of via the Atlantic for the already-planned landfall of Fernandina, Florida. Fernandina, a flat coastal spit in the north of the state, had been nominated as *Catalpa*'s American landfall because it was home to an Irish-born Clan na Gael member, Senator Conover, who had helped Devoy and planned a welcome for rescuers and rescued there.

Most of the New York newspapers praised the enterprise, even the generally hostile *New York Times*. 'The affair will bring little credit to Mr Disraeli, who so easily refused to remit the penalties of these men.' When the news reached Dublin, 500 torchbearers led a procession of thousands to Grattan Bridge over the Liffey, where Disraeli and the Duke of Cambridge were burned in effigy.

*

As *Catalpa* rounded Africa and entered the Atlantic, sperm whales were occasionally seen and boats were lowered. Captain Anthony had proposed to Breslin that the vessel should hunt for whales for a time, for this was again the whaling season in the Western Grounds off North Africa. Seeing a chance to defray the cost of the enterprise, Breslin agreed. The released prisoners, however, noticed that the ship was heading north instead of crossing the Atlantic diagonally. In their quarters forward, Brennan had told them that the purpose of the journey was to get them ashore as soon as possible. Brennan claimed that he was, in the eyes of Clan na Gael, the overall leader, with power to decide where the ship should go and that John Breslin had been nothing but a plausible interloper. Duggan, the carpenter, supported Brennan in this, and added another grievance: delicacies specially brought on for the escapees had been sold to other vessels or consumed by the crew. By delicacies, Duggan, who held a grudge against Anthony for having been confined to the ship after going on a bender in Bunbury, meant whiskey. In reality, John Devoy had been opposed to the idea of putting liquor aboard – it would be unwise for men who had been deprived of drink for ten years to start bingeing on board a whaler. Besides, Anthony and Smith were New England teetotallers.

Encouraged by Brennan, the men decided to protest at the idea that they should now endure a conventional whaling expedition. Breslin would discover that long imprisonment, frequent despair, delayed rescue, fraught and arduous escape, and, above all, new freedom, tended to encourage petulance rather than grandeur of spirit. The escapees' uneasiness grew also from a genuine fear, stoked perhaps by Brennan, of being retaken at sea by a British warship. Between then and July, the *Catalpa*, which should have been – in tune with Irish sentiment everywhere – a triumphant whaler, was beset by a strange atmosphere of let-down and rankling anxiety. On 10 July, when *Catalpa* crossed the equator into the North Atlantic, Anthony told the absconders, 'You're almost American citizens now.' The truth was they wanted to be Americans as soon as possible. At one time they told him that they had been better treated aboard the convict ship, where they got a glass of wine for scurvy every day. On a morning when the flapjacks were burned, Cranston said he wished he was back in Fremantle. James Wilson – the man whose letter had initiated the rescue – argued that because of his heart condition he would die if he were not put ashore soon. He probably believed himself near death, and perhaps it should not have surprised Breslin and Anthony that men whose ability to express even minor annoyance had been suppressed for ten years should now break out in complaint. Sergeant Darragh was the only one of the six whom Breslin exempted from the charges of poor behaviour.

Some 100 miles off the West Indies, *Catalpa* sighted a ship flying

American colours and steering in towards the Caribbean. Captain Anthony wanted to board her to get some molasses, stores of which were running low, but while he was in his whaleboat chasing the ship Wilson came up to Breslin and cried, 'You refuse to put me on board. Life is life. My health is getting worse every day. I want to be put on shore.' As Anthony returned with a handful of newspapers from the ship, he informed the company that the ship was the *Kentuckian* of Boston, bound for New Orleans but with barely enough provisions for her own crew.

That afternoon, Duggan, Brennan and Desmond requested a private talk with Breslin in the cabin aft. Brennan demanded that they be put ashore at Fernandina or some other port without delay. With perhaps more percipience than Breslin, Brennan said that until they were landed on American soil, the men would not feel gratitude. And it would give the organisation greater benefit for the whaler to put in at once than to remain out longer on the off-chance of taking $14,000 worth of oil. Breslin, profoundly hurt, challenged the delegation to name where they had not been treated as passengers should be. He had eaten the same rations as they. To get aboard in Fremantle, they would all have been willing to face much harsher conditions. The two men complaining of ill health had been in ill health for some years, Breslin argued, and their appearance had improved during their voyage.

Tom Desmond was caught in the middle in this debate. Bunking forward with them, he could understand the prisoners' anxieties. He knew too that unless they could be got to land in good time, life on board *Catalpa* would be rendered intolerable. Desmond had therefore argued that if they could convince Anthony that by going into port he would be satisfying the owners, Breslin would probably consent too. That evening, Breslin received a note signed by all the prisoners as well as by John King, Brennan, Duggan and Desmond, requesting on a number of grounds that *Catalpa* go into port: 'the innutricious quality of the food' was mentioned, as was the ill health of some of the ex-prisoners, all of whom repeated that they would not believe themselves free until they stood on American soil.

Breslin read each paragraph back to the signatories, and then took the document to Anthony, pointing out Brennan's argument that he, not Breslin, represented the desires of the owners. The captain and John Breslin drafted a tough and unconditional document for the prisoners and the others to sign. It stipulated for a start that the food on *Catalpa* was sound ship's food; 'the water is good and in sufficient quantity. The ex-prisoners are in as good a state of health today as when they came on board.' But: 'The ex-prisoners are anxious to get on shore.' So they were to take 'responsibility of all loss to the owners incurred by my compliance with their request to go into port'. As Anthony and Breslin intended, this gave the men pause. How was a penniless rescued convict such as Michael Harrington able to assume such crushing shipping debts? But Brennan passionately assured the escapees that the Clan would never think of seeking recompense from them. So they all signed it. It was endorsed too by Tom Desmond and John King. On seeing this, Anthony suggested that since landfall was to be achieved as fast as possible, New York was much closer than Fernandina.

Breslin's report, praising Darragh for showing 'common sense and common decency', casting doubt on Harrington's complaint about dysentery and Wilson's claim of a heart problem, would be endorsed utterly by Clan na Gael. Clan na Gael's committee to review the escape censured Brennan and Duggan, but trod warily in judging the former prisoners. After their years of imprisonment they had had no way of knowing the relative merits of what Brennan asserted as against what Breslin said.

When the New York pilot came on board to bring *Catalpa* into harbour, he expressed surprise that a whaler would enter that port of commercial and passenger traffic. But *Catalpa* moored in the small hours on 18 August, the last entry in the log at 1.30 on Saturday morning reading: 'Went to city wharf. Made her fast. So ends this day a pleasant voyage for J. T. Richardson.' The men who looked out incredulously at the great city had given their youth to the principles for which this grand republic and its large Irish community stood. Like earlier escapees, they had been long incarcerated and must now deal with the complex freedoms of urban America. Was Michael Harrington, just under fifty years of age, too old to make the transition from Western Australian felon to shining American? What about Darragh, at forty-three years? They had little time to contemplate their dilemma. For the last time in this account, the journalists and Irish leaders of New York had been on their eager way through the streets of Lower Manhattan to find boatmen and intercept the ship before it even dropped anchor.

Clan na Gael had initiated an escapees' fund, but everything was still totally unprepared when John Breslin, hurrying from the ship, walked into O'Donovan Rossa's hotel in Chatham Square, New York. Rossa himself was away in San Francisco. But his son and the former convict William Foley – Breslin's hulking, ailing ticket-of-leave contact in the Fremantle days – were there. Foley, very ill, was so overcome with emotion on hearing the news that *Catalpa* had put in that he fainted. John Devoy lay a-bed with flu in Dr Carroll's house in Philadelphia when he got a telegram from Dennis Rossa telling him the *Catalpa* was in New York. O'Reilly was also informed by telegram.

Early on the Saturday morning, the rescued men landed and were taken to Rossa's hotel, where the green flag was run up. The *Irish World* said that a stream of visitors poured in, 'and the *Catalpan Six* would have been quickly tired out but that the satisfaction of being free men and compatriots did not allow any other feeling to affect them'. Ironically, the *World* declared them all fine-looking – Hogan, Darragh, and Wilson in particular – and 'they all looked remarkably well'.

Devoy arrived during the day, still coughing. When he got a chance to take them into one of the vacant reception rooms to speak to them, he was startled to hear a barrage of complaints against Breslin. Devoy spoke frankly to them, telling them that Breslin was the undoubted leader of the enterprise and that Brennan had been misleading them. But in his *Recollections* he would remark that he 'never succeeded in removing the feeling of positive hatred, not to speak of ingratitude, which they entertained for Breslin'. Only here at the core of the triumph was there rancour. As the former prisoners delivered themselves of complaints, in the public rooms of the hotel and in the street and the square outside, unambiguously joyous people cheered continually. Other crowds rode out into the harbour to visit the whaler and cheer its captain, something which the prisoners had not done.

Anthony had altered greatly. When he left New Bedford he had weighed 160 pounds and his hair had been jet black. He now weighed 123 pounds and there was grey in his hair. Above all else, he wanted to get home and unload his whale oil.

Predictable celebrations continued throughout America. John Kenealy, back from a buying trip for his three-storey Los Angeles dry-goods business, the People's Store, called in to a mass Clan celebration organised by Talbot in San Francisco, then jubilantly took the new Southern Pacific railway home. The Robert Emmet Association of Troy, New York, fired a salute, and more artillery salutes were fired at Woonsocket and in dozens of other Irish communities. The Emmet Society of Quebec held a celebratory meeting. In New York City, Captain Anthony presented the flag of *Catalpa* to Clan na Gael, and the Philadelphia Clan held a great fête in Rising Sun Park to honour the whaling captain. Meanwhile the rescued men, in parties of two or three, were sent to speak at celebrations. Some $15,000 was collected around the country, and divided amongst them.

Catalpa docked in New Bedford on the following Thursday, and Anthony was surprised to see a huge crowd covering the New Bedford wharves, and to hear an artillery salute of seventy-one cannon, one gun for every state of the Union, and one for every county in Ireland, pounding out across the river. The following evening, a delighted John Boyle O'Reilly made a speech to acclaim Anthony at Liberty Hall, New Bedford. Anthony's self-sacrifice and fidelity as he 'took his life in his hands and beached his whaleboat on the penal colony defying its fearful law, defying the gallows and the chain gang, in order to keep faith with the men who had placed their trust in him – this is almost beyond belief in our selfish and commonplace time'. The legend of New Bedford men circling the earth to deliver liberty to those they did not know entered the port's mythology and receives today considerable emphasis in a town whose mills are closed and whose whaling past has become a resource.

A Clan committee for the dispersal of funds from the whaling enterprise began its work. They took the *Whaleman's Shipping List* as their guide, averaged out catches taken by other whalers, and oil prices. The *lay* of each crew-member of *Catalpa* was calculated and paid out in this manner. The ship was then valued at $6,000 and made over to Richardson, Anthony and Hathaway. Devoy learned later that the price realised by the sale of the ship fell short of this figure, but neither Richardson, Anthony nor Hathaway complained. Devoy was not himself particularly easy in conscience with the settlement that was made with Anthony, but the captain's total return, including the *Catalpa* committee's *ex gratia* payment of $1,000, came to just over $4,000. The total cost of the voyage would turn out to be nearly $26,000.

British efforts to retrieve the Fenians were futile on a number of grounds. The day after the escape, Matthew Skinner-Smith, Chief Superintendent of Police in Western Australia, had addressed a communication to the police chief in *Catalpa*'s home port, New Bedford:

Officer in charge of Police Department, New Bedford.

Sir, I beg to inform you that on the 17th inst. the imperial convicts named in the margin absconded from the convict settlement at Fremantle in this colony in the American whaling bark *Catalpa*, G. Anthony, Master . . . I attach a description of each of the absconders, and have to request that you will be good enough to furnish me with any particulars you may be able to gather concerning them.

The officer on to whose desk the letter was delivered happened to be Henry Hathaway.

Anthony took his management job in the mills. In 1886 he received a letter of appointment from President Cleveland's administration as a customs officer, and the text referred admiringly to his part in the *Catalpa* rescue. That admirable vessel *Catalpa* was gone by then. After three more whaling voyages, it was sold to Central American owners in 1884, and ended as a coal barge, ultimately condemned and burned on the beach at Belize, British Honduras.

Before the year of his rescue was out, Robert Cranston, the 36-year-old ex-prisoner who had begun the escape process that Easter Monday morning by telling warders tales of potato-digging and furniture-moving, would marry and become a staunch worker for the radical O'Donovan Rossa. Martin Hogan settled in Chicago and was active in Fenian affairs. The others led relatively obscure American lives. By 1896, only three of them were still alive to be honoured as guests at a huge Clan na Gael escape twentieth anniversary, held in Rising Sun Park in Philadelphia. But in 1920, forty-four years after rescue, when Eamon de Valera – president of the unofficial Irish Republic – toured the States, 82-year-old James Wilson, sufferer aboard *Catalpa* of a suspect heart, was in New York to meet him.

As for Breslin, he went apparently unmarried, and became a trustee of O'Donovan Rossa's famous Skirmishing Fund. A disapproving Devoy liked him, and employed him at his *Irish Nation Weekly*. But aside from Fremantle, the other great mission of Breslin's life was to do with the development of the submarine. In 1876 he met a former Clare schoolmaster, a Fenian named Stephen Holland, once dismissed from the Christian Brothers for frail health. He had robust plans, though, for a viable 'Fenian ram', a vessel which could travel underwater in British ports and sink warships. Holland developed petrol engines to drive his submarine on the surface, and electrical engines to drive it underwater. He offered his invention to the Clan, while Rossa was still part of the organisation, in the early 1870s. Some $60,000, first from the Clan and then from Rossa's Skirmishing Fund, was spent between 1876 and 1881 in building three separate submarines at the Delamater Ironworks on West 13th Street, New York, with Holland as inventor and engineer-in-chief, and Breslin as project manager. The first prototype, Holland I, was a failure – improper riveting let water in, creating clouds of chlorine from the batteries. The second failed because of weight distribution. The third vessel was stored, ready for deployment, in the yard of James Reynolds, *Catalpa* Jim, in New Haven. In the end, the American government encouraged Holland to launch a version of this third 'Holland' in 1897, armed with a 'dynamite gun' and a torpedo tube, at the Crescent Shipyard in New Jersey, and ordered six more. The submarine, launched the year after Breslin's death in 1896, went into service as the USS *Holland*, with a crew of seven. The *Holland*, decommissioned by the navy in 1910, would be exhibited in Madison Square Gardens to raise money for the victims of the 1916 Easter Rising.

Anthony lived until 1913, and in 1920 Eamon de Valera placed on his grave in New Bedford the colours of the proposed Irish Republic – the same colours the youth Tom Meagher brought back from Paris in 1848. As for Devoy, he survived as a force in the politics of Ireland and the diaspora, making many enemies. He jealously refused to countenance any other revolutionary Irish organisation in the United States than Clan na Gael, and into the 1880s it remained the focus of all Irish American effort. But a corrupt political boss from Chicago, Alexander Sullivan, split the Clan into two factions. Sullivan's group – the Triangle – was much feared and condemned in both the Irish and general community. Like factions in Northern Ireland in the twentieth century, the Triangle authorised its own independent string of dynamite attacks on England, in the course of one of which, in 1884, William Lomasney, former Fenian prisoner, blew himself up while attaching a bomb to a London bridge. These operations of terror were despised and condemned by O'Reilly in the *Pilot*, and by most of the Clan membership.

Prior to America's entry into the First World War, Devoy made approaches to the German ambassador in Washington, just as John Mitchel had once approached the Russian ambassador. The arms carried by rebels in the Easter Week uprising were purchased with the Clan's – that is, Devoy's – subscriptions. Wizened but authoritarian, Devoy would die aged eighty-six in Brooklyn in 1928. *The Times* of London paid him what he would have considered a high compliment: 'As well as the most dangerous enemy of this country Ireland has produced since Wolfe Tone, for sixty years he was unremittingly engaged in conspiracies.' His body was taken to Glasnevin, and the remains of the founders of the Irish Free State surround his own.

The last person associated with *Catalpa* to die was Mrs Annie Anthony, who at the time of her death in November 1935 was still telling New Bedford the story of how John Boyle O'Reilly had found her taking down the washing when he came to tell her the news of *Catalpa*'s success.

31
Republican Christ

The vulgar show of the pompous feast
Where the heaviest purse is the highest priest;
The organised charity, scrimped and iced,
In the name of a cautious, statistical Christ . . .
John Boyle O'Reilly, *In Bohemia*, 1885

If we look at O'Reilly in the fourteen years after *Catalpa*, we see a man who in a different sense from Mitchel was a lightning rod for every significant Irish and American question. One of the influences on him was a relatively obscure fellow, former Dartmoor inmate Michael Davitt, now, like O'Reilly, in his early thirties. Davitt's liberation was a much less spectacular but ultimately more significant liberation than the *Catalpa* escape. A former weapons purchaser for the Fenians, one-armed as a result of an accident suffered as a child in the Lancashire cotton mills, he was released from Dartmoor in late 1877. A complex young man, he had spent time in his cell contemplating the débâcle of Fenianism, and had returned to the principles of Young Ireland's late Fintan Lalor: land lay at the bottom of all Irish questions. The prime objective should be the destruction of Irish landlordism, 'first, as the system which was responsible for the poverty and periodic famines which have decimated Ireland'; and secondly, but only secondly, 'because landlordism was a garrison which barred the way to national independence'.

When he travelled to the United States in 1878 to visit his mother and raise funds, he had the idea for a land reform effort, a land league, and discussed it when he met with O'Reilly in Boston. It was his strategy to drag in the old Fenians, and to get support from Irish America he believed that he needed the backing of O'Donovan Rossa. O'Reilly warned him that Rossa could not serve as a figurehead for the non-violent land agitation which Davitt wanted.

When they had finished arguing in O'Reilly's copy-cluttered office, they discussed Tom Chambers and Charles McCarthy, who were still in British prisons. O'Reilly published in the *Pilot* Davitt's account of the mistreatment of Sergeant McCarthy and Corporal Chambers of the 61st Regiment of Foot. Chambers could receive and write no letters, and 'dozens of times these officers have stripped him naked in the presence of thieves, and subjected him to insults too disgusting to describe'. In 1877, when Chambers was moved to Woking prison, John Boyle O'Reilly had written to him, urging him to hope: 'When ten more years have passed we shall both look back with pleasure – yes, as sure as you live, old friend – at the dark shadow.' It happened that a few months after Davitt and O'Reilly discussed these half-forgotten men, both Chambers and McCarthy were set at liberty. Chambers visited his family and intended catching a steamer for the United States, but O'Reilly advised him on dealing with the kinds of displays which had attended the arrival of the *Catalpa* men. 'Tell me precisely how you are situated and what you propose doing. I beg of you to avoid the kindly-meant demonstrations in your honour, either at home or here, should you come here. It is frothy excitement; there is nothing of it left after a few weeks.'

O'Reilly's literary repute had been augmented, despite some subsequent poor reviews, by his novel of Western Australia, *Moondyne Joe*. It was first published in weekly instalments in the *Pilot* beginning on 30 November 1878, and the following year appeared in book form as *Moondyne – A Story from the Under-world*, 'dedicated to all who are in prison'. 'Moondyne' was said to be a manufactured name 'from a vague Australian native cry or sound'. The book had an agenda of penal reform to it, and urged the value of compassion towards prisoners at a time when the Pentonville System – segregation of prisoners from each other, monastic silence, and tedious labour – was still the fashion even in America.

The Moondyne Joe of the novel is a mythic convict who has absconded into the bush for an entire three years. One would need, said the narrator, to see and experience Western Australia in summer to know how harsh such a wilful absence from the settled regions would be. During his life at large, Moondyne encounters the so-called 'king of the Vasse', a sort of Aboriginal Prester John.

Meanwhile, a young man named Sheraton has gone home from Western Australia to find his beloved, Alice Walmsley, and has discovered to his horror that she is in prison serving a life sentence. Sheraton takes his plea for her release to Sir Joshua Hobb, administrator of Britain's penal system. 'A tall, gaunt man of fifty with an offensive hauteur . . . His face said plainly: I know all – these gentlemen know nothing . . . *I* am the convict system.' O'Reilly satirises Hobb as having no thought on what the dark stream of criminality arose from, or where it was going. He is merely 'a dried mudbank' to keep it within bounds a little while. In his efforts to release his beloved Alice, Sheraton enjoys a number of conversations with English gentlemen technocrats concerning various forms of penitentiary. One tells Sheraton, for example, that the Separate System has increased insanity from twelve to thirty-one per thousand prisoners, and is therefore being replaced by the Public Works System. A gobbledegook-prone disciple of Sir Joshua's speaks of the mask, an eyelet-holed skullcap, designed by Sir Joshua, which comes down over the face and is designed to promote a salutary shame in the prisoners. 'He was made a Knight Commander of the Bath for that wonderful invention.'

In the midst of Sheraton's efforts to achieve Alice's release, a penal informer named Wyville arrives in England with the King of the Vasse, the Aboriginal Neggra-jil. Wyville is the escapee Moondyne Joe under an assumed identity. He appals the bureaucrats by comparing society to the tree of evil in Bunyan's *Pilgrim's Progress*, whose roots 'are born of aristocracy. They spring from the rotting luxuries that fall from the tables of kings and earls and hereditary gentry.'

By a variety of stratagems, Sheraton and Wyville manage to arrange for Alice Walmsley's release from prison on condition she accompanies a Sister of Mercy on a convict ship for males and females to Western Australia. So a version of the *Hougoumont* begins its journey, but with scenes of such vividness that one feels they must represent the real ship. Arrived in Western Australia, which O'Reilly depicts with the same ambiguous love found in his poetry, Sheraton and Alice marry, and Wyville ascends to superintendence of Fremantle prison, confusing the bullies with well-managed compassion. Moondyne Joe, despised convict, has shown the colony how to be civilised.

The novel was attacked as anti-Christian, most noticeably by J. A. McMaster, editor of New York's *Freeman's Journal*, the same McMaster who had once fired on Thomas Francis Meagher. 'It is worse than pagan . . . it breathes out principles that are not un-Christian only, but anti-Christian . . . Away with law! . . . Yes, mankind is older than the birth of Jesus Christ! If Jesus Christ will become a republican, we will adopt him! If not—'

The critic in the *Atlantic Monthly* judged the book on purely literary grounds. O'Reilly's literary strength, he said, lay in the presentation of the dramatic, done 'with a sombre power which equals Blackmore and recalls Browning'. But 'his animated narrative is incessantly interrupted and marred by asides wonderful for weak sentiment and bad writing'. The *Boston Daily Advertiser*, however, compared *Moondyne* to Dumas's *Count of Monte Cristo*.

About the time *Moondyne* appeared, a set of new alliances were created on the Irish front. In 1878, John Devoy sent a cable from New York to the Fenian journalist Charles Kickham, the Paris-exiled president of the supreme council of the residual IRB. Devoy proposed a deal between the Clan na Gael in America and the new leader of the Irish Party in the

House of Commons, Charles Stewart Parnell. The Clan and old Fenians such as Kickham should offer to support Parnell if he stopped promoting Home Rule as a mere demand for Ireland to be a self-governing province within the United Kingdom, and substituted a more general declaration in favour of self-government. Parnell should also agree to pursue Davitt's agenda: agitation on peasant ownership. Devoy hoped for a pact between himself, the celibate New Yorker, the deaf and exiled Fenian Kickham, the one-armed land reformer Davitt, and the benign but remote sphinx of a Wicklow landlord, Parnell.

This attempt at Irish unity became known as the New Departure, and the text of Devoy's offer was published prematurely in the *New York Herald* on 26 October 1878, before Davitt had even heard of it. 'It was a most imprudent proceeding,' he thought, 'amounting as it did to an open proposal through the public press, for an alliance between men avowedly revolutionist and the leaders of the constitutional party in the British House of Commons.' There was now a crucial meeting between Devoy, O'Reilly and his friend Dr Joyce at Joyce's home in Boston, at which Joyce and O'Reilly managed to persuade Devoy to forget the matter of self-government, and concentrate on the overthrow of landlordism. On the cable at the *Pilot* office in Franklin Street, O'Reilly was receiving reports that, particularly in the west, the Irish were suffering now perhaps more than at any other time since the Famine. Rain and cold weather had diminished the grain crop, produced a shortage of food for cattle and pigs, and encouraged again that old black rot of potatoes which the aged had not seen since the catastrophe of thirty years past. In Davitt's Mayo, where a cholera epidemic struck the chickens, and the blight the potatoes, the twin terrors of famine and eviction hung over people, some of whom in resisting eviction fought armed police with stones. The weather had been so torrential as to prevent the drying of turf to keep the families of the west warm. But now these despised would have a cause, O'Reilly argued, the land reform and peasant proprietary which were much closer to their hearts than was the dream of republicanism. The propaganda for the new land movement was carried on in Boston by the *Pilot* and in New York by Patrick Ford's *Irish World*. Of the two, the *Pilot* was perhaps more welcome ideologically to Davitt and to Parnell, for Davitt had already spoken to Ford, the *World*'s editor, about the distractions of explosives, their irrelevance to the present struggle. 'I believe I can lay claim to having induced Mr Ford to abandon for good his propaganda of dynamite,' Davitt assured O'Reilly.

In January 1879, Devoy and Davitt went to Paris to meet Kickham, but found he had little tolerance for a policy of co-operation with members of the House of Commons like Parnell. He conceded, though, that as individuals Fenians could support land-reform meetings. In fact, as individuals, Fenians flocked to these meetings. And so, after hesitation, did parliamentarians.

The Irish Land War, an extraordinary and largely moral struggle, began with a rally at Irishtown in County Mayo on 20 April 1879. It produced a spate of Sunday rallies which for popular enthusiasm matched the monster meetings of O'Connell. Hopeful tenants, men and women both, dressed in their best and marched in military formation behind bands and horsemen bearing pikes. They cheered speakers who condemned landlordism, often in old-fashioned militant imagery of which Mitchel and Meagher would not have been ashamed. They listened as balladeers mounted the platform to turn their grievances into rhyme. Parnell accepted Davitt's invitation to attend in June a meeting of tenant farmers at Westport, in County Mayo, where Fenians, ex-Fenians, land agitators and politicians were all on the platform, and it was this meeting which helped create a formal structure, the Land League of Mayo, and the Irish National Land League, whose American disciple and servant O'Reilly became.

O'Reilly compared the movement in Ireland to 'that wild anti-slavery agitation . . . the land of Ireland is not held by so good or just a tenure as the slave holders possessed'. He wanted not revolution but British legislation to compel 'absentee owners of large estates in Ireland to sell the land to the farmers who till the soil and who pay its produce in rents that are spent out of the country'. Parnell himself came to Boston to argue the cause in 1880. He was not quite in the mould of Irish heroes. He lacked the flamboyance of O'Connell, was solemn, or at least a little sombre. But he was eagerly greeted. Shortages of food in Ireland turned the focus of his journey through America away from land reform and into famine fund-raising. John Boyle O'Reilly, mere son of a national schoolmaster, served as one of Parnell's reliable guides. He advised Parnell not to serve on a relief committee put in place by the *New York Herald*, for that journal, which had until now been sympathetic to Irish issues, considered the Land League a manifestation of socialism. The Irish did not trust the *Herald* fund and would not subscribe to it. Wendell Phillips applauded O'Reilly's counsel to Parnell on the *Herald*. 'You may congratulate yourself on the advice you gave him.'

O'Reilly urged his old friend Devoy to use the Clan and its funds not for armed uprising but to support the Land League. To help a licit, non-violent struggle, said O'Reilly, would be good for the Clan's repute amongst those Irish Americans who now despised failed Fenianism, but, because of their childhoods in the Irish countryside, were fierce against landlordism. O'Reilly was ecstatic when his potent Boston friend Patrick Collins, soon bound for Congress, ultimately to be mayor of Boston, was in 1880 elected President of the Irish Land League of America. Collins had captured the American branch of the Land League for the pragmatists, whom Davitt and Charles Stewart Parnell felt most at home with.

We do not know to what extent O'Reilly talked of these things with his wife, Mary – she, not a political creature, was all the more understandably disengaged from politics, being pregnant with their fourth child. His favourite and most vulnerable daughter, Blanid, would be born in the summer of highest Irish hopes, 1880.

Throughout the decade, between indulging Blanid, O'Reilly agitated from platforms around the country for the Land League. 'Throw down the gage of battle to landlordism, as the source of Irish poverty, eviction, and immigration, and a mighty power will be enlisted in the fight against English rule.' He was hurt to be accused of charging fees to make speeches. Committees who wanted him to speak for nothing said, 'Oh, it will do the *Pilot* good if you come.' 'This is bosh,' commented the *Pilot* in 1881. 'The *Pilot* will be better served by constant attention. O'Reilly has literally raised tens of thousands of dollars for the Irish Fund this winter; and has sacrificed more since October in literary reputation and money, giving up his work, than he could earn by lecturing in seven years.'

Like Mitchel, he believed he needed a retreat. In 1879, the O'Reillys had bought a house in Hull, across Boston Harbor. It was in large part seventeenth-century, and ultimately he renovated it. (The building is now the Hull Public Library.) From this haven, he would commute by ferry to the *Pilot* office. His unsettled existence, his concern for the health of his wife and baby Blanid, worsened his chronic and ultimately fatal insomnia.

Influenced by his group of progressives and above all by the ageing giant Wendell Phillips, O'Reilly was by 1880 writing even in the *Pilot* of the misuse of Christianity for the subjection of the poor. His laments on the subject have a raw, sad authority, a taste of both Whitman and Marx.

Oh Christ! And Oh Christ! In thy name the law!
In thy mouth the mandate! In thy loving hand the whip!
They have taken thee down from thy cross and sent thee to scourge the people;
They have shod thy feet with spikes and jointed thy dead knees with iron,
And pushed thee, hiding behind, to trample the poor dumb faces.

There is no record of what the Archbishop of Boston thought of Christ's iron-spiked knees as part of the list of proletariat woes.

Soon the 37-year-old editor had the news, through the Irish census of 1881, that all the plans, all the hopes, captures, imprisonment, destroyed loves, violated secrets, blunted loyalties and ruined youths arising from

Irish nationalist protests, had not halted ruin. The population of Ireland had declined a further 21 per cent in the past thirty years and was now just over five million. The rest of Europe boomed; Ireland withered. Migration, as Davitt was only too happy to point out, was still the Irish way. Sligo, Mayo, Clare, Galway, Roscommon – counties where land tenure and life were most insecure – were on their way down to a third of their 1841 numbers. O'Reilly absorbed the figures with horror.

But Gladstone's Land Act was working to allay some of the defiance of Irish tenants. The act gave legal status throughout Ireland to the Ulster custom by which farmers would be paid for improvements they had made upon the land. It enabled land purchase – three quarters of the purchase price could be advanced by a land commission, to be repaid over thirty-five years at 5 per cent. But fewer than 1,000 tenants would be rich enough to buy land under this system, and the most important reform for the mass of tenants was the right to take their rents for review to a new Land Court. The Land Court was much used by farmers, who generally ended up with a reduction in rent of up to a quarter. What this first Land Act had not done, however, was give comfort to those who were already in arrears for rent, who had already been evicted, or who were either starving or under the threat of starvation. It was estimated that 280,000 Irish families, representing 1,500,000 or more people, plus those already evicted, were not helped.

For these people, nothing was altered. But the Land League had given them coherent stratagems, including the stratagem of the boycott. The method had first been proposed by Parnell at a speech in Ennis in County Clare in 1880. In some versions of the speech the first four instances of the word 'show' are rendered as 'shun'. 'When a man takes a farm from which another has been evicted, you must show him on the roadside when you meet him, you must show him in the streets of the town, you must show him at the shop-counter, you must show him at the fair and at the market-place and even in the house of worship, by leaving him severely alone, by putting him into a sort of moral Coventry, by isolating him from the rest of his kind, as if he were a leper of old, you must show him your detestation . . . if the population of a county in Ireland carry out this doctrine . . . there will be no man so full of avarice, so lost to shame, as to dare the public opinion of all right-thinking men within the county.' The first victim of this device was Captain Charles Cunningham Boycott, a land agent at Lough Mask in Mayo. Local people refused to deal with him or take his crop in. A work force of fifty Orangemen had to be escorted by 1,000 troops every day to and from Lough Mask. As a result of the Boycott affair in the early 1880s, landlords had now to deal with an Irish tenant class who would no longer speak to them, servants who would not fill their glasses, shopkeepers who turned their shoulders or closed their doors. There were few communities where instances of this moral revolt were not seen. Ordinary people had discovered their power.

One of the surprising opponents of the Land League was Pat Smyth. Before his death in 1884 he denounced the Land Leaguers as the League of Hell. His problem with it may have arisen from the trouble he had in the management of a small estate he had inherited. But the popular force of the League seemed gloriously unstoppable. In October 1881, Parnell attended a rally in Wexford, entering into the city through triumphal arches, and delivered an Irish nationalist speech full of traditional imagery. 'The Irishman who thinks he can now throw away his arms just as Grattan disbanded the volunteers in 1783, will find to his sorrow and destruction when too late that he has placed himself in the power of the cruel and perfidious English enemy.' Asked at supper afterwards in a hotel in Wexford whether he expected to be arrested for such a speech, he said, echoing O'Connell long before, that if the government suppressed the Land League, 'the people will be driven back upon secret organisations as in former times'.

The day after the Wexford meeting, Gladstone read the speech and authorised Parnell's arrest. In short order, across the Atlantic, O'Reilly published the details of how Superintendent Mallon arrested Parnell at dawn at Morrison's Hotel in Dublin. He was taken to Kilmainham gaol. Davitt, who was touring England, was also arrested and found himself once more in the dreary prison at Portland. 'England may imprison every public representative in Ireland,' said an outraged O'Reilly. 'She may break up every public meeting of the Land League. Very well. Then she drives the people to secret organisations – she plays into the hands of the revolutionists.' O'Reilly could not know that from within Kilmainham prison, Parnell was secretly sending mail to his beloved, Kitty O'Shea, still the legal wife of Captain O'Shea. Parnell's fellow prisoners included John Dillon, son of John Blake Dillon, Young Irelander political refugee to New York, and William O'Brien, a veteran Cork Fenian. In his cell on the sunny side of Kilmainham, amongst furniture provided by the Ladies' Land League, Parnell and his fellows, amidst news of authorities striking back and evictions progressing, issued a call for a general strike against rents, a 'No Rent Manifesto'. 'Every tenant farmer in Ireland is today the standard-bearer of the flag unfurled at Irishtown and can bear it to glorious victory . . . PAY NO RENT UNDER ANY PRETEXT. STAND PASSIVELY, FIRMLY, FEARLESSLY BY while the armies of England may be engaged in their hopeless struggle against a spirit which their weapons cannot touch.'

The manifesto was signed by Charles Stewart Parnell; Parnell's friend Andrew Kettle; Michael Davitt, Honorary Secretary, Portland gaol;

Thomas Sexton, Head Organiser, Kilmainham gaol; and Patrick Egan, Treasurer of the IRB, Paris. But Parnell was believed to have put his name to the document reluctantly. And Michael Davitt, in Portland prison in England, had his name attached without his permission, and later denounced it. On 20 October, the government fulfilled Parnell's *and* O'Reilly's fears, and answered the manifesto by outlawing the Land League itself.

The No Rent Manifesto was not obeyed by most tenants anyhow, in part because the 1881 Land Act had improved life so greatly for so many middling tenant farmers. Negotiations began secretly between Gladstone and the jailed Parnell to deal with the problems the No Rent Manifesto had raised. The two intermediaries on Parnell's side were his lieutenant Captain Willy O'Shea, formerly of the 18th Hussars and now Home Rule MP for County Clare, and his wife, Katherine O'Shea, who was carrying Parnell's child. An understanding was reached between Parnell and Gladstone. In return for a law to protect tenants in arrears of rent, and a repeal of the Coercion Act under which Parnell and others had been arrested, Parnell would call off land agitation and co-operate in framing a new Land Act.

There had been cheers in the House of Commons in May 1882 when Gladstone announced the name of the new Irish secretary – Lord Frederick Cavendish, his own nephew by marriage. Within a week of Cavendish's appointment, he and the Permanent Under-Secretary of Ireland, while strolling over Phoenix Park's extensive greensward, were hacked to death by 12-inch surgical knives plied by members of the group known as the Invincibles, whose leader was that old Confederate raider, John McCafferty. Hearing of the immolation of Cavendish, Parnell was so devastated that he thought of giving up politics. It was doubly depressing to hear that the surgical knives had been smuggled from London into Dublin by the wife of the secretary of the Invincibles, Frank Byrne, who had once been president of the Land League.

In Boston, Patrick A. Collins and John Boyle O'Reilly called a public meeting of outrage on the Phoenix Park murders, and sent a cablegram to Parnell. 'A reward of $5,000 is hereby offered by the Irishmen of Boston for the apprehension of the murderers, or any of them, of Lord Cavendish and Mr Burke, on Saturday, May 6th.' At first, John Boyle O'Reilly believed that the killings had been committed by government stooges. It took him some time to realise that the murders had not been a ploy of Dublin Castle.

There was at that time another challenge to the demands Ireland made on O'Reilly. Between Speranza's son, Oscar Wilde, and the solid Boston literary citizen John Boyle O'Reilly lay a gulf both as writers and as human beings. But the 27-year-old literary star and the ten years older O'Reilly were bound together by common nationality and by varying degrees of awe for Speranza, 'poetess' of the *Nation*. Although Lady Wilde had by now, like O'Reilly, disassociated herself from the Fenians, her place in the temple of the Young Ireland movement assured that any son of hers fetching up on a foreign shore came under the patronage and protection of passionate expatriates.

A measure of protection was necessary from the day Wilde's steamer, the *Arizona*, docked in New York harbour early in 1882. Here was a very different Irishman from the wary, vociferous steerage Irish who had filled the city's air with fiddle music, songs of nostalgia and defiance, snatches of Gaelic, impenetrable accents, and tubercular breath. As the author of a middling book of verse and an unsuccessful play entitled *Vera*, young, large, florid Oscar was renowned chiefly for his theory of aesthetics and his personal style.

It was on landing that he was said to have proclaimed to customs: 'I have nothing to declare except my genius.' He was probably the only Irishman landing in New York to make such a claim, standing as he was where others had declared chiefly their rude unworldliness, their economic or political desperation. In that sense, Oscar's arrival was the apogee of all Irish arrivals. Speranza's son, unmarked by Ireland's dismal statistics, had many letters of introduction, and got off to a social whirl in New York. His first lecture in that city was a sell-out. Wilde came on stage ceremonially, carrying his speech manuscript in a Moroccan leather case which he opened with a flourish. He was wearing knee breeches and silk stockings, the costume of Apollo Lodge, the Freemasons' lodge at Oxford University. With a cavalier's cloak over the shoulder, he was again setting himself up to be abominated by the sissy-hating subscribers to the Yankee ethic, and constituted a tough test for the loyalty of hard-handed American Irishdom. He ended his lecture with praise for the lily and the sunflower, 'in England the most perfect models of design, the most naturally adapted for decorative art'. In Camden, New Jersey, visiting Walt Whitman in his squalid rooms, he announced that Speranza began reading Whitman to him in childhood. Henry James, who met him in Washington, wrote, ' "Osscar" Wilde is a fatuous fool, tenth-rate cad.' He declared him 'an unclean beast'. Old friends even attacked him from England. 'It is always Judas who writes the biography,' said Oscar.

Then it came time to visit John Boyle O'Reilly in Boston, where Wilde saw Whitman's signature immediately above his own in the O'Reilly autograph book, and wrote beside it, 'The spirit who living blamelessly but dared to kiss the smitten mouth of his own century.' In Boston, and in considerable part under O'Reilly's aegis, Wilde visited Henry Longfellow, had lunch with Wendell Phillips, with Oliver Wendell Holmes, and with Julia Ward Howe, author of 'The Battle Hymn of the Republic'. Such Boston Brahmans were notches in his belt, but he was safest in the Irish fraternity of the playwright Dion Boucicault, and of Boucicault's friend John Boyle O'Reilly. Both these men had such standing in Boston that they were able to temper the hostility of editors towards the apostle of the lily and the sunflower. It worked to an extent with the *Globe*, but not so well with Higginson of the *Atlantic Monthly*. Higginson, who had commanded a coloured regiment in the Civil War, in the one article attacked Walt Whitman for being a Civil War *poseur* and Oscar for writing prurient poems.

Wilde's task with O'Reilly was to arrange the publication of his mother's poetry by the *Pilot*. 'I think my mother's work should make a great success here, it is so unlike the work of her degenerate artist son,' he wrote to O'Reilly. With unconscious irony, O'Reilly took him to see *Oedipus Tyrannus* at the Globe Theatre, and may have been the one to tip him off to the fact that at his lecture in the Boston Music-Hall on 31 January, sixty Harvard students intended to dress like him and fill the front seats. Oscar countered by wearing a normal dinner suit. The undergraduates were reduced to applauding wildly every time he drank a sip of water.

Not that Boucicault and O'Reilly were Oscar's only supporters in town. The poet Joaquin Miller was also something of a consoler and protector as the barbarians weighed in. The disadvantage of Oscar's purely Irish approval at such times was that he knew it was in part approval for his mother. In St Paul, Minnesota, Oscar heard himself praised by a priest as the son 'of one of Ireland's noblest daughters – of a daughter who in the troublous times of 1848 by the works of her pen and her noble example did much to keep the fire of patriotism burning brightly'. How Oscar must have flinched at such effulgence! In San Francisco, knowing his audience, he wisely spoke on 'The Irish Poets of 1848'. He used the term 'poet' to include most revolutionaries. He could remember some of them coming to his house – Smith O'Brien, John Mitchel, James Clarence Mangan, Charles Gavin Duffy. He called Thomas Davis the greatest of them. 'Of the quality of Speranza's poems I perhaps should not speak – for criticism is disarmed before love – but I am content to abide by the verdict of the nation.'

O'Reilly was surely pleased to see this strange young Irishman survive America – not all strange young Irishmen did. Ahead of young Wilde lay both his great works – *The Picture of Dorian Gray*, *The Importance of*

Being Earnest, *Lady Windermere's Fan* – and the disgrace which would evince from him the harrowing *De Profundis*.

From treacherous Irish and perverse American politics, O'Reilly found in his muscular late thirties an essentially American solace – canoeing in the wilderness. He made his first long canoe journey in July 1882, down the Merrimac River. The following year, on the Connecticut River, O'Reilly had a collision with a timber raft and capsized. He took on the Delaware, the Susquehanna in Virginia, and, six years after his first excursion, the immensity of the Dismal Swamp. His companion was a Boston figure named Ned Moseley, with whom he frequently took afternoon canoe excursions on Boston Harbor.

There was a particular pathos in O'Reilly's excitement on his last large excursion to the Dismal Swamp in the autumn of 1888. 'We still need good whiskey for snakes etc,' he wrote to Ned Moseley from Virginia. 'I shall bring some rare stuff, also rum. I think too it would be well if we had long rubber boots for the swamp grass.' In canoeing he found a respite from the regimen the demons of his spirit demanded of him. In his last year of life, he enthusiastically published a book on athleticism, *Athletics and Manly Sport*, in which canoeing, text by O'Reilly, photographs by Moseley, had a large place. He remained passionate about bare-knuckle prize fighting, and was 'one of the guiding spirits' of the Cribb Club of Boston, named after the English boxer Tom Cribb. But he was also an excellent fencer – for a season he coached the students at Harvard – and was sponsor for an annual O'Reilly Hurling Cup. To these sporting events, he often took his sportive brother-in-law, Mary's brother John Murphy, book-keeper of the *Pilot*.

The athlete-poet! For in 1882, in the midst of all the Land League agitation and support for Parnell, O'Reilly's next volume of verse – *Statues in the Block* – emerged. The reviewer in the *Atlantic Monthly* believed that some of the lines gained by their formlessness:

Insects and vermin, ye, the starving and dangerous myriads,
List to the murmur that grows and growls! Come from your mines and mills,
Pale-faced girls and women with ragged and hard-eyed children,
Pour from your dens of toil and filth, out to the air of heaven . . .

The reviewer said that in other passages, however, O'Reilly 'does not convey through his irregular lines the sense of a long billow-like rhythm which Whitman manages to get into his best fragments'. His muse was serviceable for lyric rhymes and the felicities of the civic verse, but was capable too of a furious eloquence not utterly dissimilar to that of

Whitman. The *New York Herald* of 3 April 1881 praised this very Whitman-ish quality. 'Petticoated Boston will, no doubt, set itself to "frown down" this wildness.'

In between verses and editorials, with a group of friends from the Papyrus Club O'Reilly wrote as a literary lark a fantastical serial which was later published as a bestselling book, *The King's Men: A Tale of Tomorrow*. The novel dealt with a period when America has cut down the wall of protection which surrounds England, and has thus made Britain such a poor country that King Albert of England emigrates to the United States. As the American experience of Boyle O'Reilly and the other authors showed, once monarchy was cut down demagoguery was the great peril. A complicated plot deals, inevitably, at least in the parts of the book for which O'Reilly was responsible, with Dartmoor prison. O'Reilly wrote so vividly of a Dartmoor evening that it is clear the salient aspects of his penal experience had never left him.

The gangs all over the farm formed into little squads and marched towards the prison . . . the warders drawing after them the light iron bridges of the canals which were locked on one side every night. By this means *The Farm*, which was intercepted by a score of the wide and deep trenches, was impassable; and as it hemmed in one side of the hill on which the prison stood, with a guard tower on either end, it was a greater safeguard even than the walls of the prison.

When *In Bohemia* was published in the fall of 1886, he was criticised as earlier for defects of grace and finish. Bohemia was cast as an ideal republic: 'I'd rather fail in Bohemia than win in another land'. Oliver Wendell Holmes wrote generously that he had 'recognised a genuine fire of inspiration in your verse . . . if they have faults which have escaped my too hasty reading, that is a small matter when a poem has life in it'. But if O'Reilly strove to be Whitman, his tragedy probably was that he strove also to be Whittier or Longfellow. After his house at Hull was damaged by an Atlantic storm in November 1888, he turned the tempest to good account in a narrative poem about heroic fishermen going out to rescue the passengers of three vessels which had foundered off the coast.

It was in that insomniac decade that he further established himself as a major American occasional poet. In 1882, at the reunion of the Grand Army of the Potomac in Detroit, he read a poem of which Grant said, 'That is the grandest poem I have ever heard.' John Greenleaf Whittier and Oliver Wendell Holmes had also written letters of appreciation.

The verse reads nicely enough now:

Here towns unguarded lie, for here alone
Nor caste, nor kin, nor privilege is known.
For home our farmer plows, our miner delves,
A land of toilers, toiling for themselves;
A land of cities, which no fortress shields,
Whose open streets reach out to fertile fields . . .

He praised the Union victory for abstaining from punishing the South.

No brutal show abased thine honoured State:
Grant turned from Richmond at the very gate!

Similarly, when Wendell Phillips, his Bostonian prophet, died in a cold November in 1885, O'Reilly – stricken and orphaned – stayed up late in the *Pilot* office writing a verse obituary.

For his life was a ceaseless protest, and his voice was a prophet's cry
To be true to the Truth and faithful, though the worlds were arrayed for the Lie.

Meanwhile, O'Reilly published some early verse of that very different poet, Oscar Wilde, who wrote to him, 'I esteem it a great honour that the first American paper I appeared in should be your admirable *Pilot*.' P. W. Rolleston, Douglas Hyde, founder of the Gaelic League, Lady Wilde, alias Speranza, Catherine Tynan and William Butler Yeats were contributors to the *Pilot* and were published by its esteemed editor.

The grail of Home Rule was by the early 1880s so beloved by the Irish diaspora that from Nevada to Western Australia mines were named to honour the idea, and a discharged political felon of an earlier generation than O'Reilly's was about to make a massive sacrifice for it.

No one seemed safer from fatal Irish enthusiasms than the former Young Irelander Kevin Izod O'Doherty of Brisbane, an admired, handsome paterfamilias and accomplished colonial surgeon, twelve or thirteen thousand miles removed from the seat of Home Rule agitation. O'Doherty's zeal seemed up to this point to have been emphatically Australian in scope. Returning to the Queensland Parliament in 1877 as a legislative councillor, a member of the state upper house, O'Doherty was able to push through this conservative forum a bill to give the Central Board of Health authority over quarantine, vaccination, drainage, sanitation and food purity. It is hard to imagine anyone opposing such reforms, but Queensland would always be an anarchically individualist state, and many of his fellow councillors opposed the measures as intrusive. These battles of his early fifties in the state legislature were fought without the comfort of his spouse, Eva. She was proudly conveying their two oldest sons, William and Edward, across the world; William, the eldest, was to study dentistry in Philadelphia, and Edward to study medicine at the Royal College of Surgeons, Dublin. The *San Francisco Monitor* announced the arrival of 'Eva of the *Nation*', and her sons looked at her with amazed delight to find their 47-year-old mother so famous so far from Brisbane! She was able to place a manuscript of her poems with a San Francisco company. The proofs of the book were ready when she returned via San Francisco to take ship for Queensland later that year, and the verses were dedicated to 'The Felons John Mitchel and John Martin', the former of whom was closer to her in politics than was her pragmatic husband. Most of the poems were of Irish revolution, but one was a climatically enthusiastic but socially cool verse named 'Queensland'.

But ah! Upon the bright expanse,
The glory of a clime Elysian,
'Tis but a cold and soulless glance
That meets the gazer's vision.

Despite Eva's ambiguity, O'Doherty now seemed entrenched for life. A premier of Queensland, Arthur Macallister, consulted O'Doherty over epileptic convulsions which he suffered. O'Doherty had also been asked to produce a special report on the Peel Island Quarantine Station, where conditions were said to be primitive. The newly arriving governor of Queensland, Sir Arthur Kennedy, was himself quarantined at Dr O'Doherty's word aboard the smallpox-stricken steamer *Brisbane*. O'Doherty exempted His Excellency's daughter and her companion from compulsory chest inspections, inspecting their hands and wrists instead.

But half the landscape of Saint Kevin's mind was still Irish. When the news of the 1879 famine in Ireland reached Queensland, O'Doherty, with John Flood, the pardoned Fenian who had settled on the gold-fields of Gympie, north of Brisbane, convened a meeting. They were hugely successful, for contribution to famine relief was not seen as political. A relief fund of £12,000 was raised, more per capita – said the *Brisbane Courier* – than other Australian states.

Yet the *Courier* ran frequent, bitter attacks on Parnell and Home Rule. O'Doherty was chairman of the Irish Land League in Brisbane, to the disapproval of the *Brisbane Courier*, who reminded him that if Parnell and his followers 'need sympathy at present, then sympathy is given to shooting landlords and bailiffs, maiming cattle, burning hayricks, poisoning coverts and establishing both in town and country the worst despotism on earth – the despotism of the mob'. When the Redmond brothers, John and William, principal lieutenants of Parnell, visited Queensland in 1883, O'Doherty innocently took them to the camp of the Queensland Volunteer Forces, which raised eyes in the officers' mess. The Redmonds suggested an Irish national convention in Melbourne, and O'Doherty attended, even though the *Brisbane Courier* repudiated it as 'a disloyal assemblage aimed against our Queen and country'.

By now the O'Doherty family had much at stake. They lived in a splendid villa named 'Frascati', after the area of Blackrock, Dublin, where Kevin's mother had lived. The lower floor of Frascati supplied Kevin and Edward with consulting rooms, and a third room was used by William for his dental practice. In 1885, O'Doherty thought himself so well established at Frascati that he decided to travel to Ireland to see the elections to be held later that year. He had been in Australia a quarter of a century, and believed himself safe from disapproval. His son Edward would run the medical practice.

At a meeting O'Doherty had with Parnell in London, the proposition of a safe Irish seat was discussed. Prodded by Michael Davitt, the Dublin corporation gave O'Doherty the freedom of the City of Dublin, and honoured him at a banquet attended by Parnell. The *Brisbane Courier* mocked him accordingly: 'Doctor O'Doherty is presently "starring it" in the Emerald Isle, or the Isle of the Saints or the "most distressful country" as it is variously known . . . all things considered, he is reaping not unpleasant remarks for the little indiscretions of his hot youth.' And at the Land League Convention in Dublin on 8 October he was selected as a candidate for North Meath. Not being required to campaign, being sure of election on his name alone, he made as brief a visit as he could back to Australia, as surgeon aboard the *Duke of Westminster*. On arrival in Australia he heard the British election results. On a new form of household electoral right in use for the first time, he had been elected to the House of Commons.

Though he was guest of honour at various functions in Brisbane, Sydney and Melbourne over the summer of 1885–6, they were largely Irish, pro-Home Rule dinners. The Brisbane banquet, attended by 300 worthies, was boycotted – to use that word which had now spread throughout the empire – by the mass of Queensland parliamentarians. There had been recent dynamitings, financed by the Skirmishing Fund and carried out by the Chicago Triangle, at the London Metropolitan Railway station near Tottenham Court Road, the Tower of London and the Houses of Parliament. All of these had been victimless, but they outraged colonial opinion. O'Doherty had to tell a public meeting that 'he had an interview with Mr Parnell shortly after arriving in Dublin, and he could assure his hearers that there was no feeling stronger in Mr Parnell's mind than his horror of dynamite and outrages of every kind'.

He returned to England by steamer and was presented to the Speaker of the House of Commons in the spring of 1886. The Irish were a bloc of eighty-six members in the House, and held the balance of power which had returned Gladstone and caused him to promise Home Rule. A Home Rule bill was being drafted when O'Doherty took his seat, and in his first speech at its second reading O'Doherty told the House, 'I have an exceptional claim to speak in this debate from the fact that I have travelled all the way from the other end of the world – from the colony of Queensland . . . The whole of the Australian colonies received this benefit of Home Rule in its fullest extent . . . In no single case of these six colonies has there been the slightest difficulty.' Two factions of the Liberals voted against the bill, and the cause was lost in a crucial late-night vote on 8 June 1886, 343 votes to 311. This defeat saw Gladstone lose office. There would in the end be three Home Rule bills, including the one for which O'Doherty had sacrificed so much. The second, in 1893, would also be defeated and the third, in 1912, would go down before the combined vote of Conservatives and Ulster Loyalists – all with dire results not fully resolved to this day.

O'Doherty declined to stand in the ensuing election, citing, 'only imperative private reasons'. According to a Queensland journalist, O'Doherty was secretly repelled by Parnell's cold character and said so to a number of his best Brisbane friends. 'He was cold, autocratic, intolerant, and without a scrap of human sentiment.' But whatever he thought of Parnell, O'Doherty had financial difficulties as well. His medical practice had suffered – to what extent due to his absence, and to what extent colonial primness, is hard to say. He had trouble with the mortgage on Frascati. His daughter Gertrude would later say, and Eva would tell a correspondent, that 'it was for financial reasons, not from any other cause, that he was obliged to resign and return to Australia'. The relentless criticism of the *Courier* and the *Brisbane Telegraph* had eroded the value of his practice. Edward had lost patients for the same reason. O'Doherty went for a time to Sydney to work as a member of the honorary staff at St Vincent's Hospital. Here he was fêted by the Irish community, who began collecting money in appreciation of his services to Ireland and in tacit acknowledgement of his present troubles.

In 1887, still a Brisbane pariah, he was appointed Government Medical Officer at a place called Croydon in North Queensland where gold had been discovered. It was no post for an eminent surgeon, and he did not choose to take Eva, since Croydon lay in equatorial country, beyond the Tropic of Capricorn, and in dry, scrubby terrain inland from the Gulf of

Carpenteria. It was a sad posting for a man approaching his sixty-fourth birthday, but he hoped – as he had in the 1850s when he and Pat Smyth had gone to the Victorian gold-field – that one spare-time bonanza would fix everything. He was on a gold-field where death from haphazard sanitation, mine disasters and lung disease was so high that by 1889 the life-insurance companies refused to issue policies there. The miners were hardy and were loath to call for medical attention until their children were already failing, or their wives already perishing of milk fever or other complications of childbirth. One man accused him of having been drunk while attending a patient, and, although there was no evidence of the fact, it could not be remarkable that a man of such qualifications on a remote gold-field would have soothed himself with liquor.

Returned to Brisbane and Eva none the wealthier in 1889, he had to sell Frascati, and his sons found consulting rooms elsewhere. Dr Edward O'Doherty was forced to declare bankruptcy as a world recession deepened and the O'Dohertys remained under a loyalist cloud. Saint Kevin was reduced to advertising medical advice at 5 shillings a consultation, and medicine and consultation at 7 shillings and 6 pence. It was harrowing for brave Eva to see her husband reduced to such medical dodges. But the government of Queensland itself came to his aid in the end by giving him three part-time jobs – secretaryship of the Board of Health, superintendency of the quarantine station, and attending surgeon at the Diamantina Orphanage. The Medical Society honoured him and his now prospering rival, Dr Bell, with honorary memberships. And he remained passionate on public health, in 1893 circularising all political candidates urging the establishment of a colonial Department of Health, compulsory reporting of infectious diseases, and the inspection of abattoirs and dairies.

But O'Doherty and his family never recovered from Parnell and Home Rule.

O'Reilly was disappointed with the contents of that first modest Home Rule Bill of 1886, the one that was defeated and helped destroy Saint Kevin. It had proposed to limit Irish control of education, ports and lighthouses, and though the Irish government would control the Metropolitan Police, the Royal Irish Constabulary would be still administered from Westminster. Above all, its legislation could be vetoed by the Lord Lieutenant, who was also to be the Chief Executive. Parnell accepted the draft bill as a first bid. But O'Reilly told Boston, and indeed America, that the proposed bill 'says life and it enacts Death . . . it grants the parliament of the people and empowers a chamber of press and landlords to veto their proceedings'.

For his stance, O'Reilly was much attacked by various Irish members, including Justin McCarthy, whom he had recently warmly welcomed to

Boston. But though in Ireland the questions were independence and land, in America the questions were to do with labour and the industrial misery of the Atlantic north-east. The blossoming of American capital since the Civil War, O'Reilly believed, was the greatest peril to the society he lived in. But even in America he saw Land League principles as a model. He wrote with increasing regularity on profit-sharing by employees, and the establishment of boards of arbitration to determine where profit ended and wage fairness began. If such arbitration processes could work for tenant farmers in Ireland, why could they not operate for American labourers? Early in his *Pilot* career, he had argued that the best response for workmen and women was to create stores and co-operatives of their own, 'and meet the masters on their own ground by becoming masters themselves'. On account of the 'irresponsible tyranny' of proprietors, he raised the concept, blasphemous to capital, of nationalising the Pennsylvania coal-mining companies, and of government control of railroads. 'Paternalism supported by state power is better than capital monopoly upheld by the private mercenaries whom Pinkerton lets up to the service of the money kings,' he wrote in 1883. His radicalism and conservatism were equally patchy, but behind both lay a humane voice; and one raised again for the natives of America.

After the Custer massacre in 1876, he described the policy of the Indian Bureau as 'methodistic cant, its protection high-handed coercion, its object plunder; and its results disgrace and death of the Indians'. Later in his life, when the infamous Dawes Act was passed in 1887, breaking up the tribal structures and offensive Indian 'communism', and taking good land in return for 'allotments' of marginal country granted to each male, O'Reilly published a letter of protest from the Lakota Chief Red Cloud, and supported it with an editorial.

The British Empire had in the meantime not forgotten O'Reilly, his treachery, escape and associations. When he was invited to Ottawa to deliver the St Patrick's Day address for 1885, he declined the invitation for fear of embarrassing his hosts, given – as he put it – that he was 'self-amnestied'. But he did write to the Secretary of State of Canada, asking if his American citizenship would protect him from arrest if he went to Canada. And by the advice of friends in the Irish Party in the House of Commons, he also wrote to the British Home Secretary, Sir William Harcourt, asking if he could safely go to Canada. A British bureaucrat replied that Sir William 'cannot accede to the request'. Thomas Sexton, a member who had been imprisoned with Parnell, made a dazzling speech in the Commons in favour of an amnesty for both James Stephens and John Boyle O'Reilly. 'Mr Boyle O'Reilly, whom he had the pleasure to meet lately at Boston, was a gentleman of very high personal qualities and of the rarest intellectual gifts, and during the years of his residence in America he had made such good use of his powers that he now filled the position of co-proprietor . . . of one of the most important journals in the United States. Mr O'Reilly was one of the most influential men in the State of Massachusetts.'

Harcourt, in answering, made a reference to O'Reilly's 'Prison Breach', and this may have helped generate a rumour that, in escaping, O'Reilly had been in violation of a parole. The journalist Roche, who had joined the *Pilot* in the early '80s, got a pithy response on the matter from Father McCabe in Waseca County, Minnesota. 'John Boyle O'Reilly never broke his parole, *never having one to break*.' But Sir William Harcourt's attitude towards John Boyle O'Reilly's case was certainly influenced by the year's dynamitings, funded from America. He saw O'Reilly as no better than the Invincibles and the Chicago Triangle.

Harcourt and others would be pleased to find that another former Fenian prisoner, O'Donovan Rossa, did not go unbloodied for his role as founder of the Skirmishing Fund. A young English woman, giving the name of Mrs Yseult Dudley, called on him in his office in New York. She told him she was anxious to help with operations against England, and Rossa organised to meet her the following morning on a corner of Chambers Street in Lower Manhattan. As Rossa came up to greet her the next day, she drew a revolver and fired five shots at him, only one of which struck home and wounded him. When asked by the New York police why she had committed the crime, Mrs Dudley said, 'Because he is O'Donovon Rossa.' Some British newspapers compared Mrs Dudley to Charlotte Corday, who had stabbed the demagogue Marat in his bath. 'When thirty million English people', wrote O'Reilly, 'wildly cheer a half insane and wholly disreputable murderess, and thirty million people of Irish blood half sympathise with the desperate lunatics who would burn down London – it is time for both sides to pause.'

Though O'Reilly could not go to Canada to address a St Patrick's Day crowd, it was consistent for him to urge Boston Irish on St Patrick's Day 1887 to consider that 'we can do Ireland more good by our Americanism than by our Irishism'; and at the same time to resist any official celebration in Faneuil Hall – a site identified with the American revolution – of Queen Victoria's jubilee. 'Irishmen should be as thankful for the reign of Victoria as they might be for the plagues of Egypt.' Still, on the eve of the jubilee, he told a meeting, 'The man who would raise a finger against an Englishman tomorrow in Boston, is unworthy to be present here today.'

He had been a Bostonian long enough now to absorb a civic pride in the holy places of the American Revolution. He had a place on the committee of a project which combined his passion for Jeffersonian republicanism with his commitment to coloured America – the committee for the construction of a memorial to those who died in the Boston Massacre on the eve of the American rebellion. To O'Reilly the most eloquent amongst the Boston dead was Crispus Attucks, the freed black man who was the first to fall to British bullets, and who symbolically linked American liberty to emancipation and the ascent of black America. In his commemorative poem for the 1888 opening of the massacre memorial on Boston Common, the Crispus Attucks Memorial, O'Reilly elevated Attucks into an American pantheon.

Where shall we seek for a hero, and where shall we find a story?
Our laurels are wreathed for conquest, our songs for completed glory.
But we honour a shrine unfinished, a column uncapped with pride,
If we sing the deed that was sown like seed when Crispus Attucks died.

Though he was still clearly in his prime, men with whom O'Reilly had been fraternally joined in revolution were dying, and death had always a particular impact on an increasingly delicately balanced spirit. On 2 December 1888, Corporal Thomas Chambers died in his early forties at the Carney Hospital in Boston. 'In his case at least,' wrote O'Reilly, 'England's vengeance was complete: the rebel's life was turned into a torture.' O'Reilly had placed him in the hospital six months before his death and had paid his medical expenses, reflecting that Chambers had once been the happiest and merriest, the youngest and strongest man he had known. 'For two years, while I was in prison in England, he and I were chained together whenever we were moved, and we generally managed to get another rebel named McCarthy, on the same chain. McCarthy's health was quite broken, and he had sunk into a melancholy . . . I remember one day, when we were marched through the streets of London . . . with the crowd staring at us, Chambers made McCarthy laugh so heartily that it brought on a fit of coughing, and we had to halt until the poor fellow got his breath.'

Though O'Reilly might have repented of Fenianism, he retained an affection and loyalty for Fenians, and indeed was sensitive to the honour of the Irish in America. Perhaps the clue to his appalling record as a political tipster lay in the fact that, as one of his modern biographers wrote: 'Political bias at times so ruled this man of passion that even an apparent affront to Irishmen or Catholics was considered a challenge.' His endorsement of political candidates combined the two requirements that they be both Democrat and pro-Irish. He had begun by endorsing Horace

Greeley's nomination for president in 1872, and, as editor in 1876, he supported Samuel J. Tilden. More than a year before the 1880 elections, O'Reilly began editorialising for Thomas Bayard of Delaware. The Democrats chose not Bayard but Meagher's old friend General Winfield Scott Hancock, whom O'Reilly then supported. When the new Republican president, Garfield, was assassinated less than a year later by an aggrieved place-seeker, Charles Guiteau, O'Reilly described the assassin as a poisoned flower of the spoils system, and pleaded for civil service reform.

In 1884 O'Reilly led a robust campaign against the Republican party's presidential candidate, James G. Blaine. For the Democrats, he liked Bayard or Ben Butler, and opposed the candidacy of Grover Cleveland. But when the Democrats in the end nominated Cleveland to face Blaine. 'We shall faithfully and earnestly work for the election of Cleveland, the Democratic standard bearer,' O'Reilly dourly pledged. For, as O'Reilly wrote, 'Irish Americans have been Democrats not by chance, but by good judgement. Tried in the fires of foreign tyranny, their instincts as well as their historical knowledge of Jeffersonian Democracy, led them to the American party that expressed and supported the true principles of republican government.'

With Cleveland elected – a rare O'Reilly success – O'Reilly himself expected that his Land League friend Patrick A. Collins would be given a senior Cabinet post – perhaps Secretary of State. The continued passing over of Collins and the appointment of Anglophile Edward Phelps to the US embassy in London turned O'Reilly into a critic of the Cleveland administration. However, in 1888 O'Reilly threw his support behind Cleveland again.

O'Reilly was now in his early forties. He was restless still, but seemed to be driven more by literary than political ambition. Not that he was displeased to have a part in the expulsion of the British ambassador to Washington, Lord Sackville-West, even if it was initiated through a tricky piece of work by the Republicans. A Republican *agent provocateur* wrote a letter, purportedly from a British-born American in Pomona, California, asking Sackville-West's advice on who to vote for in the coming elections. Sackville-West fell into the trap of suggesting that since the Republican majority had opposed what would have been for Great Britain a lenient fisheries treaty, the conciliatory Cleveland should be voted for.

When this letter appeared in the press, Irish voters – as the Republican party had hoped – deserted the cause of Cleveland. O'Reilly stayed with him, but demanded that Sackville-West be expelled. Cleveland wrote to Secretary of State Bayard saying that Sackville-West must be sent away precisely because 'John Boyle O'Reilly of the *Boston Pilot* who was doing good work will falter, or worse, if this is not done'. When Sackville-West went home, the Tory press cried for war. The *Daily Chronicle* declared: 'If President Cleveland is of opinion that it consorts with his dignified position to abase himself and his country before the O'Reillys, Collinses and other Irish demagogues, and to reserve his rudeness for accredited diplomatists of friendly powers . . . it is our duty to resent the insult put upon us as promptly as it was offered.'

O'Reilly's life was if anything too restive. Years past, in prison, someone had passed *The Imitation of Christ* under his cell door, with its intimations of the folly of human frenzy. There was a sense in which O'Reilly knew that by his activities he was evading more absolute questions. The confession had been there in *In Bohemia*.

> I am tired of planning and toiling
> In the crowded hives of men;
> Heart-weary of building and spoiling,
> And spoiling and building again.

He relished the summer house in Hull, but did not necessarily have as much of his summer there as his daughters would have liked. Part of his problem was that he now had the full credentials of a literary man. During 1888 he read at the Boston Museum with Oliver Wendell Holmes and Mark Twain. 'I am now suffering the consequence of overwork,' he wrote poignantly to a woman editor. 'My poem for your collection I have had mapped out and partially written for over a month; but now I am stopped by an attack of insomnia. I trust that in a few days I shall be able to finish the poem; but the very thought of my inability aggravates my sleeplessness.'

A Mr Burren asked him to come to Woodstock to read a poem. 'I am overworking,' wrote O'Reilly, 'and I cannot help it for a year or two more . . . a few years hence, when I shall have "eased up" on the journalistic labour, I shall have my chance of reading a poem at Woodstock.' He was telling near-strangers of his exhaustion, as if they might have suggestions of ease. He still found time, though, for great bardic events, and it might have been the apogee when in the summer of 1889 he was selected as the poet for the Plymouth celebration honouring the Pilgrim Fathers. There was considerable mumbling, since the Yankee poets Holmes and Lowell were still alive. But he had an utterly unfeigned admiration for the dissenting founders of Massachusetts, and a facility for identifying a common cause in Irish and dissenters alike against 'Norman' tyranny communally suffered.

Here, on this rock, and on this sterile soil,
Began the kingdom not of kings, but men:
Began the making of the world again.

In post-Civil War America it was a popular line, and when O'Reilly boarded the Hull ferry the morning his poem was published in the *Globe* other passengers held up their copies of the paper and cheered him. Judge Mellon Chamberlain, chairman of the Boston Public Library, was quite overwhelmed by O'Reilly's pilgrim poem. Such praise might have been evanescent, but helped confirm O'Reilly in his role of Boston literary man.

Now O'Reilly was old enough to have protégés, and one of them was the young sculptor John Donoghoe, about whom O'Reilly wrote unsolicited letters of enthusiasm to various important people, including on 2 June 1887 to Governor Ames of Massachusetts. 'Sending you a copy of *Art Review* to call your attention to the magnificent *Young Sophocles* by John Donoghoe the sculptor (he is the gentleman I introduced you to on the Lowell train).' Donoghoe, said O'Reilly, had a nymph exhibited in the Paris Salon. 'An order from you would be a great benefit at this stage of his life, and he would give you the greatest portrait of the time.'

In the late winter of 1890, O'Reilly, beginning at the Boston Theatre, embarked on what would prove to be his last lecture series, fund-raising for Home Rule. This tour would occupy the spring and early summer and add to his habitual exhaustion, while the *Pilot* operated in the safe hands of Denis Cashman and Roche. His route sounds like the sort of oratorical Stations of the Cross followed by eager young Meagher years before – Syracuse and Chicago in quick succession, then St Paul, where the Reverend Patrick McCabe was present in the audience. The priest stayed with O'Reilly at a St Paul hotel as his guest, and persuaded him that in the following fall he would return to McCabe's parish and give a series of public speeches. Since McCabe had saved his life and his soul, he could hardly plead exhaustion and insomnia. After a lecture in Minneapolis, he went on to Butte in Montana, a considerably Irish mining city, barely a village in the days of Governor Meagher. On 14 March O'Reilly spoke in Spokane Falls in the east of Washington State, and then in Seattle. In Tacoma for St Patrick's Day, he participated in the procession in an open barouche drawn by four white horses. After his speech, a dinner was given by the Ancient Order of Hibernians, who kept him up until 4.00 a.m. The following evening he appeared in Portland.

Like others before him, he thought that this north-western region was the country to which the Irish urban poor should come. 'That matchless country, as large as an empire, and filled with all kinds of natural wealth, contains only about as many people as the city of Boston.' From Portland the steamer *Oregon* took him to San Francisco. By now he was surprised to find himself utterly exhausted, but mentioned in his journal that he had got a 'great rest' aboard the *Oregon*. Every other night he had suffered insomnia.

After central California, he returned by way of the great, admirable western vacancies to Boston to take up the active editorship of the *Pilot* again throughout a busy summer. He took time to go with his daughters to Revere Beach, north of Boston, where on 6 August he was the guest of honour at the Gaelic Athletic Association Sports Day. The day was very hot and a crowd of 4,000 Irish hemmed him in. O'Reilly collapsed and returned by the ferry to his house in Hull, where he rested all the next day on a sofa in a sitting-room – O'Reilly liked to call it the Tower Room – next door to his wife's bedroom. But the next morning, a Friday, he was back in the *Pilot* office, complaining again to Cashman of insomnia. He had some committee work to attend to – he was involved in the organisation of a Grand Army of the Republic convention which was due to muster on Boston Common and would march past the *Pilot* building the following Tuesday.

On Saturday afternoon he left sweltering Franklin Street and went to catch the ferry to Hull, out past the light of Deer Island where the Famine Irish had been quarantined, and snugly in between Peddocks Island and the Nantasket Peninsula near whose head stood the town. He was met at the pier by his youngest daughter, Blanid, a fragile but mentally lively child who would not long outlive her father and with whom, playing word games, he went laughing home.

A little after midnight on that Saturday night, Mrs O'Reilly called out to her husband, who was reading and smoking in the family sitting room. She said she felt very ill and feverish. She asked him to get some medicine for her from Dr Litchfield, the family physician. O'Reilly walked a few blocks to the doctor's house. The medicine Litchfield prescribed had no effect on Mary O'Reilly's discomfort. In preparing what he had given her, O'Reilly had spilled a portion. He therefore made a second visit to the doctor, who renewed the prescription and said, 'Mr O'Reilly, you should take something yourself.' Back home, after administering the mixture to his wife, O'Reilly himself went to the medicine closet, looking for a sleeping draft.

Mrs O'Reilly woke in the small hours after a short sleep. She found her husband on a couch in the sitting room, still reading and smoking. She insisted on his getting some rest. He said, 'Yes, Mamsie dear, I've taken some of your sleeping medicine.' As she watched he stretched out on the couch he was sitting on and looked unusually pallid. He seemed to grow comatose very quickly. She spoke to him and tried to rouse him, and he murmured, 'Yes, my love!'

She became worried about his condition, and sent for Dr Litchfield. The doctor spent fifty minutes trying to revive him, but O'Reilly died at ten minutes to five that Sunday morning, 10 August. The death certificate, signed by Litchfield, indicated 'Heart Failure, superinduced, perhaps, by an overdose of chloral, taken for insomnia.' As a modern writer says, the insomniac O'Reilly, with many physician friends, must have used chloral before. The overdose might have been a mixture error of Litchfield's or of a pharmacist. But the possibility that O'Reilly may have committed suicide was tentatively raised. Obviously O'Reilly had the necessary streak of morbidity, having tried it in Western Australia.

When his heart stopped, O'Reilly was forty-six years old. Mary O'Reilly, desperately grieving, travelled with her daughters to her widowed mother's house in Boston. Her brother John Murphy, and O'Reilly's eldest daughter, Mollie, took the body across to the family's town house in Winthrop Street, Charlestown. Former President Cleveland sent his condolences, as did Cardinal Gibbons – 'It is a public calamity,' said the Cardinal. Oliver Wendell Holmes wrote, 'John Boyle O'Reilly was a man of heroic mould and nature; brave, adventurous, patriotic, enthusiastic, with the *perfervidum ingenium* which belongs quite as much to the Irish as the Scotch . . . His poems showed us what he might have been had he devoted himself to letters.'

At the close of the National Encampment of the Grand Army of the Republic, a resolution unanimously carried mourned his death. A meeting of Parnellite members from the House of Commons sent their sympathies and testified to the great services of the dead patriot. On Tuesday, his body was taken from Winthrop Street to St Mary's, Charlestown, for the funeral service. His pallbearers included O'Donovan Rossa, with whom he had quarrelled but who nonetheless came up from New York for the event, and Denis Cashman, fellow prisoner in Western Australia, fellow journalist in Boston. Amongst his honorary pallbearers were a number of former generals and Captain Henry C. Hathaway of New Bedford. Then the family and mourners endured a considerable train ride through Boston to Roxbury, where O'Reilly was buried.

There followed eulogies preposterous for a former convict. A memorial service was held in the Tremont Temple, and there Mayor Hart, Judge Woodbury, Father William Byrne, Vicar-General of Boston, General Ben Butler, Thomas Wentworth Higginson, and the Honorable Patrick A. Collins all spoke. In regretting O'Reilly's inability ever to return to the sites of his childhood or his parents' graves, Collins himself called on all the gifts of the bardic orator to evoke the countryside around the Boyne:

'By the banks of that lovely river, where the blood of four nations once commingled, in sight of the monument to the alien victor, hard by the great mysterious Rath, over one sanctified spot dearer than all others to him, where the dew glistened on the softest green, the spirit of O'Reilly hovered, and shook the stillness of the Irish dawn on its journey to the stars.'

The most authentic voice raised at that meeting may well have been that of Mr Edward G. Walker, black lawyer and orator, President of Tufts College. 'With his pen John Boyle O'Reilly sent through the columns of a newspaper that he edited in this city, words in our behalf that were Christian, and anathemas that were just.' He had taken up the slack, said Walker, after the death of the great Wendell Phillips.

A Pontifical requiem mass was celebrated by the Archbishop of Boston at the Cathedral of the Holy Cross on 10 September 1890. At a memorial service in the Metropolitan Opera House in New York, the speakers included Meagher's friends Generals Hancock and Howard, the governor of the state, a number of serving and former Senators, and the president of Columbia University. A letter of condolence from President Harrison was read.

A Boston committee endowed an Alcove of Celtic Literature in his honour in the Boston Public Library. A commissioned bust was placed in the library. A fine monument, engraved with two harps and displaying his features as Bostonians knew them, also stands on the Fenway. His remains were exhumed from Calvary Cemetery, Roxbury, in November, and then moved to what his supporters considered a more august grave in Holywood Cemetery in Brookline. Marked by a huge glacial rock, the grave was simply inscribed.

O'Reilly was by death at least saved the odious side-taking which took place when Parnell was cited as co-respondent in a divorce suit Captain O'Shea filed against his wife Katherine, a woman thereafter doomed to proceed into history under the soubriquet 'Kitty'.

As we have already seen, many of his less frenetic fellow prisoners in British prisons and passengers on *Hougoumont* lived considerably longer. The more obscure, competent, honourable, temperamentally positive Denis Cashman, who had tempered O'Reilly's rashness on *Hougoumont*, would survive him by twelve years, and at his death was still employed by the *Pilot*.

John Kenealy, former Western Australian prisoner now of Los Angeles, had made a place for himself in California as spacious as, but less lustrous than, that achieved by O'Reilly in Boston. Devoy remembered much later that Kenealy had 'moved to Los Angeles before it became famous, except as a health resort'. The rail link assured that the tuberculosis sufferers of the East and Midwest teemed to Pasadena and Los Angeles in tens of thousands to be cured by the pure, dry, warm air, and old Fenian dry-goods men benefited accordingly.

The People's Store of Dillon and Kenealy, 86 Main Street, 'opposite the Temple Block', on what is now the corner of Market Street, bespoke Kenealy's respect for enterprise and property. The company was a regular advertiser in the *Los Angeles Daily Star* and later in the *Los Angeles Times*, particularly throughout spring and autumn. The *Los Angeles Daily Star* of 14 March 1878, for example, asserted: 'This space is reserved for Dillon and Kenealy, who are in receipt of a LARGE consignment of Foreign and Domestic Dry Goods.' There followed a long list of the goods Mr Kenealy had shipped back from his annual buying trips: black and coloured silks, shawls, dress goods, figured and plain piques, printed linen, lawns, ladies and children's hosiery, 20,000 yards of beautiful embroideries.

Kenealy and his wife May Dillon had two children, James F. Kenealy, who became a noted Los Angeles attorney, and May Kenealy. He resided from 1875 in a cottage on the east side of Fort and Second Street, Fort later becoming Broadway. Nearby was the music school of Mary E. Hoyt, the town's best-known music teacher, from whose house could be heard children working their way through 'Listen to the Mocking Bird' and 'The Rippling Brook'. Los Angeles looked for all the world like a little town in Australia, and not at all unlike a slightly inland Fremantle minus the gaol. Boyle Workman, memoirist of Los Angeles and son of one of the oldest Californian Irish families, had been a schoolboy with Kenealy's son James at St Vincent's College on Sixth Street between Fort and Hill. 'There was no Seventh Street in those days . . . Our baseball field was on the Fort Street side.'

'Every year,' wrote Boyle Workman, 'Kenealy went to Ireland to buy the finest laces and linens.' Obviously the Los Angeles Irish attached their own mythology to these buying trips. 'Had the British government known his political background, it might have halted these buying trips.' And perhaps there was a political component to Kenealy's travel, as there had been when he was a buyer for the Queen's Old Castle. For after *Catalpa*, Kenealy remained an activist of the Clan. In 1882 a British agent sent to the Foreign Office a circular from the Clan na Gael Council which showed that John Kenealy of Los Angeles, California, was one of the council members elected in Chicago on 3 August 1881. This was only a little prior to the period when Chicago would be rendered unacceptable for moderate Clan members such as Kenealy by the emergence of the Chicago Triangle.

From companies of the stature of the People's Store came much of the resources of the Clan and monetary support for the Land League. Indeed, on his journeys to Ireland to buy linen Kenealy would have witnessed defiance towards landlords in his native North Cork. In the mid-1880s, the tenants of Arthur Langford's estate, twenty-five families, were on rent strike. Appearing before the court of land judges in November 1888 in order to oppose the demand made by some of his tenants for a 30 per cent rent remission, Langford complained bitterly that he was 'reduced to such a picture of poverty' by these people boycotting and rent-striking that he could not afford counsel. In Kanturk, in Kenealy's family area, the Reverend N. D. Kennedy, a young Columban priest, was the highly effective leader of the League.

Kenealy's business flourished as the town enlarged and assumed a civic pride. On 29 August 1888, in the *Los Angeles Herald*, along with the announcement of the National Democratic ticket for President of Winfield Scott Hancock of Pennsylvania and William A. Tinglish of Indiana for Vice-President, another typical Dillon and Kenealy summer advertisement indicated the People's Store was doing massive business. 'Compulsory sale of dry goods at Dillon and Kenealy's in order to make way for immense quantities of goods purchased by Mr Kenealy in the European and Eastern markets. Stock has to be reduced by at least $40,000.' These advertisements, proud of newly purchased merchandise, a little boastful of their enormous surplus stock, continued to appear under the masthead of the *Herald* each day for a month.

Later, Kenealy branched out. He had shares in the Los Angeles Cable Railway Company, a business which failed, but then went into partnership with young Boyle Workman in the fire insurance business, an interesting vocation for a man who, at his trial, had been accused of desiring to put Cork to the torch. 'Our offices', Workman remembered decades later, 'were at 207 South Broadway in the YMCA building.' W. H. Workman, Boyle's father, who had been Democratic mayor of Los Angeles a number of times, in 1903 was elected City Treasurer. Irish Democrat politics in the City of Angels took its style from the party machines of the East, at least according to a disgruntled Republican, Stinson, who later complained, 'At that time, 1903, the political machine controlled all of the political offices from Governor to Constables.' False names were placed on the voting registers; men were fraudulently registered as living on vacant blocks, in Japanese lodging houses and so on. Stinson organised young Republicans to go to polling booths and supervise the crossing off of the electoral roll and the signatures of electors.

John Kenealy appeared in the Los Angeles Auditor's Report of 1903 as the appointed city treasury clerk under Workman's fairly or foully elected incumbency as Treasurer. The photograph in the report resembles Kenealy's mug shot as a Fenian. Broad in the forehead, benign, he was bearded and was still – as a witness had said at his trial – stout. Kenealy's son, James F. Kenealy, was by that time caught up in the city's larger drama: not Ireland, but water. He worked as a lawyer for the Board of Arbitration established to judge the crucial southern Californian matter of water ownership between the city and the Crystal Spring Water Company. No doubt the attention even of ageing Irish activists was – in a desert coast town – sometimes galvanised by the question of water, a case which the city won in the end in the Supreme Court.

Before Fenian John Kenealy was of advanced age, notices for the Elmore, the Packard, which cost $3,500, and the Pierce Straight Arrow Six, costing a considerable $4,000, appeared side by side with dry-goods advertisements in the Sunday editions of the *Los Angeles Times*. Middle-aged Fenians' grandchildren read the new comic strips – *Little Memo in Slumberland*, *Waggles in Wonderland* and *Buster Brown*. One Colonel Selig had in 1908 rented a boom-time mansion at Eighth and Old Streets and shot the first motion picture for exhibition purposes in Los Angeles. It was entitled *In the Sultan's Power*. But though the world had altered, Irish faction and sect had not, and Home Rule had still not been achieved. Without seeing it, far less an Irish Republic, Kenealy died on 9 September 1908 at the age of seventy-one, at his then residence, 1121 West Ninth Street. The next day the *Los Angeles Times*, serving a city which had increased tenfold since the Fenian first arrived, carried on its front page the headline 'Revolutionist Irish Leader has Passed On'. Kenealy's picture appeared side by side with that of the winner of the first Los Angeles marathon, a red-headed boy named Edward Dietrich. The report said Kenealy had been confined to his house for many months. His Fenian remains had the honour of a High Mass at the Cathedral.

In the parallel universe of Australia, the ageing and poetry-fated couple Saint Kevin and Eva now suffered a hecatomb of their children. Their son Vincent, a manager of the National Bank, left a wife and small son when in 1890 he was run down at night, while crossing George Street, Brisbane, by a horse-drawn public carriage. Rushed to Brisbane Hospital, he died of a fractured skull. In 1892, Dr Edward O'Doherty's 4-year-old daughter died. William, their first son, perished after a long illness the next year. Still there was young Kevin, and the energetic Dr Edward, who had fought his way back from bankruptcy and was a physician at Brisbane Hospital. But both would die within a few months of each other in 1900, at the end of that unfulfilled century. Far from home, on the sun-blasted gold-field of Kalgoorlie in Western Australia, Kevin was taken by pneumonia at the height of a desert summer. Then, during winter, Dr Edward O'Doherty fell entering a coach outside his house in Wickham Terrace, Brisbane, and died before night of a brain haemorrhage. Saint Kevin and Eva had begotten eight children, and now only their youngest, Gertrude, remained.

Kevin and Eva waited out that fatal decade in a superior boarding-house in Wickham Terrace, Brisbane. Undefeated, Dr O'Doherty devoted himself to research on a safe defrosting and preservation method for previously frozen meat, which was brought to the attention of Queensland legislators in 1897. 'The process is the conception of Dr K. I. O'Doherty and Mr Henderson, a government analyst. On Wednesday, a brisket of corn beef treated by it was boiled by Mr Baldwin and submitted to the opinion of the legislators.' The dried beef was served in the parliamentary dining room, and though a patent for the process was applied for, it did not restore the O'Doherty fortunes.

About the turn of the century, Kevin and Eva moved to a suburb named Rosalie, to a characteristic little Queensland, wide-verandahed wood-frame house on stilts. Eva's intelligence and courage still blazed under the banality of that ceiling. She did not publicly reflect on how much more plebeian than Killeen House in Portumna, or even than Frascati, this plain cottage was. Soon, complete blindness descended on Kevin and prevented him from carrying out his duties. He was irked and bored, but three young colleagues who held the ageing doctor in esteem performed his work and gave him the fees.

He died in July 1905 at eighty-one years, and was buried in suburban Toowong Cemetery. His place of death was nominated as 'His residence, Westholme, Heussler Terrace', a Queensland cottage floridly named. The *Brisbane Courier* now asked, 'Who knowing such men as Doctor O'Doherty can link them with the darker crimes of great agitations?' One observer would call him 'the genial medico, Kevin Izod O'Doherty', and said that 'no man was better known in his day'. Such cordial appraisals came too late to do Saint Kevin any good.

Eva survived another five years in hard circumstances. Her only surviving child, Gertrude, lived with her, and Gertrude's wages as a state government typist, and a small insurance policy on Kevin's life, were her mainstay. Mother and daughter, the residue of furious hopes and hearty clans, moved to a modest cottage near Toowong. Eva was a forthright woman and was offended that the Redmond brothers had not sent her condolences for the loss of a man who had twice sacrificed all for Ireland, and all the more offended since William Redmond was in Queensland at the time. But a literary priest from Settle, Yorkshire, Father William Hickey, who had a passionate interest in the Young Irelanders, communicated with her, asked her for any Young Ireland memorabilia she might care to send him and, hearing of her circumstances, suggested a new edition of her works. To him she wrote of her late husband that when he went to join Parnell, 'It was a very losing game for a professional man, but the doctor was not one to count the cost.'

Father Hickey undertook to look after the cost of printing her works. There were editorial delays in 1908 as he asked for more material, including her prose pieces. In August 1908 he wrote of raising a subscription to the publication, and also of a fund-raising concert which would be held in Dublin in October to meet the expenses. He told her that friends to whose judgement he paid attention strongly urged him not to publish every poem, but to select them. This, he felt, 'would be better for your *great* reputation as the worthy *soror poetica* of Mary and Speranza'. In September 1908, the Irish publishers Gill accepted the collected works for publication, and offered to pay the author on the day of publication the sum of £20 and a royalty of 10 per cent. This meant that the £140 Hickey had raised for printing costs could now be sent to maintain Eva.

The poems appeared in December, and in congratulating her at her re-emergence, Eva of the *Nation* redivivus, Father Hickey urged her to write pen sketches of the ultimately knighted Sir Charles Gavan Duffy, of Smith O'Brien, Thomas Francis Meagher, John Mitchel, John Martin, Father Kenyon, and the *Nation* poets Mary and Speranza. The ageing rebel Eva sat down in her little cottage in Toowong and made vivid and sometimes acerbic notes absolutely in character with the brisk poetry she had written as Ireland's virgin muse. Her notes indicate again that Eva had not moved from her opinions in 1848. 'The rising misnamed – no rising. No plans or order – no leader. The hour had come in all probability, *but not the man.* Certainly there was one man who had been suffered to be seized as a felon – John Mitchel – who held practical views.' She defended Father Kenyon, who, she wrote, had always said that the time for striking the blow came when Mitchel was brought as a convicted felon through the streets of Dublin. She had believed that sixty years before, and now, in the humidity of Brisbane, in the walls of timber, she still believed it. 'The people were then ready – or filled with rage and enthusiasm. They were held back by their leaders.'

She denied that it was Speranza who stood up in court at Duffy's trial and tried to proclaim herself the writer of those treasonable articles, '*Alea Jacta Est*' and 'The Tocsin of Ireland'. In fact she implied cowardice on the part of Speranza and others in not taking responsibility for the seditious material they had written. The heroine who did own up in the public gallery in Green Street courthouse was Mrs Callan, Duffy's sister-in-law, later a resident of Melbourne.

Not that Eva showed much tolerance for Duffy, who had died in retirement in France in 1903. In tune with Mitchel, she felt that Duffy had dishonoured himself by calling on too many character witnesses. 'When first I met Sir C. G. Duffy, he seemed to me full of an abounding vitality, something wild and eerie in speech and laughter.' She described him a little snobbishly as possessing 'a Dublin-like physiognomy'. Then, 'In later years, as he passed through the mill of modern social conventionalism, his physiognomy was in marked contrast . . . it had been moulded into the expression of a man of society and letters.' She disclosed that whenever she wrote an item for the *Nation* on the subject of Smith O'Brien's treatment in exile, Charles Gavin Duffy received an angry protest from Lucy O'Brien, denying the truth of the inflammatory reports of her husband's poor health.

Under a mocking Queensland sun, she took pride in her descent from the O'Flahertys and the O'Kellys of Hy Many, Hugh Larkin's country, and as the last of all the actors of Young Ireland she revived the particularity of all the others in that little house in the bush-bound suburbs of a raw city, and their ghosts glittered, postured and revived her.

Hickey wrote of her collected works, 'All the reviews of your book that I have seen since its publication give instinctive praise to your verses; so you have, I think, left to the reading world of your countrymen a work that will last many a day and year.' But Eva was not immune in her last years from the normal publication blues. She complained that the book had not been adequately advertised in Australia. Though it might not have been much literary consolation, Eva received about £400 from special events held throughout the Irish communities in various states, including an 'Eva of the *Nation*' fund in Queensland.

Her memoirs unfinished, she died of complications from influenza at eighty years of age on 21 May 1910. Saint Kevin and Eva of the *Nation* lie in Toowong Cemetery under a handsome monument built by the Irish community.

Physician and Muse, man and wife!
They came from Ireland's shores.
Through adversity their light shone brightly,
Inspiring all on whom it shone.

The O'Doherty male line did not survive. The only grandson of Saint Kevin and Eva, Willy O'Doherty, son of the tragic Vincent, was killed in France in 1918 fighting with the Australian forces, struggling for a different cause than his grandparents', another set of myths – antipodean ones.

*

In 1912, Home Rule seemed likely, but the Loyalists of the North armed themselves against the possibility and, along with Loyalist officers in the British army who threatened to mutiny, dissuaded the British government from proceeding. As the First World War began, an understanding existed that Home Rule would be broached again once the war was won, and decided in the light of Irish participation in the British forces. The Irish enlisted, fought lustily, suffered plentiful casualties. But even amongst the Anglo-Irish gentry, in the case of Lady Gregory's flying-ace son, Major Robert Gregory, as depicted by Yeats, there prevailed a detached stoicism.

Those that I fight I do not hate,
Those that I guard I do not love;
My country is Kiltartan Cross,
My countrymen Kiltartan's poor,
No likely end could bring them loss
Or leave them happier than before.

Stephens's old Irish Republican Brotherhood had at the start of the war taken over control of the Irish Volunteers, a force founded in response to the Ulster Volunteer Force who had armed themselves in 1912 to thwart Home Rule. In the late summer of 1914, the Volunteers numbered 80,000. They were supported by Clan na Gael in the United States. MacManus was revisited – when O'Donovan Rossa died in New York in 1915, the Volunteers organised a splendid funeral for him in Glasnevin at which a young poet and schoolmaster, Patrick Pearse, assumed Rossa into the tradition of resistance. 'The Defenders of this Realm . . . think that they have pacified Ireland . . . but the fools, the fools, the fools! – they have left us our Fenian dead, and while Ireland holds these graves, Ireland unfree shall never be at peace.'

The Easter Rising of 1916 was ill-managed, the chief of staff of the Irish Volunteers delaying orders for a general uprising because arms had not arrived on the Kerry coast from Germany. But 1,500 Dublin Volunteers were led out by Pearse, and supplemented by more than 200 of James Connolly's Irish Citizen Army. The failure of the uprising and the execution of its leaders led to what Smith O'Brien had failed to arouse, popular resistance to British rule. The bitter era known as 'the Troubles' ended in an Irish Free State, made up of twenty-six counties, including two Ulster ones, Monaghan and Donegal, and Meagher's flag flew over those counties, as it still does. The treaty was narrowly passed by the Irish Cabinet, and a civil war between pro-treaty (Free State) and anti-treaty (Republican) resulted. Meanwhile, behind the northern border itself, the ancient quarrel between Catholic Republicans and Protestant Loyalists proceeded through the twentieth century, with a fixation and denial of civil fraternity which would have appalled Davis, Meagher or O'Reilly.

This book is entitled *The Great Shame* because in spite of all the struggles and travails of the Australian-transported activists with whom we have shared our hours, the population of Ireland had by the time of the founding of the Irish Free State in 1922 shrunk to barely more than half the population of 1841. Such a phenomenon made Ireland unique in Europe, where, despite the imperial follies of the major European powers, population had uniformly risen. This great loss is believed by some to have created in the Irish themselves a certain amount of that survival shame which characterises victims of the Holocaust. The title might also be seen as referring to the misgovernment of Ireland under British rule, and the continuing discrimination against northern Catholics in the decades following the treaty. At the time of writing, through the goodwill of the governments of the Republic of Ireland, Britain, the United States, of the mass of Republicans and Loyalists, and in the context of an increasingly unified Europe where Davis's or Mitchel's nineteenth-century concept of sovereignty seems less and less realistic, there is hope of peace in Ulster, and an end to shame.

Again, and in a more intimate sense, the title has reference to the failures of all the principals of this tale to produce by agitation, constitutional or otherwise, a successful nineteenth-century state in a Europe where many other states were emergent. And, finally, it might stand for a redolence of the shame of transportation itself, without which, of course, we would have been deprived of the tales here told, and Australia deprived of the piquant blood, and potent ghosts, of the characters to whom we now bid goodbye.

ACKNOWLEDGEMENTS

At the close of this book, it is an especial pleasure to thank all those who gave aid and comfort in the writing of it.

In Australia, I am indebted to the Librarian of the Mitchell Library, Sydney, Alan Ventress, and his staff; to the Director of the Archives Office of New South Wales, David Roberts, the Manager of Reference Services, Christine Yeats, and their staff; to the Curator and staff of the Archives Office of Tasmania, Hobart; to the Librarian and staff of the John Oxley Library in Brisbane; and, via the skilled researcher Helene Charlesworth, to the Librarian and staff of the Battye Library and to the Curator and staff of the Western Australian Archives in Perth.

In the United States I found vast and material help at the Huntington Library, San Marino, California, from its Director of Research, Dr Robert Ritchie, from Catherine Babcock, Jennifer Watts, Curator of Photographs, Olga Tsapina, Curator of American Historical Manuscripts, and from all the staff. The delightful Huntington was for several months my second home. But I must also thank the Curator and staff of the Manuscripts and Archives Division of the Public Library of New York, especially Wayne Furman of the Office of Special Collections, and the Curator and staff of Special Collections at the Boston Public Library. I remember the welcome extended to me by Steve Cotham, Head of the McClung Historical Collection at the East Tennessee Historical Center, Knoxville, Tennessee, and by his people. In Thomas Francis Meagher's Montana, the Society Librarian of the Montana Historical Society Archives, Mr Robert Clark, his colleague Brian Shovers, the Curator of Photographs, Lory Morrow, and their assistants provided me, without my having to consult any catalogue, with every document they held on Meagher's extraordinary Montana gubernatorial career. Ellie Arguimbau, Archivist, later helped me with the necessary references.

In Ireland, where the tale begins, I received genial aid from Michael Flynn, Curator, National Museum of Ireland, the Librarian, curators and staff of the National Library of Ireland, the Librarian of Trinity College Library, the Librarian of the Royal Irish Academy, Siobhán O'Rafferty, and the Director and staff of the National Archives of Ireland. Patrick Melvin, Librarian of the Oireachtas Library at the Irish Dial, gave considerable help.

I was also fortunate to have splendid research assistants. Gillian

Johnston and David Chan, then graduate students at the University of California, Irvine, respectively hunted out sources on the impact on the United States of the Irish, the Famine and Fenianism, and on the influence of the Irish question upon Canada. Mark Duncan, then a Tutor at the University College, Dublin, provided further valuable research from the National Archives of Ireland and the National Library of Ireland. Helene Charlesworth, a professional researcher from Perth, Western Australia, scrupulously gathered documentation from the Western Australian Archives and the Battye Library, Perth, on Western Australia's Fenian prisoners, and their connections with the authorities and free society. My daughter Jane Keneally applied her remarkable skills as as researcher at various Irish archives, at the National Archives in Washington, DC, and at the Boston Public Library. In many of my own researches in Australia, the United States and Ireland, I had the robust help and companionship of my wife, Judy.

At the end of the process, the unedited manuscript was read for solecisms by the Professor of Anglo-Irish Literature, University College Dublin, Declan Kiberd, whose input, encouragement, scholarship and suggested strategies for dealing even-handedly with controversial phases of Irish history had a large and creative impact on the book. Needless to say, none of its errors, if they exist, are Declan's fault. His predecessor in the chair of Anglo-Irish Literature, the late Augustine Martin, and his wife Clair, were cherished supporters of the project. Professor Cormac O Gráda, also of University College Dublin, and an economic historian of great distinction, gave me the use of his wonderful article on oral sources, and answered some of my anxious questions.

Other notable friends of this narrative include Senator Edward Kennedy of Massachusetts, who successfully lobbied for a monument to Thomas Francis Meagher and the Irish Brigade to be erected on Antietam battlefield, whose forebears knew John Boyle O'Reilly, and who was throughout a splendid patron to *The Great Shame*. Michael Larkin of Lismany, County Galway, descended from Larkin contemporaries of Hugh Larkin, shared with me the fruits of his extraordinary memory of East Galway history, and introduced me to the direct descendants of Hugh who still live in Galway. In Australia, my sister-in-law Therese Johnson, also a descendant of Hugh Larkin, generously offered her research to me. The well-informed Leon O'Donnell of New Norfolk, Tasmania, accompanied Judy and I on a pilgrimage of Young Ireland sites in that state, and selflessly pointed me to various fascinating documentary and physical traces of Smith O'Brien and his fellow prisoners. Jack McGee of St Clair, New South Wales, another Young Ireland enthusiast, assisted through indefinite loans of rare sources on these extraordinary convicts. Professor

Richard Davis of the University of Tasmania, the leading Australian expert on Young Ireland, and his wife and fellow researcher, Marianne, gave consistent guidance and encouragement. Professor Alex Castles of Adelaide, South Australia, spaciously shared information on John Mitchel's sons, and handed me an article he had written on John Mitchel junior, commander of Fort Sumter. Professor Patrick O'Farrell of the University of New South Wales kindly sent me his article on the Famine as cultural property. John Boyle O'Reilly's most recent biographer, A. C. Evans, historian Anne-Maree Whitaker and Young Ireland enthusiast Peter O'Shaughnessy offered open-handed counsel.

For their generous agency services, and their enthusiasm, I thank three exceptional women: Jill Hickson, Deborah Rogers and Amanda Urban. I also have an unpayable debt to my editors, Penelope Hoare and Roger Cazalet of Random House UK, and Nan Talese of Nan Talese/Doubleday. Penelope Hoare read the unmanageable 2000-page version of this book, and, despite all the research clogging the veins of the narrative, discerned something of potential value there. Roger Cazalet managed an extensive editing-down with great skill, fraternity, understanding and generosity. Nan Talese dealt with the early, inchoate book and proposed many of the devices by which it might be reduced to readable form. If you enjoy this book, much of praise belongs to these three editors.

It is to state mere fact to say that I could not have survived this exercise in non-fiction without the love, nurture and protection offered by my wife, Judy, and by my daughters, Margaret and Jane. Friends also carried the burden, listening to repeated versions of the narrative and to reiterated biographies of its leading characters. I promise all of them I shall now behave more normally.

The writing of *The Great Shame* was an experience akin to being locked in a cupboard with a tyrannosaurus rex, and I could not have finished without the kindnesses of all those mentioned above, and of many who go unmentioned, who – I hope – will excuse the oversight.

NOTES

Abbreviations

ADB, *Australian Dictionary of Biography*
AONSW, Archives Office of New South Wales
BPL, Boston Public Library
BPP, *British Parliamentary Papers*
HRA, *Historical Records of Australia*
HRNSW, *Historical Records of New South Wales*
ML, Mitchel Library, Sydney
NAI, National Archives of Ireland
NLI, National Library of Ireland
NYPL, New York Public Library
PRO, Public Record Office
TSA, Tasmanian State Archives
WAA, Western Australian Archives

Abbreviations relating to newspapers, groups or individuals:

CGD, Charles Gavan Duffy
FB, Fenian Brotherhood
ILN, *Illustrated London News*
IRB, Irish Republican Brotherhood
JBOR John Boyle O'Reilly
N, *Nation*
NYT, *New York Times*
SMH, *Sydney Morning Herald*
SOB, Smith O'Brien
TFM, Thomas Francis Meagher
TL, *Times* of London
YI, Young Ireland

Newspaper reports to which a date is explicitly appended in the text are generally not referred to in these notes.

Preface

xii The Kennedys and Thomas Francis Meagher: Conversation between the author and Senator Ted Kennedy, April 1995.
xii Esther Larkin Petition: The Irish Gift, FS 23/1840, National Library of Australia.

Notes

1 Hugh Larkin's Ireland

3 Mount Street accident: *Galway Weekly Advertiser*, 20 July 1833.

4 Hugh Larkin's appearance: Ship's Indent, *Parmelia* (2), 4/7076, MF reel 2426, AONSW.

4 Larkin's temperament and oral remembrance of Larkin: Letter of Michael Larkin, Lismany, Galway, Irish descendant of Larkin and Tully, to Therese Johnson, Australian direct descendant of Larkin and Shields, undated, c. 1992; interview of Michael Larkin by author, July 1995; September 1997.

4 Hugh Larkin's locality: O Lorcáin, David, *Larkin Family History: Ireland to Illawarra*, Brisbane, 1983; MacLochlainn, Tadg, *A Signpost of Ballinsloe and District*, n.d.; parish, barony and other maps of East Galway Family History Society, Woodford Heritage Centre, Woodford, Co. Galway; *Annala Muinter Lorcáin*, Journal of Larkin Clan Association, Burpengary, Queensland, Vol. 6, 1990.

4 Expectation of resurrection of old Gaelic system: Clark, Samuel and Donnelly Jr, James S. (eds), *Irish Peasants: Violence and Political Unrest, 1780–1914*, Dublin, 1983.

4 Hugh's marriage and children: Ship's Indent, *Parmelia*, AONSW; Returns of Applications, 1837–43, 21 December 1841, 4/4492, MF reel 700, AONSW; Parish of Clontuskert, Church Records of Baptisms, Volumes 6 and 11 (8 August 1830; 19 February 1833), supplied by Woodford Heritage Centre, Woodford, Co. Galway.

4 The Gaelic-speaking West: O Tuathaigh, Gearóid, *Ireland before the Famine, 1798–1848*, Dublin, 1972.

4–5 Irish courtship and marriage: Tocqueville, Alexis de, *Alexis de Tocqueville's Journey in Ireland, July–August, 1835*, trans. and ed. Emmet Larkin, Dublin, 1990; Donnelly, S. J., *Priests and People in Pre-Famine Ireland 1780–1845*, Dublin, 1982.

5 Gaelic love poem: John Montague (ed.), *The Faber Book of Irish Verse*, London, 1974.

6 Earlier threat against Seymour, and Terry Altism generally: *Galway Free Press*, 31 March 1932.

6 Clancarty estates, Ballinasloe, Co. Galway: Inglis, Henry D., *A Journey Throughout Ireland During the Spring, Summer and Autumn of 1834*, Volume II, London, 1835.

6 Seymour's ultimate landlord and acreages: *Griffith's Valuation Lists*, Clontuskert, Co. Galway, 1855.

6 Seymour's status and East Galway wool breeding: Royal Society survey, East Galway, 1824, in O Gráda, Cormac, *Ireland Before and After the Famine: Explorations in Economic History, 1800–1925*, Dublin, 1993; indirect evidence of Seymours found in *Householder's Index*, Co. Galway, 1823–6 and 1852–5, NLI, and in *Griffith's Valuation Lists*, Clontuskert, Co. Galway, 1855.

6 Earlier prosperity and post-Napoleonic slump: O Gráda, O Tuathaigh, as above; Otway, C. G., *A Tour in Connaught*, Dublin, 1839; Kinealy, Christine, *This Great Calamity: The Irish Famine 1845–52*, Dublin, 1994; Hoppen, K. Theodore, *Ireland Since 1800: Conflict and Conformity*, London and New York, 1989.

6–7 Emancipation and O'Connell: MacDonagh, Oliver, *O'Connell*, London, 1991; O'Faolain, Sean, *King of the Beggars*, Dublin, 1980.
8 Shrinkage of franchise: Foster, R. F., *Modern Ireland 1600–1972*, London, 1988.
8 Class III families: O Gráda, as above.
8 Conacre: O Gráda, as above; Salaman, Redcliffe N., *The History and Social Influence of the Potato*, Cambridge, 1949; Mokyr, Joel, *Why Ireland Starved*, London, 1983.
9 Pressure on landlords and their attitudes to eviction: O Gráda, O Tuathaigh, as above.
10 Labourers in Ballinasloe area: Inglis, as above.
10 The Penal Laws and their impact on the native Irish: Moody, T. W. and Martin, F. X., *The Course of Irish History*, Niwot, CO, 1994; Smith, Cecil Woodham-, *The Great Hunger*, London, 1962.
11 Landlords and their behaviour: Lewis, George Cornwall, *On Local Disturbances in Ireland*, London, 1836; Johnson, James, *A Tour in Ireland with Meditations and Reflections*, London, 1844.
11 Peasant meals: Póirtéir, Cathal, *Famine Echoes*, Dublin, 1995.
12 Irish diet: First quotation from O Gráda, Cormac, *The Great Irish Famine*, Dublin, 1989; second from Salaman, Redcliffe N., FRS, 'The Influence of the Potato on the Course of Irish History', Tenth Finlay Memorial Lecture, Dublin, 1943.
13 Whiteboyism, Ribbonism, Terry Altism, including derivation of terms: McCartney, Donal, *The Dawning of Democracy: Ireland 1800–1878*, Dublin, 1987; Clark, Samuel and Donnelly, James S. (eds), *Irish Peasants: Violence and Political Unrest, 1780–1914*, Dublin, 1983; Beames, Michael, *Peasants and Power: The Whiteboy Movements and Their Control in Pre-Famine Ireland*, New York, 1983.
13 Presence of troops and story of Ned Lohan: Flynn, John S., *Ballymacward: The Story of an East Galway Parish*, Galway, 1982.
13 Switching of terms 'Ribbonism' and 'Terry Altism': *Galway Free Press* and *Galway Advertiser*, 1832–3, *passim*.
13–14 Ribbon activism in Clontuskert: *Galway Advertiser*, 24 March 1832.
Tithes: O Tuathaigh, as above; Hickey, D. J. and Doherty, J. E., *A Dictionary of Irish History 1800–1980*, Dublin, 1980.
14 The Lord Courtown case: *TL*, 18 July 1833.
15 Mining of Four Courts: Hickey and Doherty, as above.
15 Protest criminals: Rude, G., *Protest and Punishment*, Oxford, 1978.
15 Hugh's attack on Somerset House: Michael Larkin; *Galway Weekly Advertiser*, 3 August 1833; *Galway Free Press*, 31 July, 1 August 1833; *Connaught Journal*, 1 August 1833.
16 Troops in Laurencetown: Referred to later in Outrage Papers (Galway), 1846, 1398, NAI.
16 Hugh's capture: Interview with Michael Larkin; and newspapers as for attack.
16 Kilkenny assizes: *Galway Free Press*, 17 July 1833.
16 Prisons: O Tuathaigh, as above; Hill, Matthew Davenport, *A Paper on the Irish Convict Prisons*, London, 1857; and for the better conditions of paying prisoners, see later history of O'Connell and Young Irelanders.

17 Hessian and Strahanes: *Galway Free Press*, 31 July 1833; and Ship's Indent, *Parmelia*, 4/7076, AONSW.
17 Percentage Irish speakers: O Tuathaigh, as above.
17 The Orange Order: Pakenham, Thomas, *The Year of Liberty: The History of the Great Irish Rebellion of 1798*, London, 1969.
17 12 July parades, 1833: *TL*, 3 July 1833; 18 and 19 July 1833.
17–18 Coote Hill affray: *TL*, 22 July 1833.
19 Lohan story: Michael Larkin; tale occasionally reiterated in Galway. Researched by author and comprehensively by Dublin researcher, Mark Duncan. Contemporary newspapers, and other sources of NLI, and reports and documents, NAI, yielded no confirmation of tale.
19 Papal condemnation of secret societies: *Ad Graviora*, 1826, noted in O'Shea, James, *Priests, Politics and Society in Post-Famine Ireland: A Study of County Tipperary 1850–1891*, Dublin, 1981.
20 Demand for Coercion Act to operate in Longford: Colonial Secretary's Office, RP 1911, NAI.
20 Graftings in oral history: O Gráda, Cormac, 'The Great Famine in Folk Memory and in Song'. Unpublished at time of writing, kindly provided by author.
20 Turf: Mokyr, as above.
20–1 Ribbon song: Montague, as above.
21–2 Wakes, also animist mysteries, customs, mores, feast days: Doyle, Martin, *Irish Cottagers*, Dublin, 1833; Keenan, Desmond, *The Catholic Church in the Nineteenth Century*, Dublin, 1983; Donnelly, as above.
22 Hugh's departure, Galway gaol: *Galway Free Press*, 24 August 1833.
23 Esther remains in Lismany: Oral record confirmed by Returns of Applications, 1837–43, 4/4492, reel 700–1, 41/1333, AONSW.
23 Cholera: *Galway Weekly Advertiser*, 20 July 1833.
23–4 Strahanes and others: Ship's Indent, *Parmelia*.
24 Sodomy rare: Governor Sir George Gipps to Lord Stanley, 1843, quoted in O'Farrell, Patrick, *The Irish in Australia*, Sydney, 1986.
24 Hugh's scar: Ship's Indent, *Parmelia*.
24 Spike Island: Mitchel, John, *Jail Journal*, published with addenda and appendices from original text, *Irish Citizen*, New York, 1854.

2 The Shipping of Ireland, and the Exile of Chains

Chapter heading: Bateson, Charles, *The Convict Ships, 1787–1868*, Sydney, 1983.

26 *Parmelia*, Master Gilbert and career: Bateson, as above; Ship's Indent, *Parmelia*.
26 Major Anderson: Anderson, Joseph, *Recollections of a Peninsular Veteran*, London, 1913; Pike, Douglas (General Editor), *ADB*, 1788–1850, Volume 1, Melbourne, 1966–7.
27 Lloyd's classification of ships: Bateson, as above.
27 Surgeon Donoghoe, and his management of convicts: Bateson, as above; Surgeon-Superintendent's Journals, PRO 3206, 2/8272, reel 2426, AONSW.
27 Ship numbers, convict management: As for previous note.
27–8 Convict deck: Surgeon Peter Cunningham, quoted in Bateson, as above.

29–30 Hugh's details, and those of other prisoners: Ship's Indent, *Parmelia*, 4/7076, AONSW.

29 Hedge schools: O Tuathaigh, as above; Hickey and Doherty, as above.

31 Proportion of Ribbon offences: Ship's Indent, *Parmelia*, 4/7076, AONSW.

31 Lord Lieutenant's warrant, *Parmelia*: Musters and Papers, 2/8272, reel 2426, AONSW.

33 Convict sodomy: O'Farrell, as above.

33–4 Irish immigrants to North America, 1825–45: Miller, Kerby A., *Emigrants and Exiles: Ireland and the Irish Exodus to North America*, New York, 1985.

34 Immigrants, London, Upper Canada: Houston, Cecil J. and Smith, William J., *Irish Emigration and Canadian Settlement*, Toronto, 1990.

34 Irish immigrants to Britain, and Marx quotation: Davis, Graham, *The Irish in Britain 1815–1914*, Dublin, 1991.

34 Irish immigration to Australia: O'Farrell, as above.

34–6 Journey of *Parmelia*: Surgeon-Superintendent Donoghoe's Journal, 2/8272, AONSW.

36 Length of journey: Bateson, as above.

3 Assigning Ireland

Chapter heading: *BPP*, Volume XX, 1822, quoted in Robson, L. L., *The Convict Settlers of Australia*, Melbourne, 1965.

37 *Parmelia* anchors down-harbour: *Sydney Gazette*, 6 March 1834.

37 *Fairlie*: Bateson, as above; *Sydney Herald*, *Sydney Gazette*, *Sydney Monitor*, 6 March 1834.

37 Colonists' questions about convict behaviour aboard ship: Mudie, James, *The Felonry of New South Wales*, London, 1837.

37 Early landing of troops: *Sydney Gazette*, 8 March 1834.

38 Landing before 25 March 1834: *Parmelia* convicts no longer mentioned, *Sydney Gazette*, *Sydney Monitor*, *Sydney Herald* of that date.

38 Defenders and United Irishmen: Pakenham, O'Farrell, as above; Whitaker, Anne-Maree, *Unfinished Revolution*, Sydney, 1994; Kiernan, T. J., *The Irish Exiles in Australia*, Dublin, 1954; O'Donnell, Ruan, 'General Joseph Holt', in Reece, Bob (ed.), *Exiles from Erin*, Dublin, 1991; Holt, Joseph, *A Rum Story: The Adventures of Joseph Holt, Thirteen Years in Australia*, ed. P. O. O'Shaughnessy, Sydney, 1988.

39 Australian Vinegar Hill, 1804: Whitaker, as above; Clark, C. M. H., *A History of Australia*, Volume I, Melbourne, 1962.

40 Sir Richard Bourke: Clark, as above; *ADB*, Volume 1.

40 John Hubert Plunkett: O'Farrell, as above; *ADB*, Volume 2.

40 Roger Therry: *ADB*, Volume 2; Therry, Roger, *Reminiscences of Thirty Years' Residence in New South Wales and Victoria*, London, 1863.

41 Disrepute of convict women: *Sydney Herald*, 10 March 1834.

41 Eliza Burns tale: *Sydney Herald*, 3 March 1834.

42 Sydney and its society: Mudie, as above; Roberts, Stephen H., *The Squatting Age in Australia, 1835–1847*, Melbourne, 1935; Harris, Alexander, *Settlers*

and Convicts: Recollections of Sixteen Years' Labour in the Australian Backwoods, by an Emigrant Mechanic, Melbourne, 1969.

43 The barracks and E. A. Slade: *ADB*, Volume 2; *Return of Corporal Punishment inflicted by sentence of the Sydney Police bench, from the 4th to 30th September, in the presence of E. A. Slade, JP, Superintendent, Hyde Park Barracks, BPP*, Volume VI; *Reports from Select Committee on Transportation, BPP*, Volume XIX, E. A. Slade evidence, Sessions 1837; Hirst, John, *Convict Society and Its Enemies*, North Sydney, 1983.

43 Ullathorne's observations: Ullathorne, William, *The Horrors of Transportation Briefly Unfolded to the People*, Dublin, 1838, quoted in Hughes, Robert, *The Fatal Shore*, New York, 1987; *ADB*, Volume 2.

43 John Lhotsky: Heney, H. M. E., *In a Dark Glass: The Story of Paul Edmund Strzelecki*, Sydney, 1961.

43 New South Wales floggings: Hirst, as above.

44 Demand for labour, 1834; Roberts, as above.

44 Study of protest criminals: Rude, as above.

44 The Assignment system, Wakefield's tract: Hirst, as above; *HRNSW*, Volume 1, Part 2; Volume 5; Select Committee on Transportation, *BPP*, Volume XIX, 1837.

44 Assignment of Larkin and others: Memoranda Book, 1829–37, 2/8208, reel 2664, AONSW; 1837 Muster, HO 10/30, reel 70, AONSW.

45 The Nineteen Counties: Roberts, as above.

45 William Bradley: *ADB*, Volume 3; Brodribb, W. A., *Recollections of an Australian Squatter*, Sydney, 1883; Hancock, W. H., *Discovering Monaro*, Cambridge, 1972.

45 Convict muster 1837: As above.

45 Convict wages: *Butts of Tickets of Private Employment, 1841–42*, 4/4287, reel 592, AONSW; also reel 2664, AONSW.

46 'On the Plains of Emu', in Reece, *Exiles from Erin*, Appendix 1, as above.

46 Convict system seen as national disgrace: Hirst, as above; Shaw, A. G. L., *Convicts and the Colonies*, London, 1966; Select Committee on Transportation, *BPP*, 1837.

46 Norfolk Island mutiny: Anderson, as above.

47 Foster Fyans: Hughes, as above; *ADB*, Volume 1.

47 Anderson on Norfolk Island: Anderson, Hughes, as above.

47 Private employment tickets: Examples exist at 4/4287, reel 592, AONSW.

47 Absconders: *New South Wales Government Gazette*, 5 March 1834.

47 Hunter River desperadoes: *Sydney Herald*, same date.

48 Bold Jack Donahue (also Donohoe): Hughes, as above; Ward, Russell, *The Australian Legend*, Melbourne, 1958.

48 Brodribb in Monaro: Brodribb, as above; *ADB*, Volume 3.

48–9 View of Aborigines: Ward, as above.

49–52 Squatter pastoralists and their shepherds: Roberts, Ward, Harris, as above.

50–1 Shepherds and hut-keepers: Roberts, Harris, Mudie, Ward, as above.

53 Mudie's assigned convicts: Therry, Hirst, as above.

54 Currency lads and patriotism: Clark, C. M. H., *A Short History of Australia*, Melbourne, 1993.

4 The Limits of Location

Chapter heading: Ingleton, Geoffrey Chapman (ed.), *True Patriots All, or News from Early Australia*, Sydney, 1952.

56 Commissioners of Crown lands: Roberts, as above.
57 Conditions of wool marketing: Roberts, as above.
57 Ned Ryan, Ribbonman squatter: Barnett, M., *King of Galong Castle*, Sydney, 1978, quoted in Robertson, Sir Rutherford, *The Three Societies Lecture: Penal Settlement to High Technology and the Future*, 1988; Brennan, Niamh, 'The Ballagh Rioters Barracks "Rioters" ', in Reece, *Exiles from Erin*, as above.
58 Ngarigo tribe: Hancock, as above.
58 Early contact, terms used, cohabitation: Byrne, J. C., *Twelve Years' Wanderings in the British Colonies from 1835 to 1847*, 2 volumes, London, 1848, quoted in Ward, as above; Select Committee on Transportation, *BPP*, Volume XIX, evidence of Mudie and others, 1837.
60 Protectors of Aborigines: Roberts, Ward, as above.
60 Governor Gipps: Roberts, as above; *ADB*, Volume 1.
61 Meagher family history, and character, Thomas Meagher senior: Gavan Duffy manuscript collection, MS 12, Royal Irish Academy; Duffy, Charles Gavan, *Four Years of Irish History, 1845–1849*, Melbourne, 1883.
61 P. J. Smyth on Meagher: Smyth, P. J., *The Life and Times of Thomas Francis Meagher*, ed. J. C. Waters, Dublin, 1867.
61–2 Thomas Francis Meagher, early life: narrated by Meagher in *Irish American*, 5 January 1856; Cavanagh, Michael, *The Memoirs of General Thomas Francis Meagher*, Worcester, MA, 1892.
62 William Smith O'Brien: *Smith O'Brien's Retrospect, 1848*, MS 464, NLI; O'Brien, William Smith, *To Solitude Consigned: The Tasmanian Journal of William Smith O'Brien, 1849–1853*, ed. Richard Davis (General Editor), Sydney, 1995; O'Brien, Grania, *These My Friends and Forebears: The O'Briens of Dromoland*, Whitegate, Co. Clare, 1991; Adam-Smith, Patsy, *Heart of Exile*, Melbourne, 1986; Davis, Richard, *The Young Ireland Movement*, Dublin, 1987.
64 Smith O'Brien's mistress: Weir, Hugh W. I., 'William Smith O'Brien's Other Family', *The Other Clare*, Vol. 20, April 1996.
65–6 First Irish Poor Law: O'Connor, John, *The Workhouses of Ireland – The Fate of Ireland's Poor*, Dublin, 1995; MacDonagh, as above; Kinealy, as above; O'Brien, Grania, as above.
66 Good harvest 1837: Mokyr, O Gráda, as above.

5 Ireland and the *Whitby* Women

Chapter heading: Robinson, Portia, *The Women of Botany Bay*, Sydney, 1993.

67 O'Connell's doldrums: *Dublin Protestant Guardian*, reproduced in *TL*, 3 October 1838.
67–8 Mary Shields's crime and those of co-condemned: *Limerick Chronicle*, 9 January 1839.

68 Mary Shields's wedding: Marriage records of the parish of St John's, Limerick, 2 May 1834, Entry No. 593.
68 Baptismal records: St Michael's, Limerick. Michael, 10 May 1835; Bridget, 12 May 1837.
68 Pipe or *dudeen*-smoking: Harris, as above.
69 Children sharing prison with mothers: List of children on *Whitby*, 2/8282, reel 2428, AONSW.
69 Criminal records of Irish women convicts: Robinson, as above.
69 Summer seasonal hunger: *Report of the Commissioners Appointed to take the Census of Ireland for the year 1841*, *BPP*, Volume XXIV, 1843. And apart from early mentioned works, Crawford, Margaret (ed.), *Famine: The Irish Experience, 900–1900, Subsistence Crises and Famines in Ireland*, Edinburgh, 1989; the chapter by Margaret Crawford, 'Subsistence Crises and Famines in Ireland: A Nutritionist's View', in her *Famine: The Irish Experience, 900–1900*, as above.
69 Poor Laws and workhouses, George Nicholls, Thackeray: O'Connor, as above.
71 *Roslin Castle* surgeon, *Neva*: Bateson, as above.
71 Shields in Kilmainham: might equally have been Newgate, but Kilmainham suggested by proximity to the Grand Canal.
71 People and articles shipped on *Whitby*: Ship's Indent, 2/8282, reel 2428, AONSW (also on Microfiche 739); Lord Lieutenant's Warrant, *Whitby*, 4/7078, AONSW; O'Connor, as above.
71–2 John Kidd and health of convicts: Surgeon's Log, *Whitby*, PRO 3212, reel 2428, AONSW.
72 Surgeon Cunningham: Bateson, Robinson, as above.
72 New Rules, Surgeon's behaviour: *BPP*, Volume XLVII, 1834.
72 Special disadvantages of Irish convict women: Robinson, as above.
72 Children's clothing: As above, 2/8282, AONSW.
73 *Whitby*'s children: As above, 2/8282, AONSW.
73 Names of women's relatives in NSW: As above, 2/8282, AONSW.
73 Inferior victualling: Sir George Gipps to Glenelg, 25 May 1838, *HRA*, Volume XIX.
74 *Whitby* meets *Freak*: *Sydney Gazette*, 25 June 1839.

6 The Lass from the Female Factory

Chapter heading: Mudie's evidence, Select Committee, *BPP*, Volume XIX, 1837.

75 Whitby's cargo: *Sydney Gazette*, 26 June 1839.
75 Attacks on female assignment: Hirst, as above; *Report of Select Committee on Transportation*, *BPP*, Volume XXII, 1838.
75 Opinion of Colonial Secretary: 25 September 1841, Colonial Secretary's Correspondence, Female Factory, Female Factory Papers, 4/3691, reel 1053, AONSW.
75 Labourers to Valparaiso: Roberts, as above.
76 Landing of *Whitby* women and children: *Sydney Monitor*, 2 July 1839.

76 Landing of women described: Mudie, as above.
76 Sisters of Charity in Sydney: Reid, Richard and Mongan, Cheryl, *A Decent Set of Girls*, Yass, NSW, 1996.
76 Taking women upriver: Salt, Annette, *These Outcast Women – The Parramatta Female Factory, 1821–1848*, Sydney, 1984; Colonial Secretary's Memoranda Book, 1829–37, 13 August 1829, 2/8208, reel 2664, AONSW.
77 Female Factory: Salt, as above; Returns of Female Factory, 4/7327, reel 702, and Colonial Secretary's file, 4/2610–1, AONSW.
78 'The Lass from the Female Factory': Ingleton, as above.
78 Mudie's view of Factory: Select Committee on Transportation, *BPP*, Volume XIX, 1837.
78–9 Governor and Lady Gipps: Salt; *ADB*, Volume 1, as above.
79 Factory needlework: *Government Gazette*, 18 June 1839.
79 Orphanages: Salt, Therry, as above.
79–80 TFM, Stonyhurst and Belgium: Smyth, as above; *Irish American*, 5 January 1856.
80 Factory women's grievances: Gipps to Lord Stanley, 20 May 1843, *HRA*, Series 1, Vol. XXII.
81 Factory women's insurgency: Therry, as above.
81 Women protect Corcoran: *BPP*, Volume XXII, 1843.
81 Scandal at Factory: Deputy Commissary-General Miller to the Colonial Secretary, 20 October 1843, *BPP*, Volume XIX.
81–2 Trevelyan's orders for Female Factory: *BPP*, Volume XX, 1843.
82 Assignment of well-conducted women: 30 June 1843, Colonial Secretary's Correspondence, Female Factory, 4/3691, reel 1053, AONSW.
82 Women leaving Factory: Gipps to Stanley, 20 May 1843, *HRA*, Volume XXII.
83 Children travelling with mothers: Salt, as above, quoting Rules and Regulations of Female Factory, drawn up by Governor Darling.
83 Descriptions of Shields, Carthy and Conelly: Tickets-of-Leave, 4/4178, reel 949, AONSW; Conelly (spelled Connelly here) 43/1821; Carthy 43/1826; Shields 43/1816. The side of Shields's ticket is marked 'Per the Gov. Minute on a Ticket on the Matron of the FF Parramatta R No 43/7214'.
83 General nature of travel in New South Wales: Harris, Roberts, Ward, as above.
84 The emancipists' bank and Samuel Terry: *ADB*, Volume 2.
84 Depression: Brodribb, Roberts, Hancock, as above.
84 Tallow: Roberts, as above.
84 Bradley's interests: Brodribb, Hancock, as above; *ADB*, Volume 3.
84 Brodribb's manner of life (and planned marriage): Brodribb; *ADB*, Volume 3.
85–6 Hugh's application, and others noted: Returns of applications, 1837–43, 4/4492, reel 700–1, AONSW. In Hugh's case 41/1333, 21 December 1841.
86 Other applications: 4/4492, reel 700–1, AONSW.
86 Men approved for family reunion: Minute of Colonial Secretary, 5 May 1842, copies of letters sent re: convicts, 4/3689, reel 1053, AONSW.
87 Order-in-Council ending transportation, and plans to revive it: Hirst, as above.
87 Hugh's ticket-of-leave: 4/4163, reel 944, 42/1457, AONSW.
88–90 Brodribb's and Hugh's adventures: Brodribb, as above.

7 Ireland Young and Old

Chapter heading: From *The Irish Sketch Book*, Thackeray, quoted in O'Faolain, as above.

91 TFM and Inns of Court: Smyth, MacDonagh, as above; Molony, John N., *A Soul Came into Ireland: Thomas Davis 1814–1845*, Dublin, 1995.
91 Dublin of the period: McCall, Seamus, *Irish Mitchel*, Dublin, 1938.
91 Repeal and O'Connell: MacDonagh, O'Faolain, as above, and for all subsequent O'Connell references unless otherwise noted.
92 O'Connell and slavery: Ignatiev, Noel, *How the Irish Became White*, New York, 1995.
93 Maintenance of Repeal rent amongst peasants: O Tuathaigh, as above.
93 Founding the *Nation*: Molony, as above; Doheny, Michael, *The Felon's Track*, Dublin, 1920; Davis, Richard, *The Young Ireland Movement*, Dublin, 1987; Pearl, Cyril, *The Three Lives of Gavan Duffy*, Kensington, NSW, 1979.
93 First edition, *Nation*: *N*, 15 October 1842.
94 'Faugh-a-Ballagh': *N*, 29 October 1842.
94 Davis verses: *The Poems of Thomas Davis*, ed. Thomas Wallace, Dublin, 1848.
94 Farmer–Agitator dialogue: *N*, 7 January 1843.
95 Monster meetings: Apart from O'Connell sources above, *N*, *passim*, summer 1843; Davis, Richard, *Young Ireland*; Owens, Garry, 'Hedge Schools of Politics: O'Connell's Monster Meetings', *History Ireland*, Vol. 2, No. 1, 1994.
96 New York Repeal meeting: *N*, 1 July 1843.
98 SOB's letter on joining Repeal: *N*, 28 October 1843.
98 Lady O'Brien to SOB over joining Repeal: 24 October 1843, O'Brien Papers, MS 443, NLI.
99 SOB and Repeal: O'Connell sources, Davis, Richard, *Young Ireland*, and O'Brien, Grania, as above; Adam-Smith, as above.
100 TFM's speeches and opinions: Meagher, Thomas Francis, Brevet Major-General, United States Army, *Speeches on the Legislative Independence of Ireland*, New York, 1870; Griffith, Arthur (ed.), *Meagher of the Sword*, Dublin, 1916; Lyons, W. F., *Brigadier General Thomas Francis Meagher*, New York, 1870; Athearn, Robert G., *Thomas Francis Meagher: An Irish Revolutionary in America*, Boulder, CO, 1949.
100 Young TFM's confession of dandyism: Duffy, as above.
100 Origins of term 'Young Ireland', and subsequent Young Ireland material: Davis, Richard, *Young Ireland*, Doheny, Duffy, as above.
100 'Letters of a Protestant on Repeal': *N*, 15 and 22 June 1844.
101 Mitchel's youth, John Martin, and subsequent Mitchel material unless otherwise noted: McCall, as above; Dillon, William, *Life of John Mitchel*, Volume 1, London, 1888; Sillard, P. A., *The Life of John Mitchel*, Dublin, 1908.
102 'The Anti-Protestant Catholics': *N*, 27 May 1843.
102 Repeal meeting over colleges: usual sources, YI; Doheny, as above.
102 '82 Club: Davis, Richard, *Young Ireland*, Doheny, Duffy, as above.
103 SOB on '82 Club uniform: Davis, Richard, *Young Ireland*, as above.

103 Mitchel meets TFM: *Irish Citizen*, 2 November 1867. For first meeting, Smyth, as above.
104 Shields bears Larkin a child: Baptismal Records, St Peter and St Paul's Cathedral, Goulburn, 22 August 1844.
104 Brodribb's marriage: Brodribb; *ADB*, Volume 3.

8 A Fond Farewell to the White Potatoes

Chapter heading: *Béaloideas*, Irish Folklore Commission, quoted in O Gráda, Cormac, 'The Great Famine in Folk Memory and in Song', unpublished at time of writing and kindly provided by author.

105 Courtship and death of Davis: Molony, Pearl, Duffy, as above.
106 Mitchel on railways and their destruction: *N*, 22 November 1845.
106 Onset of blight and subsequent Famine material unless otherwise noted: Mokyr, *Why Ireland Starved*, and O Gráda, *Ireland Before and After the Famine*, as above; Edwards, R. Dudley and Williams, T. Desmond (eds), *The Great Famine: Studies in Irish History, 1845–52*, Dublin, 1956; Smith, Woodham-, as above; O'Rourke, Canon John, *The Great Irish Famine*, Dublin, 1989; Kinealy, as above; Póirtéir, Cathal (ed.), *The Great Irish Famine*, Dublin, 1995; Daly, Mary E., *The Famine in Ireland*, Dublin, 1986.
107 Peasant reaction to rotting potatoes, East Galway: Póirtéir, *Famine Echoes*, as above; *Béaloideas*, quoted in O Gráda, 'The Great Famine', as above.
107 Liberator expresses concern to SOB: MacDonagh, as above.
108 Benthamite Utilitarianism: Kinealy, as above.
108 Malthus on Ireland: Mokyr, as above.
109 Trevelyan on Irish: Trevelyan, Charles, *The Irish Crisis*, London, 1848.
109 Connubiality figures: Mokyr, as above.
109 Attitude to Indian corn, and names: As well as standard sources, Póirtéir, *Famine Echoes*, as above.
110 No grounds for apprehension: *Galway Mercury*, 20 September 1845.
110 Irish names of Famine: O Gráda, 'The Great Famine', as above.
110 Survey of five townlands in Longford barony: Relief Commission Papers, 1, 2/441/16, NAI.
110–11 Ballinasloe area: Egan, Patrick K., *The Parish of Ballinasloe*, Galway, 1994.
111 Visitor to Ballinasloe: Nicholson, Asenath, *Ireland's Welcome to a Stranger*, London, 1847.
111 Attributing Famine to census: O Gráda, 'The Great Famine', as above.
111–12 Famine fevers, cause and impact: MacArthur, Sir William P., 'Medical History of the Famine', in Edwards and Williams, as above.
111 T. Harrison, Ballinasloe Dispensary, and Loughrea Dispensary: *BPP*, Volume XXXVII, 1846.
112 Ballinasloe workhouse fever wards: O'Connor, as above.
113 Prophecy of worse things: *N*, 11 April 1846.
113 SOB's view of Famine: MacDonagh, and SOB, *To Solitude Consigned*, as above.
113–14 SOB's parliamentary imprisonment: *ILN*, 9 May 1846; *TL*, 8 May 1846.
114 East Galway evictions: *Freeman's Journal*, 9 April 1846; *ILN*, 4 April 1846.

114 SOB disappointed by Repeal: CGD, as above.
114–15 YI's visit to O'Connell and SOB: Davis, Richard, *Young Ireland*, as above; *Thomas Francis Meagher Reminiscences*, J. M. (John Martin), *Weekly Times*, Dublin, 16 November 1867.
115 Whig alliance: CGD, Doheny, MacDonagh, as above; Davis, Richard, *Young Ireland*, as above.
115 CGD's view of the emergent TFM: CGD, as above.
115 This and later speeches, TFM, unless otherwise noted: Meagher, Brevet Major-General, *Speeches on Legislative Independence*, as above; Griffith, as above.
117–18 Mitchel on Famine: *N* article, reproduced in Mitchel, John, *History of Ireland from the Treaty of Limerick to the Present Time*, Volume II, Dublin, n.d.
118 O'Connell and his tenants: MacDonagh, as above.
118 O'Briens and their tenants: O'Brien, Grania, as above, based on Distress Papers, NAI, and O'Brien Papers, NLI; Smith, Woodham-, as above.
119 Lord Monteagle: Smith, Woodham-, as above; O'Mahony, Christopher and Thompson, Valerie, *Poverty to Promise: The Monteagle Emigrants, 1838–58*, Sydney, 1994.
119 Trial, and all subsequent trials of CGD: Duffy, Pearl, as above; Davis, Richard, *Young Ireland*, as above.
120–3 Crisis in Repeal, and subsequent O'Connell material unless otherwise noted: MacDonagh, CGD, as above; Davis, Richard, *Young Ireland*, as above.
123 Speranza on TFM: *N*, 8 August 1846.
123 Impact of Davis's death on Speranza: Yeats, William Butler, quoted in *Thomas Davis Centenary Address*, Oxford, 1947.
123 Speranza's life and career: Ellmann, Richard, *Oscar Wilde*, London, 1987; Pearson, Hesketh, *The Life of Oscar Wilde*, London, 1954.
123 'Liberty's torch . . .': Speranza, *It Was the Lark*, *N*, 25 April 1846.
123–4 Poems and career of Eva: Patrick, Ross and Patrick, Heather, *Exiles Undaunted: The Irish Rebels Kevin and Eva O'Doherty*, University of Queensland, St Lucia, Brisbane, 1989.
124 Eva on TFM: *N*, 22 August 1846.
125 Killimor Relief Committee: Plea from Killimor Relief Union, Relief Commission Papers, 3/2, Galway, 2/441/43, NAI.
125 Conditions in East Galway: Egan, as above.
125 Outrages, Eyre, Lawrence: Outrage Papers (Galway), 1398, 1846 and 1466, 1847, NAI.

9 A Thousand Farewells to You, Island of St Patrick

Chapter heading: Quoted in O Gráda, 'The Great Famine', as above.

126 'Weary men, what reap ye?': Speranza, *N*, 23 January 1847.
126 Mitchel on visit to village family: *N*, 16 January 1847.
127 Dr Donovan on Taureen: *Cork Southern Reporter*, 23 January 1847.
127 People's hunt for food sources: Póirtéir, *Famine Echoes*, as above.

127–8 Further Famine diseases and practices adopted to contain them: MacArthur, in Edwards and Williams, as above.
128 Thomas Burke to sister: Fitzpatrick, David, 'Flight from Famine', in Póirtéir, *The Great Irish Famine*, as above.
128 Death rate and workhouses: O'Connor, as above.
128 People bear 'worst privations' rather than accept relief: *BPP*, Volume XXXVII, 1846.
128 'O King of Glory . . .': 'Song of the Black Potatoes', O Gráda, 'The Great Famine', as above.
129 Gregory clause: Kinealy, Smith, Woodham-, as above.
129 'young crows . . .': As for 'O King of Glory . . .'.
129 Food sources: Póirtéir, *Famine Echoes*, as above.
129 Closing of depots and founding of relief committees, and all subsequent issues: Standard Famine sources, as above, unless otherwise stated.
130 Maria Edgeworth: Standard Famine sources, as above.
130 Soup kitchen described by Mitchel: McCall, as above.
130 Lord Clancarty on outdoor relief: *BPP*, Volume XV, 1849.
131 Soup riot in Ballinasloe: Outrage Papers (Galway), 1466, 1847, NAI.
131 British Association: Standard sources, as above; *Report of the British Association for the Relief of Extreme Distress in Ireland and Scotland*, London, 1849.
131 Cummins visiting Skibbereen: *TL*, 24 December 1846.
131 Trevelyan warns Association: Standard sources, as above.
132 Queen Victoria's contribution: British Association, *Report*, as above.
132 James Mahony on West Cork: *ILN*, 13 and 20 February 1847.
132 American contribution: Smith, Woodham-, as above.
132 Kevin Izod O'Doherty: Patrick and Patrick, as above.
132 Cry for reform with Jesus's help: O Gráda, 'The Great Famine', as above.
133 Potato blight from Atlantic to Caspian: CGD, as above.
133 Confederation and other YI developments: Doheny, CGD, Davis, as above.
134 O'Connell's last Commons speech: Standard O'Connell sources; *Hansard*, 8 February 1847, Volume LXXXIX.
135 Emigration: Davis, Graham, *Irish in Britain*, as above; Houston and Smyth, Miller, as above; Mackay, Donald, *Flight from Famine: The Coming of the Irish to Canada*, Toronto, 1990; Gallagher, Thomas, *Paddy's Lament: Ireland 1846–7*, New York, 1982; Whyte, Robert, *Famine Ship Diary* (originally, *The Ocean Plague*), ed. James Managan, Dublin, 1994.
135 Emigrant and hurley stick: O Gráda, 'The Great Famine', as above.
136 Chances for pilferage, East Galway: Outrage Papers (Galway), 1398, 1846 and 1466, 1847, NAI.
136 Arrival, Famine emigrants, River Mersey: *ILN*, 15 March 1847.
136 Engels on Irish in England: Kinealy, as above.
136 Board of Commissioners of Emigration, New York: Bayor, Ronald H. and Meagher, Timothy J. (eds), *The New York Irish*, Baltimore, MD, 1996.
137 Castle Garden: Standard sources, as above; Ernst, Robert, *Immigrant Life in New York City, 1825–1863*, Syracuse, NY, 1994.
137 Landing fever patients: Keegan, Gerald, *Famine Diary – Journey to a New World*, Dublin, 1991.
138 Grosse Ile, summer 1847: Standard sources, as above; Whyte, Keegan, as

above; Jordan, J. A., *The Grosse-Isle Tragedy and the Monument to the Irish Famine Victims, 1847*, Quebec, 1909.

138 Voyage of *Ajax*: Whyte, as above.

139 Partridge Island: Standard sources, Jordan, as above.

139 Irish at St Catherine's: Whyte, as above.

140 *Nation* advises emigrants: *N*, 8 January 1847.

140 Birth and death of Larkin-Shields daughter: O Lorcáin, as above.

141 Irish convict marriage, New South Wales style: Therry, as above.

141 Marriage of Larkin and Shields: Marriage Register, St Peter and St Paul's Cathedral, Goulburn, 24 December 1848 (2197, Vol. 65), 16 March 1848.

142 Governor FitzRoy: *ADB*, Volume 1.

142 Hugh's conditional pardon: 4/4459, reel 788, 48/1224, 1 June 1848, AONSW.

142 Land Deed, Cowper Street: Land Deeds, 48/11967, 25 October 1848, Land Title Office, NSW.

142 Birth of Anne Larkin: Baptismal Register, St Peter and St Paul's Cathedral, Goulburn, 24 December 1848 (2197, Vol. 65), in O Lorcáin, as above.

142 Brodribb family tragedy: Brodribb, as above.

142 Bradley's loss: *ADB*, Volume 3.

143 Warrant to pay Hugh: 4/4548, reel 597, March 1849, AONSW.

143 Hugh's bank account: 2/8391, reel 58, copied from PRO, AONSW.

143 Land Deed, Grafton Street: Land Deeds, 49/3963, 18 April 1849.

143 *Sydney Morning Herald* celebrates political liberties of New South Wales: *SMH*, 26 July 1848.

143 Anti-transportation successes: Hirst, as above; Pearl, Cyril, *Brilliant Dan Deniehy*, Melbourne, 1972.

10 Fiasco and Noble Gesture: The Rebellion of Young Ireland

Chapter heading: TFM, *N*, 15 February 1851.

144 YI developments and movements, and subsequent movements and developments unless otherwise noted: CGD, Doheny, Pearl, as above; Davis, Richard, *Young Ireland*, as above.

144 Balfe: Petrow, Stefan, 'Judas in Tasmania', from Davis, Richard, *et al.* (eds), *Irish-Australian Studies, Papers Delivered at the Irish-Australian Conference*, Hobart, 1995.

145 Emergence of Lalor: CGD, Doheny, Davis, Richard, *Young Ireland*, as above.

145 Mitchel's expectations of peasants' fighting power: CGD, as above.

146 Affection of family for Mitchel: Dillon, Volumes 1 and 2, as above.

147 *United Irishman*: Dillon, and standard Mitchel and CGD sources, as above.

147 Mitchel's 'Letters to Ulster Protestants': Reproduced as Mitchel, John, *An Ulster Man for Ireland*, Dublin, 1917.

148 CGD's excitement over French revolution: *N*, 14 March 1848.

148 Lord Clarendon calls on 'striplings': CGD, as above.

149 Chartist march: Davis, Graham, as above.

150 Mitchel on his trial: Mitchel, John, *Jail Journal*, as above.

151 Eva's 'For one . . .': Davis, Richard, *Young Ireland*, as above.

153 Mitchel, on 'pauper appetite': *N*, quoted in McCall, as above.

153 Martin's view of Mitchel's transportation: *Irish Felon*, 24 June 1848.
153 *Felon* quotes *Castlebar Telegraph*: *Irish Felon*, 1 July 1848.
154 '*Alea Jacta Est*' and 'Silken Thomas': 15 July 1848. (Verse begins: 'The banners wave . . .')
155 Dublin press on TFM and SOB: Davis, Richard, *Young Ireland*, as above.
155–6 Arrest of TFM and Doheny: CGD, Doheny, as above.
156 Slievenamon meeting: Doheny, as above; Davis, Richard, *Young Ireland*, as above; *Tipperary Vindicator*, 22 July 1848.
157 TFM departs Waterford, goes to Dublin: *N*, 8 February 1851.
157–8 TFM's movements on hearing of suspension of Habeas Corpus, and journey with Dillon: *N*, 15 February 1851.
158 Finding SOB, and TFM's argument for move to Kilkenny: *N*, 22 February 1851.
159 Movements of YI rebels: As well as standard sources, especially Doheny, CGD, as above; Adam-Smith, as above.
159–62 O'Donohoe's adventures, SOB's call for respect for property: O'Donohoe manuscript, 'The Rising of 1848', MS 770, NLI.
162 MacManus: CGD, Doheny, as above.
163 Cavalry permitted to pass, quotation: O'Donohoe MS, as above.
163–4 YI's further movements and conferences: Standard YI sources, as above; TFM, *N*, 1 March 1851.
164 MacManus: CGD, as above.
164–5 Account of battle: Usual sources; *ILN*, 5 August 1848.
165 Father Fitzgerald's version of Ballingary: Fitzgerald, Reverend P., *Personal Recollections of the Insurrection of Ballingarry*, Dublin, 1861.
166 The military encampments at Ballingarry: *TL*, 5 August 1848.
166 O'Gorman's adventures: Doheny, as above.
167 McGee's adventures: *N*, 15 March 1851.

11 Young Ireland on Trial

Chapter heading: Grace O'Brien to Anne Martineau, O'Brien, Grania, as above.

170 Mitchel in Bermuda: Mitchel, *Jail Journal*, as above; Shaw, as above.
172 TFM, O'Donohoe, Doheny on run: Doheny, as above.
173 Robert O'Brien's admiration for his brother's nobility: O'Brien, Grania, as above.
173 Duffy and O'Doherty trials: Doheny, CGD, as above.
173 'Our Harvest Prospects': *Irish Tribune*, 8 July 1848.
174 Eva and O'Doherty: Patrick and Patrick, as above. See also Eva O'Doherty's notes, OM-71, John Oxley Library, Brisbane.
175 Martin's trial: Doheny, CGD, as above.
176 Sir Lucius following SOB's arrest: O'Brien, Grania, as above.
176 Reproach of Smith O'Brien: Examples from this book include letters from Lucius and Lady O'Brien to SOB in MS 443, NLI, and Thomas Chisholm Anstey to SOB: 4 April 1850, MS 443, NLI, copied to NS553/1, TSA. (This letter also had the further motivation of urging SOB to take a ticket-of-leave.) Similar sentiments expressed by Fitzgerald, as above. Of the not so gentle variety: *TL*, 30 August 1848.

176 The O'Brien family following O'Brien's arrest and during trial: From O'Brien Papers, NLI, quoted in O'Brien, Grania, Adam-Smith, as above.
176–7 Visit to TFM's cell: Lyons, as above.
177 Charges and trial: Doheny, CGD, as above; *ILN*, 7 October, 14 October 1848.
178 Grace to Anne Martineau: O'Brien Papers, NLI, Adam-Smith, as above.
179 Briskness of O'Brien's trial: *TL*, 2 October 1848.
179 Form of sentence for high treason: Mitchel, *History of Ireland*, Volume II.
179 Grief of women at O'Brien's sentence: *ILN*, 14 October 1848.
179 Robert O'Brien's opinion of verdict and his brother's mind: O'Brien Papers, NLI, quoted in O'Brien, Grania, as above.
180 Trial of MacManus and O'Donohoe: Standard YI sources.
180 Report on TFM: *TL*, 18 October 1848, quoting from *Cork Examiner*.
180 Women at TFM's trial: *TL*, 20 October 1848.
181 Old policeman as witness, and subsequent details: *N*, 22 February 1851.
182 TFM's speech from the dock: CGD, Lyons, Griffith, as above.
182 Other prisoners greet condemned Meagher: O'Donohoe, *N*, 15 December 1850.
182 CGD and O'Doherty plan escape: CGD, as above.
183 *Warder* on SOB's death sentence: *Warder*, 14 October 1848, quoted in Davis, Richard, *Young Ireland*, as above.
183 Lady O'Brien's *Political Duty*: MS 2655, NLI.
183 Dr O'Hanlon to SOB: 5 January 1849, O'Brien Papers, MS 443, NLI.
183 SOB invokes Thermopylae: SOB, *To Solitude Consigned*, as above, hereafter cited as SOB, *Journal*, and also found at MS 3923, NLI.
184 Michael Shaughnessy and child convicts: Smith, Woodham-, as above.
184 Arrival of child convicts, VDL: Indents and Papers of ships sent to Van Diemen's Land, D12, Mitchel Library.
184 Revival of blight, 1848, and increased suffering, East Galway: Egan, as above; *BPP*, Volume XLVIII, 1849; *Poor Law Commissioners, Second Report*, London, 1849.
185 Ireland's ingratitude: *TL*, 30 August 1848.
185 Turnip stealing: Póirtéir, *Famine Echoes*, as above.
185 Esther's resources of food: As for previous note; Póirtéir, *Great Irish Famine*, as above.
185–6 British Association and Strzelecki: Heney, as above; Captain Mann, *Report of the British Association*, as above.

12 Shipping Young Ireland

Chapter heading: TFM, *N*, 27 July 1850.

187 Denison, his orders and relations with State prisoners: Denison, Sir William, *Varieties of Vice-Regal Life*, London, 1870.
188 TFM to Doheny: Lyons, as above.
188 SOB to Anne Martineau: O'Brien Papers, MS 443, NLI.
188 Costs of trial: As for previous note.
188 Life led by prisoners: CGD, as above.

188 Mitchel in Bermuda, and subsequent Mitchel experiences unless otherwise noted: Mitchel, *Jail Journal*, as above.
189 SOB's Christmas invitation to Lady O'Brien: O'Brien Papers, MS 443, NLI.
189 O'Brien women find TFM amusing: O'Brien, Grania, as above.
189 Creation of trust arrangement for Cahirmoyle: As for previous note.
189 The bounty of the Australian table: Harris, Russell Ward, as above.
189 Letter of Robert to SOB: O'Brien Papers, MS 443, NLI.
189 Onset of cholera: MacArthur in Edwards and Williams, as above; Geary, Lawrence M., 'Famine, Fever, and the Bloody Flux', in Póirtéir, *Famine Echoes*, as above.
189 East Galway, wearing apparel: *BPP*, Volume XLVIII, 1849.
189–90 Cremation of Garveys: O Gráda, 'The Great Famine', as above.
190 Shrinkage of houses and population, East Galway: *Report of Census Commissioners, 1851*, as above.
190 Later movements of Esther Larkin: Oral record.
191 TFM's invitation to O'Farrell: Michael O'Farrell Papers, 5 May 1849, MS 9786, Trinity College Library, Dublin.
191 Mitchel in Bermuda: Mitchel, *Jail Journal*, as above.
192 Struggle of SOB and lawyers against transportation, meeting with Lady O'Brien, etc.: SOB to O'Farrell, 20 June 1849, Michael O'Farrell Papers, MS 9786, as above.
193 TFM's beliefs on monarchy and republic: Gavan Duffy manuscript collection, MS 12, document headed 'Meagher's Politics', Royal Irish Academy.
193 Transportation of O'Doherty and Martin: Patrick and Patrick, as above.
194 MacManus to O'Farrell: O'Farrell Papers, 18 June 1849, MS 9786, as above.
194 O'Doherty and Martin nicknames: Kiernan, as above.
194–5 Grey's assurance to Sir Lucius: Touhill, Blanche M., *William Smith O'Brien and His Revolutionary Friends in Penal Exile*, Columbia, MO, 1981.
195 SOB poem: O'Brien Papers, MS 443, NLI.
195 TFM's shopping list before transportation: TFM's invoices, June 1849, MS 7410, NLI.
195–6 Transporting YI across the city and aboard ship: Quoted from *Freeman's Journal*, *TL*, 11 July 1949.
196 SOB's exhilaration at being on the water and all other unnoted references to do with transportation: SOB, *Journal*, Part 1, as above.
196 O'Farrell goes to harbour and boards *Swift*: O'Farrell Papers, MS 9786, as above.
196 SOB's version of *Swift* and its voyage: SOB, *Journal*, as above.
196 TFM's version: *N*, 27 July 1850.
196 SOB's accommodation: O'Brien to family, MS 443, NLI.
197 O'Donohoe's experience on *Swift*: *N*, 15 December 1850.
197 Readings on board: O'Donohoe, *N*, as for previous note; TFM, *N*, 27 July 1850; SOB, *Journal*, as above.
197 O'Donohoe to his wife: *Nation* (New York), 26 January 1850.
198 SOB's Sergeant Perry verse, and most subsequent SOB verses: SOB, *Journal*, as above.
199 O'Doherty and Martin arrive Sydney: Patrick and Patrick, as above.
199 Meagher's impressions of Hobart: *Nation* (New York), 25 May 1850.

199–200 *Courier*'s advice to State prisoners: *Hobart Town Courier*, 31 October 1849.
200 Details of conditions of ticket-of-leave, and subsequent SOB treatment, unless otherwise noted: SOB, *Journal*, as above; Denison, Sir William, as above.
200 TFM, Nairn, and later descriptions of VDL: *Nation* (New York), 25 May 1850.
201 Lt Governor's choice of Maria Island for SOB: MS 443/1, NLI, copied to NS553/1, TSA.
202 Eva's poem 'Ever, Ever': *N*, 17 November 1849.
202 Meagher on the VDL countryside, and experiences in Campbell Town: *Nation* (New York), as above.
203 Movements of O'Doherty, Martin, MacManus: Standard YI sources, including Touhill, as above; Cullen, Rev. J. H., *Young Ireland in Exile*, Dublin and Cork, 1928.
203 Dr John Stephen Hampton: Standard YI sources and *ADB*, Volume 1, pp. 508–9.
203 O'Donohoe's VDL career: Davis, Richard, 'Patrick O'Donohoe, Outcast of the Exiles', in Reece, Bob (ed.), *Exiles from Erin*, Dublin, 1991.
204 SOB on Maria Island, all aspects: SOB, *Journal*, as above.

13 By Order of Great Denison

Chapter heading: SOB to TFM, 23 November 1849; O'Brien Papers, MSS 443, 444, NLI.

206 SOB's correspondence on Maria: SOB, *Journal*, as above; and MS 443, 444, NLI.
206 SOB on his situation, Maria Island: SOB, *Journal*, as above.
207 SOB to Sir Lucius: 15 December 1849, O'Brien Papers, MS 443, NLI.
207 SOB poem to TFM: 11 January 1850, O'Brien Papers, MS 444, NLI.
207 SOB to Robert O'Brien: 1 January 1850, O'Brien Papers, MS 443, NLI.
208 SOB orders rice and curry, Carter's reply, mock-heroic verse: SOB to TFM, 23 November, 1849, O'Brien Papers, MS 443, NLI.
208 '6/7 week of my solitary confinement': for example, SOB to O'Doherty, 27 December 1849, O'Brien Papers, MS 443, NLI.
208 TFM to SOB about delightful solitude: 12 December 1849, O'Brien Papers, MS 443, NLI.
208 Dr Dawson reports meeting SOB: Denison, Sir William, as above.
209 O'Donohoe: Kiernan, Curren, as above: Davis, Richard, 'Outcast', in Reece, *Exiles from Erin*, as above.
209 O'Donohoe to his wife, Anne: *N*, 27 April 1850.
209 O'Donohoe's picnic adventure: Martin to O'Doherty letters, and vice versa, unless otherwise noted, MS 10,522, NLI; Kiernan, as above.
210 O'Donohoe's first edition: *Irish Exile*, 26 January 1850.
210 O'Donohoe on colonial Pharisees: *Irish Exile*, 9 March 1850.
210–11 The McDonnell case, and gold: *Irish Exile*, 16 February 1850.
211 Impact of Californian gold rush on VDL: *Irish Exile*, 23 February 1850.
211 Limerick support for SOB: *Irish Exile*, 9 March 1850.

211 SOB to Edward, partly in Latin: December 1849, O'Brien Papers, MS 444, NLI.
211 Lady O'Brien to SOB: 1 May 1850, O'Brien Papers, MS 444, NLI.
211 SOB to Rev. Gabbett: 7 March 1850, O'Brien Papers, MS 443, NLI.
211 Lucy senior to SOB: 7 May 1850, O'Brien Papers, MS 444, NLI.
212 Lucy junior to SOB: 17 October 1849, MS 443, NLI.
212 SOB to Grace: September 1850, O'Brien Papers, MS 444, NLI.
213 Mitchel in VDL: Kiernan, Cullen, as above; Mitchel, *Jail Journal*, as above.
214 TFM's experiences: TFM to SOB, 21 February 1850, O'Brien Papers, MS 443, NLI; Kiernan, Cullen, as above.
214 TFM and O'Doherty dine on Blackman bridge: TFM, *Meagher of the Sword*, as above.
215 The *Speranza*: Mitchel, *Jail Journal*, as above.
215 Martin to O'Doherty: Kiernan, as above.
215 'Yes, pale one . . .': Eva, *N*, 15 September 1849.
216 Gregson's 'Case for Opinion': 19 February 1850, O'Brien Papers, MS 443, NLI.
216 Anstey to SOB: 14 April 1850, O'Brien Papers, MS 444, NLI.
217 Martin to SOB about Lake Sorell meeting: 23 December 1849, O'Brien Papers, MS 443, NLI.
217 TFM on remonstrance to Denison: *N*, 3 August 1850.
217 TFM on meetings with O'Doherty: *N*, 27 July 1850.
217 O'Doherty's description of meetings: Kiernan, as above.
217–18 Mitchel riding: Mitchel, *Jail Journal*, as above.
218 Reids of Ratho: Brown, P. L., *Clyde Company Papers*, Volume 6, Oxford, 1968.
218 Martin to the Connells: Cullen, as above.
219 Attack on O'Donohoe: *Sydney Morning Herald*, 2 April 1850.
219 YI rallies to O'Donohoe: *Irish Exile*, 13 and 20 April 1850.
220 *Cork Examiner* and *Sligo Champion* on SOB situation: both quoted, *N*, 22 June 1850.
220 Sympathy meeting, New York: *N*, 15 October 1850.
220–1 SOB to Edward: n.d., O'Brien Papers, MS 444, NLI.
221 SOB to Lucy junior: 25 January 1850, O'Brien Papers, MS 444, NLI.
221 SOB to Lucy senior: 4 July 1850, O'Brien Papers, MS 444, NLI.
221–3 Evidence of Smart and convict constables on SOB and Susan Lapham, and all correspondence: MM62/29, Volumes A1131/2, Comptroller-General's correspondence, ML; SOB, *Journal*, as above.
223 'Moneyed' Clarke: *ADB*, Volume I.
224 O'Doherty and the Medical Board: Patrick and Patrick, Kiernan, as above; O'Doherty to SOB, 27 May 1850, O'Brien Papers, MS 444, NLI.
224 O'Doherty's interpretation of Medical Board's request: Kiernan, as above.
224 O'Doherty resigning ticket-of-leave: Patrick and Patrick, as above.
224 'Come, wild deer of the mountainside!': *N*, 15 June 1850
225 Contact between TFM and McCarthy: TFM to SOB, 9 October 1852, O'Brien Papers, MS 445, NLI.
225–6 SOB's experience of escape attempt: SOB, *Journal*, as above.
226 Denison and Lady Denison on SOB's escape attempt: Denison, Sir William, as above.

14 Young Ireland and the Profane Colonists

Chapter heading: O'Donohoe to TFM; *N*, 5 July 1851.

228 SOB to Anne Martineau: Sixteen letters from SOB to Martineau, Miscellaneous Collections, MS 18301, NLI.
229 SOB writes to Nixon: SOB, *Journal*, as above; 11 September 1850, O'Brien Papers, MS 444, NLI.
229–30 Denison reacts to offer, and all subsequent Denison unless otherwise noted: Denison, Sir William, as above.
230 SOB appeals to Sir Lucius over Lapham: 2 October 1850, O'Brien Papers, MS 444, NLI.
230 Nairn to SOB: 2 October 1850, O'Brien Papers, MS 444, NLI.
230 MacManus to SOB: 4 November 1850, O'Brien Papers, MS 444, NLI.
230 O'Donohoe warns of Baron de Bhere: *Irish Exile*, 2 November 1850.
230 SOB informs Lucy: 14 November 1850, O'Brien Papers, MS 8653, NLI.
231 Human railway and ring-bolting: Hughes, as above; SOB, *Journal*, as above.
232 SOB to Lucy on Derwent settlers: 25 December 1850, MS 8653, NLI.
232 MacManus relates visiting SOB: *N*, 10 May 1851.
232 TFM relates visiting SOB: *N*, 5 July 1851.
232–3 O'Donohoe visit: Touhill, as above; Davis, Richard, 'Outcast', in Reece, *Exiles from Erin*, as above.
233 Sympathetic *Courier*: *Hobart Town Courier*, 4 January 1851.
233 TFM asks SOB whether he should surrender parole: Christmas Day 1850, MS 444, NLI.
233 Career of Brian Bennett, and his VDL property: Cullen, as above.
233 Earlier policy of no Irish convicts in VDL: Robson, as above.
233 SOB visits Bennetts: SOB, *Journal*, as above.
234 MacManus writes from Hobart convict depot to TFM, and from Cascades: Cullen, as above.
234 O'Donohoe at Port Arthur and Salt Water River: Davis, Richard, 'Outcast', in Reece, *Exiles from Erin*, as above; *N*, 8 November 1851.
234 O'Donohoe's work in Port Arthur: *Hobart Town Guardian*, 2 April 1851, quoted in Davis, Richard, 'Outcast', in Reece, *Exiles from Erin*, as above.
234 MacManus on his Cascades experience: MacManus to SOB, 29 January 1851, O'Brien Papers, MS 444, NLI.
234 Martin to O'Doherty on TFM's courtship: Kiernan, as above.
234 TFM's rationale for marriage: Kiernan, as above.
235 Meagher senior foots attempted escape bill: Touhill, as above; Mitchel to SOB, 26 June 1851, O'Brien Papers, MS 444, NLI.
235 SOB sees TFM and Catherine, goes on to work in Avoca, and subsequent SOB unless noted: SOB, *Journal*, as above.
235 Lady Denison and the MacManus case: Denison, Sir William, as above.
236 TFM's wedding invitation to MacManus: Undated, Meagher Papers, MS 3900/1, NLI.
236–7 MacManus escape: SOB, *Journal*, as above; Touhill, as above.
237 The *Exile* appeals for payment of debts: *Irish Exile*, 22 February 1851.
237 O'Donohoe's financial position after his imprisonment: Touhill, Cullen; Davis, Richard, 'Outcast', in Reece, *Exiles from Erin*, as above.

237–8 O'Doherty to Martin on severity of Impression Bay: Patrick and Patrick, as above.
238 Martin asks O'Doherty why he gave up dispensary: Kiernan, as above.
239 Mitchel's reunion – his movements: Mitchel, *Jail Journal*, as above.
239–40 Jenny to Miss Thompson: 21 July 1851, 11 September 1851, Mrs Jane Mitchel's Letters to Miss Mary Thompson, Manuscripts and Archives, NYPL.
240 Gold discoveries, Australia: Clark, C. M. H., *A History of Australia*, Volume 4, 1978.
240 MacManus in San Francisco: Bisceglia, Louis R., 'The MacManus Welcome, San Francisco, 1851', *Eire-Ireland*, Vol. 16, No. 1, 1981.
241 Widespread news of the MacManus escape: Bisceglia, 'The MacManus Welcome', as above.
242 Monteagle emigrants in Goulburn area: O'Mahony and Thompson, as above.
242 Deniehy and *Goulburn Herald*: *ADB*, Volume 3; Pearl, *Deniehy*, as above, quoted.
243 John and Jenny's excursion to meet SOB *et al.*: Mitchel, *Jail Journal*, as above; Mrs Jane Mitchel to Miss Mary Thompson, 6 December 1851, Manuscripts and Archives, NYPL.
244 Balfe: Petrow, in Davis, *Irish-Australian Studies*, as above.
245 Jenny writes of Mrs Meagher, and other things: Mrs Jane Mitchel to Miss Mary Thompson, 6 December 1851, Manuscripts and Archives, NYPL.
247 A witness writes of TFM's escape: Adam-Smith, as above.
247 A further witness defends TFM's escape: *NYT*, 16 January 1857.
248 Jenny Mitchel on TFM's escape: Mrs Jane Mitchel to Miss Mary Thompson, 25 February 1852, Manuscripts and Archives, NYPL.
248 TFM's conflict with the Halls, and his vile entanglements: Martin to O'Doherty, 13 August 1851, Hickey Papers, MS 3226, NLI.
248 Concern about TFM's escape: Martin to O'Doherty, 11 January 1852, John Martin Papers, MS 10,522, NLI.
248 Martin investigates O'Meagher's mode of escape: 18 January 1852, John Martin Papers, MS 10,522, NLI.
248 Mitchel asks SOB if they should appeal to TFM to return: Mitchel to SOB, 19 January 1852, MS 444, NLI.
249–50 TFM's account of escape: TFM, 'Six Weeks in the South Pacific', *Irish News*, 9 and 14 April, 21 May 1859.
250 Kate Meagher to friend: Cullen, as above.

15 Locked Within the Pyramid

251 Senator Foote's motion on State prisoners: *Congressional Globe*, 32nd Congress, Session One, Volume 21, Part 1, quoted in Athearn, as above.
251 Activities of Fillmore and others on State prisoners' behalf: Athearn, Touhill, as above.
251 *Pilot* reports TFM's escape: *Pilot*, Boston, 15 May 1852.
252 Details of TFM's welcome and American career: Athearn, Cavanagh, Lyons, as above, unless otherwise noted.
252 TFM's first full day in New York: *Irish American*, 6 June 1852.
252 TFM's speech and demeanour: *New York Herald*, 29 May 1852.

252 More praise for TFM: *NYT*, 31 May 1852.
253 Irish in New York: Bayor and Meagher, as above.
253 Irish, population level 1850s, illicit naturalisation, saloon politics: Roberts, Edward S., *Ireland in America*, New York, 1931; Potter, George, *To the Golden Door*, Boston, 1960; Levine, Edward, *The Irish and Irish Politicians*, Notre Dame, IN, 1966.
254 McGee's American career: Skelton, Isabel, *The Life of Thomas D'Arcy McGee*, New York, 1925.
254 SOB visits Bennetts: Catherine Meagher to TFM, Cullen, as above.
254–5 Death of TFM's child: Cullen, Athearn, as above; Mrs Jenny Mitchel to Miss Mary Thompson, 12 July 1852, Manuscripts and Archives, NYPL.
255 TFM, received at Astor House, rejects further receptions: *NYT*, 9 June 1852.
255 TFM at Irish military event, the Battery: *NYT*, 28 July 1852.
255 TFM's speech at military event: *New York Tribune*, 28 July 1852.
255 The Metropolitan: McKay, Ernest A., *The Civil War and New York City*, Syracuse, 1990.
256 *Herald*'s boast: *New York Herald*, 5 November 1852.
256 TFM's first New York lecture: *NYT*, 26 November 1852.
257 TFM's profit from speech: *Irish American*, 4 December 1852.
257 TFM lectures upstate: *Albany Atlas*, quoted in *Irish American*, 11 December 1852.
257 TFM and St Louis toast to Australian republic: *NYT*, 15 January 1853.
257 TFM's admission to SOB: Ahearn, as above.
257 SOB sees dilemma in accepting pardon: SOB to Lucy, 2 May 1852, MS 8653, NLI.
257 Rev. Henry O'Brien's Memorial not fully subscribed: Henry O'Brien to SOB, 26 May 1852, O'Brien Papers, MS 444, NLI.
258 SOB anxious over Lapham: SOB to Lucy, 19 February 1853, O'Brien Papers, MS 8653, NLI.
258 SOB upbraids Lucy: SOB, *Journal*, as above.
258 O'Donohoe's exposé on Port Arthur: Davis, Richard, 'Outcast', in Reece, *Exiles from Erin*, as above.
258 The treadmill: Hughes, as above.
258 Balfe's career: Petrow, in Davis, Richard, *Irish-Australian Studies*, as above.
258–9 O'Donohoe attacks Balfe: *Launceston Examiner*, 14 August 1852.
259 O'Donohoe attempts escape on *YY*: *N*, 9 July 1853.
260 O'Donohoe in Melbourne and final escape: N, 9 July 1853; Touhill, Cullen, as above.
260 O'Shanassy: Pearl, *CGD*, as above; *ADB*, Volume 5.
260 Abolition of transportation, last ship, Home Office to Denison: Denison, Bateson, Shaw, Hirst, as above.
260–1 O'Donohoe's sad American career: Athearn, as above; Davis, Richard, 'Outcast', in Reece, *Exiles from Erin*, as above.
261 Pat Smyth in VDL: Mitchel, *Jail Journal*, as above.
261 Keep Smyth away from O'Donohoe: TFM to Deas, 12 September 1852, NS1376/5, TSA.
262 Mitchel's attitude to child born in VDL: Mrs Jane Mitchel to Miss Mary Thompson, 31 January 1853, Manuscripts and Archives, NYPL.
262 TFM meets Pierce and has Washington success: *Irish American*, 10 March 1853.

263 Career of General Cass: *Dictionary of American Biography*.
263 General Shields: Athearn, Cavanagh, Lyons, as above; Daly, Maria Lydig, *Diary of a Union Woman, 1861–65*, ed. Harold Earl Hammond, New York, 1962.
263 New York speech condemning Irish clergy: *NYT*, 26 May 1853.
264 Mrs Meagher reaches London: *N*, 4 June 1853; arrives in Waterford: *N*, 9 July 1853.
266–71 Mitchel escape: Mitchel, *Jail Journal*, as above; P. J. Smyth in *N*, 24 October 1884.

16 The Skeleton at the Feast

Chapter heading: *NYT*, 20 December 1853.

272 Martin on Mitchel's escape: Martin to O'Doherty, 29 April 1854, in Kiernan, as above.
272 SOB's Tasmanian constitution: SOB, *Journal*, as above, Appendix 1.
272 Edward wants to attend English university: Edward to SOB, 6 November 1853, O'Brien Papers, MS 8656, NLI.
272 SOB's reaction: SOB to Lucy, 17 April 1854, O'Brien Papers, MS 8653, NLI.
273 Charles Murrough to SOB: O'Brien Papers, undated, MS 8656, NLI.
273 The Mitchels in San Francisco: Mitchel, *Jail Journal*, as above; Kiernan, Touhill, as above.
273 Jenny tempted to remain in San Francisco: Mrs Jane Mitchel to Miss Mary Thompson, 14 December 1853, Manuscripts and Archives, NYPL.
273 R. K. Nuttall to Mrs Williams: 15 November 1853, Brown, *Clyde Company*, Volume 6.
274 Mitchel in New York: *NYT*, 30 November 1853.
274 Jenny on furore: Mrs Jane Mitchel to Miss Mary Thompson, 14 December 1853, Manuscripts and Archives, NYPL.
275 Mitchel banquet: *NYT*, 20 December 1853.
275 First edition, *Citizen*: *Irish Citizen*, 7 January 1854.
276 Mitchel against Know-Nothingism: *Irish Citizen*, 14 January 1854; and *Irish Citizen*, *passim*.
276 Mitchel on Bishop of Rome: *Irish Citizen*, 11 February 1854; and *Irish Citizen*, *passim*.
276–7 *Irish American* on O'Donohoe's death: *Irish American*, 11 February 1854.
277 Mitchel on O'Donohoe: *Irish Citizen*, 11 February 1854.
277 *Citizen* publishes pro-Southern letters, attacks Stowe and Rev. Beecher: *Irish Citizen*, 25 March, 1 April, 8 April 1854, and *passim*.
278 Attacks on Mitchel: Reprinted *NYT*, 18 February 1854.
278 Jenny on slavery: Mrs Jane Mitchel to Miss Mary Thompson, 20 April 1854, Manuscripts and Archives, NYPL.
278 Pardon of SOB and others: Touhill, as above; SOB, *Journal*, as above.
279 Mr Elwin sells hotel: SOB to Lucy, 6 March 1854, O'Brien Papers, MS 8653, NLI.
279 Jenny pities Catherine Meagher: Mrs Jane Mitchel to Miss Mary Thompson, 14 December 1853, Manuscripts and Archives, NYPL.
280 Death of Catherine Meagher: *N*, 13 May 1854.

280 Mitchel on Catherine's death: *Irish Citizen*, 20 May 1854; Cullen, as above.
280 The McMaster brawl: *NYT*, 19 July 1854.
280 Stonington: Mitchel to Miss Thompson, Dillon, Volume 2, as above.
280 Jenny despairs of Ireland: Mrs Jane Mitchel to Miss Mary Thompson, 2 December 1854, Manuscripts and Archives, NYPL.
281 Smyth's movements: Mitchel, *Jail Journal*, as above; Dillon, Kiernan, as above.
281 Pardons and other orders arrive at Hobart: Denison, Sir William, as above.
281 SOB tells Lucy of his spirits and New Norfolk celebrations: SOB to Lucy, 28 June 1854, O'Brien Papers, MS 8653, NLI.
281 SOB to Lucy, Geelong, Melbourne: 12 July 1854, O'Brien Papers, MS 8653, NLI.
281 State prisoners welcomed in Melbourne: *Irish Citizen*, 4 November 1854.
281 Nature of Criterion Hotel clientele: Kiernan, as above.
282 SOB from Point de Gable: SOB to Lucy, 21 August 1854, O'Brien Papers, MS 8653, NLI.
282 Martin in Paris to Eva: Kiernan, as above.
283 SOB to Lucy from Vittoria, Paris, Brussels: 16, 21, 24, 25, 29 November 1854, O'Brien Papers, MS 8653, NLI.
283 TFM rail smash: Athearn, as above; Mrs Jane Mitchel to Miss Mary Thompson, 2 December 1854, Manuscripts and Archives, NYPL.
284 Samuel Mitchell Barlow: *Dictionary of American Biography*; Barlow Papers, Huntington Library, California.
284 Townsend asks Barlow to approach Sickles: 4 June 1855, Box BW 24, Barlow Papers, Huntington Library, CA.
284 Townsend asks Barlow to chase a steel sample: 11 March 1855, Box BW 9, Barlow Papers, Huntington Library, CA.
284 TFM to Miss Townsend: 2 January 1855, Meagher Papers, Small Collection 309, Folder 2: General Correspondence, N–V 1849–1867, Montana Historical Society Archives, Helena, Montana.
284–5 Libby's ancestry: Diamant, Lincoln, *Chaining the Hudson*, New York, 1989.
285 TFM's St Patrick's Day speech: *NYT*, 19 March 1855.
285 Smyth and O'Doherty on the gold-fields: Patrick and Patrick, as above.
285 Peter Lalor and miners' rights: Cullen, Kiernan, as above.
286 O'Doherty's movements, etc.: Kiernan, as above.
286 O'Doherty visiting the Kellys: 9 July 1855, T. Arthur, Sub-Inspector of Police, Portumna, County Galway, to Inspector General of Police, Dublin, Home Office, ERE9115, PRO, quoted in Patrick and Patrick, as above.
286 O'Doherty marriage and movements: Kiernan, Patrick and Patrick, as above. Eva's French Passport: No. 1054, OM71-6, Envelope 1, O'Doherty Papers, John Oxley Library.
287 Mitchels' move South: Mitchel, Dillon, as above.
288 Mitchel's new Southern friends: Samuels, William C., *John Mitchel, the Irish Patriot, Resident of Tennessee*, East Tennessee Historical Society's Publications, No. 10, 1938.
288 Jenny tired of moving: Mrs Jane Mitchel to Miss Mary Thompson, 21 March 1855, Manuscripts and Archives, NYPL.
288 Dr Esperandieu: Williams, as above.

288 Tuckaleechee: Burns, Inez, *History of Blount County Tennessee, 1795–1955*, East Tennessee Historical Society, 1957.
288–9 Jenny's scepticism: Mrs Jane Mitchel to Miss Mary Thompson, 21 March 1855, Manuscripts and Archives, NYPL.
289 Farm deed: Deeds, Blount County, 1855, Volume Y, East Tennessee Historical Center, Knoxville, Tenn.
289 *NYT* mentions disinheritance of Elizabeth Townsend: *NYT*, 15 November 1855.
289 Peter Townsend's tender feelings: Townsend to Barlow, 11 March 1855, Box BW 9; 30 September 1857, Box BW 14, Barlow Papers, as above.
290 Duffy leaves Ireland; CGD, Pearl, as above.
290 Duffy's departing judgement: *N*, 15 August 1855.
291 Cornelius Sheahan and family: O Lorcáin, as above.
291 *SMH*, day of Mary's death: *SMH*, 1 November 1854.
291–2 Mary's grave: Mortis Street Cemetery, Goulburn.
292 State of Australia at Hugh's death: Clark, Volume IV, as above.
293 Australia, Queen's birthday: *SMH*, 22 May 1857.
294 Hugh's death certificate: 1 June 1857, Number 118, Goulburn District Death Register.
294 Sale of Larkin's effects: *Goulburn Herald*, 23 May 1857, for Wednesday 27 May 1857, by order of executor, John Sheahan.
294 Larkin's children: O Lorcáin, as above.
294 John Larkin's body is sent by train to Goulburn: *Goulburn Herald*, 13 September 1887.
295 Irish children of Larkin: Michael Larkin, Lismany; Woodford Heritage Centre, East Galway, marriage records.

17 Young Ireland and the Isms of Yankeedom

Chapter heading: TFM, *Meagher of Sword*, as above; Athearn, as above.

299 Population and other Irish statistics, 1850s: Edwards, Ruth Dudley, *The Atlas of Irish History*, London, 1981.
299–300 Kavanagh's 'The Great Hunger': Montague (ed.), as above.
300 O'Brien family separates, and movement for full pardon: Touhill, as above.
300 Desirability of full pardon: SOB to Lucy, 17 March 1856, O'Brien Papers, MS 8653, NLI.
300 Full pardon for SOB, O'Doherty, Martin: Touhill, as above.
300 SOB's distress over lack of economic independence: SOB to Lucy, 17 June 1856, O'Brien Papers, MS 8653, NLI.
300 The gold cup: O'Brien, Grania, as above.
300 SOB's happiness approaching Ireland: As for previous note.
300 SOB blithe in Cahirmoyle: SOB to Lucy, 12 September 1857, O'Brien Papers, MS 8653, NLI.
301 SOB states his disenchantment with politics: *N*, 26 July 1856.
301 SOB petitioned by 10,000 people, his answer, his warning against boasting: *N*, 20 September 1856.
301 SOB on what should have been done to save Ireland: *TL*, 29 December 1856.

301 Meagher founds *Irish News*, and Mitchel as warning to TFM: *New York Herald*, 11 April 1856.
302 New York's Irish poor: Bayor and Meagher, as above.
302 American filibustering: Stout, Joseph Allen, *The Liberators: Filibustering Expeditions*, Los Angeles, 1973; Roche, James Jeffrey, *The Story of the Filibusters*, London, 1891.
303 TFM, and *Irish News*, supporting Walker and defending Farbins: Athearn, as above.
304 TFM supports Buchanan: *Irish News*, 18 October 1856.
305 TFM praises South: *Irish News*, quoted by *New York Daily Tribune*, 27 August 1856.
305 *NYT* questions TFM's escape: *NYT*, 30 December 1856.
305 Further *NYT* judgement on escape: *NYT*, 14 January 1857.
305 TFM asks Buchanan for a South or Central American consulship: Letter to President James Buchanan, 28 January 1857, notated by Buchanan, 15 March 1857 in Appointment Papers, Department of State, National Archives, Washington DC, quoted Athearn, *TFM*.
306 Mitchel to Miss Thompson and to his sister Matilda, William Mitchel, and subsequent letters of Mitchel: Dillon, Volume 2, as above.
306 Texture of rural life, Tuckaleechee: Burns, Inez, *History of Blount County Tennessee, 1795–1955*, East Tennessee Historical Society, Knoxville, 1957.
307 Mitchel's town site: Isabella French to John Mitchel, Deeds of Conveyance, March 1856, East Tennessee Historical Society, Lawson McGee Library, Knoxville, Tenn.
307 Mitchel's friendships with McAdoo and Swan: Williams, Samuel C., *John Mitchel, the Irish Patriot, Resident of Tennessee*, East Tennessee Historical Society's Publications, No. 10, 1938.
308 *Southern Citizen*: Eighteen copies, Miscellaneous File A, Knoxville Newspapers, 1840–58, Lawson McGhee Library, Knoxville, Tenn.
308 Kenyon, Miss Thompson, Mitchel and *Southern Citizen*: Dillon, Volume 2, as above.
308–9 Attitude towards Kansas: *Southern Citizen*, 11 February 1858.
309 Benefits of African slavery: *Southern Citizen*, 18 March 1858.
309 *Susquehanna* incident: *Southern Citizen*, 21 January 1858.
309 O'Doherty's medical career, and correspondence, Eva to Martin: Kiernan, Patrick and Patrick, as above; O'Doherty Papers, OM71–6, Medical Certificates in Envelope 7, John Oxley Library, Brisbane, Queensland.
310 Eva's poems in exile: Cuttings in O'Doherty Papers, Envelopes 2 and 3, as for previous note; Patrick and Patrick, as above.
311 TFM defends Walker and Mrs Meagher visits Ireland: Lyons, W. F., Cavanagh, Athearn, as above.
311 Defence of Walker by Stephens: *Southern Citizen*, 21 January 1858.
312 TFM to Roche: Athearn, as above.
TFM goes to Costa Rica: 'Holidays in Costa Rica', Part I, *Harper's Monthly Magazine*, Vol. XX, December 1859.
312 San José; the president and the Frenchman; the hospital: 'Holidays in Costa Rica', Part II, *Harper's Monthly Magazine*, Volume XX, January 1860.
313 To the Atlantic coast: 'Holidays in Costa Rica', Part III, *Harper's Monthly Magazine*, Vol. XX, February 1860.

313 TFM to Daly: Daly, Maria Lydig, *Diary of a Union Woman, 1861–65*, ed. Harold Earl Hammond, New York, 1962, Introduction.
313 SOB's bill for gold cup: SOB letter of 10 September 1857, ML.
314 Visit to Mitchel by Stephens: Dillon, Volume 2, as above; Ryan, Desmond, *The Fenian Chief*, Coral Gables, 1967.
314 Mitchel to Mrs Williams: Brown, *Clyde Company Papers*, Volume 6, as above.
314 SOB on the Mitchels in Washington: To Lucy, 10 March 1859, O'Brien Papers, MS 8653, NLI.
315 SOB writing aboard riverboat: SOB to Lucy, 27 March 1859, as for previous note.
315 From the *Mississippi*: SOB to Lucy, 7 April 1859, as for previous note.
315 Chicago visit (writing from Niagara Falls): SOB to Lucy, 3 May 1859, as for previous note.
315 SOB delighted to be absent for election: SOB to Lucy junior, 16 May 1859, as for previous note.
315–17 The Key murder: Swanberg, W. A., *Sickles the Incredible*, New York, 1956; Fontaine, Felix, *De Witt's Special Report: Trial of the Hon. Daniel E. Sickles*, Washington, 1859.
317 Relationship between TFM and Dalys: Daly, *Union Woman*, as above; Daly Papers, Manuscripts and Archives, NYPL.
318 Judge Daly's career: As for previous note, and Hammond, Harold Earl, *A Commoner's Judge: The Life of Charles Patrick Daly*, Boston, 1954.
319 Chiriqui grant: *Charter and Statutes, or By-Laws*: Chiriqui Improvement Co., 1864, copy in Rare Books, Huntington Library, CA.
319 TFM's journey to Chiriqui: Meagher, Thomas Francis, 'The New Route through Chiriqui', *Harper's Monthly Magazine*, Vol. XXI, January 1861.
320–1 Closing of *Southern Citizen*, and Mitchel and family go to Paris: Standard Mitchel sources, including Mitchel, *Jail Journal*, as above.
322 *Irish News* applauds TFM: Athearn, as above.
322 Collapse of Chiriqui enterprise: Usual TFM sources, as above.

18 Ireland and the Bloody Arena

323 Death of MacManus: Standard YI sources, as above.
323 Barlow's solution to crisis: *A Private Citizen's Proposal for the Settlement of all Differences between the Northern and Southern States*, Barlow Papers, Huntington Library, CA.
324 Feelings of New York towards Lincoln and South: McKay, *Civil War and New York City*, as above.
324 O'Mahony, Stephens, Fenian Brotherhood, IRB: D'Arcy, William, *The Fenian Movement in the United States, 1858–1886*, Washington, 1947; Harmon, Maurice, *Fenians and Fenianism*, Seattle, 1970; Neidhardt, W. S., *Fenianism in North America*, Pittsburgh, PA, 1975; Walker, Mabel Gregory, *The Fenian Movement*, Colorado Springs, 1969; Ryan, *Fenian Chief*, as above.
325 TFM to Daly, about Irving Hall lecture: 21 January 1861, Daly Papers, Box 2, Manuscripts and Archives, NYPL.
325 Meagher's speech on MacManus, Irving Hall: *Irish American*, 4 April 1861.

325–7 McGee and Canada: Senior, Hereward, *The Fenians and Canada*, Toronto, 1978; Skelton, as above.

327 John Mitchel junior at bombardment of Sumter: Castles, Alexander C., 'From Van Diemen's Land to Fort Sumter: Captain John C. Mitchel of the First South Carolina Artillery', kindly provided by author, unpublished at time of writing.

327 Transformation of New York Democrats after Sumter: McKay, *Civil War and New York City*, as above.

327 TFM chastises his father-in-law, and general reaction to outbreak of war: Cavanagh, Athearn, as above.

328 Departure of 69th Militia: *Irish American*, 11 May 1861.

329 General Scott's regard for the 69th: *Irish American*, 18 May 1861.

329 TFM and Zouaves at Fort Corcoran: Corcoran to Daly, 8 July 1861, Daly Papers, Manuscripts and Archives, NYPL.

329 Corcoran to Daly: 8 July 1861, Daly Papers, Manuscripts and Archives, NYPL.

329–30 TFM's speech to 69th NYSM: *Irish American*, 13 July 1861.

330 TFM to Barlow: 15 July 1861, Barlow Papers, Huntington Library, CA.

330 69th NYSM in Virginia, including campaign and relationship to Sherman: Meagher, Thomas Francis, Captain, Company K ('Irish Zouaves'), *The Last Days of the Sixty-Ninth in Virginia*, New York, 1861; and Athearn, Lyons, W. F., Cavanagh, as above.

334 Maria Lydig Daly on TFM, here and subsequent: Daly, *Union Lady*, as above.

335 Russell on TFM: *New York Tribune*, 23 July 1861.

335 Russell's version: Russell, W. H., *My Journeys North and South*, Volume 2, London, 1862.

335 SOB on Civil War, and O'Brien family matters: O'Brien, Grania, as above.

335–6 SOB bereavement and health: Davis, Epilogue, in SOB, *Journal*.

336 Mitchel in Paris: Dillon, Volume 2, as above.

336 Mitchel on workers of New York: *Irish American*, 19 January 1861.

336 SOB's visit: Mitchel, *Jail Journal*, as above.

337 Lincoln visits 69th and subsequent: TFM, *Last Days*, as above.

337 *Tribune* pushes TFM's colonelcy: *New York Daily Tribune*, 6 August 1861.

19 Faugh-a-Ballagh

339 Fund raiser program, 69th New York Militia: Huntington Library, CA.

339 Shields: Hammond (ed.), Introduction, in Daly, *Union Lady*.

340 TFM to Daly on Shields: 23 August 1861, Daly Papers, Manuscripts and Archives, NYPL.

340 Shields's wary response to Daly: 8 June 1861, Daly Papers, Manuscripts and Archives, NYPL.

341 Gathering at Jones's Wood and TFM speech: *New York Daily Tribune*, 28 August 1861.

341 The Irish Brigade, its initiation, recruitment, campaigns: Jones, Paul, *The Irish Brigade*, Washington and New York, 1969; Conyngham, Captain D. P., *The Irish Brigade and Its Campaigns*, New York, 1867.

342 MacManus's remains in New York: *New York Herald*, 19 September 1861.

342–3 MacManus's remains in Ireland: Denieffe, Joseph, *A Personal Narrative of the Irish Republican Brotherhood*, New York, 1906.
343–4 MacManus funeral: *Freeman's Journal* (Dublin), 11 November 1861; *Irish Times*, 11 November 1861.
345–6 TFM's communications with Secretary of War: Generals Papers and Records, Adjutant General's Office, Department of War, Volume IV, M344, National Archives, Washington, DC.
345–6 TFM military papers: Memorandum of Papers in Case of Thomas Francis Meagher, M1064, Roll 187, National Archives, Washington; Index of Letters received by Secretary of War from Generals, L–Z, M455, Roll 1 (1861), Roll 3 (1862), Roll 5 (1863), Roll 7 (1864), Roll 9 (1865); Military Telegrams, M698, Index to General Correspondence received by the Assistant Secretary of War, all in National Archives, Washington, DC.
346 Edwin Vose Sumner: Conyngham, Jones, as above; Sears, Stephen W., *To the Gates of Richmond*, New York, 1992.
346–7 Life in camp: Corby, Reverend William, *Memoirs of Chaplain Life*, Chicago, 1893.
347 TFM accepts commission: 2 March 1862, Generals Papers and Records, Secretary of War, Volume IV, M344, National Archives, Washington, DC.
347 Telegram, Libby to her mother: 3 March 1862, as previous note.
348 'A certain carpet bag . . .': Generals Papers and Records, Secretary of War, 31 March 1862, M344, National Archives, Washington, DC.
349 TFM to Barlow: 4 March 1862, Barlow Papers, Huntington Library, CA.

20 The Chickahominy Steeplechase

Chapter heading: Athearn, Conyngham, Cavanagh, as above.

350 The war situation and McClellan's strategy: McPherson, James M., *The Battle Cry of Freedom*, New York, 1988.
350 General outline of Peninsula campaign: Sears, *Gates of Richmond*, as above.
352–4 Fair Oaks battle, and subsequent brigade engagements: Lyons, W. F., Cavanagh, Conyngham, Jones, as above.
354 TFM as littérateur: Conyngham, as above.
354 Surgeon Ellis: As for previous note.
356–7 Gaines's Mill engagement: Report of Brigadier-General Meagher, in US Department of War, *War of the Rebellion: A Compilation of the Official Records of the Union and Confederate Armies*, Series 1, Volume 11, Part 2, Washington, DC, 1880–1901, hereafter *War of the Rebellion.*
357 TFM's tipsiness, Brigade's valour, Sumner: Sears, *Gates of Richmond*, as above.
358 TFM praises Nugent's command, Savage's Station: Brigadier-General Meagher, Report, *War of the Rebellion*, Series 1, Volume 11, Part 2.
358 Surgeon Ellis: Conyngham, as above.
359 Lieutenant Turner: Conyngham, as above.
360 A Union officer describes end of engagement: Sears, *Gates of Richmond*, as above.
360–2 Brigade at Malvern Hill: Meagher's Report, Harrison's Landing, 2 July

1862, *War of the Rebellion*, Series 1, Volume 11, Part 2; Conyngham, as above.

362 Kearny's outburst: Sears, *Gates of Richmond*, as above.

363 TFM's appeal to War Department: Athearn, as above.

363 Mitchel in Paris still: Mitchel, *Jail Journal*, as above; Dillon, Volume 2, as above.

21 Woefully Cut Up

366 Northern Virginia campaign, McClellan and Pope: McPherson, *Battle Cry*, as above.

367 McClellan desires to keep Irish close to Washington: Conyngham, Jones, as above.

367–8 Antietam campaign: Sears, Stephen W., *Landscape Turned Red*, New York, 1983.

369 Reynolds, O'Mahony, and soldier Fenians: D'Arcy, as above.

370–1 Stephens, Luby and Civil War: Ryan, D'Arcy, as above.

372 Tom Connors and Lieutenant Bernard O'Neill: http://www.thewildgeese-.com.

372 *Tribune* announces TFM wounded: *New York Daily Tribune*, 21 September 1862.

372 Strother and Cox on TFM: Sears, *Landscape Turned Red*, as above.

372 TFM cocktail: Kelly, Bernard B., 'The Fighting 69th', *The World of Hibernia*, New York, Summer 1995.

373 General McClellan on Irish Brigade at Antietam: McClellan's Report, *War of the Rebellion*, Series 1, Volume 19, Part 1.

373 TFM in Sumner's dispatch: Sumner's Report, 1 October 1862, in *War of the Rebellion*, Series 1, Volume 19, Part 1.

373 Colonel Barlow's report, TFM at Antietam: Daly, *Union Lady*.

374 TFM discusses burial truce after Antietam: Meagher's Report, in *War of the Rebellion*, as above.

374 Lee abandons Antietam lines: Meagher's Report, in *War of the Rebellion*, as above.

374 Meagher to Libby on Antietam: Copied by Libby to Barlow, 1 October 1862, Barlow Papers, Huntington Library, CA.

374 Captain Gosson incident: Conyngham, as above.

375–6 Mitchel re-enters South: Mitchel, *Jail Journal*, as above; Dillon, Volume 2, as above.

377 John Dooley remembers Antietam: Sears, *Landscape Turned Red*, as above.

377 Mitchel's editorial style: *Daily Enquirer*, 8 October 1862.

378 McCarter's experience of Meagher, Bolivar Heights to Fredericksburg: McCarter, William, *My Life in the Irish Brigade: The Civil War Memories of Private William McCarter, 116th Pennsylvania*, ed. Kevin O'Brien, Campbell, CA, 1997.

380 TFM on relief of McClellan: TFM to Barlow, 10 November 1862, Barlow Papers, Huntington Library, CA.

381–2 Fredericksburg Campaign: McPherson, as above.

382 TFM's telegram: TFM to Senior Officer, Recruiting Office, undated, Generals

Papers and Records, Secretary of War, Volume IV, M344, National Archives, Washington, DC.

383 Sergeant McClelland's version, TFM's Fredericksburg speech: *Irish American*, 10 January 1863.

385 Thomas F. Galwey on Irish Brigade: Conyngham, as above.

385 Officer writes of widows and orphans: Lieutenant Nagle to his father, *Irish American*, 17 December 1862.

386 Singing of 'Ireland Boys Hurrah': Jones, as above.

386 Reynolds's medical certificate: Reynolds to Assistant Adjutant-General, 15 December 1862, Generals Papers and Records, Secretary of War, Volume IV, M344, National Archives, Washington, DC.

387 Military telegram to Major Horgan's sister: 21 December 1862, as for previous note.

22 Let Me Have Idaho

Chapter heading: D'Arcy, as above

388 Conscription notices: *Richmond Enquirer*, 2 January 1863.

388 Irish perceptions of the war: *Richmond Enquirer*, 10 January 1863.

388 Union's use of Irish symbols: *Richmond Enquirer*, 10 January 1863.

389 All Mitchel's letters to Miss Thompson: Dillon, Volume 2, as above.

389 Requiem Mass for Brigade dead, and subsequent dinner and speeches: *NYT*, 17 January 1863.

389 Halpine verse: Lyons, W. F., as above.

389 Halleck's order to Adjutant-General: 30 January 1863, Generals Papers and Records, Secretary of War, Volume IV, M344, National Archives, Washington, DC.

390 TFM's certificates from Surgeon Edgar: Edgar to Adjutant-General, 11 January, 3 February 1863, as for previous note.

390 TFM requests Irish Brigade be relieved: TFM to Secretary Stanton, 19 February 1863, and to Assistant Adjutant-General, 26 February 1863, as for previous note.

390 Hooker returns letter: Hooker to Hancock and TFM, 26 February 1863, as for previous note.

390 TFM requests leave to go to Congress: TFM to Hooker and Halleck, 4 March 1863, as for previous note.

391 TFM's apology to Major O'Beirne: 24 March 1863, 'Some Letters of Meagher to Captain James R O'Beirne', *American-Irish Historical Society Journal*, Vol. 30, 1932.

391 The Irish crisis of 1863: Jordan, Donald E., Jr, *Land and Popular Politics in Ireland – County Mayo from the Plantation to the Land War*, Cambridge, 1994; O'Neill, Tim, 'The Persistence of Famine in Ireland', from Póirtéir, *Great Irish Famine*, as above.

391 TFM's telegram to Hancock: 20 April 1863, Generals Papers and Records, Secretary of War, Volume IV, M344, National Archives, Washington, DC.

392–3 Chancellorsville campaign in general: McPherson, as above.

393 TFM on Chancellorsville: Report, *War of the Rebellion*, Series 1, Volume 25, Part 1, as above.

393–4 Irish Brigade's part in battle: Lyons, W. F., Cavanagh, Corby, Conyngham, as above.
394 TFM's resignation: TFM to Assistant Adjutant-General, 8 May 1863, Generals Papers and Records, Secretary of War, Volume IV, M344, National Archives, Washington, DC.
394 Response from Adjutant-General, War Department: 15 May 1863, as for previous note.
395 Mitchel on TFM's resignation: *Richmond Enquirer*, 18 May 1863.
395 Lincoln's 3-year enlistees: *Richmond Enquirer*, 24 April 1863.
396 Call for strong Southern measures in North: *Richmond Enquirer*, 22 June 1863.
396 Site of Willy's fall and burial; Captain Haverty: http://www.thewildgeese-.com.
397 Minimising meaning of Gettysburg, and warning to Confederates: *Richmond Enquirer*, 5 August 1863.
397 TFM post-resignation: Lyons, W. F., Cavanagh, Athearn, as above.
397 TFM asks to withdraw resignation: TFM to Stanton, 13 July 1863, Generals Papers and Records, Secretary of War, Volume IV, M344, National Archives, Washington, DC.
397–8 Draft riots: McKay, *Civil War and New York City*, as above; Bernstein, Iver, *The New York Draft Riots*, New York, 1990.
399 TFM to O'Beirne: 'Some Letters', as above.
400 TFM and Fenian pledge: D'Arcy, as above.
400 SOB on Civil War: *N*, 7 November 1863.
401 TFM to Daly on Corcoran's death: 23 December 1863, Generals Papers and Records, Secretary of War, Volume IV, M344, National Archives, Washington, DC.
401 *Irish American* attacks TFM for pro-Lincoln bias: *Irish American*, 19 January 1864.
401 Hancock to Daly on 'Irish general': Athearn, as above.
401 John Mitchel junior, including friendship with Rhetts, military career, death: Castles, 'From Van Diemen's Land', as above; http://www.thewildgeese.com.
402 Jenny and her two daughters run the blockade: Dillon, Volume 2, as above.
402 John Daniel: His listing in *Dictionary of American Biography*; Frederick S. Daniel (ed.), *The Richmond Examiner During the War, or The Writings of John M. Daniel*, New York, 1868.
402 John Daniel's Southern spelling: McCall, as above.
402 The one vice of the Confederacy: *Richmond Examiner*, 19 July 1864.
403 Mary Pegrim Anderson: Dillon, Volume 2, as above; McCall, as above.
404 The *Examiner* on Atlanta campaign: *Richmond Examiner*, 8 November 1864.
404–5 SOB's last general letter on Ireland: SOB to Archdeacon O'Brien, *Limerick Chronicle*, 7 January 1864.
405 Death of SOB: *Freeman's Journal*, 20 June 1864.
405 Mourners meeting SOB's body, Dublin: *TL*, 24 June 1864.
405 Martin mourns O'Brien: *N*, 9 July 1864.
406 TFM's quarrel with *Irish American*: Athearn, as above.
406 Sherman's view of Meagher: Athearn, Robert G., *Sherman and the Settlement of the West*, Norman, OK, 1956.

406 General Thomas's orders for TFM: Thomas to Steedman, 16 November 1864, *War of the Rebellion*, Series 1, Volume 45, Part 1.
407 TFM in Chattanooga, Christmas 1864, and Steedman's praise for TFM: Athearn, *TFM*, Lyons, W. F., as above.
407 Grant's concern TFM's men might desert, New York: Grant to Halleck, 23 January 1865, *War of the Rebellion*, Series 1, Volume 47, Part 2.
407 Halleck to Grant: 25 January 1865, as for previous note.
408 TFM too drunk to comprehend orders: Report of Captain Scott, 9 February 1865, Generals Papers and Records, Secretary of War, Volume IV, M344, National Archives, Washington, DC.
408 Dismissing TFM: Grant to Halleck, 14 and 20 February 1865, *War of the Rebellion*, Series 1, Volume 47, Part 2.
408 TFM dismissed: HQ of the Department of North Carolina, Army of the Ohio, Wilmington, NC, 24 February 1865, Special Order No. 13, as for previous note.
409 *Examiner* dissents from Davis's speech in Confederate Congress: *Richmond Examiner*, 27 February 1865.
409 Is Lee a good Southerner?: *Richmond Examiner*, 16 February 1865.
409 Inevitable war between France and Britain: *Richmond Examiner*, 24 March 1865.
410–11 Mitchel, post-war and imprisonment: Dillon, Volume 2, as above; Mitchel, *Jail Journal*, as above.
411 TFM resigns commission: TFM to Adjutant-General, 12 May 1865, Generals Papers and Records, Secretary of War, Volume IV, M344, National Archives, Washington, DC.
411 Acceptance of resignation: Adjutant-General to TFM, 15 May 1865, as for previous note.
411 Apparent reversal of resignation: Undated, as for previous note. (In Meagher's hand.)
411–12 TFM petitions for second star and governorship: Meagher to Major O'Beirne, 20 June 1865, in 'Some Letters', as above.
412 TFM to Colonel Browning: Athearn, *TFM*, as above.
412 TFM to his father: No date, Meagher Papers, MS 3227, NLI.
413 Fortress Monroe imprisonment: Mitchel, *Jail Journal*, as above; Dillon, Volume 2 as above; McCall, as above.
414 TFM's journey to Montana: Athearn, *TFM*, as above.
414–15 Colonel O'Keefe's journey: Colonel Cornelius O'Keefe, 'Rides through Montana (Thomas Francis Meagher)', *Harper's Monthly Magazine*, Vol. XXVII, October 1867.

23 Glorio, Glorio, to the Bold Fenian Men

Chapter heading: S. L. Anderson to Lord Naas, undated, 1867, Box 4, Fenian Police Reports, 1857–1880, NAI.

416 Population and other figures, Ireland: Edwards, as above.
416 Kenealy's family and townland of Glenlara: *Griffith's Valuation List*, Parish of Glenlara, Co. Cork, 1855.

416 Newmarket area: Duhallow Heritage Project, *Newmarket Court (1725–1996)*, Newmarket, Cork, 1994.
417 Kenealy's background and Fenian career: Kenealy, John, *Recollections of the Irish Republican Brotherhood, Written in the Year 1908*, privately published, Los Angeles, 1908.
417 North Cork in the Famine: O'Connor, as above; Donnelly, James S., Jr, *The Land and the People of 19th-Century Cork*, London and Boston, MA, 1975.
417 Tyrannous landlords: Denieffe, as above.
417–18 Tenant Rights Movement, Sadleir and Joint Stock Bank: Keneally, Denieffe, as above; Hickey, D. J. and Doherty, J. E., *A Dictionary of Irish History, 1800–1980*, Dublin, 1980.
418 Mitchel catechism: Rutherford, as above.
418–19 Stephens and founding of IRB: Ryan, as above.
420 John Devoy on Kenealy: Devoy, John, *Devoy's Post Bag (1871–1928)*, Volume 1, ed. William O'Brien and Desmond Ryan, Dublin, 1948.
420 Landlords evicting in the Fenian era: Davitt, Michael, *The Fall of Feudalism in Ireland*, New York, 1904.
421 Cork Fenians and absolution: Kenealy, as above.
421 Fenianism, the Church, the timbre of Cork Fenians, etc: O'Leary, John, *Recollections of Fenians and Fenianism*, Volumes 1 and 2, Dublin, 1896.
421 Founding of *Irish People* and its contents: O'Leary, as above.
421 Kickham and other *Irish People* personnel: Denieffe, O'Leary, as above; Comerford, R. V., *Charles J. Kickham*, Portmarnock, 1979.
422 *Irish People* and parish priest of Skibbereen: *Irish People*, 7 January 1865.
422 Priest approves of *Irish People*: as for previous note.
422 Kickham anti-clerical articles: O'Leary, as above.
422–3 Mrs O'Donovan Rossa's verse: *Irish People*, 20 May 1865.
423 Eva's verse, and place of women: O'Leary, as above.
423 Stephens's marriage: Denieffe, Ryan, as above.
423 Fenian fair and American fund-raising: Ryan, as above.
424 Fenian arms notation: Denieffe, as above.
424 Mission of Meehan and Dunne to Ireland: Rutherford, Denieffe, as above.
424–5 Loss of table of organisation: Rutherford, Denieffe, Kenealy, as above.
425 Table of organisation: Fenian Briefs, 1865–69, Carton 3, Envelope 1, NAI, seems to be the lost document.
425 How Kenealy reacts to Dunne's offer of 30,000 men: Kenealy, as above.
425 Loyalist fear of Cawnpore-style uprising: Cork to Dublin Castle, 9 September 1865, Fenian Police Reports, Box 3, NAI.
425 Fenian drill, Newburgh Street: Thomas Saunders to Metropolitan Police, 5 September 1865, as for previous note.
425–6 Constable Meagher on Midland railway employees: Meagher to Superintendent, Metropolitan Police, 7 September 1865, as for previous note.
426 Mitchelstown report: Mitchelstown, 5 September 1865, as for previous note.
426 American in Cork City: Second head constable Patrick Phelan to Constabulary Office, Dublin Castle, 14 September 1865, as for previous note.
426 Saint-Nazaire shells: British Consul to Secretary of State for Foreign Affairs, 21 September 1869, as for previous note.
426 *Fenianos non esse . . .* : Copied from British Foreign Office to Superintendent, Metropolitan Police, 21 September 1865, as for previous note.
426 Nagle report: Nagle to Superintendent, Metropolitan Police, 15 October 1865, Fenian Police Reports, Box 4, NAI.

428–9 Arms proclamation and raid on Heggarty: *ILN*, 30 September 1865.
429–30 Stephens's escape: Denieffe, Ryan, as above.
430 Republic Bond crisis in USA, emergence of Senate, and General Sweeny: D'Arcy, as above.
431 'The Finians': Ward, Artemus, *Artemus Ward and the 'Finians'*, New York, 1866.
431 The special commission: Chemney, William G., *The Fenian Conspiracy: Report of the Trials of Thomas F. Burke and Others for High Treason and Treason-Felony at the Special Commission, Dublin*, Dublin, 1869.
431 Seditious manuscript: Fenian Briefs, 1865–69, Carton 3, Envelope 5, NIA.
432 O'Leary, Luby, Kickham, Rossa in court: Chemney, as above.
432 Trial of Kenealy: Kenealy, as above; *Cork Examiner*, 2 January 1866.
432–3 Warner's history: *TL*, 20 December 1865.
433 Kenealy chairs Fenian meetings: *Weekly News*, 23 December 1865.
433 Dowse baiting the informer Nagle: Denieffe, as above.
433–5 Remainder of Kenealy trial: Kenealy, as above; *Cork Examiner*, 2 January 1866.
435–6 Mountjoy, Pentonville, prison experience: Rossa, Jeremiah O'Donovan, *Irish Rebels in English Prisons*, New York, 1882.
437–8 John Boyle O'Reilly (hereafter JBOR), childhood and subsequent: Schofield, William G., *Seek for a Hero – The Story of John Boyle O'Reilly*, New York, 1956; Roche, James Jeffrey, *John Boyle O'Reilly: His Life, Poems and Speeches*, New York, 1891; Evans, A. G., *Fanatic Heart: A Life of John Boyle O'Reilly, 1844–1890*, A. G. Evans, Perth, 1997.
438 Pagan O'Leary, William Roantree: Denieffe, as above.
439 Devoy meets JBOR: Devoy, John, *Recollections of an Irish Rebel*, Dublin, 1869.
439 McCafferty amongst the Irish: D'Arcy, Kee, *Bold Fenian Men*, London, 1972.
439–40 Arrest and imprisonment of JBOR and others: Roche, Evans, as above; D'Arcy, Kee, as above; Amos, Keith, *The Fenians in Australia, 1865–1880*, Sydney, 1988.
440 Fenian soldiers' careers: Amos, as above.
441–2 Trial of JBOR, and subsequent imprisonment: Roche, Schofield, Evans, as above.

24 Re-Making Montana; Violating Canada

Chapter heading: Athearn, *TFM*, as above.

444 Decision to call the legislature: *Montana Post*, 7 February 1866; Meagher, Thomas Francis, *Lectures of Governor Thomas Francis Meagher in Montana*, Helena, MT, 1867.
444–5 TFM informs President and Seward: Athearn, *TFM*, as above; TFM, *Lectures of Governor*, as above.
445 TFM's Montana career, relationship with Sanders and others: Rayma, Robert George, *Montana: The Land and the People*, 3 volumes, Chicago and New York, 1930; Burlingame, Merrill G., *The Montana Frontier*, Helena, MT, 1842; Malone, Michael P., Roeder, Richard B. and Lang, William J., *Montana: A History of Two Centuries*, Seattle, WA, 1991; Spence, Clark C.,

Territorial Politics and Government in Montana, 1864–89, Chicago, 1975; Sanders, Helen Fitzgerald, *A History of Montana*, Chicago and New York, 1913; Miller, Joaquin, *An Illustrated History of the State of Montana*, Chicago, 1894; *Contributions to the Historical Society of Montana*, Vol. VIII, Helena, MT, 1917.

446 The legislature meets: *Montana Democrat*, 8 March 1866.

446 Chumasero accusations: Athearn, *TFM*, as above.

447 TFM's St Patrick's Day speech: TFM, *Lectures of Governor*, as above.

447 TFM's problems with judges: Duice, John D. W., *The Rocky Mountain Bench: The Territorial Supreme Courts of Colorado, Montana and Wyoming*, New Haven, CT, 1972.

448 Meagher to Johnson on long tours: Athearn, *TFM*, as above.

448 Kuppens and TFM: Kuppens, SJ, Father, 'Memoirs', *Mid-America*, Vol. XIV, No. 2, October 1931.

449 TFM's Irish vision for Montana: Emmons, David N., *The Butte Irish – Class and Ethnicity in an American Mining Town, 1875–1925*, Chicago, 1990.

449 Dimsdale and Vigilantes: Dimsdale, Professor Thomas J., *The Vigilantes of Montana*, Helena, MT, 1915.

450 Daniels's petition and TFM's reaction: TFM's proclamation, 22 February 1866, Small Collection 1634, Montana Historical Society Archives, Helena, MT.

451 FB instructions to Mitchel, and enthusiastic reports from Stephens and other Fenians: D'Arcy, as above; Dillon, Volume 2, as above; Mitchel, *Jail Journal*, as above.

452 Hunters' Lodges: Senior, as above.

453 Elgin complains of Canadians: Beamis, S. F., *A Diplomatic History of the United States*, New York, 1942.

453 Anti-British feeling in the United States: Beamis, as above.

453 Calls for Union to send troops to Canada: *Chicago Tribune*, 14 December 1864.

453 McGee dumped from cabinet, joins Conservatives: Senior, Skelton, as above.

454 Campobello: D'Arcy, Senior, Neidhardt, as above.

454 Canadians on verge of invasion: *New York Daily Tribune*, 15 April 1866.

455 Fenians disband: *New York Daily Tribune*, 20 April 1866.

455 Canadian invasion, June: Denison, Major George T., Jr, *History of the Fenian Raid on Fort Erie, with an account of the Battle of Ridgeway, June 1866*, Toronto, 1866; Canada, Department of the Secretary of State, *Correspondence Relating to the Fenian Invasion*, Ottawa, 1869; Somerville, Alexander, *Narrative of the Fenian Invasion of Canada*, Hamilton, 1866.

455 Sweeny's Canada plan: *Irish American*, 3 February 1866.

455 *Address to the People of British Canada*, and Fenian Anthem: Senior, as above.

456 O'Neill: D'Arcy, as above; LeCaron, Henri, *Twenty-Five Years in the Secret Service: the Recollections of a Spy*, London, 1892.

456–8 O'Neill's campaign: Denison, Somerville, *Correspondence*, as above; Owen, David, *The Year of the Fenians*, Buffalo, 1990.

458 Mistaken burial: Senior, as above.

459 Chief glory of Fenian invasion: *New York Daily Tribune*, 7 June 1866.

459 McGee's reaction to invasion: Slattery, T. P., *The Assassination of D'Arcy McGee*, Toronto, 1968.

459 Potential of executions: *Rochester Union* reported in *Toronto Globe*, 10 October 1866.
460 Father McMahon's and other trials: Gregg, G. and Roden, E., *Trials of the Fenian Prisoners at Toronto*, Toronto, 1867.
460 Roberts's letter to Lynch: *Toronto Globe*, 17 December 1866.
460–1 Mitchel returns from Paris; and Mitchel family: Mitchel, *Jail Journal*, as above; McCall, Dillon, Volume 2, as above.
461 Mitchel criticises Fenianism: *Irish Citizen*, 25 April 1868.
461 Lieutenant Hogan, letters to O'Connell: 21 July 1866, 6 January 1867, 18 January 1873, Martin E. Hogan Papers, Small Collection 864, Montana Historical Society Archives, Helena, MT.
462 Green Clay Smith: Montana histories, as above.
463 TFM to Barlow: 26 October 1866, Barlow Papers, Box BW 62, Huntington Library, CA.
463 Nullification of TFM's legislatures, and rewards for federal officials: Athearn, *TFM*, Duice, as above.
464 Sherman refusing troops to TFM: *Montana Post*, 17 March 1866.
464 Blackfoot Treaty: *Montana Democrat*, undated clipping, Montana Historical Society Archives, Helena, MT.
464 TFM at Fenian Library: TFM, *Lectures of Governor*, as above.
465 Request to raise militia: Athearn, *TFM*, as above; Athearn, *Sherman and Settlement*, as above.
465 Bozeman killing: *Helena Herald*, 3 February 1867.
466 Sherman to Stanton: Athearn, *TFM*, as above; Athearn, *Sherman and Settlement*, as above.
466 *Herald* on TFM as pacifier: *New York Herald*, 31 May 1867.
467 Invisible not invincible militia: TFM to Barlow, 30 January 1867, Barlow Papers, Box BW 64, Huntington Library, CA.
467 TFM commends Major Vielé's plans: TFM to Barlow, as for previous note.
468–70 O'Doherty's defence of Quinn, and other aspects of the lives of Kevin and Eva in Queensland: Patrick and Patrick, as above; Patrick, Dr P. Ross, 'From Convict to Doctor', the Clem Mack Memorial Oration, 1981, *Royal Historical Society of Queensland*, Vol. XI, No. 2, 1981.
469 Martin's description of Smyth: Kiernan, as above.
470 Dipsomaniacal TFM: Athearn, *Sherman and Settlement*, as above.
471 I. G. Baker's account: Rayma, as above.
471–2 John Doran's account: *New York Sun*, 8 June 1913.
473 Lyons's version: Lyons, as above.
473 Chris Stephens accuses the Vigilantes: *Irish Times*, 8 May 1973.
473 TFM denounces Sanders: Meagher to Seward, 20 February 1866, Territorial Papers of Montana, Volume 2, Department of Missouri, File M25, 1866, National Archives, Washington, DC.
474 Enquiry concerning TFM's rank: John C. Foley to Adjutant-General, 9 July 1867, Generals Papers and Records, Secretary of War, Volume IV, M344, National Archives, Washington, DC.
474 Walch's patent: TFM to O'Connell, 5 January 1867, Andrew O'Connell Papers, SC175, Montana Historical Society Archives.
475 Petrified man: *Helena Independent*, 26 November 1899.
475 Millar and Mack: *Anaconda Standard*, 2 June 1913.

25 Fenians Transported

Chapter heading: Amos, as above.

476–7 The 1867 uprising: Kee, D'Arcy, Neidhardt, Ryan, as above.
477–8 Kelly's contempt for Stephens: Kelly to Rossa, 12 March 1867, O'Donovan Rossa Papers, Manuscripts and Archives, NYPL.
479 Manchester Martyrs: Kee, as above; Quinlivan, Patrick and Rose, Paul, *The Fenians in England 1865–1872: A Sense of Insecurity*, London and New York, 1982.
479 Engels and Marx on English proletariat and Fenians: Dixon, R. (ed.), *Marx and Engels on Ireland*, London, 1971.
479–80 Clerkenwell: Quinlivan and Rose, as above.
480 Rossa approached about Australia: Rossa, as above.
481 Departure from Portland, and *Hougoumont*: Roche, Evans, Amos, as above.
481 Cashman joins *Hougoumont*: Diary, Denis B. Cashman, MSS 1636, ML.
482 *Hougoumont* dimensions: Bateson, as above.
482 Burges's fear: Governor's Despatch to Buckingham, 24 December 1867, Colonial Office Despatches, Item 10, PRO, copied by Australian Joint Copying Project to 41 WAA.
482 Hampton's Western Australian career: *ADB*, Volume 1.
482 Hampton finds out Fenians coming: Buckingham to Governor, 17 October 1867, Colonial Office Despatches, Item 70, PRO, copied by Australian Joint Copying Project to 41 WAA.
482 Colonial fears: Governor to Buckingham, 24 December 1867, Colonial Office Despatches, Item 10, PRO, copied by Australian Joint Copying Project to 41 WAA.
483 Manning's fears, and sending of *Brisk*: Amos, as above.
483 Infantry from Tasmania: Buckingham to Governor, 26 February 1868, Colonial Office Despatches, Item 72, PRO, copied by Australian Joint Copying Project to 41 WAA.
483 JBOR plans mutiny, and subsequent Cashman: Diary, Denis B. Cashman, MSS 1636, ML.
483 Pensioner Guards: Buckingham to Governor, 17 October 1867, Colonial Office Despatches, Item 70, PRO, copied by Australian Joint Copying Project to 41 WAA.
483 Casey: Diary, John Sarsfield Casey, MSS 1447, ML.
484 Concert parties: Diary, Denis B. Cashman, MSS 1636, ML.
484 JBOR verses: Roche, as above.
485 *Moondyne*: O'Reilly, John Boyle, *Moondyne: A Story from the Underworld*, Boston, MA, 1879.
485 The *Wild Goose*: MSS 1542, ML; McGrath, Walter, 'The *Wild Goose*, Convict Ship Newspaper, Re-discovered', *Cork Historical and Archaeological Society*, Part 1, Vol. LXXIV, No. 219, January–June 1969.
486 Contributors: Diary, Denis B. Cashman, MSS 1636, ML.
487 Appearance of town: JBOR, *Moondyne*, as above.
488 Continuing loyalist fears of Fenians: Bolton, G. C., 'The Fenians Are Coming, the Fenians Are Coming', *Studies in Western Australian History*, Vol. IV, December 1981.
488 Hampton moves to Fremantle and reports anxiety diminished: Governor to

Buckingham, 29 January 1867, Colonial Office Despatches, Item 70, PRO, copied by Australian Joint Copying Project to 41 WAA.

26 The Fenians of the Desert Coast

Chapter heading: Roche, as above.

489 Walle, and other convict letters unless otherwise stated: Amos, as above.
489 Hampton reports policy with Fenians: Governor to Buckingham, 29 January 1868, Colonial Office Despatches, Item 70, PRO, copied by Australian Joint Copying Project to 41 WAA.
490 McGarry's gang: Carroll, Martin C., *Behind the Lighthouse: A Study of the Australian Sojourn of John Boyle O'Reilly*, dissertation, Perth, 1954; in Keneally's case confirmed by *Personal and Other Descriptions of 280 Convicts received per ship 'Hougoumont' on the 10th January, 1868*, Acct. 1156 V 10, Convict Establishment, Convict Department No. 40, Comptroller General's Office, Miscellaneous Volume, WAA.
490–1 JBOR's treatment and movements ashore: Amos, Roche, Evans, Carroll, as above.
491 'Here the aisle . . .': O'Reilly, John Boyle, *Songs from the Southern Seas*, Boston, 1873.
492 Attempted assassination, Prince Alfred: *SMH*, 13 March 1868; Amos, as above; Travers, Robert, *The Phantom Fenians of New South Wales*, Sydney, 1986.
492 Lord Belmore does not want witch-hunt: Governor to Buckingham, 1 July 1868, Belmore Papers, A 2542–2, ML.
492 Charles Miller dispatched: Colonial Secretary's Bundle, 4/7680/1, AONSW.
493 Miller's insufficient funds: Miller to Inspector-General of Police, 12 May 1868, as for previous note.
493 Boggis: Informant to Principal Under-Secretary of Police, 10 June 1868, as for previous note.
493 Detective McGlone, Fenian railwaymen, McBurnie, Stoneman: All 4/7680/1, ML.
493 McGee before assassination: Skelton, Senior, as above; MacKay, *Flight from Famine*, as above.
493 McGee's Wexford speech: Skelton, Senior, Slattery, as above.
495 McGee's assassination, and pursuit of killer: Slattery, as above; *Trial of Patrick J. Whelan for the murder of Thos Darcy McGee*, Ottawa, 1868.
495 McGee's letter to Peggy: Slattery, as above.
495 Macdonald commemorates McGee: 7 April 1868, House of Commons Debates, First Session – First Parliament, 31 Victoria.
495 McGee's last speech: 6 April 1868, House of Commons Debates, First Session – First Parliament, 31 Victoria.
496 Hogan, JBOR after attempt on Prince Alfred, and Fullams and other Fenians: Amos, as above.
497 Casey imprisoned: Diary, John Sarsfield Casey, MSS 1447, ML.
497–8 Hampton suggests early tickets-of-leave: Governor to Buckingham, 13

October 1868, Colonial Office 19–159, PRO 1658, copied by Australian Joint Copying Project to WAA.

498 Howard mutiny and results: Amos, Carroll, as above; Bruce to Buckingham, 11 February 1869, Colonial Office 18–163, PRO 1661, copied by Australian Joint Copying Project to WAA.

498–9 Visit by Prince Alfred: Amos, as above.

499 Bruce attacked for influencing Prince: *Fremantle Herald*, 13 February 1869.

499–500 Possible free pardons: *Fremantle Herald*, 27 February 1869.

500 JBOR and Miss Woodman: Roche, Amos, Evans, Carroll, as above.

500 Notebook: Evans, as above.

501 Abandonment of escape precautions, Fremantle: *Fremantle Herald*, 23 November 1867.

501 JBOR attempts suicide: 17 December 1869, Timperley, Interview Diary, 2892A, Battye Library, Perth, Western Australia.

501–4 Escape plans and escape: Carroll, Amos, Roche, as above.

504 Escape reported: 18 February 1869, Timperley, Interview Diary, 2892A, Battye Library, Perth, Western Australia.

504 Timperley's Report on Thompson and O'Reilly's escape: 20 February 1869, Colonial Police Records, AN5/6, Accession No. 129, Item 12/962, WAA.

504–5 Hare's response: 27 February 1869, as for previous note.

505–9 Further escape details, whaling journey, relationship with Gifford and Hathaway: Roche, Amos, Evans, Carroll, as above.

509 JBOR's first book of verse and dedication: JBOR, *Songs from Southern Seas*, as above.

510 *Bombay* verse: JBOR Papers, MSS ACC 247, Special Collections, BPL.

510–12 JBOR in US: Roche, Evans, Schofield, as above; McManamin, Francis G., *The American Years of John Boyle O'Reilly, 1870–1890*, New York, 1976.

27 Fenians at Large

513 Fenian pardons: Granville to Bruce, 30 April 1869, Colonial Office Despatches, Item 74, PRO, copied by Australian Joint Copying Project to 41 WAA.

514 Kenealy stays with group in Fremantle, and later developments: Kenealy, John, 'Reminiscences', *Gaelic American*, 17 and 24 December 1904.

515 Samuel Winter and other Melbournians: Amos, as above.

515 *Argus* takes note of Kenealy's arrival: *Melbourne Argus*, 9 July 1869.

516 Campaign of the *Argus*, and Kenealy accedes to Irish community: Kenealy, 'Reminiscences', as above.

517 Supreme Court decision interpreted as gesture of independence: Amos, as above.

518 Casey and other pardoned Fenians journey to Albany and eastern Australia: John Sarsfield Casey, *Irishman*, 5 March 1870.

520 Sydney committee: *Freeman's Journal* (Sydney), 9 October 1869; Kenealy, 'Reminiscences', as above.

520 *SMH* on Clontarf picnic: *SMH*, 16 October 1869.

520 Problem of picnic and Jack Robertson proscription: 16 October 1869, enclosure in Governor to Colonial Secretary, and reply by Granville, 24

January 1870, Colonial Office Despatches 1860–70, 4/784/1, AONSW.

521 Arrival of Fenian 'escapees' in San Francisco: *New York Daily Tribune*, 27 January 1870.

522 Arrival of Casey and others, Ireland: *Irishman*, 16 and 19 February 1870.

522 Walsh to JBOR: Amos, as above.

522 Kenealy's position with Talbot: Devoy, *Devoy's Post Bag*, Volume 2, as above.

522–3 Pardoned men remaining in Western Australia: Amos, as above.

523–4 Preparations for, and course of, 1870 invasion: Senior, D'Arcy, Neidhardt, as above.

523–4 O'Neill's chief failing, and other aspects of 1870 campaign: LeCaron, as above.

523 Papal Decree, January 1870: D'Arcy, as above.

524 Grant's reaction: Grant's anti-invasion proclamation: *New York Daily Tribune*, 25 May 1870.

524–9 The campaign: Senior, Neidhardt, as above: Toner, P. M., 'The "Green Ghost": Canada's Fenians and the Raids', *Eire-Ireland*, Vol. 16, No. 4, 1981; *Fenian Raid of 1870, The*. By Reporters at the Scene, Montreal, 1871; O'Neill, John, *Official Report of General John O'Neill, President of the Fenian Brotherhood, on the Attempt to Invade Canada, May 25, 1870*, New York, 1870.

525–6 JBOR's account: *Pilot*, 4 June 1870.

529 Home Rule: Kee, Robert, *The Laurel and the Ivy*, London, 1993; Foster, R. F., *Modern Ireland 1600–1972*, London, 1988; Foster, R. F. (ed.), *The Oxford History of Ireland*, Oxford, 1989.

529 Parnell: Kee, *Laurel and Ivy*, as above; Abels, Jules, *The Parnell Tragedy*, New York, 1966; Callaghan, Mary Rose, *'Kitty O'Shea'*, London, 1994.

529 JBOR articles: Roche, as above.

529 Amnesty Association: Kee, *Bold Fenian Men*, as above.

530 Rossa's election: Rossa, as above; Kee, *Bold Fenian Men*, as above.

530 Careers of newly pardoned Fenians, Western Australia: Amos, as above.

530–1 Kimberley's warning: Kimberley to Belmore, 17 February 1871, Secretary of State's Despatches, 4/1360, AONSW.

531 Fergusson's mistake: Kimberley to Belmore, 24 May 1871, as for previous note.

531 Enquiry into Fergusson's error and Kimberley's all-clear: Kimberley to Belmore, 21 March and 16 June 1871, Belmore Papers, A2542–2, ML.

531–2 Destiny of Goulding and others here and subsequent in chapter: Amos, as above.

531–2 Flood's career: Marriage Certificate and other documents, MSS 1636, ML, from the O Lúing Papers, M2048, NLI.

28 Home Rule and Dynamite

Chapter heading: JBOR to Devoy, *Devoy's Post Bag*, Volume 1, as above.

535 *Cuba* Five: D'Arcy, Neidhardt, as above; Devoy, *Recollections*, as above; Golway, Terry, *John Devoy and America's Fight for Ireland's Freedom*, New York, 1998; *Irish People* (New York), 28 January 1871.

536 Mass of Irish have never belonged to nationalist bodies: Roche, as above; Devoy, *Devoy's Post Bag*, Volume 1, as above.
536 Communists visit Fenians: Devoy, *Recollections*, as above; Golway, Neidhardt, as above.
536 JBOR denounces name of Fenianism: Roche, as above; Devoy, *Devoy's Post Bag*, as above.
537 '*Friend to the Irishman*': Roche, as above.
537 Ambiguities of immigration: Miller, Kerby A., as above; Bayor and Meagher, as above.
537 Charlotte O'Brien visits New York: As for previous note.
538 Founding and history of Clan na Gael: D'Arcy, Neidhardt, Golway, as above; Devoy, *Recollections* and *Devoy's Post Bag*, as above.
538 Hogan's and other letters from Fenian prisoners: Roche, Amos, Devoy (both works), as above.
539 Death of JBOR's father, JBOR courtship and other subsequent JBOR matters: Roche, Schofield, Evans, McManamin, as above.
540 Fire at *Pilot*: *Pilot*, 14 June 1873.
540 Whipple's 'Sunday evenings': His listing in *Dictionary of American Biography*.
540 Phillips, Wendell and Anne: Listings in *Dictionary of American Biography*; Schofield, McManamin, Roche, as above.
540–1 A freed slave writes to Garrison: 22 June 1874, Garrison Letters, MS A1. 2, Volume 37, Special Collections, BPL.
541 Phillips's moral status: 1 March 1874, Garrison Letters, as previous note.
541 Lydia Maria Child: Her listing, *Dictionary of American Biography*; MS 1092, Special Collections, BPL.
541 JBOR on the future of black Americans: Roche, as above.
541 Massachusetts politics: Baum, Dale, 'The Irish Vote and Party Politics in Massachusetts, 1860–1876', *Civil War History*, Vol. 26, No. 2, 1980.
541 JBOR's first volume of verse: JBOR, *Songs from Southern Seas*, as above.
542 JBOR to Whipple: 20 March 1878, O'Reilly Papers, MS 219, Special Collections, BPL.
542 Aldrich: Roche, as above; Aldrich listing, *Dictionary of American Biography*.
543 Letter to Aunt: Roche, as above.
543 Mrs O'Reilly's health: Evans, as above; Whipple to JBOR, 23 January 1883, O'Reilly Papers, MS ACC 623, Special Collections, BPL.
544 Acquisition of *Pilot*: Roche, Schofield, McManamin, Evans, as above.
544 JBOR verse unless otherwise noted: Roche, as above.
545 Soldier Fenians and their letters: Amos, as above.
545–6 'Voice from the Tomb' and Clan na Gael convention: Devoy, *Devoy's Post Bag*, Volume 2, as above; Devoy, *Recollections*, as above; D'Arcy, Amos, as above; O Lúing, Seán, *Fremantle Mission*, Tralee, 1965.
546 McCafferty's plan: D'Arcy, O Lúing, as above.
547 Talbot to Devoy: Devoy, *Post Bag*, Volume 2, as above.
547 Mitchel returns $100: Mitchel to Rossa, 8 December 1874, Rossa Papers, Maloney Collection of Irish Historical Papers, Manuscripts and Archives, NYPL.
548 Patrick Collins and John 'Honey' Fitzgerald: Their listings, *Dictionary of American Biography*.
548 JBOR's aphorism on freedom: *Wexford People*, 31 March 1962.

548–51 All Devoy's movements and letters in relation to rescue: Devoy, *Post Bag*, Volume 2, and *Recollections*, as above; Golway, Amos, as above.
550–1 Anthony, Richardson, Hathaway, as well as previous sources: Pease, Zephaniah W., *The Catalpa Expedition*, New Bedford, 1897.
551–2 Mitchel's last years: Usual Mitchel sources, as above.
552 The Wildes: Ellmann, Richard, *Oscar Wilde*, London, 1987; Pearson, Hesketh, *The Life of Oscar Wilde*, London, 1954.

29 The Fenian Whaler

Chapter heading: Devoy, *Post Bag*, Volume 2, as above.

555 *Catalpa* expedition: Pease, O Lúing, as above; Anon., *The Rescue of the Military Fenians from Western Australia, with a memoir of John Devoy*, Dublin, 1929.
555 Devoy does not put himself aboard: *Gaelic American*, 27 August 1904.
557–8 Breslin's movements, USA and Australia, and Desmond: Amos, O Lúing, Anon., *Rescue of Military Fenians*, as above.
559 King and Sydney Fenians: Amos, O Lúing, as above.
562 Sir William Cleaver Robinson: *ADB*, Volume 6.
563 Warning from Carnarvon: Confidential report from the Earl of Carnarvon to the Governor of Western Australia, 20 January 1876, Colonial Office 18–185, copied by Australian Joint Copying Project to WAA.
565–6 O'Doherty's parliamentary and surgical career: Patrick and Patrick, as above; Patrick, 'From Convict to Doctor', as above.
566 O'Doherty on Lilley: *Brisbane Courier*, 19 February 1870.
567 Speech as president of the Hibernian Society: *Brisbane Courier*, 8 September 1871.
567 O'Doherty to his daughter: O'Doherty Papers, OM71–6, Envelope 1, John Oxley Library, Brisbane.
569 Doonan records Fauntleroy conversation: Superintendent Fremantle Prison, AN35B, ACC 1156/35AC, enclosed in Governor's Correspondence, No. 264, 26/6/1869–27/8/1886, 92 WAA.
570 King meets McCarthy: King's account, *Gaelic American*, 8–22 October 1904.
570–1 Breslin visits Bunbury: Sub-Inspector Wisby to Hare, WA Police Department, AN5/6, ACC 129, Item 23/164, enclosed as for note p. 569 above, 92 WAA.
571–5 All telegrams, Breslin/Anthony: Copy made 18 April 1876, Escape of Fenians in American Whaler, File AN5/6, ACC 129, Item 23/164, enclosed as for previous note, 92 WAA.

30 Perth Regatta Day

Chapter heading: Ballad from Ward, Russell, *Three Street Ballads*, Russel Ward, Fentree Gully, Victoria, 1957.

577–8 Keilley: Roche, as above; General account of the rescue, *Gaelic American*, 16 July 1904; *Personal and Other Descriptions of 280 Convicts received per ship 'Hougoumont' on the 10th January, 1868*, Acct. 1156 V 10, Convict Establishment, Convict Department No. 40, Comptroller-General's Office, Miscellaneous Volume, WAA.

578–80 Movements of Fenian convicts on morning of escape: Western Australian Police Records, Report by Doonan and others, AN5/6, ACC 129, Item 23/164, 92 WAA.

580 Between cemetery and piggery: *Perth Inquirer*, 21 April 1976.

581 Breslin verse: Anon., *Rescue of Military Fenians*, as above.

582 All steps taken to pursue escapers: Report by Doonan and others, and Governor's Despatch to Secretary of State, 19 April 1876, 1/1/74–7/8/77, Item 13, WAS 1166, WAA.

582 Mr Tondut's regatta success: *Western Australian Times*, 21 April 1876.

582–3 Further movements and operations in response to escapes: *Western Australian Times*, 21 April 1876; *Fremantle Herald*, 22 April 1876.

583 Lord Stowell, quoted in Governor's Despatch, as above.

583 Irish letter from Fremantle: *Munster News*, reprinted in the *Irishman*, 15 July 1876.

583–4 Robinson's telegraph: 15 May 1876, Governor's Letterbook, 27/7/1872–14/12/1876, Item 4, WAS 1232, WAA.

585 Sam Smith's answer to Stone: *Fremantle Herald*, 21 April 1876.

585 Robinson's report: Governor's Despatches to Secretary of State, 19 April and 15 May 1876, 1/1/74–7/8/77, Item 13, WAS 1166, PRO, WAA.

586 Reasons HM's government could ask the American government to take actions: As for previous note.

587 Governor would not have sent *Georgette* out again: As for previous note.

589–90 Final exchange, *Catalpa* and *Georgette*: *Fremantle Herald*, 22 April 1876.

591 Keilley's destiny: Amos, as above.

591–2 Remainder of *Catalpa* journey: Various accounts, *Gaelic American*, 1904; Anon., *Rescue of Military Fenians*, as above; Pease, O Lúing, as above.

592 McAuliffe on behaviour of McCarthy: 12 May 1876, enclosed in Governor's Correspondence, No. 350, 392 WAA.

592 Rowe, McCarthy, Walsh: Amos, as above.

592 Invincibles: Kee, *Bold Fenian Men*, Neidhardt, Amos, as above.

592 Rowe on Tondut: Amos, as above.

593 Doonan condemns Lindsey and Booler: Doonan to Fauntleroy, 27 April 1876, G10/605, WAA.

593 Doonan attacks Fauntleroy for keeping Keilley at his quarters: 10 May 1876, Doonan to Governor, enclosed in Governor's report, as above, WAA.

593 Enquiry recommends removal of Lindsey: 13 May 1876, Governor's Correspondence, No. 350, 392 WAA.

593 Warder Lindsey puts up fight: Lindsey's Memorial to His Excellency, 22 May 1876, M12143/12, WAA.

593 Fauntleroy sacked: Home Office to Governor, 13 August 1877, Home Office Despatches, No. 377, WAA.

593 Robinson's behaviour approved by Home Office: Colonial Office from Home Office, 14 December 1876, No. 100, copied by Australian Joint Copying Project to WAA.

594 Little credit to Disraeli: O Lúing, as above.

595–7 Problems on *Catalpa*: Breslin's report in Clan na Gael, *Report of the Eighth*

Annual Convention, Cleveland, Ohio, September 4, 1877, Catholic University of America, Washington, DC.

597 The escapees at Rossa's hotel: *Irish World*, 25 July 1876.

598 Kenealy's store: Workman, Boyle, *The City That Grew, 1840–1936*, Los Angeles, 1936; Newmark, Harris, *Sixty Years in Southern California, 1853–1913*, New York, 1926.

598 American jubilation at escape: Amos, as above.

599 O'Reilly praises Anthony: *Irishman*, 16 September 1876.

599 Calculating rewards for Anthony and crew: Devoy, *Recollections*, as above; O Lúing, as above.

599 Request to New Bedford police: 18 April 1876, AN5/6, ACC 129, Item 23/164, enclosed as for earlier note, 92 WAA.

599–600 Fate of *Catalpa*: O Lúing, as above.

600 American careers of escapers: Devoy, *Post Bag*, Volume 2, as above; O Lúing, Amos, as above.

600 Breslin's later career: D'Arcy, O Lúing, as above; Devoy, *Post Bag*, Volume 2, as above.

600 Holland submarine: Devoy, *Post Bag*, Volume 2, as above; http/www.subnet-.com.

601 Devoy's later life: Devoy, *Recollections*, as above; Golway, as above.

601 Devoy's death: *TL*, 1 October 1928.

601 Life of Anthony and Mrs Anthony: O Lúing, as above.

31 Republican Christ

602 Davitt's life and Land League: Kee, *Bold Fenian Men* and *Laurel and Ivy*, Davitt, as above.

602 McCarthy and Chambers, letters: Roche, as above.

604 JBOR attacked in *Atlantic Monthly*: *Atlantic Monthly*, January 1880.

605–10 Parnell's oratory, arrest, downfall: Kee, *Laurel and Ivy*, as above; Lyons, F. S., Abels, Callaghan, as above.

605 New Departure: Golway, as above.

605 The catastrophe in Ireland, and Mayo Land League meetings: Jordan, Donald E., Jr, as above.

606 O'Reilly in relation to Davitt, Land League and Parnell: Roche, McManamin, Schofield, as above.

606 Phillips to JBOR concerning Parnell: 18 June 1880, MSS Acc 623, Special Collections, BPL.

606 JBOR applauds Land League: *Pilot*, 15 November 1879.

608 Land Act: Kee, *Laurel and Ivy*, as above; Lyons, as above.

608 Parnell's boycott speech: As for previous note.

609 Nicaragua Smyth and difficulties as landlord: Smyth Papers, 28 November 1881, 11 June 1882, and elsewhere, MS 8216, NLI.

609 JBOR denounces treatment of Parnell: *Pilot*, 3 December 1881.

609 Catherine O'Shea: Callaghan, and usual Parnell sources, as above.

609 *No Rent Manifesto*: Usual Parnell sources, as above.

610 Phoenix Park murders: As for previous note.

610 JBOR's reaction: Roche, Schofield, McManamin, as above.

610–12 Oscar Wilde's American tour: Roche, Ellmann, as above.

613 JBOR takes on Dismal Swamp with Ned Moseley: O'Reilly Papers, 26 November 1888, MSS ACC 2537, Department of Rare Books, BPL.
613 JBOR's irregular lines praised: *Atlantic Monthly*, June 1882.
614 *The King's Men*: O'Reilly, John Boyle (co-author), *The King's Men*, with Robert Grant, Frederic Stimson, John T. Wheelwright, New York, 1884.
614 Holmes praises *In Bohemia*: Roche, as above.
615–19 O'Dohertys in later life: Patrick and Patrick, as above.
617 *Courier* attacks Irish National Convention: *Brisbane Courier*, 6 November 1883.
617 *Courier* remarks O'Doherty 'starring it': *Brisbane Courier*, 22 October 1885.
618 *Courier* attacks O'Doherty for accepting Irish seat: *Brisbane Courier*, 7 December 1885.
618 O'Doherty repelled by Parnell: Brown, Spencer, *Journalist's Memories*, Brisbane, n.d.
618 Eva says O'Doherty resigned from Commons for financial reasons: O'Doherty Papers, OM71–6, Envelope 4, John Oxley Library, Brisbane.
618–19 Croydon goldfield: Maurie, Arthur, 'History of the Croydon Goldfield', *Historical Society of Queensland*, Vol. 4, No. 4, December 1951.
619 JBOR attacks Home Rule Bill: *Boston Pilot*, 15 May 1886.
620 JBOR's first expression of belief in workers' co-operatives: *Pilot*, 10 May 1873.
620 Paternalism vs Monopoly: *Pilot*, 1 September 1883.
620 JBOR on America's indigines: Roche, Schofield, as above.
620 JBOR and Harcourt: Usual JBOR sources, as above.
621 JBOR on Rossa wounding: As for previous note.
621 Americanism vs Irishism, and Queen Victoria Jubilee: Roche, as above.
622 JBOR's Irish defensiveness: McManamin, as above.
622 JBOR's record in backing politicians: Roche, as above.
623 JBOR dutifully backs Cleveland: *Pilot*, 19 July 1884.
623 Irish Americans and Democrats: Roche, as above.
624 JBOR exhausted: JBOR to Frances Bowen, 13 June 1887, O'Reilly Papers, MS AM 1662, Special Collections, BPL.
624 JBOR overworked: JBOR to Mr Burren, 24 January 1888, as for previous note.
625 JBOR as patron: JBOR to Governor Ames, 2 June 1887, Merle Johnson Papers, Manuscripts and Archives, NYPL.
625 Last lecture tour: Roche, Schofield, McManamin, as above.
627 Death and mourning: Roche, Evans, as above.
627 Chance of prescription error: Evans, as above.
628 Devoy on Kenealy: Devoy, *Post Bag*, Volume 2, as above.
629 Kenealy in Los Angeles: Workman, as above: obituary, *Los Angeles Times*, 10 September 1908.
629 People's Store: Workman, Newmark, as above.
629 Kenealy a member of Clan na Gael Council: 25 October 1882, Foreign Office Correspondence, FO5, PRO 5779, copied by Australian Joint Copying Project to ML.
630 Land defiance, North Cork: Donnelly, *Land and People*, as above.
630 Political practice in Los Angeles: Stinson, Marshall, *Fun, Fight, and Fiestas in Old Los Angeles*, Los Angeles, 1966.

630–1 Kenealy's later Los Angeles career: *City of Los Angeles Auditor's Report, 1903*, Los Angeles, 1904.

631 James F. Kenealy's career, and the water impasse: Workman, as above; Caughey, John and Caughey, LaRee, *Los Angeles: Biography of a City*, Los Angeles, 1977; Davis, Margaret Leslie, *Rivers in the Desert: William Mulholland and the Inventing of Los Angeles*, New York, 1993.

631 Kenealy's death, and *In The Sultan's Power*: Spalding, William A., *History and Reminiscences, Los Angeles, City and County, California*, Volume 1, Los Angeles, n.d.

631 Kenealy obituary: *Los Angeles Times*, 10 September 1908.

631–2 O'Dohertys – final years: Patrick and Patrick, as above.

632 O'Doherty's obituary: *Brisbane Courier*, 28 July 1905.

632 'Genial medico': Bernays, C. A., *Queensland Politics During Sixty Years (1858–1919)*, Brisbane, n.d.

633 Eva tells Hickey it was losing game for O'Doherty to join Parnell: O'Doherty Papers, Eva O'Doherty to Father Hickey, February 1906, OM71–6, Envelope 4, John Oxley Library, Brisbane.

633 *Soror poetica* letter: Hickey to Eva, as for previous note.

633 Hickey congratulates Eva: O'Doherty Papers, 14 March 1909, OM71–6, Envelope 4, John Oxley Library, Brisbane.

633 Eva's notes on the people of 1848: O'Doherty Papers, OM71–6, Envelope 5, John Oxley Library, Brisbane.

634 Poems inadequately advertised in Australia: Eva to Father Hickey, 12 November 1909, as for previous note.

635 Irish attitudes to the war: 'An Irish Airman Foresees his Death', in Yeats, W. B., *The Wild Swans at Coole*, London, 1919.

635 Pearse's speech for Rossa: Kee, *Bold Fenian Men*, as above.

635–6 Developments leading to 1916, and following it: Kee, *Bold Fenian Men*, as above; Foster, *Modern Ireland*, as above.

BIBLIOGRAPHY

Contemporary sources

This section includes some works published later but of contemporary provenance.

Anderson, Joseph, *Recollections of a Peninsular Veteran*, London, 1913.

Anon., *The Irish Cause on the Pacific: John Savage in California*, New York, 1870.

Bernays, C. A., *Queensland Politics During Sixty Years (1858–1919)*, Brisbane, n.d.

British Association, *Report of the British Association for the Relief of the Extreme Distress in Ireland and Scotland*, London, 1849.

Brodribb, W. A., *Recollections of an Australian Squatter*, Sydney, 1883.

Brown, Spencer, *Journalist's Memories*, Brisbane, n.d.

Canada, Department of the Secretary of State, *Correspondence Relating to the Fenian Invasion*, Ottawa, 1869.

Canada, *House of Commons Debates, First Session, First Parliament*, Ottawa, 1868.

Cavanagh, Michael, *The Memoirs of General Thomas Francis Meagher*, Worcester, Mass., 1892.

Chemney, William G., *The Fenian Conspiracy: Report of the Trials of Thomas F. Burke and Others for High Treason and Treason-Felony at the Special Commission, Dublin*, Dublin, 1869.

Chiriqui Improvement Co., *Charter and Statutes, or By-Laws*, 1864.

Cox, Samuel S., *Irish Prisoners and English Prisoners*, Washington, 1870.

Cullen, Reverend J. H., *Young Ireland in Exile*, Dublin and Cork, 1928.

Daly, Maria Lydig, *Diary of a Union Woman, 1861–65*, ed. Harold Earl Hammond, New York, 1962.

Daniel, Frederick S. (ed.), *The Richmond Examiner during the War, or The Writings of John M. Daniel*, New York, 1868.

Davin, Nicholas Flood, *The Irishman in Canada*, London, 1877.

Davis, Thomas, *The Poems of Thomas Davis*, ed. Thomas Wallis, Dublin, 1846.

Davitt, Michael, *The Fall of Feudalism in Ireland*, New York, 1904.

Denieffe, Joseph, *A Personal Narrative of the Irish Revolutionary Brotherhood*, New York, 1906.

Denison, Major George T., *History of the Fenian Raid on Fort Erie, with an account of the Battle of Ridgeway, June 1866*, Toronto, 1866.

Denison, Sir William, *Varieties of Vice-Regal Life*, Volumes 1 and 2, London, 1870.

Devoy, John, *Recollections of an Irish Rebel*, New York, 1928.

Devoy's Post Bag (1871–1928), Volumes 1 and 2, ed. William O'Brien and Desmond Ryan, Dublin, 1948–53.

Dillon, William, *Life of John Mitchel*, Volumes 1 and 2, London, 1888.
Doheny, Michael, *The Felon's Track*, Dublin, 1920.
Doyle, Martin, *Irish Cottagers*, Dublin, 1833.
Duffy, Charles Gavan, *Four Years of Irish History, 1845–1849*, Melbourne, 1883.
Fenian Raid of 1870, The. By Reporters at the Scene, Montreal, 1871.
Fitzgerald, Reverend P., *Personal Recollections of the Insurrection at Ballingarry*, Dublin, 1861.
Fontaine, Felix, *De Witt's Special Report: Trial of the Hon. Daniel E. Sickles*, Washington, 1859.
Gregg, G. and Roden, E., *Trials of the Fenian Prisoners at Toronto*, Toronto, 1867.
Harris, Alexander, *Settlers and Convicts: Recollections of Sixteen Years' Labour in the Australian Backwoods*, by an Emigrant Mechanic (Alexander Harris), Melbourne, 1969.
Hill, Matthew Davenport, *A Paper on the Irish Convict Prisons*, London, 1857.
Holt, Joseph, *A Rum Story: The Adventures of Joseph Holt, Thirteen Years in Australia*, ed. P. O'Shaughnessy, Sydney, 1988.
Inglis, Henry D., *A Journey Throughout Ireland During the Spring, Summer and Autumn of 1834*, Volumes I and II, London, 1835.
Johnson, James, *A Tour in Ireland with Meditations and Reflections*, London, 1844.
Jordan, J. A., *The Grosse-Isle Tragedy and the Monument to the Irish Fever Victims, 1847*, Quebec, 1909.
Keegan, Gerald, *Famine Diary – Journey to a New World*, Dublin, 1991.
Kenealy, John, *Recollections of the Irish Republican Brotherhood, Written in the Year 1908*, privately published, Los Angeles, 1908.
LeCaron, Henri, *Twenty-Five Years in the Secret Service: The Recollections of a Spy*, London, 1892.
Lewis, George Cornwall, *On Local Disturbances in Ireland*, London, 1836.
Los Angeles, *City of Los Angeles Auditor's Report, 1903*, 1904.
Lyons, W. F., *Brigadier General Thomas Francis Meagher*, New York, 1870.
McCarter, William, *My Life in the Irish Brigade: The Civil War Memories of Private William McCarter, 116th Pennsylvania*, ed. Kevin O'Brien, Campbell, CA, 1997.
Meagher, Thomas Francis, Captain, Company K ('Irish Zouaves'), *The Last Days of the Sixty-Ninth in Virginia*, New York, 1861.
Meagher, Thomas Francis, Brevet Major-General, United States Army, *Speeches on the Legislative Independence of Ireland*, New York, 1870.
Meagher, Thomas Francis, *Lectures of Governor Thomas Francis Meagher in Montana*, Helena, MT, 1867.
Mitchel, John, *Jail Journal*, published with addenda and appendices from original text, *Irish Citizen*, New York, 1854.
An Ulster Man for Ireland, Dublin, 1917.
History of Ireland from the Treaty of Limerick to the Present Time, Volume II, Dublin, n.d.
Mudie, James, *The Felonry of New South Wales*, London, 1837.
Newmark, Harris, *Sixty Years in Southern California, 1853–1913*, New York, 1926.

Nicholson, Asenath, *Ireland's Welcome to the Stranger*, London, 1847.
O'Brien, William Smith, *To Solitude Consigned: The Tasmanian Journal of William Smith O'Brien, 1849–1853*, ed. Richard Davis (General Editor), Sydney, 1995.
O'Leary, John, *Recollections of Fenians and Fenianism*, Volumes 1 and 2, Dublin, 1896.
O'Neill, John, *Official Report of General John O'Neill, President of the Fenian Brotherhood, on the Attempt to Invade Canada, May 25, 1870*, New York, 1870.
O'Reilly, John Boyle, *Songs from the Southern Seas*, Boston, MA, 1873.
Moondyne: A Story from the Underworld, Boston, MA, 1879.
(co-author), *The King's Men*, with Robert Grant, Frederic Stimson, John T. Wheelwright, New York, 1884.
Otway, C. G., *A Tour in Connaught*, Dublin, 1839.
Pease, Zephaniah W., *The Catalpa Expedition*, New Bedford, 1897.
Poor Law Commissioners, Second Report, London, 1849.
Report of the Proceedings in the case of the Queen versus O'Connell and Others, Dublin, 1844.
Report of the Proceedings for the First Sitting of the Special Committee for the County of the City of Dublin held at Green Street, Dublin, for the Trial of Thomas Clarke Luby and others for Treason-Felony, 'The Fenian Conspiracy', Dublin, 1866.
Roche, James Jeffrey, *The Story of the Filibusters*, London, 1891.
John Boyle O'Reilly: His Life, Poems and Speeches, New York, 1891.
Rossa, Jeremiah O'Donovan, *Irish Rebels in English Prisons*, New York, 1882.
Russell, W. H., *My Journeys North and South*, 2 volumes, London, 1862.
Rutherford, John, *The Secret History of the Fenian Conspiracy, Its Origins, Objects and Ramifications*, 2 volumes, London, 1877.
Scrope, G. Poulett, *The Plan of the Poor Law for Ireland*, London, 1833.
Shaw, A. G. L., *Convicts and the Colonies*, London, 1966.
Smyth, P. J., *The Life and Times of Thomas Francis Meagher*, ed. J. C. Waters, Dublin, 1867.
Somerville, Alexander, *Narrative of the Fenian Invasion of Canada*, Hamilton, 1866.
Spalding, William A., *History and Reminiscences, Los Angeles, City and County, California*, Volume 1, Los Angeles, n.d.
Stinson, Marshall, *Fun, Fight, and Fiestas in Old Los Angeles*, Los Angeles, 1966.
Therry, Roger, *Reminiscences of Thirty Years' Residence in New South Wales and Victoria*, London, 1863.
Tocqueville, Alexis de, *Alexis de Tocqueville's Journey in Ireland, July–August, 1835*, trans. and ed. Emmet Larkin, Dublin, 1990.
Trevelyan Charles, *The Irish Crisis*, London, 1848.
Trial of Patrick J. Whelan for the murder of Thos Darcy McGee, Ottawa, 1868.
US Department of War, *War of the Rebellion: A Compilation of the Official Records of the Union and Confederate Armies*, Washington, 1880–1901.
Ward, Artemus, *Artemus Ward and the 'Finians'*, New York, 1866.
Whyte, Robert, *Famine Ship Diary* (originally *The Ocean Plague*), ed. James Managan, Dublin, 1994.

Wiggins, John, *The 'Monster' Misery of Ireland*, London, 1844.
Workman, Boyle, *The City That Grew, 1840–1936*, Los Angeles, 1936.

Secondary sources

Abels, Jules, *The Parnell Tragedy*, New York, 1966.
Adam-Smith, Patsy, *Heart of Exile*, Melbourne, 1986.
Adams, William Forbes, *Ireland and Irish Emigration to the New World from 1815 to the Famine*, Baltimore, MD, 1980.
Amos, Keith, *The Fenians in Australia, 1865–1880*, Sydney, 1988.
Anon., *The Rescue of the Military Fenians from Western Australia, with a memoir of John Devoy*, Dublin, 1929.
Athearn, Robert G., *Thomas Francis Meagher: An Irish Revolutionary in America*, Boulder, CO, 1949.
Sherman and the Settlement of the West, Norman, OK, 1956.
Atkinson, Donald Harman, *The Irish Diaspora: A Primer*, Toronto, 1993.
Bateson, Charles, *The Convict Ships, 1787–1868*, Sydney, 1983.
Bayor, Ronald H. and Meagher, Timothy J. (eds), *The New York Irish*, Baltimore, MD, 1996.
Beames, Michael, *Peasants and Power: The Whiteboy Movements and Their Control in Pre-Famine Ireland*, New York, 1983.
Beamis, S. F., *A Diplomatic History of the United States*, New York, 1942.
Bernstein, Iver, *The New York Draft Riots*, New York, 1990.
Bisceglia, Louis, *Irish Identity in the Mother Lode: The Hibernian Benevolence Society, Columbia, California, 1857–71*, San Jose, 1986.
Black, R. D. C., *Economic Thought and the Irish Question 1817–1870*, Cambridge, 1960.
Brown, P. L., *Clyde Company Papers*, Volume 6, Oxford, 1968.
Brown, Thomas M., *Irish-American Nationalism 1870–1890*, Philadelphia, PA, and New York, 1996.
Burlingame, Merrill G., *The Montana Frontier*, Helena, MT, 1842.
Burns, Inez, *History of Blount County Tennessee, 1795–1955*, East Tennessee Historical Society, Knoxville, 1957.
Callaghan, Mary Rose, *'Kitty O'Shea'*, London, 1994.
Campbell, John H., *History of the Friendly Sons of St Patrick and of the Hibernian Society for the Relief of Immigrants from Ireland*, Philadelphia, PA, 1892.
Caughey, John and Caughey, LaRee, *Los Angeles: Biography of a City*, University of California, 1977.
Clark, C. M. H., *A History of Australia*, Volume I, Melbourne, 1962.
A History of Australia, Volume IV, Melbourne, 1978.
A Short History of Australia, Melbourne, 1993.
Clark, Dennis, *Hibernia America: The Irish and Regional Cultures*, New York, 1986.
Clark, Samuel and Donnelly Jr, James S. (eds), *Irish Peasants: Violence and Political Unrest, 1780–1914*, Dublin, 1983.
Cole, J. A., *Prince of Spies: Henri LeCaron*, London, 1984.

Coleman, Terry, *Going to America*, New York, 1972.
Comerford, R. V., *Charles J. Kickham*, Portmarnock, 1979.
Conyngham, Captain D. P., *The Irish Brigade and its Campaigns*, New York, 1867.
Corby, Reverend William, *Memoirs of Chaplain Life*, Chicago, 1893.
Crawford, Margaret (ed.), *Famine: The Irish Experience, 900–1900, Subsistence Crises and Famine in Ireland*, Edinburgh, 1989.
Daly, Mary E., *The Famine in Ireland*, Dublin, 1986.
D'Arcy, William, *The Fenian Movement in the United States, 1858–1886*, Washington, 1947.
Davis, Graham, *The Irish in Britain, 1815–1914*, Dublin, 1991.
Davis, Margaret Leslie, *Rivers in the Desert: William Mulholland and the Inventing of Los Angeles*, New York, 1993.
Davis, Richard, *The Young Ireland Movement*, Dublin, 1987.
William Smith O'Brien Ticket-of-Leave New Norfolk, Hobart, 1995.
Diamant, Lincoln, *Chaining the Hudson*, New York, 1989.
Dimsdale, Professor Thomas J., *The Vigilantes of Montana*, Helena, MT, 1915.
Dixon, R. (ed.), *Marx and Engels on Ireland*, London, 1971.
Donnelly, James S., Jr, *The Land and the People of 19th-Century Cork*, London and Boston, MA, 1975.
Donnelly, S. J., *Priests and People in Pre-Famine Ireland 1780–1845*, Dublin, 1982.
Duhallow Heritage Project, *Newmarket Court (1725–1996)*, Newmarket, Cork, 1994.
Duice, John D. W., *The Rocky Mountain Bench: The Territorial Supreme Courts of Colorado, Montana and Wyoming*, New Haven, CT, 1972.
Edwards, Ruth Dudley, *The Atlas of Irish History*, London, 1981.
Edwards, R. Dudley and Williams, T. Desmond (eds), *The Great Famine: Studies in Irish History, 1845–52*, Dublin, 1956.
Egan, Patrick K., *The Parish of Ballinasloe*, Galway, 1994.
Ellmann, Richard, *Oscar Wilde*, London, 1987.
Emmons, David N., *The Butte Irish – Class and Ethnicity in an American Mining Town, 1875–1925*, Chicago, 1990.
Ernst, Robert, *Immigrant Life in New York City, 1825–1863*, Syracuse, NY, 1994.
Evans, A. G., *Fanatic Heart: A Life of John Boyle O'Reilly, 1844–1890*, Perth, 1997.
Flynn, John S., *Ballymacward: The Story of an East Galway Parish*, Galway, 1982.
Foster, R. F., *Modern Ireland 1600–1972*, London, 1988.
(ed.), *The Oxford History of Ireland*, Oxford, 1989.
Gallagher, Thomas, *Paddy's Lament: Ireland 1846–7*, New York, 1982.
Gibson, Reverend C. B., *The History of the County and City of Cork*, Volume II, Cork, 1861.
Golway, Terry, *John Devoy and America's Fight for Ireland's Freedom*, New York, 1998.
Griffith, Arthur (ed.), *Meagher of the Sword*, Dublin, 1916.
Hammond, Harold Earl, *A Commoner's Judge: The Life of Charles Patrick Daly*, Boston, MA, 1954.

Hanchett, William, *Charles G. Halpine in Civil War America*, Syracuse, NY, 1970.
Hancock, W. H., *Discovering Monaro*, Cambridge, 1972.
Harmon, Maurice, *Fenians and Fenianism – Centenary Essays*, Seattle, WA, 1970.
Heney, H. M. E., *In a Dark Glass: The Story of Paul Edmund Strzelecki*, Sydney, 1961.
Hickey, D. J. and Doherty, J. E., *A Dictionary of Irish History 1800–1980*, Dublin, 1980.
Hirst, J. B., *Convict Society and Its Enemies*, North Sydney, 1983.
Hoppen, K. Theodore, *Ireland Since 1800: Conflict and Conformity*, London and New York, 1989.
Houston, Cecil J. and Smyth, William J., *Irish Emigration and Canadian Settlement*, Toronto, 1990.
Hughes, Robert, *The Fatal Shore*, New York, 1987.
Ignatiev, Noel, *How the Irish Became White*, New York, 1995.
Ingleton, Geoffrey Chapman (ed.), *True Patriots All, or News from Early Australia*, Sydney, 1952.
Jones, Paul, *The Irish Brigade*, Washington and New York, 1969.
Jordan, Donald E., Jr, *Land and Popular Politics in Ireland – County Mayo from the Plantation to the Land War*, Cambridge, 1994.
Kee, Robert, *The Laurel and the Ivy*, London, 1993.
The Bold Fenian Men, London, 1972.
Keenan, Desmond, *The Catholic Church in the Nineteenth Century*, Dublin, 1983.
Kiernan, T. J., *The Irish Exiles in Australia*, Dublin, 1954.
Kilpatrick, Hugh J., *The Irish Soldier and the War of the Rebellion*, Princeton, NJ, 1880.
Kinealy, Christine, *This Great Calamity: The Irish Famine 1845–52*, Dublin, 1994.
Laubenstein, William J., *The Emerald Whaler*, Indianapolis, 1960.
Leeson, M. A., *The History of Montana 1739–1885*, Chicago, 1885.
Levine, Edward, *The Irish and Irish Politicians*, Notre Dame, IN, 1966.
Lyons, F. S. L., *Charles Stewart Parnell*, London, 1977.
McCall, Seamus, *Irish Mitchel*, Dublin, 1938.
McCartney, Donal, *The Dawning of Democracy: Ireland 1800–1878*, Dublin, 1987.
MacDonagh, Oliver, *O'Connell*, London, 1991.
McInnis, Edward William, *The Unguarded Frontier: A History of American–Canadian Relations*, New York, 1942.
MacKay, Donald, *Flight from Famine: The Coming of the Irish to Canada*, Toronto, 1990.
McKay, Ernest A., *The Civil War and New York City*, Syracuse, NY, 1990.
MacLochlainn, Tadg, *A Signpost of Ballinasloe and District*, n.d.
McManamin, Francis G., *The American Years of John Boyle O'Reilly, 1870–1890*, New York, 1976.
McPherson, James M., *The Battle-cry of Freedom*, New York, 1988.
Maguire, James G., *Ireland and the Pope – A Brief History of Papal Intrigue Against Irish Liberty*, San Francisco, 1888.
Malone, Michael P., Roeder, Richard B. and Lang, William J., *Montana: A*

History of Two Centuries, Seattle, WA, 1991.
Marlow, Joyce, *Captain Boycott and the Irish*, New York, 1973.
Miller, Joaquin, *An Illustrated History of the State of Montana*, Chicago, 1894.
Miller, Kerby A., *Emigrants and Exiles: Ireland and the Irish Exodus to North America*, New York, 1985.
Mokyr, Joel, *Why Ireland Starved*, London, 1983.
Molony, John N., *A Soul Came into Ireland: Thomas Davis 1814–1845*, Dublin, 1995.
Montague, John (ed.), *The Faber Book of Irish Verse*, London, 1974.
Moody, T. W., *Davitt and the Irish Revolution, 1846–1882*, Oxford, 1981.
Moody, T. W. and Martin, F. X., *The Course of Irish History*, Niwot, CO, 1994.
Nairn, Bede (General Editor), *Australian Dictionary of Biography*, Volume 6, Melbourne, 1976.
Neidhardt, W. S., *Fenianism in North America*, Pittsburgh, PA, 1975.
Nicolas, Stephen (ed.), *Convict Workers*, Cambridge, 1988.
O'Brien, Grania, *These My Friends and Forebears: The O'Briens of Dromoland*, Whitegate, County Clare, 1991.
O Broin, Leon, *Fenian Fever – An Anglo-American Dilemma*, New York, 1971.
O'Connor, John, *The Workhouses of Ireland – The Fate of Ireland's Poor*, Dublin, 1995.
O'Driscoll, Robert and Reynolds, Lorna, *The Untold Story: The Irish in Canada*, Toronto, 1988.
O'Faolain, Sean, *King of the Beggars*, Dublin, 1980.
O'Farrell, Patrick, *The Irish in Australia*, Sydney, 1986.
Ireland's English Question: Anglo-Irish Relations, 1534–1970, London, 1971.
O Gráda, Cormac, *The Great Irish Famine*, Dublin, 1989.
Ireland Before and After the Famine: Explorations in Economic History, 1800–1925, Dublin, 1993.
O'Leary, John, *Recollections*, Volumes 1 and 2, Dublin, 1896.
O Lorcáin, David, *Larkin Family History: Ireland to Illawarra*, Brisbane, 1983.
O Lúing, Seán, *Fremantle Mission*, Tralee, 1965.
O'Mahony, Christopher and Thompson, Valerie, *Poverty to Promise: The Monteagle Emigrants, 1838–58*, Sydney, 1994.
O'Regan, Cathal and Jones, John (eds), *Moylough: A People's Heritage*, Moylough, 1993.
O'Rourke, Canon John, *The Great Irish Famine*, Dublin, 1989.
O'Shea, James, *Priests, Politics and Society in Post-Famine Ireland: A Study of County Tipperary 1850–1891*, Dublin, 1981.
O Tuathaigh, Gearóid, *Ireland before the Famine, 1798–1848*, Dublin, 1972.
Owen, David, *The Year of the Fenians*, Buffalo, 1990.
Pakenham, Thomas, *The Year of Liberty: The History of the Great Irish Rebellion of 1798*, London, 1969.
Palmer, Norman Dunbar, *The Irish Land League Crisis*, New Haven, CT, 1940.
Patrick, Ross and Patrick, Heather, *Exiles Undaunted: The Irish Rebels Kevin*

and Eva O'Doherty, University of Queensland, St Lucia, Brisbane, 1989.
Pearl, Cyril, *The Three Lives of Charles Gavan Duffy*, Kensington, NSW, 1979.
Brilliant Dan Deniehy, Melbourne, 1972.
Pearson, Hesketh, *The Life of Oscar Wilde*, London, 1954.
Phelan, E. J., *Ardent Exile*, Toronto, 1951.
Pike, Douglas (General Editor), *Australian Dictionary of Biography*, Volumes 1–5, Melbourne, 1966–7.
Póirtéir, Cathal (ed.), *The Great Irish Famine*, Dublin, 1995.
Famine Echoes, Dublin, 1995.
Pomfret, John E., *The Struggle for Land in Ireland, 1800–1923*, Princeton, NJ, 1930.
Potter, George, *To the Golden Door*, Boston, MA, 1960.
Quigley, Dr Hugh, *The Irish Race in California and on the Pacific Coast*, San Francisco, 1878.
Quinlivan, Patrick and Rose, Paul, *The Fenians in England 1865–1872: A Sense of Insecurity*, London and New York, 1982.
Rayma, Robert George, *Montana: The Land and the People*, 3 volumes, Chicago and New York, 1930.
Reece, Bob (ed.), *Irish Convicts: The Origins of Convicts Transported to Australia*, Dublin, 1989.
Exiles from Erin, Dublin, 1991.
Reid, Richard and Mongan, Cheryl, *A Decent Set of Girls*, Yass, NSW, 1996.
Reynolds, James A., *The Catholic Emancipation Crisis in Ireland, 1823–1829*, Newhaven, 1954.
Roberts, Edward S., *Ireland in America*, New York, 1931.
Roberts, Stephen H., *The Squatting Age in Australia, 1835–1847*, Melbourne, 1935.
Robinson, Portia, *The Women of Botany Bay*, Sydney, 1993.
Robson, L. L., *The Convict Settlers of Australia*, Melbourne, 1965.
Rossa, Jeremiah O'Donovan, *Irish Rebels in English Prisons*, New York, 1882.
Rude, G., *Protest and Punishment*, Oxford, 1978.
Ryan, Desmond, *The Fenian Chief*, Coral Gables, 1967.
Salaman, Redcliffe N., *The History and Social Influence of the Potato*, Cambridge, 1949.
Salt, Annette, *These Outcast Women – The Parramatta Female Factory, 1821–1848*, Sydney, 1984.
Sanders, Helen Fitzgerald, *A History of Montana*, Chicago and New York, 1913.
Schofield, William G., *Seek for a Hero – The Story of John Boyle O'Reilly*, New York, 1956.
Sears, Stephen W., *Landscape Turned Red*, New York, 1983.
To the Gates of Richmond, New York, 1992.
Senior, Hereward, *The Fenians and Canada*, Toronto, 1978.
Sillard, P. A., *The Life of John Mitchel*, Dublin, 1908.
Skelton, Isabel, *The Life of Thomas D'Arcy McGee*, New York, 1925.
Slattery, T. P., *The Assassination of D'Arcy McGee*, Toronto, 1968.
Smith, Cecil Woodham-, *The Great Hunger*, London, 1962.
Spence, Clark C., *Territorial Politics and Government in Montana, 1864–89*, Chicago, 1975.

Stout, Joseph Allen, *The Liberators: Filibustering Expeditions*, Los Angeles, 1973.
Swanberg, W. A., *Sickles the Incredible*, New York, 1956.
Touhill, Blanche M., *William Smith O'Brien and His Revolutionary Friends in Penal Exile*, University of Missouri, Columbia, MO, 1981.
Travers, Robert, *The Phantom Fenians of New South Wales*, Sydney, 1986.
Walker, Mabel Gregory, *The Fenian Movement*, Colorado Springs, 1969.
Ward, Russell, *The Australian Legend*, Melbourne, 1958.
Watson, John (ed.), *Catalpa 1876*, Perth, 1976.
Whitaker, Anne-Maree, *Unfinished Revolution*, Sydney, 1994.
Woodham-Smith, see Smith, Cecil Woodham-.
Yeats, W. B., *The Wild Swans at Coole*, London, 1919.

Theses, articles and chapters

Baum, Dale, 'The Irish Vote and Party Politics in Massachusetts, 1860–1876', *Civil War History*, Vol. 26, No. 2, 1980.
Bisceglia, Louis R., 'The McManus Welcome, San Francisco, 1851', *Eire-Ireland*, Vol. 16, No. 1, 1981.
Bolton, G. C., 'The Fenians Are Coming, the Fenians Are Coming', *Studies in Western Australian History*, Vol. IV, December 1981.
Brennan, Niamh, 'The Ballagh Rioters Barracks "Rioters" ', in Bob Reece (ed.), *Exiles from Erin*, Dublin, 1991.
Carroll, Martin C., *Behind the Lighthouse: A Study of the Australian Sojourn of John Boyle O'Reilly*, dissertation, Perth, 1954.
Castles, Alexander C., 'From Van Diemen's Land to Fort Sumter: Captain John C. Mitchel of the First South Carolina Artillery'. Unpublished at time of writing, kindly provided by author.
Contributions to the Historical Society of Montana, Vol. VIII, Helena, MT, 1917.
Crawford, Margaret, 'Subsistence Crises and Famines in Ireland: A Nutritionist's View', in Margaret Crawford (ed.), *Famine: The Irish Experience, 900–1900, Subsistence Crises and Famine in Ireland*, Edinburgh, 1989.
Davis, Richard, 'Patrick O'Donohoe, Outcast of the Exiles', in Bob Reece (ed.), *Exiles from Erin*, Dublin, 1991.
Fitzpatrick, David, 'Flight from Famine', in Cathal Póirtéir (ed.), *The Great Irish Famine*, Dublin, 1995.
Geary, Lawrence M., 'Famine, Fever and the Bloody Flux', in Cathal Póirtéir (ed.), *Famine Echoes*, Dublin, 1995.
Gwynn, Denis, 'Thomas Francis Meagher', the O'Donnell Lecture, Cork, 1961.
Kelly, Bernard B., 'The Fighting 69th', *The World of Hibernia*, New York, Summer 1995.
Kuppens, SJ, Father, 'Memoirs', *Mid-America*, Vol. XIV, No. 2, October 1931.
MacArthur, Sir William P., 'Medical History of the Famine', in R. Dudley Edwards and Desmond T. Williams (eds), *The Great Famine: Studies in Irish History, 1845–52*, Dublin, 1956.
McGrath, Walter, 'The *Wild Goose*, Convict Ship Newspaper, Re-discovered',

Cork Historical and Archaeological Society, Part 1, Vol. LXXIV, No. 219, January–June 1969.

Maurie, Arthur, 'History of the Croydon Goldfield', *Historical Society of Queensland*, Vol. 4, No. 4, December 1951.

Meagher, Thomas Francis, 'Holidays in Costa Rica', Part I, *Harper's Monthly Magazine*, Vol. XX, December 1859.

'Holidays in Costa Rica', Part II, *Harper's Monthly Magazine*, Vol. XX, January 1860.

'Holidays in Costa Rica', Part III, *Harper's Monthly Magazine*, Vol. XX, February 1860.

'The New Route through Chiriqui', *Harper's Monthly Magazine*, Vol. XXI, January 1861.

'Some Letters of Meagher to Captain James R. O'Beirne', *American-Irish Historical Society Journal*, Vol. 30, 1932.

Murray, Frank, 'The Irish and Afro-Americans in US History', *Freedomways*, Vol. 22, No. 1, 1982.

O'Donnell, Ruan, 'General Joseph Holt', in Bob Reece (ed.), *Exiles from Erin*, Dublin, 1991.

O'Farrell, Patrick, 'Whose Reality?: The Irish Famine in History and Literature', *Historical Studies*, April 1982.

O Gráda, Cormac, 'The Great Famine in Folk Memory and in Song'. Unpublished at the time of writing, kindly provided by author.

O'Keefe, Colonel Cornelius, 'Rides through Montana (Thomas Francis Meagher)', *Harper's Monthly Magazine*, Vol. XXVII, October 1867.

O Laighin, Pádraic, 'Grosse-Ile: The Holocaust Revisited', in Robert O'Driscoll and Lorna Reynolds (eds), *The Untold Story: The Irish in Canada*, Toronto, 1988.

O'Neill, Tim, 'The Persistence of Famine in Ireland', in Cathal Póirtéir (ed.), *The Great Irish Famine*, Dublin, 1995.

Owens, Garry, 'Hedge Schools of Politics: O'Connell's Monster Meetings', *History Ireland*, Vol. 2, No. 1, 1994.

Patrick, Dr P. Ross, 'From Convict to Doctor', the Clem Mack Memorial Oration, *Royal Historical Society of Queensland*, Vol. XI, No. 2, 1981.

Petrow, Stefan, 'Judas in Tasmania', in Richard Davis *et al.* (eds), *Irish-Australian Studies, Papers Delivered at the Irish-Australian Conference*, Hobart, 1995.

Robertson, Sir Rutherford, *The Three Societies Lecture: Penal Settlement to High Technology and the Future*, Canberra, 1988.

Salaman, Redcliffe N., FRS, 'The Influence of the Potato on the Course of Irish History', Tenth Finlay Memorial Lecture, Dublin, 1943.

Sarbaugh, Timothy J., *Post-Civil War Fever and Adjustment*, dissertation, Gonzaga University, 1992.

Solar, Peter, 'The Great Famine Was No Ordinary Subsistence Crisis', in Margaret Crawford (ed.), *Famine: The Irish Experience, 900–1900, Subsistence Crises and Famines in Ireland*, Edinburgh, 1989.

Toner, P. M., 'The "Green Ghost": Canada's Fenians and the Raids', *Eire-Ireland*, Vol. 16, No. 4, 1981.

Walter, Dave, 'Montana's Sensational Petrified Man', *Montana Magazine*, March–April 1984.

Weir, Hugh W. I., 'William Smith O'Brien's Other Family', *The Other Clare*, Vol. 20, April 1996.

Whalen, James M., ' "Almost as Bad as Ireland": The Experience of the Irish Famine Immigrant in Canada, Saint John, 1847', in Robert O'Driscoll and Lorna Reynolds (eds), *The Untold Story: The Irish in Canada*, Toronto, 1988.

Williams, Samuel C., *John Mitchel, the Irish Patriot, Resident of Tennessee*, East Tennessee Historical Society's Publications, No. 10, 1938.

Yeats, William Butler, *Thomas Davis Centenary Address*, Oxford, 1947.

Newspapers principally consulted

Boston Pilot
Connaught Journal
Cork Examiner
Galway Advertiser
Galway Free Press
Hobart Courier
Irish American
Irish Citizen
Irish Exile
Irish Felon
Irish News
Irish People
Irish Times
Illustrated London News
Los Angeles Times
Melbourne Argus
Montana Democrat
Montana Post
Nation
New York Herald
New York Times
New York Daily Tribune
Southern Citizen
Sydney Gazette
Sydney Herald and, later, *Sydney Morning Herald*
Sydney Monitor
The Times of London
United Irishman

INDEX